Gay and Lesbian Rights

A Question:
Sexual Ethics or Social Justice?

Richard Peddicord, O.P.

Sheed & Ward
Kansas City

Sheed & Ward™ is a service of The National Catholic Reporter Publishing Company.

◆

Library of Congress Cataloguing-in-Publication Data

Peddicord, Richard, 1958-
     Gay and lesbian rights : a question—sexual ethics or social justice/
Richard Peddicord.
       p.   cm.
     Includes bibliographical references and index.
     ISBN: 1-55612-759-6 (alk. paper)
     1. Gay rights—Religious aspects—Catholic Church. 2. Homosexuality—
Religious aspects—Catholic Church. I. Title.
BX1795.H66P43   1996
261.8'35766'08822—dc20   95-44315
                                                      CIP

◆

Published by: Sheed & Ward
                115 E. Armour Blvd.
                P.O. Box 419492
                Kansas City, MO 64141-6492

To order, call: (800) 333-7373

In Memoriam

Professor André Guindon, O.M.I. (1933-1993)
Mentor and Friend

Justice pour moi, Seigneur,
moi j'ai marché en mon integrité,
je m'appuie sur Toi et ne dévie pas.
(Ps. 26:1)

In Gratitude

To Professors Hubert Doucet, Richard Hardy, Jean-Marc Larouche, Kenneth Melchin, and Gregory Walter (St. Paul University, Ottawa); Professor Bernard East, O.P. (Collège dominicain de philosophie et de théologie, Ottawa); and to my Dominican brothers in the Province of St. Albert the Great (Chicago).

Contents

Introduction vii

Part I
The Gay and Lesbian Movement in the United States

Chapter One: A History of the Gay Liberation Movement
    in the United States 3
1. Introduction 3
2. The Stonewall Rebellion 7
3. The Mattachine Society 9
4. The Daughters of Bilitis 14
5. Early Successes on the Legal Front 16
6. Confrontation with the Medical Establishment 18
7. Courting the Christian Churches 19
8. Conclusion: What Do Gays and Lesbians Want? 24

Chapter Two: The Secular Debate on Gay and Lesbian Rights . 27
1. Contemporary U.S. Attitudes on Gay Liberation 28
2. Michael Novak: "Homosexuality is Harmful to Society" . . . 34
3. Roger Magnuson: "Are Gay Rights Right?" 37
4. Milton Gonslaves: "Right and Reason" 45
5. Richard Mohr: "Gays/Justice" 51
6. Conclusion 58

Part II
Catholic Teaching on Gay and Lesbian Rights

Chapter Three: Responses to the Gay Liberation Movement
    by the American Catholic Hierarchy 63
1. John Cardinal O'Connor 64
2. Joseph Cardinal Bernardin 69
3. Archbishop John R. Quinn 76
   3.1 "A Pastoral Letter on Homosexuality" 79
   3.2. Archbishop Quinn on Violence Against Homosexuals . . 88
   3.3. A New Problematic: Gay and Lesbian Partnership Laws . 91
4. Conclusion 92

Chapter Four: Catholic Sexual Ethics and Homosexuality . . . 96
1. The Traditional Case Against Homosexuality 97
   1.1 The Bible and Homosexuality 105
   1.2 Two Competing World Views 109

2. Soteriological Implications: The Damnation Factor 112
3. PCHP, the Revisionists, and Gay Rights 116
4. Conclusion 118

Chapter Five: Catholic Social Teaching and Homosexuality . 119
1. Catholicism and Human Rights 120
2. The C.D.F.'s 1992 Intervention on Gay Rights 123
3. Critiques of SCC 130
4. Conclusion 140

Coda: Catholic Sexual Ethics v. Catholic Social Teaching . . . 141

Part III
Catholic Support for Gay and Lesbian Rights

Chapter Six: John Courtney Murray on the Church-State
    Relationship 147
1. Murray on Religion and Society; Church and State 147
2. Indebtedness to Thomistic Political Theory 152
    2.1 A Necessary Dualism 153
    2.2 Art v. Deductive Reasoning: Murray on Contraception . . 156
3. Conclusion 163

Chapter Seven: John Courtney Murray on Religious Freedom 164
1. Tolerance Revisited. 164
2. The Rights of Conscience 170
3. *Dignitatis humanae* 171
4. Conclusion 175

Chapter Eight: A Catholic Case for Supporting Gay and
    Lesbian Rights Ordinances 178
1. Introduction: On Extending the *Modus Vivendi* 178
2. Indebtedness to JCM's Work on Church-State Relations . . 179
3. Justice as a Univocal Term 180
4. Indebtedness to JCM's Work on Religious Liberty 184
5. Conclusion 185

Abbreviations 187

Bibliography 188

Index 206

Introduction

In the mid 1970s, as the Gay Liberation Movement (GLM) gained momentum, a number of municipalities in the United States were faced with the question of gay rights ordinances. The framers of these ordinances sought to ensure that lesbians and gay men would not suffer the loss of their jobs, or their housing, or other social benefits offered to all citizens, should their sexual orientation come to light.[1] The American Catholic hierarchy was faced with a decision: would they advocate the legal sanctioning of their position on the human dignity and the basic human rights of homosexual people?[2] A few bishops voiced their support for these civil ordinances; others were reticent or refused to do so.

---

1. See E. Carrington Boggan, Marilyn G. Haft, Charles Lister, John P. Rupp, and Thomas B. Stoddard, *The Rights of Gay People* (New York: Bantam Books, 1975), pp. 171-178 for examples of such municipal ordinances. The anti-discrimination law of Minneapolis, Minnesota is representative: "It is determined that discriminatory practices based on race, color, creed, religion, national origin, sex, or affectional or sexual preference, with respect to employment, labor union membership, housing accommodations, property rights, education, public accommodations, and public services, or any of them, tend to create and intensify conditions of poverty, ill health, unrest, civil disobedience, lawlessness, and vice and adversely affect the public health, safety, order, convenience, and general welfare; such discriminatory practice threaten the rights, privileges, and opportunities of all inhabitants of the city and such rights, privileges, and opportunities are hereby declared to be civil rights, and the adoption of this Chapter is deemed to be an exercise of the police power of the City to protect such rights." [Amending Chapter 945 of the Minneapolis Code of Ordinances Relating to Civil Rights (99-68). In Boggan, et al, *The Rights of Gay People*, pp. 171-172].

2. See especially the National Conference of Catholic Bishops' document, "To Live in Christ Jesus" in Robert Nugent and Jeannine Gramick (eds.), *A Time to Speak: A Collection of Contemporary Statements from U.S. Catholic Sources on Homosexuality, Gay Ministry and Social Science* (Mt. Rainier, MD: New Ways Ministry, 1982), p. 6. The bishops write that gays and lesbians, "like everyone else, should not suffer from prejudice against their basic human rights. They have a right to respect, friendship and justice. They should have an active role in the Christian community. Homosexual activity, however, as distinguished from homosexual orientation, is morally wrong." The bishops conclude their reflection by adding that the Christian community ought to provide homosexuals "a special degree of pastoral understanding and care."

Before long, a clear bipolarity, based on the Church's sexual ethic and its social teaching, developed in reference to this issue. From the vantage point of Catholic sexual morality, some argued that the Church could not support such legislative proposals. Homosexual behavior is taken to be objectively immoral[3] and the Church should work to keep it from becoming "legalized." On the other hand, guided by nearly a century of papal involvement in the cause of social justice throughout the world, the contemporary social teaching of the Church seemed to call for nondiscrimination vis-à-vis the homosexual minority. Moreover, it did not appear to preclude the incorporation of gay and lesbian rights into civil statures.

THE C.D.F.'S INTERVENTIONS ON GAY AND LESBIAN RIGHTS

Among the directives contained in the C.D.F.'s "Letter to the Bishops of the Catholic Church on the Pastoral Care of Homosexual Persons" (henceforth, PCHP) is one which advises the bishops to distance themselves from groups within the Church whose unspoken agenda includes pressuring the Church to change its moral evaluation of homosexuality. It points out that "a careful examination of their public statements and the activities they promote reveals a *studied ambiguity* by which they attempt to mislead the pastors and the faithful."[4] Such groups "use the word 'Catholic' to describe either the organization or its intended members, yet they do not defend and promote the teaching of the magisterium; indeed, they openly attack it."[5] The bishops should offer them no support.

This directive of PCHP had a chilling effect on the ministry of the Church to homosexual persons. One of the most obvious results was the distancing that took place between the American episcopate and Dignity, the largest organization of gay and lesbian Catholics. Dignity was deemed one of the groups which had consistently cultivated a "studied ambiguity" on the question of the moral valence of homosexual acts.[6]

---

3. Although it morally distinguished the homosexual orientation from homosexual genital expression, the C.D.F.'s (Confraternity for the Doctrine of the Faith [henceforth C.D.F.]) *Declaration on Certain Questions Concerning Sexual Ethics* (December 29, 1975), Vatican translation, *L'Osservatore Romano* (Boston: Daughters of St. Paul, no date given) represented an unambiguous reaffirmation of the Church's traditional evaluation of "homosexual acts."

4. C.D.F., PCHP, #14 in Jeannine Gramick and Pat Furey (eds.), *The Vatican and Homosexuality: Reactions to the "Letter to the Bishops of the Catholic Church on the Pastoral Care of Homosexual Persons"* (New York: Crossroad, 1988), p. 7. Emphasis added.

5. C.D.F., PCHP, #14, p. 8.

6. See Bishop Francis Mugavero's "Withdrawing Support from Certain Homosexual Groups," in *Origins,* 16 (1987), p. 651.

In July of 1992, the C.D.F.'s "Some Considerations Concerning the Catholic Response to Legislative Proposals on the Non-Discrimination of Homosexual Persons"[7] (henceforth, SCC) appeared in the American press. The cornerstone of this document is the insistence that there are times when society *ought* to discriminate against homosexual persons. When gay people attempt employment which would put them in close contact with children or when they try to adopt children, they should be opposed. Moreover, as a rule of thumb, the civil rights of gays and lesbians are dependent upon their remaining invisible to society at large. For SCC, the Church's negative moral evaluation of "homosexual acts" is the principle from which all else flows.

THE PRESENT REALITY

SCC notwithstanding, the bipolar nature of the question of Catholic support for gay and lesbian rights has not been transcended. A bishop's evaluation of the possibility of Catholic moral teaching sanctioning non-discrimination legislation for gay people still turns upon his decision to view the question under the rubric of sexual ethics or social ethics.[8]

From the perspective of Catholic sexual ethics, support for gay rights seems to be ruled out. Homosexual behavior is an intrinsic evil: the law should not grant people "rights" to gravely immoral behavior. Moreover, homosexuality is sometimes taken to have a deleterious effect on the institutions of marriage and the family; therefore certain forms of discrimination against gays and lesbians are justifiable.

However, if one starts from the perspective of Catholic social teaching, with its emphasis on human dignity, human rights, and inviolability of the individual conscience and the respect that is owed to the conscientious judgments of others, a society's decision to give the force of law to nondiscrimination relative to its gay and lesbian minority appears to be within the ambit of the Catholic moral tradition.

Sexual morality versus the Church's social teaching: such is the impasse at which one finds the Catholic hierarchy in the United States on the question of gay and lesbian rights ordinances. The fact that this impasse has been allowed to fester for several years shows that the American Catholic Bishops are involved in fostering a "studied ambiguity" of their own: they insist upon affirming the dignity of homosexual persons (this is a refrain that one hears from even the most ardent opponents of gay

---

7. The first version of this Instruction can be found in *The National Catholic Reporter* (July 31, 1992), p. 10; the revised version is in *Origins,* 22 (August 6, 1992), pp. 173, 175-177.

8. As we shall see, several U.S. bishops have publicly supported gay and lesbian rights ordinances since the appearance of SCC.

rights legislation) yet they do not insist upon the codification of this dignity into protective legislation for the homosexual minority.[9]

Our thesis is not only that the moral tradition of the Catholic Church can endorse the movement whereby the human and civil rights of gays and lesbians are protected through civil legislation and (or) municipal "gay rights" ordinances; we argue that if the Church does not support such measures, it risks infidelity to its fundamental moral principles.[10]

METHODOLOGY

This work is composed of three precise moments: the historical (chapters 1-5), the metaethical (chapters 6-7), and the normative (chapter 8).

In Part I (chapters 1 and 2) we set the stage for a Catholic reflection on the issue of gay and lesbian rights. Toward this end, the first chapter examines the history of the GLM in the United States from 1945 to the present. It documents the process by which gays and lesbians identified themselves as a distinct cultural minority and it touches upon the successes of the GLM and its contemporary agenda.

The second chapter provides a summary statement on the state of the question in the secular literature. Here the position of four representative voices on the advisability of gay and lesbian rights ordinances are presented. This secular debate will provide the specific context out of which to analyze the originality of the Catholic debate.

In Part II (chapter 3-5), the terms of the "studied ambiguity" in the Church's teaching are examined. Chapter 3 presents the positions of Archbishop Quinn and Cardinals O'Connor and Bernardin. (The thought of these three Church leaders creates the parameters of the discussion for most of Catholic America.) At the end of this chapter we will be in a position to comment on the distinctiveness of the Catholic debate on the moral advisability of gay and lesbian rights ordinances.

---

9. We will show, moreover, that the decision to broach this subject from the perspective of the Church's social teaching is more in line with the tradition of Catholic morality than is its alternative. Here, an added dimension of the episcopacy's "studied ambiguity" comes to the surface: it has allowed the impression to be given that viewing the question of gay rights under the rubric of sexual ethics has as much merit as viewing it as a question for the Church's social teaching.

10. I am indebted to John Coleman's "Two Unanswered Questions," in Jeannine Gramick and Pat Furey (eds.), *The Vatican and Homosexuality: Reactions to the "Letter to the Bishops of the Catholic Church on the Pastoral Care of Homosexual Persons"* (New York: Crossroad, 1988), pp. 59-65, for the impetus to pursue this particular problem. Particularly helpful was his observation that the C.D.F.'s PCHP leaves unanswered the following question: "What is the relation of law and morality, and, in particular, the status of a Catholic case for supporting, in law, the civil rights of homosexual persons?" (p. 64).

In the fourth chapter, through and extended look at PCHP, the first partner in ambiguity comes to the fore – Catholicism's traditional moral evaluation of homosexuality. This discussion serves to explain the stance of a number of U.S. bishops and the position adopted by the C.D.F. in SCC.

Against the backdrop of SCC, the fifth chapter entails a review of the second partner in ambiguity – Catholic social teaching's espousal of the cause of global human rights. It concludes by critiquing the teaching of SCC and by showing that SCC is not the last word on Catholic support for civil protections for homosexual persons.

In chapters 6 and 7 we interpret traditional Catholic positions with a view toward finding a basis for deciding whether the question of gay rights ordinances should be considered under the rubric of sexual ethics or social ethics.

Based upon support from the theological contribution of John Courtney Murray, S.J., we argue that the issue of gay rights does not belong in the ambit of the Church's sexual ethics: the Church's social teaching must take priority.

Having made the case that the question of gay liberation is most properly one for the Church's social teaching and that this source would not by definition be obliged to render a negative judgment concerning protective legislation for gays and lesbians, we move in chapter 8 to make a Catholic case for supporting the civil rights of gays and lesbians.

In the first place, we appeal to the present *modus vivendi* that the Church has accepted relative to social policy on other sexual issues. For instance, the contemporary Church leadership, while maintaining the immorality of fornication, adultery, and artificial means of birth control, has not advocated that these practices be criminated. No good reasons keep adult, consensual homosexual relations from being added to the current *modus vivendi*.

Secondly, we apply the work of Murray to the question. Murray's reflections on the Church-State relationship and on religious liberty provide a strong foundation for Catholic support for gay and lesbian rights in civil society.

In the end, this work intends to show that a Catholic case for supporting non-discrimination legislation for gays and lesbians can be made on traditional principles of moral theology and that such a case has more merit than those which argue otherwise.

Part I

The Gay and Lesbian Movement
in the United States

CHAPTER ONE

A History of the Gay Liberation Movement in the United States

1. INTRODUCTION

The definitive history of the GLM in the United States is probably years away from being written. Indeed, it is only in the last few years that substantive histories of the movement have become available.[1] There is a paucity of published works on the history of gay liberation; at the same time, the GLM is still very much in process. Within these parameters, this chapter will provide a general introduction to the GLM in the United States. We will note the fundamental aims of this movement and the successes that it has known. As a means of setting the stage for what will follow in the rest of this work, we will conclude with a brief statement on the controverted relationship between the GLM and the Roman Catholic Church in the United States.

Homosexuality is a topic that few people can address without some degree of emotional response.[2] It is not surprising, then, that the American civil discourse on homosexuality tends to be benighted. By and large, it is fraught with myths, half-truths, and sweeping generalizations.

---

1. See, for instance: Margaret Cruikshank, *The Gay and Lesbian Liberation Movement* (New York: Routledge, Chapman & Hall, 1992); Martin Duberman, *About Time: Exploring the Gay Past* (New York: Meridian, 1991); Jonathan Katz, *Gay American History. Lesbians and Gay Men in the U.S.A.* (New York: Meridian, 1992); and Eric Marcus, *Making History: The Struggles for Gay and Lesbian Equal Rights, 1945-1990. An Oral History* (New York: Harper Collins, 1992). John D'Emilio's *Sexual Politics, Sexual Communities: The Making of a Homosexual Minority in the United States, 1940-1970* (Chicago: University of Chicago Press, 1983) remains the standard-bearer for gay studies in the United States.

2. Milton A. Gonsalves puts it this way: "Homosexuality, whenever it is discussed, generates a variety of reactions ranging from lurid curiosity to passionate hostility. For persons not quite secure in their own sexual identity, . . . (the) discussion . . . becomes highly emotional with little possibility for being objective. Even people who are more secure in their heterosexual self-identity often have irrational fears concerning homosexual persons." [See: *Fagothey's Right & Reason: Ethics in Theory and Practice* (Columbus, OH: Merrill Publishing Co., 1989), p. 401.]

For instance, Marshall Kirk and Hunter Madsen, in their study, *After the Ball: How America Will Conquer its Fear and Hatred of Gays in the 90's*, identify "seven hallowed public myths of homosexuality." To the minds of many Americans, gay people are:

(1) Hardly worth thinking about
(2) Few in number
(3) Easy to spot
(4) Homosexual because of sin, insanity, or seduction
(5) Kinky, loathsome sex addicts
(6) Unproductive and untrustworthy members of society
(7) Suicidally unhappy.[3]

Kirk and Madsen show that the gay and lesbian reality bears little resemblance to the various stereotypical formulations; throughout the chapters that follow, we will have occasion to reinforce this point. What will be highlighted shortly is that gays and lesbians have been – and continue to be – the recipients of a fair amount of vilification. Kirk and Madsen claim that much of the blame for this can be laid at the feet of ignorance.

People who "have a predominant erotic attraction to others of the same sex,"[4] i.e., gay men and lesbians, are found in every social grouping in American society. They come from no particular social class, from no particular racial background or ethnic stock, from no particular geographic region. On the surface, gays and lesbians are indistinguishable from everyone else.[5]

The question of the percentage of the population who are homosexually oriented is rife with controversy. The estimates run anywhere from less than two percent to more than ten percent.[6] In a nation the size of the United States, obviously, even a fraction of a percentage point involves a significant number of people. If the homosexual population of the United States were but one percent, gays and lesbians would outnumber the populations of several of the smaller states. The size of the homosexual minority alone is enough to discredit the first two operative myths identified by Kirk and Madsen.

---

3. Marshall Kirk and Hunter Madsen, *After the Ball: How America Will Conquer its Fear and Hatred of Gays in the 90's* (New York: Plume, 1990), p. 61.

4. Richard A. Isay, M.D. *Being Homosexual: Gay Men and Their Development* (New York: Avon Books, 1989), p. 11.

5. Some gay men and lesbians are adept at "passing" in heterosexual society, i.e., they are skilled at keeping their sexual orientation secret. Others, including the effeminate gay man and the masculine lesbian, are either less gifted or simply do not find passing worth their while.

6. For a balanced discussion, see Richard A. Posner, *Sex and Reason* (Cambridge, MA: Harvard University Press, 1992), pp. 294-295.

The etiology of same-sex attraction admits of as much controversy. Is homosexuality innate or an acquired characteristic? Is it communicable – a possible contagion – or is the average person's sexual orientation more or less unaffected by the presence of gays and lesbians in society and even impervious to instances of homosexual solicitation? As Margaret Cruikshank ponders: "Is it an essence, a core self, or is it the product of social forces? Did homosexuals exist before sexologists gave them a label, or were homosexuals an invention of sexologists?"[7]

The sciences – physical and human – have not pronounced definitively on any of these questions. One point, however, seems incontrovertible: the true homosexual orientation – regardless of its cause(s) – is all but unchangeable.[8] The question of whether one's sexual orientation is shaped more by biology or more by culture is all but rendered moot by its sheer fixity.

The scientific research on the etiology of homosexuality[9] damages the third myth identified by Kirk and Madsen. Gays and lesbians do not experience erotic attraction to members of the same sex because of personal sin, mental defect, or because of the malevolence of others. Whereas anyone could be implicated in "homosexual acts," same-sex erotic attraction is experienced by homosexual people as a given. (The last three myths are equally untenable. For them, however, personal knowledge of a law-abiding, community-minded, and God-fearing homosexual is enough to demonstrate their discontinuity with reality.)

Persecution of gay people – or, at least, people who have been found guilty of committing homosexual acts – has been a perennial feature of Western civilization. The Mosaic law demanded the death penalty for anyone caught in a homosexual liaison; much of European jurisprudence continued to follow suit into the nineteenth-century.[10] The ideological framework of the Third Reich's war against homosexuals,[11] although out of step

---

7. Cruikshank, *The Gay and Lesbian Liberation Movement*, p. 25.

8. This point is discussed further below. See *infra*, pp. 40-42.

9. The scientific data is discussed below. See especially p. 40, n. 49.

10. See especially, David F. Greenberg, *The Construction of Homosexuality* (Chicago: University of Chicago Press, 1988), pp. 301-346. Greenberg highlights that when sodomy was removed from the list of capital offenses in a given society, it nonetheless usually remained a criminal offense.

11. Cf., Michael Burleigh and Wolfgang Wippermann, *The Racial State: Germany, 1933-1945* (Cambridge: Cambridge University Press, 1991), pp. 136-197. Nazi ideology held homosexuals – especially gay men – to be dangers to the 'purity of the State,' their presence in society, it was argued, would weaken ('feminize') and eventually lead to the downfall of the Fatherland. All campaigns against homosexuals – and the very existence of criminal statutes against private consensual homosexual relations between adults – assume that homosexuality has a deleterious effect on the common good. See also Heinz Heger, *The Men with the Pink Triangle* [trans. by David Fernbach] (Boston: Alyson Press, 1980) and

with the European practice of its time, is all but indistinguishable from the various medieval and early modern purges of homosexuals.

In the main, throughout Christian history, gays and lesbians have been targeted for persecution and treated as criminals. "The history of social policy toward homosexuals in Western culture since Christ is one of strong disapproval, frequent ostracism, social and legal discrimination, and at times ferocious punishment."[12] An in-depth accounting for this hostility is beyond the scope of this work; it is clear, however, that the Christian churches have provided much of the ideological foundation for what can be called a war on homosexual men and women. The most damning arguments – literally and figuratively – against homosexual people have come from conservative Christian theology, founded upon a literal interpretation of the Scriptures, and, in the case of Catholicism, buttressed by a static conception of natural law.

Derrick Sherwin Bailey's *Homosexuality and the Western Christian Tradition*[13] is the classic work on this topic. Bailey examined "the historical and theological factors which have contributed to the formation of the traditional Western Christian attitude to homosexual practices."[14] He concentrated on the legislation and injunctions of the Bible that bear upon homosexuality[15] and the Roman laws on the subject. He concluded that these were "only the proximate or immediate determinants of the traditional Western view of homosexual practices – those which most readily lend themselves to historical investigation."[16]

Bailey surmised that other, more subtle factors account for the West's hostility toward gay people. For example, he commented favorably upon G. Rattray Taylor's contrasting of patrist and matrist societies on the question of the treatment of homosexuals. Taylor had found that patrist societies tend to be "repressive, authoritarian, conservative, strongly subordinationist in its view of woman, and horrified at homosexual practices," while matrist societies tend to be "liberal, enquiring, democratic, inclined to enhance the status of woman, and tolerant of homosex-

---

Richard Plant, *The Pink Triangle: The Nazi War Against Homosexuals* (New York: Henry Holt and Company, 1986).

12. Posner, *Sex and Reason*, p. 291. Greenberg's, *The Construction of Homosexuality* and John Boswell's *Christianity, Social Tolerance, and Homosexuality: Gay People in Western Europe from the Beginning of the Christian Era to the Fourteenth Century* (Chicago: University of Chicago Press, 1980) offer several important exceptions to Western civilization's historic hostility to homosexuals.

13. (London: Longmans, Green and Co., 1955).

14. Bailey, *Homosexuality. . .*, p. 153.

15. As we will have occasion to see, these are few in number and pose difficult problems for the exegete. See *infra*, pp. 105-109.

16. Bailey, *Homosexuality. . .*, p. 159.

ual practices."[17] In sum, the entire blame for Western Christendom's draconian treatment of homosexual persons cannot be held by its Judeo-Christian foundation alone.[18] Cultural anthropology, sociology, and psychology may play a greater role in producing hostility to homosexuals than one might be inclined to think.[19]

2. THE STONEWALL REBELLION

The centuries-old tradition of hostility and violence against homosexual persons records no concerted effort on their part to join together to protect themselves until one summer's night in 1969.

In the early morning hours of June 28, 1969, an unlikely group of gays broke the cycle of victimization. At the Stonewall Inn, a gay bar in New York's Greenwich Village, they took a forceful and violent stand against police harassment. This night witnessed the beginning of a new moment: the birth of gay *liberation*.[20]

> The riot at the Stonewall Inn sent shock waves through New York's small homophile circles and the wider but inchoate community of uninvolved gay men and women. The shock waves did not end at the city's boundaries. Because of New York's role as the nation's communications center, the riot at the Stonewall Inn was reported and broadcast across the nation. Although much of the news coverage was negative, the startling word of gay people fighting back inspired the formation of new, and newly radical, 'gay liberation' organizations in cities large and small and on university campuses from Berkeley to Harvard.[21]

Rey Rivera was present at the Stonewall Inn when the police entered at about 2 a.m. on Saturday, June 28, 1969. He reports:

---

17. In Bailey, *Homosexuality. . .*, p. 159.

18. One notes that any number of non-Jewish and non-Christian societies have also been unaccepting of homosexuals.

19. See, for example, Joseph Aguero, Laura Bloch, and Donn Byrne, "The Relationships Among Sexual Beliefs, Attitudes, Experience, and Homophobia," in John P. De Cecco, ed., *Bashers, Baiters & Bigots: Homophobia in American Society* (New York: Harrington Park Press, 1985), pp. 95-108.

20. Up to this time, the homophile organizations that existed in the U.S. had been, by and large, conformist. Their goals were to show that homosexual people could be respectable members of American society. They tended to downplay any differences that might be thought to exist between homosexuals and heterosexuals. Above all, they longed to be left alone by society. "Liberation" entails a completely different ideology. Its battle cry, "Gay is Good," would have sounded either impudent or heretical to the members of the older organizations. See John Lauritsen and David Thorstad, *The Early Homosexual Rights Movement, 1864-1935* (New York: Times Change Press, 1974).

21. Marcus, *Making History. . .*, pp. 171-172.

> I don't know if it was the customers or if it was the police, but
> that night everything just clicked. Everybody was like. . . . 'Why
> should we be chastised? Why do we have to pay the Mafia all this
> kind of money to drink in a lousy . . . bar? And still be harassed
> by the police?'[22] It didn't make any sense. . . .

> When they ushered us out, they very nicely put us out the door.
> Then we were standing across the street in Sheridan Square Park.
> But why? Everybody's looking at each other. 'Why do we have to
> keep on putting up with this?' Suddenly, the nickels, dimes, pen-
> nies, and quarters started flying. I threw quarters and pennies and
> whatnot. 'You already got the payoff, and here's some more!'[23]

The police were surprised by the crowd which had gathered: its intentions were not compliant. The police officers themselves retreated into
the Stonewall Inn, whereupon the establishment was bombarded with pro-
jectiles and set on fire. "Reinforcements rescued the shaken officers from
the torched bar, but their work had barely started. Rioting continued far
into the night, with Puerto Rican transvestites and young street people
leading the charges against rows of uniformed police officers and then
withdrawing to regroup in Village alleys and side streets."[24]

Rioting continued through the next evening. That night the New
York Mattachine Society put together a special edition of its newsletter
and "characterized the events, with camp humor, as 'The Hairpin Drop[25]
Heard Round the World.'"[26] John D'Emilio continues:

> It scarcely exaggerated. Before the end of July, women and men
> in New York had formed the Gay Liberation Front, a self-pro-
> claimed revolutionary organization in the style of the New Left.
> Word of the Stonewall riot and GLF spread rapidly among the
> networks of young radicals scattered across the country, and
> within a year gay liberation groups had sprung into existence on
> college campuses and in cities around the nation.[27]

If "Stonewall" brought to the surface gay people's deep frustration
with police harassment and their willingness to fight for the recognition of

---

22. At this time, gay bars were usually owned by the Mafia. The mobsters, who charged
their clientele more than other bar owners, in turn bribed the police for a *laissez-faire* approach. See D'Emilio, *Sexual Politics.* . ., p. 51.

23. "The Drag Queen: Rey 'Sylvia Lee' Rivera," in Marcus, *Making History.* . ., p. 191.

24. D'Emilio, *Sexual Politics.* . ., p. 232.

25. Thomas Michael Thurston, *Homosexuality and Contemporary Catholic Ethical Discussion* (Ann Arbor, MI: U.M.I. Dissertation Services, 1990), p. 281, n. 64, explains that in
the gay argot of the time, "'dropping hairpins' meant dropping clues that one was homosexual."

26. Thurston, *Homosexuality.* . ., p. 281.

27. D'Emilio, *Sexual Politics.* . ., pp. 232-233.

their civil rights, it also represented the death of the operative strategies that had guided the two largest homophile organizations – the Mattachine Society (MS) and the Daughters of Bilitis (DOB).

3. THE MATTACHINE SOCIETY

It is impossible to underestimate the importance of the Second World War in furthering the cause of gay liberation in the United States. Military service brought together gay men and women from across the country.[28] Whereas a young gay adult in a small Midwestern town might have thought that he was the only one of his kind, his "uniqueness" was destroyed upon entering the armed forces. For even though the military intended to keep homosexuals out, its methods were far from effective. John D'Emilio explains:

> Given the patriotic fervor that the war elicited and the stigma attached to a rejection for neuropsychiatric reasons, few gay men willingly declared themselves in order to avoid service. Moreover, the medical questioning averaged only a few minutes in duration and depended upon the most superficial signs of homosexuality. As their means of identification, doctors often relied on body type or recruits' recognition of homosexual slang. In general, only the most effeminate, those with arrest records, or those especially worried about the strain of living in an all-male environment with stringent sanctions against homosexual behavior found themselves rejected because of their sexuality.[29]

The young gay recruit was usually relieved of his fantasy of uniqueness early on:

> The sex-segregated nature of the armed forces raised homosexuality closer to the surface for all military personnel. Soldiers indulged in buffoonery, aping in exaggerated form the social stereotype of the homosexual, as a means of releasing the sexual tensions of life in the barracks. Such behavior was so common that a towel company used the image of a GI mincing with a towel draped around his waist to advertise its product. Army canteens witnessed men dancing with one another, an activity that in peacetime subjected homosexuals to arrest. Crowded into port cities, men on leave or those waiting to be shipped overseas shared

---

28. "The Selective Training and Service Act of 1940 led to the immediate registration of more than 16,400,000 males between the ages of twenty-one and thirty-five. . . . Although the military cast a wide net in order to meet its manpower needs, it preferred men who were young, single or with few dependents: a population group likely to include a disproportionate number of gay men." [D'Emilio, *Sexual Politics*. . ., p. 24.]

29. D'Emilio, *Sexual Politics*. . ., pp. 24-25. [In *ibid.*, D'Emilio also reports that Dr. William Menninger concluded that, "for every homosexual who was referred or came to the Medical Department, there were five or ten who never were detected."]

beds in YMCAs and slept in each other's arms in parks or in the aisles of movie theaters that stayed open to house them. Living in close quarters, not knowing whether they would make it through the war, and depending on one another for survival, men of whatever sexual persuasion formed intense emotional attachments. In this setting, gay men could find one another without attracting undue attention and perhaps even encounter sympathy and acceptance by their heterosexual fellows.[30]

The same dynamic held true for the young lesbian. The Women's Army Corps played a prominent – though unwitting – role in "fostering a lesbian identity and creating friendship networks among gay women."[31] And, the officials in the women's division of the armed forces were equally ill-equipped at screening out lesbian recruits.

Nonetheless, it would be going much too far to claim that the military was supportive of homosexuality or that it usually cast a blind eye on transgressions of the military code. Purges of gay people are well-documented.[32] What ought to be kept in mind is that in spite of the military's antihomosexual policy, "wartime conditions . . . offered a protective covering that facilitated interaction among gay men."[33] And after the war, many homosexual veterans, more secure in their sexual identities and unwilling to renounce their newly-found freedom, decided to remain in the major military ports – particularly New York and Los Angeles. Thomas Thurston describes this dynamic:

> After the War, ports of entry swelled with gay people. For one thing, those stigmatized often found it difficult to return to their home towns and face neighbors and relatives. Furthermore, other veterans were loathe to abandon the freedom they found in the big cities. Gay ghettos fostered camaraderie and openness. Although police harassed . . . (the clients) of gay bars and meeting places, the conflict fostered efforts at collective self-protection by gay people.[34]

One of the first such efforts was the founding of the Mattachine Society (MS).[35] In 1950, in Los Angeles, a small group of gay men[36] – all

---

30. D'Emilio, *Sexual Politics. . .*, pp. 25-26.

31. D'Emilio, *Sexual Politics. . .*, p. 27.

32. See D'Emilio, *Sexual Politics. . .*, pp. 28-30. Randy Shilts' recently published *Conduct Unbecoming: Gays & Lesbians in the U.S. Military* (New York: St. Martin's Press, 1993) offers a host of examples.

33. D'Emilio, *Sexual Politics. . .*, p. 26.

34. Thurston, *Homosexuality. . .*, p. 265.

35. "According to historian John D'Emilio, the name *Mattachine* was taken from mysterious masked medieval figures, who, one of the organization's founders speculated, might

members of the Communist Party or other left-wing groups – came together to discuss the oppression of gay people and the possibility of doing gay community organizing. Chuck Rowland, one of the founders of MS, describes its beginnings:

> We started having regular meetings. We had been saying, 'We'll just have an organization.' And I kept saying, 'What is our theory?' Having been a communist, you've got to work with a theory. 'What is our basic principle that we're building on?' And Harry (Hay) said, 'We are an oppressed cultural minority.' And I said, 'That's exactly it!' That was the first time I know of that gays were referred to as an oppressed cultural minority.[37]

But few homosexuals in the 1950s could conceive of themselves as an oppressed cultural minority. For the most part, they simply did not want minority status. They wanted to be seen as no different than everyone else. They wanted their sex lives to be understood as falling under the rubric of privacy: it's nobody's business what goes on between adults behind closed doors. They were more than willing to keep their sexuality secret, all the while hoping that such a strategy would win them at least tacit protection from discrimination in the workplace and from the more overt forms of social coercion.[38]

The original MS members couldn't have been farther from this grassroots stance. Thurston provides a succinct synopsis of the motivating ideology of the founders:

> Hay and his followers focused on organizing a gay constituency capable of militant cohesive action. As Marxists, they believed injustice was deeply rooted in the structures of society, and therefore they rejected pragmatic, reformist methods. They held that homosexuals' ignorance of the fact that they were a social minority kept homosexuals imprisoned within the dominant culture. Because of this false consciousness, imposed by the hegemonic ideology, homosexuals labelled their eroticism as an individual aberration. Hay and his followers hoped that consciousness-raising would bring homosexuals to recognize their common interests. From their awareness of their status as an oppressed minority, homosexuals could evolve a 'highly ethical homosexual culture,' and 'lead well-adjusted, wholesome, and socially productive lives.' They would thus develop a new pride from participating in the cultural growth and achievements of the homosexual minority.[39]

---

have been homosexuals." [Marcus, *Making History*. . ., p. 26, n. 1.]

36. The founders were Harry Hay, Rudi Gernreich, Bob Hull, Dale Jennings, and Chuck Rowland. See Marcus, *Making History*. . ., p. 32.

37. "The Organizer: Chuck Rowland," in Marcus, *Making History*. . ., p. 32.

38. See Marcus, *Making History*. . ., pp. 32-36.

Chuck Rowland, at the first constitutional convention of MS (1953) made a speech in which he remembers saying: "The time will come when we will march arm in arm, ten abreast down Hollywood Boulevard proclaiming our pride in our homosexuality."[40] He recalls, as well, the less than rousing reception such an idea received: "One of my friends . . . said he almost had a coronary at such an outrageous thought. . . . I deliberately built this speech up to what I hoped would be a rousing climax. I got some applause, but people were more in shock than anything else. To me, it seemed perfectly reasonable."[41]

With such an ideological split, it wasn't long before MS was in crisis. The radical leadership – unable to convince much of the membership of the importance of working toward the day when American society would recognize and accept gay people as equals – found itself out of office after the convention of 1953.[42] MS from that point onward belonged to Harold L. ("Hal") Call.

Hal Call had a modest, though not uncontroversial, agenda. He believed that the one goal worth fighting for was sexual freedom; indeed, to his way of thinking, "gay rights" were identical to "sexual rights." To this day, Call remains a controversial figure. His supporters "admire him for being a tireless advocate of gay sexual freedom in the face of brutal police repression. Others accuse him of stealing the Mattachine Society from its founders and turning it into a sex club and personal profit center."[43]

Under Call, MS adopted an accommodationist position. Gay people should present themselves as unobtrusively as possible; they were to make no waves, ruffle no feathers. In the struggle for (homo)sexual freedom, MS "looked to professionals and to individual efforts rather than mass action to advance . . . (its) cause."[44] Perhaps most significantly, the discussion groups of MS, which had earlier been the basis for consciousness-raising, were now better classified as fulfilling a therapeutic role: members were encouraged to share their difficulties with being gay and with fitting into heterosexual society.[45] MS had lost the vision of its founders; interestingly enough, it also lost many members.[46]

---

39.   Thurston, *Homosexuality. . .*, pp. 268-269.

40.   "The Organizer: Chuck Rowland," in Marcus, *Making History. . .*, p. 34.

41.   "The Organizer: Chuck Rowland," in Marcus, *Making History. . .*, p. 34.

42.   Their undoing was the decision to make MS a fully democratic organization. See Chuck Rowland's account in Marcus, *Making History. . .*, pp. 34 ff.

43.   Marcus, *Making History. . .*, p. 59.

44.   Thurston, *Homosexuality. . .*, p. 271.

45.   See Thurston, *Homosexuality. . .*, p. 271.

46.   In 1953, MS had upwards of 2000 members; by 1960 it had about 200 members. See Thurston, *Homosexuality. . .*, pp. 269, 273.

In a 1992 interview with Eric Marcus, Call explained his side of the story:

> I didn't just disagree with how the original Mattachine was run. I also disagreed with the philosophy of the Mattachine founders. I felt that they were sort of pie in the sky, erudite, and artistically inclined. Take Harry Hay, the kingpin of the original founders. You could never talk to him very long without him going way back in history to some ancient Egyptian cult or something of that sort. He was always making Mattachine and the homosexual of today a parallel to some of those things he found out in his historical research. . . .
>
> We saw Mattachine as a here-and-now, practical thing. . . . I felt that education and getting the word out was the best thing we could do, so the whole society could ultimately say, 'Homosexuals are human beings in our midst. They're only different in certain ways from the rest of us. Leave them alone.' We wanted to see those goals achieved by evolutionary methods, not revolutionary methods. We were pretty pure and bland, really. By today's standards, we were a bunch of limp-wrist pussyfoots. But we were out of the closet, and that was a very courageous thing in those days. . . .[47]

Hay and the other founders of MS had refused to accept the medical establishment's approach to homosexuality.[48] This approach classified homosexuality as a sickness – a mental disorder whose sufferers could be helped by medical treatment.[49] It did not matter to the partisans of the "medicalization of homosexuality"[50] that they were never able to reach a consensus on the etiology of their newly found disease;[51] what was important was believing they could be of help in either curing the disease or in alleviating its most disturbing manifestations.[52]

---

47.   "Gay Sexualist: Hal Call," in Marcus, *Making History. . .*, pp. 62-63.

48.   John Coleman reminds us that in the nineteenth century, medicine had "displaced religion as the key *social* source for defining homosexual orientation and behaviors." See his "The Homosexual Revolution and Hermeneutics," in Gregory Baum and John Coleman, eds., *The Sexual Revolution* [*Concilium*, (June 1984)] (Edinburgh: T. & T. Clark, 1984), p. 55.

49.   The parallel to alcoholism is noted by David F. Greenberg: "In 1852 . . . the Swedish physician Magnus Huss coined the word 'alcoholism,' a new 'disease' that medical research claimed to have discovered; before that there had only been drunkenness, condemned from the pulpit and managed by the policeman. By calling heavy drinking a disease, Huss was reclassifying it as a condition that physicians should treat." See *The Construction of Homosexuality*, p. 403.

50.   See especially Greenberg, *The Construction of Homosexuality*, pp. 397-433.

51.   Like contemporary theorists, which tend to allow for a mysterious admixture of genetic and environmental factors, the progenitors were apt to accept some type of degeneracy theory. Some of these were more weighted toward heredity, others toward social influences. See Greenberg, *The Construction of Homosexuality*, pp. 397-433.

Without the original leadership at the helm and with its new accommodationist strategy, MS was helpless in the face of the medicalization of homosexuality. John D'Emilio describes the scheme that developed:

> Fear, along with the lack of confidence in their own ability to speak with authority about homosexuality, created a crippling dependency. In their search for allies and their quest for legitimacy in the eyes of the establishment, movement leaders often bowed to an apparently superior professional wisdom that was part of the problem they needed to confront. It led them to open their publications to articles classing homosexuals with rapists, child molesters, and exhibitionists as sexual psychopaths, articles arguing that homosexuals were 'almost invariably neurotic or psychotic' and advising gays at least to 'try to get cured.'[53]

4. THE DAUGHTERS OF BILITIS

Although they were always a relatively small minority, women had been members of MS from the beginning. With the change of leadership in 1953 and the turn toward focusing primarily on sexual freedom, the lesbian contingent felt more and more left out.[54] The scene was set for the founding of an organization specifically for lesbians.

In 1955 in San Francisco, a group of four lesbian couples formed a group which they called the Daughters of Bilitis (DOB).[55] The inspiration came primarily from one of the couples: Del Martin and Phyllis Lyon. Their vision was for an organization which would help to educate the public and provide support and answers for lesbians. Billie Tallmij,[56] an early member of DOB, describes its earliest objectives:

---

52.   From our vantage point, much of this "help" appears to be quackery. See, for instance, "The Therapy of C. M. Otis (1911)," in Martin Duberman, *About Time: Exploring the Gay Past* (New York: Meridian, 1991), pp. 80-88; and Jonathan Ned Katz, *Gay American History: Lesbians and Gay Men in the U. S. A. A Documentary History* (New York: Meridian, 1992), pp. 129-208. [Among other things, Katz documents the use of electroshock therapy in attempts to "cure" homosexuals. This type of therapy was in use well into the 1960s.]

53.   D'Emilio, *Sexual Politics. . .*, p. 125. We shall see below (pp. 18-19) how the tables were turned on the medical establishment with the revolutionary experiments and analyses of Dr. Evelyn Hooker.

54.   Indeed, as D'Emilio makes clear, many lesbians wished to distance themselves from their gay brothers. DOB, for instance, would find "gay male promiscuity and the police harassment that accompanied it an encumbrance that seemed to make lesbians guilty by association in the eyes of society." See *Sexual Politics. . .*, p. 105.

55.   Marcus explains the allusion: Bilitis was the "heroine of the fictional *Song of Bilitis*, which was written by the late nineteenth century author Pierre Louys, who portrayed Bilitis as a sometime lesbian and contemporary of Sappho." See *Making History. . .*, p. 70.

56.   Billie Tallmij is a pseudonym.

The better known the Daughters became, the more letters and phone calls we got. We had people in Podunk, Iowa, writing letters that would break your heart. 'Here I am. I'm the only one in the world. What do I do? How do I make contact? Where do I find people? Who can I talk to? What books can I read?' Every one of them felt like she was the only voice crying out in the wilderness.

If the Daughters did nothing else – and we did a lot else – we were able to bring some sense of solace to these women. Just knowing that we were there would sometimes keep them from cracking up or from suicide. I talked more than one person out of suicide in those early days. The women were so frightened because they didn't understand why they were so . . . different from everybody else.[57]

Despite the antagonisms that existed between gay women and men, the DOB did collaborate from time to time with MS. One of the most significant examples of this collaboration was with the publication of *The Ladder*, the DOB's newsletter.[58]

Like MS, the DOB adopted a strictly accommodationist approach. The political atmosphere, highly charged by the machinations of Senator Joseph McCarthy,[59] did not seem to admit of any other tactic. Even into the 1960s, the DOB held to this policy.[60]

5. EARLY SUCCESSES ON THE LEGAL FRONT

Before the Stonewall riots, the GLM – as exemplified in the efforts of MS and the DOB – knew some significant successes. Many of them, of course, were inchoate: they would come to fruition many years later. Others were incapable of being fully appreciated: the support a young, suici-

---

57. "The Teacher: Billie Tallmij," in Marcus, *Making History. . .*, pp. 75-76.

58. Although *The Ladder* was the newsletter of the first lesbian organization, it was not the first lesbian newsletter. That distinction goes to *Vice Versa*. In 1947, Lisa Ben (a pseudonym) single-handedly published the newsletter from her office typewriter and distributed it to a circle of friends. See "'Gay Gal' – Lisa Ben," in Marcus, *Making History. . .*, pp. 5-15.

59. It is a little-known fact that during the "McCarthy era," more people lost their jobs for allegedly being homosexual than those who were accused of communist sympathies. See D'Emilio, *Sexual Politics. . .*, chapter 3: "The Bonds of Oppression: Gay Life in the 1950s," pp. 40-56.

60. The DOB even had a dress code for its members who wished to join pickets or other protests. Members had to wear dresses or skirts. Barbara Gittings explains: "We decided that we were the bearers of a message. To keep attention on the message, not on ourselves, we had to look unexceptional and blend into the landscape. So the order went out, and everybody followed it. The stirrings to disobey the dress code didn't really come up until 1969." See "The Rabble Rousers: Barbara Gittings and Kay Lahusen," in Marcus, *Making History. . .*, p. 123.

dal gay person found in *The Ladder* or the *Mattachine Review*; the impact a picket or a protest might have had on those who witnessed it; or the undocumented acts of courage that were inspired by the knowledge that two fledgling gay organizations had been established "out there" in California.[61]

One of the first and most fundamental successes concerned the legal protection of the publications of the gay organizations. It was illegal to send obscene material through the mail; anything that mentioned homosexuality in a favorable light was generally regarded as obscene. John D'Emilio describes the successful challenge made against this position by the editors of *ONE* magazine:[62]

> In October 1954 the Los Angeles postmaster seized copies of *ONE* and refused to mail the magazine on the grounds that it was 'obscene, lewd, lascivious and filthy.' The editors decided to contest the government's view. In 1956 a federal district judge sustained the postmaster's action, and the following year, an appeals court dealt *ONE* another blow when it characterized the magazine as 'cheap pornography.' But in January 1958 the United States Supreme Court unanimously reversed the findings of the lower courts. . . . (From then on) homophile publications escaped any further legal action by postal authorities or local law enforcement agencies.[63]

The homophile organizations also made progress in overcoming police harassment of gay and lesbian bars and the entrapment strategies of some police departments. Herb Selwyn, one of the first lawyers who worked for MS, recounts a case that reveals one aspect of what gay liberation was up against in the early years of the movement:

> I'll never forget one case in the late fifties, in which the state tried to revoke the license of a hairdresser, a cosmetologist, for being gay. I think the hairdresser had a lewd conduct arrest for propositioning an undercover policeman or something like that. But it was a misdemeanor, and it wasn't something that affected his work. It wasn't as if he was a crook or a person who might

---

61. It bears noting that the groups were covered by San Francisco's mainline press in the 1950s – albeit unfavorably. More objective reporting became the trend as the 1960s began. *Life* magazine's exposé on gay life in San Francisco (June 26, 1964) ought to be seen as the definitive break with the national media's decades-old "conspiracy of silence" concerning homosexuality. [See D'Emilio, *Sexual Politics. . .*, pp. 120-122, 159-160, 165, 195.]

62. *ONE* was the brainchild of Martin Block, a disaffected member of the MS. "Writers in *ONE* magazine projected an image of defiant pride in their identity; they intentionally tried to shake their readers out of a resigned acceptance of the status quo." [D'Emilio, *Sexual Politics. . .*, p. 108; see also "The Editor: Martin Block," in Marcus, *Making History. . .*, pp. 37-42.]

63. D'Emilio, *Sexual Politics. . .*, p. 115.

assault somebody. It was simply that he was a homosexual, and therefore the prosecutor believed he should be stripped of his cosmetologist's license.

When we got to court, I suggested to the administrative law judge, who I knew was a married man, that he should ask his wife how many of the male hairdressers she had gone to in her life she thought might be gay. And I jokingly asked him how all of our wives and girlfriends would look if all the gay hairdressers had their licenses removed. He chuckled at that one. The prosecutor frowned. The whole thing was very amusing, but not for the poor guy whose license was at stake. . . . If he had lost his license, it would have caused a great deal of harm to him and to the people who depended on him.[64]

Probably the most significant legal battle began in 1957 when Frank Kameny was dismissed by the United States Army Map Service because of his homosexuality. Kameny was a Ph.D. in astronomy from Harvard University. "Within the small pre-NASA world of professional astronomers, everyone knew Frank was a homosexual;"[65] he would never again be able to work in his field of specialization.

Kameny decided to fight his firing. He recalls his thinking at the time and the eventual outcome of his struggle:

I had decided that my dismissal amounted to a declaration of war against me by my government. First, I don't grant my government the right to declare war against me. And second, I tend not to lose my wars. So that started an eighteen-year war, which is this country's longest. It was fought by every possible means and ultimately ended on July 3, 1975, when the then-Civil Service Commission issued its surrender documents – in the form of a news release – saying, in effect, but not in these words, that the government was changing its policy to suit me. The commission said that they would no longer exclude homosexuals from government employment.[66]

Part and parcel of Kameny's war was his founding the Washington, D.C., chapter of the Mattachine Society in November 1961. The Washington MS, unlike most other chapters and unlike the official leadership of MS, did not adopt an accommodationist approach; it refused to be bullied by the prevailing "sickness discourse" of the medical profession; it saw itself as "the homosexual equivalent of the National Association for the Advancement of Colored People, and decided to adopt the strategies of the Southern Christian Leadership Conference: demonstrations and picket-

---

64. "The Attorney: Herb Selwyn," in Marcus, *Making History. . .*, p. 57.
65. Marcus, *Making History. . .*, p. 93.
66. "The Very Mad Scientist: Frank Kameny," in Marcus, *Making History. . .*, pp. 94-95.

ing."[67] In many ways the Washington MS was a precursor to the more militant wing of the GLM which was to appear after Stonewall.

6. CONFRONTATION WITH THE MEDICAL ESTABLISHMENT

Thomas Thurston, following the lead of Ronald Bayer's *Homosexuality and American Psychiatry: The Politics of Diagnosis*,[68] advances the notion that "the gay rights movement created the conditions for the human sciences to view homosexuality more positively."[69] This conviction is certainly true when it comes to discussing the role of Dr. Evelyn Hooker in the nascent gay liberation movement.

Evelyn Hooker's "The Adjustment of the Overt Male Homosexual"[70] sounded the death knell for the conceptualization of homosexuality as a mental disorder. Her experiment was strikingly simple: she found 30 gay men (who were not in therapy) and then matched them with 30 heterosexual men for age, education, and I.Q. These 60 men were given a standard battery of psychological tests and were asked to give a considerable amount of information about their life histories. Hooker then gave the test results to several of her colleagues and asked them to analyze the data with an eye to determining who were the homosexuals and who were the heterosexuals. These colleagues, skilled in reading test results, could not accomplish the task with any degree of accuracy. Hooker concluded that "there is no inherent connection between homosexual orientation and clinical symptoms of mental illness."[71]

Gay liberation simply could not have had any success without the work of Evelyn Hooker and those that have followed in her steps. Psychiatry's labelling of gays and lesbians as "sick" kept them from social participation and social equality better than any civil statute had ever been able to do.

The story that must be told, according to Dr. Hooker, is that the inspiration to do her ground-breaking study came from a gay couple, "Sammy" and "George." On Thanksgiving Day, 1945, Sammy and George invited Hooker and her husband to San Francisco's "Finocchio's," to see the female impersonators' show. . . .

> After the show, we came back to the Fairmont Hotel on Nob Hill
> for a snack. I was unprepared for what came next. Sammy turned

---

67. Thurston, *Homosexuality*. . ., p. 274.

68. (New York: Basic Books, 1981).

69. Thurston, *Homosexuality*. . ., p. 306.

70. In *The Journal of Projective Techniques*, 21 (1957), pp. 1-31.

71. Quoted in Martin Hoffman, "Homosexual," in *Psychology Today*, 3 (1969), p. 43; cited by Donald Goergen, *The Sexual Celibate* (Garden City, NY: Image Books, 1979), pp. 101-102.

to me and said, 'We have let you see us as we are, and now it is your scientific duty to make a study of people like us.' Imagine that! This bright young man, somewhere in his early thirties, had obviously been thinking about this for a long time. And by 'people like us' he meant, 'We're homosexual, but we don't need psychiatrists. We don't need psychologists. We're not insane. We're not any of those things they say we are.'[72]

Dr. Hooker continues:

I had a colleague with whom I shared an office. . . . His name was Bruno Klopfer. Bruno was one of the world's greatest experts on the Rorschach test. So I went to Bruno and I told him about this suggestion. He jumped out of his chair and said, 'You must do it, Eee-vah-leeeen! You must do it! Your friend is absolutely right. We don't know anything about people like him. The only ones we know about are the people who come to us as patients. And, of course, many of those who come to us are very disturbed, pathological. You must do it!' So I told Bruno I would do it. Bruno later served in my research as a judge. Unfortunately, Sammy was killed in a tragic automobile accident and never learned the outcome of what he urged me to do.[73]

Because of the trust and the persistence of one gay man and the tireless and meticulous work of one psychologist, homosexuality would eventually be removed from the American Psychiatric Association's *Diagnostic and Statistical Manual of Mental Disorders*. "Gay men and women no longer had to live with the burden of the abhorrent official 'sickness' label."[74]

7. COURTING THE CHRISTIAN CHURCHES

Three institutions in modern Western society had effectively demonized homosexuality: law, medicine, and religion. The early leaders of the GLM targeted all three. We have seen some of the effects on the legal and medical fronts. We now move to a discussion of the dialogue initiated with the Christian churches.

In 1964 the Council on Religion and the Homosexual (CRH) was founded in San Francisco. This organization was the joint effort of the

---

72. "The Psychologist: Dr. Evelyn Hooker," in Marcus, *Making History*. . ., p. 18.

73. "The Psychologist: Dr. Evelyn Hooker," in Marcus, *Making History*. . ., p. 19.

74. Marcus, *Making History*. . ., p. 173. The decision of the APA to remove homosexuality from its list of mental disorders was hotly contested and the object of much political maneuvering. Bayer's *Homosexuality and American Psychiatry* includes a frank discussion of the gay community's efforts in lobbying the APA to change its official designation of homosexuality as a sickness.

MS, the DOB, and several Christian congregations in the city. Billie Tallmij remembers the initial meeting:

> With Mattachine, we (the DOB) wrote to as many ministers as we could from as many different faiths as existed. We got representatives from the Episcopalians, the Quakers, and the Baptists. We held the conference in Marin over a three-day weekend. We had about twenty gays. . .and seven women. . . . Del (Martin) and I deliberately arranged it so all the participants were brought there and dropped off. We did it that way so no one could leave. To put it bluntly, they came to convert us, and we came to convert them.[75]

The upshot was that a remarkable dialogue was initiated. Most of the ministers had never had someone say to them, "I am a homosexual;" most found that they needed more understanding of the reality of homosexuality. The eagerness of the church representatives is probably best explained by an admixture of evangelical outreach and the ambience of the burgeoning civil rights movement. The cause of racial justice in American society provided a ready-made paradigm for gay and lesbian liberation; society's complicity in injustice was *the* insight of the age.

The MS and the DOB were able to capitalize upon this prevailing *Zeitgeist*. Tallmij recounts a particularly successful strategy:

> . . .we took some of these ministers to some of the gay bars. We started with the pits – these places were toilets; they were filthy – and then we moved up to some of the better ones. Our point was, 'Because you will not allow us to be open, this is where we have to meet. Would you bring your wife here? Would you want your son to go here? Do you know that your son isn't going here?' It really jarred the living hell out of a lot of them.[76]

One of the first ministers to reconsider his church's moral evaluation of homosexuality in light of his involvement with CRH was the Episcopalian priest, Robert Warren Cromey.[77] Cromey was also deeply offended by the police harassment of homosexual people (harassment that he witnessed even on the occasion of a social gathering of the CRH) and the necessity most gays and lesbians felt for keeping their true identities hidden. His

---

75. "The Teacher: Billie Tallmij," in Marcus, *Making History. . .*, p. 78. The question of who initiated the first contact is discussed in D'Emilio, *Sexual Politics. . .*, pp. 192 ff. It seems clear that the honor goes to the Reverend Ted McIlvenna, assistant at Glide Memorial Methodist Church. In 1962, McIlvenna had contacted the MS in an effort to get help in understanding the issues surrounding sexual identity: in his social outreach ministry he had encountered a number of gay male runaways who were involved in street hustling.

76. "The Teacher: Billie Tallmij," in Marcus, *Making History. . .*, p. 79.

77. See Robert Warren Cromey, *In God's Image: Christian Witness to the Need for Gay/Lesbian Equality in the Eyes of the Church* (San Francisco: Alamo Square Press, 1991).

first-hand experience with CRH and his ministry with gay people as rector of Trinity Episcopal Church in San Francisco no doubt greatly influenced his ability to make the following statement:

> I am outraged that so many people in our society and Church hate 'faggots, queers, and dykes.' My stomach turns when I hear Christian people condemn homosexuality as a sin and homosexual people as perverts. I weep when I think of the long road ahead for full freedom. I pray for the souls of my fellow church people who continue to block full freedom for God's children who were given the gift of being drawn in loving and sexual communion with people of the same gender.[78]

Beginning in the late 1960s, many Protestant churches began a reappraisal of the traditional condemnation of homosexuality. One commentator argues that this reappraisal was based on three basic criteria:

> First, a better informed pastoral care had revealed much unnecessary suffering. Second, the issues of civil rights could not be ignored. Third, even though scholarly work on the tradition was small in quantity, it pointed in the direction of inadequate scholarly bases for the traditional positions.[79]

To speak of "traditional positions" on homosexuality in Protestantism is to speak almost exclusively of the traditional interpretations of the handful of biblical texts which deal with homosexuality. Derrick Sherwin Bailey's seminal study, *Homosexuality and the Western Christian Tradition* raised what for many would become *the* critical question for biblical hermeneutics: How could the biblical authors have condemned realities which would come into existence only centuries later?[80] The biblical authors were cognizant of a limited range of homosexual behaviors: pederasty (following the Greek pedagogical model)[81] or male prostitution (rit-

---

78. Cromey, *In God's Image. . .*, pp. 19-20.

79. S. Hiltner, "Homosexuality and the Churches," in J. Marmor, ed., *Homosexual Behavior: A Modern Reappraisal* (New York: Basic Books, 1980), pp. 222-223. Cited in Robert Nugent and Jeannine Gramick, "Homosexuality: Protestant, Catholic, and Jewish Issues; A Fishbone Tale," in R. Hasbany, ed., *Homosexuality and Religion* (New York: Haworth Press, 1989), p. 15.

80. In reference to the anti-homosexual verses in the Pauline corpus, Bailey asks: "(D)o the Apostle's strictures apply to the homosexual acts of the genuine invert, and in particular to those physical expressions of affection which may take place between two persons of the same sex who affirm that they are 'in love'? To such situations it can hardly be said that the New Testament speaks, since the condition of inversion, with all its special problems, was quite unknown at that time." See Bailey, *Homosexuality. . .*, p. 157.

81. The definitive study is K. J. Dover, *Greek Homosexuality* (Cambridge, MA: Harvard University Press, 1989).

ual or not).[82] They show no awareness of the "homosexual orientation" or that adult persons of the same sex might share an intimate relationship marked by mutuality, erotic passion, tenderness, and fidelity.

Robin Scroggs, in his magisterial *The New Testament and Homosexuality,* offers the following conclusion on the "homosexuality" that would have been known to the authors of the New Testament:

> I do not wish to . . . force all male homosexual activities in the Greco-Roman world to a simple form of pederasty. Obviously there were many different avenues pederasty could and did take, and, no doubt, many subtle nuances in concrete cases that would never be reflected in our texts. Nor do I wish the syllogism to be: All homosexuality was pederastic; all pederasty was constitutive of inequality and thus evil; therefore all homosexuality was evil. I do not doubt that friendships of good passion and tender caring existed. I *am* suggesting that if we interpret pederasty supplely enough to include the continuation of that model into these borderline cases, then it is certain that pederasty was the only *model* in existence in the world of this time. That proposed by twentieth-century gay liberation movements was, without question, entirely absent.[83]

This type of historical-critical interpretation, with an emphasis on social and cultural contexts, has played an immense role in the liberalizing of the stances on homosexuality in mainline Protestantism. It would no longer be possible to say that 'the Bible has taken care of the problem once and for all.' This factor, added to a growing willingness of religious people to enter into dialogue with gays and lesbians, ensured that changes would be forthcoming in the official positions of several Christian churches.

It is beyond our scope to present detailed documentation on the changes that have occurred in American Protestantism's moral evaluation of homosexual behavior. Let Gabriel Moran's remarks provide a summary statement for the broad lines of the developments:

> Until about 1970 there was almost total silence. With the emergence of a gay rights movement, one wing of Christianity turned vocally negative. The only difference today is that their condemnation has become more strident. A visitor from another planet listening to these preachers would assume that homosexuality is listed as the number one sin in the New Testament.
>
> In the rest of Christianity much of the writing moved to a second stage. Here it is said that gays should not be treated badly or le-

---

82. Tom Horner, *Jonathan Loved David: Homosexuality in Biblical Times* (Philadelphia: Westminster Press, 1978), pp. 90-99, provides a thorough discussion of male prostitution in New Testament times.

83. Robin Scroggs, *The New Testament and Homosexuality: Contextual Background for Contemporary Debate* (Philadelphia: Fortress Press, 1983), p. 139.

gally harassed – despite their acting contrary to God's will. A third stage that seems to have arrived in some quarters removes gay sex from the paragraph listing sexual problems. These books acknowledge that an aspect of some people's lives is their homosexual orientation. There is fourth stage, which I find in no textbooks but which is suggested by some writers today. They would view homosexuality as a necessary corrective to present heterosexual attitudes. The human race will never understand power, love, and transcendence so long as it fails to embrace gay sexuality.[84]

Most mainline Protestant churches in the United States are somewhere between stages two and three. While one would be hard put to find the leadership of any major Protestant denomination advocating discrimination against gay people, to find a Protestant minister who would agree (say) to bless publicly a gay union may be just as difficult.[85] The Moravian Church, The Friends ("Quakers")[86] and the United Universalist Association are among the few denominations which have "endorsed same-sex genital expressions as fully compatible with Christian morality and human sexuality."[87] Most Protestant churches find themselves in the same situation as the Lutheran Church in America (LCA) – continuing to study the many interrelated issues.

The LCA issued a study document on homosexuality – "A Study of Issues Concerning Homosexuality" – in 1986. This study acknowledged that the church is in an interim situation as regards homosexuality, and, "far from being able to instruct the world about the meaning of homosexuality," the LCA "finds itself with the world struggling to understand and to know where to praise and where to judge."[88] The interim nature of the church's reflection was reaffirmed strikingly in 1987 at the LCA's national convention: The governing board determined that the local churches

---

84. Gabriel Moran, "Education: Sexual and Religious," in Robert Nugent, ed., *A Challenge to Love: Gay and Lesbian Catholics in the Church* (New York: Crossroad, 1989), pp. 161-162. It is to be noted that Moran's discussion is not limited to American Protestantism. His remarks concern the entire Christian reality in the United States.

85. A striking exception is John Shelby Spong, the Episcopal bishop of Newark, New Jersey. He writes: "If they (a gay couple) want to have a liturgy, a service, in which the holiness of their relationship is liturgically proclaimed in the company of people with whom they're comfortable, then I'm willing to do that for them." See "The Bishop: John Shelby Spong," in Marcus, *Making History. . .*, p. 498.

86. See especially Alastair Heron, ed., *Toward a Quaker View of Sex* (London: Friends Home Service Committee, 1963). This work was remarkable – and shocking – for its time. It proposed that mutual love, commitment, and fidelity are the only categories by which a Christian's sexual relationship ought to be judged. It was posited, therefore, that some homosexual relationships could be judged morally good.

87. Nugent and Gramick, "A Fishbone Tale," p. 26.

88. Quoted in Nugent and Gramick, "A Fishbone Tale," p. 24.

should be given the authority to decide whether or not they will ordain homosexual candidates for the ministry.[89]

There are a number of religious organizations that have been established along denominational lines for gay and lesbian Protestants. Among these groups are Affirmation (United Methodist), American Baptists Concerned, Brethren/Mennonite Council for Gay Concerns, Evangelical Outreach Ministries, Evangelicals Concerned, Friends for Lesbian and Gay Concerns (Quakers), Lutherans Concerned/North America, Presbyterians for Gay/Lesbian Concerns, and the United Lesbian and Gay Christian Scientists.[90] The existence of a support group ought not to be taken as evidence that a particular denomination's leadership has ruled that homosexual behavior can be undertaken morally. Such is most likely *not* the case. What is important to note is that in mainline Protestantism a great deal of pastoral leeway exists for ministering to gay men and lesbians. The above organizations have not had to deal with the same kind of challenges that Dignity and New Ways Ministry (NWM) have had to face from members of the American Catholic hierarchy.[91]

8. CONCLUSION: WHAT DO GAYS AND LESBIANS WANT?

The goals of the contemporary GLM are not easily synthesized. "Gay liberation" is, in the end, an umbrella term which comprises many groups with potentially conflicting ideologies, value systems, and general aims. In the early years of the movement, many were satisfied with working toward the day when gay people would be "left alone," when their same-sex attraction and (private) sexual practices would have no bearing on their participation in American society. After the Stonewall Rebellion, however, the movement took on a more radical mentality; social tolerance would no longer be enough. "Lesbians and gay men wanted to be recognized as equal to heterosexuals in their sexuality, creativity, and social usefulness."[92]

At our present historical juncture, the goals of the GLM can be generalized to include the following five points:

(1) an end to all forms of social control of homosexuals;
(2) civil rights legislation to prevent housing and job discrimination;

89. See Nugent and Gramick, "A Fishbone Tale," p. 24.

90. See Richard Woods, O.P., *Another Kind of Love: Homosexuality and Spirituality* [Third edition] (Ft. Wayne, IN: Knoll Publishing, 1988), pp. 189-191.

91. Jeannine Gramick and Robert Nugent, co-founders of NWM, detail the difficulties they faced in establishing NWM and in staging some of its programs in *Building Bridges: Gay & Lesbian Reality and the Catholic Church* (Mystic, CT: Twenty-Third Publications, 1992), pp. 195-207. Bishop Francis Mugavero's "Withdrawing Support from Certain Homosexual Groups" [in *Origins*, 16 (1987), p. 651] is a good example for the problematic nature of Dignity's relationship with some members of the American hierarchy.

92. Cruikshank, *The Gay and Lesbian Liberation Movement*, p. 9.

(3) repeal of sodomy laws;

(4) acceptance of lesbian and gay relationships;

(5) accurate portrayal in the mass media.[93]

From the vantage point of the contemporary American Catholic Church, all of these points are controversial. Although one would be hard-pressed to find official Catholic support for imprisoning – or even fining – those who indulge in private, adult to adult, consensual, homosexual relations, one is not going to find many Catholic leaders demanding that sodomy laws be repealed. Indeed, one might find them arguing that it is best to keep such laws in place – even if they're unenforceable – because they send a necessary message to society at large concerning the immorality of homosexual practices.

Points 1, 4, and 5 are even more contentious. The moral tradition of the Catholic Church is at odds with a completely secularist[94] understanding of human sexual relating. The Church cannot bless the "sexual freedom movement" (for lack of a better term) if its only ethical norm is the mutual consent of all involved parties.

"Acceptance" of gay and lesbian relationships is an ambiguous concept. For some, it might mean that gay couples ought to receive all the socio-economic benefits that are afforded married couples. For others, it entails equating moral qualms over gay relationships with the basest forms of bigotry. On this reading, gay people are not merely to be tolerated, they are to be affirmed precisely in reference to their sexual selves. In other words, the message is: "Love me; love my (sexual) lifestyle."[95] Nothing short of a theological paradigm shift (the likes of which one cannot even begin to fathom) could move the Church to "accept" gay and lesbian relationships if "acceptance" is so defined.[96]

The fifth point is not without its own set of difficulties. What is to count as an "accurate" portrayal of gays and lesbians? For that matter, what is an accurate portrayal of heterosexually-oriented people? The gay

---

93. Cruikshank, *The Gay and Lesbian Liberation Movement*, p. 9. (It should be noted that while not strictly pertaining to "liberation," most every contemporary gay and lesbian organization strongly advocates AIDS education, research, funding, etc.)

94. "Materialist" or "rationalist" can be readily substituted here.

95. See the editorial "Live & Let Live," in *Commonweal*, 120 (January 15, 1993), p. 4.

96. Archbishop John Quinn pulled no punches on this issue in his commentary on the C.D.F.'s "Letter to the Bishops of the Catholic Church on the Pastoral Care of Homosexual Persons:" ". . .those who entertain the hope that the Church will alter its moral teaching on homosexuality or that it can be forced to do so through various forms of pressure are soaring into the realms of fantasy." See "Toward an Understanding of the Letter 'On the Pastoral Care of Homosexual Persons,' " in Jeannine Gramick and Pat Furey, eds., *The Vatican and Homosexuality: Reactions to the "Letter to the Bishops of the Catholic Church on the Pastoral Care of Homosexual Persons"* (New York: Crossroad, 1988), p. 15.

and lesbian experience is as varied as human experience itself: it includes people of every conceivable background; it includes people with the moral sensibilities of a Neanderthal, of a Gandhi, and everything betwixt and between. On this point, one gets the impression that the GLM's definition of an "accurate portrayal" is anything that presents gay people and homosexuality in a positive and affirming manner.

The bulk of this present study will be concerned with the second goal as enunciated by Cruikshank: "civil rights legislation to prevent housing and job discrimination." We will attempt to show that not only is this plank of the GLM compatible with Catholic moral teaching, it ought to be accepted by the Catholic conscience as normative. In other words, contemporary Catholicism ought to bear witness to the unacceptability of social and economic discrimination against gay people.

CHAPTER TWO

The Secular Debate on Gay and Lesbian Rights

In the preceding chapter, it became clear that one of the strategies of the GLM involved entering into a dialogue on the issues surrounding homosexuality with representatives of the legal profession, the medical establishment, and organized religion. The hope was that this dialogue would eventually succeed in softening American society's negative attitudes toward gay people. If laws could be changed, if gays and lesbians could get a clean bill of mental health, and if homosexuality could be proclaimed a natural variant in God's good creation, then, it was felt, the ancient fears and hatreds of heterosexual culture would fade into acceptance and appreciation.

It hardly needs commenting that the longed for acceptance and appreciation have not been completely forthcoming. For one thing, not all the laws have been changed; not all the members of the medical profession have assented to the APA's decision to remove homosexuality from its list of mental disorders; few Christian denominations can use the terms "gay" and "good" in the same utterance. The GLM has faced numerous obstacles – not the least of which has been the AIDS epidemic.[1]

---

1.   It is impossible to completely account for the impact of AIDS on the GLM. One statistic, however, is telling: since 1980, 91,789 gay and bisexual men have died from AIDS. [See Bill Turque, et al, "Gays Under Fire," in *Newsweek* (September 14, 1992), p. 39.] The sheer loss of manpower is staggering. Moreover, whereas AIDS has brought out the very best in some people, it has also brought out some of the most vicious examples of human behavior. For every member of society who feels sympathy for a gay man who is HIV positive, there are still significant numbers who would claim that he got exactly what he was asking for. [Richard Davenport-Hines' "Hurting Others: AIDS," in his *Sex, Death, and Punishment: Attitudes to Sex and Sexuality in Britain Since the Renaissance* (Glasgow: William Collins Sons, 1990), pp. 330-383, offers a thoughtful discussion of the dynamics involved in blaming the homosexual community for the appearance of the AIDS virus.]

1. CONTEMPORARY U.S. ATTITUDES ON GAY LIBERATION

Nevertheless, the idea that the vast majority of Americans either fear or hate gay people cannot be substantiated. All impressions to the contrary notwithstanding, the American people have accepted bits and pieces of the GLM's objectives. Much ambivalence, however, remains. Bill Turque describes this ambivalence as a feeling of being "torn between a basic impulse to be tolerant and a visceral discomfort with gay culture."[2]

On an issue that has traditionally been paramount for gay and lesbian political organizations – equal rights in job opportunities and job protection – Americans believe, by an overwhelming majority,[3] that sexual orientation should not figure in the equation. It is interesting to note that when pushed to be specific, a majority feel that most occupations should allow homosexuals into their ranks.[4] Most Americans are opposed to discriminating against their fellow gay and lesbian citizens in the marketplace.

Other gay issues touching upon the marketplace also find a significant level of support among Americans. The majority support health insurance and social security coverage for gay "spouses" (67% to 27% and 58% to 35% respectively) and inheritance rights for same-sex partners (70% to 25%). However, the American public is still unwilling to allow the legal sanctioning of "gay marriages" (58% to 35%) and is opposed to adoption rights for homosexual couples (61% to 32%).[5] In the face of these statistics, it seems safe to say that Americans are willing to admit that gay men and lesbians have been – and continue to be – the victims of injustice in American society. At the same time, most do not believe that society's heterosexual norm is unjust; it is not unfair, in other words, to restrict the definition of marriage to one man/one woman. Concurrently, since homosexuality is still so little understood, it seems best to reserve adoption and child-rearing to heterosexual couples. But, all things being equal, it is clear that Jerry Falwell's "national battle plan" to oppose gay rights with its rallying cry – "We must awaken to their wicked agenda for America!"[6] – is not attractive to most Americans.

The GLM has effected modest changes on the state and local fronts. At present there are 23 states which have overturned their anti-sodomy

---

2. Turque, et. al., "Gays Under Fire," p. 36.

3. I.e., 78% to 17%. See Turque, et. al., "Gays Under Fire," p. 36.

4. And so, according to the *Newsweek* poll, 83% saw no problem with hiring homosexuals as salespersons; 64% thought that they could be a member of the president's cabinet; 59% saw no reason why they shouldn't be allowed into military service or in the medical profession; 54% would welcome gays and lesbians as high-school teachers; 51% for elementary-school teachers. See Turque, et. al., "Gays Under Fire," p. 36.

5. See Turque, et. al., "Gays Under Fire," p. 37.

6. Quoted by Turque, et. al., "Gays Under Fire," p. 37.

laws; "six states and about 110 municipalities have statutes barring discrimination against gays."[7] Nowhere are "gay marriages" recognized, but about a dozen cities provide some sort of benefit package for the same-sex partners of city employees.[8] "A handful of private companies, including Levi Strauss and software giant Lotus Development, provide health benefits to gay partners."[9]

However, without a federal law barring discrimination on the basis of sexual orientation, "homosexuals have little legal recourse against even blatant bias."[10] In many places in the United States, there is nothing to protect gays and lesbians from losing their jobs, from being evicted from their homes, or from being denied a bank loan because of their sexual orientation.[11]

In this, the experience of Cheryl Summerville is telling. Bob Cohn explains:

> She was among a dozen or more gay and lesbian workers fired last year from a Cracker Barrel restaurant, a chain with headquarters in Tennessee. Out of the blue, the company announced that it would no longer employ people 'whose sexual preferences fail to demonstrate normal heterosexual values which have been the foundation of families in our society.' With no gay anti-discrimination laws on the Georgia books, even the ACLU refused to represent Summerville in court. 'What do you mean, I don't have a case?,' she asked them. 'How can they do this to me?'[12]

Since the Second World War, homosexuals have been explicitly barred from serving in the United States Armed Forces; the military's records show that about 1000 gay men and lesbians are expelled each year after their sexual orientation comes to light.[13] The rationale for this overt discrimination is found in the following policy statement from the U.S. Department of Defense:

> Homosexuality is incompatible with military service. The presence in the military environment of persons who engage in homosexual conduct or who, by their statements, demonstrate a propen-

---

7. Bob Cohn, "Discrimination: The Limits of the Law," in *Newsweek* (September 14, 1992), p. 38.

8. Among these are San Francisco, Seattle, and Ithaca, New York. See Cohn, "Discrimination. . .," p. 38.

9. Cohn, "Discrimination. . .," p. 38.

10. Cohn, "Discrimination. . .," p. 38.

11. See William B. Rubenstein, ed., *Lesbians, Gay Men, and the Law* (New York: The New Press, 1993) for a masterful accounting of the legal difficulties gays and lesbians continue to face in many American locales.

12. Cohn, "Discrimination. . .," p. 39.

13. See Cohn, "Discrimination. . .," p. 39.

sity to engage in homosexual conduct, seriously impairs the accomplishment of the military mission. The presence of such members adversely affects the ability of the military services to maintain discipline, good order, and morale; to foster mutual trust and confidence among service members; to insure the integrity of the system of rank and command; to facilitate assignment and worldwide deployment of service members who frequently must live and work under close conditions affording minimal privacy; to recruit and retain members of the military services; to maintain the public acceptability of military service; and to prevent breaches of security.[14]

Under this policy, gay people must lie about their sexual orientation if they wish to be inducted into the Army, Navy, Air Force, Marines, Coast Guard, or college campus ROTC (Reserve Officer Training Corps) programs. "Many do lie in order to serve, and military investigators vigorously seek out and discharge . . . service members . . . because of their sexual orientation."[15]

In 1988, Dr. Ted Sarbin and Dr. Ken Karols were commissioned by the Defense Department to study homosexuality in the military as "a condition related to trust violation."[16] Their report, "Nonconforming Sexual Orientations and Military Suitability," was delivered to the Pentagon in December of that same year.

Sarbin and Karols went beyond the rather narrow topic which had been assigned to them: they also addressed the general question of whether or not gay men and lesbians are appropriate candidates for military service. On this, their conclusion was that systematic exclusion of gay people from the Armed Forces is counter-indicated. Such exclusion is based on an amalgam of stereotypes, unfounded fears, and slanderous misconceptions of gays and lesbians.

It comes as no surprise that "Nonconforming Sexual Orientations and Military Suitability" was unacceptable to the Pentagon. It thereupon commissioned a second study. Michael A. McDonald, the chosen researcher, was told to stay within the confines of the following question: "whether homosexuality is an indicator that a person possesses characteristics, separate from sexual orientation, that make one unsuitable for

---

14. U.S. Department of Defense, "Enlisted Administrative Separations," Appendix A, Part 1, Section H, 47. [Federal Regulation 10,162; 10,179 (1982).] Quoted in Thomas B. Stoddard, E. Carrington Boggan, Marilyn G. Haft, Charles Lister, and John P. Rupp, *The Rights of Gay People: An American Civil Liberties Union Handbook* (New York: Bantam Books, 1983), pp. 32-33.

15. Kate Dyer, ed., *Gays in Uniform: The Pentagon's Secret Reports* (Boston: Alyson Publications, 1990), pp. xiv-xv.

16. Dyer, *Gays in Uniform*, p. xvi.

positions of trust."[17] McDonald's conclusion, too, would be deemed unacceptable by the Defense Department:

> In summary, this report has provided limited but cogent evidence regarding the preservice suitability of homosexuals who may apply for positions of trust. Although this study has several limitations, the preponderance of the evidence presented indicates that homosexuals show preservice suitability – related adjustment that is as good or better than the average heterosexual. Thus, these results appear to be in conflict with conceptions of homosexuals as unstable, maladjusted persons. Given the critical importance of appropriate policy in the national security area, additional research attention to this area is warranted.[18]

It is only due to the tenacity of Congressman Gerry S. Studds and his legislative assistant, Kate Dyer, that these two reports have come to light. Studds, acting on a tip, was able, with the assistance of House Armed Services Subcommittee Chairwoman Patricia Schroeder (U.S. Representative from Colorado), to get the Pentagon to release the two documents. It had been the intention of the Defense Department to keep them from being published. Given their conclusions, Schroeder is of the opinion that "the real question is how long the military can maintain a personnel policy based solely on prejudice."[19]

The GLM suffered a significant setback in the 1986 Supreme Court ruling *Bowers v. Hardwick*. The case was a challenge to the constitutionality of the state of Georgia's anti-sodomy law. The Court ruled in a 5 to 4 decision that prosecuting a gay couple "for engaging in consensual sex in their own bedroom did not violate the federal right to privacy."[20]

---

17. See Michael A. McDonald, "Preservice Adjustment of Homosexual and Heterosexual Military Accessions: Implications for Security Clearance Suitability," in Dyer, *Gays in Uniform*, pp. 111-135, at p. 114.

18. McDonald, "Preservice Adjustment. . .," p. 134.

19. Quoted in Dyer, *Gays in Uniform*, p. i. It bears reporting that when President Harry Truman desegregated the Armed Forces, he was told that it would be "bad for morale." "Until 1948 the U.S. Armed Forces were racially segregated on exactly the same grounds as those adduced now for barring gays, and especially on the ground that whites could not work with blacks." [Richard D. Mohr, *Gays/Justice: A Study of Ethics, Society, and Law* (New York: Columbia University Press, 1988), p. 196.] Mohr also reminds his readers that most Western European nations allow gays and lesbians to serve in their armed forces with no adverse effects. (See *ibid.*, p. 196.)

20. Cohn, "Discrimination. . .," p. 39. The Georgia law in question reads as follows: "A person commits the offense of sodomy when he performs or submits to any sexual act involving the sex organs of one person and the mouth or anus of another." See The Editors of the Harvard Law Review (EHLR), *Sexual Orientation and the Law* (Cambridge, MA: Harvard University Press, 1989), p. 11.

A number of commentators have signalled the fact that the majority opinion in *Bowers* is out of step with the Court's other privacy rulings. In this vein, Justice Blackmun, in his dissenting opinion

> . . . criticized the majority opinion's focus on the particular act rather than the underlying right to freedom from government intrusion. . . . (He) found that private consensual sodomy is protected under the right to privacy as a decision properly left to individuals and as involving places afforded privacy regardless of the particular activities taking place there. According to Justice Blackmun, a fair reading of the Court's prior privacy cases discloses a commitment to individual autonomy in matters of personal choice – a principle that should apply with full force to the decision to engage in sodomy. Justice Blackmun also criticized the majority's state-interest analysis and concluded that Georgia's interest in enforcing private morality could not sustain the statute.[21]

The majority opinion, as framed by Justice White, claimed that the privacy rights recognized by other Supreme Court cases[22] encompassed only those that are "integral to procreative choice and family autonomy."[23] White argued that the recognition of a fundamental right requires that the right "be either 'deeply rooted in this nation's history and tradition' or implicit in the concept of ordered liberty."[24] White found homosexual sodomy to be unprotected by either standard.

The majority opinion in *Bowers v. Hardwick* focused on the historical condemnations of homosexuality in the Judeo-Christian tradition. Its historical exposition, however, is contentious:

> Judges have no special insight to *Geschichte*; their job neither allows them time nor invokes the talents required for honing historical skills to a level that might permit impartial findings; not even professional historians usually achieve that. Even for experts, *Historie* is controversial and as ideologically laden as any of the humanities and social sciences. Judges are as likely as any amateurs to pick and choose its variety in ways that fit their preconceived ends. Justice Burger's concurrence in *Bowers* provides a particularly clear instance of this vice. He claims that 'homosexual conduct. . .(has) been subject to state intervention throughout the his-

---

21. Ehlr, *Sexual Orientation. . .*, pp. 12-13. Justice Stevens joined Blackmun in criticizing the majority opinion for analyzing the Georgia law as if it only applied to homosexual sodomy. As written, the law criminalizes even marital sodomy. (See *ibid.*, p. 13.)

22. See especially, *Griswold v. Connecticut* (1965) which overturned Connecticut's prohibition of the use of contraceptives by married couples and *Roe v. Wade* (1973) which established constitutional protection for abortion. See EHLR, *Sexual Orientation. . .*, p. 12.

23. Ehlr, *Sexual Orientation. . .*, p. 12.

24. Ehlr, *Sexual Orientation. . .*, p. 12.

tory of Western Civilization' and that to protect homosexual acts 'would be to cast aside millennia of moral teaching.' He cites but one historian and makes no reference to John Boswell's magisterial *Christianity, Social Tolerance, and Homosexuality. . . .* which thoroughly criticizes Burger's one source and shows that far from a uniform condemnation of gay sex 'throughout the history of Western Civilization,' over the largest stretch of that civilization – the sixth-century B.C. to the twelfth-century A.D. – there was a large variety and considerable flux in the moral, legal, and religious evaluation of gays and gay acts.[25]

The majority of Supreme Court justices were swayed by a particular reading of Western history. It seems not to have dawned on them that the incidences of Western civilization's bias against homosexual persons might be analogous (say) to its treatment of the Jews. How free would Jewish people be in American society today if American law had to mirror the laws and practices of Western civilization down through the ages? Perhaps the animus that has been directed against gays and lesbians – like that directed against the Jews – reflects the meanest form of bigotry.

As this brief survey of contemporary American attitudes and "trouble spots" indicates, many controversies surround the place of gay men and women in American society. The general aims of the GLM are at least problematic for most Americans. In the remainder of this chapter, we will present the positions of four American thinkers who have addressed the question of gay and lesbian rights. These four thinkers – Michael Novak, Roger Magnuson, Milton Gonsalves, and Richard Mohr – have been chosen because of the representative nature of their work. Two are opposed to gay rights (Novak and Magnuson); two are supportive (Gonsalves and Mohr). Two (Magnuson and Mohr) are so strongly involved in the discussion that they can be called "activists;" the other two are professional philosophers who represent the "conservative" (Novak) and "liberal" (Gonsalves) spectrums of thought on the question. Specifically, Mohr and Magnuson were chosen because their works are outstanding examples of the "pro" and "con" genres within the literature surrounding gay rights. On the other hand, any number of thinkers could have been chosen over Novak and Gonsalves. In the end, Novak's stature within American Catholicism and Gonsalves' use of the Aristotelian-Thomistic synthesis in his argument accounts for the consideration of their thought here.

The discussion which is about to unfold will reveal the intellectual context within which the Catholic debate on gay rights is situated. Focusing attention now on the work of Novak, Magnuson, Gonsalves, and Mohr will eventually help us to appraise the originality of the Catholic debate.

---

25. Mohr, *Gays/Justice*, p. 78.

2. MICHAEL NOVAK: "HOMOSEXUALITY IS HARMFUL TO SOCIETY"

Michael Novak, an American theologian, philosopher, and conservative theorist, is on record as a proponent of the view that homosexuality is abnormal and a detrimental force in society.

In his article, "Homosexuality is Harmful to Society,"[26] Novak limits his discussion to male homosexuality: "society is in a more troubled state about male homosexuality than about female homosexuality. Lesbianism may suggest infantile pleasure and regression, but it does not threaten the public, at least not to the same extent that male homosexuality does."[27] In his decision to avoid speaking of lesbianism and in his belief that lesbians pose no serious threat to society, Novak is in good company. The vast majority of legal codes – ancient to modern – have been surprisingly silent on the issue of female homosexuality. Historical study, being so long the domain of men who were concerned with recounting the exploits of "great men," paid scant attention to women – let alone "deviant" women.[28] Concurrently, most of the psychological study of homosexuality has been concerned with the etiology of male homosexuality; the Freudian theory, for instance, is noticeably maladroit in handling lesbianism. One is not surprised, then, that feminists explain the lack of scientific interest in lesbianism by reference to the preexisting male bias in society and in the sciences in particular. In a word, male homosexuality is seen as threatening because it challenges the gender-identity of the ones doing the theorizing.

Novak provides ample ammunition for a feminist critique of his position. He goes so far as to say that "female homosexuality seems somehow more natural, perhaps harmless. Male homosexuality seems to represent a breakdown of an important form of socialization."[29] Novak explains this with what strikes him as a paradox. As the sex-role stereotypes continue to change in modern society, it does not seem alarming to him that women are playing roles that once belonged solely to men; the problematic development is the weakening of the "male principle:" "Women becoming more like men" pales in significance when it is also a question of "men becoming more like women."

---

26. Michael Novak, "Homosexuality is Harmful to Society," in Bruno Leone and M. Teresa O'Neill, eds., *Sexual Values: Opposing Viewpoints* (St. Paul, MN: Greenhaven Press, 1983), pp. 71-74.

27. Novak, "Homosexuality is Harmful. . .," p. 72.

28. Lillian Faderman, against this backdrop, has published two significant histories of lesbianism. See her *Surpassing the Love of Men: Romantic Friendship and Love Between Women from the Renaissance to the Present* (New York: William Morrow, 1981) and *Odd Girls and Twilight Lovers: A History of Lesbian Life in Twentieth-Century America* (New York: Penguin, 1991).

29. Novak, "Homosexuality is Harmful. . .," p. 72.

Novak provides an explanation for this paradox by attempting to put the matter in historical context:

> In past ages, homosexuality was sometimes construed as a danger to the human race because it meant a) a decline in population, or b) a decline in those masculine qualities essential for survival. What happened in the socialization of the young male was perceived to be of greater significance, and of greater risk, to the race than what happened to the female.[30]

Unfortunately, Novak does not move beyond the level of generalities. For the sake of argument, however, it probably ought to be conceded that tribal societies, for instance, seem more interested in the socialization of the young male. The existence of more or less elaborate male initiation rites witnesses to this rather forcefully.

However, the problem that underlies Novak's thought is a lack of clarity on how he constructs the etiology of male homosexuality. All that he has to say implies an absolutely anti-essentialist position; he has opted for social constructionism (or, personal degeneracy) as a complete explanation for the existence of homosexually-oriented men. They exist because of a deficiency in their upbringing; they were improperly socialized.[31] This is the gist of the following rhetorical question:

> Is it true that the number of homosexuals is multiplying in our day? Who could marvel if it were? Men find it perplexing to be male. . . .[32]

It seems more than plausible to Novak that men are opting for the homosexual alternative because modern, post-industrial society has blurred the differences between the sexes and has thus made the dynamics of the progression toward full-fledged adult heterosexuality problematic for many.

Such an explanation, however, cannot hold up in the face of numerous empirical studies. Sexual orientation is not a matter of choice; one does not choose to be sexually aroused in this way or that. The number of homosexuals who have not received a "cure" after years under the care of a psychiatrist adds pathos to the situation. Moreover, one is justified in wondering – given the signs of rampant homophobia in American society – how Novak can conceive of the "homosexual option" as the one which

---

30. Novak, "Homosexuality is Harmful. . .," p. 72.

31. It seems unlikely, therefore, that Novak would be able to incorporate into his position the institutionalized homosexuality that exists in some societies. The "socializers" in question feel that they are responding to the preexistent dispositions of the young person: they do not see themselves as "creating homosexuals." See especially Greenberg, *The Construction of Homosexuality*, chapter 2: "Homosexual Relations in Kinship-Structured Societies," pp. 25-88.

32. Novak, "Homosexuality is Harmful. . .," p. 72.

affords the individual *less* psychic struggle. If it were all a matter of personal preference, choosing to be like the majority would be the sensible option, the course of least resistance.

In Novak's thought, male homosexuality harms society by disrupting the "male principle," by tempting men away from full human development. This development calls for the entering into communion with a woman and establishing the basic unit of society – the "traditional" family. He writes:

> From my point of view, homosexuals absent themselves from the most central struggles of the individual, the struggle to enter into communion with a person of the opposite sex. That is the battle most at the heart of life. Excluded from this struggle, whether by choice or by psychic endowments, the homosexual is deprived of its fruits. Those fruits are a distinctive honesty, realism and wisdom taught by each sex to the other: that complementarity in which your humanity is rejoined and fulfilled. Apart from this civilizing struggle there is a lack, an emptiness, a loss of realism. . . .[33]

Novak cannot conceive of same-sex relationships as humanizing for those involved or as even remotely beneficial to society.[34] Society has an overriding interest in promoting heterosexuality and in discouraging homosexuality; as he explains: "The future depends on it."[35] Heterosexuality and homosexuality ought not to be treated as equals; neither should one's sexual orientation be treated as a matter of indifference.

In "Homosexuality is Harmful to Society," Novak is wearing the hat of a philosopher: he does not propose specific public policy initiatives that would be consonant with his theses. He claims to favor "a tolerant and open system" of government, one that does not put "undue coercion upon those who do not, or who cannot" share the majority's moral vision.[36] However, he is quick to add, "for the good of all of us, homosexuals included, it is well that society should prefer heterosexuality and specially nourish it."[37]

In the end, Novak does not reveal whether he would consider something like equal opportunity in employment for gay people as weakening society's commitment to heterosexuality. It seems likely, however, that he would oppose gay partnership laws which put gay couples on the same economic footing as married couples.

---

33. Novak, "Homosexuality is Harmful. . .," p. 73.

34. Cf. "Homosexual love is . . . apart from the fundamental mystery of bringing life into the world, and sharing in the birth and death of generations. It is self-centered in a way that is structural, independent of the good-will of the individual. Marital love has a structural role in continuing the human race that is independent of the failures of the individuals who share it." (Novak, "Homosexuality is Harmful. . .," p. 73.)

35. Novak, "Homosexuality is Harmful. . ., " p. 74.

36. Cf. Novak, "Homosexuality is Harmful. . .," p. 74.

37. Novak, "Homosexuality is Harmful. . .," p. 74.

3. ROGER MAGNUSON: "ARE GAY RIGHTS RIGHT?"

Roger Magnuson's work on the question of gay and lesbian rights[38] is a passionate plea for American society to halt the progress made by the GLM. In his "Introduction," he appeals to the slippery slope upon which the United States now finds itself:

> If we extrapolate from the last two decades, we must ask where we will be two decades from now. If the breathtaking pace of acceptance of perverted sexual behavior continues, the world of the early twenty-first century will hardly be imaginable from the perspective of today. . . . Coming into view is the homosexual vision of a world where all sexual activity is placed beyond the rule of moral norms. The final destination for this ideology is a city of polymorphous and perverse sexuality where anything goes.[39]

Magnuson's work sets out legal, medical, sociological, economic, and psychological arguments against gay rights. He recognizes that "to fight successfully against gay rights proposals, citizens must arm themselves with facts that serve as objective confirmation of their moral reservations about homosexual behavior."[40] In this fight, religious arguments such as "the Bible says homosexuality is wrong" or "God did not create the human sexual faculty for homosexual uses" have no overt role to play: "A majority which does not acknowledge these arguments is often unmoved, and the arguments are easily stigmatized as a moralistic intrusion into the political process."[41] If a consensus is to be built around opposition to gay rights ordinances and (or) special privileges for homosexual people, it is necessary to focus on the lowest common denominator. For Magnuson, this is the natural revulsion that the heterosexual majority feels toward homosexual behavior.

In this regard, Magnuson pulls no punches. In chapter two ("Who Are the Gays? The Image and the Reality"), he offers sections entitled "What Do Homosexuals Do?," "Where Do Homosexuals Do It?," "With Whom Do Ho-

---

38. Roger J. Magnuson, *Are Gay Rights Right? Making Sense of the Controversy* (Portland, OR: Multnomah, 1990).

39. Magnuson, *Are Gay Rights Right?*, p. 13.

40. Magnuson, *Are Gay Rights Right?*, p. 19.

41. Magnuson, *Are Gay Rights Right?*, p. 19. However, this does not preclude the presence of a chapter entitled "Gay Rights and Religion" wherein Magnuson addresses such topics as "The Biblical View of Homosexual Behavior," "The Damaging Consequences of Homosexual Behavior" [Where Magnuson writes: "The sodomite is trapped in a lust that is destroying him by inches and yards. To tell him that he cannot help himself, to tell him to rejoice in his fatal disease, is to consign him forever to unhappiness. Much better the simple message of Christian grace. You are a responsible moral being who has sinned grievously against God. God loves you but hates your lifestyle. You are headed for judgment, but there is a way out" (In *ibid.*, pp. 122-123).], and "The Need for Repentance." See *ibid.*, pp. 109-126.

mosexuals Do It?," and "Homosexuals and Violent Crime." Magnuson focuses on the most destructive and degrading examples of gay sex. In the section entitled, "Where Do Homosexuals Do It?," for instance, he enumerates a long list of sites for homosexual activity: public parks, public restrooms, shopping malls, public libraries, bus stations, automobiles, pornographic bookstores, peep shows, and movie houses.[42] Magnuson gives no indication that heterosexual coupling also takes place in these locales; nor does he entertain the possibility that a gay couple might prefer the privacy of their own home for their sexual relating.

There is no denying that degrading sexual behavior takes place in the gay community.[43] Magnuson paints a portrait, however, where degradation is a way of life and self-destruction is the ultimate goal of all concerned parties. He provides the following rationale for viewing the gay community in this way:

> Frustrated by the biological impossibility of natural sexual relations between members of the same sex, homosexuals must use body apertures not constructed for sexual penetration or bring the mouth into contact with areas designed for the elimination of human waste, either of which causes serious hygienic and health risks. . . . Once the natural reluctance to come into contact with human waste is broken down, a significant proportion of homosexuals go further. . . .[44]

This "going further" ultimately entails losing even the natural instinct for self-preservation.

Magnuson holds the homosexual community guilty for the AIDS epidemic. Their perverse and promiscuous sexual activity – health risks in and of themselves – are taken as the reason that much of the general population is now at risk of being infected. He is, accordingly, content to speak of "innocent" and "guilty" persons with AIDS.[45]

As the actual or potential carriers of a deadly disease, homosexuals[46] ought not to be allowed to win special societal privileges. In this, Magnuson finds an analogy with alcoholism *à propos*:

---

42. Magnuson, *Are Gay Rights Right?*, p. 42.

43. Kirk and Madsen, *After the Ball*, represents a frank discussion by two gay activists.

44. Magnuson, *Are Gay Rights Right?*, p. 40. Magnuson does not address the reality of anal and oral sex among heterosexuals.

45. Cf. "The medical community was confronted with a frightening prospect: a gruesome disease from which there was no known cure and a group of recklessly promiscuous carriers. The disease was horrible enough when confined to the homosexual community, but equally disturbing were increasing reports of the transmission of AIDS to innocent parties: to heterosexual partners of bisexuals, to hospital patients receiving transfusions of AIDS-contaminated blood, to hemophiliacs dependent on regular infusions of new blood for life, to infants born to mothers with AIDS." See Magnuson, *Are Gay Rights Right?*, pp. 50-51.

46. Magnuson uses "homosexual" and "homosexuals" throughout his text. Most of what he has to say is in reference to gay men, however. It is clear that lesbians are extremely low-risk candidates for HIV infection.

Just as it would be ludicrous to call for alcoholics' rights or to have a day celebrating drunkenness, it is equally ludicrous to call for gay rights legislation or to have a day celebrating perversion. The alcoholic discovers in AA (i.e., Alcoholics Anonymous) that the fault is not with others but with himself; likewise the responsibility for change lies not with others, but with himself. Those enablers who accepted him – made up excuses for his absence from work, explained away the bruises he left on his children, rationalized his behavior as inherited – were facilitating his collapse. So too the public acceptance of homosexuality expressed in gay rights laws and gay pride days provides an easy way out for those who want to appear tolerant and loving, but in actuality it promotes conduct destructive to the homosexual himself.[47]

Magnuson's analogy can be criticized on a number of levels. Let the most basic suffice: since it allows for no distinction between alcoholics and the majority who partake of alcoholic beverages without addiction or compulsion, it intimates that all homosexuals are perverted sex addicts bent on self-destruction who will, by way of the AIDS virus, take many innocent lives with them.

In a somewhat curious treatment of the issues, Magnuson writes:

Homosexuals are made, not born. They are responsible for their conduct. But no person of good will should use this as a justification for personal acts of cruelty, violence, or insult. On a personal as well as a legal basis, homosexuals are entitled to respect as human beings, as persons with immortal souls. But this respect does not require the provision of special privileges that would infringe on the rights or liberties of others. A concern for homosexuals as people will lead, paradoxically, to withholding social acceptance of their behavior.[48]

Magnuson will not entertain the validity of studies which point to a biological basis for homosexuality;[49] to do so would seriously undercut his qualifying homosexuality as perverse, abnormal, and unnatural. (Only a theological argument would be left to so qualify homosexuality.) Moreover, these studies could conceivably turn the tide in favor of viewing gay people as a "valid" minority and lead to special minority status.

---

47. Magnuson, *Are Gay Rights Right?*, pp. 60-61.

48. Magnuson, *Are Gay Rights Right?*, pp. 61-62.

49. See, for instance, Marcia Barinaga, "Is Homosexuality Biological?," in *Science*, 253 (1991), pp. 956-957; Ann Gibbons, "The Brain as 'Sexual Organ,' " in *ibid.*, pp. 957-959; and Simon LE VAY, "A Difference in Hypothalamic Structure Between Heterosexual and Homosexual Men," in *ibid.*, pp. 1035-1037. The work of Dr. Le Vay in identifying differences between the sizes of various brain structures in gay and straight men is probably the closest a researcher has come to demonstrating an organic basis for homosexuality. Chandler Burr's "Homosexuality and Biology," in *The Atlantic*, 271 (March 1993), pp. 47-65 is a helpful summary of the present state of the question.

Instead, Magnuson relies heavily on the work of two controversial psychiatrists – Irving Bieber and Charles Socarides. Bieber and Socarides are among a minority of psychiatrists who argue that the homosexual orientation is a mental disorder; moreover, they claim success in changing the sexual object choice of homosexuals. Magnuson reports: "Irving Bieber's study of 72 patients revealed that 38% had become heterosexuals or bisexuals and 27% had shifted from homosexuality and bisexuality to exclusive heterosexuality."[50] 'Where there's a will, there's a way' seems to be the message in all of this; gays and lesbians who are not "cured" are castigated as having entered therapy with bad will. Here, Magnuson follows Socarides' provocative thesis: "psychotherapy appears to be unsuccessful in only a small number of patients in any age in whom a long habit is combined with . . . lack of desire to change."[51]

It must be acknowledged that Bieber and Socarides are on the fringe of the psychiatric community; their alleged transformations of homosexuals into heterosexuals are afforded little scientific credence. Richard Isay provides the rationale for skepticism:

> Kinsey and his co-workers for many years attempted to find patients who had been converted from homosexuality to heterosexuality during therapy, and were surprised that they could not find one whose sexual orientation had been changed. When they viewed persons who claimed they had been homosexuals but were now functioning heterosexually, they found that all these men were simply suppressing homosexual behavior, that they still had an active homosexual fantasy life, and that they used homosexual fantasies to maintain potency when they attempted intercourse.[52]

What is more, Wardell Pomeroy, a co-author of the Kinsey Report, "has maintained a standing offer to administer the Kinsey research questionnaires to any of the patients who were reported cured."[53] Irving Bieber acknowledged to Pomeroy that he had only one case that would qualify (i.e., a person who had been *exclusively* homosexual who successfully switched to heterosexuality), "but he was on such bad terms with the patient that he could not call on him."[54]

---

50. Magnuson, *Are Gay Rights Right?*, p. 59. Bieber's best known work is *Homosexuality* (New York: Basic Books, 1962); its publication date ought to be signalled: much work has been done on the topic in the more than thirty years since its appearance.

51. Magnuson, *Are Gay Rights Right?*, p. 59; Quoting Charles Socarides, "Homosexuality: Basic Concepts and Psychodynamics," in *International Journal of Psychiatry*, 10 (1972), p. 124.

52. Isay, *Being Homosexual*, pp. 111-112.

53. Isay, *Being Homosexual*, p. 112.

54. Isay, *Being Homosexual*, p. 112.

Richard Posner sets out a balanced presentation on the controversy surrounding psychoanalytic cures for homosexuality:

> The genuine bisexual is more dissuadable than a true homosexual from engaging in homosexual intercourse, because he has a good substitute; it is presumably from the ranks of the bisexuals that the occasional 'cures' of homosexuality that the literature reports are drawn. Whether his preferences are altered is another matter. Recall the analogy to left- and right-handedness. Most people are right-handed (about 93 percent); almost all the rest are left-handed; there are very few genuinely ambidextrous people. But if there are heavy costs to writing with the left hand, then left-handed people will, though with difficulty, force themselves to write with their right hand.[55]

Concurrently, it is well to recall that the father of psychoanalysis – Sigmund Freud – was less than optimistic concerning the prospects of changing a true homosexual. In a well-known letter to an American mother worried about the sexual orientation of her son, Freud holds out no extravagant claims. What he does offer to bring the young man is "harmony, peace of mind, full efficiency, whether he remains a homosexual or gets changed."[56]

It should be clear that Magnuson's decision to build a case upon the questionable findings of two maverick psychiatrists severely impairs the credibility of his argument. If true homosexuals cannot be changed into heterosexuals and if there are at least good possibilities that homosexuality has organic as well as social foundations, then much of what Magnuson has to say loses its force. It simply becomes problematic to call all homosexual behavior "unacceptable," "perverse," "abnormal," and "disgusting" outside a purely confessional context.[57] The scientific studies counsel against such designations.

Herein lies the serious flaw in Magnuson's presentation on gay and lesbian rights: he purports to be establishing his argument on the scientific (e.g., medical, psychological, sociological, etc.) evidence, but ultimately he is inspired by an *a priori* condemnation of gay sex along traditional Christian lines. Because of this, he is unable to entertain the very topic he set out to study, viz., the rights of *gay people*. Magnuson cannot see the

---

55. Posner, *Sex and Reason*, p. 298.

56. Quoted in Peter Gay, *Freud: A Life for Our Time* (New York: Anchor Books, 1989), p. 610. Freud's personal views on homosexuality were also shared in this letter (written in 1935). He wrote: "Homosexuality is assuredly no advantage, but it is nothing to be ashamed of, no vice, no degradation, it cannot be classified as an illness; we consider it to be a variation of the sexual function, produced by a certain arrest of sexual development. . . . It is a great injustice to persecute (sic) homosexuality as a crime – and a cruelty, too." In *ibid.*, p. 610.

57. Magnuson's text is liberally peppered with such terms.

people; he can only see *vile behavior.* Gay and lesbian rights, then, do not protect the rights of persons; they protect perversions that do not deserve protection.

In this, he comments on the GLM's unwillingness to enter into public debate on the topic of homosexual behavior. He says that its strategy is simple: "Keep the discussion as abstract as possible – civil rights, discrimination, minority status. . . . If someone brings up embarrassing facts about the homosexual lifestyle, accuse the person of being obsessed with sex and the merely physical dimension of human relationships."[58] It is, of course, a questionable bit of semantics for Magnuson to brand civil rights, discrimination, and minority status as "abstract" while arguing that "concrete" sexual practices are at the heart of the matter.

Nowhere is Magnuson's bias in this regard more evident than in the following passage:

> Jesus talked of people who would not come. . .(into the) light because their deeds were evil. Light exposes the darkness and what is done there. Although there is a natural and wholesome reluctance on the part of decent people to explore the details of deviant behavior, that reluctance must be tempered by a need to give society a common sense understanding about the nature and public costs of perverted sexual behavior. While the most egregious and detailed description of perverse acts is well left in darkness, society needs to know which behavior it is being asked to accept as socially legitimate.[59]

With this quotation, Magnuson's overall position comes into full view. Homosexual activity is always and everywhere wrong because it is unnatural, abnormal, and perverse. A frank discussion of the lurid goings-on between (male) homosexuals ought to convince one of this; if not, a biblically based argument is offered (chapter 4) as verification. Society has much to lose – and nothing to gain – in affording legal protection to homosexual behavior; prominent here is the inevitable rise in the death toll from AIDS and the threat posed to the sexual integrity of America's young people.[60] Confronted by the slick methodology of gay and lesbian rights activists, "those who believe that 'righteousness exalteth a nation' need both courage and good cheer. Because they walk in the light, they need not fear nor apologize for recognizing a difference between the normal and the deviant, the precious and the vile, in sexual expression."[61]

---

58. Magnuson, *Are Gay Rights Right?*, p. 142.

59. Magnuson, *Are Gay Rights Right?*, p. 145.

60. Cf. Magnuson, *Are Gay Rights Right?*, p. 137: "The fabric of society is damaged by a subgroup of citizens with serious psychological and medical problems who, because they cannot procreate, must recruit."

61. Magnuson, *Are Gay Rights Right?*, pp. 145-146.

Magnuson is able to put the matter in these terms – sexual norms versus antinomianism – because he has concentrated on exposing the ideologies of the most extreme and fringe gay organizations. The very existence of the North American Man/Boy Love Association (NAMBLA) is lamentable; but to cite its ideology as representative of the GLM is unfair. The fact of the matter is that NAMBLA is far outside the mainstream of the GLM and an embarrassment for many in the movement.[62] To concentrate on the objectives of NAMBLA at great length[63] and to pass over the goals of the leading gay and lesbian organizations leaves the reader with the impression that NAMBLA is a serious example of what gays really want. In any event, it is helpful to know that most of the activities that NAMBLA advocates are criminal offenses in all fifty states and that no serious attempts to change this are conceivable.

In focusing such attention on NAMBLA and in detailing some of the more lurid instances of child molestation,[64] Magnuson is offering a not-so-subtle argument against gay rights. He gives the impression that gay rights ordinances will protect the perpetrators of sexual abuse of minors; he intimates that the open presence of gays and lesbians (and their inevitable seduction of youth) will lead to a rise in the homosexual population of the country. Given his decision to view the etiology of homosexuality under the rubrics of "education," "example," and "choice," this prediction is not without its merits.

But, again, Richard Posner's work puts to rest Magnuson's most extravagant fears:

> When we consider how difficult – how well-nigh impossible – it appears to be to convert a homosexual into a heterosexual, despite all the personal and social advantages to being a heterosexual in this and perhaps in any society, the issue of homosexual seduction, recruitment, or propaganda is placed in perspective. How *much* more difficult it must be for homosexuals to convert a heterosexual into one of themselves![65]

Moreover, there is no evidence that those youths whose sexual identity seems uncertain or ambiguous can be swayed to the homosexual side of the spectrum by associating with gay people.[66]

---

62. See, for instance, Kirk and Madsen, *After the Ball*, p. 43.

63. See Magnuson, *Are Gay Rights Right?*, pp. 13-14, 46.

64. See Magnuson, *Are Gay Rights Right?*, p. 47.

65. Posner, *Sex and Reason*, pp. 298-299.

66. Posner remarks that the evidence that we do have ("the twin evidence, the comparisons between tolerant and intolerant societies, the child-development evidence") points away from such an idea. If they have not been swayed by the omnipresent heterosexual bias in society to become "straight," why would we consider a relatively weak minority to be powerful enough to make them "gay"? See *Sex and Reason*, p. 299.

In conclusion, Magnuson's argument against gay rights legislation turns on two related points. The first is that homosexual genital behavior is morally wrong and medically dangerous. For two people of the same sex to be involved with each other genitally offends the Judeo-Christian values upon which the United States was established; because of this, it offends the moral sensibilities of a majority of Americans.[67] Robert Beatty, in a letter to the editor of *Newsweek*, put it this way:

> Though it may be a difficult concept for the liberal mind to grasp, there are people in this nation who are as morally offended by homosexuality as liberals are by racism and sexism. Shouldn't they be accorded the same right as liberals not to have a practice that offends them shoved in their faces? Or are people allowed to take offense only in the areas that liberals declare politically correct?[68]

Magnuson, moreover, is convinced that if people knew the details of the mechanics of gay sex they would oppose special protective legislation for homosexuals by even greater margins than they do already.[69]

Since the sexual activity of homosexuals is immoral, society has an obligation to keep it illegal. Magnuson sharply draws the lines of demarcation:

> Put plainly, gay rights laws are meant to protect men and women who practice oral and anal copulation with members of the same sex. . . . Homosexuals can be characterized by what they do (sodomy) and with whom they do it (their own sex). What gay rights laws ask for is a special privilege for homosexuals not generally available to other groups, such as those who commit incest, adultery, bestiality, pedophilia, or, for that matter, any other criminal or antisocial behavior.[70]

To support gay rights legislation or protective, anti-discrimination municipal ordinances implicates one in sanctioning the immoral behavior of a deviant class of people.

4. MILTON GONSALVES: "RIGHT AND REASON"

A good part of Magnuson's argument relies on denying gay people minority status. He argues that they are simply people who indulge in perverted practices; the homosexual cannot claim that her sexual preference

---

67. A recent *Newsweek* poll asked, "Is homosexuality an acceptable alternative lifestyle?" 41% said "Yes," 53% said "No." See Turque, et. al., "Gays Under Fire," p. 36.

68. Robert Beatty, "Letter to the Editor," in *Newsweek* (October 5, 1992), p. 19.

69. See Magnuson, *Are Gay Rights Right?*, pp. 16-19.

70. Magnuson, *Are Gay Rights Right?*, p. 31.

is comparable to her race or ethnicity. Milton Gonsalves takes an opposing position.

Gonsalves' *Right and Reason*[71] is a textbook for university ethics courses. It is, however, unique in its class: it is written from the Aristotelian-Thomistic perspective. Whereas most authors of texts of an introductory nature are content to present an historical overview of the chief ethical questions and the responses given by the major schools of thought, Gonsalves believes that mastering one school of thought is beneficial for the beginner; this is especially true if it happens to have the credentials of Aristotelianism-Thomism. In his preface, Gonsalves fills out his rationale:

> Since everyone must begin somewhere to learn to think clearly about the moral problems we face daily at every level of our lives, the Aristotelian-Thomistic synthesis is an admirable base from which to make this start. Even in a pluralistic setting such as our own, moral positions are seen to be the result of a process of right reasoning and not the pure subjectivism of a 'gut' reaction. Whether or not the reader is convinced by the Aristotelian-Thomistic synthesis as it is presented here, at the very least he or she has an excellent point of departure from which to discover something better or more adequate for life.[72]

To be sure, Aristotle and Thomas Aquinas did not comment on many of the ethical issues which face our age. The Aristotelian-Thomistic synthesis, however, offers tools for critical discussion of these issues as well as principles upon which to build resolutions.

Gonsalves succinctly sets out the tradition's arguments against the morality of homosexual behavior.[73] Paramount here is the conviction that homosexuality – as sexual behavior – "is a perversion of the order of nature willed by God, because it can never be procreative of a new human being. . . ."[74] Homosexual genital sex falls hopelessly short of the ideal inherent in sexual communion and the fullness of human love.[75]

Gonsalves recognizes that the public consensus on the absolute immorality of homosexual activity is breaking down. The intrinsic perversity of gay and lesbian sex and the unnaturalness of the homosexual orienta-

---

71. Milton A. Gonsalves, *Fagothey's Right and Reason: Ethics in Theory and Practice* (Columbus, OH: Merrill Publishing Co., 1989).

72. Gonsalves, *Right and Reason*, p. iii.

73. See Gonsalves, *Right and Reason*, pp. 349-357. It is to be kept in mind that the "tradition" is not a static one. It has had to grapple with new concepts and perspectives. One of the most significant is the complex issue of "sexual orientation." St. Thomas, for instance, comments on the immorality of sodomy [cf. *Summa theologica*, 2a 2ae, Q. 154, aa. 11-12] but shows no understanding that a person might be "constitutionally" homosexual.

74. Gonsalves, *Right and Reason*, pp. 356-357.

75. See Gonsalves, *Right and Reason*, p. 357.

tion are being challenged on many fronts. A statement from "the opposition," he says, would look something like this:

> The tradition assumes, but does not prove, that the order of nature demands human genital expressions of love be heterosexual because only heterosexual intercourse is open to the creation of a new human being; sex organs can have more than one purpose other than procreation; the Judeo-Christian tradition has institutionalized heterosexuality as the only normal sexual orientation, but other cultures have accepted both orientations as good and valuable; to expect homosexuals to live celibate lives is a kind of persecution carried on by the heterosexual majority, but no one's sexual orientation gives him or her any special privileges; the law of nature merely enables us to predict what will be the case, not what morally ought to be the case. . . .[76]

Depending upon one's prior convictions, homosexuality can be taken as either a serious perversion of the order of nature or a natural variant in the world in which we live. Beyond a doubt, the Aristotelian-Thomistic synthesis as expressed in Catholicism has opted for the former. This choice is predicated upon *a priori* decisions on questions concerning proper biblical hermeneutics and the binding force of ecclesiastical pronouncements. A purely descriptive, cross-cultural (including the data on animal behavior) study would not know how to adjudicate the question of the "naturalness" of homosexuality. Reason itself cannot say that what is ought not to be; without an appeal to an authority which stands above human reason, one cannot say definitively that all homosexual behavior is perverse.[77]

Thinkers like Roger Magnuson, as we have seen, argue against gay and lesbian rights by an appeal to the immorality of homosexual practices. Gonsalves is unwilling to say that the Aristotelian-Thomistic synthesis – in order to be internally consistent – must concur in designating homosexual behavior as immoral. It seems clear that the contemporary discussion within Catholic sexual ethics on the Church's natural law tradition[78] bears out Gonsalves' hesitancy on this matter.

Given this recognition in *Right and Reason*, it is significant that it plays no part in Gonsalves' discussion of the GLM. One might have ex-

---

76. Gonsalves, *Right and Reason*, p. 357.

77. That sexual relating between adults of the same sex cannot be summarily categorized as immoral on purely rational grounds is one of the theses of Posner's "Moral Theory of Sexuality" [chapter 8 of *Sex and Reason*, pp. 220-242].

78. The Church's natural law tradition and a modern ("revisionist") retrieval of it is at the heart of Anthony Battaglia's *Toward a Reformulation of Natural Law* (New York: Seabury, 1981). Michael B. Crowe, in *The Changing Profile of the Natural Law* (The Hague: M. Nijhoff, 1977), discusses the competing interpretations of natural law in ancient, medieval, and modern thought.

pected him to argue that since the immorality of homosexual behavior cannot be demonstrated in a fully satisfactory manner even within a system of thought like the Aristotelian-Thomistic one, it would follow that civil society has no grounds in discriminating against its gay and lesbian citizens. If one cannot say that their sexual behavior is objectively perverse and despicable – outside a specifically religious vantage point – then it would seem that one ought to reconsider the grounds of society's bias against gay people and its hostility to their full participation in social life.

Rather than taking this tack, Gonsalves' reflection on the GLM[79] is much more direct. He addresses the issue from the perspective of justice. And in no time he has condemned discrimination against gays and lesbians: "Discrimination based on sexual orientation is unjust, for this gives an unfair advantage to the heterosexual majority."[80]

Justice, in the Aristotelian-Thomistic view, is the virtue by which one is disposed to give to the other his or her due.[81] "It supposes at least two persons between whom there can be some sort of equality, so that each person receives what really belongs to him or her."[82]

The tradition distinguishes two types of justice: general and particular. Gonsalves offers the following clarifications:

> *General* justice is so broad as to cover all virtue that has any social significance and is therefore not the specific cardinal virtue of justice. *Particular* justice, which is the cardinal virtue. . .(is divided) into *distributive* and *corrective*. The latter is now more commonly called *commutative*, a name derived from the commutation or exchange of goods.[83]

Commutative justice exists between two individuals; it is the basis of all contracts. One party agrees to do something for another or to give something to another in exchange for a mutually agreed upon good. However, it is not limited to explicit contracts; it also exists "in those situations in which nature itself demands the balance of equality. One who has injured another by depriving that person of something rightfully his or hers is obliged in justice to restore it to that person."[84] Until such restitution is made, justice remains violated.

---

79. See Gonsalves, *Right and Reason*, pp. 401-402.

80. Gonsalves, *Right and Reason*, p. 401.

81. Cf. Thomas Aquinas, *Summa theologica*, 2a 2ae, Q. 58, a. 1. Here St. Thomas defines justice as the perpetual and constant will to render to each one his right. Later in this question (a. 12), he will say that (particular) justice stands foremost among all the moral virtues.

82. Gonsalves, *Right and Reason*, p. 208.

83. Gonsalves, *Right and Reason*, p. 208.

84. Gonsalves, *Right and Reason*, p. 208.

Distributive justice is a relation between society and its members. It refers to a "fair and proper distribution of public benefits and burdens among the members of the community."[85] As such, it applies chiefly to the state. "It does not exist between equals, but between a superior and his or her subordinates; the equality, implied in all justice, here means that each subordinate should get a proportionate or fair share, a share equal to his or her just desserts."[86]

Gonsalves argues that discrimination against gay people violates both commutative justice and distributive justice. A person's sexual orientation ought to have no bearing on that person's employment or housing. For an employer to fire a gay employee solely on the basis of having discovered her sexual orientation is a serious blow to commutative justice. The same holds true for a landlord who would discriminate against gays and lesbians. In the face of such open violations of justice, writes Gonsalves, "it is quite proper to use the sanction of civil law to put an end to such unjust practices."[87] He remarks that "homosexuals have the same rights to friendship, association, and community as heterosexuals."[88]

As should be clear, Gonsalves sees no good reason to hold that homosexuals do not make up a distinct minority group. The fact that in individual cases the distinctions are not always clear-cut does not diminish the reasonableness of saying that human society is made up of a heterosexual majority and a homosexual minority. The dictionary definition for "minority" offers a perfect fit for gay people: "a part of a population differing from others in some characteristics and often subjected to differential treatment."[89] A certain percentage of Americans can be distinguished by a more or less exclusive erotic attraction to members of their own sex; if this characteristic were to become common knowledge they very well might find themselves to be objects of scorn, contempt, and harassment. Confronted with this state of affairs, Gonsalves writes:

> If society continues to deny homosexuals their civil rights and to treat homosexuals as the objects of scorn, cruel jokes, and contempt, then the homosexuals have every right to protest just as any other minority group. The homosexual needs friendship and association with other homosexuals to share, like heterosexuals, their deepest feelings, fears, and emotions. They need friendship

---

85. Gonsalves, *Right and Reason*, p. 208.

86. Gonsalves, *Right and Reason*, p. 209. It should be noted that under distributive justice, the citizen is obliged to contribute to the common good – he or she is called to give to the state its due.

87. Gonsalves, *Right and Reason*, p. 402.

88. Gonsalves, *Right and Reason*, p. 402.

89. *Webster's New Collegiate Dictionary*, 7th edition (Springfield, MA: G. & C. Merriam Company, 1974), p. 733.

to construct their lives meaningfully, and so they need the kind of association that they cannot find except with one another. As long as they are alienated from the largest segment of society, they will need their protest movement.[90]

As we have mentioned, the stance that Gonsalves takes on gay and lesbian rights is not dependent upon the morality of concrete sexual practices.[91] The sexual practice of homosexual persons cannot cancel out the moral obligation to treat them justly. Gonsalves' approach does depend, however, upon the recognition that many people have accepted slanderous myths about gay people. It is precisely on the weight of these myths that they are led to discriminate against gays and lesbians; or, more seriously, to lash out in violence against them. Justice demands that these myths be exposed and discredited. Gonsalves provides the following examples of common myths:

1. Every homosexual is attracted to children and adolescents and wishes to have genital sex with them.

2. Male homosexuals look and act effeminate, while female homosexuals look and act masculine.

3. Homosexuals can recognize one another easily.

4. Homosexuals invariably tend toward particular professions, for example, music, theatre, other fine arts, interior decorating.

5. All homosexuals are promiscuous and unable to form enduring relationships.

6. Homosexuals, having deliberately chosen their sexual orientation, can correct their situation by an act of will or by getting to know some member of the opposite sex intimately.[92]

On the force of these sweeping generalizations, gay people are taken as a threat to human society and are often denied equality of opportunity and equal rights.

Richard Posner concurs: many of the hardships that gays and lesbians face have been built upon a collective character assassination campaign. He makes his case in reference to the attitudes of heterosexual men:

---

90. Gonsalves, *Right and Reason*, p. 402.

91. He will say, moreover, that "the sanction of civil law should not be used for the purpose of restraining sexual activity between consenting adults in private" (see *Right and Reason*, pp. 401-402). It bears mentioning in this context that St. Thomas taught that the civil law need not repress all vice (cf. *Summa theologica*, 1a 2ae, Q. 96, a. 2); civil legislation ought to be primarily concerned with the common good – the basic structures of justice which make human society possible (cf. *Summa theologica*, 1a 2ae, Q. 104).

92. Gonsalves, *Right and Reason*, p. 349.

If you ask men who are disgusted by homosexuals what it is, precisely, about homosexual men that makes them disgusting, the answer will not be confined to the fact of erotic attraction and expression between two men, although that is part of it. The objection is to an entire homosexual lifestyle, involving what are believed to be characteristic demeanors, behaviors, attitudes, destinies that the heterosexual (and no doubt many a homosexual) abhors: a lifestyle believed to be pervaded with effeminacy, including physical weakness and cowardice; with promiscuity and intrigue, prominently including seduction of the young; with concentration in a handful of unmanly occupations centered on fashion, entertainment, decoration, and culture – such occupations as the theatre (above all the ballet) and the arts, hairdressing, interior decoration, women's fashions, ladies' shops, library work; with furtiveness and concealment; with a bitchy, gossipy, histrionic, finicky, even hysterical manner; with a concern with externals (physical appearance, youth, dress); with bad health, physical and mental, including suicide and alcoholism; with a wretched old age; with a general immorality and unreliability; with an above-average I.Q., education, and income (qualities that make homosexuals even more threatening, more insidious, more seductive and manipulative); and, of course, with narcissism.[93]

With such understandings of gay men abroad, it is no wonder that many people seem to have no qualms about refusing them fair treatment. Based on this data, it would seem that society would do well to treat gays differentially; perhaps there could be a moral obligation to keep their social advancement at bay.[94]

As we mentioned at the outset of this chapter, the AIDS crisis has played a supporting role in this dynamic. Gonsalves himself observes:

The AIDS epidemic has aroused a great deal of antihomosexual sentiment around the country. Physical and verbal attacks on gay men are on the increase, fuelled by fear that the disease is going to be spread from the initially infected gay community and intra-

---

93. Posner, *Sex and Reason*, pp. 300-301.

94. One should not underestimate, for example, the impact of a case like Jeffrey Dahmer's in galvanizing public opinion against gay rights. See Tom Mathews, et. al., "Secrets of a Serial Killer," in *Newsweek* (February 3, 1992), pp. 45-49. Mathews quotes the criminologist Eric Hickey's frightening opinion: "There are other Dahmers out there. And they're busy" (in *ibid.*, p. 49). For his part, Magnuson gets a lot of mileage from the example of John Wayne Gacy (see *Are Gay Rights Right?*, pp. 54, 119). He tramples upon the canons of civility when, in criticizing revisionist interpretations of Scripture, he writes: "to say that inhospitality was the essential sin of Sodom is equivalent to saying the essential offense of John Gacy, the Chicago contractor who invited scores of adolescents to his home, sodomized them, and buried them in his basement, was inhospitality" (in *ibid.*, p. 119).

venous drug users to the general population. This, of course, is not going to happen unless the majority of the population chooses to risk becoming infected. Nevertheless, the upsurge in scapegoating of gay people by members of the heterosexual majority is in some measure an indication of how threatened, frustrated, and helpless the majority feels in the face of the AIDS epidemic.[95]

Of course, understanding the causes of injustice does not absolve one of the obligation to denounce it. For Gonsalves, the issue of gay and lesbian rights is crucial. His argument is designed to elicit a sobering reflection from those who would be loathe to grant gay people protective legislation:

> Freedom and the rights that stem from it are an all or nothing affair. No one can be free if all are not free. Unless all people are justly treated, no one can be sure that he or she will be justly treated by others.[96]

5. RICHARD MOHR: "GAYS/JUSTICE"

At the time of its appearance in 1988, Richard Mohr's *Gays/Justice*[97] was a first: a work by a gay academic[98] which set out cogently the case for gay and lesbian rights. To date, it remains the most substantial work in support of justice for gay people.

Mohr argues that justice calls for fairness; it calls for non-differential treatment of classes of people. Fair treatment and equal treatment under the law – in short, justice – have not been afforded gays and lesbians in American society:

> Gay justice does not exist and does not nearly exist. The nation's institutional means for establishing justice – the courts – have completely failed in their duty when it has come to the plight of gays. Indeed, they have now become a major part of the mechanisms of gay oppression. The problem is not merely that the courts are now regularly upholding antigay laws – that alone would be reason for pointed protest. The problem chiefly is that the very procedures which the courts have adopted to address – or more accurately, to fail to address – gay issues reinforce the social view that gays are not worthy of equal respect.[99]

---

95. Gonsalves, *Right and Reason*, p. 401.

96. Gonsalves, *Right and Reason*, p. 401.

97. Richard D. Mohr, *Gays/Justice: A Study of Ethics, Society, and Law* (New York: Columbia University Press, 1988).

98. Mohr is a philosophy professor at the University of Illinois (Urbana).

99. Mohr, *Gays/Justice*, p. 315.

Mohr, like Gonsalves, considers the morality of adult, consensual gay sex in private to have no bearing upon the place of gay people in society and the protection of their human and civil rights. Judging the morality of instances of genital relating is difficult enough from within one distinct school of thought – it becomes hopelessly controverted within a pluralistic society. It seems to make little sense to sanction behavior where "no one gets hurt" on the grounds that some people object to it.

Of course, one might find the courage to argue that the practitioners of homosexuality *are* being hurt – not physically, perhaps, but psychologically and spiritually. Concurrently, one might take offense at the underlying moral relativism which inspires any number of gay and lesbian initiatives in public policy. Neither of these tacks, however, gets one very far. In the absence of a self-evident criteriology for judging the morality of genital relating among adults, homosexual behavior will remain controversial and a source of significant division between sincere partisans of all spectrums of opinion.

No participant in this debate can be demonized effectively. It makes no sense to categorize gay people as filthy, perverted sex addicts whose immoral behavior has blinded them to the most basic standards of ethical living. Likewise, only the most biased observer could advance the opinion that the opponents of gay and lesbian rights are simply religious bigots trapped by their own sexual fears and inadequacies. People of good will and intellectual vigor can, and do, disagree on the moral valence of the genital manipulations which lead to homosexual orgasm between consenting adults in private. In addition, one cannot get very far in questioning the internal logic of the partisan positions; the critical issue lies with the choice of first principles – a choice which cannot be established by an appeal to anything resembling self-evident truth.

For Mohr, all of this amounts to an argument in favor of gay and lesbian rights. This issue cannot be satisfactorily decided in relation to the morality of particular sex acts; it must be seen as an issue of social justice. Whereas secular society on its own terms cannot decide the morality of gay sex, it can decide to treat gay people as equals under the law. Whereas society cannot arbitrate between those who would call homosexual behavior sinful and those who would celebrate it as humanizing, it can decide that discrimination against gays and lesbians will be unlawful. At present, American society is evenly divided on the issue of the rightness or wrongness of particular sexual practices between consenting gay adults.[100] At the very least, systematic discrimination against people who have a homosexual orientation cannot be justified in the face of this lack of consensus.

---

100. Turque, as we have seen, reports that Americans are evenly divided on this question. See "Gays Under Fire."

The key point in Mohr's argument is his conviction that sexual relations[101] are a private matter; the state has no business monitoring the bedrooms of the nation. It is not necessarily that no immoral behavior takes place there; it is that the state has no mandate to stamp out all vice. Moreover, sexual relating manifests several significant characteristics that demand that it not be subject to governmental regulation. In chapter 4 of *Gays/Justice*, Mohr sets out four arguments as to why sex is private – and thus "invokes a substantive right from prosecution."[102]

Mohr's first observation is that from a purely cultural point of view, Americans consider sexual relating to be a supremely private affair. And as far as the sexual act itself goes, there is a strict obligation to keep it private. Acts of copulation must not take place in public. This requirement holds for *all* sexual intercourse – even, of course, that which "has society's highest commendation – heterosexual intercourse with benefit of clergy for procreation."[103]

Mohr argues that where there is an obligation to privacy, there is in turn a right to privacy. This is seen in the fact that "society cannot consistently claim that. . . (certain) activities must be carried out in private. . . and yet retain a claim to investigate such activity and so, to that extent, make it public behavior."[104] This applies specifically to homosexual genital behavior: "People don't want to see it and especially don't want to hear about it."[105]

There is something of a problem with this argument. Traditionally, gay sex has been understood as something which should *never* take place – neither in public nor in private. In a number of U.S. states, private, consensual sodomy between adults is still a criminal offense. It would seem that one cannot invoke "privacy" if the behavior in question has been socially condemned. But Mohr explains:

> To say that something ought not to occur at all is not to say that it ought not to be carried out in private when it does occur. In society's judgment, homosexuality is an evil of this sort. Now not all evil ought to be practiced in private if practiced at all. Murders, rapes, and child abuse, if they must occur, would be better to take place in public – to facilitate arrest. But the plaint from conservative quarters that gays objectionably 'flaunt' themselves would have no force if this were the sort of evil involved. So, in

---

101. In what follows, 'sexual relating,' 'sexual behavior,' 'gay sex,' and any such synonyms, must be understood in terms of adult consensual relations in private. Rape, seduction, public indecency, and pedophilia are not part of Mohr's argument.

102. Mohr, *Gays/Justice*, p. 94.

103. Mohr, *Gays/Justice*, p. 97.

104. Mohr, *Gays/Justice*, p. 96.

105. Mohr, *Gays/Justice*, p. 96, n. 9.

general, the argument here does not presuppose tolerance, let alone acceptance of gays, nor does it beg the question by presuming that gay sex acts are already legal. Disgust will do. So when gay sex does occur in private, it cannot be rightfully spied on – especially by the police.[106]

From this reflection on privacy from a cultural point of view, Mohr's second argument moves to a philosophical discussion of the inherent privacy of sex. His thesis here is that "the privacy of sex acts is not only culturally based but also inherent to them."[107] He explains:

> Sex acts are what I shall call 'world excluding.' Custom and taboo aside, sexual arousal and activity, like the activities of reading a poem or praying alone, are such as to propel away the ordinary world, the every day workaday world of public places, public function, and public observation.[108]

The dynamics of successful sexual relating points to the privacy of sex. It calls for the willingness to enter another world of consciousness and, concurrently, it provides the pathway to this other world. The presence of an intruder is enough to destroy this fundamental meaning of sexual relating. For "such observation brings crashing in its train the everyday world of duration and distance, function and duty, will and action. Further, the gaze of others injects into sex the waking world of vision, not the submerged and submerging world of flesh. Most importantly, it judges – even if sympathetically – causing self-reflection."[109] Self-reflection, Mohr reminds us,[110] is a virtual guarantor of impotence.

A phenomenological study of human sexual behavior reveals the necessity of privacy for its success and shows that it produces a "world excluding" experience in its practitioners. Mohr concludes that "any moral theory that protects privacy as sanctuary and as repose from the world must presumptively protect sexual activity."[111]

Mohr's third argument turns on viewing sex as "a central personally-affecting value."[112] It is far from complicated: "an impartial examination of sex's role in an individual's life would show first that, far from having any imaginable value or at most a nugatory one, sex is in general a central personal concern, and second that for those people with a sex drive, ad-

---

106. Mohr, *Gays/Justice*, p. 97.

107. Mohr, *Gays/Justice*, p. 100.

108. Mohr, *Gays/Justice*, p. 100.

109. Mohr, *Gays/Justice*, pp. 103-104.

110. Citing William H. Masters and Virginia E. Johnson, *Human Sexual Inadequacy* (Boston: Little, Brown, 1970), pp. 198-199, 202-203. See *Gays/Justice*, p. 103, n. 17.

111. Mohr, *Gays/Justice*, p. 104.

112. See Mohr, *Gays/Justice*, pp. 106-114.

dressing sex as central and appropriating it to oneself in some way or another is probably necessary for a fulfilled life."[113]

Given his first three points, Mohr's concluding position brings no surprises. If sex is so very central to one's self-understanding and one's being in the world, it is simply cruel for the state to bar (or attempt to bar) gay people from having sex. Such a campaign would be enough "to cast . . . (the gay person) automatically into a perpetual despair analogous to that of those whose plans are frustrated daily by ghetto, prison, or disease. But worse still, at least in prison, ghetto, or illness, one can achieve the consolation of the resigned, the comparative happiness of those who have reduced their expectations to match their prospects, or even the finality of giving up."[114]

This fourth point is drawn from a reflection on bodily privacy. First of all, it bears noting that

> the body is not just one more . . . thing in the world that one
> might have or own, but rather has a special value and standing, as
> that in virtue of which one possesses other things and as the chief
> means by which other things come to have their value.[115]

The body is "the primitive precondition and foundation for a person's being in the world at all, for his projection of himself into the world through actions and for his instilling value in things."[116] One cannot speak of human freedom in any sense of the term without recognizing the prerequisite nature of executive control over one's own body.[117]

Mohr argues that human freedom presupposes the right to do *to* one's body what one wishes. The human person possesses a strong presumptive right

> to feed one's body, to manipulate it, to exercise it, to dress it as
> one sees fit, to seek medical treatment, to inject foreign bodies
> into it, to permit others to do so, to touch it, to have others touch

---

113. Mohr, *Gays/Justice*, p. 109. In the discussion that follows, he is quick to point out that the personal appropriation (probably) necessary for a fulfilled life does not by definition keep one from deciding to refrain from engaging in genital activity. Religious celibates, then, are not by definition "unfulfilled" as human beings. Their free decision to take a vow of celibate chastity, Mohr argues, "support(s) a belief that one's sexual choices are as central as any aspect of one's life. For vows of chastity are as central to their religious life – their most meaningful life – as any vows they take" (in *ibid.*, pp. 109-110).

114. Mohr, *Gays/Justice*, p. 110.

115. Mohr, *Gays/Justice*, p. 119.

116. Mohr, *Gays/Justice*, p. 117.

117. Mohr is not remiss in making necessary qualifications here. He writes: "No one would claim that a person has even a *prima facie* right, let alone an absolute right, to do *with* his body as he pleases or that such use of the body grounds a right to privacy or any other. One does not have even a *prima facie* right to smash one's fist unprovokedly into another's face however much one might enjoy doing so" (see *Gays/Justice*, pp. 116-117).

it, to allow others to present their bodies to it, and to be the chief governor and guarantor of one's own feelings, emotions, and sensations – compatible with a like ability on the part of others and with other requirements for civil society.[118]

It comes as no surprise that Mohr sees the person's immunity from bodily coercion as pointing toward a general right to enter into consensual genital relations with others. He says that "consensual sex engages and nearly exhausts the core protections of the general right to bodily based privacy. Indeed it comes close to being a perfect or complete exemplification of its provisions."[119]

For the state to bar individuals from acting upon themselves is to destroy their status as free agents in any of their projects.[120] A society which has expressly condemned the use of torture as "cruel and unusual punishment"[121] – and does not claim the power to inflict "wounds to advance its projects (even as punishment) – *a fortiori* . . . cannot bar one from acting upon oneself in consensual sex."[122]

Mohr's bodily freedom argument has two rather obvious drawbacks. First, it seems wedded to a strict dualistic account of the human person – whereby the "body" is clearly distinct from the "person." Second, it is at present the basis for a "pro-choice" (or, "pro-abortion") political philosophy.[123] How much do these factors detract from Mohr's position?

On the first score, the problem appears to be one of semantics. Where Mohr speaks of "body," one might prefer to speak of "self." Thus, "to feed one's body" is equivalent to "feeding oneself." But whether one "has" a body or "is" an animated body is beside the point.[124] The question

---

118. Mohr, *Gays/Justice*, pp. 121-122.

119. Mohr, *Gays/Justice*, p. 122.

120. Mohr, *Gays/Justice*, p. 122.

121. Cf. *Weems v. United States* (U.S. Supreme Court, 1910), cited by Mohr, *Gays/Justice*, p. 122, n. 54

122. Mohr, *Gays/Justice*, p. 122. Mohr is not necessarily asserting that all instances of adult consensual sex in private are to be taken as perfectly moral. An analogy from eating is appropriate here. It would be an outrage to personal freedom if the state were to criminalize gluttony or to attempt to enforce a mandatory daily menu for all its citizens. Even if gluttony is offensive and many people's diet is nutritionally irresponsible, the value of personal freedom in these matters must take precedence. Moreover, in this hypothetical example, one can imagine competing groups developing around different interpretations of what is to constitute "gluttony" and "good nutrition." [Posner, *Sex and Reason*, p. 123 suggests an analogy between sexual relations and consumption of food.]

123. The majority opinion in *Roe v. Wade* (U.S. Supreme Court, 1973) identified a constitutional right to privacy and determined that a woman's decision to abort is guaranteed by this right.

124. And Mohr at least makes clear that "having" is used equivocally in his presentation. One "has" a body like one "has" nothing else. See *Gays/Justice*, p. 119.

revolves around one's freedom to act; positing, for example, a "substantial unity of body and soul," does not necessitate abandoning Mohr's insight into a bodily-based privacy (or, freedom).

The second charge, that Mohr's argument is substantially that of the pro-abortion lobby is true enough. Indeed, he argues that if the Supreme Court accepted this line of reasoning in *Roe v. Wade*, then *a fortiori* complete decriminalization of consensual gay sex between adults cannot be impeded logically.

Be that as it may, the acceptability of abortion as an instance of "the body and privacy" is much more problematic than that of gay sex. The pro-abortionist is at pains to discredit any "rights" the fetus may be said to possess, and to show that its continuance in existence is under the executive jurisdiction of its female host. Both of these tasks are involved when it is advanced that the fetus is all but indistinguishable from the woman's body. No such task must be performed in protecting homosexual behavior as an instance of bodily privacy; Mohr's argument does not depend upon doing away with second and (or) third party claims.

This brief exposition ought to be enough to demonstrate that placing consensual gay sex under the rubric of bodily privacy is not necessarily tied to being in favor of legal abortions, let alone being of the opinion that abortion raises no moral questions. What is more, one can be convinced of Mohr's conclusion that gay people ought not to be stopped from entering into sexual communion with other gay adults and still be of the opinion that such sexual relating is always immoral.

Mohr's four points go a long way in showing that sexual relating between adults, whether heterosexual or homosexual, commands a significant claim to privacy. Thus, governments of free societies would do well to view the consensual sexual relating of their adult citizens as off-limits. One is at a loss to articulate a social value which could conceivably trump the individual's liberty to enter into an intimate partnership of this nature. In the end, the state is patently incompetent for deciding such matters for its people.

After this discussion of sex and privacy, it comes as no surprise that Mohr identifies himself as a disciple of John Stuart Mill. One commentator on the thought of Mill says that Mill's overarching thesis in his *On Liberty* can be summarized in seven words: "Your rights end where his nose begins."[125] It follows, then, that "government interference with adult consensual activities is unjustified unless it can be shown to be necessary for the protection of the liberty or property of other persons."[126] Concurrently, Mohr will use Mill's philosophy to show that state coercion in the

---

125. Posner, *Sex and Reason*, p. 3.
126. Posner, *Sex and Reason*, p. 3.

form of civil rights legislation is warranted as the most effective means of promoting and protecting individual liberty.[127]

Also central to Mohr's presentation, as in that of Gonsalves, is that gay people are a true minority; the record shows, moreover, systematic attempts to discriminate against gays and lesbians on the basis of the group characteristic which constitutes them as a minority – same-sex erotic attraction. He explains:

> . . .(I)f sexual orientation is something over which an individual has virtually no control, either for genetic or psychological reasons, then sexual orientation becomes relevantly similar to race, gender, and ethnicity. Discrimination on these grounds is deplorable because it holds a person accountable without regard for anything *he himself* has done. And to hold a person accountable for things over which she has no control is a central form of prejudice.[128]

6. CONCLUSION

Through the study of the positions of Novak, Magnuson, Gonsalves, and Mohr, one can postulate the existence of four basic options for determining the moral advisability of gay and lesbian rights legislation. Two of these options produce a positive response; two produce a negative response. Concurrently, each option is comprised of two components – the first, theoretical considerations; the second, practical considerations. The theoretical component consists of the prior ideological commitments that a person brings to the question. Simply put, depending upon one's philosophical and (or) religious allegiances, one will be inclined either to support or to oppose gay rights legislation. The practical component consists in a reflection upon the effects to be produced by such legislation.

The four basic options can be outlined in the following manner: the first option (I) consists of theoretical support for gay rights legislation with practical support for the same; the second option (II), theoretical opposition with practical opposition; the third option (III), theoretical support with practical opposition; the fourth option (IV), theoretical opposition with practical support. Options I and II are the pure positions; III and IV are mixed.

Gonsalves and Mohr are advocates of I. Their philosophical commitments lead them to support the human and civil rights of gay people; they see nothing on the practical plane which would make them back away from supporting gay and lesbian rights legislation. Moreover, discrimina-

---

127. See Mohr, *Gays/Justice*, pp. 144-161.
128. Mohr, *Gays/Justice*, p. 188.

tion against gays and lesbians based upon their sexual orientation is seen as a clear-cut injustice.

Magnuson represents II. His philosophical and religious allegiances lead him to oppose gay rights; moreover, his hypotheses concerning the negative effects of such legislation lead him to voice practical opposition as well.

Novak's position is not as easily classified. He is more than likely an advocate of IV. His work does not leave many questions about his theoretical opposition to gay rights – the questions are found more in how he reads the practical ramifications. His preference for an "open society" where all share the same basic rights leads us to postulate a willingness on his part to support some instances of legislative protection for gay people.

One notes that we have not identified any defenders of III (theoretical support with practical opposition) in the secular literature. It may be that once one accepts the idea that gays and lesbians deserve (and need) legislative protection against discrimination that one cannot then conceive of any possible negative effects as being significant enough as to entail practical opposition.

In the next chapter, we move to a discussion of the American Catholic debate on the question of the moral advisability of gay and lesbian rights ordinances. We will see that while this debate has much in common with its secular counterpart, it is not simply the same debate under a religious mantle. The Catholic debate in the United States will be shown to possess an originality all its own.

Part II

Catholic Teaching
on Gay and Lesbian Rights

CHAPTER THREE

Responses to the GLM by the American Catholic Hierarchy

The GLM in the United States has posed a powerful dilemma for the American Catholic hierarchy. On the one hand, the hierarchy is obliged to uphold the magisterium's evaluation of "homosexual acts" as always and everywhere gravely sinful. On the other hand, the GLM's push for the civil rights of gays and lesbians has not met complete opposition from the U.S. hierarchy: as we shall see, a number of American bishops have issued calls for the protection of the human and civil rights of homosexual persons. These bishops hold that such a program is consonant with Catholic social teaching.

As a rule, there is warrant for claiming that the average American bishop would feel comfortable with (say) issuing a statement on the necessity of respecting the humanity of homosexual persons and on the obligation of wishing them no harm. However, this same bishop is apt to be skittish when it comes to a question of his supporting a specific piece of legislation designed to protect homosexual persons from discrimination. Often the choice is made to oppose the legislation with a view toward publicly upholding the Church's sexual ethic and keeping at bay the trend toward a more benign interpretation of homosexuality.

The inconsistency inherent in such an approach is lost on no one. An editorial in the Newark, New Jersey diocesan newspaper, angry at hierarchical opposition to a gay rights ordinance, clearly grasped the problem. Citing other clergy support for the measure, the author wrote: "these are people who support a proposal like this NOT because they waver in their allegiance to Christ and his Gospel, but precisely because they adhere so courageously to his Gospel of human rights based on the principle of charity."[1]

---

1. Quoted in Robert Nugent and Jeannine Gramick, eds., *A Time to Speak: A Collection of Contemporary Statements from U.S. Catholic Sources on Homosexuality, Gay Ministry, and Social Science* (Mt. Rainier, MD: New Ways Ministry, 1982), p. 2.

In this chapter, we discuss the contributions of three American Catholic Churchmen to the question of the moral advisability of gay and lesbian rights legislation. These three – Archbishop John R. Quinn and Cardinals Joseph Bernardin and John O'Connor – have made extensive contributions to this question and have articulated stances with which other American bishops have allied themselves. From the outset it bears noting – *mutatis mutandis* – that Bernardin espouses III, O'Connor is a proponent of II, and Quinn supports I.[2]

1. JOHN CARDINAL O'CONNOR

As we have seen, New York City witnessed the birth of the more militant wing of the GLM. On June 28, 1969, a group of young gay men, a few lesbians, and a handful of drag queens stood up to the New York police department and held their ground. Within the year, it was proposed that "sexual orientation be added to the groups protected by the city's human rights law. At that time, this was a new idea and the New York City Council was the first legislative body anywhere to consider such legislation."[3] However, the City Council failed to adopt the bill; indeed, New York City would not have a gay and lesbian rights ordinance until 16 years later, after "some 50 cities and the State of Wisconsin had adopted such legislation."[4]

The birthplace of the contemporary GLM was long embroiled over the issue of non-discrimination legislation. It is no secret that the two most powerful opponents were "the Orthodox Jewish community and the Roman Catholic Archdiocese of New York. Conservative and fundamentalist Protestantism . . . (was) not strong enough and visible enough in the city to be a significant barrier."[5]

The religious community of New York, however, did not present a united front on this issue. The Orthodox Jews and the Catholic archbishop voiced their disapproval, but the Episcopal bishop, Paul Moore, Jr., and the Reform Jews, under the leadership of Rabbi Balfour Brickner, openly backed the bill. One commentator went so far as to call Moore and Brickner "stalwart supporters" of the gay rights law.[6]

---

2.   We have not located an American bishop who is on record as supporting IV (i.e., theoretical opposition to gay rights proposals with practical support for the same).

3.   Arthur J. Moore, "Gay Rights and the Churches," in *Christianity and Crisis,* 46 (April 21, 1986), p. 127.

4.   Moore, "Gay Rights. . .," p. 127.

5.   Moore, "Gay Rights. . .," pp. 126-127.

6.   Moore, "Gay Rights. . .," p. 128.

The opponents had their way over and over again; but the issue never went away. Finally, Mayor Edward Koch, a strong proponent of the legislation, devised a way of implementing part of the desired program. In 1980 he issued Executive Order Number 50 (EO 50) which banned discrimination against gays and lesbians by agencies holding contracts with New York City.

At first, the New York Catholic Archdiocese offered no resistance to the order. But this changed with the death of Cardinal Terence Cooke and the accession of John O'Connor as archbishop. Joined with the Salvation Army, O'Connor brought a complaint to the New York State Court of Appeals.[7] They claimed that EO 50 was an instance of interference with the free exercise of religion: under the terms of the order, religious bodies were not exempt (unless, of course, they held no contracts with the city.) The archbishop argued that a Catholic institution or agency ought not to be forced to hire practising homosexuals.

The Court of Appeals agreed with the plaintiffs: EO 50 was struck down. It ruled that only explicit legislation could accomplish the goals of the order. Koch's action was deemed an abuse of his executive powers.

Arthur Moore recounts the subsequent chronology:

> Meantime, Majority Leader Cuite retired and another bitter opponent of the legislation died. The new leader, though personally opposed, promised the mayor that he would allow the full council to vote on the bill. The drafters of the latest version of the bill had reworked it to meet past objections: Religious organizations were specifically exempted; sexual orientation was defined; affirmative action quotas were ruled out; there was explicit denial of endorsing 'any particular behavior or way of life' and of making lawful any act that violates the penal code of the State of New York.[8]

---

7. It is important to note that Bishop Francis Mugavero of Brooklyn did not join with O'Connor in this process. In a joint memoir with Mayor Koch, Cardinal O'Connor attempted an explanation: "The issues in the EO 50 case were complex, and the fact that the Bishop of Brooklyn and I took different approaches added to the confusion. I can certainly understand the confusion on the part of the press and their question: 'If it's acceptable to Bishop Mugavero, why isn't it acceptable to you?' That's a fair question. Its answer would require an analysis of circumstances that would take too much space. . . . Suffice it to say, Bishop Mugavero and I are committed to the same Church doctrine. If at times we take differing approaches on how best to preserve that doctrine, such is to be expected of men of different temperaments, and in differing sets of circumstances, even though we are both headquartered in the same city." See John Cardinal O'Connor and Mayor Edward I Koch, *His Eminence and Hizzoner: A Candid Exchange* (New York: William Morrow, 1989), pp. 123-124.

8. Moore, "Gay Rights. . .," p. 128.

Even with these emendations, Cardinal O'Connor's position remained constant. In no uncertain terms he voiced the archdiocese's disapproval. Looking back on the issue, he explained:

> This is an excellent example of the complexities of Church-State
> relationships when it comes to the formation of public policy. I
> see the churchman's responsibility primarily in terms of the moral
> dimensions of any policy. I do not believe in a 'human right' to
> practice homosexual behavior. I believe that constituting such be-
> havior as either a 'civil' or a 'protected' right can have a severely
> damaging effect on society at large, in the long run, adversely af-
> fecting marriage, family life and young people in a particularly
> grave way. I see it, further, as one of the many efforts to impose a
> national religion of civil rights on our entire society.[9]

For Cardinal O'Connor, the issue of civil rights protection for gay
people falls squarely under the rubric of the Church's sexual ethic. "Homosexual behavior" (i.e., the genital manipulations of homosexual persons) is an intrinsic evil and the law should not grant people "rights" to
gravely immoral behavior. In O'Connor's vision, the Catholic position on
the moral valence of homosexual acts inspires opposition to measures
which attempt to ensure fair treatment for gay men and lesbians. Since
gay and lesbian sexual relating is deemed immoral, it follows logically
that if it were to fail to receive social disapproval, society must be said to
have taken a turn for the worse. A "live and let live" attitude on homosexuality contributes to the further erosion of the strength and vitality of
American marriages and family life. Young people are particularly at risk;
they are all but defenseless in the wake of militant gay ideology.

Given his past forays into this battle, few expected O'Connor to support the newly proposed legislation. However, the Coalition for Lesbian
and Gay Rights believed that it had received a pledge of neutrality from
the neighboring diocese of Brooklyn. Representatives from the coalition
had met with auxiliary bishop Joseph Sullivan, counsel Mildred Shanley,
and canonist Monsignor William Varvaro; "(i)t was reported that Bishop
Sullivan had told Catholic Charities that they had no problem with the
bill."[10]

However, Brooklyn's ordinary, Francis Mugavero, did not remain
neutral. He joined Cardinal O'Connor in issuing a public statement which
attacked the proposal as " 'exceedingly dangerous to our society' and said
that 'what the bill primarily and ultimately seeks is the legal approval of
homosexual conduct and activity.'[11] To this, they added the interesting

---

9.   O'Connor and Koch, *His Eminence and Hizzoner,* p. 311.

10.   Moore, "Gay Rights. . .," p. 128.

11.   It is unclear whether "conduct" and "activity" constitute a rhetorical parallelism or if
two distinct realities are envisioned.

thought that 'it is a common perception of the public that whatever is declared legal by that very fact becomes morally right.' "[12]

It is important to note that Bishop Mugavero's pastoral letter, "Sexuality: God's Gift," which was published on February 11, 1976 in *Origins,* was hailed at the time by Catholic progressives. In a survey of developments in Catholic sexual ethics, Philip Keane was to write: "Individual leaders such as Bishop Mugavero of Brooklyn have tried to develop sensitive positions on issues such as homosexuality."[13] James Hanigan remarked that Mugavero's letter had "won wide acclaim for its positive, compassionate and supportive tone, as well as its direct language."[14] Richard McCormick, too, joined in hailing "Sexuality: God's Gift:"

> Mugavero's language and tone meet people where they are. Tone in moral matters, is not everything, but it is enormously important; for it reveals attitudes towards persons, norms, conflicts, God, the human condition. Because this is so, tone not only affects communicability; at some point it also cuts close to the basic value judgments themselves. . . . That is why a document that is tonally inadequate risks being substantially incomplete or even wrong.[15]

To give a picture of Mugavero's 1976 stance on homosexuality and gay rights, the following excerpt from "Sexuality: God's Gift" is relevant:

> We urge homosexual men and women to avoid identifying their personhood with their sexual orientation. They are so much more as persons than this single aspect of their personality. That richness must not be lost. . . It is not homosexuality which should be one's claim to acceptance or human rights or to be loved by us all: it is the fact that we are all brothers and sisters under the Fatherhood of God. Our community must explore ways to secure the legitimate rights of all our citizens regardless of sexual orientation, while being sensitive to the understanding and hopes of all involved.[16]

Some of the Bishop's concerns here might strike the careful analyst as somewhat contrived. Does anyone *really* identify their very personhood with

---

12. · Moore, "Gay Rights. . .," p. 128.

13. Philip S. Keane, *Sexual Morality: A Catholic Perspective* (New York: Paulist Press, 1977), p. 98. On p. 206, n. 26, Keane describes Mugavero's letter as "an excellent pastoral approach to homosexuals."

14. James P. Hanigan, *What Are They Saying About Sexual Morality?* (New York: Paulist Press, 1982), pp. 65-66.

15. Richard A. McCormick, *Notes on Moral Theology, 1965 Through 1980* (Washington, D.C.: University Press of America, 1980), pp. 679-670. Cited in Hanigan, *What Are They Saying. . .,* p. 66.

16. Quoted in Nugent and Gramick, *A Time to Speak,* pp. 2-3.

their sexual orientation? Surely the overwhelming majority of people can distinguish between their humanity and an aspect of their personality. Similarly, it seems that one would have to search far and wide to find an individual who holds that an aspect of her psychic composition is the source of her claim to 'acceptance or human rights or to being loved by us all.'

However, Mugavero had good reason to frame the issues in this way. If one's rights flow from one's humanity – not from one's sexual orientation – then homosexuals who act upon their sexual drives do not thereby forfeit their human or civil rights. When it is further recognized that all sorts (quantitatively the vast majority if over 90% of human society is heterosexually oriented) of intrinsically disordered and gravely immoral conduct flow from people's *hetero*sexual orientation, the desire to discriminate against homosexual persons – even the most flamboyant – is revealed as arbitrary and unjust.

Given his pastoral letter and the repudiation of its principles implied by joining Cardinal O'Connor in opposing the new non-discrimination legislation, Bishop Mugavero was assumed to have been pressured into the stand he took. He denied any such thing, but as Arthur Moore remarks:

> This denial was not widely believed, the only question being where the pressure came from. Informed sources say that O'Connor got the apostolic nuncio to the United States, Archbishop Pio Laghi, to do the job for him.[17]

Cardinal O'Connor continued his attack on the legislation. The culmination of his campaign took place in a Sunday homily at St. Patrick's Cathedral, just a few days before the vote . . .

> He called the measure an affront to Judeo-Christian values that would offer legal protection to sexual behavior that is 'abnormal' and 'a sin.' He warned, 'Let not any legislature impose anyone's morality on society or on the Catholic Church.'[18]

The Orthodox Jews, too, continued their public opposition. They targeted Mayor Koch for their displays of disapproval. On several occasions, when "Mayor Koch testified for the bill at public hearings, some 50 to 75 Hasidic Jews stood up, turned their backs on him and began jeering and booing. As the mayor left the room, they shouted, 'Shame! Shame! Shame!' Rabbi Yehuda Levin of Brooklyn said that the bill was supported by 'your corrupt mayor and his Greenwich Village buddies.' "[19]

---

17. Moore, "Gay Rights. . .," p. 128. Moore informs his readers that after the O'Connor-Mugavero statement, the Bishop of Brooklyn made no further public comments on the issue.

18. Moore, "Gay Rights. . .," p. 128. This last statement was a masterful piece of rhetoric. It was, after all, exactly what the gay and lesbian community had been accusing Cardinal O'Connor of trying to do.

Bishop Moore and Rabbi Brickner versus Rabbi Levin and Cardinal O'Connor. As the time came for the vote, the situation had all the makings of a religious war. Ideologies were in high gear; tempers flared. After O'Connor's appearance in the pulpit at St. Patrick's,

> Moore . . . held a press conference with Rabbi Brickner, the Rev. William Sloan Coffin, Jr., of Riverside Church, and Roman Catholic Father Bernard Lynch endorsing the bill. Later he (Moore) went so far as to publicly snipe at Cardinal O'Connor's motives, which drew an equally irritated reply from O'Connor. Both Moore and Brickner testified for the bill at the public hearings and held a second news conference to declare passage 'a simple and urgent matter of justice' and say that 'it is high time we eliminated this last vestige of discrimination.'[20]

"Amid great public clamor, vituperative exchanges and near-physical combat hardly observant of Marquis of Queensberry rules, the gay rights legislation passed,"[21] is how Cardinal O'Connor described the final resolution of the conflict.

The Cardinal has remained convinced of the rightness of his stance. Indeed, he gives the impression that the only possible Catholic approach to gay and lesbian rights ordinances is active opposition:

> What . . . can I say . . . to those I hurt because of my own belief in and attempted fidelity to Church teaching? I cannot bring myself to believe that they could ever have even a shred of respect for an archbishop, the primary teacher of Church doctrine in this or any other archdiocese, should he be unfaithful to what the Church holds and what he personally believes. Nor could they respect an archbishop who teaches or condones what he believes is ultimately damaging to homosexual persons themselves, simply for his own popularity, or so that he may be perceived as compassionate. Popularity *is* a heady intoxicant, but as every intoxicant, it can destroy the life of one who thirsts for it above all else.[22]

2. JOSEPH CARDINAL BERNARDIN

By all accounts, Cardinal Joseph Bernardin, archbishop of Chicago, is possessed of a temperament very much unlike that of Cardinal O'Con-

---

19. Moore, "Gay Rights. . .," p. 128. Moore deems the Orthodox Jewish opposition as having been clearly counter-productive: "its reliance on the Levitical Code and its near advocacy of stoning homosexuals scared most of those not already committed to its point of view. As one bystander put it, he never believed that there was any need for a gay rights bill until he heard Rabbi Levin" (in *ibid.*).

20. Moore, "Gay Rights. . .," p. 128.

21. O'Connor and Koch, *His Eminence and Hizzoner,* p. 311.

22. O'Connor and Koch, *His Eminence and Hizzoner,* p. 310.

nor. Bernardin is "the man in the middle," the great conciliator, the voice for the moderate wing of the American episcopacy.[23] Bernardin has never been accused of grandstanding; he is a man of well-measured speech and action. The adoption by the Catholic bishops of his approach to human life issues – "The Seamless Garment" – reflects well on Bernardin's insight and persuasiveness.

On the issue of gay rights, Cardinal Bernardin has taken a highly nuanced position. In his "Letter to the Illinois Gay and Lesbian Task Force"[24] (January 2, 1985), he clearly spelled out his policy. In the first place, he remarked: "Let me state clearly at the outset that I am not afraid to take an unpopular position in defense of human or civil rights. However, I know you understand that any leadership I might provide in regard to such issues would have to be exercised within the parameters of the Catholic Church's teaching."[25]

From the dichotomy drawn between human and civil rights on the one hand, and the Catholic Church's teaching on the other, the Illinois Gay and Lesbian Task Force must have seen the handwriting on the wall: no support for protective legislation from the archbishop of Chicago. Since the publication of Pope John XXIII's encyclical *Pacem in terris,* however, it might seem counterintuitive that Catholic teaching can find itself in conflict with human or civil rights. What accounts for Bernardin's position?

The Cardinal enumerated four principles which guided his decision not to support a gay and lesbian rights ordinance for the city of Chicago. First, he affirmed the human dignity of homosexual persons. Quoting the 1976 U.S. Bishops' pastoral letter, "To Live in Christ Jesus,"[26] he wrote: "Homosexuals, like everyone else, should not suffer prejudice against their basic human rights. They have a right to respect, friendship, and justice. They should have an active role in the Christian community."[27]

---

23. Such a role has exacted a certain price from the Cardinal and from the Archdiocese of Chicago. See Robert J. McClory, "Bernardin's Chicago Adrift in a Sea of Malaise," in *National Catholic Reporter* (February 14, 1992), pp. 6-9; and Robert J. McClory, "Interview with Cardinal Bernardin," in *ibid.*, pp. 10-11. Bernardin responded to the first of these articles in an editorial in *National Catholic Reporter* (March 6, 1992), p. 2, as did Eugene Kennedy (in *ibid.*, pp. 2, 18).

24. Joseph Cardinal Bernardin, "Letter to the Illinois Gay and Lesbian Task Force," in John Gallagher, ed., *Homosexuality and the Magisterium: Documents from the Vatican and the U.S. Bishops, 1975-1985* (Mt. Rainier, MD: New Ways Ministry, 1986), pp. 103-104.

25. Bernardin, "Letter. . .," p. 103.

26. It is interesting to note that Cardinal Bernardin got the name of the bishops' letter wrong: he referred to the pastoral as "The Gift of Sexuality." This is a close approximation of the title of Bishop Mugavero's pastoral letter of the same year.

27. Bernardin, "Letter. . .," p. 103.

Secondly, Bernardin affirmed:

There is no place for arbitrary discrimination and prejudice against a person because of sexual attraction. We especially deplore violence and harassment directed against such persons. Moreover, all human persons, including those with a homosexual orientation, have a right to decent employment and housing.[28]

There is nothing in these first two principles which would demand that the Archbishop oppose a gay rights ordinance for Chicago. Gays and lesbians are said to have a right to 'respect, friendship, and justice.' Moreover, they should not be denied 'decent employment and housing.' At this point, *not* supporting anti-discrimination legislation sounds like a violation of the Church's teaching and the Cardinal's responsibility as a bishop.

In the third principle, Bernardin rehearsed the Church's moral evaluation of "homosexual acts." "Homosexual *activity*, as distinguished from homosexual orientation, *is* morally wrong." He then affirmed that "a corollary of this traditional teaching of the Church is that patterns of life, sometimes referred to as 'lifestyles,' which encourage immoral behavior are also morally objectionable. . . . As a Church, we do not approve of those patterns of life or lifestyles which encourage, promote, or advocate homosexual activity."[29]

The corollary enunciated by the Cardinal is problematic. Notice that he does not speak of "lifestyles wherein immoral behavior is practised," but rather "lifestyles which encourage immoral behavior." A lifestyle, being by definition any pattern of life of fallible human beings prone to immorality, can never be free from the potential of wickedness. Sin is found in the lives of the devotees of every conceivable lifestyle. And since genital manipulations conducive to orgasm[30] make up only a fraction of all that might go into a "homosexual lifestyle," it would seem to be unjust to allow discrimination against gays and lesbians.

No doubt this is why the Cardinal moves the discussion to lifestyles which "encourage, promote, or advocate homosexual activity." However, the language used is unfortunate: it is vague and, therefore, potentially misleading. No indication is given as to which types of homosexual life patterns are implicated in promoting, encouraging, and advocating homosexual activity. Surely one would want to say that the homosexual prostitute (although he may not be a true homosexual) is involved in encouraging gay sex. The same would have to be said of the proprietor of a

---

28. Bernardin, "Letter. . .," p. 103.

29. Bernardin, "Letter. . .," p. 103.

30. Technically, this is all that the Catholic Church has against the "practising homosexual" as such. "Camp" and interest in *haute couture* (following the stereotypical image of the gay male), for instance, have never been defined as immoral.

"sex shop" whose wares facilitate homosexual orgasms. (This business-man, too, of course, might not be gay.) However, is the celibate, lesbian, Catholic religious who works in advocacy for gay and lesbian rights guilty of advocating immoral behavior? Is the gay couple who do not "wear their lifestyle on their sleeve" guilty of encouraging others to go and do likewise?

At the same time, one is justified in questioning how much "encouragement" is thought to be necessary before the average gay man or lesbian "breaks down" and commits immoral acts. PCHP, for instance, warns against downplaying the average homosexual's will power.[31] Moreover, no amount of encouragement, promotion, or advocacy seems likely to entice the constitutional heterosexual to adopt a "homosexual lifestyle."[32]

Bernardin's third principle, then, is much too ambiguous to be helpful in judging concrete circumstances. One is given no guidance on who is to be taken as an advocate or promoter of sinful behavior.[33]

Bernardin's fourth principle, being highly controversial, warrants a full citation:

> Parents have the right to keep their children free during their formative years of any person(s) or influence(s) which might draw them toward homosexual practice or condoning homosexual activity.[34]

The danger of such a principle ought to be apparent. Adult-child sexual activity is rightly a criminal offense in all fifty states; the Cardinal had

---

31. Cf. "What is at all costs to be avoided is the unfounded and demeaning assumption that the sexual behavior of homosexual persons is always and totally compulsive and therefore inculpable. What is essential is that the fundamental liberty which characterizes the human person and gives him his dignity be recognized as belonging to the homosexual person as well. As in every conversion from evil, the abandonment of homosexual activity will require a profound collaboration of the individual with God's liberating grace." PCHP, #11, in Gramick and Furey, *The Vatican and Homosexuality*, p. 6.

32. As we have seen (*supra*, pp. 40-41), a person's sexual orientation is not prone to change. However, it bears noting that, given the right set of circumstances (especially the unavailability of the opposite sex), a significant percentage of the population can be enticed into isolated instances of homosexual behavior. Such activity, however, cannot be termed a "homosexual lifestyle."

33. The traditional category of "scandal" would appear to be preferable to Bernardin's awkward use of "encourage, promote, and advocate." Scandal, moreover, entails a judgment concerning the intention of the person under question. One is guilty of scandal who *intends* the sin of another. This distinction could get the above-mentioned Catholic religious "off the hook" as well as the gay couple. See, for instance, Bruno Schuller, "Direkte Totung – indirekte Totung," in *Theologie und Philosophie*, 47 (1972): 341-357; cited in his "The Double Effect in Catholic Thought: A Reevaluation," in Richard McCormick and Paul Ramsey, eds., *Doing Evil to Achieve Good: Moral Choice in Conflict Situations* (Chicago: Loyola University Press, 1978), pp. 165-192, at p. 166.

34. Bernardin, "Letter. . .," p. 104.

to know that non-discrimination legislation for gays and lesbians contains no hidden clause which would decriminalize the seduction of children and (or) the corruption of minors. What, then, is the right that parents are said to have which would trump the rights of a gay person? How might society be structured so that children in their formative years do not receive a favorable impression of homosexuality?

The Cardinal, for instance, would surely not wish to claim that Catholic parents have the right to keep their children free from (say) Jehovah's Witnesses and that because of this, Jehovah's Witnesses must be made to forfeit some of the civil rights they would normally have had if they weren't such a threat to the orthodoxy of young Catholics. Even though it is clear that Roman Catholics and Jehovah's Witnesses operate in radically different dogmatic and liturgical worlds, and even though it is well-known that a significant percentage of Jehovah's Witnesses are people who have been actively recruited from Catholicism, it is inconceivable that a Catholic leader would advocate the diminishment of Jehovah's Witnesses' civil rights.

To return directly to Bernardin's fourth principle, it should be noted that the myth of homosexual recruitment seems to be lurking not far below the surface. The impression is given that gays and lesbians are likely to draw young people toward homosexual practice and the belief that there is nothing about homosexuality which raises any moral qualms. Why else would parents have a right to keep their children from the presence of such people?[35]

Bernardin gave no explanation; but in the next paragraph he explicitly stated: "We do not assume that many homosexuals are child abusers or seducers of young people."[36] Moreover, he precised: "We have not recommended the firing of any persons of homosexual orientation from Church-related positions where they may be simply disliked."[37] The archdiocesan hiring procedures did not allow for questioning potential employees about their sexual orientation. Finally, the Cardinal said that anyone

---

35. It is important to note in this context that in at least one survey, Catholic teenagers appear rather intolerant of gays and lesbians. Michael Maher conducted a survey among Catholic confirmation candidates for parishes in Kansas City (the research was incorporated into a master's thesis accepted by the Faculty of Education at the University of Kansas). Among his findings: "More than one of three Catholic young men . . . did not agree with a statement that physical violence against homosexuals is not acceptable. . .; almost half of the entire group . . . did not agree that Church leaders should speak out against derogatory terms, jokes, and physical violence directed against homosexual people. . .; nearly one out of four young women . . . and three out of five young men . . . did not agree that the Church should treat homosexual people with understanding" [See Kevin Kelly, "Catholic Teenagers 'Intolerant of Gays,'" in *Bondings*, 14 (1991), pp. 1, 11].

36. Bernardin, "Letter. . .," p. 104.

37. Bernardin, "Letter. . .," p. 104.

acting in a non-professional manner on the job or who publicly advocates behavior that is contrary to Catholic morality would be subject to disciplinary action. And, significantly, "that would include anyone who promotes or advocates a *heterosexual* lifestyle which we would consider immoral, as, for example, people living together without benefit of marriage."[38]

Where, then, did this leave Bernardin in terms of *civil* legislation which would protect gays and lesbians from discrimination? By all accounts, the archdiocesan policies were moderate – not likely to anger the homosexual community nor inflame a more traditional and conservative Catholic. Toward the end of his letter, Cardinal Bernardin showed that he appreciated the bipolar nature of the question. One senses a certain ambivalence as he clarified his position:

> My own position, then, is this: I firmly deplore acts of violence, degradation, discrimination, or diminishment of any human person – including anyone with a homosexual orientation. I am especially concerned that such attitudes or acts might be found at times in institutions of this archdiocese. At the same time, I am equally bound to teach that homosexual activity and patterns of life which promote it are immoral.[39]

These last three sentences are a perfect accounting of the dilemma that has faced the Catholic hierarchy in the United States since the beginning of the GLM. There is no way that the Gospel and the Church's social teaching of the last 100 years could advocate remaining silent – and thus being an accomplice – when human persons are subject to violence, degradation, discrimination, or diminishment. At the same time, the Church's magisterium has, on several occasions in recent years, vigorously reaffirmed the objective immorality of homosexual behavior. On the one hand, there is the Church's social ethic; on the other hand, its sexual ethic: how is one to resolve this dilemma in terms of concrete policy?

In the following passage, Cardinal Bernardin came to a resolution:

> My specific concern about gay rights legislation is its implications. If it implies acceptance or approval of homosexual activity *or* advocacy of a lifestyle which encourages homosexual activity, we will have no choice as a Church but to oppose the legislation. If it merely provides needed legal protection for people with a homosexual orientation and *explicitly* does not approve homosexual activity or endorse the kind of lifestyle which would promote it, we could support it.[40]

Less than a year after the Illinois Gay and Lesbian Task Force received Bernardin's letter, the Chicago City Council was faced with the

---

38. Bernardin, "Letter. . .," p. 104.
39. Bernardin, "Letter. . .," p. 104.
40. Bernardin, "Letter. . .," p. 104.

question of a municipal gay rights ordinance.[41] As had been the experience in New York and in many other cities, this issue inflamed the passions of many Chicagoans. To the chagrin of the homosexual community, Cardinal Bernardin went on record as opposing the ordinance.[42] He began an explanation of his opposition in the following manner:

> In the case of gay rights legislation, I seek to balance two values: (1) the fact that no person should be discriminated against because of his or her sexual orientation; and (2) the normativeness of heterosexual marital intimacy as the proper context for intimate genital encounters.[43]

In this particular instance, Bernardin judged that the proposed ordinance would compromise the normativity of heterosexual marital intimacy.[44] Unfortunately, he did not specify how such a compromise would have been effected. Since the ordinance did not say that anyone who is so inclined *ought* to partake of gay sex, and since the ordinance did not state that all Chicagoans must consider a homosexual way of life to be as valid as a heterosexual one, one is justified in surmising that the Cardinal would see heterosexuality compromised in *any* ordinance or *any* piece of legislation that purported to protect gays and lesbians. Bernardin's position seemed to have

---

41. See the following for a summary of the controversy: "Gay Rights Ordinance Fails," in *The Chicago Tribune,* July 30, 1986, p. 1; "Chicago City Council Defeats Gay Rights Bill," in *The Advocate,* no. 454 (September 2, 1986), p. 13; "Homosexual Sex is (Objectively) Immoral," *The* Chicago Tribune, July 17, 1986, p. 1. [This last headline, of course, is a reference to Catholic moral teaching. It was unambiguously reaffirmed by Cardinal Bernardin. However, for a respected daily newspaper to put it in bold print on its front page counts as a serious failure to grasp the delicate nuances of the Cardinal's position. One can only imagine how the headline would have read if the Cardinal had *supported* the ordinance.] These sources are cited by Mohr, *Gays/Justice,* pp. 330-331.

42. Richard Mohr's exasperation is palpable: "Gays would do well to appeal to the traditional American value that religion is not to be the fount of public policy, for it is just exactly religious opposition to gays that gives their average opponent the false appearance of being himself principled in his opposition. Here the grandeurs of Catholicism are much more dangerous than Protestant fundamentalism, Bernardin more dangerous than Falwell. Catholicism's natural law theology . . . has an air of intellectual respectability, of transferable universality, underwritten for good measure by tradition, an air that fundamentalists and their recent and revealed gods have not. It is perfectly respectable and indeed the principled thing to do for gays to remind the nation that it is not a Catholic country; few would disagree with that. It is perfectly respectable, indeed the thing to do to remind political conservatives of what the National Conference of Catholic Bishops has to say about capitalism. To do that might just get them to reconsider the role of God in public policy. But in any case, it is time for gays to stop pandering to un-American religious immorality, to stop begging for rights from religious bigots and using religious do-gooders as their own front men." See *Gays/Justice,* p. 331.

43. Joseph Cardinal Bernardin, "I, Too, Struggle," in *Commonweal,* 111 (December 26, 1986), p. 683.

44. See Bernardin, "I, Too, Struggle," p. 684.

been that no matter how ordinances are phrased, if they become law, the average person is going to get the impression that "gay is now good."[45]

In the end, the Cardinal was to realize that his opposition to the city's proposed gay rights ordinance produced much ambivalence. His malaise concerning this issue was clear:

> I know that I have angered some in the homosexual community who would argue . . . that to protect orientation but not activity is unacceptable because it partitions the human person. I have angered others who feel that it is wrong to grant *any* rights to homosexuals. Moreover, I have learned how difficult it is in our legal system for legislators who agree with my position to draft appropriate legislation.[46]

Nonetheless, the Cardinal had had his way: the ordinance failed to pass the City Council on July 29, 1986, by a vote of 30 to 18.[47] By most accounts, Bernardin's opposition was critical to its defeat.[48]

3. ARCHBISHOP JOHN R. QUINN

With relations between the Catholic and gay communities invariably running from bad to worse, John R. Quinn has the unenviable task of being the Catholic archbishop of San Francisco – the city which is indisputably "the capital of gay life."[49] Archbishop Quinn has issued several important pastoral letters on the constellation of issues surrounding homosexuality. These letters will eventually be the focus of this section. First, however, we will discuss the political backlash that the GLM faced by the end of the 1970s, culminating in California's Proposition 6, the so-called "Briggs Initiative."

Throughout much of the 1970s, the GLM scored modest gains. A number of municipalities enacted non-discrimination ordinances, the courts were more inclined to provide equal treatment under the law, and generally American society seemed more accepting of the aspirations of its gay and lesbian citizens.[50]

All was not well, however. By the late 1970s a political backlash was gaining momentum. One of its key players was a rather unlikely figure who held minor celebrity status: Anita Bryant. Bryant had for quite some time been identified with conservative causes[51] and when Miami be-

---

45.   See, especially, Stephen Elred, "Gay Rights/Gay Plight: An Open Letter to Cardinal Bernardin," in *Commonweal*, 113 (December 26, 1986), pp. 680-682.

46.   Bernardin, "I, Too, Struggle," p. 684.

47.   See Leigh W. Rutledge, *The Gay Decades* (New York: Penguin/Plume, 1992), p. 260.

48.   Elred, "Gay Rights/Gay Plight," p. 680.

49.   Edmund White, *States of Desire: Travels in Gay America* (New York: Penguin/Plume, 1991), p. 32.

50.   See Marcus, *Making History. . .*, pp. 172-173.

came the first major Southern city to enact a gay rights ordinance – prohibiting housing and employment discrimination against gay men and lesbians, she organized "Save Our Children" (SOC). Her intention was to overturn the protective legislation. On March 20, 1977, SOC took out a full-page advertisement in *The Miami Herald*. It read as follows:

> Homosexuality is nothing new. Cultures throughout history have dealt with homosexuals almost universally with disdain, abhorrence, disgust – even death. . . . The recruitment of our children is absolutely necessary for the survival and growth of homosexuality. Since homosexuals cannot reproduce, they *must* recruit, *must* freshen their ranks. And who better qualifies as a likely recruit than a teenage boy or girl who is surging with sexual awareness.[52]

The *non sequiturs* in this advertisement notwithstanding, SOC made great strides in the polls. It was able to get six times the required number of signatures to put the ordinance up for a city-wide vote. To the shock of gay activists throughout the country – who had, by and large, underestimated SOC and its coalition of religious conservatives[53] – the gay rights ordinance was overturned on June 7, 1977 by a margin of more than two to one.[54]

A year later, revelling in international notoriety, Anita Bryant spelled out some of her most basic beliefs in an interview in *Playboy* (June 1, 1978). Bryant, the interviewer reported:

- insists that homosexuality inevitably leads to sadomasochism, drug abuse, and suicide
- claims that homosexuals are called 'fruits' because they eat 'the forbidden fruit of the tree of life' (i.e., semen)
- reveals that if the gay rights ordinance had passed in Dade County there was 'a group of prostitutes who were going to initiate similar legislation permitting whores to stand up in front of kids in the classroom and then ply their trade'

---

51. In 1970, for instance, she was "honored by the Freedom Foundation for her part in organizing . . . (the) 'Rally for Decency' at Miami's Orange Bowl. The rally – whose themes were 'We Believe in God,' 'We Love Our Families,' and 'Down With Obscenity' – drew over thirty thousand participants. . . ." See Rutledge, *The Gay Decades*, p. 15.

52. Quoted in Rutledge, *The Gay Decades*, p. 103. It is important to note that SOC quickly gained national attention. Shortly after its formation, "the Arkansas State House of Representatives unanimously. . .(passed) a special resolution commending Bryant for her antigay crusade." The lawmaker who introduced the resolution explained the rationale: "When you go against God's law, you have no human rights" (quoted in *ibid.*).

53. Bryant styled herself a Christian activist and much of the rhetoric of SOC under her leadership involved the religious condemnation of homosexuality. Although it sounds like part of a stand-up comedian's routine, one of her favorite slogans was: "If homosexuality were normal, God would have created Adam and Bruce." See Rutledge, *The Gay Decades*, p. 101.

54. See Rutledge, *The Gay Decades*, p. 108. Within six months, voters in St. Paul, Minnesota; Wichita, Kansas; and Eugene, Oregon repealed gay rights ordinances (see *ibid.*, pp. 122-123).

- objects to people using the terms 'queer' or 'faggot,' but says that 'homo' isn't really all 'that bad'
- acknowledges that she's never read the Bible cover to cover
- advocates homosexual behavior being classified as a felony punishable by at least twenty years in prison, even for young first-time 'offenders'
- says that all Jews and Muslims are 'going to hell' because they haven't embraced Jesus Christ as their personal savior
- asserts that no matter what happens in her marriage, divorce isn't 'in my vocabulary'[55]

It is no wonder that Anita Bryant became *the* American homosexuals loved to hate.[56]

Less than a week after Bryant's interview appeared on the newsstands, the Briggs Initiative ("Proposition 6") qualified for the November ballot in California. This proposition, named for its author – state senator John Briggs – was designed to "bar gay people, or 'anyone advocating a homosexual lifestyle,' from teaching in California's public schools."[57] What was remarkable in this instance was how the *opposition* constituted a "popular mobilisation which extended beyond normal political boundaries."[58] The Catholic archbishop of San Francisco joined his voice in opposition to the measure. In a statement issued on October 11, 1978, Archbishop Quinn wrote:

> Proposition 6 involves moral, justice and civil rights issues . . .
> (T)he civil rights of persons who are homosexual must also be our
> concern. Hence, the American bishops affirmed the following
> principles in a national pastoral letter on moral values: 'Homo-
> sexuals, like everyone else, should not suffer from prejudice
> against their basic human rights. They have a right to respect,

---

55. In Rutledge, *The Gay Decades*, p. 124.

56. However, "after the breakup of her marriage a few years later, Bryant expressed regret over her previous actions in a dramatic about-face." See Woods, *Another Kind of Love*, p. 62, n. 6. In the December, 1980 issue of *The Ladies' Home Journal*, Bryant would claim that "she no longer feels as militantly as she once did about gay rights. 'The answers don't seem so simple now,' acknowledges the singer, who also admits to having been unfaithful to her ex-husband. 'I'm more inclined to say live and let live.'" See Rutledge, *The Gay Decades*, p. 161.

57. Rutledge, *The Gay Decades*, p. 120.

58. Jeffrey Weeks, *Sexuality and Its Discontents: Meanings, Myths, & Modern Sexualities* (New York: Routledge, 1985), p. 265, n. 1. It is noteworthy that even ex-governor Ronald Reagan went on record as opposing the Briggs Initiative. Randy Shilts, in *The Mayor of Castro Street: The Life and Times of Harvey Milk* (New York: St. Martin's Press, 1982), p. 243, reports: "Former Governor Ronald Reagan. . .went on record against Prop 6, observing, 'Whatever else it is, homosexuality is not a contagious disease like measles.'"

friendship and justice.' There is serious reason to believe that the proposed amendment in this initiative would tend to violate and would limit the civil rights of homosexual persons.[59]

It is important to call attention to the *form* of legislation that was opposed by Archbishop Quinn. The Briggs Initiative would have excluded homosexuals from teaching in the public schools. To be against it meant, then, that one did not believe that gays and lesbians – as a category of persons – should be declared unfit for employment by California school boards. It could not be construed as meaning that one wishes to promote the social acceptance of homosexual behavior. In other words, it would seem likely that Cardinal Bernardin's approach would not have differed from Archbishop Quinn's. In any event, supporting a "positive" ordinance is more problematic than opposing a "negative" one. The latter appears as a clear-cut instance of injustice; the former can easily be interpreted as affording "special treatment" to an undeserving minority.

In the end, the Briggs Initiative was defeated rather handily: 59% to 41%.[60] Charles Brydon, a gay rights activist, remarked: "That was an incredible achievement: a state-wide ballot issue coming through as well as it did in a state with such a diverse population."[61] It is safe to say that the opposition of the Catholic Church had an important role to play in the defeat of Proposition 6.[62]

3.1 *"A Pastoral Letter on Homosexuality"*

On May 5, 1980, Archbishop Quinn issued a pastoral letter on homosexuality. This document received wide attention and would eventually serve as the foundation of at least one other bishop's attempt to write cogently on homosexuality.[63]

Quinn's pastoral letter is remarkable for its grasp of the issues involved and its willingness to tackle the difficult issues of biblical exegesis and ethical normativity. The tone that is struck throughout is clearly *pastoral*: sincere, serious, understanding.

In the first section, entitled "The Present-Day Situation," Quinn recognizes that much has changed in American society's understanding of homosexuality; indeed, in the not-so-distant past most people would have

---

59. Quoted in Nugent and Gramick, *A Time to Speak*, p. 14.

60. See Rutledge, *The Gay Decades*, p. 129.

61. "The Insider: Charles Brydon," in Marcus, *Making History. . .*, p. 308.

62. Bishops John Cummins (Oakland) and Juan Arzube (Los Angeles) also issued strongly-worded denunciations of Proposition 6, as did the Directors of the California Conference of Catholic Charities and *America* magazine's editor. See Nugent and Gramick, *A Time to Speak*, pp. 14-15 for the documentation.

63. Cf. Bishop Stanislaus Brzana (Ogdensburg, New York), "Homosexuality and Human Dignity," in *Origins*, 13 (February 2, 1984), pp. 75-76.

considered a public discourse on homosexuality to be unthinkable. Many homosexual people, too, have changed their tactics: they are unwilling to remain hidden from society, forever lurking in the shadows of polite company. No, they acknowledge who they are and they claim minority status – and the civil protection that this status ought to afford them. What is more, within and without the Church, people are clamoring for change in the traditional Catholic moral evaluation of homosexual behavior. Some see no good reasons why it shouldn't take a place beside heterosexual coupling as a valid human expression of love and commitment.

> In short, we are being besieged to move from a non-prejudicial attitude toward individuals to a point of view of total acceptance of homosexuality as a legitimate personal and public choice. Thus homosexuality is seen as a legitimate alternative to heterosexuality and the society is asked to support this position. Does this warrant our agreement?[64]

It will come to no one's surprise that this question will eventually be answered by the Archbishop with a resounding "No." Even at a distance of more than a decade, it is unimaginable that an American Catholic archbishop might argue for the moral legitimacy of a "homosexual lifestyle."[65] Be that as it may, it is necessary to highlight an exaggeration in Quinn's statement of the problem and a subtle *non sequitur*.

In the first place, the Archbishop claims that the Catholic Church is being asked to take on an attitude of "total acceptance of homosexuality as a legitimate personal and public choice." Insofar as the Church has not granted "total acceptance" to heterosexuality – if, for instance, one includes adultery, fornication, and rape under the umbrella of "heterosexuality" – it goes without saying that a "total acceptance of homosexuality" is out of the question. There are, however, no serious calls for the Church to bless the homosexual seduction of minors, to celebrate the S & M scene, to sanction gay promiscuity; in other words, no one is really asking for *total* acceptance of all that might be taken to comprise "homosexuality." At the time of Quinn's writing, as in the present-day, those who are "besieging" the Church ("beseeching" is perhaps more accurate) are doing so in the name of an extremely circumscribed range of "homosexual behaviors." Most are not even willing to put this highly limited version of "homosexuality" on the same pedestal as "heterosexuality."[66]

---

64. Archbishop John R. Quinn, "A Pastoral Letter on Homosexuality," in Gallagher, *Homosexuality and the Magisterium*, p. 22.

65. Emphasis here is placed equally on "American" as on "Catholic." [For an example of a French bishop who is willing to reconsider this question, see "Interview with Bishop Jacques Gaillot of Evreux, France: A Welcoming and Listening Church," in *Bondings*, 15 (Winter, 1992-1993), p. 1. The interview originally appeared in *Gai Pied* (October 8, 1992). It was written by Eric Lamien and translated by Joe Orndorff.]

As for the *non sequitur*, Quinn gives the impression that homosexuality is the object of choice when he writes: "Thus homosexuality is seen as a legitimate alternative to heterosexuality and the society is asked to support this position." The wording here is unfortunate. The true lesbian, for instance, does not have two alternatives between which to choose, one "gay" and the other "straight." Homosexually oriented people cannot seriously opt for the "heterosexual alternative." They can choose, of course, whether to engage in this or that sexual act, but they cannot choose their sexual feelings. The Archbishop would have done well to have said something like "thus some homosexual behavior is seen as a legitimate alternative to perpetual continence[67] and society is asked to support this position." "Homosexuality versus heterosexuality" is by no means the choice that presents itself to the homosexually oriented man or woman.[68]

Archbishop Quinn's pastoral letter is a reaffirmation of contemporary Catholic magisterial teaching on homosexuality. It unhesitatingly recognizes the *justesse* of the distinction between the homosexual orientation (morally blameless because it is unchosen) and homosexual behavior (morally blameworthy if freely chosen). It counsels gay people under the same rubrics as those that apply to unmarried persons:

> . . . just as unmarried persons are not exempt from the moral teaching of the Scriptures and of the Church which has to do with sexual conduct, so homosexual persons are not exempt from this teaching either. Thus despite the difficulties, homosexual persons who wish to receive the Eucharist must be honestly following the moral teaching of the Church or at least striving to live up to that teaching. This implies that like other Christians they must take advantage of the powerful graces that come from the reverent and frequent recourse to the Sacrament of Penance. In addition, of

---

66. We will have occasion to discuss the proposals of revisionist Catholic moral theologians in the next chapter. It is worth stating now, however, that none of them call for a blanket approbation of "homosexuality."

67. Perpetual continence is, of course, how the Church conceives of the homosexual person's moral obligation in the matter of sexuality. This was reiterated in the C.D.F.'s *Declaration on Certain Questions Concerning Sexual Ethics* (PH) (Boston: Daughters of St. Paul, n. d.), #7, p. 10: "every genital act must be within the framework of (heterosexual) marriage."

68. André Guindon wonders: "Does a gay's moral dilemma consist in choosing between being a gay (the immoral choice) and not being a gay (the moral choice)? Is this a reasonable choice for one who is irreversibly a homosexual?" He will conclude: "There are enough gay bibliographies nowadays to convince anyone who is not incurably prejudiced that for many persons gayness is their only sane choice." The *real* question, then, is whether gays may morally act in accord with who they are – whether the common-sense maxim *agere sequitur esse* holds for the gay man and the lesbian. See André Guindon, *The Sexual Creators: An Ethical Proposal for Concerned Christians* (Lanham, MD: University Press of America, 1986), pp. 160-161.

course, the natural aids they may need such as counseling, psy-chological help, etc., should and must be used where indicated and as needed. In any case there is nothing to justify a departure from the Church's normative pastoral and doctrinal teaching that one who has sinned gravely cannot approach the Eucharist until he has been absolved from that sin in the Sacrament of Penance and this of course implies the firm amendment on the part of the penitent and his conscious intention to avoid that sin in the fu-ture.[69]

When it comes to the question of the social life of gay people in American society – a society which is, by all accounts, democratic, secu-lar, and pluralistic – Archbishop Quinn does not argue that the Church's belief in the ethical normativity of heterosexuality carries with it the obli-gation to deny gays and lesbians their human and civil rights. At the same time, the tension on this point is unmistakable: ". . . the Church holds that there is no place for discrimination and prejudice against a person because of sexual attraction. But this does not mean that there is nothing wrong with homosexual conduct."[70]

This two-point theme is repeated throughout Quinn's letter.[71] How-ever, with just this document in hand, it is not possible to determine

---

69. Quinn, "A Pastoral Letter. . .," p. 33. It should be noted that the Archbishop effec-tively rules out any "internal forum" solutions for the "practising homosexual." Bruce Wil-liams, O.P., in his "Gay Catholics and Eucharistic Communion: Theological Parameters," in Robert Nugent, ed., *A Challenge to Love: Gay and Lesbian Catholics in the Church* (New York: Crossroad, 1989), pp. 205-215, takes a different tack. On pp. 213-214, he writes: "Precisely in view of the singular importance of the Eucharist for the strengthening of im-perfect Christians, as repeatedly underlined by the Church, gay Catholics involved in a life-style they honestly do not recognize as sinful should not be discouraged from this unique means of grace any more severely than other seriously errant believers who are presumably in good faith. This would seem to be the very least that is entailed in the American bish-ops' collective acknowledgement that homosexual persons require 'a special degree of pas-toral understanding and care' from the Church."

70. Quinn, "A Pastoral Letter. . .," p. 33.

71. Cf., among other examples: "Homosexual persons cannot, merely because they are homosexual, be visited with harassment and contempt. The lynch gang approach cannot be justified. At the same time, however, opposition to homosexuality as a form of conduct, opposition to homosexuality as an acceptable lifestyle, by the Church or by society, cannot be regarded as a prejudice" (p. 26); "To agree that the persecution and harassment of ho-mosexuals is incompatible with the Gospel is . . . not to say that the Church and society should be neutral about homosexual activity" (p. 26); ". . .there is a clear difference be-tween the acceptance of homosexual persons as worthy of respect and as having human rights, and the approval of the homosexual lifestyle (p. 30);" "(The Church) must tirelessly try to help homosexual men and women accept and live up to the moral teaching which the Church has received from Christ. But in no case can such acceptance or recognition of the homosexual imply recognition of homosexual behavior as an accepted lifestyle (p. 31)." One might fear that this repetitive juxtaposition subtly undermines the teaching that gay people, as fully human, possess the same rights as others.

where the Archbishop would stand in relation to a specific instance of gay rights legislation. As we have seen, Cardinals O'Connor and Bernardin, while upholding the human rights of gay people, saw support for municipal gay rights ordinances as incompatible with their episcopal ministry. And since the city of San Francisco had already enacted positive, protective legislation well before Quinn's letter, it is understandable that he did not directly address it.[72] Moreover, his pastoral letter primarily entailed a discussion of the morality of homosexual expression and the Church's ministry to gay people – not a social analysis of the proper place of homosexuals in American society.

Be that as it may, the Archdiocese of San Francisco's Senate of Priests' "Ministry and Homosexuality in the Archdiocese of San Francisco,"[73] which appeared in May 1983 with the approbation of Archbishop Quinn, implicitly reveals the archbishop's stance. Although this document, too, is primarily concerned with the ministry of the Church to the gay community and ways in which this ministry might be more effective, there is a significant clause in the section entitled "Education" which bears on the subject of gay rights. The authors see an important connection between education and the social well-being of gay men and lesbians. They write:

> The Church in the Archdiocese of San Francisco is blessed with an outstanding educational system. Through its schools, religious education programs, and youth activities, it brings the message and values of the Gospel to some seventy-five thousand young men and women each year. The schools and the catechetical programs of the Archdiocese are a rich resource, and one which can give the Church a unique opportunity to assist in the value formation of our young people. Because of this, the Church has a special responsibility to educate young people about the issues of homosexuality: about the realities of a homosexual orientation, about the teachings of the Church, about the prejudice often directed against homosexual persons, and about the Gospel imperative to respect the human and civil rights of all people.[74]

The following statement amounts to a strong counterpoint to the SOC campaign:

> . . . the grammar schools and religious education programs of the Archdiocese should make efforts to foster in their students a full

---

72. On March 20, 1978, the San Francisco Board of Supervisors passed a gay rights ordinance. See Rutledge, *The Gay Decades*, p. 121.

73. Senate of Priests, "Ministry and Homosexuality in the Archdiocese of San Francisco," in Gallagher, *Homosexuality and the Magisterium*, pp. 55-78. See p. 56 for Archbishop Quinn's approval of this document.

74. Senate of Priests, "Ministry and Homosexuality. . .," p. 74.

and deep respect for the human and civil rights of homosexual persons. Prejudicial attitudes are developed all too young in our society, and we have an obligation to work against intolerance at all ages. Thus teachers should be careful to deal effectively in their classes with any overt incidents of homophobia; and in teaching about the nature of Christian community, they should endeavor to promote respect for and acceptance of people of all sexual orientations.[75]

These proposals, made in the context of educating Catholic youth, are remarkable for their sensitivity and compassion. Even one as "moderate" as Cardinal Bernardin felt compelled, as we have seen, to speak of parents' rights to keep their children away from those who might give them a favorable impression of homosexuality.[76] What might account for the appearance of such a teaching in the Archdiocese of San Francisco?

In this regard, one should not discount the violence which gay people (especially gay men) increasingly became subject to in the 1980s and especially the cold-blooded murders in San Francisco of Robert Hillsborough and later, of gay politico, Harvey Milk.

During the public debate surrounding the Briggs Initiative, violent acts against gay men increased sharply in San Francisco's Castro Street district. These were not robberies or muggings, they were simply violent attacks. As a result, "gays started carrying police whistles and organized street patrols."[77] Sadly, this mobilization would not be enough to save the

---

75. Senate of Priests, "Ministry and Homosexuality. . .," p. 75.

76. It is to be noted that Bernardin was not the first to speak of such a "right." The Archdiocese of New York, under Terence Cardinal Cooke, issued "The Rights of Homosexuals v. Parental Rights" on January 11, 1978 [In *Origins*, 7 (January 26, 1978), pp. 498-500]. The gist of this document is as follows: ". . .Catholics maintain unequivocally that homosexual activity is immoral and that patterns of life that encourage immorality are gravely wrong. Without encouraging any unkindness toward homosexuals, the Catholic moral position strongly reinforces parents' and their surrogates' determination to keep all children in their formative years free of any persons or influences that might draw them toward homosexual sympathies or practice. Parent's rights are unchallengeable in this regard. . . . When parents' rights conflict with the rights of another person (e.g., an active homosexual) to specific housing or employment, then, in the balance of rights that inspires our laws, the basic human right to protect children from immoral influences, as their parents so determine, must prevail" (pp. 498-499). It doesn't take much thought to come up with a rather perplexing Catch-22 situation based on this principle: What of the parental rights of those who consider discrimination against homosexuals to be vile behavior and desire to keep their children away from any influences which could paint this discrimination in a positive light?

77. Shilts, *The Mayor of Castro Street. . .*, pp. 161-162. For an in-depth study of the phenomenon of violence against homosexuals in American society, see Comstock, *Violence Against Lesbians and Gay Men*; he discusses the Hillsborough case on pp. 78-82; Harvey Milk's murder is treated on pp. 27-29, 88-89, 113-114, 137, and 172. Another significant study is John P. De Cecco, ed., *Bashers, Baiters & Bigots: Homophobia in American Society* (New York: Harrington Park Press, 1985).

life of Robert Hillsborough. Randy Shilts provides the following chronology:

> No sooner had Robert Hillsborough and Jerry Taylor climbed from their car on that warm night of June 21 [1977] than the four attackers were upon them. The slight, thin Taylor scrambled over an eight-foot fence and hid behind garbage cans, convinced the huskier Hillsborough could handle himself.
>
> Then came the screams: 'Faggot, faggot, faggot.' A Latino youth, later identified as John Cordova, was kneeling over the prostrate body of Robert Hillsborough, stabbing him passionately, thrusting the fishing knife again and again into the gardener's chest, then into his face. Blood stained his hand, spurted into the streets and still he sank his blade into the fallen man; fifteen times he lashed out, sinking the steel into flesh, shouting 'Faggot, faggot, faggot.'[78]

A shock wave went through the gay community of San Francisco with the news of the murder. "Mayor Moscone ordered the city's flags flown at half-mast and angrily blamed the killing on the anti-gay campaigns of Anita Bryant and John Briggs."[79] Helen Hillsborough, Robert's 78-year-old mother, came to the city from San Diego. In a public statement, she said: "Now that my son's murder has happened, I think about the Bryant campaign a lot. Anyone who wants to carry on this kind of thing must be sick. My son's blood is on her hands."[80]

With passions riding high over the Briggs Initiative, the San Francisco police had been fearing that the Gay Freedom Day Parade (scheduled for June 26th) might erupt into violence. With the Hillsborough murder, such a possibility seemed all the more likely. However, the memorial service for Robert Hillsborough and that year's parade were surprisingly peaceful. Shilts provides the following commentary:

> Nearly 250,000 assembled . . . along the wide Market Street Boulevard, more people than had come together in the city for nearly a decade. . . . Television stations had to rent helicopters to get a high enough vantage point to film the entire parade. Contingents came from as far away as Denver and Alaska. Vast crowds lined the streets. Hour after hour, the demonstrators poured into the Civic Center plaza. The largest group carried uniform placards: 'Save Our Human Rights.' One row of picketers stretched the breadth of a street holding aloft large portraits of Adolf Hitler, Joseph Stalin, Idi Amin, a burning cross – and the smiling face of Anita Bryant.

---

78. Shilts, *The Mayor of Castro Street. . .*, pp. 162-163.
79. Shilts, *The Mayor of Castro Street. . .*, p. 163.
80. Quoted in Shilts, *The Mayor of Castro Street. . .*, pp. 163-164.

As the thousands passed the wide stairs of the majestic City Hall, one marcher dropped a flower over the headline announcing Robert Hillsborough's murder. Several more followed, the flowers falling for a man few had ever heard of a week ago. A small mound grew and, by the end of the day, thousands upon thousands of blossoms rested silently at the golden-grilled doors of City Hall, all in remembrance of a mild-mannered gardener. . . .[81]

At the 1977 Gay Freedom Day Parade, Harvey Milk announced his candidacy for the San Francisco Board of Supervisors. Milk, openly gay, had long been involved in city politics.[82] In the speech announcing his candidacy, he struck deep chords with the embattled gay community: ". . . it's not my election I want, it's yours. It will mean that a green light is lit that says to all who feel lost and disenfranchised that you can now go forward. It means hope and we – no – you and you and you and, yes, you, you've got to give them hope."[83]

On November 8, 1977, Milk was "elected supervisor from the newly created 5th District, encompassing the heart of the city, including the Castro area."[84] He was the first openly gay man elected to public office in San Francisco. Anne Kronenberg, his campaign manager, explained the jubilation that swept the area: "The feeling there was just one of total joy. . . . And it was more than just a candidate winning. It was the fact that all of these lesbians and gay men throughout San Francisco who had felt they'd had no voice before now had someone who represented them."[85]

Harvey Milk was to serve as a city supervisor in the administration of Mayor George Moscone for less than one year. On November 17, 1978, both the mayor and the gay supervisor were assassinated. Leigh Rutledge provides the basic outline:

Informed that San Francisco mayor George Moscone is about to announce a replacement for him on the city's Board of Supervisors, Dan White straps a snub-nosed .38 pistol to his shoulder, tosses ten extra cartridges into his pocket, and then has a friend drive him to City Hall, where he sneaks in through a side window to avoid the metal detectors. A few minutes later, he pumps two bullets into Mayor Moscone's chest, and then two more . . . into the mayor's skull. White then reloads his gun, crosses City Hall, and uses five bullets to assassinate gay city supervisor Harvey Milk.[86]

---

81. Shilts, *The Mayor of Castro Street.* . ., pp. 164-165,

82. He had run unsuccessfully for public office three times. See Rutledge, *The Gay Decades*, p. 115.

83. Quoted in Shilts, *The Mayor of Castro Street.* . ., p. 165.

84. Rutledge, *The Gay Decades*, p. 115.

85. Quoted in Rutledge, *The Gay Decades*, p. 115.

Dan White had been San Francisco's "major anti-gay politico;"[87] in particular, there had been a history of bad blood between White and Milk. Indeed, the credit for Moscone's decision not to reappoint White (after he had resigned)[88] belongs largely to Milk. "In a conversation (he) boastingly repeated to his friends, Milk bullishly gave the mayor an ultimatum. 'You reappoint Dan White to the board and you won't get elected dogcatcher,' Harvey told him."[89]

White, a former fireman and policeman of Irish extraction and a practising Catholic, gave an interview to Charles Morris, the publisher of a local newspaper, a short time before the assassinations. He was confident that he would be reappointed to the Board of Supervisors. When he was asked if he would characterize himself as being anti-gay, White said: "Let me tell you right now, I've got a real surprise for the gay community – a real surprise."[90]

White did not specify what he meant. If it referred to the assassinations, he did much more than surprise the gay community: he shocked and stunned *all* San Franciscans. Acting Mayor Dianne Feinstein addressed the citizenry: "'I think we all have to share the same sense of sorrow and the same sense of anger.' Feinstein urged the public to 'go into a state of very deep and meaningful mourning and to express its sorrow with a dignity and an inner examination.'"[91]

The public mourning for Moscone and Milk was peaceful and respectful. Thousands participated in memorial services. The city was a model of level-headedness in the midst of tragedy.

The peace was broken, however, when the jury announced its verdict on Dan White's culpability. In what many consider to be a miscarriage of justice, White was found guilty of violating section 192.1 of the penal code: voluntary manslaughter. Whereas he could have received life imprisonment had he been convicted of first-degree murder, the most he could receive for two charges of voluntary manslaughter was seven years, eight

---

86. Rutledge, *The Gay Decades*, p. 130-131.

87. Shilts, *The Mayor of Castro Street. . .*, p. 254.

88. Dan White had resigned his seat three days after the defeat of the Briggs Initiative – citing financial reasons (the salary for city supervisors was but $9600 per year). Shortly thereafter, however, he asked for his position back. Shilts shows that White received pressure to do this from the San Francisco Police Officers' Association and the city's Board of Realtors – two groups who consistently opposed the political aims of the gay community. See *The Mayor of Castro Street. . .*, pp. 249-254.

89. Shilts, *The Mayor of Castro Street. . .*, p. 258.

90. Quoted in Shilts, *The Mayor of Castro Street. . .*, p. 258.

91. In Shilts, *The Mayor of Castro Street. . .*, p. 274. President Jimmy Carter also expressed his outrage at the killings. He made a point to praise Harvey Milk as "a hard-working and dedicated supervisor, a leader of San Francisco's gay community, who kept his promise to represent all constituents" (in *ibid.*, p. 274).

months. "With time off for good behavior, White would probably be out of jail in less than five years."[92]

The indignation in the gay community was at fever-pitch and it soon erupted into rioting. This was the beginning of the so-called "White Night Riots."[93] "Ten years after the Stonewall Rebellion and on the opposite coast, lesbians and gay men continued to act and organize against, rather than retreat from, the violence directed at them."[94] And in this instance, the gays lashed out against the San Francisco police department: the same department which had, along with the fire department, raised $100,000 for White's defense fund and some of whose members had been seen sporting "Free Dan White" t-shirts.[95]

3.2 Archbishop Quinn on Violence Against Homosexuals

This brief overview of two of the most infamous gay murder cases helps to understand Archbishop Quinn's great emphasis on the human and civil rights of gay people; it also helps to put in context his two statements on the Church's reaction to violence against homosexuals.

Quinn published his "Letter on Violence to Archdiocesan Deans"[96] on August 2, 1984; his "Homily on Violence Against Gays,"[97] appeared on August 6, 1989. In both, his intention is crystal clear: to address the growing problem of violence against homosexuals and to denounce "gay-bashing" as morally reprehensible – something which is diametrically opposed to the Gospel of Jesus Christ.

In the 1984 letter, he begins by announcing: "Nothing can justify these attacks on homosexual persons and the Church must clearly repudiate all such acts."[98] The Archbishop is at pains to highlight the incompati-

---

92. Shilts, *The Mayor of Castro Street.* . ., p. 325. Shilts reports that a "gallows humor pervaded the city's newsrooms as journalists started shaping their verdict reaction stories. 'Sara Jane Moore got life for *missing* Gerald Ford,' a reporter commented. . . . Gay journalist Randy Alfred wondered aloud why the jury had not just gone ahead and convicted Milk of 'unlawful interference with a bullet fired from the gun of a former police officer'" (in *ibid.*, p. 326).

93. Comstock reports that this amounted to the largest gay and lesbian riot in history. In the end, it would result in the destruction of eleven police cars and the damaging of sixteen others. See *Violence Against Lesbians and Gay Men*, p. 28.

94. Comstock, *Violence Against Lesbians and Gay Men*, pp. 28-29.

95. Shilts, *The Mayor of Castro Street*. . ., p. 302.

96. Archbishop John Quinn, "Letter on Violence to Archdiocesan Deans," in Gallagher, *Homosexuality and the Magisterium*, p. 100.

97. Archbishop John Quinn, "Homily on Violence Against Gays," in *Origins*, 19 (September 21, 1989), pp. 260-262.

98. Quinn, "Letter on Violence. . .," p. 100.

bility of gay-bashing with life in Christ.[99] But to many, this might be taken as gratuitous – much like an episcopal pronouncement condemning theft or "taking the name of the Lord in vain." It is arguable, however, that something much more subtle was behind Quinn's statement.

Quinn was undoubtedly aware that the Catholic Church's moral discourse on homosexuality can – given the right set of circumstances and a seriously deficient hermeneutic – be an accomplice in violence against gay people. The subtlety of the "hate the sin/love the sinner" approach[100] can be lost on many; in practice, finding the moral wherewithal to love someone who does what one considers to be reprehensible acts seems more the work of a saint than that of an "ordinary" Christian. The Church's forceful, public denunciations of homosexual behavior can incite vigilantism.[101] Just as Quinn was quick to explain that supporting gay rights does not mean that the Church has changed its judgment on the "homosexual lifestyle," so, too, is it necessary to explain that the Church's condemnation of "homosexual acts" does not mean that gays and lesbians can be bashed with impunity.

Archbishop Quinn's "Homily on Violence Against Gays" was preached at Most Holy Redeemer Church in San Francisco's Castro Street neighborhood on August 6, 1989. The context was the annual 40-Hours adoration dedicated to people with AIDS. Before all else, his homily is an eloquent testimony to his commitment to the Church's ministry to people with AIDS. It also reveals Quinn's personal contact with the afflicted:

> I will always remember Jim Stolz of this parish, whom I visited just two days before he died. His hope in the resurrection shone in the way he prepared spiritually for death. Through the grace of his daily prayer and meditation, he carefully brought closure to his affairs on earth and peacefully let go in the hope of the promise of eternal life with God. And there was Julio, who could not

---

99. Cf. "I ask you (i.e., archdiocesan deans) to communicate to the priests and those who collaborate with them in roles of leadership and responsibility the utter incompatibility of such acts of violence with a witness to the Gospel." See Quinn, "Letter on Violence. . .," p. 100. One might hope that this was merely a rhetorical device: Did the Archbishop seriously believe that some of his priests and their co-workers needed reminding about the moral valence of violence against gays?

100. Cf. "Our role as priests is a difficult one. We must be faithful to the moral teaching of the Church concerning homosexual acts. At the same time we must unfailingly have the compassion and kindness of Christ in our pastoral service." See Quinn, "Letter on Violence. . .," p. 100.

101. Gary Comstock reports that it is not uncommon for the perpetrators of violence against gays and lesbians to justify their activity on religious grounds. A full 39% of victims of such violence report that their attacker(s) referred to "God, religion, or the Bible" during the attack. See *Violence Against Lesbians and Gay Men* (New York: Columbia University Press, 1991), p. 142.

speak but whose smile communicated his peace and trust in God.[102]

Quinn's eloquence in speaking of his own experience is matched when he turns his attention to the issue of violence against homosexuals. . .

All that I have said, all that we have heard from the word of God, makes it clear, then, how utterly foreign violence is to the way of Christ, for the sources of violence are fear and desperation, not faith and hope. And so once again in the name of Christ, I raise my voice to affirm that

- Those who perpetrate violence against others cannot call themselves followers of Christ;

- Acts of violence such as those experienced during these past weeks by men in the Sunset . . . and even one of the members of this parish, are absolutely incompatible with the name of Christian or Catholic;

- Those who perform these acts of violence cannot consider themselves true sons or daughters of the Church. They make themselves the instruments of evil and enter into solidarity with the powers of darkness. They are the witnesses of an anti-Gospel calculated to tarnish and distort the authentic Gospel handed down in the Church from the beginning;

- In the name of Christ and of his Church, I unequivocally condemn these kinds of acts and support all efforts of the civil authority and others to control and eliminate this outrage.[103]

For the Archbishop to speak expressly "in the name of Christ and his Church" shows the seriousness with which he has invested this issue.[104] One cannot find a clearer statement on the moral evil of gay-bashing.[105]

---

102. Quinn, "Homily. . .," p. 261.

103. Quinn, "Homily. . .," p. 261.

104. Sadly, many did not feel that this was the case with the C.D.F.'s PCHP. At #10, after condemning violence against homosexuals, it is stated: "But the proper reaction to crimes committed against homosexual persons should not be to claim that the homosexual condition is not disordered. When such a claim is made and when homosexual activity is consequently condoned, or when legislation is introduced to protect behavior to which no one has any conceivable right, neither the Church nor society at large should be surprised when other distorted notions and practices gain ground, and irrational and violent reactions increase" (in Gramick and Furey, *The Vatican and Homosexuality*. . ., p. 6).

105. And in all due respect to the balance that usually characterizes episcopal statements, it is refreshing that Archbishop Quinn did not feel the need to reaffirm the Church's negative moral evaluation of "homosexual acts" at any point in this homily.

3.3 *A New Problematic: Gay and Lesbian Partnership Laws*

Archbishop Quinn has spoken out strongly in defense of the human and civil rights of lesbians and gay men; his condemnation of violence against homosexual persons has been unsurpassed by any American prelate.[106] Recently, however, he felt compelled to express his profound disagreement with an ordinance approved by the San Francisco Board of Supervisors.

On May 22, 1989 the Board unanimously enacted a domestic partnership ordinance. The ordinance allowed homosexual couples as well as unmarried heterosexuals "to register with the city as domestic partners, similar to the filing of marriage licenses by conventional couples."[107] One of the key objectives of the ordinance was to provide health insurance benefits, sick leave, and bereavement leave for the partners of gay and unmarried city workers.

For Archbishop Quinn this was an unacceptable assault on marriage. In a strongly-worded letter addressed to San Francisco mayor Art Agnos, Quinn expressed his sympathy for the idea of extending benefits to the partners of gay and unmarried city workers, but, as he explained,

> the legislation passed unanimously by the Board of Supervisors last night is a serious blow to our society's historic commitment to supporting marriage and family life, and equates domestic partnerships with marriage. Such legislation, as I wrote to Mayor Feinstein in 1982, 'imperils the deepest values of our common, public moral heritage and damages the fundamental well-being of society. . . . Injury to individual rights should be redressed by means other than the radical repudiation of fundamental values and institutions which have profound significance for a present and future viable and well-ordered society.'[108]

Quinn held that the goal of the ordinance was acceptable but that the means chosen to achieve the goal was not. He claimed that its passage set the Board on "a clear path of connivance with the erosion and destruction of the rock-bottom institutions of both religion and society."[109]

---

106. In a letter to San Francisco mayor Art Agnos dated May 23, 1989 (which will shortly be subject to our consideration), Quinn explained: "I . . . believe that the establishment and protection of the legitimate rights of homosexual men and women is one of the important challenges we face as a city. Indeed, I have spoken out repeatedly in the past condemning violence directed against the gay and lesbian communities. And I have vigorously and publicly opposed ballot initiatives which would result in unjust discrimination against them." See Archbishop John Quinn, "Letter to Mayor Art Agnos," in *Origins*, 19 (June 8, 1989), p. 50.

107. "On File," in *Origins*, 19 (June 8, 1989), p. 50.

108. Quinn, "Letter to Mayor Art Agnos," p. 50.

109. Quinn, "Letter to Mayor Art Agnos," p. 50.

He ended his intervention by highlighting his "grave concern for the true well-being of our city."[110]

Archbishop Quinn's intervention was ill-received by San Francisco's gay community. An editorial in the *San Francisco Examiner* said that opponents of the bill "will have to argue from outdated, narrow-minded, self-serving views of morality. They will call themselves religious, but theirs is a religion of hate."[111]

Archbishop Quinn responded to this attack in a letter to the Editor of the newspaper. He wrote:

> We are all grateful for a free press and for our democratic society. The *Examiner* certainly has the right to voice its opinion in favor of Proposition K. But to inject this provocative and unfounded element expressive of religious bigotry is a great disservice to the public good and exceeds acceptable bounds.[112]

Quinn concluded by reminding the *Examiner* that he has "repeatedly called for civility in public discourse and spoken against violence and violent rhetoric."[113] In the end, his letter was a renewal of that appeal.[114]

Archbishop Quinn, as we have seen, worked for the defeat of the Briggs Initiative and has been an outspoken opponent of violence against gay people. He has consistently supported the civil rights of gays and lesbians. However, he has taken exception with legislative proposals which might end by putting gay and lesbian couples' legal status on an equal footing with married couples. He has deemed such a development dangerous to the foundation upon which society rests.

4. CONCLUSION

Three high-profile American Catholic churchmen have taken significantly different positions on gay and lesbian rights legislation. Cardinal O'Connor has strongly opposed all such legislation; his opposition is founded on the maxim that one has no "right" to homosexual behavior. Moreover, he argues that legislation which would protect homosexuals

---

110. Quinn, "Letter to Mayor Art Agnos," p. 50. It is to be noted that shortly after the Board of Supervisors passed the ordinance, a petition was filed to force the issue to a city-wide vote. On November 7, 1989, the domestic partnership law was rejected by a margin of only 1700 votes. However, the ordinance made it back on the ballot in 1990 (as "Proposition K") due to the efforts of city Supervisor Harry Britt. Archbishop Quinn reiterated his opposition, along with other of the city's religious leaders.

111. See "Bishop, Newspaper Clash Over Partnership Law," in *Bondings*, 13 (1990), p. 3.

112. Quoted in "Bishop, Newspaper Clash. . .," p. 3.

113. Quoted in "Bishop, Newspaper Clash. . .," p. 3.

114. On November 6, 1990, San Franciscans approved the domestic partnership law. At the same time, two openly lesbian women were elected to the city's Board of Supervisors. See Rutledge, *The Gay Decades*, p. 361.

from discrimination is bound to have a deleterious effect on the institutions of marriage and the family.

Cardinal Bernardin has opposed gay rights ordinances for the city of Chicago, but in theory he supports equal rights for gay people and advocates not discriminating against them. His problem with specific instances of non-discrimination legislation revolves around the conviction that once something is "legalized," people will get the impression that it is "moral." His Christian intuition is that the rights of gays and lesbians need protection; his adherence to the Church's condemnation of "homosexual acts" makes him skittish about protective legislation. Moreover, the potentially liberalizing effect acceptance of such legislation on society's understanding of homosexuality as a valid "alternative lifestyle" calls for the Church's opposition.

Archbishop Quinn has been a strong supporter of legislation which would protect gays and lesbians from economic and social discrimination. While he has often reaffirmed the Church's negative evaluation of "homosexual behavior," he does not see the necessity of this teaching leading to a campaign to deny gays and lesbians their human and (or) civil rights. Moreover, from the standpoint of the Church's social justice teaching, discrimination against homosexuals is counter-indicated. Of course, this is not to say that every demand of the gay and lesbian community is to be regarded as involving a human and (or) civil right.

The positions of O'Connor, Bernardin, and Quinn represent the possibilities open to members of the American hierarchy who wish to publicly confront the issue of gay and lesbian rights legislation. Following the approach of Cardinal O'Connor, they might oppose such legislative measures in the name of the Church's sexual ethic. Taking their cues from Cardinal Bernardin, they might oppose such legislation primarily because of the negative effects that are supposed to follow in its wake. Or, they might support the legislation in the name of the Church's social teaching, as has Archbishop Quinn.[115]

---

115. Among those who have issued statements supporting non-discrimination legislation are Archbishop John R. Roach (St. Paul-Minneapolis) [See his "The Rights of Homosexual Persons," in *Origins*, 21 (November 7, 1991), pp. 356-357]; Archbishop John F. Whealon (Hartford, CT) [See his "The Church and the Homosexual Person," in *Bondings*, 13 (1991), p. 11; and the article, "Archbishop Gives OK to Gay Rights Bill," in *Bondings*, 13 (1991), p. 11]; Archbishop Rembert Weakland (Milwaukee) [See his "Who Is Our Neighbor?," in Gallgher, *Homosexuality and the Magisterium*, pp. 34-35]; and the Washington State Catholic Conference (under the leadership of Archbishop Raymond Hunthausen) [See their "The Prejudice Against Homosexuals and the Ministry of the Church," in Gallagher, *Homosexuality and the Magisterium*, pp. 46-54]. Among those who have come out against protective legislation (emphasizing either the Church's teaching on gay sex or the potential harm to society) include the Massachusetts Catholic Conference (under the leadership of Bernard Cardinal LAW) [See "Bishops Oppose Homosexual Rights Bill," in *Origins*, 14 (June 14, 1984), pp. 73-74]; Archbishop Daniel Kucera (Dubuque, IA) [See Charles Isenhart, "Dubuque Archbishop Latest to Oppose Gay Rights," in *National Catholic Register*, 64 (December 18, 1988), p. 1]; and Archbishop Edward McCarthy (Miami) [See "News Releases," *Bondings*, 13 (1991), p. 11].

All things being equal, it is unremarkable to find bishops of the Catholic Church disagreeing among themselves. However, when it comes to matters of great importance, disagreement in the hierarchy *does* become remarkable – and troublesome. A cursory look at the state of the "homosexual question" in contemporary American civil society is enough to convince anyone that it is a 'matter of great importance;' the fact that the stances taken by Cardinal O'Connor and Archbishop Quinn are mutually exclusive *is* problematic. Indeed, that such a state of affairs has been allowed to persist amounts to a "studied ambiguity."

In the end, when one compares the Catholic and the secular debates on gay and lesbian rights, one is struck by the number of similarities. In both discourses, for instance, questions of justice and fairness loom large, as do conjectures about the impact legislative proposals will have on American society. The question of the moral status of homosexual conduct cannot be avoided in either debate; nor can either debate assume that gay people will suddenly stop asserting what they believe to be their rights as human beings and as American citizens.

At the same time, each of the Churchmen that we have studied can be easily classified according to the framework be developed in chapter 2. Archbishop Quinn is an advocate of I; Cardinal O'Connor sides with II; Cardinal Bernardin tends to support III.

Nevertheless, the Catholic debate should not be considered as a religious extension of the secular debate. Although the argumentation used by Gonsalves and Quinn is all but indistinguishable and although Magnuson and O'Connor share many of the same concerns, the originality of the Catholic debate is found in the self-understanding of its protagonists.

It should be clear from our study that when members of the hierarchy comment on the moral advisability of gay and lesbian rights legislation they do not believe that they are offering simply their personal opinions on the matter; nor do they consider that they are acting as spokesmen for a particular philosophical school of thought. *Rather, they hold that they are interpreting the exigencies of official Catholic doctrine for their contemporaries.* By definition, they take this doctrine as normative; they do not feel free to build their arguments on other grounds.[116] In other words, unlike those debating in the secular arena, the members of the Catholic debate all start from the same set of premises and argue from within a specific moral tradition.

In this regard, the disagreements in the Catholic debate are more problematic than those between the "seculars." One expects disagreements between Mohr and Magnuson – their ideological starting points are vastly dissimilar. But in the Catholic debate, to have three mutually exclusive

---

116. In contrast, one notes Gonsalves' freedom to opt for the Aristotelian-Thomistic synthesis and Mohr's decision to side with John Stuart Mill.

positions (i.e., I, II, and III) come from the same foundational principles raises questions about the clarity of these principles and (or) the strength of the debating partners' grasp of these principles.

In the next two chapters, then, we will examine the general parameters of Catholic sexual ethics and Catholic social ethics. These two "partners" provide the starting-point for the Catholic debate on gay and lesbian rights. We will see that each possesses a considerable amount of ambiguity and that failure to specify a hierarchy of values to be safeguarded accounts for the divergent stances of members of the American hierarchy.

CHAPTER FOUR

Catholic Sexual Ethics and Homosexuality

The American Catholic bishops have serious disagreements on the moral advisability of gay and lesbian rights ordinances. From the perspective of Catholic sexual ethics, Cardinal O'Connor, for instance, has opposed non-discrimination legislation for the city of New York. From the vantage point of Catholic social ethics, however, Archbishop Quinn has fought for the rights of gay people. It does not take much reflection to realize that these positions are mutually exclusive: one cannot reconcile support for gay and lesbian rights ordinances with opposition to the same. We have argued that this state of affairs amounts to a studied ambiguity: as a body, the American bishops have not resolved a troublesome moral issue with wide-ranging social ramifications. And, since both an Archbishop Quinn and a Cardinal O'Connor would hold that they are interpreting "official Catholic doctrine" in the positions which they have taken, this "official Catholic doctrine" will be the focus of the next two chapters of this work.

Clearly, there are two partners in the bishops' studied ambiguity: Catholic sexual ethics and Catholic social ethics. In this chapter we discuss the Church's moral evaluation of homosexuality and, as a means of focusing this teaching, we examine some of the critiques which followed the C.D.F.'s "Letter to the Bishops of the Catholic Church on the Pastoral Care of Homosexual Persons" (PCHP). There has been much dissent from this teaching; by the end of this chapter we will see that this dissent has an important impact on the question of Catholic support for gay and lesbian rights.

1. THE TRADITIONAL CASE AGAINST HOMOSEXUALITY

John F. Harvey has devoted much of his academic and pastoral career to the question of the morality of homosexuality. He has written several articles on the topic[1] and the book, *The Homosexual Person: A New Thinking in Pastoral Care*.[2] Quite simply, Harvey "is a pioneer in the area of moral studies and research concerning homosexuality."[3] Concurrently, his conclusions are strictly in line with the Church's official teaching: "He takes a strongly negative view of homosexual relationships, believing them to be contrary to God's will as revealed in Scripture and, from his own pastoral experience, humanly destructive."[4] Father Harvey is also the founder of Courage – a "twelve-step" support group for Catholic homosexuals. Courage accepts the ideal of absolute sexual continence for gays and lesbians, an ideal which flows from recognizing the homosexual orientation as disordered and destructive of true humanity. Just as the alcoholic must abandon alcohol, so must the gay man and lesbian abandon genital relating.[5]

Harvey was the author of the article on homosexuality in the *New Catholic Encyclopedia*; its section on the morality of homosexual behavior remains one of the most succinct expositions of Catholic teaching on the subject. To begin, Harvey writes: "Contrary to popular opinion, a person does not become a homosexual because he wants to be one."[6] The homosexual person, therefore, bears no moral responsibility for his or her same-sex erotic attraction. Although the etiology of this attraction has yet to be fully determined, it is clear that the individual's choice does not play a role: "The condition develops gradually over many years as a result of complex influences not under the control of the potential homosexual. He

---

1.   See, for instance, John Harvey, "Homosexuality as a Pastoral Problem," in *TS*, 16 (1955), pp. 86-108; "Attitudes of a Catholic Priest towards Homosexuality," in *Bulletin of the National Guild of Catholic Psychiatrists* (December 1972), pp. 52-58; "The Controversy Concerning the Psychology and Morality of Homosexuality," in *American Ecclesiastical Review*, 167 (1973), pp. 602-629; "Chastity and the Homosexual," in *The Priest*, 33 (1977), pp. 10-16; "An In-Depth Review of *Homosexuality and the Christian Way of Life*," in *The Linacre Quarterly*, 50 (1983), pp. 122-143.

2.   (San Francisco: Ignatius Press, 1987).

3.   John J. McNeill, *The Church and the Homosexual* [3rd edition, updated and expanded] (Boston: Beacon Press, 1988), p. 8.

4.   McNeill, *The Church and the Homosexual*, p. 8.

5.   See Woods, *Another Kind of Love*, p. 117. Woods also reports that similar groups, "such as Exodus International, Homosexuals Anonymous, Metanoia Ministries, Outpost, and Regeneration exist in conservative Protestant denominations" (p. 117). It is to be noted that "these groups reflect a fundamentalistic approach to homosexuality and aim at 'curing' or reorienting homosexual persons towards heterosexuality with a view to marriage" (p. 119, n. 11). Harvey, however, warns: "Considering the poor prognosis of redirection of the deviate's sexual drive into normal channels (according to current research), it would be imprudent to counsel matrimony for any homosexual" [John F. Harvey, "Homosexuality," in *New Catholic Encyclopedia* (NCE), vol. VII (Washington, D.C.: The Catholic University of America, 1967), p. 119.].

6.   Harvey, "Homosexuality" (NCE), p. 117. Harvey defines a homosexual as "anyone who is erotically attracted to a notable degree toward persons of his or her own sex and who engages, or is psychologically disposed to engage, in sexual activity prompted by this attraction" (p. 116).

cannot reasonably be expected to foresee the outcome of these influences, or to alter their course."[7]

Nevertheless, the homosexual *act* represents "a grave transgression of the divine will."[8] This is due to the fact that "by its essence (it) excludes all possibility of transmission of life; such an act cannot fulfil the procreative purpose of the sexual faculty and is, therefore, an inordinate use of that faculty."[9] Simply put, homosexual genital activity is a serious abuse of the divinely willed purpose of human sexual relating, viz., the fostering of the intimate union of husband and wife, and the propagation of the species.

This approach, based on a reflection upon the human sexual faculty,[10] cannot in any way condone instances of gay and lesbian sex. The quality of the relationship, say, its stability, exclusivity, tenderness, and honesty, is a moot point. *All* homosexual acts are objectively evil.[11]

On the question of the individual's subjective guilt for homosexual behavior, Harvey cautions that prudence demands that one not be quick to judge that the active homosexual has committed mortal sin. He writes:

> Only truly free consent involves moral guilt; many homosexuals simply do not know whether they have given consent to the desires incessantly besieging them. Their unhappiness suggests that they have not. At times they are conscious of guilt, but more often than not they seem to act under compulsion, at least in the interior realm of erotic fantasy and desire.[12]

Harvey's approach to the question of homosexuality in his article in the NCE was strongly validated by the C.D.F.'s *Persona humana* of 1975.[13] Specifically, PH was the first Roman magisterial document to recognize the distinction between constitutional and situational homosexuality:

---

7. Harvey, "Homosexuality" (NCE), p. 117.

8. Harvey, "Homosexuality" (NCE), p. 117.

9. Harvey, "Homosexuality" (NCE), p. 117.

10. While it is true that Harvey accepts the idea that Scripture has definitively condemned "homosexual acts," his argument is not precisely biblical. This is due to the fact that if there were no scriptural passages that dealt with homosexuality, the condemnation of homosexual behavior would still hold. Witness the Catholic case against artificial means of birth control and masturbation. That Scripture is silent on these two issues has not kept the Church from determining that they represent serious abuses of the human sexual faculty.

11. Of course gay promiscuity is "worse" than sexual relating within a stable gay relationship. But ultimately that is not to say very much. The operative analogy would be something like comparing killing ten people with killing just one person. Certainly killing ten is "worse" than killing one; but this does not change the fact that killing one innocent person is absolutely despicable.

12. Harvey, "Homosexuality" (NCE), p. 118.

13. See *supra*, p. viii, n. 3 for bibliographic citation.

> A distinction is drawn, and it seems with some reason, between
> homosexuals whose tendency comes from a false education, from
> a lack of normal sexual development, from habit, from bad exam-
> ple, or from similar causes, and is transitory or at least not incur-
> able, and homosexuals who are definitively such because of some
> kind of innate instinct or a pathological constitution judged to be
> incurable.[14]

PH, like Harvey's presentation, assumes that the constitutional homosexual ought not to be considered at fault for his or her same-sex attraction.
One's psychic and emotional constitution – at least as regards the impulse of sexual attraction – is beyond one's executive power; one does
not decide to be sexually attracted this way or that. Because of this, homosexuals ought to be afforded a compassionate pastoral care.[15] However, "no pastoral method can be employed which would give moral justification to . . . (homosexual) acts on the grounds that they would be
consonant with the conditions of such people."[16] The reason for this is
two-fold:

> . . . according to the objective moral order, homosexual relations
> are acts which lack an essential and indispensable finality. In Sa-
> cred Scripture they are condemned as a serious depravity and
> even presented as the sad consequence of rejecting God. This
> judgment of Scripture does not of course permit us to conclude
> that all those who suffer from this anomaly are personally respon-
> sible for it, but it does attest to the fact that homosexual acts are
> intrinsically disordered and can in no case be approved of.[17]

It is only within marriage that genital sex is morally good: "All deliber-
ate exercise of sexuality must be reserved for this regular relationship."[18]

---

14.   PH, #8, p. 12.

15.   Cf., "In the pastoral field, these homosexuals must certainly be treated with understanding and sustained in the hope of overcoming their personal difficulties and their inability to fit into society." [PH, #8, pp. 12-13.]

16.   PH, #8, p. 13.

17.   PH, #8, p. 13. It would have been extremely helpful to the discussion if PH had been
clear about the principles upon which this position is founded. If, for example, Scripture
says that homosexuality results when people turn away from God (the allusion is undoubtedly to Romans 1:18-32), how is one to judge that Scripture is "wrong" on this point, or at
least that it ought not to be taken in its literal sense? If Scripture can be "wrong" or if it
sometimes must not be taken literally, then how does one confidently ground 'the fact that
homosexual acts are intrinsically disordered' in the self-same Scripture? Moreover, the
scriptural passages that are taken to teach the intrinsic evil of all homosexual acts do not
seem to warrant a pastoral program which would treat homosexuals with understanding,
patience, and compassion: it is well known that Leviticus prescribed the death penalty for
people who were caught in same-sex liaisons.

18.   PH, #9, p. 14.

Outside marriage, sexual relating is vitiated of its divinely ordained purposes and is gravely wrong.

On October 31, 1986, the C.D.F. released its "Letter to the Bishops of the Catholic Church on the Pastoral Care of Homosexual Persons" (PCHP).[19] One of its chief objectives was to undermine the trend in Catholic moral theology which affords some instances of homosexual behavior a favorable ethical analysis. Of particular importance was what was determined to have been a misuse of its own PH. At issue was PH's recognition of the "homosexual condition" as distinct from "homosexual actions:"

> In the discussion which followed the publication of the Declaration (i.e., PH) . . . an overly benign interpretation was given to the homosexual condition itself, some going so far as to call it neutral, or even good. Although the particular inclination of the homosexual person is not a sin, it is a more or less strong tendency ordered toward an intrinsic moral evil; and thus the inclination itself must be seen as an objective disorder.[20]

This passage is absolutely key. One could even say that the desire to declare the homosexual orientation an objective disorder precipitated the writing of PCHP.[21] It is clear that this teaching represents a significant development in the magisterium's reflection on homosexuality. It is equally clear that a constellation of critical issues surrounds this declaration – all of which bear directly upon the morality of homosexual behavior.

In the first place, PCHP places itself squarely in the camp which refuses to see homosexuality as a natural variant of human sexual response. Simply stated, homosexuality (with or without genital contact between persons) is an aberration that has entered the human community. As such, it has to be the result of sin – original sin and (or) actual sin as the particular case may be. It is not proper to claim that God creates homosexually oriented people; the fact that a certain percentage of humankind is erotically attracted to members of the same sex cannot be attributed to God's will for such persons.

An analogy can be drawn, then, between homosexuals and those unfortunates who are born with physical deformities and (or) mental defi-

---

19. See *supra*, p. viii, n. 4 for bibliographic citation.

20. PCHP, #3, p. 2.

21. William H. Shannon, in his "A Response to Archbishop Quinn," in Jeannine Gramick and Pat Furey, eds., *The Vatican and Homosexuality: Reactions to the "Letter to the Bishops of the Catholic Church on the Pastoral Care of Homosexual Persons"* (New York: Crossroad, 1988), pp. 20-27, at p. 26, writes: "This letter clearly attaches great importance to this declaration. Indeed, it would not be unfair to say that the letter was written primarily in order that this declaration might be made."

ciencies. All such persons are not as they should be; but they are not at fault for their handicap. For reasons which ultimately elude human comprehension, God *permits* these evils which have entered his good creation because of human sin. In Eden, one would have encountered no blindness, no withered limbs, and no same-sex attraction.[22] And, if the truth be told – undoubtedly a hard truth for some – one can neither say that "blindness is as good as sightedness" nor that "homosexuality is as good as heterosexuality." Benedict Ashley writes:

> Current propaganda and the mistaken compassion of certain psychiatrists and theologians have encouraged many homosexuals to deny their disability by arguing that homosexuality is just a legitimate variation of human sexuality, or even that it is the will of God. But sex was not created only for pleasure or to provide companionship. The Bible and Christian tradition have always taught that sex is for marriage only, and marriage is not only for the couple but for their children as well. Hence the Congregation for the Doctrine of the Faith calls homosexual acts 'disordered,' that is, not ordered to marriage and children.[23]

Honesty – and *true* compassion – demand that gay and lesbian people be counselled to a life of sexual continence. There is no justification for thinking that they may enter into sexual partnerships with like-oriented individuals. The objective moral order rules this out:

> To choose someone of the same sex for one's sexual activity is to annul the rich symbolism and meaning, not to mention the goals, of the Creator's sexual design. Homosexual activity is not a complementary union, able to transmit life; and so it thwarts the call to a life of that form of self-giving which the Gospels say is the essence of Christian living.[24]

Gay men and lesbians ought to be seen as people who are suffering from a significant disability. Those who recognize their disability for what it is (viz., "a more or less strong tendency toward an objective moral evil") and take the necessary measures to keep it in check (for example: self-denial, prayer, frequent celebration of the Sacrament of Reconciliation[25]) are to receive the warm welcome and support of the Church. Those who revel in their disability – unlike the blind person, who, think-

---

22. Benedict M. Ashley, O.P., explains: "God never wills anyone to suffer from the disability through impotence, sterility, or homosexuality of entering into marriage or of having children. He only permits such troubles, so that we will use our creativity to find their remedy or courageously bring spiritual good out of misfortune." See "Compassion and Sexual Orientation," in Gramick and Furey, *The Vatican and Homosexuality. . .*, p. 106.

23. Ashley, "Compassion. . .," pp. 105-106.

24. PCHP, #7, p. 4.

25. Cf., PCHP, #12, pp. 6-7.

ing he has no problem, is to be pitied – are beyond the pale. Their revelry is not only immoral, it is supremely dangerous: "Even when the practice of homosexuality may seriously threaten the lives and well-being of a large number of people, its advocates remain undeterred and refuse to consider the magnitude of the risks involved."[26] Because of all of this, PCHP advises the bishops to distance themselves from any organization which has cultivated a "studied ambiguity" on the issue of the moral valence of homosexuality. It is a matter of justice that the Church keep the "deceitful propaganda" of the "pro-homosexual movement" at bay: it "has a direct impact on society's understanding of the nature and rights of the family and puts them in jeopardy."[27]

The C.D.F. was compelled to classify the sexual orientation of gays and lesbians as objectively disordered because PH had given people the impression that a homosexual orientation is "neutral" and that "homosexual acts" are the real moral problem for the Church. In other words, the received teaching was something like "it's OK to be gay, just don't act like a gay person." Before long people were saying that it's OK to be gay because God made them that way. If God made them that way, then "gay must be good." And, finally, if "gay is good," then the arguments used to keep gay people from acting on their erotic attractions must be seriously mistaken.[28]

One of the difficulties with PCHP's stance however, is that it tends to make gay people feel like their personhood itself is under attack. Some ten years earlier, PH had spoken of sexuality as profoundly significant for human personality. Its opening lines read:

> According to contemporary scientific research, the human person is so profoundly affected by sexuality that it must be considered as one of the factors which give to each individual's life the principal traits that distinguish it. In fact it is from sex that the human person receives the characteristics which, on the biological, psychological and spiritual levels, make that person a man or a

---

26. PCHP, #9, p. 5.

27. PCHP, #9, p. 5.

28. Peter Hebblethwaite offers the following explanation: "I would suggest that the reason it has been abandoned (i.e., "orientation is OK; acts are not OK") is because it was unworkable. For it put into the hands of gay persons an extremely powerful and indeed, on one level, irrefutable argument. All *theologos* is ultimately talk about God. But what "orientation is OK; acts are not OK" said was that God created human beings who were doomed to frustration in the whole of their lives since, as *Persona humana* asserts, sexuality "is the source of the biological, psychological and spiritual characteristics that make a person male or female." A God who can create such frustrated creatures has to be a sadistic monster." See "Please Don't Shoot the Bearer of Bad Tidings: An Open Letter on Cardinal Ratzinger's Document," in Gramick and Furey, *The Vatican and Homosexuality. . .*, p. 139.

woman, and thereby largely condition his or her progress towards maturity and insertion into society.[29]

Few would quarrel with this position. If anything, some might insist even more strongly on the critical nature of the relationship between a person's gender, sexual self-understanding, and sexual orientation and her self-identity and personhood. To claim then, that the sexual orientation of a gay person is itself objectively disordered is qualitatively different than arguing that (say) anorexia is objectively disordered because it is structured toward an end which is itself disordered. On this point, Archbishop Quinn's defense of PCHP[30] is on shaky ground. Quinn wrote:

> . . . we should advert to two things. First, every person has disordered inclinations. For instance, the inclination to rash judgment is disordered, the inclination to cowardice, the inclination to hypocrisy – these are all disordered inclinations. Consequently, homosexual persons are not the only ones who have disordered inclinations. Second, the letter does not say that the homosexual person is disordered. The inclination, not the person, is described as disordered.[31]

In the first place, no unbiased student of Catholic moral teaching could ever get the impression that the Church holds that only homosexuals have been adversely affected by the Fall. That all people have disordered inclinations is a self-evident truth. Therefore, to remind gays and lesbians of this is to raise a moot point. The problem is that *their* inclination is said to be disordered because it tends toward disordered acts which seriously threaten their salvation.[32] Moreover, the coward, the hypocrite, and those disposed to rash judgment can always work on acquiring the virtues which would effectively do away with their "disorder;" the gay person can never know such victory.

William Shannon, in an article written in response to Archbishop Quinn's defense of PCHP, grasped the full import of the "disordered inclination" teaching:

> What this statement is saying is *that a person who is not heterosexual is a person whose sexuality is an 'objective disorder.'*

---

29. PH, #1, p. 3.

30. See Archbishop John R. Quinn, "Toward an Understanding of the Letter 'On the Pastoral Care of Homosexual Persons,'" in Gramick and Furey, *The Vatican and Homosexuality. . .*, pp. 13-19.

31. Quinn, "Toward an Understanding. . .," pp. 16-17.

32. Cf. "Just as the Cross was central to the expression of God's redemptive love for us in Jesus, so the conformity of the self-denial of homosexual men and women with the sacrifice of the Lord will contribute for them a source of self-giving which will *save them from a way of life which constantly threatens to destroy them.*" PCHP, #12, p. 7; emphasis added.

Since our sexuality is part of what constitutes us as persons, the letter is really saying that part of what constitutes the homosexual person as a person is an 'objective disorder.' Further it is said – and this would follow logically from the 'objective disorder' evaluation – that the condition of being a homosexual person is itself 'a more or less strong tendency ordered toward an intrinsic moral evil.' Whether one agrees with this position or does not, it is not difficult to see the psychological damage that could be done to a person by telling him or her that his or her very person was ordered toward intrinsic moral evil. It would be like telling someone that he or she is carrying a moral time bomb. It would be to say that such a person is a constant proximate occasion of sin to himself or herself.[33]

There are two inter-related points to underscore in the context of this particular discussion. In the first place, calling the homosexual orientation disordered flows directly from the prior moral judgment that homosexual orgasmic behaviors are immoral. This entails a unidirectional movement: gay sex is not immoral because the sexual orientation of gays is disordered. As such, the disordered designation is something of a faith stance: it can be neither verified nor falsified by scientific methodologies.[34]

Secondly, then, if one were to claim (say) to know a well-adjusted lesbian couple who are every bit as happy, fulfilled, responsible, faithful, and socially conscious as their heterosexual contemporaries, it would be beside the point. The experience of faithful and faith-filled gay and lesbian couples has no bearing on the moral evaluation of their "lifestyles."[35]

The guiding principle of PCHP is a negative moral evaluation of "homosexual acts." The genital manipulations of gays and lesbians which are conducive to orgasm are declared – always and everywhere – to be gravely immoral. If one were to engage in such activity with the requisite knowledge and freedom, one would be guilty of mortal sin: one would destroy the life of grace and become an enemy of God. Because of this

---

33. Shannon, "A Response. . .," p. 26.

34. This is arguably the gist of the following passage from PCHP; ". . . the Catholic moral viewpoint is founded on human reason illumined by faith and is consciously motivated by the desire to do the will of God our Father. The Church is thus in a position to learn from scientific discovery but also to transcend the horizons of science and to be confident that her more global vision does greater justice to the rich reality of the human person in his spiritual and physical dimensions, created by God and heir, by grace, to eternal life." See #1, p. 1.

35. And, given the insistence that Church teaching on this matter "transcends the horizons of science," the fact that the American Psychiatric Association and the American Psychological Association no longer accept the idea that a homosexual orientation is a manifestation of psychological pathology can have no role in a discussion of the morality of homosexual behavior.

drastic consequence of choosing intrinsically evil behavior, same-sex erotic attraction in and of itself raises serious concerns.

What is the basis for the Church's condemnation of "homosexual acts"? Upon what foundation does such a condemnation rest? Most would agree that this negative evaluation has two basic foci: biblical passages hostile to ranges of homosexual behavior and a time-honored philosophical world view. In the next two sections we undertake a brief examination of these two sources.

1.1. *The Bible and Homosexuality*

Modern biblical studies has played a significant role in liberalizing the approaches to homosexuality in several mainline Protestant denominations. Many of these churches have a difficult time in accepting the idea that the Bible has settled the question of the morality of all homosexual behaviors for all time. Given the fact that Roman Catholicism has little in common with the many small groups of Christian fundamentalists in the United States, it is ironic that on the question of Scripture and homosexuality PCHP unambiguously affirmed that the Bible condemns all possible homosexual behaviors and that this condemnation is for all time. PCHP comments on the two condemnations in Leviticus' Holiness Code (at 18:22 and 20:13) with one sweeping generalization: "in the course of describing the conditions necessary for belonging to the Chosen People, the author excludes from the People of God those who behave in a homosexual fashion."[36]

The C.D.F. is well aware that its exegesis of the handful of biblical texts which are said to bear upon homosexuality[37] is contentious. It recognizes that not a few biblical scholars find its approach unacceptable:

> An essential dimension of authentic pastoral care is the identification of causes of confusion regarding the Church's teaching. One is a new exegesis of Sacred Scripture which claims variously that Scripture has nothing to say on the subject of homosexuality, or that it somehow tacitly approves of it, or that all of its moral injunctions are so culture-bound that they are no longer applicable to contemporary life. These views are gravely erroneous. . . .[38]

PCHP's position on what Scripture has to say on the morality of homosexuality is clear; its biblical hermeneutics, however, are far from clear. The problem can be boiled down to the following perplexity: If one were to grant that (say) the two verses of Leviticus condemn all homosexual

---

36. PCHP, #6, p. 3.

37. I.e., Genesis 19:1-11; Leviticus 18:22, 20:13; 1 Corinthians 6:9; Romans 1:18-32; and 1 Timothy 1:10.

38. PCHP, #4, p. 2.

behavior for all times and in all places, by what principle(s) are contemporary men and women said to be able to forgo fulfilling (say) the dietary proscriptions found in the same book? In a word, the Bible contains a great deal of ancient legislation and practical advice that moderns intuitively determine to be presently counter-indicated. How is one to determine which scriptural injunctions are still in force?

PCHP makes reference to a "new exegesis of Sacred Scripture." And the tone of this reference is that this new exegesis threatens good morals. However, the exegesis that is implicated here is none other than that which was canonized by the Second Vatican Council. In Vatican II's *Dei verbum* (DV), we read the following on the interpretation of biblical texts:

> Seeing that, in Sacred Scripture, God speaks through men in human fashion, it follows that the interpreter of Sacred Scriptures, if he is to ascertain what God has wished to communicate to us, should carefully search out the meaning which the sacred writers really had in mind, that meaning which God had thought well to manifest through the medium of their words.

> In determining the intention of the sacred writers, attention must be paid, *inter alia*, to 'literary forms for the fact is that truth is differently presented and expressed in various types of historical writing, in prophetical and poetical texts,' and in other forms of literary expression. Hence the exegete must look for that meaning which the sacred writer, in a determined situation and given the circumstances of his time and culture, intended to express and did in fact express, through the medium of a contemporary literary form. Rightly to understand what the sacred author wanted to affirm in his work, due attention must be paid both to the customary and characteristic patterns of perception, speech and narrative which prevailed at the age of the sacred writer, and to the conventions which the people of his time followed in their dealings with one another.[39]

The principles enunciated in DV have led to an assault on the idea that one can find an all-inclusive ban on "homosexual behaviors" in the Bible.

Let St. Paul's reflection in the first chapter of his letter to the Romans (1:18-34) serve as an example. Paul speaks of women who "exchanged natural relations for unnatural" (v. 26b) and of men who "gave up natural relations with females and burned with lust for one another" (v. 27). He continues: "Males did shameful things with males . . . . And since they did not see fit to acknowledge God, God handed them over to their undiscerning mind to do what is improper" (vv. 27-28).[40] If one were to

---

39. DV, c. 3, #12; in Austin Flannery, O.P., ed., *Vatican Council II: The Conciliar and Post Conciliar Documents* (Collegeville, MN: Liturgical Press, 1975), pp. 757-758.

follow the guidelines of DV with a view toward applying Paul's reflection in Romans to the modern reality of homosexuality, numerous problems would surface.

In the first place, what did Paul's age know of homosexuality?[41] Does the context of the passage, viz., a condemnation of pagan worship, have a bearing on what Paul wished to affirm? Does the fact that Paul is not elaborating a full-blown sexual ethic and is using particular homosexual behaviors as an example of the debauchery òf the pagans militate against taking these verses as an out-right condemnation of all homosexual expression for all times and places? It is certain that Paul and his era knew nothing of what we call a "homosexual orientation" or "constitutional homosexuality."[42] Does Paul's understanding that homosexual activity must therefore be the product of people intentionally perverting their natural drives provide a solid foundation for determining that homosexuality is "unnatural"? Finally, doesn't the fact that in "the original language of the Bible, the terms *homosexual* and *homosexuality* are never used . . . (leave) homophobic fundamentalists much room for creativity?"[43]

Archbishop Quinn, in his defense of PCHP, is not swayed by the reasoning involved in these questions. He is satisfied that the understanding of the six texts cited (seven, if one includes PCHP's general remarks on 'the order of creation' in reference to Genesis 1-3)[44] "has been a constant in the moral tradition of the Church."[45]

Dan Grippo, however, claims that when PCHP says that the Scriptures present a unified and clear condemnation of homosexuality and homosexual behavior, "nothing could be further from the truth."[46] He explains:

---

40. This translation of the text is that of the *New American Bible* [revised New Testament edition] (Wichita, KS: Catholic Bible Publishers, 1987).

41. Lillanna Kopp maintains that is beyond dispute that when the Bible touches upon same-sex sexual relating, it is always within one or more of the following contexts: "(1) as acts of violence, (2) as acts of lust, and (3) as acts of sacred ritual in fertility cults." See "A Problem of Manipulated Data," in Gramick and Furey, *The Vatican and Homosexuality.* . ., p. 42.

42. "Homophilia or constitutional homosexuality defined in the scientific community as a fixed, unalterable orientation toward same-sex love, was never mentioned in either Scripture or early church tradition for the simple reason that it was an unknown, unnamed phenomenon in prescientific times." [Kopp, "A Problem of Manipulated Data," p. 42.]

43. Kopp, "A Problem of Manipulated Data," p. 42. André Guindon's remarks on this topic are germane: "Since the Congregation does not indicate what methods *it* applies to discover what Scripture really says and what this could mean for us, the letter (i.e., PCHP) bears all the trappings of a fundamentalist approach. The text serves as a pretext for upholding positions which are grounded on extrabiblical criteria." ["Homosexual Acts or Gay Speech?," in Gramick and Furey, *The Vatican and Homosexuality.* . ., p. 208.]

44. See PCHP, #6, p. 3.

45. Quinn, "Toward an Understanding. . .," p. 14.

The six scripture passages cited by the Vatican authors are interpreted in a distorted and woefully inadequate fashion that will
only serve to perpetuate time-honored prejudices. The fact is that
the Bible says very little about homosexual behavior, and nothing
at all about persons with a homosexual orientation.[47]

Grippo is certainly right that the Bible has very little to say about
homosexuality and nothing to say about the homosexual orientation. Six
terse and somewhat enigmatic verses can not pass for a complete treatment of homosexuality. Only by way of anachronism can the homosexual
orientation be found in any of the biblical writers' work. In this, Archbishop Quinn overstated the case by employing the "constant teaching of
the Church" formula.[48] In truth, before PH, one would have been at a loss
to find even six explicit references to homosexuality in Roman magisterial
teaching. Moreover, one simply cannot have a clear and constant teaching
of the Church on a reality that continues to admit of new data and whose
very etiology has yet to be determined.

The most that can be said is that a handful of biblical authors condemned certain homosexual couplings in particular contexts for less than
clear reasons. No biblical author set out to write a treatise on sexual ethics; no biblical author ever revealed the slightest awareness that two adult
gay people might be able to relate genitally out of love for each other in a
relationship marked by tenderness, fidelity, and stability.

1.2. *Two Competing World Views*

The hermeneutic used by those who have lined up against PCHP's
blanket condemnation of "homosexual acts" admits "that the moral dis-
cernments of specific practices made by Jewish or Christian communities
never definitively resolve our own moral perplexities."[49] This statement

---

The Vatican and Homosexuality. . ., p. 33.

47. Grippo, "The Vatican Can Slight Scripture. . .," p. 33.

48. It has to be conceded that John Boswell's *Christianity, Social Tolerance, and Homosexuality: Gay People in Western Europe from the Beginning of the Christian Era to the
Fourteenth Century* (Chicago: University of Chicago Press, 1980) successfully demonstrated the vagarious nature of Church teaching on the issues attendant to homosexuality.
James P. Hanigan puts it this way: ". . . critical historical studies have a way of showing
that the tradition was often less uniform, less consistent and less certain than might appear
to many in the present day. . . . Such studies also reveal that some positions were adopted
due to incomplete or inaccurate biological or psychological or philosophical knowledge,
knowledge which is available to us today." [*What Are They Saying About Sexual Morality?*
(New York: Paulist Press, 1982), p. 15.]

49. Guindon, "Homosexual Acts or Gay Speech?," p. 208.

by André Guindon succinctly reveals the heart of the problem: The C.D.F. and its critics are operating out of two competing world views.[50]

Robert Francoeur, in an insightful critique of PCHP claims that

(t)he philosophical mainspring behind today's conflict is that the Vatican has never resolved its centuries-old tension between the Judaic biblical world vision in which time is linear, a developmental arrow, and the Platonic-Aristotelian world view in which time is cyclic. . . . In the linear time of the biblical vision, creation is an epigenetic evolutionary process in which the very nature and essence of things is in the process of being created. In the archetypical world of the Vatican, all change is superficial illusion because the nature of everything was established 'in the beginning' and creation is nothing more than the unfolding of eternal archetypes (*eidoi*) already preformed within a cosmic duration that is nothing more than a ceaseless repetition, an *anakyklesis*, and a shadowy incarnation of eternal *eidos*.[51]

These two world views, the "classical" and the "historically conscious,"[52] yield strikingly different sexual moralities. The classical world view tends toward a code morality. The virtuous person follows the sexual laws as they are found in the Scriptures and in Church teaching. Never mind that "such a model of ethics leads almost inevitably to a childish and primitive pattern of taboo morality, a morality that sees certain acts as forbidden apart from any consideration of intentions and circumstances."[53] The goal is to stay within the sexual guidelines believed to have come

---

50. On second thought, perhaps "sexual world views" is better nomenclature: the Roman magisterium's approach to moral issues other than sexual ones is strikingly like the "dissenting" approach. Charles Curran explores this conundrum in his "Catholic Social and Sexual Teaching: A Methodological Comparison," in *Theology Today*, 44 (1988), pp. 425-440. (Much earlier Curran had hinted at this in his "Homosexuality and Moral Theology: Methodological and Substantive Considerations," in *The Thomist*, 35 (1971), pp. 447-481.) See also Richard A. McCormick, S.J., "Human Sexuality: Toward a Consistent Ethical Method," in John A. Coleman, S.J., ed., *One Hundred Years of Catholic Social Thought: Celebration and Challenge* (Maryknoll, NY: Orbis Books, 1991), pp. 189-197. At p. 190, McCormick characterizes PCHP (and PH, *Humanae vitae*, *Donum vitae*, and *Inter insigniores*) as "deductive, nontentative, authoritarian, noncollaborative, heavily reliant on past statements." This is in sharp contrast to the documents which make up contemporary Catholicism's social teaching.

51. Robert Francoeur, "Two Different Worlds, Two Different Moralities," in Gramick and Furey, *The Vatican and Homosexuality. . .*, p. 189.

52. This terminology is Bernard Lonergan's; see his "A Transition from a Classicist Worldview to Historical Mindedness," in James E. Biecher, ed., *Law for Liberty: The Role of Law in the Church Today* (Baltimore: Helicon Press, 1967). [Cited by Charles Curran, "Natural Law in Moral Theology," in Charles E. Curran and Richard A. McCormick, S.J., eds., *Readings in Moral Theology, No. 7: Natural Law and Theology* (New York: Paulist Press, 1991), pp. 247-295, at pp. 263 and 292.]

53. Hanigan, *What Are They Saying. . .*, p. 85.

directly from the unchanging will of God; for the faithful Catholic any uncertainties about these guidelines are settled by interventions from the Church's magisterium.

Francoeur characterizes the conflict in the Church between the classical and historically-conscious world views in the following manner:

> The Vatican's world view is clearly rooted in a fixed Aristotelian philosophy of nature and a creator who has created from above and outside. The hierarchy thus become the custodians of divine creation, the curators awaiting the return of the Infinite Museum Owner. (Remember the careful servant who dug a hole and hid the master's money in Matthew 25.) On the other hand, many Catholics struggle to be good and faithful servants who risk in order to return more than they were entrusted with. They take their inspiration from the Spirit and Word who move through matter. They are the creators who through faith, human experience, and risk strive to make considered judgments and take responsible actions which contribute to the unfolding of the ultimate kingdom. While the curators make rules for behavior in the museum, the creators strive to bring forth the living art works which will decorate the kingdom.[54]

Francoeur does not mention any indebtedness to André Guindon for this poetic vision, but the fact is that 'the curators versus the creators' is one of the subtexts which runs throughout Guindon's *The Sexual Creators: An Ethical Proposal for Concerned Christians*[55] and it is founded upon understanding human sexuality as language.[56] James Hanigan provides a helpful summary:

> It is Guindon's proposal . . . that sexual behavior should be regarded as a form of language, as one basic way human beings have of saying what they mean, or, of course, of misleading themselves and others. The authentic expression of meaning and the integrity of human communication would then be the framework for evaluating the morality of sexual behavior.[57]

In his contribution to *The Vatican and Homosexuality: Reactions to the "Letter to the Bishops of the Catholic Church on the Pastoral Care of Homosexual Persons,"* Guindon is cognizant of the fact that his approach to human sexuality, as well as those of other Catholic ethicists, has been undervalued by the C.D.F. Just as PCHP sidesteps the findings of contem-

---

54. Francoeur, "Two Different Worlds. . .," p. 190.

55. (Lanham, MD: University Press of America, 1986).

56. See Guindon's earlier work, *The Sexual Language: An Essay in Moral Theology* (Ottawa: University of Ottawa Press, 1976).

57. Hanigan, *What Are They Saying. . .*, p. 86.

porary biblical scholars, so too does it refuse to consider the validity of much of the work of modern Catholic moral theologians. "It once again takes up a pre-Vatican II discourse on human activity understood as a biopsychical function directed toward a 'complementary union, able to transmit life' (#7) and endowed with immutable 'intrinsic' and 'objective' laws of operation."[58]

The problem with this approach lies in its undeniable implication, viz.,

> that there are specific instances of 'physical behavior' or 'material performances' which, independently of any user's meaning-making operation, have an evil meaning. Meanings would exist in the world before a community of speaking persons has structured them. Since they would be in the things themselves, 'intrinsically,' and not in the sayings of those who constitute their human world by speaking, such meanings, true or false, good or bad, never change. Human persons would not be free to create their world of meanings. They would find the world all figured out. Their task would consist merely in forming a mental replica of what is out there.[59]

If human sexual relating is about the communication of meaning from one person to another, then strictly human criteria for adjudicating questions of sexual morality are demanded.[60] In other words, it does not make sense to evaluate human sexual behavior on purely "physicalist" terms or to claim that the physical dimension of the behavior in question is *the* morally decisive factor.

This is precisely what PCHP opted for in its discussion of the morality of "homosexual acts." And, in a very real sense the scriptural condemnations that are adduced are simply "icing on the cake:" they are welcome props for an evaluation grounded elsewhere. PCHP "does not stand or fall upon the woefully inadequate scriptural exegesis found in number 6 . . . . For this document is based . . . on the sexuality-for-procreation approach."[61]

---

58. Guindon, "Homosexual Acts or Gay Speech?," p. 209.

59. Guindon, "Homosexual Acts or Gay Speech?," pp. 210-211.

60. Guindon's following point is irrefutable: "Animals, when they 'perform' sexually with a heterosexual partner for the reproduction of the species are not more moral than when they use sex, as they often do, for satisfying other individual and collective needs. Open to the transmission of life or not, animal sex is amoral because it is not meaning-creating speech. Animal sex produces nothing in terms of the historical meaningfulness of the relationship." ["Homosexual Acts or Gay Speech?," p. 212.]

61. Hebblethwaite, "Please Don't Shoot the Bearer. . .," p. 137. Hebblethwaite adds in the same place: "And the document still stands erect though tattered when you have proved that it is uncompassionate, unevangelical, unjust, fraudulent, biased, and discriminatory." (We should mention that Hebblethwaite considers all of these to be fair characterizations of PCHP.)

2. SOTERIOLOGICAL IMPLICATIONS: THE DAMNATION FACTOR

Many critics of PCHP point to the image of God that is presupposed by the Church's condemnation of all instances of gay sex. Bernard East's reflection in "L'Église et l'homosexualité" is a good summary statement of this dynamic:

> It seems to me to be possible for one to be homosexual, to live a privileged relationship with a person of the same sex, and that this would not automatically offend God. What kind of image of God would we have if he, the Creator of all things, permits the existence of homosexuals and at the same time refuses to allow them to live according to their nature? Would we not end up with an image of a sadistic God who takes pleasure in the suffering and the torments of his sons and daughters?[62]

An intimately related problematic is what can be called the "damnation factor" in Catholic sexual ethics.

> Ever to be in hell, never to be in heaven; ever to be shut off from the presence of God, never to enjoy the beatific vision; ever to be eaten with flames, gnawed by vermin, goaded with burning spikes, never to be free from those pains; ever to have the conscience upbraid one, the memory enrage, the mind filled with darkness and despair, never to escape; ever to curse and revile the foul demons who gloat fiendishly over the misery of their dupes, never to behold the shining raiment of the blessed spirits; ever to cry out of the abyss of fire to God for an instant, a single instant, of respite from such awful agony, never to receive, even for an instant, God's pardon; ever to suffer, never to enjoy; ever to be damned, never to be saved; ever, never; ever, never.[63]

Such is the image of hell that is afforded James Joyce's protagonist, Stephen Dedalus, by his Jesuit retreat master. Stephen, who is in the midst of his sexual awakening, soon finds himself at wits end. He has been led to believe that his sexual nature and the inclinations of his flesh toward sexual pleasure are evil. He comes to consider that to embrace the way of Christ would have to mean denying himself on a most profound level.

---

62. Bernard East, O.P., "L'Église et l'homosexualité," in *Présence*, 2 (février 1993), pp. 21-22. [*"Il me semble qu'il est possible d'être homosexuel, de vivre une relation privilégiée avec une personne du même sexe, et ce faisant de ne pas automatiquement offenser Dieu. Quel image avons-nous de Dieu si, lui, le Créateur de toutes choses permet qu'il y ait des homosexuels à qui il refuserait de vivre selon leur nature? N'aboutissons-nous pas à une image d'un Dieu sadique qui se complait à la souffrance et aux tourments de ses fils et de ses filles?"*]

63. James Joyce, *A Portrait of the Artist as a Young Man* (London: Minerva, 1992, p. 137. [First published in 1924 by Jonathan Cape.]

It is a dilemma as old as Christianity itself. From the outset, Christian preachers had pitted the physical against the spiritual and especially the sensual against the holy; the All-Holy One was understood as ever ready to avenge the sins of the flesh. The paradoxical nature of this vision of the Christian God is not lost on Jean Delumeau, whose research leads him to speak of "an infinitely kind God, who nonetheless gives terrible punishments."[64]

Delumeau's *Sin and Fear* is a *tour de force*; he documents in minute detail and with great panache the development of a "guilt culture" in the West. The thirteenth through the eighteenth century witnessed what Delumeau calls a *surculpabilisation* – an "intensification of guilt."[65] One finds treatise after treatise on the tortures of the afterlife (Joyce's attempt to capture the horrors of the damned pales in comparison) and innumerable examples of sermons which counselled contempt for the world and its allurements. Beyond a doubt, the greatest danger that faced humankind was thought to be lust, the sins of the flesh, impurity. As an example, Delumeau quotes Hyacinthe de Montargon's *Dictionnaire apostolique*:

> Impurity encompasses all other sins. . . . This vice . . . is not only a sin like the rest, (it) is the epitome of all sins; it is sin itself. . . . A sin is more weighty according to the extent to which it outrages and injures God. Now, the sin of lust is all the greater because the thing preferred to God is more vile and contemptible. For such is the voluptuary: he prefers the pleasures of the flesh, a moment of desire, to God and a blessful eternity. . . . (I)mpurity profanes the entire faith of a Christian. . . . Those who have just a smattering of our holy books will note that God has always punished the sin of impurity more severely than all others.[66]

In *The Portrait of the Artist as a Young Man*, Stephen Dedalus' dilemma, which stands as a cipher for Joyce's own, will eventually be resolved by breaking with the Catholic Church. The Church, which had earlier been implicated negatively in Irish politics,[67] would be revealed as espousing an inhuman and draconian sexual ethic.

---

64. Jean Delumeau, *Sin and Fear: The Emergence of a Western Guilt Culture, 13th-18th Centuries* [trans. by Eric Nicholson] (New York: St. Martin's Press, 1990), p. 401.

65. See the "Translator's Preface" to *Sin and Fear*, p. ix.

66. Hyacinthe de Montargon, *Dictionnaire apostolique*, v. 3, a. 2, pp. 91-100; cited by Delumeau, *Sin and Fear*, p. 439.

67. Mr. Casey, joined in debate with Stephen's father and Dante, asks: "Didn't the bishops of Ireland betray us in the time of the union when Bishop Lanigan presented an address of loyalty to the Marquess Cornwallis? Didn't the bishops and priests sell the aspirations of their country in 1829 in return for Catholic emancipation? Didn't they denounce the Fenian movement from the pulpit and in the confession box? And didn't they dishonour the ashes of Terence Bellew MacManus?" (p. 35). Key to this scene is the Irish bishops' condemnation of the Irish nationalist Charles Stewart Parnell following the revelation of an adulterous affair. Their intervention effectively ended Parnell's political career.

In our day, one might find it sad, and perhaps even quaint, that the Church's sexual ethic could raise such qualms of conscience in such a sincere, and at the time of the scene in *Portrait*, innocent young man. One might even feel the urge to take Stephen aside and calm his fears and reassure him that the Church's teaching isn't *that* harsh, or (say) that with the findings of modern psychology the Church is not holding to such a strict interpretation these days, *et cetera*. However, such a pastoral approach was explicitly ruled out by PH.

For instance, PH warned the faithful that certain sexual acts (especially premarital sexual relations, masturbation, and homosexual relations) are to be understood as grave moral disorders. If one engages in these actions with sufficient reflection and wilful consent, then one has committed *mortal sin*.[68]

On the subject of masturbation, for instance, PH reads:

> . . . both the magisterium of the Church – in the course of a constant tradition – and the moral sense of the faithful have declared without hesitation that masturbation is an intrinsically disordered act.[69]

> On the subject of masturbation modern psychology provides much valid and useful information for formulating a more equitable judgment on moral responsibility and for orienting pastoral action. . . . But, in general, *the absence of serious responsibility must not be presumed*; this would be to misunderstand people's moral capacity.[70]

Many expositions of Catholic sexual morality fail to present clearly the soteriological consequences that the magisterium envisages for those who engage in "intrinsically and seriously disordered acts." These consequences are simple: mortal sin (if the requisite conditions pertain, i.e., knowledge, freedom, and consent) – which makes one an enemy of God – and eternal damnation if one never repents of the evil done. It bears stating here that the magisterium holds that two men who knowingly and willingly engage in consensual sexual relations with each other have committed mortal sin.[71] Unless they turn away from such behavior, they will

---

68. See PH, #10, pp. 17-18: "A person . . . sins mortally not only when his action comes from direct contempt for love of God or neighbor, but also when he consciously and freely, for whatever reason, chooses something which is seriously disordered. For in this choice . . . there is already included contempt for the divine commandment: the person turns himself away from God and loses charity."

69. PH, #9, p. 14.

70. PH, #9, p. 15.

71. Might not one claim that *if* persons so involved sincerely do not believe that they are doing anything wrong, then they are not subjectively guilty of wrong-doing? It is difficult to imagine the magisterium validating such an approach; indeed, it is probable that its response would be that such persons have malformed consciences *for which they are morally*

be eternally cut off from God. The same goes for the cohabitating hetero-sexual couple, the practitioners of artificial birth control, and the mastur-bator.

Now of course no one can ever judge the subjective guilt of those involved in sexual relating outside the marriage bond. One cannot read their hearts; nor can one know the extent of their freedom or the quality of their consent. At the same time, however, one must not presume that mortal sin *has not* been committed.

One of the chief problems with this teaching is its aforementioned damnation factor. Joyce found it ridiculous; few Catholic moralists ever directly discuss it. These latter are content to speak of "normative" and "non-normative behavior" without consigning the wilful doers of the non-normative to an eternity in the Abyss.[72] Neither do most seem willing to say that those so implicated have chosen, *ipso facto*, behavior diametri-cally opposed to Love.

As long as the Church holds that in matters of sexuality there is no parvity of matter,[73] the damnation factor is firmly in place. As long as all infractions of the Church's sexual ethic are considered to be serious by their very nature, most contemporary people's salvation must be believed to be in jeopardy. It is probable that the damnation factor has played a role in leading modern Catholic moral theologians to reconsider the

---

responsible. It is, after all, a serious moral obligation to form one's conscience according to Church teaching. [This in turn leads to a Catch-22 situation whereby one is morally obli-gated to follow one's (malformed) conscience and is thereby guilty of serious sin (for hav-ing a malformed conscience in the first place).] For the ambiguities that Vatican II did not settle relative to conscience and Church authority, see especially Judith A. Dwyer, S.S.J., "Vatican II and the Dignity of Conscience," in Lucien Richard, O.M.I., ed., with Daniel T. Harrington and John W. O'Malley, *Vatican II, The Unfinished Agenda: A Look to the Fu-ture* (New York: Paulist Press, 1987), pp. 160-173.

72.   Lisa Sowle Cahill offers a good case-in-point. In "Moral Methodology: A Case Study" [in *Chicago Studies*, 19 (1980), p. 182] she writes: "The consistent positive contribution to the Christian tradition on sexuality is that 'normative' human sexuality is heterosexual, marital, and has an intrinsic relation to procreation, love and commitment. Hence the tradi-tional condemnation of homosexual acts as not truly expressive of the meaning of human and Christian sexuality. . . . However, the sticky task of Christian ethics is determining when, why and how to make exceptions to norms." On pp. 183-184, she explains that "a normative judgment that the homosexual orientation is a less than fully human and Chris-tian form of sexual preference does not necessarily entail a corollary prohibition of those genital acts through which confirmed homosexuals express and strengthen a committed re-lationship."

73.   This is done implicitly when all sexual behavior outside marriage is deemed "intrinsi-cally and seriously disordered." Even an 'impure thought' is, in and of itself, an instance of grave matter – one of the requisite components for positing a mortal sin. (André Guindon, in *The Sexual Language*, offers an in-depth look at the tradition concerning sexual fantasies on pp. 223-249.)

Church's teaching on homosexuality. Quite simply, it is difficult for many to hold that the sexual relating within a committed gay relationship is by definition seriously evil and a probable indicator that those involved are opting for an eternity outside the love of God.[74]

3. PCHP, THE REVISIONISTS, AND GAY RIGHTS

PCHP cast a pall over the question of Catholic support for gay and lesbian rights.[75] The following passage, for example, leaves one with the impression that the Roman magisterium is opposed to any civil legislation which would protect homosexual persons from discrimination:

> There is an effort in some countries to manipulate the Church by gaining the often well-intentioned support of her pastors with a view to changing civil statutes and laws. This is done in order to conform to these pressure groups' concept that homosexuality is at least a completely harmless, if not an entirely good, thing. . . .
>
> (The Church's) clear position (on the morality of homosexuality) cannot be revised by pressure from civil legislation or the trend of the moment. But she is really concerned about the many who are not represented by the pro-homosexual movement and about those who may have been tempted to believe its deceitful propaganda. She is also aware that the view that homosexual activity is equivalent to, or as acceptable as, the sexual expression of conjugal love has a direct impact on society's understanding of the nature and rights of the family and puts them in jeopardy.[76]

Clearly PCHP fears that changing civil statutes and laws concerning homosexuality will have a deleterious impact on marriage and family life. It believes that the GLM uses justice arguments for ulterior motives, viz., to achieve societal approbation for homosexuality and a concomitant silencing of those who consider homosexual behavior to be immoral.

This reticence in supporting gay and lesbian rights is not found among a number of Catholic thinkers. The authors of the Catholic Theo-

---

74. Edmund Hill, O.P., in *Being Human: A Biblical Perspective* (London: Geoffrey Chapman, 1984), pp. 160-161, writes that homosexuality "is manifestly not oriented to marriage, and thus is, of its nature, defective sexual behaviour. But it does not seem to be, of its very nature, necessarily against love or charity; it may even be, like heterosexual activity, expressive of genuine love or charity. So on this line of reasoning I would argue that it is not necessarily of its nature a mortal sin."

75. It is not beyond the pale to suggest that the prefect of the Congregation for the Doctrine of the Faith believed that some U.S. bishops had been duped by the GLM – that they were unwitting pawns in attempts to discredit Catholic sexual morality. See the "Introduction" to Gramick and Furey, *The Vatican and Homosexuality. . .* , pp. xiii-xxi.

76. PCHP, #9, p. 5.

logical Society of America's *Human Sexuality: New Directions in American Catholic Thought*, for instance, state that

> (i)t should not be too much to expect that the Church and its leaders serve as more than a barometer of public moral opinion, that they take a lead in advance of the civil courts in championing the civil rights of homosexuals by working to change unjust social conditions, even when this is not a particularly popular cause. Eliminating discrimination on the basis of race and religion should extend logically to eliminating discrimination and injustice on the basis of sexual orientation.[77]

The authors advance the opinion that gays and lesbians can validly appeal to Catholic teaching on justice for protection; however, given the fact that this statement comes in the context of a discussion of the morality of certain *homosexual acts* and given the fact that it comes after certain of these acts are said to be morally justifiable, one might get the impression that gay people deserve social protection because there really isn't anything wrong with their sexual lives in the first place.

This is a significant problem for the present state of the Church's teaching on gay and lesbian rights. Since many of the calls for Catholic support for such rights are made in the context of criticizing the Church's condemnation of all instances of gay sex, the impression is given that justice for gay people is dependent upon a benign interpretation of at least some of their sexual practices.[78] In the end, it becomes arguable that the C.D.F.'s hesitancy on this question can be traced to this problematic; in other words, one witnesses to the immorality of homosexual behavior by

---

77. Anthony Kosnik, William Carroll, Agnes Cunningham, Ronald Modras, and James Schulte, *Human Sexuality: New Directions in American Catholic Thought* [A Study Commissioned by The Catholic Theological Society of America] (New York: Paulist Press, 1977), p. 218. Other Catholic thinkers who have endorsed this approach include Gregory Baum, "Human Rights for Homosexuals," in *Catholic New Times*, January 11, 1987, p. 10; John Coleman, "Two Unanswered Questions," in Gramick and Furey, *The Vatican and Homosexuality. . .*, pp. 59-65; André Guindon, "Gais et lesbiennes dans l'Église. Pour un déplacement de la problématique," in *Nouveau Dialogue*, 47 (1982), pp. 25-28; and Gordon Zahn, "The Human Rights of Homosexuals: Let Catholics Be Consistent," in *Commonweal*, 116 (1989), pp. 462-465 and "Let's Support Civil Rights for Homosexuals," in *U.S. Catholic*, 54 (1989), pp. 13-15.

78. A notable exception to this trend is Benedict Ashley's "Compassion and Sexual Orientation," in Gramick and Furey, *The Vatican and Homosexuality. . .*, pp. 105-111. After having strenuously supported the teaching of PCHP on the morality of homosexual acts, Father Ashley writes: "Generally speaking, one's sexual orientation is a private matter. I believe the Church should support the civil rights of homosexuals and should preach that no one has any right to judge same-sex companions living privately. Such companionship without sex can be quite suitable for homosexuals and was common enough even in Victorian society without public suspicion. Nor should sexual orientation be a ground for discrimination in employment, provided that it not be made evident by public acts" (pp. 108-109).

speaking of this behavior as "something to which no one has any conceivable right."[79]

4. CONCLUSION

The C.D.F. and revisionist moral theologians are at loggerheads on the morality of homosexuality.[80] To the chagrin of the former, the latter tend to allow for the moral goodness of some instances of homosexual behavior. This debate has important ramifications for a Catholic stance on non-discrimination legislation for gays and lesbians. By and large, the revisionists see no good reason to sanction discrimination against people who may be doing nothing wrong; the C.D.F. is committed to witnessing to the immorality of all instances of homosexual behavior by frowning upon Catholic support for any of the planks of the GLM. Neither, however, seem to have grasped the fact that Catholic sexual ethics is not suited to answer what is most precisely a question for the Church's social teaching.

---

79. Cf. PCHP, #10, p. 6: ". . .the proper reaction to crimes committed against homosexual persons should not be to claim that the homosexual condition is not disordered. When such a claim is made and when homosexual activity is consequently condoned, or when civil legislation is introduced to protect behavior to which no one has any conceivable right, neither the Church nor society at large should be surprised when other distorted notions and practices gain ground, and irrational and violent reactions increase." Beyond a doubt, the more benign an evaluation one posits for "homosexual acts," the more likely one is to support gay and lesbian rights. One has no compelling reason to criminalize all the possible ranges of gay and lesbian sexual relating if some of these behaviors can be called morally good, or at least morally justifiable. *A fortiori*, one has lost strong reasons for campaigns to limit the social, cultural, and economic participation of gay people if their "lifestyles" are not *ipso facto* morally reprehensible.

80. This state of affairs dramatically highlights the ambiguities present within Catholic sexual ethics. It bears noting that the "studied ambiguity" under question in this work is not only because one may give priority to one of the two partners (sexual or social ethics) in the debate on gay and lesbian rights, but because the "sexual ethics partner" is itself less than clear . . . unless, of course, one holds that nothing which is proposed in the Church has any value and credibility except the Vatican's discourse.

CHAPTER FIVE

Catholic Social Teaching and Homosexuality

By most accounts, Catholic social teaching admits of much ambiguity. David J. O'Brien's evaluation is typical: "Internal inconsistencies, disconti- nuities, and sharply differing positions on key questions make it very diffi- cult to generalize about Catholic social teaching. . . ."[1] In this regard, it is unwise to deny that John Mahoney's way of characterizing Christian theol- ogy applies *par excellence* to the social teaching of the Church:

> Much, if not all, of Christian theology is a theology *ex convenientia,* of exploring the fittingness and the intrinsic coherence of why God is as he is and why he has acted in history as he has done. It is an act of faith in the ultimate intelligibility and self-consistency of God, and a stumbling attempt to comprehend something of the mystery which one believes is not at heart an intellectual absurdity or sheer caprice.[2]

Concurrently, one would not be overstating the case if one were to argue that Catholic social teaching provides a prime example for demonstrating Church teaching on the "development of doctrine."[3] In fact, Catholic so- cial teaching has witnessed dramatic developments on any number of questions.[4]

---

1.   David J. O'Brien, "A Century of Catholic Social Teaching: Contexts and Comments," in John A. Coleman, S.J., ed., *One Hundred Years of Catholic Social Thought: Celebration and Challenge* (Maryknoll, NY: Orbis Books, 1991), p. 13.

2.   John Mahoney, S.J., *The Making of Moral Theology: A Study of the Roman Catholic Tradition* (Oxford: Clarendon Press, 1987), p. 246.

3.   It is to be granted, however, that "development" as applied to the Church's social teaching is a loaded term; it presupposes a modicum of internal consistency and continuity through time. It is well to heed John Coleman's warning concerning the social teaching enunciated in the papal encyclical tradition: "The logical unity of the teaching still needs to be shown." [John A. Coleman, S.J., "Development of Church Social Teaching," in Charles E. Curran and Richard A. McCormick, S.J., *Readings in Moral Theology, No. 5: Official Catholic Social Teaching* (New York: Paulist Press, 1986), p. 176; cited by Michael J. Schuck, *That They Be One: The Social Teaching of the Papal Encyclicals, 1740-1989* (Washington, D.C.: Georgetown University Press, 1991), p. x.]

It is not our intention here to provide anything even remotely resembling a synthetic account of the Church's social teaching.[5] Nor are we prepared to take sides in the debate surrounding the ultimate theological grounding for contemporary Catholic social ethics.[6] We will be content to call attention to contemporary Catholicism's espousal of the cause of global human rights and how the Church's present self-understanding entails acting as universal guardian of these rights. Ultimately, this discussion will serve to highlight how the C.D.F.'s "Some Considerations Concerning the Catholic Response to Legislative Proposals on the Non-Discrimination of Homosexual Persons" (1992) is taken by many to be seriously out of sync with a fundamental trajectory of modern Catholicism.

1. CATHOLICISM AND HUMAN RIGHTS

The Roman Catholic Church is a relative newcomer to the cause of human rights.[7] It is well-known that the Church "was a vigorous opponent

---

4.   Schuck's *That They Be One* offers an army of examples. On p. 155, summarizing the teaching of the post-Leonine popes, he writes: "Like their predecessors, the popes consider mistaken concepts to be the solvent causing communal erosion. Again, Enlightenment atheism, naturalism, and rationalism are spurned and their varieties identified: the 'death of God' movement, the Enlightenment notion of progress, ethical hedonism. However, some social ideas considered troublesome in earlier periods are not repeated: freedom of conscience in religion, Roman Catholic collaboration with socialists, ecumenism, the religiously neutral state, the centrality of sentiment in marriage, socialism (as distinct from communism, or 'Marxist collectivism'), freedom of speech and press, artistic verism and relativism, freedom of instruction, and pedagogical naturalism. Many other social ideas thought dangerous by prior popes are repeated, with new candidates offered: the superpower 'logic of blocs' and both liberal capitalist and Marxist theories of development."

5.   This would entail a herculean task. One notes, however, that Karen Lebacqz, in her *Six Theories of Justice: Perspectives from Philosophical and Theological Ethics* (Minneapolis: Augsburg, 1986), claims that following points would have to be considered in any such synthetic account: "(1) the inviolable dignity of the human person, (2) the essentially social nature of human beings, and (3) the belief that the abundance of nature and of social living is given for all people" (p. 67).

6.   Schuck, *That They Be One*, chapter 4 ("Theories of Coherence"), pp. 173-189, succinctly spells out the parameters of this debate – at least as regards the papal encyclical tradition. David Hollenbach's contention that "(t)he dignity of the human person . . . (is) the thread that ties all these (papal and conciliar) documents together" [See his *Claims in Conflict: Retrieving and Renewing the Catholic Human Rights Tradition* (New York: Paulist Press, 1979), p. 42; cited by Schuck, *That They Be One*, p. 178] is at the heart of the debate.

7.   The specific content of "human rights" admits of a certain fluidity. David Hollenbach (following John Langan) defines human rights as "moral claims that human persons can make independently of and prior to their acknowledgment by particular societies;" they are the immunities and entitlements which are due every person "simply by virtue of being a human person, irrespective of his or her social status, cultural accomplishments, moral merits, religious beliefs, class memberships, or contractual relationships." [David Hollenbach, S.J., "Global Human Rights: An Interpretation of the Contemporary Catholic Understanding," in Alfred Hennelly and John Langan, eds., *Human Rights in the Americas*

of both the democratic and socialist revolutions which were the chief proponents of the civil and social rights enshrined in twentieth-century human rights declarations."[8] In this regard, Bernard Plongeron reminds his readers that, confronted with the Declaration of 1789 (revolutionary France's "Rights of Man"), the Catholic hierarchy "roundly declared (it) to be a work of the devil and not of the Gospel."[9]

The Second Vatican Council and the pontificates of John XXIII and Paul VI effectively put an end to this tradition of hostility. Indeed, Church teaching and praxis had so radically changed that in his eulogy for Pope Paul VI, the ecumenical patriarch Dimitrios could reverently speak of the deceased pontiff as the "defender of human dignity, herald of the rights of man and of the ending of all social discrimination, upholder of religious liberties, champion of peace in the world."[10] In the same vein, François Refoulé offers the following assessment of Paul VI's work on behalf of global human rights:

> Anyone who takes the trouble to glance through the late pope's output – encyclicals, addresses to the diplomatic corps, letters to secretaries-general of the UNO or to various international agencies, messages to the world, homilies, etc. – cannot but be impressed by the place occupied by the defence of the dignity and rights of man. And the words he spoke at the UNO in 1965 are unforgettable: 'We make our own the voice of the poor, the disinherited, the wretched, those who long for justice, a dignified life, freedom, well-being and progress.' The same goes for the letter he wrote to Kurt Waldheim, Secretary-General of the UNO in 1972: 'The Church feels wounded in her own person whenever a man's rights are disregarded or violated, whoever he is and whatever it is about.'[11]

Refoulé, moreover, judges it highly significant that Paul VI often referred the attention of the world to the United Nations' 1948 declaration on human rights. The Pope wanted to make the "Universal Declaration of the Rights of Man" the "corner-stone of all his work, and that is why he always commended it."[12]

(Washington, D.C.: Georgetown University Press, 1982), p. 14.]

8.   Hollenbach, "Global Human Rights. . .," p. 9.

9.   Bernard Plongeron, "Anathema or Dialogue: Christian Reactions to Declarations of the Rights of Man in the United States and Europe in the Eighteenth Century" (trans. by Lawrence Ginn), in Aloïs Müller and Norbert Greinacher, *The Church and the Rights of Man* (New York: Seabury Press, 1979), p. 39. [Cf. *Concilium*, 124 (4/1979).]

10.   Quoted in François Refoulé, "Efforts Made on Behalf of Human Rights by the Supreme Authority of the Church" (trans. by John Maxwell), in Müller and Greinacher, *The Church and the Rights of Man*, p. 77.

11.   Refoulé, "Efforts Made on Behalf of Human Rights. . .," p. 77.

12.   Refoulé, "Efforts Made of Behalf of Human Rights. . .," p. 78. One notes with Refoulé that Pope John XXIII had voiced some reservations about the UN's declaration. In

How is one to account for this "qualitative transformation" of the Church's involvement in social and political affairs?[13] David Hollenbach's thesis seems irrefutable: "[the Second Vatican Council] launched this new phase through its recognition that the context for Christian social ministry is an inherently pluralistic world. The reality of religious, ideological, and cultural diversity was taken with great seriousness by the Council, particularly in the two most important conciliar documents dealing with the social role of the church: the Pastoral Constitution on the Church in the Modern World and the Declaration on Religious Liberty."[14]

In the main, following Vatican II's understanding of the Church's role in guarding and guaranteeing human rights, "the central institutional organ of the Catholic Church, the Holy See, has adopted the cause of human rights as the prime focus of its ethical teaching and pastoral strategy in the domain of international justice and peace."[15]

In the years since Vatican II, any number of aggrieved minority groups have appealed to the Church in their struggles for justice. Groups as disparate as the United Farm Workers and particular Native American tribes have received solace and support from the Catholic Church in the United States. Since the Church's contemporary self-understanding includes being a champion of human rights, logical consistency might lead one to apply the Church's social teaching to the question of discrimination against gay people. As Archbishop Quinn has repeatedly argued, nothing in the Church's social ethics sanctions hating and vilifying gay men and lesbians; nor does the Church's social teaching provide the rationale for opposing gay people's active participation in society at large. As human beings, gay people possess the same rights as everyone else; as American citizens, there is no reason they should have to endure discriminatory treatment by employers or landlords. Quinn argues that faithfulness to the Church's social teaching calls for protecting the gay and lesbian minority from harassment.

Pacem in terris, he sought "to redress the imbalances of the . . . (Declaration), forcefully stressing man's social being and, in consequence, the reciprocity of rights and duties." Moreover, *Gaudium et spes'* warning about the 'need to go beyond an individualistic ethic' (#30) was a not-so-subtle critique of the Declaration. Nonetheless, Paul VI was able to hail the Declaration not only " 'as a step towards the establishment of a juridico-political organization of the world community' but also as a meeting-place of Church and state." [In *ibid.,* p. 79.]

13. This characterization is David Hollenbach's. See his "The Church's Social Mission in a Pluralistic Society," in Lucien Richard, ed., with Daniel T. Harrington and John W. O'Malley, *Vatican II, The Unfinished Agenda: A Look to the Future* (New York: Paulist Press, 1987), p. 113.

14. Hollenbach, "The Church's Social Mission. . .," p. 113.

15. Hollenbach, "Global Human Rights. . .," p. 9.

Nevertheless, the C.D.F. recently questioned the legitimacy of using Catholic social teaching to support gay and lesbian rights. We move now to examine this challenge of the C.D.F. and the controversy which followed in its wake. We conclude this chapter by appraising the authoritative nature of the C.D.F.'s intervention.

2. THE C.D.F.'S 1992 INTERVENTION ON GAY RIGHTS

In July 1992, the C.D.F.'s "Some Considerations Concerning the Catholic Response to Legislative Proposals on the Non-Discrimination of Homosexual Persons" (SCC) made its appearance in the American press.[16] Its public appearance, however, had not been planned by the C.D.F.; the text of SCC was made available to the American media on July 15, 1992 by New Ways Ministry (NWM), a Catholic organization involved in gay and lesbian ministry. The pro-nuncio had sent SCC to the American bishops; one or more of the bishops passed it to NWM.[17]

On July 23, 1992, the C.D.F. issued a second version of the text. Joaquin Navarro-Valls, a Vatican spokesman, in a statement attached to the revised version of SCC, explained the rationale:

> With the idea that the publication of the observations would be something beneficial, a slight revision of the text was undertaken and a second version prepared. In the meantime, various references to and citations from the considerations have appeared in the media. For the sake of an accurate report on the matter, the revised text . . . is made public today.[18]

The editors of *Origins* remark that an official at the C.D.F. told them that "both texts were valid, but issued for different purposes: the first for bishops to use however they saw fit, the second for wider publication."[19] Given the unusual existence of two valid texts of the same document in the same language, one might think that a comparative study would produce deeper insights into the teaching. However, such is not the case here; Navarro-Valls' characterization of the differences as "slight" is no understatement. The editors of *Origins* explain that the differences are

---

16. The first version of SCC can be found in the *National Catholic Reporter* (July 31, 1992), p. 10; the revised version is found in *Origins*, 22 (August 6, 1992), pp. 173, 175-177.

17. It seems safe to say that the bishop(s) doing the passing knew that NWM would make the document public and that the public reaction would not reflect positively on the C.D.F.'s position. See Laura Sessions Stepp, "Vatican Supports Bias Against Gays," in *Bondings,* 14 (1992), pp. 1, 6, 9.

18. Joaquin Navarro-Valls, "Statement," in *Origins*, 22 (August 6, 1992), p. 175.

19. See "Introduction to SCC," in *Origins*, 22 (August 6, 1992), p. 173.

generally insignificant: most amount to "matters of rewording or of drop-ping or adding words."[20]

The only significant addition comes at #14. The revised text adds the following paragraph:

> In addition, there is a danger that legislation which would make homosexuality a basis for entitlements could actually encourage a person with a homosexual orientation to declare his homosexual-ity or even to seek a partner in order to exploit the provisions of the law.[21]

In the end, the existence of two texts which are so strikingly similar is mysterious. The bishops' version and the version for the wider public are all but indistinguishable and the changes in the latter hardly seem worth the trouble of creating a second, equally valid document.[22]

As we have seen, the question of Catholic support for legislative proposals which would protect gays and lesbians from discrimination has been a divisive issue for American Catholics and their bishops. We have examined the varied approaches of Cardinals O'Connor and Bernardin and Archbishop Quinn and have seen how these different approaches entail different public stands. It should be noted here that not infrequently the accusation of official Catholic hatred for gay people is one of the results of the stands taken by Catholic hierarchs.[23]

The appearance of SCC had to have confirmed the above perception for many gays and lesbians. SCC pulled no punches: it set out to enumer-ate cases where discrimination against homosexuals is not only *just*, but *morally required*. SCC set the stage for this development in Catholic re-flection on homosexuality by quoting favorably PCHP (#9): "One tactic used (by those who would subvert Catholic teaching on the morality of homosexuality) is to protest that any and all criticism of or reservations

---

20. See *Origins,* 22 (August 6, 1992), p. 175.

21. SCC, revised text, #14, in *Origins,* 22 (August 6, 1992), p. 176.

22. For the sake of clarity, all references in this work to SCC will be to the revised version as it appears in *Origins,* 22 (August 6, 1992), pp. 173, 175-176.

23. The bad blood between the Archbishop of New York and ACT-UP is notorious. See John A. Coleman, S.J., "ACT-UP Versus the Church," in *Commonweal,* 118 (September 27, 1991), pp. 533-535. On p. 533, Coleman recounts that "(o)n December 10, 1989, ACT-UP (AIDS Coalition to Unleash Power) demonstrators disrupted Sunday Mass at New York's St. Patrick's Cathedral by shouting and lying down in the aisle; drowned out Cardinal John O'Connor's sermon with shouts of 'bigot' and 'murderer;' and desecrated the Eucharist." Because of his stance on gay rights and his opposition to AIDS education which includes any discussion of "safe sex," ACT-UP has targeted the Cardinal as a major opponent. Cole-man reports that ACT-UP's video, *Stop the Church,* "gives viewers a full dose of hateful and demonstrably untrue statements about the Catholic Church and about Cardinal O'Con-nor" (p. 533).

about homosexual people, their activity and lifestyle are simply diverse forms of unjust discrimination."[24]

Specifically, SCC teaches that sexual orientation "does not constitute a quality comparable to race, ethnic background, etc., in respect to non-discrimination. Unlike these, homosexual orientation is an objective disorder and evokes moral concern."[25] Gay people are not to be considered "entitled minorities," i.e., as minorities which deserve social protection and (or) special treatment of any kind. It is not that they fail to live up to a scientific definition of "minority" – sociologists are quite willing to accord gays and lesbians this status – it is rather that the catalyst which constitutes them as a minority is an objective disorder which evokes moral concern. Homosexual people are an "undeserving minority"; the factor which bestows minority status on them is something that cannot be given social approval. Consequently, to try to construe gays and lesbians as a "deserving minority" is taken to be the same as saying that homosexuality does not raise any moral qualms.

This reasoning is programmatic for SCC. The reason that one would discriminate against a gay person in the first place is precisely in reference to her sexual identity and the genital behaviors that she is likely to undertake. There are, of course, stereotypic assumptions underlying this, but since the orientation is itself a disorder and since any and all genital relating outside marriage is wrong, to grant rights to homosexuals *qua* homosexual is to enter into collusion with their (objectively) immoral lifestyle. SCC follows PCHP closely: "There is no right to homosexuality, which therefore should not form the basis for judicial claims."[26]

SCC's argumentation thus far might appear unassailable. A legal right to homosexual behavior does sound outlandish; would most people undertake an effort to have (say) fornication or adultery recognized as legal rights for all Americans? However, the C.D.F.'s manner of proceeding pays scant attention to the history of systematic oppression of gay people. The modern homosexual movement, as we have shown in broad strokes, has been primarily concerned with protecting gay *people* – not the variety of their sexual activities. As long as a company, for instance, can maintain a policy of terminating the employment of anyone discovered to be homosexual, an injustice is present; even SCC is willing to concede this point.[27]

---

24. SCC, #4, p. 175.

25. SCC, #10, p. 176; the reference to "objective disorder" is to PCHP, #3.

26. SCC, #13, p. 176; PCHP, #10, p. 6, as we have seen, referred to "behavior to which no one has any conceivable right."

27. In #12 (p. 176), we read: "Homosexual persons, as human persons, have the same rights as all persons, including the right of not being treated in a manner which offends their personal dignity. Among other rights, all persons have the right to work, to housing, etc."

At this point, an analogy might be helpful. Fornication is a disvalue in official Catholic sexual ethics. It is in no way to be approved of, let alone to be advocated as morally upright behavior. Fornication is a misuse of the sexual faculty, an intrinsically evil act, and, if certain conditions obtain, it is also seriously sinful. However, fornication is not a criminal offense in the United States. Does this mean that the unmarried American has a "right" to fornication? Not at all. *It simply means that she has a right not to be prosecuted and punished for her acts of fornication.*

Staying with this same analogy, let us say that the fornicator is a university student who has secured a substantial loan from the government. If the governmental agency were to cancel her loan upon learning that she regularly has sexual intercourse with her boyfriend, what are we to conclude? Would this be unjust discrimination? Or, would it send a much needed message to today's youth that sex outside the marriage bond can in no way be afforded society's approval?

It seems unlikely that one would wish to give fornication *per se* legal protection, to make it legally protected behavior. However, it doesn't follow that one would necessarily want fornicators to face the systematic loss of their jobs, their housing, or their enjoyment of the numerous social goods that are open to all citizens by virtue of their birthright. And, in the face of a campaign to deny fornicators these rights, it might strike many as reasonable to enact legislation which would make discrimination on the basis of "sex outside of marriage" illegal. One can, in other words, accept unequivocally the objective immorality of fornication while refusing to make it a criminal offense.

One of the most controversial set of guidelines in SCC concerns the obligatory nature of some discriminatory practices against gay people. At paragraph 11 we read:

> There are areas in which it is not unjust discrimination to take sexual orientation into account, for example, in the placement of children for adoption or foster care, in employment of teachers or athletic coaches, and in military recruitment.[28]

In the next paragraph, it is recognized that homosexuals *qua* human are the possessors of human rights. These rights, however, are not absolute: "They can be legitimately limited for objectively disordered external conduct."[29] Moreover, "this is sometimes not only licit but obligatory."[30]

The analogy that is used to defend this conclusion concerns society's treatment of the physically and (or) mentally ill. As regards the contagious and mentally ill, "it is accepted that the state may restrict the exer-

---

28. SCC, #11, p. 176.
29. SCC, #12, p. 176.
30. SCC, #12, p. 176.

cise of rights . . . in order to protect the common good."[31] The common good demands that society be protected from the carriers of contagious diseases and from the potentially dangerous behavior of those who suffer from mental disorders. It is not unjust to deny these groups of people the full exercise of their inherent human rights – a greater good is at stake.

Obviously the argument turns upon the appropriateness of identifying the average gay man and lesbian with the bearers of contagious disease or the potentially dangerous mentally ill. No one would argue that social restrictions ought to be applied to the homosexual who is incidentally criminally insane. It is reasonable to curtail the activities of the homosexual who happens to have a disease that admits of airborne transmission. But SCC goes much further: it advocates *systematic* discrimination against gays and lesbians under the rubric of protecting society from danger.

What specifically does SCC see as the danger posed to society by homosexual people? The exclusionary list enunciated at #11 is revelatory: gay men and lesbians are taken to be threats to children. Homosexuals are improper guardians of youth; they must not be allowed to be adoptive or foster parents; they should not enter into the teaching profession nor be employed as athletic coaches.

Unfortunately, SCC does not explain the threat posed to young people who find themselves in the presence of a lesbian or who are placed under the supervisory care of a gay man. However, three more or less common positions readily found among the opponents of gay liberation can be adduced. First, in the above situations children might be led to conclude that there is nothing wrong with being homosexual; second, this conclusion could lead them to homosexual experimentation and the choice of homosexuality as a lifestyle; and finally, children might be seduced and sexually molested by their gay parents, teachers, or coaches.

And so, NWM's response to SCC, "Human Dignity and the Common Good: A Response of New Ways Ministry to the Vatican Document on Lesbian and Gay Rights" (HDCG), is quick to call attention to the 1983 declaration of the Catholic bishops of the state of Washington:

> A number of Catholics are concerned about the role of homosexuals in professions which have care of their children. There are those who think that gays and lesbians inevitably impart a homosexual value system to children or that they molest children. This is a prejudice and must be unmasked as such. There is no evidence that exposure to homosexuals, of itself, harms a child. . . . Accordingly, there is no need to make efforts to screen out all homosexually oriented persons from our educational system.[32]

---

31. SCC, #12, p. 176.

32. NWM, HDCG (unpublished manuscript available from NWM).

One has to assume that the choice of singling out teaching and coaching as improper vocations for gay people was not done arbitrarily. And, in the absence of any explanation, it is reasonable to conclude that SCC accepts the stereotype of the homosexual as corruptor of youth and as sexually attracted to the young. The most basic psychology textbook counsels restraint in this regard: gay men and women are not to be identified with pedophiles; a homosexual orientation does not mean that one is desirous of sexual contact with children.[33]

It is equally possible that a variation on the "recruitment theory" is operative in SCC's claim that teaching and coaching ought to be off-limits to homosexuals. The classic parameters of this theory are found in the following quotation by Jerry Falwell: "Please remember, homosexuals do not reproduce! They recruit! And many of them are out after my children and your children."[34]

SCC is openly dependent upon PCHP – its whole first section (at least half of the document) consists of direct quotations from the 1986 letter. As we have seen, the new theological element introduced by PCHP was the understanding that the homosexual orientation is itself an objective disorder. This understanding accounts for a subtle dynamic in SCC: to designate the homosexual orientation as a disorder tempts one to look for signs of external verification. In the main, disordered things produce disordered effects. And so, it could be taken as calling into question the decision to name the homosexual orientation a disorder (a decision made on philosophical grounds) if one could not find any disordered effects which flow from it. In this regard, the C.D.F. shows that it is unwilling to be satisfied with the idea that the only disordered effects are the immoral genital manipulations produced by gays and lesbians. To stop the search for disordered effects here could be construed as stopping with something of a tautology: if one designates homosexuality as a disorder, homosexual acts must be disordered by definition.

And so, SCC hypothesizes about the negative effects which society would experience should gay rights legislation be enshrined in civil statutes.[35] Beyond the supposed harm such legislation would have on chil-

---

33. See Kirk and Madsen, *After the Ball*. On p. 43, they write: "the statistics suggest no disproportionate homosexual involvement in pederasty: about 10% of all detected child molesters are gay, just as 10% of the general population is thought to be gay; the other nine-tenths of this vile business is monopolized by heterosexual men (and, to a lesser extent, women)."

34. Quoted in Kirk and Madsen, *After the Ball*, p. 42.

35. In this regard, it is telling that SCC does not make reference to the experience in Europe. Most of the nations of Western Europe have recognized gay and lesbian rights for a number of years. (Homosexual couples have even been able to "marry" in Denmark since 1989.) The negative effect of their policies in this regard is far from being evident. See Neil Miller, *Out in the World: Gay and Lesbian Life from Buenos Aires to Bangkok* (New York: Random House, 1992). Miller's treatment of the Danish experience (pp. 336-356) is particularly illuminating.

dren, the Church's responsibility to promote family life is cited as reason to oppose legal protection for lesbians and gay men. The connections, however, are never explicitly made. How would (even) conferring equivalent family status on homosexual unions harm the traditional family?[36] Is the family done a serious disservice if the partners of homosexuals are allowed to share in the medical benefits of their "spouses"?[37]

SCC simply assumes that homosexually oriented people are in an adversary relationship with marriage and family life. Moreover, the homosexual person is the designated aggressor – she is out to get things to which she has no right, things which have a deleterious effect on the good of husbands and wives and their children. How else can one explain the following guideline: "In assessing proposed legislation, the bishops should keep as their uppermost concern the responsibility to defend and promote family life"?[38] SCC concludes with a similar point:

> . . . where a matter of the common good is concerned, it is inappropriate for church authorities to endorse or remain neutral toward adverse legislation even if it grants exceptions to church organizations and institutions. The Church has the responsibility to promote family life and the public morality of the entire civil society on the basis of fundamental moral values, not simply to protect herself from the application of harmful laws.[39]

The assumption is clear: homosexuality has a negative impact on marriage and family life. This is, moreover, advanced as a statement of fact – it is not a philosophical stance nor a theological utterance. As such, it is open to scientific verification or nullification. It is difficult to refrain from charging SCC with recklessness on this point – the scientific evidence to support its claims are simply not forthcoming.

In this regard, HDCG remarks:

> What is harmful to family life is the rejection of gay and lesbian members by parents and families, the pressures on homosexual people to hide their identity and enter into heterosexual marriages, and the pain and disruption of divorces which result from such unions.

> The definition and experience of 'family' continue to evolve. The fear that the heterosexual family will no longer be the dominant mode of socialization if society supports civil rights for homosexual people is groundless. Empirical evidence indicates that cities, towns, and municipalities which have enacted civil rights for homosexual people remain predominantly heterosexual.[40]

---

36. See SCC, #15, p. 176.
37. See SCC, #15, p. 177.
38. SCC, #9, p. 176; see PCHP, #17, p. 10.
39. SCC, #16, p. 177.
40. NWM, HDCG.

3. CRITIQUES OF SCC

The American presidential election of 1992, by all accounts, was one of the most unusual in many years.[41] A sitting president was defeated and the Democrats gained the White House for the first time since 1976; an independent candidate garnered 19% of the popular vote; and four women were elected to the Senate. The polls gave conflicting reports on how the various candidates were doing – right up to election day.

Of all the ballot measures that voters had to consider, none was more controversial than Oregon's Ballot Measure 9 (M9). If accepted, M9 would have had homosexuality classified as " 'abnormal, wrong, unnatural, and perverse' and would (have) required the state government to be assertive in discouraging homosexuality, teaching that it is a moral offense similar to pedophilia, sadism, and masochism."[42]

M9 was sponsored by the Oregon Citizens Alliance (OCA) – an affiliate of the Reverend Pat Robertson's Christian Coalition. The OCA had to collect over 89,028 valid voter signatures in order to get the measure of the state ballot. This proved to be no problem: the OCA presented 115,000 signatures to qualify for admission on the November 3, 1992 ballot. Scott Lively, a spokesman for the OCA, enunciated the underlying goal of M9: "We want to prevent government from promoting homosexual behavior and from teaching our children that homosexuality is a good choice."[43] Many Oregonians found the proposal compelling enough to agree that it ought to be put to a statewide vote.

At face value, M9 could be taken as more than compatible with Catholic moral teaching.[44] From the vantage point of Catholic sexual ethics, the Church would have little quarrel with labelling homosexuality as 'abnormal, wrong, unnatural, and perverse.' Both PH and PCHP teach as much. While the Church preaches compassion for the homosexual, her

---

41. Russell Baker, a columnist for the *New York Times* and a long-time political reporter, wrote: "For pure gaudy, obscene, hilarious, unnatural, shameful and silly politicking, the present campaign beats them all, hands down." See his "The '92 Follies: A Show with Legs," in *The New York Times Magazine* (November 1, 1992), pp. 27-29, 58-59, at p. 27.

42. Timothy Egan, "Violent Backdrop for Anti-Gay Measure," in *New York Times* (November 1, 1992), p. A40. The precise ramifications of accepting M9 were not clear. The editorial staff of the *New York Times* explained: "Ballot Measure 9 might, for example, be used to justify firing openly gay teachers or police officers, or to deny homosexuals licenses to practice medicine or law. Librarians might be pressured to purge their shelves of works that portray homosexuality in a favorable light." See "The Oregon Trail of Hate," in *New York Times* (October 26, 1992), p. A26.

43. Quoted by Charles E. Beggs, "Proposed Anti-Gay Law Creates Tumult in Oregon," in *Detroit Free Press* (July 21, 1992), p. A4.

44. Indeed, the OCA had planned to release a statement on the Catholic Church's moral evaluation of homosexuality just before the election. See Katrin Snow, "Oregon Anti-Gay Measure Escalates Violence," in *National Catholic Reporter* (October 30, 1992), p. 30.

sexual orientation and same-sex attraction is disordered: it can not be called 'natural' as it is contrary to God's will for human beings.

At the same time, the Church would instinctively oppose any governmental initiative which would encourage people to engage in homosexual experimentation or to adopt a homosexual lifestyle. One can imagine the Church's hostility if the state were to order (say) that all public schools must teach children that homosexuality is as good as heterosexuality or that homosexual behavior must not be called immoral.

With a strong tradition of opposition to homosexuality and a recent Vatican statement warning against the social agenda of the homophile movement, one might have expected the Catholic Church in Oregon to join forces with the OCA to deny "special rights" to gay people and to amend the Oregon state constitution to be explicitly anti-gay. Yet the two bishops of the state of Oregon (William Levada, archbishop of Portland; and Thomas Connolly, bishop of Baker City) were the first religious leaders in the state to *oppose* M9. In a letter subsequently approved by the Oregon Catholic Conference, Archbishop Levada and Bishop Connolly explained to their priests "that they felt the measure could lead to an increase in hate crimes, as well as the denial of basic rights to lesbians and gays."[45]

Bishop Connolly was later to explain:

I feel this initiative could produce very bad results. It's an overreaction by a right-wing group. It's not fair, or just, or appropriate. While the gospel (sic) says it's not right to act out homosexual behavior, it doesn't say it's wrong to be homosexual. I feel that people are not homosexual by choice . . . . We cannot condemn them for who they are, and it's wrong to deny them basic human rights . . . . This group (i.e., OCA) wants to obliterate homosexuals from the community. That's simply wrong.[46]

Archbishop Levada was active in his opposition to M9. He argued that the proposed constitutional amendment was "potentially harmful and discriminatory to homosexual citizens."[47] What is more, Levada asked the parish priests of the archdiocese to prohibit circulation of the petitions for M9 on church property.

Official Catholic opposition to M9 was warmly welcomed by Linda Welch, the executive director of the political action committee "Right to Privacy" – one of the groups which had mounted a counter-offensive against OCA. She was grateful for the bishops' involvement, but couldn't

---

45. "Bishops Urge Ban on OCA Petition in their Domain," in *Bondings*, 14 (1991), p. 5.

46. Quoted in "Bishops Urge Ban. . .," p. 5.

47. Quoted by Mark Kirchmeier and Patricia Lefevere, "Archbishop Opposes Anti-Gay Measure," in *Bondings*, 13 (1991), p. 6.

help expressing some astonishment: "I must admit we're a bit surprised the Catholic bishops are . . . the first to speak out against the measure."[48]

Levada and Connolly proved to be prophetic in their linking violence and hate crimes with the proposed constitutional amendment. Timothy Egan reports that the incidence of arson, vandalism, and verbal threats – from both proponents and opponents of M9 – went up sharply as the campaign reached election day.[49] In the most publicized incident, a gay man and a lesbian were killed when a Molotov cocktail hit their Salem apartment.[50]

In a passionate editorial against the Oregon measure, *New York Times* columnist Anna Quindlen lamented the death of the two gay people:

> Trickle-down homophobia is what happens when government and community leaders trash gay people crudely or subtly, purse their lips and talk about 'lifestyle choice' or open their mouths wide to use Scripture to justify their prejudice. The folks who cooked up the anti-gay referendum let loose a message of hatred and, lo and behold, it turned into a skinhead's firebomb.[51]

Suzanne Pharr, a spokesperson for "No on 9," voiced a similar concern: "What Ballot Measure 9 has done is open up a window for people who are bigoted to display those feelings, and that's what happened in the Salem slayings. Measure 9 has lit a match to a fuse that was already there."[52]

It is significant that at least one Catholic parish was the target of anti-gay violence. In early October 1992, St. Matthew's Church in Hillsboro was vandalized. Inside the church, intruders painted a swastika with the phrases "Catholics love gays" and "Kill gays and Catholics," and an office in the rectory was set on fire. The Reverend Carl Flach, pastor of St. Matthew's, later revealed that an anonymous caller had warned him not to say anything about the Oregon bishops' opposition to M9. Nonetheless, Flach had published the bishops' statement in the parish bulletin.[53]

---

48. Quoted in "Bishops Urge Ban. . .," p. 5. It seems safe to conclude that Ms. Welch considered the Church's sexual ethic to be problematic for opposition to M9.

49. Egan, "Violent Backdrop. . .," p. A40.

50. See Egan, "Violent Backdrop. . .," p. A40; Snow, "Oregon Anti-Gay Measure. . .," p. 9; and Anna Quindlen, "Putting Hatred to a Vote," in *New York Times* (October 28, 1992), p. A21.

51. Quindlen, "Putting Hatred to a Vote," p. A21. She concludes by saying: "For too long we dared not speak its (i.e., homosexuality's) name. Now, too often, people speak it and then lie, making monsters where there are only men and women. This puts an enormous responsibility on the leaders of this country. Trickle-down homophobia cannot exist if they speak out, loud and clear, for the rights of all people. If they speak the name, and pronounce it right. Call it gay. Call it human."

52. Quoted in Egan, "Violent Backdrop. . .," p. A40.

53. See Snow, "Oregon Anti-Gay Measure. . .," p. 9.

After months of rancorous debate, the citizens of Oregon voted down M9; 56% of the voters opposed the anti-gay constitutional amendment.[54] For its part, the OCA vowed to bring the question back to the voters at the next statewide election.[55]

The battle over M9 is a valuable indicator of the reception of SCC by the American hierarchy. Although Archbishop Levada's opposition to M9 predated SCC by several months,[56] he had to take it into consideration when it made its appearance in the final months before election day. Nevertheless, he and Bishop Connolly assured the Catholics of Oregon that opposition to M9 was consistent with papal teaching on homosexuality.[57] The Oregon Catholic Conference believed that the anti-gay measure would have been harmful and discriminatory to gay and lesbian citizens; it argued that M9 would have contributed "to attitudes of intolerance and hostility directed at homosexuals."[58] These potentialities were deemed significant enough to work toward blocking a ballot initiative which would have enshrined in the state's constitution that which is substantially the Church's moral evaluation of homosexual practice. Both PH and PCHP are in accord with designating homosexuality as 'abnormal, wrong, unnatural, and perverse;'[59] SCC deemed it obligatory to work against the social acceptance of the "gay lifestyle." In spite of all of this, considerations of social justice were taken to trump the exigencies of Catholic sexual ethics. The C.D.F.'s observations on gay rights legislation were not considered germane to the situation in Oregon.

Ultimately, the bishops of the state refused to accept the ideology of the Christian Right, an ideology that commentators refer to as "dominion theology."[60] This ideology entails the conviction that all of the nation's legislation and public policy measures must be explicitly in line with (what is taken to be) the orthodox Christian position. Moreover, government positions must be filled by practising Christians. In the main, dominion theology revolves around refusing to accept the fact that the United States of America is a pluralistic society.[61]

---

53. See Snow, "Oregon Anti-Gay Measure. . .," p. 9.

54. See Jeffrey Schmalz, "Gay Areas are Jubilant over Clinton: Oregon Defeats Bid to Curb Gay Rights," in *New York Times* (November 5, 1992), p. B8.

55. See Timothy Egan, "Oregon G.O.P. Faces Schism Over Agenda of Christian Right," in *New York Times* (November 14, 1992), p. A6.

56. Levada first spoke out against the measure in September, 1991. See Kirchmeier and Lefevere, "Archbishop. . .," p. 6.

57. See Snow, "Oregon Anti-Gay Measure. . .," p. 9.

58. Quoted in Snow, "Oregon Anti-Gay Measure. . .," p. 9.

59. It is unimaginable that the antonyms for this group – 'normal, right, natural, and innocent' – would ever be used in the magisterium's discourse on homosexuality.

60. See Egan, "Oregon G.O.P. Faces Schism. . .," p. A6.

Archbishop Levada and Bishop Connolly have not been the only members of the American episcopate who have distanced themselves from SCC. Three bishops[62] were among the more than 1500 signers of a statement opposing the teaching that discrimination against gays and lesbians is sometimes obligatory.[63] One of these bishops, Thomas Gumbleton of Detroit, also issued a public statement recording his opposition to SCC. Gumbleton wrote that he could not in good conscience accept SCC as consistent with the Gospel: "It is . . . in conflict with Gospel values that condemn discrimination and insist that we recognize the dignity inherent in all persons. . . . (I)t is impossible to imagine Jesus supporting this call to discrimination."[64]

Archbishop Quinn has offered the most substantive critique of SCC by a member of the American hierarchy.[65] Putting the question in context, Quinn begins by saying:

> I myself, the bishops of California and the national conference of bishops have over a period of many years affirmed the human and civil rights of gay and lesbian persons, including the right to be free of unjust discrimination in housing and employment. It was precisely because those rights were placed in jeopardy that I publicly opposed the Briggs initiative several years ago.[66]

Ultimately, Quinn judged that SCC does not have the kind of binding force that would demand a change in his present opinion or a retraction his earlier stances.[67] He wrote that this judgment is founded upon "the canons of interpretation approved and used by the Vatican itself. According to those canons, this document is not a mandate but is a document

---

hind Patrick Buchanan's bid to wrestle the Republican Party's nomination from George Bush. See, for instance, Michael Duffy, "How Bush Will Battle Buchanan," in *Time*, 139 (March 2, 1992), pp. 15-16. Buchanan's televised prime-time speech at the Republican National Convention wherein he called for a "cultural war" was at heart an instance of dominion theology. In this speech, Buchanan suggested that "God . . . was on the Republicans' side; that Clinton had thrown in with the criminals, deviates, and baby-killers. The speech opened the proceedings on a note of intolerance, a smallness of spirit from which it never really recovered." [Peter Goldman and Tom Mathews, "Rocky Road to Houston," in *Newsweek*, 120 (November/December 1992; special edition), pp. 65-69, at p. 69.]

62. They were Thomas Gumbleton (auxiliary, Detroit, MI), Walter Sullivan (Richmond, VA), and Charles Buswell (retired, Pueblo, CO).

63. The statement, "A Time to Speak: Catholics for Gay and Lesbian Civil Rights," was sponsored by NWM. It appeared in the *National Catholic Reporter* (November 13, 1992). pp. 13-16.

64. Bishop Gumbleton's statement appeared in *Bondings*, 14 (1992), p. 3.

65. See Archbishop John Quinn, "Civil Rights of Gay and Lesbian Persons," in *Origins*, 22 (August 20, 1992), p. 204.

66. Quinn, "Civil Rights. . .," p. 204.

67. For instance, SCC, as we have noted, says that society is obliged to keep homosexuals from employment as teachers. This was exactly the goal of the Briggs initiative which Archbishop Quinn strongly condemned.

intended as an informal aid to bishops looking for some assistance in dealing with problems of legislation."[68]

Archbishop Quinn does not cite the pertinent "canons" which would establish his position (it is not clear, even, if he means to make reference to canon law). Even if he had done so, however, SCC is not easily classified.[69] Unhappily, the C.D.F. did not clarify its canonical significance. The problematic issue, of course, is that few American Catholics – bishops included – seem to be able to believe that a document from a Roman congregation – especially the Congregation for the Doctrine of the Faith – could have been issued without any binding force on the designated recipients. It is difficult for many to imagine that the prefect of the C.D.F. or one of his assistants would issue any document with a "take it, or leave it" attitude.

Yet, this seems to be the case for SCC. The editors of *The Tablet* report that the Vatican's spokesman, Joaquin Navarro-Valls said as much. Navarro-Valls explained that SCC was "not intended to be an official and public instruction on the matter from the congregation but a background resource offering discreet assistance"[70] for bishops perplexed about gay rights legislation. At the same time, SCC was not intended to pass judgment on any responses to such legislation that individual bishops had made in the past.[71]

Navarro-Valls' statement makes the canonical classification of SCC a moot point. SCC is understood to (merely) put forward some "observations" of the C.D.F. which may or may not be helpful for bishops who must decide on a stand to take in regard to protective legislation for lesbians and gay men.

As a result, Archbishop Quinn could announce with impunity:

> . . . my policy and the policy of the archdiocese will continue to be what it has been: to affirm and defend the human and civil rights of gay and lesbian persons; to oppose unjust or arbitrary discrimination in housing or employment; to affirm and defend the church's teaching on marriage and the family; to affirm and defend the church's teaching on the distinction between sexual orientation and behavior, but especially *always* to remember that 'there are three things that last, faith, hope and charity. And the greatest of these is charity' (1 Cor. 13).[72]

---

68. Quinn, "Civil Rights. . .," p. 204.

69. For instance, following Francis G. Morrisey's *Papal and Curial Pronouncements: Their Canonical Significance in Light of the 1983 'Code of Canon Law'* (Ottawa: St. Paul University, 1992), SCC could arguably be designated an "instruction," a "declaration," or a "circular letter." See pp. 27-34.

70. Quoted in "Angry Reaction to Vatican Observation on Homosexuals," in *The Tablet,* 246 (August 1, 1992), p. 967.

71. See "Angry Reaction. . .," p. 967.

Learning that SCC has no binding force on the American episcopate – that it represents just one opinion among others – may take away much of the sting initially felt by Catholic advocates of gay and lesbian civil rights. But the deeper issue – the problematic question – is how the C.D.F. was able to countenance direct discrimination against lesbians and gay men in the first place. Upon what theological or philosophical principles is such a proposal thought to rest? At the same time, it is supremely important to recognize that the C.D.F. has not retracted its opinion in SCC; it has not admitted to an erroneous judgment nor to a misapplication of general principles. The C.D.F. stands by its belief that gays and lesbians ought to be barred from certain vocations and that it is not unjust discrimination to delimit where they may be permitted to live. Moreover, the congregation continues to hold that marriage and family life are seriously threatened by the presence of homosexuals who are "out," and by the concessions that some municipalities have given to same-sex partners. The C.D.F. may have decided not to force its position on the American bishops; nonetheless, the obligatory nature of discrimination against homosexual persons in some instances remains its "official" position.

This, too, amounts to a studied ambiguity. If it is a moral obligation to keep homosexuals away from children in their formative years, then one would expect that the Church would not allow dissent on this issue. If, moreover, the sexual orientation of young people is so fluid that knowing an openly gay person could influence them to adopt a "gay lifestyle," then Catholics might not only expect, but demand that the Church use its political clout to keep the social advancement of gay men and lesbians at bay. If, finally, the presence of homosexual persons in society does have a detrimental effect on the stability of marriage and family life, then OCA is right and an all-out cultural war can be morally justified by way of the canons on self-defense. If the C.D.F. is convinced of these propositions, then it is irresponsible to allow its teaching in SCC to have only the force of "one opinion among many."

On the other hand, if the C.D.F. is not fully convinced of the underpinnings of its pro-discrimination stance, or if it cannot verify them empirically, then it is irresponsible to advocate measures that are prejudicial to gay people. It then becomes impossible to keep the applicability of the charge of homophobia – or "homohatred"[73] – from the Roman congrega-

---

72. Quinn, "Civil Rights. . .," p. 204.

73. Kirk and Madsen prefer this term when one is not speaking of a pathological fear of homosexuals, but instances of bias against gay people. They write that homophobia "suggests that our enemies, all who oppose, threaten, and persecute us . . . are actually scared of us! If we must be hated, it's comforting to imagine that we have, at the very least, the power to inspire fear. The very term 'phobia' ridicules our enemies (and intentionally so), evoking images many would find comical, such as the old lady standing on the dining-room table, hiking up her skirts, and shrieking – at a mere mouse. . . . (I)s it phobia, or is it

tion. Many letters to the Editor in *The Tablet* and the *National Catholic Reporter* after the appearance of SCC made this point.[74] If the Vatican cannot produce evidence that self-accepting gay men and lesbians are harmful to the common good, it ought to refrain from urging society to deny them certain rights. To persist in such a stance would be not only irrational but unjust.[75]

Richard Posner convincingly argues that down through the ages, Western society has punished homosexual behavior and has been unwelcoming to gay people in view of what is ultimately an unattainable goal: to destroy same-sex attraction and desire. He writes:

> If you say that you would like to kill X but of course will not because you are a civilized, law-abiding person, no one is apt to think much worse of you; but if you (being male) say that you'd like to have sex with that nice-looking man but of course will not because you are law-abiding, afraid of AIDS, or whatever, you will stand condemned in the minds of many as a disgusting faggot. *Homosexual acts are punished in an effort, however futile, to destroy the inclination.*[76]

In this view, SCC would be nothing more than the latest foray in a battle that cannot be won.

Without evidence to support its claims, SCC is patently unjust. It would be advocating none other than the systematic oppression of an already undervalued social minority.

It has to be noted that SCC never makes a direct cause and effect argument. It simply says that gay rights ordinances *may* prove to be harmful.[77] For the sake of argument, let us grant the point: it is possible that

---

hatred? Common sense tells us that many of our enemies come by their queerbashing actions the old-fashioned way: by hating. Fear need have nothing to do with it" (*After the Ball*, p. xxiv).

74. Cf. *The Tablet*, 246 (August 8, 1992), p. 984; (August 15, 1992), p. 1015; (August 29, 1992), pp. 1071-1072; (September 5, 1992), p. 1101; and the *National Catholic Reporter*, (July 31, 1992), p. 24; (August 14, 1992), p. 20; (August 28, 1992), pp. 20-21; (September 4, 1992), p. 17. The remarks of a priest from the Chicago archdiocese are representative: "Institutional homophobia is not new to this age or to institutional church leadership. However, current research into homosexuality and its origins, as well as contemporary scriptural exegesis, point to the dignity and self-worth of lesbian and gay people and their unique contributions to society and the church. Many in the church hierarchy are simply unwilling to listen or pay attention to it." [See Edward Harasim, "Letter to the Editor," in *National Catholic Reporter*, (August 28, 1992), pp. 20-21.]

75. This seems to be the opinion of Archbishop Rembert Weakland of Milwaukee. He wryly confessed that he was "unaware of any other group against which the Church condoned discrimination." [Quoted in "Angry Reaction. . .," p. 967.]

76. Posner, *Sex and Reason*, p. 233; emphasis added.

77. Cf. "Such initiatives (i.e., gay rights ordinances) . . . even where they seem more

protective legislation for gay people might one day be shown to have a harmful effect on some aspect of society. Nonetheless, the Catholic moral tradition would consider it an unwarranted leap to undertake a campaign to undermine people's civil rights because of what "may" happen.

This lack of concordance with the Catholic moral tradition is the heart of John Tuohey's argument in "The C.D.F. and Homosexuals: Rewriting the Moral Tradition."[78] Tuohey, an assistant professor of moral theology at the Catholic University of America, writes:

> Even if those moralists who have been criticized by the C.D.F. for suggesting that the presence or absence of proportionate reason is sufficient to judge the appropriateness of an act would never justify the performance of evil simply on the grounds that doing so might prevent some other harm that 'may' result. Even these so-called revisionist theologians insist on hard evidence to support a claim that a lesser evil is being tolerated or performed for a greater good. By calling on 'conscientious' persons (Foreword) to engage in direct discrimination on the grounds that failure to do so 'may' result in harming the goods of family and community life, the C. D. F. has rewritten the rules of moral theology: It is so opposed to homosexuality it will sometimes make obligatory the performance of a direct evil and require no proportionate reason to justify it.[79]

Tuohey explains that since at least 1950 Catholic morality has been referring to discrimination as a social evil. "Discrimination, as it has been understood in the tradition, is a moral evil when it is directly intended."[80] This teaching, he reminds his readers, was forcefully affirmed in the 1989 declaration of the Pontifical Justice and Peace Commission, *The Church and Racism: Toward a More Fraternal Society.*

Tuohey's critique of SCC is ultimately founded upon what all commentators would take as one of the principle pillars of Catholic morality: it is never licit to perform moral evil directly; one is never justified in doing evil – even if one's intentions were the best. Traditionally, to deal with a particular set of conflict situations wherein a contemplated action is known to produce both good and bad effects, the principle of "double effect" is invoked. In such a situation, it is said that one can justifiably posit the action as long as four conditions are met:

(1) The action is good or indifferent in itself; it is not morally evil.

---

directed toward support of basic civil rights than condonement (sic) of homosexual activity or a homosexual lifestyle, may in fact have a negative impact on the family and society." [SCC, "Foreword," p. 175.]

78. In *America*, 167 (September 12, 1992), pp. 136-138.
79. Tuohey, "The C.D.F. and Homosexuals. . .," pp. 136-137.
80. Tuohey, "The C.D.F. and Homosexuals. . .," p. 136.

(2) The intention of the agent is upright, that is, the evil effect is sincerely not intended.

(3) The evil effect must be equally immediate causally with the good effect; for otherwise it would be a means to the good effect and would be intended.

(4) There must be a proportionately grave reason for allowing the evil to occur.[81]

As Richard McCormick explains: "If these conditions . . . (are) fulfilled, the resultant evil is referred to as an 'unintended byproduct' of the action, only indirectly voluntary and justified by the presence of a proportionately grave reason."[82]

The principle of double effect has had great practical importance in Catholic moral theory. It has been applied in cases involving the taking of human life (self-defense, suicide, abortion, euthanasia, and warfare), wounding the human body (surgical procedures, sterilization), scandal, and cooperation in the wrong-doing of another. Peter Knauer goes so far as to claim that the principle of double effect, since "it responds to the question of whether the causing or permitting of an injury is morally evil," is really at the heart of what morality is all about; it is "the principle of all morality."[83] Is SCC's proposal of denying certain rights to gay people justifiable in light of the principle of double effect?

SCC does not explicitly call attention to the Catholic tradition's use of the double effect principle. However, at #12, it seems to be implied: here SCC stated, as we have seen, that it is "accepted that the state may restrict the exercise of rights, for example, in the case of contagious or mentally ill persons, in order to protect the common good."

Certainly all self-accepting gay people whose sexual partnerships are marked by conscientious decision-making would find the analogy in this passage odious; it is incendiary to identify such persons with the insane or with the bearers of contagious disease. Nevertheless, the principle that one's rights can be legitimately limited for "objectively disordered external conduct"[84] is one of the bedrock principles of most every governmen-

---

81. Richard A. McCormick, S.J., "Ambiguity in Moral Choice," in Richard A. McCormick and Paul Ramsey, eds., *Doing Evil to Achieve Good: Moral Choice in Conflict Situations* (Chicago: Loyola University Press, 1978), p. 7.

82. McCormick, "Ambiguity in Moral Choice," p. 7.

83. Peter Knauer, "The Hermeneutic Function of the Principle of Double Effect," in Charles Curran and Richard McCormick, eds., *Readings in Moral Theology, No. 1: Moral Norms and Catholic Tradition* (New York: Paulist Press, 1979), p. 1.

84. This phraseology is patently awkward. It seems, moreover, to be tailored to fit the homosexual problem (the use of "objectively disordered" – from the vantage point of Catholicism – most often calls to mind issues in sexual morality). Surely SCC would have to

tal arrangement ever devised. The "many" have to be protected against the dangerous "few." The problem is that in free societies the "external conduct" which will result in the loss of some of one's rights are spelled out in codes of law. That all homosexual behaviors ought to be criminated and that their practitioners ought to be punished by having certain rights rescinded is precisely what is in question. How does one go about arguing that gay people ought to be penalized for their "objectively disordered external conduct" in societies where sodomy has been decriminalized? This question brings us full circle: SCC argues against gay rights ordinances in view of their (unsubstantiated) harmful effects. In light of this, one must grant Professor Tuohey's point: SCC has rewritten the rules of Catholic moral theorizing by "sometimes making obligatory the performance of a direct evil without requiring a proportionate reason to justify it."[85] What is more, in no way can such a programme find support by way of the principle of double effect: it does not fulfil even one of the four requirements as outlined by Richard McCormick.

4. CONCLUSION

SCC has not settled the question of the moral advisability of Catholic support for gay and lesbian rights ordinances; indeed, as the Vatican spokesman pointed out, its proposals do not rise above the level of "opinion." Because of this, Archbishop Quinn, along with others in the American hierarchy, has argued that SCC provides no mandate for working against the rights of gay people. Indeed, with Catholic social teaching as one's point of departure, it is all but impossible to see such work as consonant with the fundamental trajectories of Church teaching since the Second Vatican Council.

---

accept that *subjectively* disordered conduct is sometimes as harmful as the objectively disordered variety: indeed, doing a good deed with vicious intentions is usually thought to be worse than doing a bad deed with the best of intentions. Moreover, the use of "external conduct" appears redundant; its antonym, "internal conduct," would apparently refer to one's thoughts and few moderns would classify a person's mental states as "conduct."

85. See Tuohey, "The C.D.F. and Homosexuals. . .," p. 137.

CODA

Catholic Sexual Ethics
v. Catholic Social Teaching

It is evident that SCC does not offer the last word on the propriety of Catholic support for gay and lesbian rights ordinances. Indeed, the impasse as we have described it – whether to broach the question from the vantage point of sexual or social ethics – remains firmly in place. For instance, at the time that Archbishop Quinn reaffirmed his support for social justice for gay people, Archbishop Daniel Pilarczyk voiced his opposition to a proposed gay rights ordinance in Cincinnati.[1] In a letter addressed to the City Council, Pilarczyk wrote that the ordinance would indirectly promote the homosexual lifestyle and that it would "seriously undermine the stability of the family in our society and the moral education and values of our youth."[2] The drama of Pilarczyk's intervention is heightened when one recognizes that at the time he was serving as president of the National Conference of Catholic Bishops.

The lack of "official" clarity on the issue of gay rights legislation became even more pronounced when, in response to SCC, Cardinal Bernardin wrote in his regular column in Chicago's archdiocesan newspaper: "I affirm the fundamental human and civil rights of persons who are gay or lesbian. . . . Bigotry towards persons because of race, creed, national origin, gender, or sexual orientation must be rooted out of our society."[3] Robert McClory reports on the Cardinal's article:

> Although 'affirming the inviolable dignity of a gay or lesbian person and the goodness of their stable, loving, and caring relationships,' the cardinal added: 'I cannot endorse homosexual genital expression. Intimate sexual relations are appropriate only in the context of heterosexual marriage.'[4]

---

1. See "Cincinnati Archbishop Opposes Gay Rights Ordinance," in *Bondings*, 14 (1992), p. 5.

2. Quoted in "Cincinnati Archbishop. . .," p. 5.

3. Quoted in Robert McClory, "Rome Document on Gays No 'Mandate,' Bernardin Says," in *National Catholic Reporter* (November 20, 1992), p. 8.

141

How is the American Catholic to adjudicate between the demands of the Church's sexual morality and the ideal of "liberty and justice for all"? How is one to determine which American prelate's position has a stronger claim on one's conscience? Lacking empirical evidence which would demonstrate that non-discrimination legislation adversely affects society's foundational institutions, how can the Church be justified in sanctioning and, in some instances, advocating policies which are prejudicial to gay people? In a word, what ought to be the Church's goals in influencing the body politic in a secular, pluralistic nation such as the United States?

These questions revolve around the relationship between religion and society, or more specifically, between Church and State. Their likes have bemused clerics and public servants for generations. Although Jesus' admonition to "repay to Caesar what belongs to Caesar and to God what belongs to God,"[5] has been used to support the idea that there are specific and delimited domains for God and Caesar, he did not catalogue the just claims of Caesar on the Christian's conscience nor did he say what is to be taken as belonging specifically to God. Minimally, we in the West – as heirs of the Enlightenment – have come to accept the idea that the State has no business in proselytizing and that, all things being equal, religious institutions would do well to keep their clergy "in the sanctuary."[6] The model which often commends itself is that of the United States, where the "separation of Church and State" has become something of a secular article of faith.[7]

In this arrangement, the State allows for the freedom of the religious bodies within its boundaries and does nothing to impede their flourishing.

---

4. McClory, "Rome Document on Gays. . .," p. 8. It should be highlighted that it is not clear whether this latest foray into the question of gay rights by the Cardinal amounts to a reversal of his earlier position. Does he still hold, for example, that any legislation which explicitly protects gays and lesbians from discrimination amounts – *ipso facto* – to an unacceptable endorsement of the "homosexual lifestyle"? Or, might the "inviolable dignity" and the "fundamental human and civil rights" of gay people be such that gay rights ordinances are not only tolerable but also morally required? Since Chicago accepted a non-discrimination ordinance on February 17, 1989 [See Rutledge, *The Gay Decades*, p. 310], it is conceivable that Bernardin no longer considered these questions germane. However, their importance to the Catholic debate on gay and lesbian rights cannot be denied.

5. See Matthew 22:15-22, at v. 21.

6. The modern Catholic Church has incorporated this understanding in its *Code of Canon Law*. Canon 285, no. 3 reads: "Clerics are forbidden to assume public offices which entail a participation in the exercise of civil power." [See *Code of Canon Law. Latin-English Edition*. (Washington, DC: Canon Law Society of America, 1983), p. 101. The Latin text reads: *"Officia publica, quae participationem in exercitio civilis potestatis secumferunt, clerici assumere vetantur."*]

7. This characterization is John Courtney Murray's. See *We Hold These Truths: Catholic Reflections on the American Proposition* [henceforth, Whtt] (New York: Sheed & Ward, 1960).

In turn, there is an unspoken understanding that these bodies will encourage good citizenship and vilify sedition.

The State's side of the bargain is relatively clear: it ought to maintain a "hands-off" policy towards the religious groups within its borders. Conversely, the Church's involvement in the life of the State is fraught with many conceptual difficulties. Catholicism and mainline Protestantism, for instance, preach a gospel of social *engagement:* the object of one's religious life is not to become less involved in the working of the everyday world, but more involved. "Feed the hungry," "clothe the naked," "instruct the ignorant," and similar injunctions have concrete referents – they are not to be taken in some "spiritual" sense. And, all things being equal, Christians with at least a moderately developed social conscience will denounce governmental policies which would increase the number of "hungry," "naked," or "ignorant" citizens. It is impossible to remove the sociopolitical dimension of the Christian message.

The practical difficulty in all of this arises when one grants that "things are never equal." The issues which confront modern democratic societies call for *political* solutions – not *theological* ones. In the main, one can hardly imagine finding such solutions without at least a modicum of compromise. At its best, politics is the "art of the possible," the art of creating alliances based on compromise. This dynamic raises further questions concerning the Christian churches' involvement in the political life of modern society: it must be underlined that "compromise" is usually a dirty word for the devout of all religious traditions.

The experience of countless individual Christians demonstrates that there is a permanent and fundamental tension between gospel and culture, between religion and society, between Church and State. To be a Christian is to be, in certain respects, "counter-cultural." The bewildering question, however, revolves around how radically counter-cultural one is obliged to be.

If we concentrate attention on the Catholic Church in the United States in the last decade or so, it becomes clear that the Church's official policies are, by and large, selectively counter-cultural. The Church's most uncompromising stances have tended to revolve almost exclusively around a constellation of sexual issues.[8] The U.S. bishops' pastoral letters on war and peace and on the American economy are, by most accounts, less

---

8.   In this regard, see especially Kenneth A. Briggs, *Holy Siege: The Year that Shook Catholic America* (San Francisco: Harper, 1992). The "year" to which Briggs refers ran from August 18, 1986 to September 19, 1987. During this time, the Vatican silenced Father Charles Curran, stripped Seattle's Archbishop Raymond Hunthausen of five areas of responsibility (notably, dealing with Seattle's gay and lesbian community), and released PCHP to the world's bishops. See also the in-depth review of Briggs' work by John C. Cort in *Commonweal,* 119 (November 6, 1992), pp. 37-38.

"hard-line," more nuanced examples of Catholic teaching. The fact that the pastoral letter on war and peace did not go so far as to condemn the morality of producing nuclear weapons for the sake of deterrence is a case in point.[9]

To return the discussion to the issue of a Catholic stance on gay rights ordinances, one wonders if a way out of the sexual ethic/social ethic dilemma can be found. Is there anything in the Catholic tradition which might clarify, for instance, which ethic ought to take precedence on this question? Is there any way to determine which choice may have a greater claim on the Catholic conscience?

In Part Three we turn to the work of John Courtney Murray, S.J., for guidance on this question. Choosing Murray's work for this task will surprise no one. Murray, an American theologian of international repute, spent his professional life dealing with the issues surrounding the relationship between Catholic theology and American civil life. What is more, with Vatican II's acceptance of *Dignitatis humanae* ("Declaration on Religious Liberty"), Murray became one of the few theologians to have seen his own work become part of the Catholic Tradition.

In the chapters that follow, we argue that choosing justice for gay people rather than demanding that every instance of public policy witness to the immorality of homosexual behavior can be grounded in the thought of John Courtney Murray. Murray's contribution to Catholic theological reflection, then, will be shown to validate the approach to gay and lesbian rights that has been advocated by Archbishop Quinn (and Milton Gonsalves). In the main, Murray's work on the Church-State relationship, on Thomistic political theory, and on religious liberty provide a strong rationale for insisting that the Church's social teaching – specifically its teaching on human rights and justice – ought to take priority over its sexual ethic as regards the moral advisability of protecting gay and lesbian people from discrimination.

---

9. See National Conference of Catholic Bishops, *The Challenge of Peace: God's Promise and Our Response. A Pastoral Letter on War and Peace* (Washington, D.C.: United States Catholic Conference, 1983), pp. 52-56.

Part III

Catholic Support for
Gay and Lesbian Rights

CHAPTER SIX

John Courtney Murray
on the Church-State Relationship

John Courtney Murray, S.J., (JCM), is generally regarded as the most important theologian the Catholic Church in the United States has yet to produce.[1] Born in 1904,[2] he joined the Society of Jesus and embarked upon a theological career. He was professor of theology at Woodstock College (Maryland) for three decades, as well as the founding editor of the prestigious *Theological Studies*. He was the author of several books and numerous scholarly articles. Above all, JCM is known for his pivotal role in the Second Vatican Council's acceptance of *Dignitatis humanae* (DH) – the "Declaration on Religious Liberty;" indeed, as we shall see, DH is substantially his work. JCM died in 1967, just two years after the closing session of the Council.

1. MURRAY ON RELIGION AND SOCIETY; CHURCH AND STATE

JCM spent his adult life grappling with the issues surrounding the place of religion in modern, pluralistic societies. Specifically, he was drawn to reflect upon his own experience as a committed Christian living in the archetypical pluralistic society – the United States of America. JCM became convinced that the U.S. Constitution's guarantee of religious freedom and its insistence that the State should recognize no "State Church" are "justifiable" in light of the history of the United States and in light of the religious diversity that has existed from the founding of the Thirteen Colonies.

---

1.   See James Bacik, "John Courtney Murray: Living as a Christian in a Pluralistic Society," in his *Contemporary Theologians* (Chicago: Thomas More Press, 1989), p. 139. David Hollenbach enthusiastically concurs with this judgment: "John Courtney Murray's contributions to Christian life and thought qualify him to be called the most outstanding theologian in the history of American Catholicism." [See his "The Growing End of an Argument," in *America*, 153 (November 30, 1985), p. 363.]

2.   It is a curiosity that four of modern Catholicism's greatest thinkers were born in 1904: Karl Rahner, S.J.; Yves Congar, O.P.; Bernard Lonergan, S.J.; and JCM.

The desire to justify the individual's religious liberty or, for that matter, the separation of Church and State may strike one as odd; most Americans have come to see these tenets of the United States' civil life as self-evident truths. Not only is the existence of a State Church unimaginable, it is unsavory. Before the Second Vatican Council, however, the generally accepted Catholic position was that the American arrangement on these issues could not be taken as a model; all things being equal, the Catholic Church was taken to have a *right* – as the one, true Church of Christ – to be officially recognized by secular society.[3]

The syllogisms underlying this proposition tended to proceed as follows: one ought to belong to the Church established by Jesus Christ; the Catholic Church alone was established by Jesus Christ; therefore, one ought to belong to the Catholic Church. At the same time, because the State must submit to God – its Author and Guarantor – it ought to grant official standing to the Church established by Christ; the Church established by Christ is the Catholic Church; therefore, the State ought to officially recognize the Catholic Church. Finally, anything which might confuse people about the claims of the Catholic Church should not be tolerated; "religious liberty" and the presence of non-Catholic religious bodies confuse people concerning the claims of the Catholic Church; therefore, religious liberty as a public policy ought not to be tolerated and non-Catholic groups have no right to exist in the (well-ordered) State.

Depending upon one's ideological commitments, these propositions will elicit a range of responses from heartfelt agreement, to amusement over the quaint thought forms of the Catholic past, to horror over the Catholic triumphalism of days gone by. But when JCM began his theological career, these propositions were firmly entrenched in the Catholic consciousness. In this regard, the opening line of his "The Problem of State Religion"[4] is revelatory: "Courteous objection was recently raised against my suggestion that the legal establishment of Catholicism as the religion of the state need not be considered a permanent and unalterable exigence of Catholic principles governing Church-State relations."[5] Any number of Catholic theologians were unwilling to grant that the separation of Church and State was anything more than a lamentable necessity, a

---

3. In *Longinqua oceani* (1895), Pope Leo XIII had "declared it erroneous to teach that American-style separation of church and state is the ideal situation or that it would be good for church and state to be separated everywhere." [William A. Herr, *Catholic Thinkers in the Clear: Giants of Catholic Thought from Augustine to Rahner* (Chicago: Thomas More, 1985), p. 234.]

4. In TS, 12 (1951), pp. 155-178.

5. JCM, "The Problem of State Religion," p. 155. The "courteous objection" had been raised by George W. Shea in his "Catholic Doctrine and 'The Religion of the State,'" in *American Ecclesiastical Review*, 123 (1950), pp. 161-174.

"lesser evil."[6] In other words, in societies where Catholicism was the majority religion, an obligation to "establish" the Church was said to obtain.

The article on *tolerance* in the influential *Dictionnaire de théologie catholique*, written in 1946, is an important indicator of the state of the question before Vatican II. In the first place, the very framing of the question is telling: " . . . it amounts to knowing just at what point the Catholic Church, without infidelity to its mission, can, in the exercise of its power of governing (magisterium), tolerate speculative doctrines (dogma) or practices (morals) which are opposed to orthodoxy."[7] The Catholic Church is the guardian of Christian orthodoxy and orthopraxis; it belongs to the Church, as a sacred mission, to ensure that heresy and heterodoxy do not gain adherents.

Consequently,

> . . . the Church is unable to tolerate that which spreads teachings harmful to the faith of its members. From the earliest days of her existence, the Church has had to profess this intolerance: to the high priests who gave the order to be quiet, Saint Peter responded: 'Whether it is right in the sight of God for us to obey you rather than God, you be the judges. It is impossible for us not to speak about what we have seen and heard.' (Acts 4:19-20; translation from the *New American Bible*)[8]

This approach is, beyond a doubt, unproblematic as long as the Church has minority status and is fighting to keep its doctrinal purity in the midst of syncretic tendencies within its own ranks. It is quite another matter when the Church can count on the power of the State to enforce its campaign for doctrinal purity and when the objects of such a campaign are religious outsiders. One needs no more than a passing acquaintance with the general parameters of the history of the Inquisition to question the ethics of this type of intolerance.

By the time of the publication of the *Dictionnaire de théologie catholique*, of course, the Church had long repudiated the use of force in

---

6. The "greater evil" was understood to be the social disharmony which would result in religiously diverse societies if Catholicism were to be made the religion of the state.

7. A. Michel, "Tolérance," in *Dictionnaire de théologie catholique*, volume XV (Paris: Librairie Letouzey et Ane, 1946), p. 1209. [" . . . *il s'agit de savoir jusqu'à quel point l'Église catholique, sans manquer à sa mission, peut, dans l'exercice de son pouvoir de gouvernement (magistère), tolérer des doctrines speculatives (dogme) ou pratiques (morale) opposées, à quelque titre que soit, à l'orthodoxie.*"]

8. Michel, "Tolérance," p. 1209. [" . . . *l'Église ne saurait tolérer que se propage un enseignement nocif pour la foi des fidèles. Dès les premiers jours de son exisitence, il lui a fallu professer cette intolérance: aux princes des prêtres qui lui intimaient l'ordre de se taire, saint Pierre repond: 'Jugez vous-mêmes s'il est juste devant Dieu de vous obéir plutôt qu'à Dieu. Pour nous nous ne pouvons pas ne pas parler' "* (Actes 4:19-20).]

this regard; however, it had not backed down from its theoretical hegemony on the religious question:

> While recognizing that from a theoretical point of view the Catholic Church alone has rights and because of this merits special privileges, the civil legislator has the right and the duty – as regards the good order of society and the general welfare – not to impede the free exercise of other religious bodies.[9]

In other words, the Catholic Church claimed that it alone had any right to exist; the other Christian bodies – because schismatic and (or) heretical – could not validly make such a claim. Their existence, in the Catholic mind, was tied to the benevolent tolerance of the Church and to the fact that a campaign of suppression would jeopardize the good order of society.

The conclusion of the article on *tolerance* is worthy of a full quotation: it sets the stage for a discussion of one of JCM's theses:

> Ecclesiastical intolerance might be an unpopular term, but the reality underlying it is in harmony with that which is the highest and most generous in our nature. It speaks of conviction and confidence, where toleration speaks of skepticism and despair; it reveals strength, where toleration reveals only weakness; it inspires a saving zealotry, while toleration inspires an egotistical indifference. The Catholic Church cannot hate anyone, nor can she be indifferent to any human suffering. She is the most intransigent, the most intolerant of Churches, but she is also the most loving. According to the expression of a French archbishop, 'the Church has the intransigence of truth and of love.'[10]

JCM's rejoinder to this particularly controversial dichotomy between tolerance and intolerance as it bears on Church-State relations, begins with the following reflection: "It is not the direct function of the Church to create a social order, any more than it is the direct function of the state to save souls. The contribution of each to the work of the other is indirect

---

9. Michel, "Tolérance," p. 1221. [*"Tout en reconnaissant que l'Église catholique a seule théoriquement tous les droits et en lui manifestant, de ce chef, une déférence toute particulière, le législateur civil a le droit et le devoir, pour des motifs suffisants de bon ordre et d'intérêt général, de ne pas empêcher le libre exercise d'autres cultes."*]

10. Michel, "Tolérance," p. 1222. [*"L'intolérance ecclésiastique peut être un mot impopulaire, mais la réalité sympathise avec ce que nous avons en nous de plus élevé et de plus généreux. Elle dit conviction et confiance, là où la tolérance dit scepticisme et désespoir; elle prouve une force, là où la tolérance n'accuse que faiblesse et impuissance; elle inspire un zèle sauveur tandis que la tolérance engage plutôt à une indifférénce égoïste. L'Église catholique ne peut haïr personne ni passer indifférente à côté d'une seule misère. Elle est la plus intransigeante, la plus intolérante des Eglises, mais aussi la plus aimante. Suivant l'expression d'un archévêque français, 'l'Église a l'intransigeance de la vérité et de la charité.'"*]

but indispensable; the Church creates a Christian spirit within the temporal order, and the state aids in creating a temporal structure that may be a proper milieu of the Christian spirit."[11]

In this, a rootedness in, for lack of a better term, "historical consciousness" is absolutely required. While it is true that the overarching principles in the matter of the Church's relation to the state are unchangeable, "the reality to which she must relate herself is a variable, not only in its institutional forms but also in the idea that men make of it."[12] Ultimately, it cannot be denied that the "history of Church-State relations is the history of . . . adaptive application. It records many compromises, but no ideal realizations."[13]

An historical study of the question reveals that the "institution of the state-church was an adaptation to a particular historical context."[14] Given the etiology of the state-church, it does not "represent a permanent and unalterable exigence of Catholic principles"[15] – other "institutionalizations of Church-State relationships . . . (can be regarded as) *aequo iure* valid, vital, and necessary adaptations of principle to legitimate political and social developments."[16]

By way of conclusion, Murray garners support from St. Thomas:

> What theory asserts, history confirms. In fact, as St. Thomas taught, and many forget, in what concerns that branch of moral science which is the science of law, history makes the first affirmations: what pertains to moral science is known mostly through experience. Here then is the place to make the decisive historical argument. . . . (T)he legal institution of the state-church and the later constitutional concept of 'the religion of the state' did not come into being as pure deductions from the nature of the Church and the nature of the state; nor do they owe their origin to a situation characterized by the sheer fact that the population, rulers and ruled, were Catholic. They owed both their origin and their justification to a necessary effort on the part of the Church to apply her permanent principles in the new historical situation. . . .[17]

---

11. JCM, "The Problem of State Religion," p. 159.
12. JCM, "The Problem of State Religion," p. 160.
13. JCM, "The Problem of State Religion," pp. 160-161.
14. Viz., "the dissolution of medieval Christendom," the "era of 'confessional absolutism' under the royal governments in the 'Catholic nations' of post-Reformation Europe," and the "monarchic restorations of the nineteenth century." See JCM, "The Problem of State Religion," p. 161.
15. JCM, "The Problem of State Religion," p. 161.
16. JCM, "The Problem of State Religion," p. 162.
17. JCM, "The Problem of State Religion," p. 178.

This new situation included, among other things, the anti-Church ideology of the French Revolution and "the institution of religious freedom, theoretically predicated on the premises of rationalist Continental Liberalism (with its absolutist concept of 'the sovereignty of the people') and practically converted into an engine of war upon the freedom of the Church. . . ."[18]

2. INDEBTEDNESS TO THOMISTIC POLITICAL THEORY

JCM's commitment to Thomism is reflected in no small measure in the overarching schema of his political theory.[19] In his article, "John Courtney Murray, S.J.: A Catholic Perspective," William R. Luckey[20] maintains that Murray's thought is substantially in accord with the following summary statement of Aquinas' teaching on politics:

> first, that the right of political authority to command derived from social needs inherent in human nature as such, and was not postulated because of corrupt proclivities due to original sin. Law was not restricted to the criminal code; power had the positive function of encouraging virtue as well as the negative function of checking vice. . . . Secondly, this authority, at least in the abstract, was distinct from and not of itself beholden to the authority of the church. . . . Third, . . . that temporal power was immediately concerned only with temporal affairs although its purpose was to promote social virtue and its commands obliged in conscience. . . . Fourth . . . government and legislation were more directly functions of art than of ethics.[21]

Luckey believes that two of these points, since they provide an insight into the distinctiveness of Aquinas' and Murray's approach, bear insisting upon. The first is the divinely sanctioned dignity of secular government. Government "receives its authority directly from God, without the mediation of the Church, for purposes that are natural and moral."[22]

---

18. JCM, "The Problem of State Religion," p. 178. These particular issues were explored further in his "The Church and Totalitarian Democracy," in TS, 13 (1952), pp. 525-563. Here, Murray suggests that Leo XIII's aversion to the "modern liberties" (freedom of speech, the press, association, and religion) came from an inability to consider whether they "could be projected on other than rationalist and Jacobin premises, and directed towards other than Jacobin purposes" (in *ibid.*, p. 562).

19. This point is made over and over again in the essays collected by Robert P. Hunt and Kenneth L. Grasso in their *John Courtney Murray and the American Civil Conversation* (*ACC*) (Grand Rapids, MI: William B. Eerdmans, 1992).

20. In Hunt and Grasso, *ACC*, pp. 19-43.

21. In Luckey, "J. C. Murray. . .," pp. 31-32. This summary statement is borrowed from Thomas Gilby, O.P. It can be found in Gilby's *The Political Thought of Thomas Aquinas* (Chicago: University of Chicago Press, 1958), pp. xxi-xxiv.

22. Luckey, "J. C. Murray. . .," pp. 32-33.

For all intents and purposes, this teaching coincides with John of Paris' contention that the prince "is not *minister ecclesiae*, but *minister Dei*. The finality of his power is determined by its origin; it is of the natural moral order."[23] Such a teaching precludes a monistic conception of the Church's competence in human affairs, it endorses a separation between the civil and the ecclesiastical domains.

The second point which Luckey is at pains to highlight, is the last: that government and legislation are more directly functions of art than of ethics. Murray, following Aquinas, would insist on the real distinction between law and morality; "political decisions ought not to be conceived as deductions from clear natural-law principles but rather as choices 'between alternatives both of which may have good moral reasons in their favor:' political decisions are arrived at by a 'kind of poetic freedom,' not by determinism proper to the deductive sciences.'"[24]

Following Luckey's lead, we will now explore in greater detail these two significant theses.

2.1. *A Necessary Dualism*

> Dualism . . . is a term very much out of favor in current discussions on many fronts. It is thought to be a virtue of almost any approach to almost anything that it is integrated, harmonious, and 'wholistic' (or 'holistic,' as in holy). . . . Most views that boast of being 'holistic,' one suspects, have achieved that status by leaving out arguments and evidences that do not fit in the scheme being advanced.[25]

Fully aware of the negative connotations of the term, Murray would argue in favor of a dualistic conception of the secular and the sacred, and of the authority invested in "the cleric" and "the prince." As Richard John Neuhaus puts it, dualism was "the unfashionable term that Murray employed to posit his challenge to ever fashionable monisms."[26]

JCM used the term "monism" to refer to any of the unitary conceptions of the human good. In particular, in his work, it refers to the perduring drive in Western culture to find *the principle* which can put to rest the competition between the "radically different concepts of how the earthly city is to be ordered."[27]

---

23. Luckey, "J. C. Murray. . .," p. 32, citing JCM, "Governmental Repression of Heresy," in *Proceedings of the Catholic Theological Society of America* (1948), p. 56.

24. Luckey, "J. C. Murray. . .," p. 33; he is once again quoting Gilby, *The Political Thought. . .*, p. xxiv.

25. Richard John Neuhaus, "Democracy, Desperately Dry," in Hunt and Grasso, ACC, p. 12.

26. Neuhaus, "Democracy. . .," p. 13.

27. Neuhaus, "Democracy. . .," p. 9.

In "The Church and Totalitarian Democracy,"[28] Murray succinctly described his definition of monism:

> (the totalitarian's) cardinal assertion is a thoroughgoing monism, political, social, juridical, religious: there is only one Sovereign, one society, one law, one faith. And the cardinal denial is of the Christian dualism of powers, societies, and laws – spiritual and temporal, divine and human. Upon this denial follows the absorption of the Church in the community, the absorption of the community in the state, the absorption of the state in the party, and the assertion that the party-state is the supreme spiritual and moral, as well as political authority and reality. It has its own absolutely autonomous ideological substance and its own absolutely independent purpose: it is the ultimate bearer of human destiny. Outside of this One Sovereign there is nothing. Or rather, what presumes to stand outside is 'the enemy.'[29]

It would be difficult to find a better description of the twentieth-century Nazi and Stalinist regimes; indeed, in this article, JCM is intent upon discussing the horrors of these particular monistic structurings of society. However, it is obvious that through the ages the Church has also attempted to foist a monistic arrangement upon Western civilization. In *We Hold These Truths*, Murray remarks that people "might share the fear of Roger Williams, that the state would corrupt the church, or the fear of Thomas Jefferson, that the church would corrupt the state."[30] History is replete with examples vindicating both Williams' and Jefferson's fears; history taught Murray the absolute necessity of insisting upon the Gelasian teaching on "the dualism of mankind's two hierarchically ordered forms of social life"[31] – the church and the state. In this, Murray argued that "the monist ambition to establish a coherent or 'integral' Christian social order is dangerously misguided."[32]

Pope Gelasius I (pope, A.D. 492-496), in his "Letter to Emperor Anastasius,"[33] taught "that before the coming of Christ, rulers assumed the function of divine worship, but after his coming, 'he distinguished between the offices of both (i.e., sacred and secular) powers according to their own proper activities and separate dignities . . . so that Christian

---

28. In TS, 18 (1952), pp. 525-563.

29. JCM, "The Church and Totalitarian Democracy," p. 531; cited by Neuhaus, "Democracy. . .," p. 9.

30. JCM, Whtt, p. 64.

31. JCM, Whtt, p. 64.

32. Neuhaus, "Democracy. . .," p. 15.

33. The "Letter" can be found in Brian Tierney, ed., *The Crisis of Church and State, 1050-1300* (Englewood Cliffs, NJ: Prentice, 1964), pp. 13-14. It is quoted from this source in Luckey, "J. C. Murray. . .," pp. 27-28.

emperors would need priests for attaining eternal life and priests would avail themselves of imperial regulations in the conduct of temporal affairs.'"[34]

Gelasius' point was far from an egalitarian conception of the sacred and secular powers; his teaching announced the superiority of the sacred power: it is more weighty than the royal power, it possesses a greater dignity. Nonetheless, it was definitely not the "political Augustinism" that Murray saw in the theories of John of Salisbury and Giles of Rome, theories which blurred "the distinction between the two powers by attributing to the civil power an excessively religious function, making it a disciplinary agent for the restraint of concupiscence and an instrument of man's supernatural redemption."[35]

JCM held that the Gelasian teaching was the "authoritative" teaching of the Church on the matter.[36] He was of the opinion that it could have served as the foundation for theologically sound policy regarding issues of "Church and State." The problem was that

> it was completely misinterpreted when it was initially delivered. Modern Roman Catholic teaching is formulated on the basis of principle – theory precedes practice. But during the Middle Ages, the process of formulating teaching regarding the proper relationship of both powers more characteristically involved moving in the opposite direction – from practice (specifically papal practice) to theory. In this case . . . the meaning of Gelasius' statement was determined on the basis of how the popes (especially the medieval popes) acted on specific occasions.[37]

In *We Hold These Truths*, Murray was to claim that the American "separation of Church and State" is *compatible* with Catholic teaching: he did not argue that the American arrangement could claim normativity for other societies. For JCM, the Catholic tradition calls one to a fundamental recognition that the church is not the state and the state is not the church. In other words, each has a competence of its own and a proper sphere of activity. Ultimately, secular attempts to dominate the church and ecclesiastical attempts to dominate the state cannot be justified by the "best" of Catholic tradition.

---

34. Luckey, "J. C. Murray. . .," p. 28; citing Gelasius' "Letter," p. 14.
35. JCM, "Governmental Repression of Heresy," p. 62; cited by Luckey, "J. C. Murray. . .," p. 29.
36. See Luckey, "J. C. Murray. . .," p. 27.
37. Luckey, "J. C. Murray. . .," p. 29.

2.2. *Art v. Deductive Reasoning: Murray on Contraception*

In her contribution to *John Courtney Murray and the American Civil Conversation*, Professor Mary Segers[38] of Rutgers University corroborates the importance of highlighting Murray's acceptance of the Thomistic preference to view politics (and hence public policy decisions) as an instance of art rather than as an instance of deductive reasoning from "first principles." In this, she reminds her readers that St. Thomas refused to identify law and morality: "legal" and "moral" were far from synonymous for Aquinas. In this same vein, she writes that Murray,

> offered four significant qualifications concerning the use of positive law to enforce standards of public morality. First, the scope of law is limited to the protection and maintenance of relatively minimal standards of public morality. A minimum of public morality is a social necessity; moreover, the force of law is coercive, and people can normally be coerced into the observance of only minimal standards. Second, this minimalist approach to the use of law to enforce moral norms holds with particular force in the case of a free society, in which government is not paternal and the jurisprudential rule obtains: as much freedom as possible; as much restriction and coercion as necessary. Third, the measure of public morality that can and should be enforced by law is necessarily a matter of public judgment, especially in a democratic society. Consensus is crucial: the people whose good is at stake have a right of judgment with regard to the measure of public virtue that is to be enforced and the manner of public evils that are to be repressed. Fourth, Murray emphasizes issues of legal efficacy and enforceability. He stressed that there must be a reasonable correspondence between the moral standards generally recognized by the conscience of the community and the legal statutes concerning public morality. Otherwise laws will be unenforceable and ineffective, and they will be resented as undue restrictions on civil personal freedom.[39]

The law ought to enforce the minimal standards of public morality; legal efficacy and enforceability preclude anything more. When a given law no longer reflects the moral consensus of the community, it becomes a source of resentment and undermines the bonds that hold people together in the project of communal living. Drawing upon unpublished materials in the John Courtney Murray Archives, Segers shows how Murray

---

38. See Mary C. Segers, "Murray, American Pluralism, and the Abortion Controversy," in Hunt and Grasso, *ACC*, pp. 228-248.

39. Segers, "Murray, American Pluralism. . .," pp. 238-239.

applied these principles to the volatile question of reforming the birth control laws in Massachusetts.[40]

The Massachusetts birth control law was one of the most restrictive in the country: it "prohibited the manufacture, sale, and distribution of contraceptives and permitted no exceptions to this rule."[41] It dated to the late nineteenth century and was enacted by the Protestant Brahmins.[42] By the early 1960s, "there was widespread noncompliance with and nonenforcement of the Massachusetts birth control law."[43] There were ever more insistent calls for the repeal of the law.

The Catholic archdiocese of Boston had long been embroiled in the controversy surrounding the question of maintaining the legal ban on contraception. Cardinal William O'Connell managed to prevent reform of the law in the 1940s. His successor, Richard Cushing, began his tenure as archbishop by upholding the archdiocese's opposition to overturning the birth control statute, but by the mid-1960s he had begun to have a change of heart.[44]

Cardinal Cushing's experience at the Second Vatican Council was the prime mover in this change of heart. At the Council, he "had come to recognize the importance of tolerance and mutual respect in a pluralist society"[45] and he was one of the Council Fathers who championed DH. Be-

---

40.   Murray would also eventually comment upon the birth control law in Connecticut. The Connecticut law read: "Any person who uses any drug, medicinal article, or instrument for the purpose of preventing contraception shall be fined no less than fifty dollars or imprisoned not less than sixty days nor more than one year or be both fined and imprisoned. Any person who assists, abets, counsels, causes, hires, or commands another to commit any offense may be prosecuted and punished as if he were the principal offender" [Connecticut General Statutes (1958 Revised), title 53, ch. 939, sec. 53-32, and title 54, ch. 959, sec. 54-196; cited by Segers, "Murray, American Pluralism . . .," pp. 233-234]. In Whtt, Murray wrote: ". . . the Connecticut statute confuses the moral and the legal, in that it transposes without further ado a private sin into a public crime" (p. 157; see Segers, in *ibid.*, pp. 233-236).

41.   Segers, "Murray, American Pluralism. . .," p. 236.

42.   Murray would use the fact that the country's birth control laws were not inspired by either Catholic sexual or social teaching against his co-religionists who argued that the laws should not be reformed. See Segers, "Murray, American Pluralism. . .," p. 235.

43.   Segers, "Murray, American Pluralism. . .," p. 237.

44.   See Segers, "Murray, American Pluralism. . .," p. 237. In 1948, Cushing's opposition was considered crucial to the failure to reform the law. Francis G. McManamin writes: "An initiative bill, seeking to reverse the state law prohibiting physicians from giving contraceptive advice, was introduced into the (Massachusetts) legislature in the spring of 1948. On April 6, the Catholic Bishops of the state presented a statement to the Joint Committee on Public Health in which they declared the bill to be ethically unsound and socially ill-advised. The opposition was effective, for the House of Representatives defeated the measure 180-84, and the Senate followed suit, 22-15. [See Francis G. McManamin, "American Bishops and the American Electorate," in *American Ecclesiastical Review*, 151 (1964), p. 224.]

45.   Segers, "Murray, American Pluralism. . .," p. 237.

tween the years 1963 and 1966, Cushing "indicated in a variety of public forums (on television, in testimony before congressional and state legislative committees, and in private correspondence) that he did not feel obligated to oppose a change in the law."[46] And this, he would add, was not because he considered contraception to raise no moral questions, but because "Catholics do not need the support of civil law to be faithful to their religious convictions, and they do not seek to impose by law their moral views on other members of society."[47]

In 1963, at the beginning of another attempt to repeal the law, Cushing said that his policy would be "just to explain our position, but not go out campaigning."[48] Francis McManamin relates the following scenario:

> When asked whether he regarded the statute as 'a bad law,' the cardinal replied that this was a particular field in which he was not proficient. 'What the considered opinion of the experts will be in the future concerning the legislation of this kind of information,' he added, 'I do not know.' He acknowledged that he would confer with the best authorities to find out how he would be obligated in the matter.[49]

Cardinal Cushing turned to JCM for advice on this most delicate issue.[50]

In his "Memorandum to Cardinal Richard Cushing,"[51] Murray presented his considered opinion on the matter of the Massachusetts birth control law. To begin, he rehearsed the Thomistic distinction between "le-

---

46. Segers, "Murray, American Pluralism. . .," p. 237.

47. Cardinal Richard Cushing, quoted by C. Dienes, *Law, Politics, and Birth Control* (Urbana, IL: University of Illinois Press, 1972), pp. 149-150; cited by Segers, "Murray, American Pluralism. . .," p. 237. McManamin, in "American Bishops. . .," pp. 224, 228-229, discusses Cardinal Cushing's change of heart on the Massachusetts law.

48. Cushing, quoted in McManamin, "American Bishops. . .," p. 224. (The reference McManamin gives is to the February 23, 1963 edition of the *Pilot*, Boston's archdiocesan newspaper.)

49. McManamin, "American Bishops. . .," p. 224; citing the February 23, 1963 edition of the *Pilot*.

50. Relying upon Timothy Bouscaren and Adam Ellis [*Canon Law: A Text and Commentary* (Milwaukee: Bruce, 1957), pp. 172-173, 725], Francis G. McManamin, in his article "Episcopal Authority in the Political Order" [in *Continuum*, 2 (1965), pp. 632-638] shows that part of the problem for Cushing was strictly canonical. The pre-1983 Code of Canon Law said that the "local ordinary has 'the right and duty to govern the diocese both in temporal and spiritual matters, with legislative, judicial, and coercive power.' In addition to his specific command to govern he also has the obligation to teach the moral law and, consequently, has the right and obligation to ensure the careful instruction and direction of his flock in conformity with the teachings of the Church" (p. 633).

51. JCM, "Memorandum to Cardinal Richard Cushing," Murray Archives, Languiner Library, Georgetown University, n.d. Quoted in Segers, "Murray, American Pluralism. . .," at pp. 238-241.

gal" and "moral." Segers offers the following commentary on this first part of the "Memorandum:"

> Appealing first to traditional notions of jurisprudence, Murray maintained that it is not the function of civil law to prescribe everything that is morally wrong. As an instrument of social order, the scope of law is limited to the maintenance and protection of public morality. Matters of private morality lie beyond the scope of law and are properly left to personal conscience. Issues of public morality arise, however, 'when an act or practice seriously undermines the foundations of society or gravely damages the moral life of the community, in such a way that legal prohibition becomes necessary in order to safeguard the social order as such. So, for instance, offenses against justice must be made criminal offenses, since justice is the foundation of civil order.[52]

The central question, then, was whether contraception ought to be viewed as an issue for public or private morality. Murray admitted that, at present, the question was disputed among Catholics. "Nevertheless, he found the case for affirming contraception a matter of private morality to be sufficiently conclusive."[53] He would argue that the scales were tipped toward private morality since so much of the discussion surrounding contraception came under the rubric of "responsible parenthood": the decision of a husband and wife to limit the size of their family through artificial means of contraception cannot easily be categorized as a practice which 'seriously undermines the foundations of society or gravely damages the moral life of the community.' Moreover, the *coup de grâce* had been delivered by mainline Protestantism: "It is difficult to see how the state can forbid, as contrary to public morality, a practice that numerous religious leaders approve as morally right. The stand taken by these religious groups may be lamentable from the Catholic moral point of view. But it is decisive from the point of view of law and jurisprudence, for which the norm 'generally accepted standards' is controlling."[54]

Next, Murray moved to a consideration based on the concept of religious freedom.[55] Segers recounts his argument in this regard:

> Here Murray held that . . . religious liberty includes a twofold immunity from coercion. 'First a man may not be coercively constrained to act against his conscience. Second, a man may not be coercively restrained from acting according to his conscience, un-

---

52. Segers, "Murray, American Pluralism. . .," p. 238; quoting JCM, "Memorandum. . .," p. 1.

53. Segers, "Murray, American Pluralism. . .," p. 239.

54. JCM, "Memorandum. . .," p. 1.

55. In chapter 7, attention will be focused on JCM's work on religious liberty.

less the action involves a civil offense – against the public peace, against public morality, or against the rights of others.'[56]

Since the practice of contraception is best understood as falling under the rubric of private morality, and since it is then by definition improper to categorize it as a civil offense, JCM held that the above "religious liberty immunities" ought to obtain. "On this reading, the Massachusetts birth control statutes were contrary to religious freedom. Thus, from the perspective of traditional jurisprudence and religious liberty, the Massachusetts statutes could not pass muster as sound law."[57]

In the end, Cardinal Cushing accepted JCM's reading of the situation. The following statement of the Cardinal is clearly indebted to the approach advocated by Murray: "In the present case, especially in the light of the position taken by other religious groups in our plural society, it does not seem reasonable for one to forbid by civil law a practice that can be considered a matter of private morality."[58]

The point of Segers' article is to apply Murray's approach to the Massachusetts birth control law to the contemporary debate surrounding the legal status of abortion. She is not blind to the controversial nature of her enterprise; she does not wish to put words in JCM's mouth, but rather desires to draw out the implications for sound abortion policy in the United States.[59] She is equally aware that Murray left nothing explicit on this topic; nonetheless, she holds that his *opera* provide much needed guidance on this issue of great social importance. Therefore, Segers asks: "(1) Were Murray with us today, would he favor the use of coercive law to prohibit or severely restrict abortion? and (2) How might he advise American Catholics to approach the question of abortion policy in the United States?"[60]

Highlighting the lack of consensus on the morality of abortion; the fact that "most Episcopalians, Methodists, Presbyterians, Lutherans, Baptists, Reform Jews, and other religious groups regard abortion as morally permissible;"[61] and the inability of many to decide whether abortion is an instance of public or private morality,[62] Segers asserts that

---

56. Segers, "Murray, American Pluralism. . .," p. 239; quoting JCM, "Memorandum. . .," p. 2.

57. Segers, "Murray, American Pluralism. . .," p. 240.

58. Cushing, quoted in Dienes, *Law, Politics, and Birth Control*, p. 201; cited by Segers, "Murray, American Pluralism. . .," p. 241.

59. See her comments on p. 231 of "Murray, American Pluralism. . .".

60. Segers, "Murray, American Pluralism. . .," p. 243.

61. Segers, "Murray, American Pluralism. . .," p. 246.

62. Segers rightly notes that this question turns on the moral status of the fetus. "If the fetus is defined as a human being from conception, then abortion is an other-regarding action that raises questions about justifiable killing." In this view, governmental restriction is

(w)ere Murray alive today, I think he would stress the Church's positive role in society rather than its political role in shaping a more restrictive abortion policy. Murray would hold that prudence dictates that the Church should not focus primarily on using coercive law to restrict abortion; rather, the Church's role in this controversy should be to exemplify Christian charity by using its resources to assist women who are involuntarily pregnant. If we assume that the Church's goal is to reduce the incidence of abortion without coercing women, then as a practical matter it would be less advantageous to endorse coercive laws and policies, the effectiveness of which is dubious, than to provide the social and economic support that many women need in order to bear and rear their children. It is possible, even probable, that in taking such measures, the Church and indeed individual Catholic Christians would play a more prophetic role and set a more convincing example of genuine respect for life than they would by using political pressure to pass coercive abortion laws.[63]

Segers' article is well-researched and well-argued; its conclusion is an "educated guess." Even though JCM was "a loyal, faithful Jesuit," it doesn't seem likely to Segers that if he were alive today that he "might be leading the charge of Catholic antiabortion activists seeking to make the nation's laws reflect Catholic moral opposition to abortion."[64] She concludes:

> Murray knew that American Catholics had to recognize that law seeks to establish and maintain only that minimum of morality necessary for a stable, functioning society. His sophisticated jurisprudence led him to recognize that not every sin need or should be a crime. He stressed legal efficacy and enforceability in approaching the question of legislating morality. Above all, he was respectful of religious liberty and tolerant of religious differences in a free society.[65]

Would JCM have emphasized "political prudence" and "religious tolerance" over the moral evil of direct abortion? Would he have been comfortable with the "I'm personally opposed to abortion, but . . ." approach to the question? Finally, would he have counselled a "non-coercive" approach to instances of involving the taking of fetal life? Segers answers each of these questions affirmatively; and, as we mentioned above,[66] much

---

required; although "issues of enforceability and legal efficacy would still influence the degree of governmental regulation" (in "Murray, American Pluralism. . .," p. 243).

63. Segers, "Murray, American Pluralism. . .," p. 247.

64. Segers, "Murray, American Pluralism. . .," p. 248.

65. Segers, "Murray, American Pluralism. . .," p. 248.

turns upon the moral status of fetal life. Faced with an instance of direct killing of human life, questions involving prudence and tolerance pale in significance. Laws restricting abortion might very well be less than efficacious and all but unenforceable, but in the end, Segers' belief that Murray would acquiesce in viewing direct abortion as a matter of private morality is less than completely convincing. Moreover, since there is simply no evidence that Murray would dissent from the magisterial teaching which accords "human status" to intra-uterine life, it is impossible to say that he would not hold abortion to be a matter of *public* morality, since it would then have to be an other-regarding action.

The fact remains that JCM held that the Church need not insist that civil law reflect Catholic opposition to contraception. Even though contraception is considered a grave moral evil – an intrinsically disordered act which implicates its agents in (objectively) serious sin – the best of the Catholic tradition would hold that it need not be the object of crimination.[67] Since Cardinal Cushing's support of legal reform in Massachusetts and the Supreme Court's ruling on the Connecticut case,[68] the American Catholic hierarchy has been quiet on the question of the legality of contraception; it has not raised problems with the legal use of contraceptives by adults. And, we should add, this silence cannot be taken as an indication that the American hierarchy has changed its mind on the moral valence of birth control. Moreover, it seems that the majority of American Catholics know that even though contraception is "legal," the official teaching of the Church is that it is "immoral."

John J. Lynch, S.J., writing in *Theological Studies'* "Notes on Moral Theology" during the height of the controversy in Massachusetts (and Connecticut), offered the following reflection:

> A year ago in these Notes the fear was expressed that scandal through misunderstanding might be occasioned by communication to the general laity of (the) . . . distinction between the demands of the natural law as regards contraception and the possible inexpediency of positive civil legislation as added sanction. Subsequent events suggest that perhaps this fear was unfounded. . . .

---

66. See *supra*, p. 162, n. 62.

67. John J. Lynch, S.J., a contemporary of Murray and a colleague at *Theological Studies*, concurred with Murray's judgment. In reference to the Connecticut ban on birth control, he wrote: "Since it cannot be proven that the private act of contraception, always a serious objective violation of the moral law is also necessarily a threat to the common good, it is difficult to see jurisprudential justification for that portion of Connecticut's law which forbids and sanctions with punishment either the contraceptive act as indulged in by husband and wife or a doctor's transmission of contraceptive instructions upon request from his patient" [John J. Lynch, "Notes on Moral Theology," in TS, 22 (1961), pp. 235-236].

68. The law was declared unconstitutional. See *Griswold v. Connecticut*, 381 U.S. 479 (1965).

In several publications intended principally for lay people, the substance of this doctrine has since been proposed in terms which seem to preclude all reasonable misinterpretation. (Even Planned Parenthood Federation prefaced with this statement its survey of Catholic opinion on the point as culled from the current literature: 'In order to avoid confusion, it should be noted clearly at the outset that all of the writers here affirm their adherence to the traditional Catholic doctrine on medical birth control.') If any untoward reaction has greeted the presentation of this thesis to the public, it has not come to attention here.[69]

American Catholics did not confuse a change in the civil law – and official Catholic support for said change – with a change in the Church's official evaluation of artificial means of birth control. They were aware that the Church's support for legal reform in the matter of contraception did not entail that contraception would henceforth be considered a moral choice.

3. CONCLUSION

Following St. Thomas, JCM distinguished between the powers appropriate to the Church and those appropriate to the State. At the same time, he maintained that there is a real difference between morality and legality. It was clear to him that it is not up to civil law to criminate all vice; every sin need not also be a crime. Civil law exists to maintain the fundamental structures of society that ensure justice and stability. Murray's approach to this complex of issues is well-exemplified in his "behind the scenes" work on the question of Catholic support for repealing anti-contraception laws.

In the next chapter, we treat JCM's greatest contribution to modern Catholicism – his work on behalf of religious liberty, a work which culminated in Vatican II's acceptance of DH. In Chapter Eight, we will have occasion to apply all of this to the contemporary question of Catholic teaching on the moral advisability of gay and lesbian rights ordinances.

---

69. Lynch, "Notes. . .," pp. 236-237.

CHAPTER SEVEN

John Courtney Murray
on Religious Freedom

1. TOLERANCE REVISITED

Demonstrating that the "State-Church" was not a theological necessity went hand in hand with JCM's work on the question of the religious freedom of the individual – a question which was no less controversial and no less fraught with conceptual difficulties.

Murray first addressed the issue of the individual's "freedom of religion" in a series of two articles published in 1945.[1] As we have seen, for a number of very practical reasons the Catholic Church had long looked askance at the idea of religious liberty. It seemed to demand the acceptance of religious indifferentism; it was often predicated upon social theories that the Church found unacceptable. By the time Murray began his first article on the question, however, it had become "a political problem of the first magnitude."[2] Here, the international community's experience with Nazism played a key role:

> Within our own memory, both open and subtle persecutions have been directed against Catholics, Protestants, and Jews by States which have claimed the right to put the human conscience in bondage to themselves and to their pagan theories of race and State and culture. And their policies in the matter of religion have powerfully contributed to the contemporary political tumult and social upheaval.[3]

When the individual is not allowed freedom of religion, his conscience is held in bondage and consequently, his human dignity is diminished. Whenever a State refuses to acknowledge the religious liberty of its citizenry and undertakes the regulation of religious beliefs and practices,

---

1. See "Freedom of Religion," in TS, 6 (1945), pp. 85-113; and "Freedom of Religion: I. The Ethical Problem," in TS, 6 (1945), pp. 229-286.
2. JCM, "Freedom of Religion," p. 87.
3. JCM, "Freedom of Religion," p. 87.

it has gravely over-stepped its bounds. One ought not to be surprised if social discord were to follow.

The Catholic Church had long demanded freedom for itself from the individual nations of Europe. The problematic issue concerned the "rights" of the *individual* in the religious domain. If, for example, one adheres to the proposition that the Catholic Church is the "one, true Church" and that the other Christian communions are, as a result, taken to be "false religions," one may be led to ask if someone can have a right to belong to one of these erroneous expressions of Christianity.[4] Can one logically maintain that a person has a "right" to hold erroneous beliefs and a "right" to concretize them in religious practices? This amounts to a claim that the human person has a right to do wrong – a proposition which is dangerously close to arguing in favor of anarchy.

And so, the Catholic solution to the problem moved, as we have seen, to a reflection on tolerance. The Church would tolerate the existence of other religious bodies and allow for their freedom – in the name of social order. Wherever repressing "false religions" would be detrimental to the peace, it ought to be left undone. JCM reports on how this position was received in the non-Catholic world:

> It is said that we are not interested in freedom, but in maintaining or acquiring political control, in order to get a free field for our 'totalitarian claims,' 'religious monopoly,' 'spiritual imperialism,' 'cultural domination,' 'ecclesiastical arrogance,' etc. . . . (O)ne of the most powerful contemporary attacks is being launched against the Church, in the attempt (conscious or unconscious) to drive a wedge between her and the modern world, which she is mightily striving to save. In this connection, I suggest that this attack will not be successfully met simply by the strenuous defense of the position that the Catholic Church is the one true Church. . . . So far as freedom of religion is concerned, what is properly at issue and what troubles a good many Catholic as well as Protestant minds is rather the political implications of our position in the present world situation.[5]

One of the problems with "tolerance" is that it bespeaks putting up with something that one cannot do much about. Therefore, 'tolerating someone's religious beliefs' can mean that one would prefer that the person pledge allegiance to a different set of beliefs (ideally, one's own) and that, if push comes to shove, one would be willing to *insist* upon it. In this context, tolerance is not indicative of respect for the dignity of the other's conscience; it is a not-so-subtle put-down. Those who are doing

---

4.   From within this ideological framework, the adherents of non-Christian religions are in an even less tenable position.

5.   JCM, "Freedom of Religion," p. 90.

the "tolerating" cannot but appear small-minded and bigoted by those who are on the receiving end of their tolerance.

Murray's strategy in his first article on religious liberty was to move the question out of the domain of ecclesiology – beyond "the hypothesis of a divine revelation whereby God, through Christ, may have determined the existence of a spiritual and juridically perfect society whose rights and freedoms are not simply the projection of the jus natural rights and freedoms of its individual members."[6] His focus would be on social ethics:

> The human person, as the image of God, is natively the equal of the other persons with whom he shares a community life; he has therefore the natural right to participate on terms of equality with others in the full political, economic, and social life of the community. Consequently, the State has a duty to respect this right, and not arbitrarily to limit it. I say, arbitrarily; for there are reasonable causes which justify its limitation, as when the State limits the right of suffrage to the literate, or inhibits the contractual competence of minors, or deprives criminals of civic rights, etc. Limitations or disabilities are reasonable and not injurious when they are necessary for the common good, and approved as such by the conscience of the community. But religious belief is not *per se* a reasonable cause for imposing such disabilities. The reason of course, is emphatically not that given by the older liberalistic individualism – the false assertion that a man's religious beliefs bear no relation to his social activities. Rather, the reason is that a man's religion will not *per se* influence his social action in such wise as to make it at all prejudicial to the common good, and thus justify the State in imposing limitations upon it. I say all this under the qualification, *per se*, since we are here speaking in terms of principle, and not in terms of the special problems created *per accidens* by peculiar religious tenets, or by the special exigencies of particular social contexts, which may qualify the concept of the common good.[7]

The question of religious liberty, then, need not call into question the Catholic Church's claim to be the "one, true Church;" nor is it necessarily predicated upon the assertion that 'one religion is as good as another.' Rather, the individual's freedom to follow the dictates of her conscience in matters of religious belief and practice is founded upon a natural-law argument: the principle of religious liberty flows from a reflection upon the nature of human life in society.[8]

---

6.   JCM, "Freedom of Religion," p. 92.

7.   JCM, "Freedom of Religion," pp. 92-93.

8.   In this regard, JCM is quick to specify that "if one chooses to stay simply on the plan of natural law, one has to admit that a protest in a particular case against disabilities, made in the name of man as the image of God and in the name of the religious conscience as

In his next article on the subject, Murray offered a further critique of the "traditional" Catholic position on religious freedom, a position that had come to be capsulized by two complementary formulae: "dogmatic intolerance" and "personal tolerance." From the outset, JCM was completely forthcoming with his dissatisfaction with this terminology: "For my own part, I feel that neither of these formulas is happy, as a formula; in fact, I should like to see both of them disappear from circulation as rapidly as possible."[9]

In this regard, the connotations raised by the terminology account for Murray's discomfort. The formula "dogmatic intolerance"

> is particularly objectionable. . . . We are normally desirous of showing that our position with regard to religious liberty, although complex, is quite reasonable. It would seem, therefore, advisable not to state it in a formula that from the outset prejudices the case against its reasonableness. As a matter of sheer fact, the word 'intolerance' is synonymous in the popular mind with all that is unreasonable, and positively hateful. In customary usage, it does not designate a considered and serene intellectual and emotional attitude, formed in the light of the full truth and impregnated with profound charity; on the contrary, it stands for the entirely detestable tone and temper of mind that is narrow, one-sided, impatient of argument, obstinate, prejudiced, aggressive, arrogant, and persecuting.[10]

Moreover, "the addition of the adjective 'dogmatic' effectually locks all the doors to understanding that were already slammed shut by the word 'intolerance;' in customary usage, it means 'opinionated; asserting a matter of opinion as if it were fact' (Webster)."[11]

Compared with "dogmatic intolerance," the formula "personal tolerance"

---

such, will always depend for its validity upon proof that the action of the State in the particular case has been arbitrary. In other words, an essential part of a case against such disabilities, as violations of individual rights, is proof that they are not demanded by the common good, and therefore are unreasonably imposed by the State. And, from the standpoint of natural law, the ultimate judge of the cogency of the proof would be the enlightened collective conscience of the community" ("Freedom of Religion," pp. 93-94).

9.   JCM, "The Ethical Problem," p. 230.

10.   JCM, "The Ethical Problem," p. 231.

11.   JCM, "The Ethical Problem," p. 231. Murray will go on to show that the effort to "purify the word 'intolerance' of its invidious connotations" (p. 231) is a waste of time. To maintain that "truth is intolerant" is an inexact metaphor; to say that "everybody is intolerant on certain subjects" merely answers one charge with another charge; and to claim that "we are not intolerant in the way that it is really intolerant to be intolerant" involves a subtlety that is lost on many (see p. 231).

is hardly more acceptable. . . . It seems to be a particularly horrid way of describing the Christian virtues of justice and charity, which are the sole norms that govern relations between persons as persons. Perhaps there is no need to say more about it. It just doesn't say what it is supposed to say; and that is rather a good test for a bad formula.[12]

Murray claimed that no double formula can capture the radical tension that ought to inform a Catholic position on religious liberty.[13] For, on the one hand, the Catholic is challenged to "love God and His Truth with a loyalty that forbids compromise of the truth, even at the promptings of what might seem to be a love of man; were it otherwise, our love both of God and man would be a *caritas ficta*."[14] But, on the other hand, the Catholic is called to "love man and his conscience with a loyalty that forbids injury to conscience, even at the promptings of what might seem to be a love of truth; were it otherwise, our love both of God and man would again be a *caritas ficta*."[15]

With the tension stated in these terms, the double formula "dogmatic intolerance" and "personal tolerance" is shown to be woefully inadequate:

At its worst, it suggests . . . that we begin with arrogant assertion and end with persecution, being withheld from the latter only by a lack of sufficient political power. Even in the minds of the more intelligent, the implications may very well be that we begin with an appeal to the authority of the Church, and end, if we can, by an appeal to the authority of the State to uphold the authority of the Church.[16]

JCM recognized that the tolerance/intolerance heuristic as regards religious liberty was, for all intents and purposes, a legacy of Pope Pius IX (pope, 1846-1878). Pius IX reigned during the solidification of the revolutionary era in Europe; given the anti-Catholic polemic rampant at the time, he anathematized the idea that the Roman pontiff ought to

---

12.   JCM, "The Ethical Problem," p. 232.

13.   He is, willing, to grant, however, that St. Francis de Sales probably came closest with his "la vérité charitable" and "la charité véritable." See "The Ethical Problem," p. 232.

14.   JCM, "The Ethical Problem," p. 232.

15.   JCM, "The Ethical Problem," p. 232.

16.   JCM, "The Ethical Problem," p. 233. This quotation helps one to understand more profoundly the difficulties that John F. Kennedy's Catholicism brought to the 1960 U.S. presidential campaign. In this regard, it is telling that the Reverend Billy Graham and the Reverend Dr. Norman Vincent Peale, two *moderate* American evangelists with a wide national following, met with 25 other leaders of American Protestantism to discuss how they might block the election of Kennedy. See Peter Steinfels' review of Carol V. George's biography of Peale – *God's Salesman* (New York: Oxford University Press, 1992) – in *New York Times* (October 31, 1992), p. A10.

accommodate himself to the spirit of the modern age.[17] Pius' profound suspicion of the so-called "modern liberties" would color much of official Catholic teaching up until the Second Vatican Council.[18]

It comes as no surprise that JCM cautions against taking Pius IX's teaching out of its historical context: it cannot be understood apart from a number of unfortunate historical events and the reactions of concrete personalities to those events. However, one is not quite prepared for the way Murray goes beyond this truism: he argues that a good part of the problem was that Pius was simply not a great philosopher. He writes: "If he had been, or if he had been surrounded by great philosophers, or, in a word, if the neo-Scholastic revival had taken place a century earlier, the whole polemic of the Church during the revolutionary era might well have had a different character, and perhaps a different outcome."[19] What was at stake were "a series of points in moral and political philosophy – what is liberty, what is conscience, what is the State, what are the 'freedoms' of conscience and of the State."[20] Religious liberty is not *per se* a theological question; in particular, it ought *not* to be seen as resting upon "the dogmatic assertion of a theology of . . . (the Church's) authority, but on a philosophical explanation of the human conscience and of the State."[21]

Even so, "the whole problem cannot be solved simply in terms of philosophy."[22] This is due to the fact that in

> the present order of the Incarnation, philosophy is not the supreme wisdom, nor is reason man's most decisive guiding light. Faith is the fuller light, and the principles of theology complete, without destroying, those of philosophy. Consequently, the problem of religious liberty must move on from its initial philosophical position and be given a theological formulation. However, when this happens, the philosophy of conscience and the State is gathered up and carried along to the new ground; and it is made· pivotal even in the theological solution to the problem. Finally,

---

17. Pius IX's *Syllabus of Errors* condemned the following proposition: *"Romanus Pontifex potest ac debet cum progressu, cum liberalismo et cum recenti civilitate sese reconciliare et componere"* [#LXXX; in *Lettres apostoliques de Pie IX, Grégoire XVI, Pie VII. Texte latin avec la traduction française en regard.* (Paris: R. Roger et F. Chernoviz, n.d.), pp. 19-35, at p. 35].

18. The formula "error has no rights," for instance, while not directly attributable to Pius IX, is certainly a reflection on his approach to the question of religious liberty. See, for example, #XV of the *Syllabus* which condemns the following assertion: *"Liberum cuique homini est eam amplecti ac profiteri religionem, quam rationis lumine quis ductus veram putaverit"* (See *Lettres apostoliques de Pie IX . . .* , p. 21).

19. JCM, "The Ethical Problem," p. 233.

20. JCM, "The Ethical Problem," p. 233.

21. JCM, "The Ethical Problem," p. 234.

22. JCM, "The Ethical Problem," p. 234.

since freedom of religion is a problem that intimately concerns the social life of man, as that life is lived in a particular set of conditions, the problem must receive its final formulation in terms of the varied and contingent realities of an individual social context. Here, too, a philosophy of conscience and of the State is still integral to its solution.[23]

2. THE RIGHTS OF CONSCIENCE

Murray's proposal begins by recognizing as absolutely foundational "the freedom of the human person to reach God, and eternal beatitude in God, along the way in which God wills to be reached."[24] At rock bottom, this is the ethical challenge that faces every human person and from which no one can claim an exemption. With a little reflection, it becomes clear that the only way to ensure the dignity of this sacred quest is to insist upon the freedom of the individual conscience – "the proximate subjective norm of human action."[25]

> . . . the nature and function of conscience are rather admirably summed up in the traditional metaphor: 'Conscience is the voice of God.' This statement immediately cuts between two extreme, and false, positions. First, it asserts that conscience is the *voice* of God; it not God Himself. Hence it is not the final arbiter of truth and falsity, right and wrong. Man is indeed judged in the light of his conscience; but it is God who judges conscience. Only God is law in its source; conscience is but law in its application. On the other hand, conscience is the voice of *God*; it is not merely a human voice. Hence its commands come to us vested with a divine authority, that may not be disregarded under penalty of sin. Conscience is a sacred and sovereign monitor; for in its utterances we hear God Himself speaking.[26]

From this reflection on the dignity of the human conscience ultimately flows JCM's proposal for compromise. As an American and cogni-

---

23. JCM, "The Ethical Problem," p. 234.

24. JCM, "The Ethical Problem," p. 236.

25. JCM, "The Ethical Problem," p. 254.

26. JCM, "The Ethical Problem," p. 255. On pp. 257-262, Murray deals with the problem of the "erroneous conscience." His discussion is openly indebted to St. Thomas' teaching (*Summa theologica*, 1a-2ae, Q. 19, a. 5, ad. 2): "When reason erroneously proposes anything as the precept of God, then to despise the dictate of reason is the same as despising the precept of God" (p. 259). However, it is important to note that JCM takes it as legitimate for the State to "forbid a man to marry more than one wife at a time, and to steal for the sake of almsgiving; and it can prosecute him as a criminal, if he disobeys. By so doing, the State violates no right of conscience, because there is no right there to violate; the erroneous conscience has no juridical status, when it issues in acts repugnant to the natural law or to the common good or to the legitimate rights of others" (p. 261).

zant of the mutual animosities between the Catholics and Protestants of his time, he explains:

> As far as I can see, the only solution . . . must be along the fol-
> lowing lines. Our subsistent theological disagreements will cease
> to generate suspicion and separatism on the level of social life,
> when both sides have the assurance that their opposing theologies
> of the Church are projected against the background of an ethic of
> conscience and a philosophy of political life that are based on
> reason, that are therefore mutually acceptable, and that are not de-
> stroyed by the disagreements in ecclesiology. This ethic of con-
> science and this political philosophy will stand guarantee that our
> respective theologies can under no circumstances have such impli-
> cations in the temporal order as would be injurious to the integ-
> rity of conscience, be it Catholic or Protestant.[27]

Rather than allowing herself to be thought an enemy of conscience, the Church ought to see her mission in the world as none other than "the protection, support, and perfecting of man to reach his eternal destiny."[28] This idea, in light of a document like *Gaudium et spes*, now seems ele- mental;[29] that the Church has a mandate to protect human dignity and to call for an end to abuses of human rights is hardly controversial. But be- fore the Second Vatican Council, Murray's ideas were hotly contested – before long he was to join an expanding list of Catholic theologians who had been "silenced" by the Roman authorities.[30]

3. *DIGNITATIS HUMANAE*

The curial officials and theologians who opposed JCM's work on re- ligious freedom were operating out of the theological perspective known

---

27. JCM, "The Ethical Problem," pp. 240-241.

28. JCM, "The Ethical Problem," p. 237.

29. Cf. *Gaudium et spes*, #21 [in Austin Flannery, O.P., ed., *Vatican Council II: The Con- ciliar and Post Conciliar Documents* (Collegeville, MN: Liturgical Press, 1980), pp. 920- 922]. In this section, the Church confronts the question of what its attitude toward atheism ought to be. It is nothing short of a revolution in official Catholic teaching for the Council to proclaim: "Although the Church altogether rejects atheism, she nevertheless sincerely proclaims that all men, those who believe as well as those who do not, should help to establish right order in this world where all live together. This certainly cannot be done without a dialogue that is sincere and prudent. The Church therefore deplores the discrimi- nation between believers and unbelievers which some civil authorities unjustly practice in defiance of the fundamental rights of the human person" (p. 922). For centuries, of course, the Church had acted as if "right order" demanded brutal campaigns to crush not only here- sies, but also heretics themselves.

30. Donald Pelotte offers an excellent overview of Murray's difficulties with the Holy Office. See his *John Courtney Murray: Theologian in Conflict* (New York: Paulist Press, 1976).

as "integrism."[31] The integrist position held that "the state is bound to promote Catholic belief, and wherever possible to establish Catholicism as the religion of the state."[32] The integrists argued that Murray's ideas on religious liberty – more than simply being poor theology – would have the deleterious effect of strengthening "the currents of secularism and indifference running through modern Western culture."[33] They held that "believing what is true is a human good that all are morally obligated to seek, . . . that this good is social in nature . . . . (and) that government has charge of enforcing this obligation."[34]

Murray accepted all but the last bit: he held that *good* government is limited government. Government ought to serve the many communities and forms of association that exist within society; its power pertains to "protecting the basic prerequisites of communal life within society, prerequisites that Murray described as 'necessary for the sheer coexistence of citizens within conditions of elemental social order.'"[35]

David Hollenbach offers the following explanation:

> There are four such prerequisites, which together define what is meant by public order: justice (which secures for people what is due them, that is, their fundamental human rights); public peace (which will only be genuine peace when it is built on justice); public morality (the minimum standards of public behavior on which consensus exists in society); and finally, public prosperity (which makes possible the material welfare of the people). Only when one or more of these fundamental prerequisites of social existence is violated should government intervene. Otherwise, freedom is to prevail.[36]

JCM's approach to religious liberty was vindicated at the Second Vatican Council when the Council Fathers accepted DH.[37] Pietro Pavan summarizes the main doctrinal points in this declaration in the following fashion:

1. Every man has a right to religious freedom because he is a person.

---

31. See Hollenbach, "The Growing End . . . ," p. 364.

32. Hollenbach, "The Growing End . . . ," p. 364.

33. Hollenbach, "The Growing End . . . ," p. 364.

34. Hollenbach, "The Growing End . . . ," p. 364.

35. Hollenbach, "The Growing End . . . ," p. 364.

36. Hollenbach, "The Growing End . . . ," p. 364.

37. It would take our study too far afield to document the course of events which would ultimately turn out to vindicate JCM. However, it is safe to say that John XXIII's inspiration to call a council of the Church and New York's Cardinal Francis Spellman's decision to name Murray as his *socius* to the Second Vatican Council figure prominently in this process.

2. The object or content of this right is freedom from coercion on the part of individuals or of social groups or any human power.

3. This freedom from coercion has a double meaning: 'in matters religious no one is to be forced to act in a manner contrary to his own beliefs'; within due limits no one is 'to be restrained from acting in accordance with his own beliefs, whether privately or publicly, whether alone or in association with others.'

4. This right has its foundation in the dignity of the human person, such as it is known in the light of revelation and by reason.

5. It is a right of the person which is to be recognized as a civil right in the constitutional law of the political society.[38]

DH announced the death knell for official Catholic support for the idea that "error has no rights." Rights are not to be understood as having their direct foundation upon spiritual values such as truth and goodness. "(R)elations involving rights are always inter-personal relations, not relations between persons and spiritual values."[39] And, "the basic rights of the person with regard to spiritual values are freedom from external coercion or the secure practice of worship and freedom to accept such values."[40]

With the acceptance of DH, the Council Fathers ratified JCM's thesis that "tolerance" is not the proper framework from which to approach religious liberty. It is not a question of tolerating non-Catholic worship; it is a question of respecting the religious conscience (and consciousness) of non-Catholics. The opening phrase of DH is programmatic for the entire document (hence its Latin title): "Contemporary man is becoming increasingly conscious of the dignity of the human person. . . ."[41]

Part and parcel of this recognition is the conviction that civil society (and *a fortiori*, the Church) has no business interfering with the individual's choice to worship God in the manner that she deems fitting. And this is *not* because the good order of society would be jeopardized or because it would entail an unjustifiable level of governmental intrusion. She is to be "left alone" on the religious question because a fundamental human right is at stake. DH states the matter succinctly:

> The Vatican Council declares that the human person has a right to religious freedom. Freedom of this kind means that all men

---

38. Pietro Pavan, "Declaration on Religious Freedom," in Herbert Vorgrimler, ed., *Commentary on the Documents of Vatican II*, volume IV (New York: Herder and Herder, 1967-1969), pp. 64-65.

39. Pavan, "Declaration . . . ," p. 82.

40. Pavan, "Declaration . . . ," pp. 82-83.

41. DH (in Flannery, *Vatican Council II . . .* , pp. 799-812), #1, p. 799.

should be immune from coercion on the part of individuals, social groups and every human power, so that, within due limits, nobody is forced to act against his convictions nor is anyone to be restrained from acting in accordance with his convictions in religious matters in private or in public, alone or in association with others. The Council further declares that the right to religious freedom is based on the very dignity of the human person as known through the revealed word of God and by reason itself. This right of the human person to religious freedom must be given such recognition in the constitutional order of society as will make it a civil right.[42]

Religious liberty is accepted by modern Catholicism as a fundamental human right. It is so basic as to demand explicit incorporation into the "constitutional order of society:" it should be recognized as a civil right. DH announces that the individual's freedom in the religious realm is predicated only upon his dignity as one created in the image and likeness of God.

Since the appearance of Pope John XXIII's encyclical *Pacem in terris* (PT) in 1961, the social doctrine of the Church had been more and more grounded upon a reflection upon human dignity.[43] In particular, the Church's teaching on human rights had been intimately linked to the inviolable dignity that inheres in each person. John XXIII expressed it this way:

Any human society, if it is to be well-ordered and productive, must lay down as a foundation this principle, namely, that every human being is a person; that is, his nature is endowed with intelligence and free will. Indeed, precisely because he is a person he has rights and obligations flowing directly and simultaneously from his very nature. And these rights and obligations are universal and inviolable, so that they cannot in any way be surrendered.[44]

John XXIII held that human reason itself could grasp the exigencies of human dignity; in this regard, faith and divinely revealed truth help one to esteem human dignity all the more, for all "are redeemed by the blood of Jesus Christ, they are by grace the children and friends of God and heirs of eternal glory."[45] John claimed for every person the rights to "life,

---

42. DH, #2, p. 800.

43. See Robert Traer, *Faith in Human Rights: Support in Religious Traditions for a Global Struggle* (Washington, D.C.: Georgetown University Press, 1991), p. 36.

44. John XXIII, PT, #9 [in David J. O'Brien and Thomas A. Shannon, *Renewing the Earth: Catholic Documents on Peace, Justice, and Liberation* (Garden City, NY: Doubleday, 1977), p. 126]. See Traer, *Faith in Human Rights*, p. 37.

45. John XXIII, PT, #10, p. 126.

to bodily integrity, and to the means which are suitable for the proper development of life; these are primarily food, clothing, shelter, rest, medical care, and finally the necessary social services."[46] Moreover, he taught that the natural law demands that every human being has the right "to respect for his person, to his good reputation; the right to freedom in searching for the truth and in expressing and communicating his opinions. . . ."[47]

Traditionally, Catholic reflection on rights entailed a concomitant plea to recognize the duties that are inseparable from rights. PT, for instance, argued that "the right of every man to life is correlative with the duty to preserve it; his right to a decent standard of living with the duty of living it becomingly; and his right to investigate the truth freely, with the duty of seeking it every more completely and profoundly."[48] Ultimately, the recognition of one person's right carries with it "a duty in all other persons: the duty, namely, of acknowledging and respecting the right in question. For every fundamental human right draws its indestructible moral force from the natural law, which in granting it imposes a corresponding obligation."[49]

DH represented a profound development in the Church's understanding of its relationship with civil society; it entailed a paradigm shift as regards the tolerance-intolerance debate. Pavån writes that "as regards religious freedom as a right of the person not to be prevented from practising one's religion whatever it may be, the Church began to recognize this only in modern times. . . ."[50] In all of this, the framework of PT was validated[51] and given even greater clarity.[52]

4. CONCLUSION

Murray wrote the commentary and notes on DH for Walter Abbott's edition of the documents of the Second Vatican Council. In this work, he is forceful in maintaining that DH contains more than practical, prudential

---

46. John XXIII, PT, #11, p. 126.

47. John XXIII, PT, #12, p. 127.

48. John XXIII, PT, #29, p. 130.

49. John XXIII, PT, #30, pp. 130-131.

50. Pavan, "Declaration . . . ," pp. 83-84.

51. JCM notes that DH is in "direct continuity with two basic doctrinal themes of John XXIII in the encyclical *Pacem in terris*: the dignity of the human person and the consequent necessity of constitutional limits to the powers of government" [See his "Religious Freedom" (a commentary on DH, henceforth RF), in Walter M. Abbott, ed., *The Documents of Vatican II* (New York: The Guild Press, 1966), p. 676, n. 2].

52. PT, #14, for instance, does not answer the following questions: "What precisely does religious freedom mean? Does it find place among the inalienable rights of man?" (JCM, RF, p. 677, n. 4).

advice for the Church. DH's content is "properly doctrinal." In particular, three doctrinal tenets are declared:

> the ethical doctrine of religious freedom as a human right (personal and collective); a political doctrine with regards to the functions and limits of government in matters religious, and the theological doctrine of the freedom of the Church as the fundamental principle in what concerns the relations between the Church and the socio-political order.[53]

While Murray acknowledged that no one would be tempted to call DH "a milestone in human history – moral, political, or intellectual"[54] – since the principle of religious liberty had long been established as a human right in the West, it was nonetheless "a significant event in the history of the Church."[55]

Murray held that the significance of DH lies in the fact that it validated the theological principle of development of doctrine[56] and that it

> opens a new era in the relations between the People of God and the People Temporal. A long-standing ambiguity has finally been cleared up. The Church does not deal with the secular order in terms of a double standard – freedom for the Church when Catholics are a minority, privilege for the Church and intolerance for others when Catholics are a majority. The Declaration has opened the way toward new confidence in ecumenical relationships, and a new straight-forwardness in relationships between the Church and the world.[57]

The ambiguity that was "cleared up" concerned the status of the integrist position. As noted above, this position rested upon "the abstract juridical maxim that error has no rights and on the correlative abstract political maxim that government is to repress error whenever possible and tolerate it only when necessary, as a concession to circumstances of relig-

---

53. JCM, RF, pp. 672-673. One notes that this tripartite doctrine was present in Murray's first two articles on religious freedom (1945).

54. JCM, RF, p. 673.

55. JCM, RF, p. 673. Murray writes in this regard: " The principle of religious freedom has long been recognized in constitutional law, to the point where even Marxist-Leninist political ideology is obliged to pay lip service to it. In all honesty it must be admitted that the Church is late in acknowledging the validity of the principle" (in *ibid.*).

56. "The notion of development, not the notion of religious freedom, was the real sticking-point for many of those who opposed the Declaration even to the end. The course of the development between the *Syllabus of Errors* (1864) and *Dignitatis humanae personae* (1965) still remains to be explained by theologians. But the Council formally sanctioned the validity of the development itself; and this was a doctrinal event of high importance for theological thought in many areas." [JCM, RF, p. 673.]

57. JCM, RF, p. 673.

ious pluralism."[58] JCM would write that the integrist theory was presented at the Council by a few of the conciliar Fathers. But

> (i)t impressed the assembly chiefly by its archaism. It obviously stands in dependence on a sociological situation, not so much of religious unity as of religious illiteracy. It also rests on the concept of government as paternal in character, charged with a duty toward the religious welfare of the 'illiterate masses,' to use the phrase of Leo XIII. It was not considered necessary at the Council to refute the theory; it was sufficient quietly to bid it good-by. Certain adversaries − as Santayana pointed out − are better treated thus. In any case, the theory was seen to be irreconcilable with the exigencies of the personal and civil consciousness at its contemporary height.[59]

DH is radically indebted to the diligent study and heroic patience of JCM; the document which Pope Paul VI termed "one of the major texts of the Council"[60] bears Murray's imprint at every turn. James Bacik notes that Murray was able to facilitate the development of Church doctrine as enunciated by DH

> by combining a brilliant historical analysis of the intent of official church teaching . . . with an insightful examination of democratic structures in the United States. Through this scholarly effort he was instrumental not only in freeing Catholics from the suspicion of being unpatriotic, but also in bringing the American political experiment with religious liberty into the official consciousness of the whole Catholic Church.[61]

---

58. JCM, "This Matter of Religious Freedom," in *America*, 112 (January 9, 1965), p. 42.

59. JCM, "This Matter of Religious Freedom," p. 42. The reference to the teaching of Pope Leo XIII is far from glib. JCM's articles on Leo's social doctrine qualify him as a Leonine scholar. See: "Leo XIII on Church and State: The General Structure of the Controversy," in TS, 14 (1953), pp. 1-30; "Leo XIII: Separation of Church and State," in TS, 14 (1953), pp. 145-214; "Leo XIII: Two Concepts of Government," in TS, 14 (1953), pp. 551-567; and "Leo XIII: Government and the Order of Culture," in TS, 15 (1954), pp. 1-33.

60. Quoted in JCM, RF, p. 674.

61. Bacik, "John Courtney Murray . . . ," p. 140.

CHAPTER EIGHT

A Catholic Case for Supporting Gay and Lesbian Rights Ordinances

1. INTRODUCTION: ON EXTENDING THE *MODUS VIVENDI*

In most U.S. states, sodomy (defined usually as both oral/genital and anal/genital contact) between consenting adults is no longer a criminal offense. In the states that continue to maintain anti-sodomy statutes,[1] it is only rarely that people are arrested and prosecuted on sodomy charges. It is germane to our study to note that the American Catholic hierarchy has been silent on this development in American jurisprudence. One looks in vain for a contemporary American bishop who teaches that private instances of genital contact between consenting adult homosexuals ought to be criminal offenses. For all intents and purposes, the Catholic hierarchy in the U.S. has acquiesced in the decriminalization of homosexuality; its silence on the issue cannot but be taken as tacit support for this development.

This is far from shocking. As our study of JCM's work revealed, the Catholic tradition – at least as represented by St. Thomas – has consistently held that the Church is under no obligation to ensure that there be a direct correspondence between what is considered immoral and what is to be considered illegal. The bishops' silence on efforts to overturn anti-sodomy legislation can be interpreted, therefore, as meaning that private, adult, consensual sexual relations between people of the same gender are not of such significance to the common good that society is strictly obligated to punish those who would become so engaged. Indeed, American Catholicism, as represented by the hierarchy, has accepted a basic *modus vivendi* with the GLM. It amounts to the following statement: "While we do not approve of your sexual practices, we see no reason why you should be imprisoned and (or) fined because of them."

---

1. It is something of an embarrassment that most outlaw *all* instances of "sodomy": heterosexual as well as homosexual; and in the case of the former, distinctions tend not to be made between the married and the unmarried.

178

This chapter brings us to our *fin ultime*, viz., the construction of a Catholic case for extending the bishops' *modus vivendi* with the GLM to include explicit Catholic support for gay and lesbian rights legislation and (or) municipal ordinances. JCM's work on the relationship between Church and State and on religious freedom will have an important part to play in this undertaking.

2. INDEBTEDNESS TO JCM'S WORK ON CHURCH-STATE RELATIONS

From all that has been said about the limited nature of human law in the Thomistic synthesis and from what we have seen of Murray's application of this tradition to the question of the legal availability of contraceptives, it seems clear that JCM would have had little trouble with decriminalizing the private sexual acts of gay men and lesbians. While nothing in Murray's theological legacy raises questions about his acceptance of the magisterium's evaluation of the objective immorality of these acts, his belief that civil law exists to protect the minimum requirements for successful social living would have kept him from advocating retribution for the private sex acts of the homosexual minority. JCM held that good government is limited government; no government is competent to tell people how to structure the intimate details of their private sexual lives. The proper aims of government are much less invasive. On the other hand, while the Church is entrusted with a divinely sanctioned moral code, she has no mandate which includes competence for producing civil legislation or public policy.

In his lecture, "Spirituality, Morality, and Our Political Life,"[2] Charles Bouchard, O.P. noted that for JCM "morality is an internal reality . . . (which) aims at personal perfection; public policy, or law, on the other hand, has the more modest goal of public order. Good laws are those which protect and enhance public order and which provide the context in which we can pursue morality."[3] Bouchard reminded his audience that morality and public policy are related, but not identical. "In a sense it is correct to say that you 'can't legislate morality.' Good laws create the context in which people can live together and pursue the moral life, but they cannot enforce morality."[4]

Given the lack of consensus in contemporary American society on the moral valence of homosexual relations between consenting adults, the more or less benign interpretations given to a range of such relations by prominent Christian thinkers, and the all but insurmountable difficulties

---

2.   Unpublished manuscript; quoted in part in *Aquinas News*, 11 (1992), p. 1. [This is a publication of the Aquinas Institute of Theology (St. Louis, MO).]

3.   Bouchard, "Spirituality, Morality . . . ," p. 1.

4.   Bouchard, "Spirituality, Morality . . . ," p. 1.

law enforcement agents face in enforcing anti-sodomy laws, it is unlikely that JCM would have held that "practising homosexuals" ought to face criminal charges. Logical consistency with his considered judgment on the Massachusetts birth control law would have precluded his taking such a tack.[5]

3. JUSTICE AS A UNIVOCAL TERM

In moving the discussion to whether or not gay people ought to be legally protected from discrimination – the heart of the question posed by this work – the following question demands to be posed: Is there a "justice" for heterosexually oriented people that stands over and above the "justice" for homosexually oriented people? Or, is "justice" a univocal term?

It goes without saying that gay people are sometimes harassed, cheated, defamed, and murdered. Sometimes their homosexual orientation is incidental to all of this; at other times knowledge of their sexual identity has a role to play in the fact of victimization. Gays and lesbians suffer injustices every day – injustices that are sometimes accidental, sometimes intentional.

From within the Christian moral tradition, a person's accidental characteristics (whether innate or acquired) do not alter the necessity of treating him fairly: justice is a univocal term. Moreover, there is no Christian warrant for the belief that a person's homosexual orientation

---

5.   Although JCM never wrote on the question of decriminalizing homosexuality, the English Dominican, Thomas Gilby, himself an expert on the Thomistic synthesis, held that there was nothing in the tradition which would demand that homosexuals ought to face civil punishment for their sexual relating. In his commentary on Thomistic political theory [i.e., *Law and Political Theory* (volume 28 of the "McGraw-Hill" *Summa theologiae*, covering 1a 2ae, QQ. 90-97) (New York: McGraw-Hill, 1966)], Gilby remarks: "Whether complete homosexual practices . . . should be penalized by human legislation is for the judgment of statemanship or political prudence" (p. 97, n. "c"). Legislation on this issue cannot be deduced from "first principles;" the objective immorality of homosexual acts is not determinative of any specific public policy.

It is noteworthy that Gilby offered this opinion at a time when British society was faced with the question of decriminalizing homosexuality. Eventually, after several years of debate, the British parliament decriminalized most homosexual acts between men (sex acts between women had never been criminal offenses in Great Britain). Just as Cardinal Cushing's role in overturning the Massachusetts law against contraceptives ought not to be underestimated, so, too, one recognizes the role of Cardinal Griffin in the demise of anti-homosexual legislation in Britain. In 1956, Griffin offered the Church's support to the voices calling for the decriminalization of adult, consensual homosexual relations. [See C. R. A. Cunliffe, "Troubled Ministry" (A review article of *Building Bridges: Gay and Lesbian Reality and the Catholic Church* by Robert Nugent and Jeannine Gramick), in *The Tablet* (August 8, 1992), pp. 986-987.] In testimony before Parliament's Wolfenden Committee, Griffin made it clear that Catholic teaching did not necessarily call for the crimination of homosexual acts – even though such acts are considered to be objectively immoral.

effectively trumps his right to be treated fairly; even if someone wilfully consented to acquiring a homosexual orientation with a view to living a life of homosexual promiscuity, the obligation that justice be done in his regard would not be countermanded.

The gay and lesbian rights ordinances that have been accepted in a number of American municipalities have a very specific aim – to punish discrimination against gay people as regards their employment, their housing, and their social participation. In view of judging the compatibility of such ordinances with Catholic moral teaching, it bears highlighting that the *Catéchisme de l'Église catholique*[6] – the "Catechism of Vatican II" – notes that

> A non-negligible number of men and women experience a deep-rooted homosexual tendency. They do not choose their homosexual condition; for most, it amounts to a burden. Such people ought to be welcomed with respect, compassion, and understanding. One ought to avoid even the semblance of unjust discrimination in their regard. They are called to fulfill the will of God in their lives, and if they are Christians, they are called to unite the sufferings associated with their condition to the sacrifice of the Cross of the Lord.[7]

It is hard to imagine a direct violation of a gay and lesbian rights ordinance as anything but 'unjust discrimination;' it ought to go without saying that if one were barred from (say) union membership because of one's homosexuality that the basic canons of 'respect, compassion, and understanding' would have been violated.

The passage quoted from the *Catéchisme* is proof-positive that calling for justice for gay people need not be grounded upon dissent from magisterial teaching condemning sexual relating between the unmarried.[8] Justice precedes sexual ethics: regardless of the private sexual acts to which adults give their consent, they are, as human beings, to be treated fairly – with the respect that is their due as children of the one God and Father of all. Thus, Benedict Ashley, O.P., the only contributor to Gramick and Furey's *The Vatican and Homosexuality* who could say that

---

6. (Paris: Mame/Plon, 1992).

7. *Catéchisme de l'Église catholique*, #2358, p. 480. [*Un nombre non négligeable d'hommes et de femmes présentent des tendances homosexuelles foncières. Ils ne choisissent pas leur condition homosexuelle; elle constitue pour la plupart d'entre eux une épreuve. Ils doivent être accueillis avec respect, compassion et délicatesse. On évitera à leur égard toute marque de discrimination injuste. Ces personnes sont appelées à réaliser la volonté de Dieu dans leur vie, et si elles sont chrétiennes, à unir au sacrifice de la Croix du Seigneur les difficultés qu'elles peuvent rencontrer du fait de leur condition.*]

8. The *Catéchisme* reiterates the magisterial teaching which condemns homosexual activity at #2357, p. 480.

he "entirely agrees with the substance of PCHP,"[9] was also able to voice support for the civil rights of gay people.[10]

Ashley concluded his article with a list of tasks that ought to be fulfilled by the Church's ministries. The first two are stated in the following terms: "(1) We should be advocates for the protection of the civil rights of homosexuals. (2) We should preach on this subject to inform Christians of the problems of the homosexual and to create respect for their human dignity and compassion for their problems."[11] Ashley argues that the Church is charged with speaking the whole truth vis-à-vis the complex reality of homosexuality. The Church cannot be satisfied, then, with simply reiterating moral condemnations against gay sex: part of her task is to promote and defend the human and civil rights of gay people. In so far as this seems controversial or even paradoxical to the average Christian, the Church has failed in her preaching of gospel justice.

We began this section with the question as to whether or not justice is to be taken as a univocal term in the Christian tradition. At this point, after having shown that justice does not mean one thing for gays and another thing for straights, a second question asks to be posed: Ought civil society penalize injustices that are perpetrated upon gay people because of their homosexuality? In other words, ought the awareness that unjust discrimination against gays and lesbians exists in American society be reflected in civil statutes?

It is difficult to envision a negative response to this question. If one grants that gay people can be the victims of injustice, how can one argue that they ought not to have recourse to the legal system? How could one maintain that their victimization must go without redress? One would be hard-pressed to call a society "just" which would knowingly cast a blind eye to the injustices suffered by a segment of its population.

Because of this, one is not unjustified in questioning the sincerity of calls for justice for gays and lesbians which would not allow recourse to the nation's courts. Such calls amount to empty exhortation: by excluding the means of ensuring compliance, they lack even a modicum of real conviction. The American Civil Rights Movement provides an important case in point. One wonders how successful this movement would have been (granting, of course, that much work remains to be done) if its leaders refused to work for legal change on the federal, state, and local levels. Without the Civil Rights Act, it is difficult to imagine the defeat of segregationist policies throughout the United States.

---

9.   Ashley, "Compassion and Sexual Orientation," p. 109.

10.   See *supra*, p. 118, n. 78.

11.   Ashley, "Compassion and Sexual Orientation," p. 109.

As we have had occasion to see a number of times, the biggest obstacle that keeps people of good will from accepting gay rights ordinances is the fear that such a change in the legal statutes will have an overall negative effect on marriage and family life. From within contemporary Catholicism, the stance of Cardinal O'Connor and SCC's reading of the situation are a strong case in point. O'Connor fears that family life will suffer if gay people are granted legal protection from discrimination;[12] SCC argues that in certain instances direct discrimination against gay people is not only licit but morally required.[13]

What bears repeating in all of this is that there is no scientific discourse which verifies that punishing instances of discrimination against gay people affects the well-being of heterosexual couples and (or) their children. The fears of a number of American churchmen in this regard do not rest upon rational grounds. What is more, there are studies which have had some success in demonstrating that the decriminalization of homosexuality and the adoption of gay and lesbian rights ordinances *do not* have an appreciable effect on the general population's willingness to enter into marriage, to raise families, and to do both of these without interference; nor do they entail more public solicitation, an increase in sexually transmitted diseases, or other "negative consequences so often detailed in parliamentary debates and arguments of opponents"[14] of the GLM. In light of this research, allowing oneself to be guided by the fear that gay rights legislation will sound the death knell for marriage and the family is at least as problematic as opposing the legal availability of contraceptives for the same reason.[15]

---

12. See *supra*, pp. 64-69.

13. See *supra*, pp. 123-130.

14. Ken Sinclair and Michael Ross, "Consequences of Decriminalization of Homosexuality: A Study of Two Australian States," in *The Journal of Homosexuality*, 12 (1985), p. 127. See also Gilbert Geis, Richard Wright, Thomas Garrett, Paul Wilson, "Reported Consequences of Decriminalization of Consensual Adult Homosexuality in Seven American States," in *The Journal of Homosexuality*, 1 (1976), pp. 419-426; and *The Journal of Homosexuality*, 13 (1986/7) which was devoted to "Interdisciplinary Research on Homosexuality in the Netherlands." David Greenberg (*The Construction of Homosexuality*) and Richard Davenport-Hines (*Sex, Death, and Punishment*) discuss the problem of attributing cataclysmic effects to the decriminalization of homosexuality and the protection of gay people at numerous points in their work.

15. This was once an argument against the legalization of contraceptives. It was feared that if people could obtain contraceptives and thus partake of sexual intercourse without the possibility of producing a child, they would forgo entering into marriage and forming families.

4. INDEBTEDNESS TO JCM'S WORK ON RELIGIOUS LIBERTY

The acceptance of DH by the Fathers of the Second Vatican Council has an indirect application to the question of civil legislation protecting homosexual persons from discrimination. If, for instance, one accepts that people have the right to follow their conscience on such an important matter as their religious affiliation and practice, *a fortiori*, it would follow that one should be free from societal and (or) governmental interference in terms of a conscientious decision to enter into an intimate relationship with a member of the same sex.

Given the fact that Catholicism has been careful in recent years to distinguish between a "homosexual orientation" and "homosexual acts," the former being blameless (though still "disordered") and the latter – defined as genital contact with another – blameworthy, and given the fact that what is condemned in the "homosexual lifestyle" is precisely the sexual acts that take place therein,[16] it follows that discrimination against lesbians and gay men on the basis that they are likely to have sex with members of their own sex is arbitrary and indefensible: a fair percentage of heterosexuals are at least as likely to indulge in illicit sexual congress.

In other words, if the Church authoritatively teaches that the adherents of all religions ought not to face discrimination because of their beliefs or practices, by what logic are gays and lesbians subject to discrimination? DH accepts the propositions that, all things being equal, one ought not to lose one's job for denying the divinity of Christ and that one ought not to lose one's lease for failing to keep the Sabbath holy. Does it not follow that people ought not to face social penalties for denying – theoretically and (or) in practice – that the sharing of sexual intimacy is only licit between a wife and her husband?

JCM was able to show that advocating religious liberty does not have to be founded upon religious indifferentism: one does not have to accept the idea that 'one religion is as good as another' in order to argue for religious freedom.[17] Likewise, to argue that gay people ought not to suffer discrimination for their homosexual orientation and (or) their decision to enter into a sexual partnership does not have to be predicated upon the acceptance of the idea that homosexuality is equal in dignity with heterosexuality; it doesn't even have to mean that one sees *any* dignity in

---

16. André Guindon puts it this way: "In ethical discussions, gay behavior is controversial as a sexual reality and in no other capacity. Lesbians and gays are not taken to task for their food preferences, their driving habits, their political views, or their working patterns" (*The Sexual Creators*, p. 160).

17. Hunt and Grasso put it this way: Murray's theological reflection "culminated in his developing a theory of religious freedom rooted not in religious indifferentism but in the exigencies of the objective moral order and Christian revelation" (see their "Introduction" to *ACC*, p. viii).

homosexuality *per se*. All that needs to be admitted is that government has no business demanding that people structure the intimate details of their private lives in this way or that. As long as we are dealing with the conscientious decisions of consenting adults in private, government has no rationale for involvement and the Church has no mandate to demand that people be coerced to accept its reading of the moral valence of such behaviors.

At the same time, protecting the individual's right to structure the intimate details of her private life *does* fall to the government. Open, democratic societies have taken measures to ensure that their citizens not be discriminated against on the basis of race or creed or ethnic background; one looks in vain for compelling reasons why sexual orientation should not to be added to this list of personal characteristics for which one ought not face penalization.

From the vantage point of the Church's insistence on human dignity, human rights, and the dignity of the human conscience, Gregory Baum writes: "Even if Catholics are convinced that homosexual love is unethical, justice demands that they defend the human rights of gay people."[18] Baum's reflection makes for a fitting conclusion to our study:

> Over the last decades, the Catholic Church has become the defender of humanity in an increasingly harsh and oppressive world. The Church has committed itself to human rights. The Church has made itself the defender of minorities suffering discrimination. This surely includes defending the dignity of homosexual men and women, a minority that suffers discrimination in our societies and is exposed to brutal repression in fascist and communist countries.[19]

5. CONCLUSION

Support for gay and lesbian rights legislation and (or) municipal ordinances is well within the parameters of Catholic moral teaching. Indeed, the theological synthesis of St. Thomas as interpreted by a thinker like John Courtney Murray, S.J. (and advanced through Murray's work on religious freedom), arguably *demands* such support. In the main, the virtue of justice, upon which civil society rests, cannot countenance treating people unfairly; it stretches the meaning of the terms to breaking point if one attempts to characterize (say) firing someone because of her sexual orientation as "fair" or "just." Concomitantly, it is inconsistent for members of the American Catholic hierarchy to call for justice for gay people and then attempt to block the legislation which would serve to ensure this justice.

---

18. Gregory Baum, "Human Rights for Homosexuals," in *Catholic New Times* (January 11, 1987), p. 10.

19. Baum, "Human Rights for Homosexuals," p. 10.

Opposing the morality of certain sexual practices ought not to entail collusion with campaigns to place social and economic obstacles in the path of an already undervalued social minority.

Abbreviations

ACC – *John Courtney Murray and the American Civil Conversation* by Robert P. Hunt and Kenneth L. Grasso (eds.)

C.D.F. – Sacred Congregation for the Doctrine of the Faith

CRH – Council on Religion and the Homosexual

DH – *Dignitatis humanae* (The Second Vatican Council's "Declaration on Religious Liberty")

DOB – Daughters of Bilitis

DV – *Dei verbum* (The Second Vatican Council's "Dogmatic Constitution on Divine Revelation")

EHLR – Editors of the *Harvard Law Review*

GLM – Gay Liberation Movement

HDCG – "Human Dignity and the Common Good" (a statement by NWM)

HM – *Homosexuality and the Magisterium: Documents from the Vatican and the U.S. Bishops, 1975-1985* by John Gallagher (ed.)

JCM – John Courtney Murray, S.J.

M9 – Oregon Ballot Measure 9 (1992)

MS – Mattachine Society

NAMBLA – North American Man/Boy Love Association

NCE – *New Catholic Encyclopedia*

NCR – *National Catholic Reporter*

NWM – New Ways Ministry

NYT – *New York Times*

OCA – Oregon Citizens' Alliance

PCHP – "Letter to the Bishops of the Catholic Church on the Pastoral Care of Homosexual Persons" (C.D.F.)

PH – *Persona humana* (C.D.F.)

PT – *Pacem in terris* (encyclical letter of Pope John XXIII)

RF – "Religious Freedom" (JCM's commentary on DH in Abbott's edition of the documents of Vatican II)

SCC – "Some Considerations Concerning the Response to Legislative Proposals on the Non-Discrimination of Homosexual Persons" (C.D.F.)

SOC – Save Our Children

TJH – *The Journal of Homosexuality*

TS – *Theological Studies*

TVH – *The Vatican and Homosexuality: Reactions to the "Letter to the Bishops of the Catholic Church on the Pastoral Care of Homosexual Persons"* by Jeannine Gramick and Pat Furey (eds.)

WHTT – *We Hold These Truths: Catholic Reflections on the American Proposition* (by JCM)

Bibliography

Abelove, Henry; Barale, Michele Aina; and Halperin, David M., eds. *The Lesbian and Gay Studies Reader*. New York: Routledge, 1993.

Adelman, Marcy R. "Sexual Orientation and Violations of Civil Liberties." TJH, 2 (1977), p. 327-330.

Altman, Dennis. *Homosexual Oppression and Liberation*. New York: E.P. Dutton, 1971.

"Angry Reaction to Vatican Observations on Homosexuals." *The Tablet*, 246 (August 1, 1992), p. 967.

Archdiocese of New York. "The Rights of Homosexuals Versus Parental Rights." *Origins*, 7 (January 26, 1978), pp. 498-500.

Ariès, Philippe and Béjin, André, eds. *Western Sexuality: Practice and Precept in Past and Present Times* [Trans. by Anthony Forster]. Oxford: Basil Blackwell, 1986.

Ashley, Benedict. "Compassion and Sexual Orientation," in TVH, pp. 105-111.

Aubert, Jean-Marie. *Droits de l'homme et libération évangélique*. Paris: Le Centurion, 1987.

_____ . "L'appel éthique de l'homme." In *Abrégé de la moral catholique: la foi vécue*. Paris: Desclée; Ottawa: Novalis, 1987; pp. 13-31.

Bacik, James J. "John Courtney Murray: Living as a Christian in a Pluralistic Society." In *Contemporary Theologians*. Chicago: Thomas More Press, 1981; pp. 139-150.

Bailey, Derrick S. *Homosexuality and the Western Christian Tradition*. London: Longmans, Green, 1955.

Baker, Russell. "The '92 Follies: A Show with Legs." *New York Times Magazine* (November 1, 1992), pp. 27-29, 58-59.

Barinaga, Marcia. "Is Homosexuality Biological?" *Science*, 253 (1991), pp. 956-957.

Battaglia, Anthony. *Toward a Reformulation of Natural Law*. New York: Seabury, 1981.

Baum, Gregory. "Catholic Homosexuals." *Commonweal*, 94 (1974), pp. 480-482.

_____ . "Human Rights for Homosexuals." *Catholic New Times* (January 11, 1987), p. 10.

188

Bayer, Ronald. *Homosexuality and American Psychiatry: The Politics of Diagnosis.* New York: Basic Books, 1981.

Beggs, Charles E. "Proposed Anti-Gay Law Creates Tumult in Oregon." *Detroit Free Press* (July 21, 1992), p. A4.

Bell, A. P. and Weinberg, M. S. *Homosexualities: A Study of Human Diversity Among Men and Women.* New York: Simon and Schuster, 1978.

_____ and Hammersmith, S. K. *Sexual Preference. Its Development in Men and Women.* Bloomington, IN: Indiana University Press, 1981.

Bernardin, Joseph (Cardinal). "Letter to the Illinois Gay and Lesbian Task Force." In HM, pp. 103-104.

_____ . "I, Too, Struggle." *Commonweal*, 111 (December 26, 1986), pp. 683-684.

"Bishop, Newspaper Clash Over Partnership Law." *Bondings*, 13 (1990), p. 3.

"Bishops Urge Ban on OCA Petition in their Domain." *Bondings*, 14 (1991), p. 5.

Black, Antony. *Political Thought in Europe, 1250-1450.* Cambridge: Cambridge University Press, 1992.

Blumenfeld, Warren J. and Raymond, Diane. *Looking at Gay and Lesbian Life.* (Updated and expanded edition) Boston: Beacon Press, 1993.

Boggan, E. Carrington; Haft, Marilyn G.; Lister, Charles; Rupp, John P.; and Stoddard, Thomas B. *The Rights of Gay People (An American Civil Liberties Union Handbook).* New York: Bantam Books, 1983.

Boswell, John. *Christianity, Social Tolerance and Homosexuality. Gay People in Western Europe from the Beginning of the Christian Era to the Fourteenth Century.* Chicago: University of Chicago Press, 1980.

Bouchard, Charles. "Spirituality, Morality, and Our Political Life." *Aquinas News*, 11 (1992), p. 1.

Briggs, Kenneth A. *Holy Siege: The Year that Shook Catholic America.* San Francisco: Harper, 1992.

Brill, Alida. *Nobody's Business: The Paradoxes of Privacy.* Reading, MA: Addison-Wesley, 1990.

Brown, Judith C. *Immodest Acts: The Life of a Lesbian Nun in Renaissance Italy.* New York: Oxford University Press, 1986.

Brzana, Stanislaus (Bishop). "Homosexuality and Human Dignity." *Origins*, 13 (February 2, 1984), pp. 75-76.

Bullough, Vern L. *Sexual Variance in Society and History.* New York: J. Wiley, 1976.

Burg, Barry R. *Sodomy and the Pirate Tradition: English Sea Rovers in the Seventeenth Century Caribbean.* New York: New York University Press, 1984.

Burgess, Faith E. R. *The Relationship Between Church and State According to John Courtney Murray, S.J.* Dusseldorf: R. Stehle, 1971.

Burghardt, Walter J. "Who Chilled the Beaujolais?" *America*, 153 (1985), pp. 360-363.

Burleigh, Michael and Wippermann, Wolfgang. *The Racial State: Germany, 1933-1945.* Cambridge: Cambridge University Press, 1991.

Burr, Chandler. "Homosexuality and Biology." *The Atlantic*, 271 (March 1993), pp. 47-65.

Buxton, Amity Pierce. *The Other Side of the Closet: The Coming-Out Crisis for Straight Spouses*. Santa Monica, CA: IBS Press, 1992.

Cahill, Lisa Sowle. "Moral Methodology: A Case Study." *Chicago Studies*, 19 (1980), pp. 171-187.

_____ . "Homosexuality," in Batchelor, E., ed. *Homosexuality and Ethics*. New York: Pilgrim Press, 1980; pp. 222-231.

_____ . *Between the Sexes: Foundations for a Christian Ethics of Sexuality*. New York: Paulist Press, 1985.

_____ . "Catholic Sexual Ethics and the Dignity of the Person: A Double Message." *TS*, 50 (1989), pp. 120-150.

_____ . "Human Sexuality," in Curran, Charles E., ed. *Moral Theology: Challenges for the Future. Essays in Honor of Richard A. McCormick, S.J.* New York: Paulist Press, 1990; pp. 193-212.

Callahan, Daniel. "An Ethical Challenge to Prochoice Advocates." *Commonweal*, 117 (1990), pp. 681-687.

Cameron, Paul and Ross, Kenneth P. "Social and Psychological Aspects of the Judeo-Christian Stance Toward Homosexuality." *Journal of Psychology and Theology*, 9 (1981), pp. 40-57.

Carlin, David R., Jr. "Two Doctrines of Privacy." *America*, 139 (1986), pp. 50-51.

_____ . "Gay Rights Laws: The Necessary Caveat." *Commonweal*, 117 (1990), pp. 568-569.

Castera, Bernard de. *Ouvrez les frontières! Introduction à la doctrine sociale de l'Église*. Preface by Cardinal Danneels. Paris: Éditions Mame, 1991.

Catéchisme de l'Église catholique. Paris: Mame/Plon, 1992.

Chauvin, Charles. *Les chrétiens et la prostitution*. Paris: Cerf, 1983.

"Cincinnati Archbishop Opposes Gay Rights Ordinance." *Bondings*, 14 (1992), p. 5.

Cohn, Bob. "Discrimination: The Limits of the Law." *Newsweek* (September 14, 1992), pp. 38-39.

Coleman, Gerald D. "The Vatican Statement on Homosexuality." *TS*, 48 (1987), pp. 727-734.

Coleman, John A. "The Churches and the Homosexual." *America*, 124 (1971), pp. 113-117.

_____ . "The Homosexual Revolution and Hermeneutics." *Concilium* (June 1984), pp. 55-64.

_____ . "Two Unanswered Questions." In TVH, pp. 59-65.

_____ . "ACT-UP Versus the Church." *Commonweal*, 118 (1991), pp. 533-534.

_____ , ed. *One Hundred Years of Catholic Social Thought: Celebration and Challenge*. Maryknoll, NY: Orbis Books, 1991.

Comstock, Gary David. *Violence Against Lesbians and Gay Men*. New York: Columbia University Press, 1991.

C.D.F. *Persona humana* ("Declaration on Certain Questions Concerning Sexual Ethics," 1975). Boston: Daughters of St. Paul, no date.

_____ . *Instruction on Christian Freedom and Liberation* (March 22, 1986). Ottawa: Canadian Conference of Catholic Bishops, no date.

_____ . "Letter to the Bishops of the Catholic Church on the Pastoral Care of Homosexual Persons" (October 1, 1986). In TVH, pp. 1-10.

_____ . "Some Considerations Concerning the Response to Legislative Proposals on the Non-Discrimination of Homosexual Persons" (July 23, 1992). In *Origins*, 22 (August 6, 1992), pp. 174-177.

Cox, Harvey. *The Secular City: Secularization and Urbanization in Theological Perspective*. Twenty-fifth Anniversary Edition. New York: Macmillan/Collier Books, 1990.

Cromey, Robert Warren. *In God's Image: Christian Witness to the Need for Gay/Lesbian Equality in the Eyes of the Church*. San Francisco: Alamo Press, 1991.

Crowe, Michael B. *The Changing Profile of the Natural Law*. The Hague: M. Nijhoff, 1977.

Cruikshank, Margaret. *The Gay and Lesbian Liberation Movement*. New York: Routledge, Chapman & Hall, 1992.

Cunliffe, C. R. A. "The Homosexual and the Vatican: An American Attempt at Dialogue." *New Blackfriars*, 69 (1988), pp. 392-399.

_____ . "Troubled Ministry" (A review article of Nugent and Gramick's *Building Bridges: Gay and Lesbian Reality and the Catholic Church*). *The Tablet* (August 8, 1992), pp. 986-987.

Curran, Charles E. "Homosexuality and Moral Theology: Methodology and Substantive Considerations." *The Thomist*, 35 (1971), pp. 447-481.

_____ . "Dialogue with the Homophile Movement: The Morality of Homosexuality." In *Catholic Theology in Dialogue*. Notre Dame, IN: Fides, 1972.

_____ . "Moral Theology, Psychiatry and Homosexuality." In *Transition and Tradition in Moral Theology*. Notre Dame, IN: Notre Dame University Press, 1979.

_____ and McCormick, Richard A. *Readings in Moral Theology, No. 1: Moral Norms and Catholic Tradition*. New York: Paulist Press, 1979.

_____ and McCormick, Richard A. *Readings in Moral Theology, No. 3: The Magisterium and Morality*. New York: Paulist Press, 1982.

_____ . "Moral Theology and Homosexuality." In Gramick, Jeannine, ed. *Homosexuality and the Catholic Church*. Chicago: Thomas More Press, 1983.

_____ and McCormick, Richard A. *Readings in Moral Theology, No. 5: Official Catholic Social Teaching*. New York: Paulist Press, 1986.

_____ . "Catholic Social and Sexual Teaching: A Methodological Comparison." *Theology Today*, 44 (1988), pp. 425-440.

_____ and McCormick, Richard A. *Readings in Moral Theology, No. 7: Natural Law and Theology*. New York: Paulist Press, 1991.

Davenport-Hines, Richard. *Sex, Death, and Punishment: Attitudes to Sex and Sexuality in Britain Since the Renaissance*. Glasgow: William Collins Sons and Company, 1990.

Dawson, Robert. "ACT-UP Acts Out." *Commonweal*, 117 (1990), pp. 476-477.

DeCecco, John P., ed. *Bashers, Baiters and Bigots: Homophobia in American Society*. New York: Harrington Park Press, 1985.

_____ and Shively, Michael G. *Origins of Sexuality and Homosexuality*. New York: Harrington Park Press, 1985.

Dei verbum ("Dogmatic Constitution on Divine Revelation," November 18, 1965). In Flannery, Austin, ed. *Vatican Council II*, pp. 750-765.

Delumeau, Jean. *Sin and Fear: The Emergence of a Western Guilt Culture, 13th-18th Centuries* (Trans. by Nicholson, Eric). New York: St. Martin's Press, 1990.

D'Emilio, John. *Sexual Politics, Sexual Communities: The Making of a Homosexual Minority in the United States, 1940-1970*. Chicago: The University of Chicago Press, 1983.

_____. *Making Trouble: Essays on Gay History, Politics, and the University*. New York: Routledge, 1992.

DeVaujuas, Arnaud. "Est-il moral de promouvoir le 'sexe sans risque'?" *Nouvelle Revue Théologique*, 110 (1988), pp. 867-878.

Dignitatis humanae ("Declaration on Religious Liberty," December 7, 1965). In Flannery, Austin, ed. *Vatican Council II*, pp. 799-812.

Dollimore, Jonathon. *Sexual Dissidence: Augustine to Wilde, Freud to Foucault*. Oxford: Clarendon Press, 1991.

Dover, K. J. *Greek Homosexuality*. Cambridge, MA: Harvard University Press, 1989.

Drane, James F. "Condoms, AIDS, and Catholic Ethics." *Commonweal*, 118 (1991), pp. 188-192.

Driver, Tom F. "Homosexuality: The Contemporary and Christian Contexts." *Commonweal*, 98 (1973), pp. 103-106.

Duberman, Martin. *About Time: Exploring the Gay Past*. Revised and Expanded Edition. New York: Meridian, 1991.

_____; Vicinus, Martha; and Chauncey, George, Jr., eds. *Hidden from History: Reclaiming the Gay and Lesbian Past*. New York: Meridian, 1991.

Dulles, Avery. *Models of the Church*. Garden City, NY: Image Books, 1978.

Dwyer, Judith A. "Vatican II and the Dignity of the Conscience." In Richard, Lucien, ed. *Vatican II, The Unfinished Agenda: A Look to the Future*. New York: Paulist Press, 1987.

Dyer, Kate, ed. *Gays in Uniform: The Pentagon's Secret Reports*. Introduced by U.S. Congressman Gerry E. Studds. Boston: Alyson Publications, 1990.

East, Bernard. "L'Église et l'homosexualité." *Présence*, 2 (1993), pp. 21-22.

Editors of the Harvard Law Review. *Sexual Orientation and the Law*. Cambridge, MA: Harvard University Press, 1989.

Egan, Timothy. "Violent Backdrop for Anti-Gay Measure." In NYT (November 1, 1992), p. A40.

_____ . "Oregon GOP Faces Schism over Agenda of Christian Right." In NYT (November 14, 1992), p. A6.

Ellacuría, Ignacio. "Human Rights in a Divided Society." In Hennelly, Alfred and Langan, John, eds. *Human Rights in the Americas: The Struggle for Consensus*, pp. 52-65.

Elred, Stephen. "Gay Rights, Gay Plight: An Open Letter to Cardinal Bernardin." *Commonweal*, 113 (1986), pp. 680-682.

Elshtain, Jean B. "Against Gay Marriage—II." *Commonweal*, 118 (1991), pp. 685-686.

Faderman, Lillian. *Surpassing the Love of Men: Romantic Friendship and Love Between Women from the Renaissance to the Present*. New York: William Morrow and Company, 1981.

_____ . *Odd Girls and Twilight Lovers: A History of Lesbian Life in Twentieth-Century America*. New York: Penguin Books, 1992.

Farrell, Edward. "What Are We Doing to our Gay People?" *The Furrow*, 41 (1990), pp. 26-33.

Fink, Peter E. "A Pastoral Hypothesis: It Was Gay Pride Week and the Church Stayed Home . . ." *Commonweal*, 98 (1973), p. 107, 110-112.

Flannery, Austin, ed. *Vatican Council II: The Conciliar and Post Conciliar Documents*. Collegeville, MN: Liturgical Press, 1980.

Foucault, Michel. *The History of Sexuality* (3 vols.) [Trans. by Robert Hurley]. New York: Vintage Books, 1990.

Fout, John C., ed. *Forbidden History: The State, Society, and the Regulation of Sexuality in Modern Europe*. Chicago: University of Chicago Press, 1992.

Francoeur, Robert. "Two Different Worlds, Two Different Moralities." In TVH, pp. 189-200.

Gallagher, John, ed. *Homosexuality and the Magisterium: Documents from the Vatican and the U.S. Bishops, 1975-1985*. Mt. Rainier, MD: NWM, 1986.

Gaudium et spes ("Pastoral Constitution on the Church in the Modern World," December 7, 1965). In Flannery, Austin, ed. *Vatican Council II*, pp. 903-1001.

Gay, Peter. *Freud: A Life for Our Time*. New York: Anchor Books, 1989.

Geis, Gilbert, *et al.* "Reported Consequences of Decriminalization of Consensual Adult Homosexuality in Seven American States." TJH, 1 (1976), pp. 419-426.

Genovesi, Vincent J. "Challenging the Legal Status of Abortion: A Matter of Moral Obligation?" *America*, 153 (1985), pp. 417-422.

_____ . *In Pursuit of Love: Catholic Morality and Human Sexuality*. Wilmington, DE: Michael Glazier, 1988.

Gibbons, Ann. "The Brain as 'Sexual Organ.'" *Science*, 253 (1991), pp. 957-959.

Gilby, Thomas. *The Political Thought of Thomas Aquinas*. Chicago: University of Chicago Press, 1958.

_____ . *Law and Political Theory* [vol. 28 of the "McGraw-Hill *Summa theologiae*"]. New York: McGraw-Hill, 1966.

Ginzburg, Carlo. *Ecstasies: Deciphering the Witches' Sabbath* [Trans. by Raymond Rosenthal]. New York: Penguin Books, 1992.

Gonsalves, Milton. *Fagothey's Right and Reason: Ethics in Theory and Practice.* Columbus, OH: Merrill Publishing Company, 1989.

Gramick, Jeannine, ed. *Homosexuality and the Catholic Church.* Mt. Rainier, MD: NWM, 1983.

Gramick, Jeannine and Furey, Pat, eds. *The Vatican and Homosexuality: Reactions to the "Letter to the Bishops of the Catholic Church on the Pastoral Care of Homosexual Persons."* New York: Crossroad, 1988.

Greenberg, David F. *The Construction of Homosexuality.* Chicago: University of Chicago Press, 1988.

Greenberg, Jerrold S. "The Effects of a Homophile Organization on the Self-Esteem and Alienation of Its Members." TJH, 1 (1976), pp. 313-317.

Griffin, Leslie. "The Church, Morality, and Public Policy." In Curran, Charles E., ed. *Moral Theology: Challenge for the Future*, pp. 334-354.

Grippo, Dan. "The Vatican Can Slight Scripture for Its Purpose." In TVH, pp. 33-39.

Guindon, André. *The Sexual Language: An Essay in Moral Theology.* Ottawa: The University of Ottawa Press, 1976.

_____ . "Après Sodome et l'Exode." *Relations*, 41 (1981), pp. 77-79.

_____ . "Gais et lesbiennes dans l'Église. Pour un déplacement de la problématique." *Nouveau Dialogue*, 47 (1982), pp. 25-28.

_____ . "Homosexualités et méthodologie éthique. À propos d'un livre de Xavier Thévenot." *Église et Théologie,* 18 (1986), pp. 57-84.

_____ . *The Sexual Creators: An Ethical Proposal for Concerned Christians.* Lanham, MD: University Press of America, 1986.

_____ . "Homosexual Acts or Gay Speech?" In TVH, pp. 208-215.

Haeberle, Erwin J. "Swastika, Pink Triangle, and Yellow Star: The Destruction of Sexology and the Persecution of Homosexuals in Nazi Germany." In Duberman, Martin, et. al. *Hidden from History*, pp. 365-379.

Hahn, Pierre. "Une sociogenèse de l'homosexualité masculine." *Lumière et Vie*, 29 (1980), pp. 29-40.

Hanigan, James P. *What Are They Saying About Sexual Morality?* New York: Paulist Press, 1982.

_____ . *Homosexuality: The Test Case for Christian Ethics.* New York: Paulist Press, 1988.

Hartinger, Brent. "A Case for Gay Marriage." *Commonweal*, 118 (1991), pp. 681-683.

Harvey, John F. "Homosexuality as a Pastoral Problem." TS, 16 (1955), pp. 86-108.

_____ . "Homosexuality." In *New Catholic Encyclopedia* (v. VII, pp. 116-119), Washington, D.C.: Catholic University of America, 1967.

_____ . "Attitudes of a Catholic Priest towards Homosexuality." *Bulletin of the National Guild of Catholic Psychiatrists* (December 1972), pp. 52-58.

_____ . "The Controversy Concerning the Psychology and the Morality of Homosexuality." *American Ecclesiastical Review*, 167 (1973), pp. 602-629.

_____ . "Chastity and the Homosexual." *The Priest*, 33 (1977), pp. 10-16.

_____ . "An In-Depth Review of *Homosexuality and the Christian Way of Life*." *Linacre Quarterly*, 50 (1983), pp. 122-143.

_____ . *The Homosexual Person: A New Thinking in Pastoral Care*. San Francisco: Ignatius Press, 1987.

Healy, P. W. J. "*Uranisme et Unisexualité*: A Late Victorian View of Homosexuality." *New Blackfriars*, 59 (1978), pp. 56-65.

Hebblethwaite, Peter. "The Popes and Politics: Shifting Patterns in Catholic Social Teaching." In Curran and McCormick, eds. *Readings in Moral Theology, No. 5*, pp. 264-286.

_____ . "Please Don't Shoot the Bearer of Bad Tidings: An Open Letter on Cardinal Ratzinger's Document." In TVH, pp. 133-144.

Hedgpeth, Judith M. "Employment Discrimination Law and the Rights of Gay Persons." TJH, 5 (1979/80), pp. 67-78.

Heger, Heinz. *The Men with the Pink Triangle*. Boston: Alyson Publications, 1980.

Hehir, J. Bryan. "The Unfinished Agenda." *America*, 153 (1985), pp. 386-387, 392.

_____ . "John Paul II: Continuity and Change in the Social Teaching of the Church." In Curran and McCormick, eds. *Readings in Moral Theology, No. 5*, pp. 247-263.

Hennelly, Alfred and Langan, John, eds. *Human Rights in the Americas*. Washington, D.C.: Georgetown University Press, 1982.

Henry, Patrick. "Homosexuals: Identity and Dignity." *Theology Today*, 33 (1976/77), pp. 33-39.

Heron, Alastair, ed. *Toward a Quaker View of Sex*. London: Friends Home Service Committee, 1964.

Hill, Edmund. *Being Human: A Biblical Perspective*. London: Geoffrey Chapman, 1984.

Holden, Constance. "Is 'Gender Gap' Narrowing?" *Science*, 253 (1991), pp. 959-960.

Hollenbach, David. *Claims in Conflict*. New York: Paulist Press, 1979.

_____ . "Global Human Rights: An Interpretation of the Contemporary Catholic Understanding." In Hennelly and Langan, eds. *Human Rights in the Americas*, pp. 9-24.

_____ . "The Growing End of an Argument." *America*, 153 (1985), pp. 363-366.

_____ . "The Church's Social Mission in a Pluralistic Society." In Richard, ed. *Vatican II, The Unfinished Agenda*, pp. 113-128.

_____ . *Justice, Peace, and Human Rights: American Catholic Social Ethics in a Pluralistic World*. New York: Crossroad, 1988.

_____ . "The Common Good Revisited." TS, 50 (1989), pp. 70-94.

Homosexuality and Social Justice: Report of the Task Force on Gay/Lesbian Issues. San Francisco: Archdiocese of San Francisco, Commission on Social Justice, 1982.

Hooker, Evelyn. "The Adjustment of the Overt Male Homosexual." *Journal of Projective Techniques*, 21 (1957), pp. 1-31.

Hooper, J. Leon. *The Ethics of Discourse: The Social Philosophy of John Courtney Murray*. Washington, D.C.: Georgetown University Press, 1986.

Horner, Tom. *Jonathan Loved David: Homosexuality in Biblical Times*. Philadelphia: The Westminster Press, 1978.

Hunt, Robert P. and Grasso, Kenneth L., eds. *John Courtney Murray and the American Civil Conversation*. Grand Rapids, MI: Eerdmans, 1992.

Isay, Richard A. *Being Homosexual: Gay Men and their Development*. New York: Avon Books, 1989.

Isenhart, Charles. "Dubuque Archbishop Latest to Oppose Gay Rights." *National Catholic Register*, 64 (December 18, 1988), p. 1.

John XXIII. *Mater et magistra* ("Christianity and Social Progress," May 5, 1961). In O'Brien and Shannon, eds. *Renewing the Earth*, pp. 50-116.

_____ . *Pacem in terris* ("Peace on Earth," April 11, 1963). In O'Brien and Shannon, eds. *Renewing the Earth*, pp. 124-170.

John Paul II. *Redemptor hominis* (March 4, 1979). Vatican Polyglot Press. Ottawa: CCCB, no date.

_____ . *Dives in misericordia* ("On the Mercy of God," November 30, 1980). Vatican Polyglot Press. Boston: St. Paul Editions, no date.

_____ . *Sollicitudo rei socialis* (For the Twentieth Anniversary of *Populorum progressio*, December 30, 1987). Vatican Polyglot Press. Ottawa: CCCB, no date.

_____ . *Centesimus annus*. ("The Social Doctrine of the Church;" On the Hundredth Anniversary of *Rerum novarum*, May 1, 1991). Vatican translation. Sherbrook, PQ: Editions Paulines, 1991.

Joyce, James. *A Portrait of the Artist as a Young Man* [1924]. London: Minerva, 1992.

Katz, Jonathan N. *Gay American History. Lesbians and Gay Men in the U.S.A.* New York: Meridian, 1992.

Keane, Philip S. *Sexual Morality: A Catholic Perspective*. New York: Paulist Press, 1977.

Kelly, James R. "A Political Challenge to the Prolife Movement." *Commonweal*, 118 (1991), pp. 696-697.

Kelly, Kevin. "Catholic Teenagers 'Intolerant' of Gays." *Bondings*, 14 (1991), pp. 1, 11.

Kirchmeier, Mark and Patricia Lefevere. "Archbishop Opposes Anti-Gay Measure." *Bondings*, 13 (1991), p. 6.

Kirk, Marshall and Madsen, Hunter. *After the Ball: How America Will Conquer Its Fear and Hatred of Gays in the 90's.* New York: Plume, 1990.

Knauer, Peter. "The Hermeneutic Function of the Principle of Double Effect." In Curran and McCormick, eds. *Readings in Moral Theology, No. 1*, pp. 1-39.

Knutson, Donald C. "The Civil Liberties of Gay Persons: Present Status." TJH, 2 (1977), pp. 337-342.

Kortge, Noretta. *Philosophy and Homosexuality.* New York: Harrington Park Press, 1985.

Kopp, Lillanna. "A Problem of Manipulated Data." In TVH, pp. 40-47.

Kosnik, Anthony; Carroll, William; Cunningham, Agnes; Modras, Ronald; Schulte, James. *Human Sexuality: New Directions in American Catholic Thought.* Paulist Press, 1977.

Kourany, Ronald F. C. "Suicide Among Homosexual Adolescents." TJH, 13 (1987), pp. 111-117.

Lamien, Eric. "Interview with Bishop Jacques Gaillot of Evreux, France: A Welcoming and Listening Church" [Trans. by Joe Orndorff]. *Bondings*, 15 (1992/93), p. 1.

Langan, John. "Human Rights in Roman Catholicism." In Curran and McCormick, eds. *Readings in Moral Theology, No. 5*, pp. 110-129.

Latourelle, René, ed. *Vatican II: Assessment and Perspectives: Twenty-five Years After (1962-1987)* (3 vols.). New York: Paulist Press, 1988/89.

Lauritsen, John and Thorstad, David. *The Early Homosexual Rights Movement (1864-1935).* New York: Times Change Press, 1974.

Lebacqz, Karen. *Six Theories of Justice: Perspectives from Philosophical and Theological Ethics.* Minneapolis: Augsburg, 1986.

LeVay, Simon. "A Difference in Hypothalamic Structure Between Heterosexual and Homosexual Men." *Science*, 253 (1991), pp. 1035-1037.

Love, Thomas T. *John Courtney Murray: Contemporary Church-State Theory.* Garden City, NY: Doubleday, 1965.

Luckey, William R. "The Contribution of John Courtney Murray, S.J.: A Catholic Perspective." In *ACC*, pp. 19-43.

Lynch, John J. "Notes on Moral Theology." TS, 22 (1961), pp. 228-269.

MacDonald, Duncan. "Intro Two: New York City's Gay Rights Law." *America*, 139 (1986), pp. 45-49.

Maddox, Robert L. *Separation of Church and State: Guarantor of Religious Freedom.* New York: Crossroad, 1987.

Magnuson, Roger J. *Are Gay Rights Right? Making Sense of the Controversy.* Portland, OR: Multnomah Press, 1990.

Mahoney, John. "The Church and the Homosexual." *Month*, 10 (1977), pp. 166-169.

_____ . *The Making of Moral Theology: A Study of the Roman Catholic Tradition.* New York: Oxford University Press, 1987.

_____ . "The Basis of Human Rights." In Curran, ed. *Moral Theology: Challenges for the Future*, pp. 313-333.

Marcotte, Marcel. "Homosexualité et morale" (1. "Les données phénoménales de base;" 2. "Préambules critiques et vues d'ensemble"). *Relations*, 36 (1976), pp. 142-146; 169-173.

Marcus, Eric. *Making History: The Struggle for Gay and Lesbian Equal Rights, 1945-1990. An Oral History*. New York: Harper Collins, 1992.

Massachusetts Catholic Conference. Statement Opposing Gay Rights Bill. *Origins*, 14 (January 14, 1984), pp. 73-74.

McClory, Robert J. "Interview With Cardinal Bernardin." In NCR (February 14, 1992), pp. 10-11.

_____ . "Bernardin's Chicago Adrift in a Sea of Malaise." In NCR (February 14, 1992), pp. 6-9.

_____ . "Rome Document on Gays No 'Mandate,' Bernardin Says." In NCR (November 20, 1992), p. 8.

McCormick, Richard A. and Ramsey, Paul, eds. *Doing Evil to Achieve Good: Moral Choice in Conflict Situations*. Chicago: Loyola University Press, 1978.

McCormick, Richard A. *Notes on Moral Theology: 1965 through 1980*. Washington, D.C.: University Press of America, 1980.

McElroy, Robert W. *The Search for an American Public Theology: The Contribution of John Courtney Murray*. New York: Paulist Press, 1989.

McManamin, Francis G. "American Bishops and the American Electorate." *American Ecclesiastical Review*, 151 (1964), pp. 217-229.

_____ . "Episcopal Authority in the Political Order." *Continuum*, 2 (1965), pp. 632-638.

McNaught, Brian. "Why Bother with Gay Rights?" *The Humanist*, 37 (1977), pp. 34-36.

_____ . "Reflections of a Gay Catholic." In Gramick, ed. *Homosexuality and the Catholic Church*, pp. 21-44.

McNeill, John J. "Response to his Silencing by the Sacred Congregation for the Doctrine of the Faith." *Origins*, 7 (1977), pp. 218-219.

_____ . "Homosexuality, Lesbianism, and the Future: The Creative Role of the Gay Community in Building a More Humane Society." In Nugent, ed. *A Challenge to Love*, pp. 52-64.

_____ . *The Church and the Homosexual*. Updated and expanded edition. Boston: Beacon Press, 1988.

_____ . *Taking a Chance on God: Liberating Theology for Gays, Lesbians and their Lovers, Families, and Friends*. Boston: Beacon Press, 1988.

Mecca, Andrew M.; Smelser, Neil J.; and Vasconcellos, John, eds. *The Social Importance of Self-Esteem*. Berkeley: University of California Press, 1989.

Melchin, Kenneth R. "Revisionists, Deontologists, and the Structure of Moral Understanding." TS, 51 (1990), pp. 389-416.

_____ . "Moral Knowledge and the Structure of Cooperative Living." TS, 52 (1991), pp. 495-523.

Menard, Guy. *De Sodome à l'Exode. Jalons pour une théologie de la libération gaie.* Montréal: Univers, 1980.

Michel, A. "Tolérance." In *Dictionnaire de théologie catholique* [v. XV, pp. 1208-1223]. Paris: Librairie Letouzey et Ane, 1946.

Miller, Neil. *Out in the World: Gay and Lesbian Life from Buenos Aires to Bangkok.* New York: Random House, 1992.

Millet, Kate. *Sexual Politics.* New York: Simon & Schuster, 1969, 1990.

Millham, Jim and Weinberger, Linda E. "Sexual Preference, Sex Role Appropriateness, and Restriction of Social Access." TJH, 2 (1977), pp. 343-358.

Mohr, Richard D. *Gays/Justice: A Study of Ethics, Society, and Law.* New York: Columbia University Press, 1988.

_____ . *Gay Ideas: Outing and Other Controversies.* Boston: Beacon Press, 1992.

Moore, Arthur J. "Gay Rights and the Churches: Social Pluralism and Christian Order." *Christianity and Crisis*, 46 (1986), pp. 127-130.

Moore, Gareth. *The Body in Context: Sex and Catholicism.* London: SCM Press, 1992.

Moran, Gabriel. "Education: Sexual and Religious." In Nugent, ed. *A Challenge to Love*, pp. 159-173.

Morrissey, Francis G. *Papal and Curial Pronouncements: Their Canonical Significance in Light of the 1983 'Code of Canon Law.'* Ottawa: St. Paul University, 1992.

Mugavero, Francis (Bishop). "Withdrawing Support from Certain Homosexual Groups." *Origins*, 16 (1987), p. 651.

Müller, Aloïs and Greinacher, Norbert, eds. *The Church and the Rights of Man.* [*Concilium*, no. 124] New York: Seabury, 1979.

Murray, John Courtney. "Christian Co-operation." TS, 3 (1942), pp. 413-431.

_____ . Review of H. C. Koenig's *Principles for Peace: Selections from Papal Documents, Leo XIII to Pius XII.* TS, 4 (1943), pp. 634-638.

_____ . "Freedom of Religion." TS, 6 (1945), pp. 85-113.

_____ . "Freedom of Religion: I. The Ethical Problem." TS, 6 (1945), pp. 229-286.

_____ . Review of M. S. Bates' *Religious Liberty: An Inquiry.* TS, 7 (1946), pp. 151-163.

_____ . "St. Robert Bellarmine on the Indirect Power." TS, 10 (1949), pp. 491-535.

_____ . "Contemporary Orientations of Catholic Thought on Church and State in the Light of History." TS, 10 (1949), pp. 177-234.

_____ . "The Problem of State Religion." TS, 12 (1951), pp. 155-178.

_____ . "The Church and Totalitarian Democracy." TS, 13 (1952), pp. 525-563.

_____ . "Leo XIII on Church and State: The General Structure of the Controversy." TS, 14 (1953), pp. 1-30.

_____ . "Leo XIII: Separation of Church and State." TS, (1953), pp. 145-214.

_____ . "Leo XIII: Two Concepts of Government." TS, 14 (1953), pp. 551-567.

_____ . "Leo XIII: Government and the Order of Culture." TS, 15 (1954), pp. 1-33.

_____ . *We Hold These Truths: Catholic Reflections on the American Proposition.* New York: Sheed & Ward, 1960.

_____ . *The Problem of Religious Freedom* (Woodstock Papers, no. 7). Westminster, MD: Newman Press, 1965.

_____ . "This Matter of Religious Freedom." *America*, 112 (1965), pp. 40-43.

_____ . "Freedom, Authority, Community." *America*, 115 (1966), pp. 734 ff.

_____ . "The Issue of Church and State at Vatican Council II." TS, 27 (1966), pp. 580-606.

_____ . "Religious Freedom" ("Commentary and Notes on the 'Declaration on Religious Liberty'"). In Abbott, Walter M. and Gallagher, Joseph, eds. *The Documents of Vatican II.* New York: Guild Press, 1966; pp. 672-696.

_____ , ed. *Religious Liberty: An End and a Beginning; The Declaration of Religious Freedom: An Ecumenical Discussion.* New York: Macmillan, 1966.

_____ . *Matthias Sheeben on Faith: The Doctoral Dissertation of John Courtney Murray.* Edited by D. Thomas Hughson. Lewiston, NY: E. Mellen Press, 1987.

National Conference of Catholic Bishops. *The Challenge of Peace. God's Promise and Our Response. A Pastoral Letter on War and Peace.* Washington, D.C.: U.S. Catholic Conference, 1983.

Navarro-Valls, Joaquin. "Statement" (on SCC). *Origins*, 22 (August 6, 1992), p. 175.

Neuhaus, Richard John. "Democracy, Desperately Dry." In ACC, pp. 3-18.

NWM. "Human Dignity and the Common Good: A Response of New Ways Ministry to the Vatican Document on Lesbian and Gay Rights" (1992). Available from NWM.

_____ . "A Time to Speak: Catholics for Gay and Lesbian Rights." In NCR (November 13, 1992), pp. 13-16.

Novak, Michael. "Homosexuality is Harmful to Society." In Leone, Bruno and O'Neill, M. Teresa, eds. *Sexual Values: Opposing Viewpoints.* St. Paul, MN: Greenhaven Press, 1983; pp. 71-74.

Nugent, Robert and Gramick, Jeannine, eds. *A Time to Speak: A Collection of Contemporary Statements from U.S. Catholic Sources on Homosexuality, Gay Ministry, and Social Justice.* Mt. Rainier, MD: NWM, 1982.

Nugent, Robert, ed. *A Challenge to Love: Gay and Lesbian Catholics in the Church.* New York: Crossroad, 1989.

_____ and Gramick, Jeannine. "Homosexuality: Protestant, Catholic & Jewish Issues; A Fishbone Tale." In Hasbany, R., ed. *Homosexuality and Religion*. New York: The Haworth Press, 1989; pp. 7-46.

_____ . *Building Bridges: Gay and Lesbian Reality and the Catholic Church*. Mystic, CT: Twenty-third Publications, 1992.

O'Brien, David J. and Shannon, Thomas A., eds. *Renewing the Earth: Catholic Documents on Peace, Justice, and Liberation*. Garden City, NY: Image Books, 1977.

O'Brien, Dennis. "Against Gay Marriage—I." *Commonweal*, 118 (1991), pp. 684-685.

O'Connor, John (Cardinal) and Koch, Edward (Mayor). *His Eminence and Hizzoner: A Candid Exchange*. New York: William Morrow, 1989.

O'Neill, Onora. "Between Consenting Adults." *Philosophy and Public Affairs*, 14 (1985), pp. 252-277.

Oraison, Marc. *La question homosexuelle*. Paris: Les éditions du Seuil, 1975.

"Oregon Trail of Hate." In NYT (October 26, 1992), p. A26.

Pagels, Elaine. *Adam, Eve, and the Serpent*. New York: Vintage Books, 1988.

Paglia, Camille. *Sexual Personae: Art and Decadence from Nefertiti to Emily Dickinson*. New York: Vintage Books, 1991.

Paul VI. *Populorum progressio* ("On the Development of Peoples," March 26, 1967). In O'Brien and Shannon, eds. *Renewing the Earth*, pp. 311-346.

_____ . *Octogesima adveniens* ("A Call to Action: Letter on the Eightieth Anniversary of *Rerum novarum*," May 14, 1971). In O'Brien and Shannon, eds. *Renewing the Earth*, pp. 352-382.

Pavan, Pietro. "Declaration on Religious Freedom, Commentary" [Trans. by Hilda Graef]. In Vorgrimler, Herbert, ed. *Commentary on the Documents of Vatican II* (5 vols.). Freiburg: Herder and Herder, 1967-1969; vol. 4, pp. 49-86.

Pelletier, Pierre. "Morale et pastorale des homosexuels." *Pastoral Sciences/Sciences Pastorales*, 5 (1986), pp. 151-162.

Pelotte, Donald E. *John Courtney Murray: Theologian in Conflict*. New York: Paulist Press, 1976.

Perry, Troy D. and Swicegood, Thomas L. P. *Profiles in Gay & Lesbian Courage*. New York: St. Martin's Press, 1991.

Peter Damian. *Book of Gomorrah* [An Eleventh Century Treatise Against Clerical Homosexual Practices]. Translated with an Introduction and Notes by Pierre J. Payer. Waterloo, ON: Wilfrid Laurier University Press, 1982.

Petit, Jean-Claude and Breton, Jean-Claude, eds. *Questions de liberté*. Montréal: Fides, 1990.

Plant, Richard. *The Pink Triangle: The Nazi War Against Homosexuals*. New York: Henry Holt, 1986.

Plongeron, Bernard. "Anathema or Dialogue: Christian Reactions to Declarations of the Rights of Man in the United States and Europe in the Eighteenth Century" [Trans. by Lawrence Ginn]. In Müller and Greinacher, eds. *The Church and the Rights of Man*, pp. 39-48.

Poulat, Émile. "Le grand absent de *Dignitatis humanae*: l'État." *Le Supplé*ment, 175 (1990), pp. 5-27.

Price, Richard M. "The Distinctiveness of Early Christian Sexual Ethics." *Heythrop Journal*, 31 (1990), pp. 257-276.

Pronger, Brian. *The Arena of Masculinity: Sports, Homosexuality, and the Meaning of Sex*. New York: St. Martin's Press, 1990.

Quindlen, Anna. "Putting Hatred to a Vote." In NYT (October 28, 1992), p. A21.

Quinn, John R. (Archbishop). "Letter on Violence to Archdiocesan Deans." In HM, p. 100.

_____ . "Toward an Understanding of the Letter 'On the Pastoral Care of Homosexual Persons'." In TVH, pp. 13-19.

_____ . "Letter to Mayor Art Agnos." *Origins*, 19 (June 8, 1989), p. 50.

_____ . "Homily on Violence Against Gays." *Origins*, 19 (September 21, 1989), pp. 260-262.

_____ . "Civil Rights of Gay and Lesbian Persons." *Origins*, 22 (August 20, 1992), p. 204.

Ranke-Heinemann, Uta. *Eunuchs for the Kingdom of Heaven: Women, Sexuality and the Catholic Church* (Trans. by Peter Heinegg). New York: Doubleday, 1990.

Rawls, John. *A Theory of Justice*. Cambridge, MA: Harvard University Press, 1971.

_____ . "Justice as Fairness: Political, not Metaphysical." *Philosophy and Public Affairs*, 14 (1985), pp. 223-251.

Refoulé, François. "Efforts Made on Behalf of Human Rights by the Supreme Authority of the Church" (Trans. by John Maxwell). In Müller and Greinacher, eds. *The Church and the Rights of Man*, pp. 77-85.

Richard, Lucien, ed., with Harrington, Daniel and O'Malley, John W. *Vatican II, the Unfinished Agenda: A Look to the Future*. New York: Paulist Press, 1987.

Richards, David A. J. "Homosexual Acts and the Constitutional Right to Privacy." TJH, 5 (1979/80), pp. 43-66.

Roach, John R. (Archbishop). "The Rights of Homosexual Persons." *Origins*, 21 (November 7, 1991), pp. 356-357.

Rohr, John A. "John Courtney Murray and the Pastoral Letters." *America*, 153 (1985), pp. 368-372.

Rubenstein, William B. *Lesbians, Gay Men, and the Law*. New York: The New Press, 1993.

Rutledge, Leigh W. *The Gay Decades*. New York: Penguin/Plume, 1992.

Scanzoni, Letha and Mollenkott, Virginia Ramey. *Is the Homosexual My Neighbor? Another Christian View*. San Francisco: Harper and Row, 1978.

Schmalz, Jeffrey. "Gay Areas Jubilant Over Clinton: Oregon Defeats Bid to Curb Gay Rights." In NYT (November 5, 1992), p. B8.

Schuck, Michael J. *That They Be One: The Social Teachings of the Papal Encyclicals, 1740-1989*. Washington, D.C.: Georgetown University Press, 1992.

Schüller, Bruno. "The Double Effect in Catholic Thought: A Re-Evaluation." In McCormick and Ramsey, eds. *Doing Evil to Achieve Good: Moral Choice in Conflict Situations*, pp. 165-192.

Scroggs, Robin. *The New Testament and Homosexuality. Contextual Background for Contemporary Debate.* Philadelphia: Fortress Press, 1983.

Segers, Mary. "Murray, American Pluralism, and the Abortion Controversy." In *ACC,* pp. 228-248.

Seidman, Steven. *Embattled Eros: Sexual Politics and Ethics in Contemporary America.* New York: Routledge, 1992.

Senate of Priests (San Francisco). "Ministry and Homosexuality in the Archdiocese of San Francisco." In HM, pp. 55-78.

Shannon, William H. "A Response to Archbishop Quinn." In TVH, pp. 20-27.

Shilts, Randy. *The Mayor of Castro Street: The Life and Times of Harvey Milk.* New York: St. Martin's Press, 1982.

_____ . *And the Band Played On: Politics, People, and the AIDS Epidemic.* New York: St. Martin's Press, 1987.

_____ . *Conduct Unbecoming: Gays & Lesbians in the U.S. Military.* New York: St. Martin's Press, 1993.

Shively, Michael G. and Hall, Marny A. "Departures from Sex Role Stereotypes of Appearance and Behavior and Violations of Civil Liberties." TJH, 2 (1977), pp. 331-336.

Showalter, Elaine. *Sexual Anarchy: Gender and Culture at the Fin de Siècle.* New York: Viking Penguin, 1990.

Siciliano, Carl. "An Epidemic of Violence Against Homosexuals." *Catholic Worker,* 54 (1987), p. 3.

Sinclair, Ken and Ross, Michael W. "Consequences of Decriminalization of Homosexuality: A Study of Two Australian States." TJH, 12 (1985), pp. 119-127.

Snow, Katrin. "Oregon Anti-Gay Measure Escalates Violence." In NCR (October 30, 1992), p. 30.

Spohn, William C. *What Are They Saying About Scripture and Ethics?* New York: Paulist Press, 1984.

Stemmeler, Michael L. and Clark, J. Michael, eds. *Homophobia and the Judeo-Christian Tradition.* Dallas, TX: Monument Press, 1990.

Stepp, Laura Sessions. "Vatican Supports Bias Against Gays." *Bondings,* 14 (1992), pp. 1, 6, 9.

Synod of Bishops (1971). *Justice in the World.* In O'Brien and Shannon, eds. *Renewing the Earth,* pp. 390-408.

_____ (1980). *Charter on the Rights of the Family* (October 23, 1983). Vatican Polyglot Press. Ottawa: CCCB, no date.

Thèvenot, Xavier. "L'action pastorale auprés des homosexuels." *Lumière et Vie,* 29 (1980), pp. 83-98.

_____ . *Homosexualités masculines et morale chrétienne.* Paris: Cerf, 1985.

Thomas Aquinas. *Summa theologica*. Complete English edition in five volumes. Translated by the Fathers of the English Dominican Province. Westminster, MD: Christian Classics, 1981 (Copyright 1948 by Benzinger Brothers, New York, NY).

Thurston, Thomas M. *Homosexuality and Contemporary Roman Catholic Ethical Discussion*. Ann Arbor, MI: U.M.I. Dissertation Services, 1990.

Timmons, Stuart. *The Trouble with Harry Hay: Founder of the Modern Gay Movement*. Boston: Alyson Publications, 1990.

Traer, Robert. *Faith in Human Rights: Support in Religious Traditions for a Global Struggle*. Washington, D.C.: Georgetown University Press, 1992.

Tuohey, John E. "The C. D. F. and Homosexuals: Rewriting the Moral Tradition." *America*, 167 (September 12, 1992), pp. 136-138.

Turque, Bill, *et al.* "Gays Under Fire." *Newsweek* (September 14, 1992), pp. 36-39.

Vacek, Edward C. "A Christian Homosexuality." *Commonweal*, 107 (1981), pp. 681-684.

Van Der Burg, Wibren. "The Slippery Slope Argument." *Ethics*, 102 (1991), pp. 42-65.

Vatican Secretariat for Non-christians. *The Attitude of the Church Towards the Followers of Other Religions* (Pentecost, 1984). Vatican Polyglot Press. Ottawa: CCCB, no date.

Vetri, Dominick. "The Legal Arena: Progress for Gay Civil Rights." TJH, 5 (1979/80), pp. 25-34.

Vilbert, J.-C. "Aux origines d'une condamnation: l'homosexualité dans la Rome antique et l'Église des premiers siècles." *Lumière et Vie,* 29 (1980), pp. 15-28.

Waaldijk, Kees. "Constitutional Protection Against Discrimination of Homosexuals (in the Netherlands)." TJH, 13 (1987), pp. 57-68.

Waldron, Jeremy. "A Right to Do Wrong." *Ethics*, 92 (1981), pp. 21-39.

_____ . "Rights in Conflict." *Ethics*, 99 (1989), pp. 503-519.

Washington State Catholic Conference. "The Prejudice Against Homosexuals and the Ministry of the Church." In HM, pp. 46-54.

Weakland, Rembert (Archbishop). "Who is Our Neighbor?" In HM, pp. 34-35.

Weeks, Jeffrey. *Sexuality and Its Discontents: Meanings, Myths, and Modern Sexualities*. London and New York: Routledge, 1989.

Whealon, John F. (Archbishop). "The Church and the Homosexual Person." *Bondings*, 13 (1991), p. 11.

Whelan, Charles M. "The Enduring Problems of Religious Liberty." *America*, 153 (1985), pp. 373, 376-379.

White, Edmund. *States of Desire: Travels in Gay America*. With a new afterword by the author. New York: Plume, 1991.

Whitehead, James D. and Whitehead, Evelyn Eaton. "The Shape of Compassion: Reflections on Catholics and Homosexuality." *Spirituality Today*, 39 (1987), pp. 126-136.

Williams, Bruce. "Gay Catholics and Eucharistic Communion." In Nugent, ed. *A Challenge to Love*, pp. 205-215.

_____ . "Homosexuality: The New Vatican Statement." TS, 48 (1987), pp. 259-277.

Woods, Richard. *Another Kind of Love: Homosexuality and Spirituality*. Fort Wayne, IN: Knoll, 1988.

Wright, Elliott. "The Church and Gay Liberation." *Christian Century*, 88 (1971), pp. 281-285.

Zahn, Gordon C. "The Human Rights of Homosexuals: Let Catholics Be Consistent." *Commonweal*, 116 (1989), pp. 462-465.

_____ . "Let's Support Civil Rights for Homosexuals." *U.S. Catholic*, 54 (1989), pp. 13-15.

Index

Abbott, Walter, 175
abortion, 57
"The Adjustment of the Overt Male Homosexual" (Hooker), 18
After the Ball: How America Will Conquer its Fear and Hatred of Gays in the 90s (Kirk and Madsen), 4
Agnos, Art, 91
AIDS, 27n1, 38, 42, 50, 89
Anastasius, Emperor, 154
Aquinas, Thomas, 45, 47, 144, 152, 156, 158, 163, 178, 185
Aristotle, 45, 47, 110
Ashley, Benedict M., OP, 101, 181-82

Bacik, James, 177
Bailey, Derrick Sherwin, 6, 21
Ballot Measure 9 (M9) (Oregon), 130-33
Baum, Gregory, 185
Bayer, Ronald, 18
Beatty, Robert, 44
Bernardin, Joseph, Cardinal, x, 69-76, 79, 83-84, 93, 124, 141
Bieber, Irving, 40
bigotry, 33, 141
birth control, 156-60, 162-63
Blackmun, Justice, 32
Boswell, John, 33
Bouchard, Charles, OP, 179
Brickner, Balfour, 64, 69
Briggs, John, 78, 85
Briggs Initiative, 78-79, 85, 92, 134
Bryant, Anita, 76-78, 85
Brydon, Charles, 79

Burger, Justice, 32-33

Caesar, 142
civil rights movement, 182
Connolly, Thomas, Bishop, 131-33
conscience, 170-71
contraception. *See* birth control
Cooke, Terence, Cardinal, 65
Cordovan, John, 85
Council on Religion and the Homosexual (CRH), 20-21
Courage, 97
Crowley, Robert Warren, 20
Cruikshank, Margaret, 5, 26
Cushing, Richard, Cardinal, 157-58, 160, 162

Daughters of Bilitis (DOB), 14-15, 20
damnation factor, in Catholic sexual ethics, 112-13, 115
Dei verbum (Vatican II), 106
Delumeau, Jean, 113
D'Emilio, John, 8, 9, 14, 16
development of Catholic social teaching, 119n3
Diagnostic and Statistical Manual of Mental Disorders, 19
Dignitatis humanae (DH) (Vatican II), 144, 147, 157, 163, 171-74, 184
Dignity, viii, 24
Dimitrios, Patriarch, 121
discrimination, 138
dualism, 153-54
Dyer, Kate, 31

East, Bernard, 112
Egan, Timothy, 132

Fallwell, Jerry, 28, 75n42, 128
Feinstein, Dianne, 87, 91
feminism, white, 81
Flach, Carl, 132
Francoeur, Robert, 109-10
Freud, Sigmund, 41, 41n56
Friends, 23

Gaudium et spes (Vatican II), 171
gay liberation movement (GLM), 3, 27-28, 42, 47, 63, 74, 76, 116, 178-79
Gays/Justice (Mohr), 51
Gelasius I, Pope, 154-55
Giles of Rome, 155
global human rights, ix
Gonsalves, Milton, 33, 44-51, 58, 94, 144
Grippo, Dan, 107-8
guilt culture, 113
Guindon, André, 109-11
Gumbleton, Thomas, Bishop, 134

Hanigan, James P., 67, 110
Harvey, John F., 96-99
Hay, Harry, 11, 13
Hillsborough, Helen, 85
Hillsborough, Robert, 85-86
Hollenbach, David, SJ, 52, 127, 172
homophobia, 136
homosexuality, 3; an aberration, viii, ix, 34-36, 45, 100-101, 114, 128; and adoption rights, 127; and the Bible, 105-8; and CDF, 123-29; condition and act, 97-98; constitutional and situational, 98-99, 184; decriminalized, 178; interim nature, 23; and the military, 29-30; right, ix; a sickness, 13
Homosexuality and American Psychiatry (Bayer), 18
Homosexuality and the Western Christian Tradition (Bailey), 6, 21
The Homosexual Person (Harvey), 96

Hooker, Evelyn, 18
Human Sexuality: New Directions in American Catholic Thought (Catholic Theological Society of America), 117

Illinois Gay and Lesbian Task Force, 70, 74
integrism, 173, 177-78
intolerance, 167-68. *See also* tolerance
Isay, Richard, 40
Is Christ the Only Way? (Heim), 320

Jefferson, Thomas, 154
Jesus Christ, 42, 142, 154, 166
John of Paris, 153
John of Salisbury, 155
John XXIII, Pope, 70, 121, 175
John Courtney Murray and the American Civil Conversation (ACC) (Hunt and Grasso), 156
Joyce, James, 112-13, 115
justice, 47-49, 51; a univocal term, 180-83

Kameny, Frank, 17
Karols, Ken, 30
Keane, Philip, 67
Kinsey, Alfred Charles, 40
Kirk, Marshall, 4-5
Klopfer, Bruno, 19
Knauer, Peter, 139
Koch, Edward, 65, 68
Krikorian, Mesron, Bishop, 220
Kronenberg, Anne, 86

The Ladder, 15
Laghi, Pio, Archbishop, 68
Leo XIII, Pope, 177
lesbianism, 34 "Letter to the Bishops of the Catholic Church on the Pastoral Care of Homosexual Persons" (PCHP), 72, 90n104, 96, 100, 102, 105-8, 109, 111, 116-18, 120, 128, 182
Levada, William, Bishop, 131-33

Levin, Yehuda, 68-69 Lively, Scott, 130

Luckey, William R., 152-53

Lutheran Church in America (LCA), 23

Lynch, Bernard, 69

Lynch, John J., SJ, 162

Lyon, Phyllis, 14

Madsen, Hunter, 4-5

Magnificat, 62

Magnuson, Roger, 33, 37-44, 59, 94

Mahoney, John, 119

Marcus, Eric, 12-13

Martin, Del, 14, 20

masturbation, 114

Mattacine Society (MS), 8, 9-14, 16-17, 20

McCarthy, Joseph, 15

McClory, Robert, 141

McCormick, Richard A., SJ, 67, 139-40

McDonald, Michael A., 30-31

McManamin, Francis G., 158

Milk, Harvey, 86-87

Mill, John Stuart, 57

Mohr, Richard, 33, 51-58, 75n42, 94

monism, 153-54

de Montargon, Hyacinthe, 113

Moore, Arthur, 65, 68

Moore, Paul, Jr., 64

Moran, Gabriel, 22-23

morality vs. legality, 158-159, 162, 179

Moravian Church, 23

Morris, Charles, 87

Moscone, George, 85-87

Mugavero, Francis, Bishop, 66-68, 65n7

Murray, John Courtney (JCM), xii, 144; in accordance with the thought of Thomas Aquinas, 151, 152-53; on church-state relationship, 147-63; on religious freedom, 164-77

Navarro-Valls, Joaquin, 123, 135

Nazism, 164

Neuhaus, Richard John, 153

The New Testament and Homosexuality (Scroggs), 22

New Ways Ministry (NWM), 24, 123, 127, 129

North American Man/Boy Love Association (NAMBLA), 43

Novak, Michael, 33, 34-36, 59

O'Brien, David J., 119

O'Connell, William, Cardinal, 157

O'Connor, John, Cardinal, x, 64-69, 83, 92, 94, 96, 124, 183

ONE, 16 On Liberty (Mill), 57

Oregon Citizens Alliance (OCA), 130, 136

Pacem in terris (PT) (Pope John XXIII), 70, 175-76

Paul, Saint, 106-7

Paul VI, Pope, 121, 177

Pavan, Pietro, 172, 175

pederasty, 22, 128

Persona Humana (PH), 98-99, 102, 130

Peter, Saint, 149

philosphy, 170

Pilarczyk, Daniel, Archbishop, 141

Pius IX, Pope, 168-69

Plato, 109

Plongeron, Bernard, 121

Pomeroy, Wardell, 40

Posner, Richard, 41, 43, 49, 137

privacy, 57

Quindlen, Anna, 132

Quinn, John R., Archbishop, x, 76-88, 93-94, 96, 103, 107, 122, 124, 134-35, 140, 144; on gay and lesbian partnership laws, 91-92; violence against homosexuals, 88-90

Refoulé, François, 121

religious freedom, 164-77

Right and Reason (Gonsalves), 45-46

Rivera, Ray, 7-8

Robertson, Pat, 130

Rowland, Chuck, 11, 12

Rutledge, Leigh, 86

Santayana, 177
Sacred Congregation for the Doctrine of the Faith (CDF), 118, 123, 135-36; intervention on gay rights, 123-29,
Sarbin, Ted, 30
Save Our Children (SOC), 77, 83
Scroggs, Robin, 22
Schroeder, Patricia, 31
Segers, Mary, 156, 159-62
Selwyn, Herb, 16
sex, private, 53-54
The Sexual Creators (Guindon), 110
sexuality, private, 53-54; and the transmission of Life, 98, 111, 115
Shanley, Mildred, 66
Shannon, William, 103
Shilts, Randy, 85
Sin and Fear (Delumeau), 113
Socarides, Charles, 40
sodomy, 25, 31, 31n20, 32, 53, 178, 178n1
"Some Considerations Concerning the Response to Legislative Proposals on the Non-Discrimination of Homosexual Persons" (SCC), ix, 123-29, 183; critique of, 130-40
"Spirituality, Morality, and Our Political Life" (Bouchard), 179
Stolz, Jim, 89

Stonewall Inn, 7-9, 88
Studds, Gerry S., 31
Sullivan, Joseph, Bishop, 66, 69
Summerville, Cheryl, 29

Tallmij, Billie, 14, 20
Taylor, G. Rattray, 6
Taylor, Jerry, 85
Thurston, Thomas, 10, 18
tolerance, 149-50, 165-66, 173. *See also* intolerance
Tuohey, John, 138, 140
Turque, Bill, 28

United Universalist Association, 23
"Universal Declaration of the Rights of Man" (UN), 121

Varvaro, William, 66
Vatican II, 122, 184
The Vatican and Homosexuality (Gramick and Furey), 181

Waldheim, Kurt, 121
We Hold These Truths (JCM), 154-55
Welch, Linda, 131
White, Dan, 86-88
White, Justice, 32
Williams, Roger, 154
world news, classical (archetypical) and historical (evolutionary, epigenetic), 109-10

Research Methods
with Gay, Lesbian, Bisexual,
and Transgender Populations

Research Methods with Gay, Lesbian, Bisexual, and Transgender Populations has been co-published simultaneously as *Journal of Gay & Lesbian Social Services*, Volume 15, Numbers 1/2 2003.

KT-377-711

The *Journal of Gay & Lesbian Social Services* Monographic "Separates"

Below is a list of " separates," which in serials librarianship means a special issue simultaneously published as a special journal issue or double-issue *and* as a "separate" hardbound monograph. (This is a format which we also call a "DocuSerial.")

"Separates" are published because specialized libraries or professionals may wish to purchase a specific thematic issue by itself in a format which can be separately cataloged and shelved, as opposed to purchasing the journal on an on-going basis. Faculty members may also more easily consider a "separate" for classroom adoption.

"Separates" are carefully classified separately with the major book jobbers so that the journal tie-in can be noted on new book order slips to avoid duplicate purchasing.

You may wish to visit Haworth's Website at . . .

Http://www.HaworthPress.com

. . . to search our online catalog for complete tables of contents of these separates and related publications.

You may also call 1-800-HAWORTH (outside US/Canada: 607-722-5857), or Fax 1-800-895-0582 (outside US/Canada: 607-771-0012), or e-mail at:

getinfo@haworthpressinc.com

Research Methods with Gay, Lesbian, Bisexual, and Transgender Populations, edited by William Meezan, MSW, DSW, and James I. Martin, MSW, PhD (Vol. 15, No. 1/2 2003). *"Must reading For all researchers concerned about vulnerable and stigmatized groups. . . . The authors raise significant methodological and ethical issues that researchers studying any vulnerable group, especially LGBT populations, must address. An excellent supplement to any social work or social science research class." (Wynne Sandra Korr, PhD, Dean and Professor, School of Social Work, University of Illinois at Urbana Champaign)*

From Here to Diversity: The Social Impact of Lesbian and Gay Issues in Education in Australia and New Zealand, edited by Kerry H. Robinson, PhD, MA, BA, DiPEd, Jude Irwin, BSW, MA, and Tania Ferfolja, MA, BEd (Vol. 14, No. 2, 2002). *"Long awaited . . . challenges the rigid binaries that are produced and reproduced through schooling. . . . A collection that will do much to keep anti-homophobia work on the educational agenda. Required reading for educators who must take seriously their responsibility to enhance the quality of school life for sexual minority students." (June Larkin, PhD, Director of Equity Studies, University of Toronto)*

Midlife and Aging in Gay America, edited by Douglas C. Kimmel, PhD, and Dawn Lundy Martin, MA (Vol. 13, No. 4, 2001). *"Magnificent. This is a topic whose time has finally come. This book fills a gaping hole in the GLBT literature. . . . Each chapter is a gem. With its coverage of elder GLBTs who are vision impaired and HIV positive as well as an important chapter on GLBT retirement planning, it makes the literature human and integrated." (Mark Pope, EdD, Associate Professor of Counseling and Family Therapy, University of Missouri, St. Louis)*

From Hate Crimes to Human Rights: A Tribute to Matthew Shepard, edited by Mary E. Swigonski, PhD, LCSW, Robin S. Mama, PhD, and Kelly Ward, LCSW (Vol. 13, No. 1/2, 2001). *An unsparing look at prejudice and hate crimes against LGBT individuals, in such diverse areas as international law, the child welfare system, minority cultures, and LGBT relationships.*

Working-Class Gay and Bisexual Men, edited by George Alan Appleby, MSW, PhD (Vol. 12, No. 3/4, 2001). Working-Class Gay and Bisexual Men *is a powerfully persuasive work of scholarship with broad-ranging implications. Social workers, policymakers, AIDS activists, and anyone else concerned with the lives of gay and bisexual men will find this informative study an essential tool for designing effective programs.*

Gay Men and Childhood Sexual Trauma: Integrating the Shattered Self, edited by James Cassese, MSW, CSW (Vol. 12, No. 1/2, 2000). *"An excellent, thought-provoking collection of essays. Therapists who work with gay men will be grateful to have such a comprehensive resource for dealing with sexual trauma." (Rik Isensee, LCSW, Author of* Reclaiming Your Life*)*

William Meezan, MSW, DSW
James I. Martin, MSW, PhD
Editors

Research Methods with Gay, Lesbian, Bisexual, and Transgender Populations

Research Methods with Gay, Lesbian, Bisexual, and Transgender Populations has been co-published simultaneously as *Journal of Gay & Lesbian Social Services*, Volume 15, Numbers 1/2 2003.

*Pre-publication
REVIEWS,
COMMENTARIES,
EVALUATIONS . . .*

"MUST READING for all researchers concerned about vulnerable and stigmatized groups. . . . The authors raise significant methodological and ethical issues that researchers studying any vulnerable group, especially LGBT populations, must address. AN EXCELLENT SUPPLEMENT TO ANY SOCIAL WORK OR SOCIAL SCIENCE RESEARCH CLASS."

Wynne Sandra Korr, PhD
*Dean and Professor
School of Social Work
University of Illinois
at Urbana Champaign*

Harrington Park Press

Midlife Lesbian Relationships: Friends, Lovers, Children, and Parents, edited by Marcy R. Adelman, PhD (Vol. 11, No. 2/3, 2000). *"A careful and sensitive look at the various relationships of [lesbians at midlife] inside and outside of the therapy office. A useful addition to a growing body of literature." (Ellyn Kaschak, PhD, Professor of Psychology, San José State University, California, and Editor of the feminist quarterly journal* Women & Therapy)

Social Services with Transgendered Youth, edited by Gerald P. Mallon, DSW (Vol. 10, No. 3/4, 1999). *"A well-articulated book that provides valuable information about a population that has been virtually ignored. . . ." (Carol T. Tully, PhD, Associate Professor, Tulane University, School of Social Work, New Orleans, Louisiana)*

Queer Families, Common Agendas: Gay People, Lesbians, and Family Values, edited by T. Richard Sullivan, PhD (Vol. 10, No. 1, 1999). *Examines the real life experience of those affected by current laws and policies regarding homosexual families.*

Lady Boys, Tom Boys, Rent Boys: Male and Female Homosexualities in Contemporary Thailand, edited by Peter A. Jackson, PhD, and Gerard Sullivan, PhD (Vol. 9, No. 2/3, 1999). *"Brings to life issues and problems of interpreting sexual and gender identities in contemporary Thailand." (Nerida M. Cook, PhD, Lecturer in Sociology, Department of Sociology and Social Work, University of Tasmania, Australia)*

Working with Gay Men and Lesbians in Private Psychotherapy Practice, edited by Christopher J. Alexander, PhD (Vol. 8, No. 4, 1998). *"Rich with information that will prove especially invaluable to therapists planning to or recently having begun to work with lesbian and gay clients in private practice." (Michael Shernoff, MSW, Private Practice, NYC; Faculty, Columbia University School of Social Work)*

Violence and Social Injustice Against Lesbian, Gay and Bisexual People, edited by Lacey M. Sloan, PhD, and Nora S. Gustavsson, PhD (Vol. 8, No. 3, 1998). *"An important and timely book that exposes the multilevel nature of violence against gay, lesbian, bisexual, and transgender people." (Dorothy Van Soest, DSW, Associate Dean, School of Social Work, University of Texas at Austin)*

The HIV-Negative Gay Man: Developing Strategies for Survival and Emotional Well-Being, edited by Steven Ball, MSW, ACSW (Vol. 8, No. 1, 1998). *"Essential reading for anyone working with HIV-negative gay men." (Walt Odets, PhD, Author,* In the Shadow of the Epidemic: Being HIV-Negative in the Age of AIDS; *Clinical Psychologist, private practice, Berkeley, California)*

School Experiences of Gay and Lesbian Youth: The Invisible Minority, edited by Mary B. Harris, PhD (Vol. 7, No. 4, 1998). *"Our schools are well served when authors such as these have the courage to highlight problems that schools deny and to advocate for students whom schools make invisible." (Gerald Unks, Professor, School of Education, University of North Carolina at Chapel Hill; Editor,* The Gay Teen.*) Provides schools with helpful suggestions for becoming places that welcome gay and lesbian students and, therefore, better serve the needs of all students.*

Rural Gays and Lesbians: Building on the Strengths of Communities, edited by James Donald Smith, ACSW, LCSW, and Ronald J. Mancoske, BSCW, DSW (Vol. 7, No. 3, 1998). *"This informative and well-written book fills a major gap in the literature and should be widely read." (James Midgley, PhD, Harry and Riva Specht Professor of Public Social Services and Dean, School of Social Welfare, University of California at Berkeley)*

Gay Widowers: Life After the Death of a Partner, edited by Michael Shernoff, MSW, ACSW (Vol. 7, No. 2, 1997). *"This inspiring book is not only for those who have experienced the tragedy of losing a partner–it's for every gay man who loves another." (Michelangelo Signorile, author,* Life Outside*)*

Gay and Lesbian Professionals in the Closet: Who's In, Who's Out, and Why, edited by Teresa DeCrescenzo, MSW, LCSW (Vol. 6, No. 4, 1997). *"A gripping example of the way the closet cripples us and those we try to serve." (Virginia Uribe, PhD, Founder, Project 10 Outreach to Gay and Lesbian Youth, Los Angeles Unified School District)*

Two Spirit People: American Indian Lesbian Women and Gay Men, edited by Lester B. Brown, PhD (Vol. 6, No. 2, 1997). *"A must read for educators, social workers, and other providers of social and mental health services." (Wynne DuBray, Professor, Division of Social Work, California State University)*

Social Services for Senior Gay Men and Lesbians, edited by Jean K. Quam, PhD, MSW (Vol. 6, No. 1, 1997). *"Provides a valuable overview of social service issues and practice with elder gay men and lesbians." (Outword)*

Men of Color: A Context for Service to Homosexually Active Men, edited by John F. Longres, PhD (Vol. 5, No. 2/3, 1996). *"An excellent book for the 'helping professions.' " (Feminist Bookstore News)*

Health Care for Lesbians and Gay Men: Confronting Homophobia and Heterosexism, edited by K. Jean Peterson, DSW (Vol. 5, No. 1, 1996). *"Essential reading for those concerned with the quality of health care services." (Etcetera)*

Sexual Identity on the Job: Issues and Services, edited by Alan L. Ellis, PhD, and Ellen D. B. Riggle, PhD (Vol. 4, No. 4, 1996). *"Reveals a critical need for additional research to address the many questions left unanswered or answered unsatisfactorily by existing research." (Sex Roles: A Journal of Research) "A key resource for addressing sexual identity concerns and issues in your workplace." (Outlines)*

Human Services for Gay People: Clinical and Community Practice, edited by Michael Shernoff, MSW, ACSW (Vol. 4, No. 2, 1996). *"This very practical book on clinical and community practice issues belongs on the shelf of every social worker, counselor, or therapist working with lesbians and gay men." (Gary A. Lloyd, PhD, ACSW, BCD, Professor and Coordinator, Institute for Research and Training in HIV/AIDS Counseling, School of Social Work, Tulane University)*

Violence in Gay and Lesbian Domestic Partnerships, edited by Claire M. Renzetti, PhD, and Charles Harvey Miley, PhD (Vol. 4, No. 1, 1996). *"A comprehensive guidebook for service providers and community and church leaders." (Small Press Magazine)*

Gays and Lesbians in Asia and the Pacific: Social and Human Services, edited by Gerard Sullivan, PhD, and Laurence Wai-Teng Leong, PhD (Vol. 3, No. 3, 1995). *"Insights in this book can provide an understanding of these cultures and provide an opportunity to better understand your own." (The Lavender Lamp)*

Lesbians of Color: Social and Human Services, edited by Hilda Hidalgo, PhD, ACSW (Vol. 3, No. 2, 1995). *"An illuminating and helpful guide for readers who wish to increase their understanding of and sensitivity toward lesbians of color and the challenges they face." (Black Caucus of the ALA Newsletter)*

Lesbian Social Services: Research Issues, edited by Carol T. Tully, PhD, MSW (Vol. 3, No. 1, 1995). *"Dr. Tully challenges us to reexamine theoretical conclusions that relate to lesbians. . . A must read." (The Lavender Lamp)*

HIV Disease: Lesbians, Gays and the Social Services, edited by Gary A. Lloyd, PhD, ACSW, and Mary Ann Kuszelewicz, MSW, ACSW (Vol. 2, No. 3/4, 1995). *"A wonderful guide to working with people with AIDS. A terrific meld of political theory and hands-on advice, it is essential, inspiring reading for anyone fighting the pandemic or assisting those living with it." (Small Press)*

Addiction and Recovery in Gay and Lesbian Persons, edited by Robert J. Kus, PhD, RN (Vol. 2, No. 1, 1995). *"Readers are well-guided through the multifaceted, sometimes confusing, and frequently challenging world of the gay or lesbian drug user." (Drug and Alcohol Review)*

Helping Gay and Lesbian Youth: New Policies, New Programs, New Practice, edited by Teresa DeCrescenzo, MSW, LCSW (Vol. 1, No. 3/4, 1994). *"Insightful and up-to-date, this handbook covers several topics relating to gay and lesbian adolescents . . . It is must reading for social workers, educators, guidance counselors, and policymakers." (Journal of Social Work Education)*

Social Services for Gay and Lesbian Couples, edited by Lawrence A. Kurdek, PhD (Vol. 1, No. 2, 1994). *"Many of the unique issues confronted by gay and lesbian couples are addressed here." (Ambush Magazine)*

Research Methods
with Gay, Lesbian, Bisexual,
and Transgender Populations

William Meezan, MSW, DSW
James I. Martin, MSW, PhD
Editors

Research Methods with Gay, Lesbian, Bisexual, and Transgender Populations has been co-published simultaneously as *Journal of Gay & Lesbian Social Services*, Volume 15, Numbers 1/2 2003.

Harrington Park Press
The Haworth Social Work Practice Press
Imprints of
The Haworth Press, Inc.
New York • London • Oxford

Published by

Harrington Park Press®, 10 Alice Street, Binghamton, NY 13904-1580 USA

Harrington Park Press® is an imprint of The Haworth Press, Inc., 10 Alice Street, Binghamton, NY 13904-1580 USA.

Research Methods with Gay, Lesbian, Bisexual, and Transgender Populations has been co-published simultaneously as *Journal of Gay & Lesbian Social Services*™, Volume 15, Numbers 1/2 2003.

Cover design by Marylouise E. Doyle

Library of Congress Cataloging-in-Publication Data

Research methods with gay, lesbian, bisexual, and transgender populations / William Meezan, James Martin, editors.
     p. cm.
     "Co-published simultaneously aas Journal of gay & lesbian social services, volume 15, numbers 1/2 2003."
Includes bibliographical references and index.
     ISBN 1-56023-320-6 (hard : alk. paper) – ISBN 1-56023-321-4 (pbk : alk. paper)
     1. Social work with gays. 2. Social work with lesbians. 3. Social service–Research–Methodology. 4. Gays–Research–Methodology. 5. Lesbians–Research–Methodology. 6. Bisexuals–Research–Methodology. 7. Transsexuals–Research–Methodology. I. Meezan, William. II. Martin, James I. III. Journal of gay & lesbian social services.
  HV1449 .R47 2002
  362.8–dc21
                                     2002014181

Indexing, Abstracting & Website/Internet Coverage

This section provides you with a list of major indexing & abstracting services. That is to say, each service began covering this periodical during the year noted in the right column. Most Websites which are listed below have indicated that they will either post, disseminate, compile, archive, cite or alert their own Website users with research-based content from this work. (This list is as current as the copyright date of this publication.)

Abstracting, Website/Indexing Coverage . . . . Year When Coverage Began

- *caredata CD: the social and community care database*
  <www.scie.org.uk> **1994**

- *CNPIEC Reference Guide: Chinese National Directory*
  of Foreign Periodicals **1995**

- *Contemporary Women's Issues* **1998**

- *Criminal Justice Abstracts* **1997**

- *ERIC Clearinghouse on Urban Education (ERIC/CUE)* **1995**

- *Family Index Database <www.familyscholar. com>* **2001**

- *Family Violence & Sexual Assault Bulletin* **1999**

- *FINDEX <www.publist.com>* **1999**

- *Gay & Lesbian Abstracts <www.nisc.com>* **1999**

- *GenderWatch <www.slinfo.com>* **1999**

- *HOMODOK/"Relevant" Bibliographic Database* **1995**

- *IBZ International Bibliography of Periodical Literature*
  <www.saur.de> **1996**

(continued)

- *IGLSS Abstracts <http://www.iglss.org>* **2000**
- *Index Guide to College Journals (core list compiled by integrating*
  48 indexes frequently used to support undergraduate programs
  in small to medium-sized libraries) **1999**
- *Index to Periodical Articles Related to Law* **1994**
- *OCLC Public Affairs Information Service <www.pais.org>* **1995**
- *Psychological Abstracts (PsycINFO) <www.apa.org>* **2001**
- *Referativnyi Zhurnal (Abstracts Journal of the*
  All-Russian Institute of Scientific and Technical Information–
  in Russian) **1994**
- *Social Services Abstracts <www.csa.com>* **1999**
- *Social Work Abstracts*
  <www.silverplatter.com/catalog/swab.htm> **1994**
- *Sociological Abstracts (SA) <www.csa.com>* **1994**
- *Studies on Women Abstracts* **1994**
- *Violence and Abuse Abstracts: A Review of Current*
  Literature on Interpersonal Violence (VAA) **1995**

Special Bibliographic Notes related to special journal issues
(separates) and indexing/abstracting:

- indexing/abstracting services in this list will also cover material in any "separate" that is co-published simultaneously with Haworth's special thematic journal issue or DocuSerial. Indexing/abstracting usually covers material at the article/chapter level.
- monographic co-editions are intended for either non-subscribers or libraries which intend to purchase a second copy for their circulating collections.
- monographic co-editions are reported to all jobbers/wholesalers/approval plans. The source journal is listed as the "series" to assist the prevention of duplicate purchasing in the same manner utilized for books-in-series.
- to facilitate user/access services all indexing/abstracting services are encouraged to utilize the co-indexing entry note indicated at the bottom of the first page of each article/chapter/contribution.
- this is intended to assist a library user of any reference tool (whether print, electronic, online, or CD-ROM) to locate the monographic version if the library has purchased this version but not a subscription to the source journal.
- individual articles/chapters in any Haworth publication are also available through the Haworth Document Delivery Service (HDDS).

Research Methods with Gay, Lesbian, Bisexual, and Transgender Populations

CONTENTS

About the Contributors   xiii

Foreword: Toward the Future of Research on Lesbian, Gay,
Bisexual, and Transgender Populations   xix
Anthony R. D'Augelli

Acknowledgments   xxiii

Exploring Current Themes in Research on Gay, Lesbian,
Bisexual and Transgender Populations   1
William Meezan
James I. Martin

When Interviewing "Family": Maximizing the Insider Advantage
in the Qualitative Study of Lesbians and Gay Men   15
Michael C. LaSala

Researching Gay and Lesbian Domestic Violence:
The Journey of a Non-LGBT Researcher   31
Joan C. McClennen

Empowering Gay and Lesbian Caregivers and Uncovering
Their Unique Experiences Through the Use
of Qualitative Methods   47
Kristina M. Hash
Elizabeth P. Cramer

Methodological Issues in Conducting Community-Based
Health and Social Services Research Among Urban Black
and African American LGBT Populations   65
Darrell P. Wheeler

Research with Gay Drug Users and the Interface with HIV:
   Current Methodological Issues for Social Work Research   79
    E. Michael Gorman

Self-Disclosure Stress: Trauma as an Example of an Intervening
   Variable in Research with Lesbian Women   95
    Marian Swindell
    Jo Pryce

Dimensions of Lesbian Identity During Adolescence
   and Young Adulthood   109
    Stephanie K. Swann
    Jeane W. Anastas

8,000 Miles and Still Counting . . . Reaching Gay, Lesbian
   and Bisexual Adolescents for Research   127
    Diane E. Elze

A Study of Sampling in Research in the Field of Lesbian
   and Gay Studies   147
    Gerard Sullivan
    Warren Losberg

Matching AIDS Service Organizations' Philosophy of Service
   Provision with a Compatible Style of Program Evaluation   163
    Sarah-Jane Dodd
    William Meezan

Applying Ethical Standards to Research and Evaluations
   Involving Lesbian, Gay, Bisexual, and Transgender
   Populations   181
    James I. Martin
    William Meezan

Index   203

ABOUT THE EDITORS

William Meezan, MSW, DSW, is the Marion Elizabeth Blue Professor of Children and Families at the University of Michigan School of Social Work, where he teaches research and policy in the Children and Youth concentration. He has served on the faculty of the Jane Addams College of Social Work at the University of Illinois at Chicago, and as the John Milner Professor of Child Welfare at the University of Southern California School of Social Work. He has been both a Fulbright Scholar in Lithuania and a Congressional Science Fellow.

Dr. Meezan is the recipient of the Outstanding Research Award from the Society for Social Work and Research, and currently serves as the Secretary of that organization. His current research includes a number of evaluations of programs that serve children and youth in Wayne County (Detroit), Michigan. His work has appeared in such journals as *Social Service Review, Children and Youth Services Review, Child Welfare, Research on Social Work Practice, Families in Society, Social Work with Groups, Administration in Social Work,* and *The Future of Children.* In addition, he has co-authored numerous monographs and five books: *Family Preservation and Family Functioning; Evaluating Family-Based Services; Care and Commitment: Foster Parent Adoption Decisions; Child Welfare: Current Dilemmas–Future Directions;* and *Adoptions Without Agencies: A Study of Independent Adoptions.*

Dr. Meezan serves or has served on the editorial boards of *Social Work, Social Work Research,* the *Journal of Social Service Research, Children and Youth Services Review,* the *Family Preservation Journal,* the *Journal of Gay and Lesbian Social Services,* and *Reflections: Narratives of Professional Helping.* He has also been a consultant to numerous social agencies and national organizations, and a number of schools of social work.

James I. Martin, MSW, PhD, is Associate Professor of Social Work at New York University, where he teaches practice and research. He previously served on the faculty of the University of Texas at Arlington.

Dr. Martin's research interests focus on the impact of self-esteem instability, coping, and other interpersonal problems, HIV prevention efforts among gay men, and other mental health issues among lesbian, gay, bisexual, and transgender populations. His work has appeared in a number of edited volumes and in *Health & Social Work*, *Social Work Research*, *Psychological Reports*, *Journal of Gay & Lesbian Social Services*, and *Focus: A Guide to AIDS Research and Counseling*. He is the co-editor of *Lesbian, Gay, Bisexual, and Transgender Issues in Social Work: A Comprehensive Bibliography with Annotations* (CSWE, 2001), and the co-author of the book *Lesbian, Gay, Bisexual Youths and Adults: Knowledge for Human Services Practice* (Sage, 1998). He serves on the editorial board of the *Journal of Gay & Lesbian Social Services*.

In addition, Dr. Martin has over 20 years of experience in clinical supervision and practice with lesbians and gay men. He is Co-Chair of the CSWE Commission on Sexual Orientation & Gender Expression, and an elected member of the 2002 NASW Delegate Assembly. He has been an evaluation consultant to the Lesbian, Gay, Bisexual, and Transgender Community Center of New York, PWA Health Group, and Chicago Teachers' Center, and a practice and supervision consultant to agencies in Dallas and Los Angeles.

About the Contributors

Jeane W. Anastas, PhD, is Professor at the Shirley M. Ehrenkranz School of Social Work at New York University. A full-time social work educator since 1980, she formerly served on the faculties of Simmons College and Smith College School of Social Work. She is the co-author of *Not Just a Passing Phase: Social Work with Lesbian, Gay and Bisexual People,* and the author of *Research Design for Social Work and Human Services.* Her recent articles have appeared in the *Journal of Social Work Education* and the *Journal of Gay & Lesbian Social Services.* Dr. Anastas serves on the editorial boards of *Affilia: The Journal of Women in Social Work* and the *Journal of Social Work Practice in the Addictions,* and as a consulting editor to *Social Work.*

Elizabeth P. Cramer, MSW, PhD, LCSW, ACSW, is Associate Professor in the School of Social Work at Virginia Commonwealth University. Her primary practice and scholarship areas are lesbian and gay issues, domestic violence, and group work. Dr. Cramer has published a number of journal articles and book chapters on educational strategies to reduce the homophobia of social work students, and she has presented on the topic at national conferences. For the past two years, Dr. Cramer has facilitated a group on sexuality and gender issues for lesbian, bisexual, trans, and questioning women at a residential substance abuse treatment program. Dr. Cramer has served as a peer reviewer for the *Journal of Gay and Lesbian Medical Association* and *Criminal Justice and Behavior.* As a commissioner on the CSWE Commission on Sexual Orientation & Gender Expression, Dr. Cramer developed and is responsible for the Mentorship Project, which matches LGBT senior faculty mentors with LGBT junior faculty members and doctoral students.

Sarah-Jane (SJ) Dodd, MSEd, MSW, PhD, is Assistant Professor and Coordinator of the Advanced Standing Program at the Hunter College School of Social Work. Her practice experience includes individual and group work within AIDS Service Organizations. She has provided evaluation workshops and consultation for a variety of health and human service agencies. Her current research focuses on the role of social workers in ethical decision-making in hospital settings. Collaborative articles have been published in *Health and Social Work, Employee Assistance Quarterly,* and the *Social Policy Journal.*

Diane E. Elze, MSSA, PhD, is Assistant Professor of Social Work at the George Warren Brown School of Social Work at Washington University, where she teaches foundation courses in human behavior and human diversity and practice courses focusing on youth and GLBT issues. Her research areas include risk and protective factors for gay, lesbian, and bisexual youths, HIV prevention interventions, and the mental health needs of adolescents with HIV infection. Her practice experience has included direct services, administration, and community education and training in areas of sexual assault and domestic violence; runaway and homeless youths; HIV case management; crisis intervention; advocacy on behalf of people with disabilities; GLBT youths; and HIV prevention for adolescents. Dr. Elze serves on the CSWE Commission on Sexual Orientation & Gender Expression and provides consultation and training to community agencies and service providers on GLBT youth issues. Her recent publications have appeared in *AIDS Education and Prevention,* the *International Journal of Adolescent Medicine & Health,* the *Journal of Lesbian Studies,* the *Journal of Psychoactive Drugs,* and *Children & Schools.*

E. Michael Gorman, MSW, MPH, PhD, is Assistant Professor at San Jose State University's College of Social Work, where he teaches research and social policy and chairs the MSW policy practice sequence. He is Principal Investigator of an NIDA-funded research project addressing the interface of HIV and drug abuse primarily among gay men. He is a consulting editor for *Social Work Research,* and serves on the editorial advisory boards of the *Journal of Social Work Practice and the Addictions* and the *Journal of Gay & Lesbian Social Services.* He also serves on the CSWE Commission on Sexual Orientation & Gender Expression. Dr. Gorman has worked in HIV/AIDS for 20 years at the University of Washington, the University of California, Berkeley, RAND, and the U.S. Centers for Disease Control and Prevention. He serves on the National AIDS Update Conference Planning Committee, and has served on the Washington State HIV Prevention Council and the NIDA Community Epidemiology Work Group. His research and policy interests include HIV/AIDS, substance abuse, gerontology, and GLBT populations. Recent publications have appeared in the *Journal of Social Work Practice and Addictions* and the *Journal of Nursing and AIDS Care.* The latter article received the JNAC research award for 2000.

Kristina Hash, MSW, PhD, LCSW, is Assistant Professor in the Division of Social Work at West Virginia University. Prior to accepting this position, she was Research Coordinator in the Department of Internal Medicine at Virginia Commonwealth University, and taught Social Work and Social Justice in the MSW Program at that university. She also has experience working in home health, residential independent living, continuing education, and research and program evaluation. She has been involved in a number of community activities including work as a hospice volunteer, a volunteer for community service agencies serving older adults, and as a board member for a variety of social service organizations. Her research interests and publications focus on aging among gay men and lesbians, caregiving for persons with chronic illnesses, geriatric social work education, and home-based social work practice. Her publications have appeared or will soon appear in the *Journal of Gay & Lesbian Social Services* and the *Journal of Gerontological Social Work.*

Michael C. LaSala, MSW, PhD, LCSW, is Assistant Professor at the School of Social Work, Rutgers University, where he teaches courses in generalist practice, family practice, and diversity and oppression. Dr. LaSala's research interests are in the area of gay and lesbian couples and families. His most recent works have appeared in *Social Work Research, Families in Society, Family Process*, and the *Journal of Marital and Family Therapy*. Before joining the faculty at Rutgers, Dr. LaSala had 15 years of direct practice, supervision, and administration experience in social work, and he currently practices part-time, seeing gay and lesbian clients at the Institute for Personal Growth in Highland Park, NJ.

Warren Losberg, M. Behave. Health Sci., is a PhD candidate at the School of Policy and Practice, Faculty of Education, University of Sydney, Australia. He teaches drug and alcohol counseling, and research analysis and design in the Faculty of Health Sciences at the University of Sydney. His research interests in lesbian and gay studies include health promotion, rehabilitation of people living with HIV/AIDS, and party culture. Mr. Losberg's background is in clinical and research psychology, and he is registered to practice psychology in New South Wales, Australia.

Joan C. McClennen, MSW, PhD, is Associate Professor at the Southwest Missouri State University School of Social Work. Her research interests focus on family violence, and over the last five years she has concentrated on domestic violence between lesbian and gay male partners. She has received a college award for her research. Some of her recent publications on this topic include the edited book, *A Professional's Guide to Understanding Gay and Lesbian Domestic Violence: Understanding Practice Interventions*, and articles in the *Journal of Gay & Lesbian Social Services* and *Research on Social Work Practice.* Dr. McClennen has also authored several book chapters on child abuse and partner abuse, and she is presently working on a book about family violence. She serves on the editorial board of the *Journal of Gay & Lesbian Social Services.* She also serves on the CSWE Commission on Sexual Orientation & Gender Expression.

Jo Pryce, MSW, PhD, is Associate Professor at the University of Alabama School of Social Work. She teaches research methods, direct practice, human behavior in the social environment, and a new course on direct and secondary traumatic stress. Her current research includes studies on the prevention of HIV transmission, the prevention of secondary traumatic stress in child welfare workers, and on military, National Guard, and veteran families. Dr. Pryce's recent publications have appeared in *Social Work Research, Tulane Studies in Social Welfare,* and *Families in Society.* She serves as a reviewer for *Families in Society* and the *Journal of Social Service Research.* She also serves on the CSWE Commission on Sexual Orientation & Gender Expression. Dr. Pryce recently received the Eagan Award for excellence in teaching and a Silberman grant for a study of the National Guard family program.

Gerard Sullivan, Dip. Ed., MA, PhD, teaches research methods in the Faculty of Education at the University of Sydney, Australia. His research interests in lesbian and gay studies include civil rights, health issues, and the social construction of homosexuality in different cultural contexts. A board member of the Australian Centre for Lesbian and Gay Research, Dr. Sullivan is co-editor of *Gay and Lesbian Asia: Culture, Identity, Community; Multicultural Queer: Australian Narratives;* and *Lady Boys, Tom Boys, Rent Boys: Male and Female Homosexuality in Contemporary Thailand.* He has just completed work on a new volume, *Gay Men's Sexual Stories,* to be published by The Haworth Press, Inc.

Stephanie Swann, MSW, PhD, LCSW, is Assistant Professor at the University of Georgia School of Social Work and an adjunct faculty member at the Smith College School for Social Work. She teaches family theory, clinical social work practice, and clinical practice with GLBT clients. In addition, she founded YouthPride, a nonprofit social service organization that serves GLBT youth in the southeastern U.S. Dr. Swann has presented nationally in the areas of ethics and clinical treatment with GLBT adolescents. In addition to several book chapters, she has published articles in the *Journal of Gay & Lesbian Social Services* and *Community Psychologist.*

Marian L. Swindell, MSW, PhD, is Assistant Professor of Social Work at Mississippi State University, Meridian Campus. Her recent research focuses on the life experiences of Native American lesbian women and infidelity in same-sex relationships. Currently, she is revising her doctoral dissertation, *Individual Differences in Cognitive Stress Associated with Self-Disclosure,* for publication. She was recently inducted into the Omicron Chapter of Alpha Epsilon Lambda and The National Library of Congress, and she is the recipient of the Dr. Leslie J. Shellhase Endowed Scholarship Award. In addition to teaching and research, she does volunteer work with abandoned, neglected, and abused children in Meridian, MS.

Darrell P. Wheeler, MSW, MPH, PhD, ACSW, is a visiting faculty member at the Hunter College School of Social Work, where he teaches community organizing and social administration methods. Dr. Wheeler has previously held faculty positions at the University of North Carolina-Greensboro, Columbia University, and the University of California, San Francisco. Dr. Wheeler is actively involved in HIV/AIDS prevention work, and he is the co-principal investigator on a CDC-funded seroprevalence study of African American gay men. Dr. Wheeler has published numerous book chapters and articles in the *Journal of Multicultural Social Work Practice,* the *Journal of Public Health Management,* and the *Journal of Applied Social Sciences.* He serves on the editorial board of the *Journal of Gay & Lesbian Social Services.*

Foreword:
Toward the Future of Research on Lesbian, Gay, Bisexual, and Transgender Populations

Social science research on lesbian, gay, bisexual, and transgender (LGBT) people has a short history indeed. The first carefully conducted studies specifically focusing on gay men, those of psychologist Evelyn Hooker that were published in the late 1950s (e.g., Hooker, 1957), demonstrated the power of traditional, even simple, scientific methods to provoke a paradigm shift in the way sexual orientation is viewed. By showing that no differences in mental health functioning could be discerned when groups of gay and heterosexual men were compared on batteries of psychological tests, Hooker's work started a chain of events culminating in the removal of homosexuality from the psychiatric nomenclature in 1973. Prior to her work, the Kinsey reports (Kinsey, Pomeroy, & Martin, 1948; Kinsey, Pomeroy, Martin, & Gebhard, 1953) were the prominent sources for information on the prevalence of different sexual behaviors, but their impact on mental health practice was not to be as profound as the impact of Hooker's research.

The impact of the Kinsey reports on the cultural normalization of same-sex sexual orientation was relatively limited, despite their evidence that same-sex sexual behavior occurred more often than most Americans would like to have thought. In later studies published in the late 1970s and early 1980s (e.g., Bell & Weinberg, 1978), the Kinsey Institute reported on the *lives* of gay men and les-

[Haworth co-indexing entry note]: "Foreword: Toward the Future of Research on Lesbian, Gay, Bisexual, and Transgender Populations." D'Augelli, Anthony R. Co-published simultaneously in *Journal of Gay & Lesbian Social Services* (Harrington Park Press, an imprint of The Haworth Press, Inc.) Vol. 15, No. 1/2, 2003 pp. xxv-xxviii; and: *Research Methods with Gay, Lesbian, Bisexual, and Transgender Populations* (ed: William Meezan, and James I. Martin) Harrington Park Press, an imprint of The Haworth Press, Inc., 2003, pp. xix-xxii. Single or multiple copies of this article are available for a fee from The Haworth Document Delivery Service [1-800-HAWORTH, 9:00 a.m. - 5:00 p.m. (EST). E-mail address: getinfo@haworthpressinc.com].

xix

bians within a sociological framework, with sexual behavior only part of their focus. These reports culminated in *Sexual Preference: Its Development in Men and Women* (Bell, Weinberg, & Hammersmith, 1981), an important work not only because its findings purported to dethrone the early parental influence model of homosexual development, but also because it suggested a biological basis for sexual orientation, since major psychological precursors did not emerge from the data. Not surprisingly, given the lack of psychological research done on homosexuality, studies based on hypotheses about biological causes, most often genetic, became increasingly influential, especially in the early 1990s. The biological basis of sexual orientation remains hotly contested today, with the studies that gained the most attention (Hamer, Hu, Magnuson, Hu, & Pattatucci, 1993; LeVay, 1991) remaining unreplicated. Indeed, while it may be premature to say that the decades-long quest for the biological cause of same-sex desire had led to a dead-end in the face of the incredible diversity of human sexual expression, it is the case that the shift of research attention has been less on why people are LGBT, and more on how LGBT people live their lives (see D'Augelli & Patterson, 1995; Patterson & D'Augelli, 1998). In many areas of LGBT life, social science research has played an important role in the simple act of documentation. For instance, descriptive research on same-sex couples, on LGBT youth, and on older adults who are LGBT helped eradicate stereotypes that such people did not exist. In addition, these studies chipped away at persistent stereotypes, such as the view that LGBT relationships are intrinsically unstable and cannot last, that sexual orientation emerges in a meaningful way in one's 20s and not before, and that older LGBT people are lonely isolates.

Some issues faced in daily living by LGBT people as they progress through the life span have stimulated studies that have generated important findings. For instance, more work has been done on the relationships LGBT people have with their biological families, but increasingly the families LGBT people create on their own have been the subject of research inquiry.

Documenting behavior patterns, psychosocial challenges, and sources of resilience of men who have sex with men (many but not all who identify as gay or bisexual) has been an important contribution of social science research to the HIV epidemic. Although social science research during these decades has been overshadowed by biomedical research, without social science research we would know little about critical psychosocial risk factors for HIV infection, and we would not know which interventions were instrumental in forestalling more infections by successfully encouraging less risky behavior.

Much knowledge has accumulated on many aspects of LGBT lives, but much remains to be learned. Research in this area is fraught with methodological difficulties, and, for many, professional and personal barriers make involvement in this work difficult. Yet, we have made dramatic progress in this area in the last few years by extracting from large representative samples people who acknowledge same-sex sexual attractions, behavior, and/or identifications, and then comparing these (relatively few) people to the presumed heterosexual remainder of the samples. Studies of adolescents and adults using this basic approach are appearing with increasing frequency; such reports are possible only because of the inclusion of questions about sexual identity and behavior in research instruments. Once sexual orientation items are routinely collected as sociodemographic characteristics required to understand any sample, progress can occur remarkably quickly. Consider, for instance, how much we would know if the U.S. Census had questions about sexual orientation.

In social science research, the effort to extract durable principles of social causality from the apparent randomness of everyday life requires the construction of reliable, if tentative, knowledge that is significantly more informative than speculation. With our ever-increasing knowledge base, increasingly sophisticated and powerful quantitative and qualitative methodologies (and, of course, the ability to process large amounts of data at a rapid rate), and with an ever-expanding cadre of researchers taking the risks associated with this kind of work, our ability to discern patterns of development of LGBT people from birth to death, the unique qualities of their relationships, and the impact of communities and cultures on the ways in which their sexualities are manifested, will come into sharper focus. In this way, research becomes a tool by which LGBT people transcend invisibility and marginalization. As new research accumulates, the unique contributions that LGBT lives make to our understanding of the nature of human development will be documented in ways never before thought possible. We do not, in fact, know where this research will take us. Early research such as Hooker's (1957) was intended to question the pathology model; more recent research has been addressing description with an eye on explanation. Future research will need to combine results from different sources of data to pose questions for the next generation of researchers.

Within the larger context of social science research on LGBT populations, this book describes the current status of social service researchers in their quest for methodological sophistication and conceptual complexity. The work of the authors in this volume exemplifies the progress that has been made since the first research reports on this topic were published. Clearly, there is much left to explore, both substantively and methodologically, as social service researchers attempt to answer more sophisticated questions in more rigorous ways, to improve the conceptualization and the delivery of human services to these populations.

Anthony R. D'Augelli
The Pennsylvania State University

REFERENCES

Bell, A.P., & Weinberg, M.S. (1978). *Homosexualities.* New York: Simon & Schuster.

Bell, A.P., Weinberg, M.S., & Hammersmith, S.K. (1991). *Sexual preference: Its development in men and women.* Bloomington, IN: Indiana University Press.

D'Augelli, A.R., & Patterson, C.J. (Eds.) (1995). *Lesbian, gay, and bisexual identities over the lifespan: Psychological perspectives.* New York: Oxford University Press.

Hamer, D.H., Hu, S., Magnuson, V.L., Hu, N., & Pattatucci, A.M. (1993). A linkage between DNA markers on the X chromosome and male sexual orientation. *Science, 261,* 321-327.

Hooker, E.A. (1957). The adjustment of the overt male homosexual. *Journal of Projective Techniques, 21,* 17-31.

Kinsey, A.C., Pomeroy, W.B., & Martin, C.E. (1948). *Sexual behavior in the human male.* Philadelphia: Saunders.

Kinsey, A.C., Pomeroy, W.B., Martin, C.E., & Gebhard, P.H. (1953). *Sexual behavior in the human female.* Philadelphia: Saunders.

LeVay, S. (1991). A difference in hypothalamic structure between heterosexual and homosexual men. *Science, 253,* 1034-1037.

Patterson, C.J., & D'Augelli, A.R. (1998). *Lesbian, gay, and bisexual identities in families: Psychological perspectives.* New York: Oxford University Press.

Acknowledgments

We wish to acknowledge the assistance of Ray Berger, Honorary Editor of the *Journal of Gay & Lesbian Social Services*, who could not have been more helpful, responsive, or supportive at each stage of our work on this volume. His guidance and flexibility helped make our editing job significantly easier as we worked toward this volume's completion.

We are also grateful for the assistance of Amanda Carlin and Yuet Lam Tong, both students at New York University. Their careful scrutiny of each manuscript ensured that every reference was cited in text correctly and every citation was accompanied by an accurate reference.

Our special thanks go to W. Michael Brittenback, who, during our work together in Ann Arbor, cooked, arranged time out for some fun, and was always supportive of our taking time from his family life to do the work right. It is no wonder that he and the first editor have been partners for nearly a quarter of a century.

Most of all, we wish to acknowledge the hard work, creativity, and cooperativeness of all of the contributing authors, whose fine scholarship enriches our field immeasurably, and whose wonderful work makes us look better than we really are.

William Meezan
Ann Arbor, MI
James I. Martin
New York, NY

Exploring Current Themes in Research on Gay, Lesbian, Bisexual and Transgender Populations

William Meezan
James I. Martin

SUMMARY. This introductory essay briefly describes each of the manuscripts in this volume. It then delineates and describes themes that cut across these works. These themes include: the usefulness of the ecological framework for research with GLBT populations; the necessity for greater complexity in the conceptualization of research with these populations; the need for more inclusive and representative samples; the need to protect GLBT research participants and ways in which this can be accomplished; the usefulness and importance of using inclusive research methods; the advantages and limitations of the insider perspective when conducting research on GLBT populations; and ways in which research with these populations can be used. It concludes with a call for research

---

William Meezan, MSW, DSW, is Marion Elizabeth Blue Professor of Children and Families, University of Michigan, School of Social Work, Ann Arbor, MI. James I. Martin, MSW, PhD, is Associate Professor, Shirley M. Ehrenkranz School of Social Work, New York, NY.

Address correspondence to: Dr. William Meezan, University of Michigan, School of Social Work, 1080 South University, Ann Arbor, MI 48109-1106 (E-mail: meezan@umich.edu).

[Haworth co-indexing entry note]: "Exploring Current Themes in Research on Gay, Lesbian, Bisexual and Transgender Populations." Meezan, William, and James I. Martin. Co-published simultaneously in *Journal of Gay & Lesbian Social Services* (Harrington Park Press, an imprint of The Haworth Press, Inc.) Vol. 15, No. 1/2, 2003, pp. 1-14; and: *Research Methods with Gay, Lesbian, Bisexual, and Transgender Populations* (ed: William Meezan, and James I. Martin) Harrington Park Press, an imprint of The Haworth Press, Inc., 2003, pp. 1-14. Single or multiple copies of this article are available for a fee from The Haworth Document Delivery Service [1-800-HAWORTH, 9:00 a.m. - 5:00 p.m. (EST). E-mail address: getinfo@haworthpressinc.com].

1

that addresses the difficult and potentially controversial issues facing GLBT populations. *[Article copies available for a fee from The Haworth Document Delivery Service: 1-800-HAWORTH. E-mail address: <getinfo@haworthpressinc.com> Website: <http://www.HaworthPress.com> © 2003 by The Haworth Press, Inc. All rights reserved.]*

KEYWORDS. Research, GLBT populations, ecological framework, sampling, protection of subjects, participatory research, insider perspective

When we decided to edit a volume addressing the current research that social workers were conducting with gay, lesbian, bisexual, and transgender populations (GLBT), and the issues faced in executing these studies, we decided to cast our net widely. We were not interested in a single type of article, but rather wanted to attract creative scholars who could share their work in a variety of ways. Toward that end, our call for papers, which was circulated widely both through personal invitations and on listserves, stated that we were looking for three types of papers: (1) those concerned primarily with research methods, including topics such as population definition, problem formulation, sampling, research design, measurement, data collection and analysis (including the appropriate uses of quantitative and qualitative data), and the ethical conduct of research; (2) those in which experiences in applying specific research strategies to GLBT populations were described, including the issues that the authors encountered in these applications and the strategies they employed to overcome them; and (3) those in which ways of conceptualizing research with these populations were described, including the specific paradigms and research approaches that were thought to be appropriate.

As we read over the abstracts that were submitted to us, we decided to choose papers that were diverse in terms of type, approach, subject, and population. With no particular conceptual scheme in mind, we decided that we would "make sense" of the papers after they were received, and order the contributions in the book only after the manuscripts were written and edited. The variety of papers we received was astounding!

Michael LaSala's paper describes the strengths and potential weaknesses of having an "inside" perspective when conducting qualitative research with gay men and lesbians. He notes that lesbian and gay investigators who study lesbians and gay men may bring special knowledge and understanding to their research, which can facilitate sample identification, data collection, and data analysis. He warns, however, that "inside" investigators might wrongfully assume common cultural understandings or fail to explore their respondents' unique perceptions, and that social desirability effects may influence responses under these circumstances. Such conditions can compromise the reliability and validity of data, and lead to the improper interpretation of findings. Throughout his article, LaSala offers a number of important suggestions to "inside" researchers that can maximize the advantages of their position while avoiding the potential biases that may occur because of it.

Joan McClennen's article provides a wonderful counterpoint to LaSala's. In her article, she describes her journey as a heterosexual woman conducting research on partner violence within a GLBT community. She presents eight strategies through which "outsiders" can overcome barriers to doing their work, the most important of which is immersion in the culture. She also presents her perceptions of the costs and benefits of conducting research with a stigmatized population to which she did not belong. Her work is clear evidence that an "outsider" can produce research that is important to GLBT populations, even when it addresses a topic as sensitive as domestic violence.

The probing of sensitive topics, with hidden and sometimes stigmatized sub-populations in GLBT communities, is the subject of a number of the articles in this volume. Kristina Hash and Elizabeth Cramer discuss the challenges of finding and studying older members of gay and lesbian communities. Their paper describes a study they conducted on the caregiving behaviors and experiences of this population. They advocate for the use of qualitative methods to uncover the unique experiences of those involved in this and other understudied populations.

Darrell Wheeler's manuscript examines factors affecting research with urban Black and African American GLBT populations, another difficult-to-reach group. He notes that this is a particularly timely topic, since reducing and eliminating racial disparities in health care has become a major national priority, and since there are no data on health outcomes or social service utilization by Black and African American GLBT persons. His article presents a case study to demonstrate the viability of the recommended research approaches described in the paper, and discusses the possible negative consequences of deviating from these methodological suggestions.

In his contribution, E. Michael Gorman discusses the special challenges that studying gay drug users pose to the researcher. He describes the methodological issues related to initiating and conducting research on this population, and discusses how such research can guide more effective prevention, treatment, and policy initiatives. He underscores the importance of conducting such research, since drug use is associated with high-risk behavior that leads to the transmission of HIV and other sexually transmitted diseases.

While all of these articles use examples from their authors' research to illustrate the points being made, other articles in this volume address the traditional stages of the research process in a more direct way. In their paper, Marian

Swindell and Jo Pryce contend that research on lesbian populations has often been simplistically conceptualized, lacking complex models with mediating and moderating variables that might help to explain the occurrence of behavioral problems that some lesbians experience. They persuasively argue that more complex conceptualizations of behavior can further our understanding of lesbians' experiences, and assert that trauma is an important intervening variable to explore when trying to understand responses to the coming out process. This conceptual article demonstrates the ways in which theory development and modeling can lead to the formulation of important research questions that deserve empirical attention.

Stephanie Swann and Jeane Anastas call for greater precision in the conceptualization and measurement of key issues explored in research. Their study examines dimensions of the construct of sexual identity among young women who identify as lesbian or questioning. Their empirical findings illustrate that more simplistic conceptualizations and measurements of this construct may not hold up under scrutiny; that the individual and social dimensions of identity development among lesbians may not be as distinct as had been previously hypothesized; and that other dimensions that were lacking in earlier models may be important to a fuller understanding of identity formation in this population.

Two articles in this volume discuss sampling issues with GLBT populations. Diane Elze discusses the major challenges of conducting research with sexual minority adolescents, and the ways in which she overcame these challenges. Her article centers upon the difficulties in finding a large sample of youth under 18 who were diverse in their stage of coming out and who were not associated with organized groups. She also discusses the issues present in dealing with Institutional Review Boards when attempting to include underage youth for whom parental consent cannot be obtained safely in research, and ethical ways to address this situation.

In their study, Gerard Sullivan and Warren Losberg examine the various types of sampling techniques used to study GLBT populations in the empirical articles that appeared in the *Journal of Gay & Lesbian Social Services* between 1997 and 2000. They describe the sample characteristics, sample sizes, response rates, and methods of obtaining samples in these studies. Using these data, they discuss sampling issues that characterize the field, and make suggestions for improving sampling and reporting practices in social service research with GLBT populations.

Sarah-Jane Dodd and William Meezan discuss the importance of the fit between the organizational characteristics and the research methodologies and approaches used in evaluation research. Their paper describes the unique features of AIDS service organizations (ASOs) that should be considered when developing an evaluation strategy, and discusses why the dominant paradigms of evaluation research are incongruent with the service delivery philosophies of these organizations. They describe an alternative, participatory evaluation approach that better matches the philosophy and service delivery approaches of ASOs to the evaluation process.

Studying stigmatized populations like members of GLBT communities, whether "out," members of "hidden" groups who are difficult to locate and engage in the research enterprise (including those who participate in illegal activities), or youth who present a host of issues not present when studying adults, can raise ethical questions and dilemmas in the conduct of research. The final manuscript in this volume, by James I. Martin and William Meezan, examines the application of ethical standards to research and evaluation on GLBT populations. They use social work's Code of Ethics and psychology's Ethical Principles of Psychologists and Code of Conduct as their organizing framework, and note that researchers may need to take additional measures to protect GLBT research participants from harm. Also, they examine heterosexist and genderist biases in the conceptualization and execution of research as additional ethical issues.

RECURRING THEMES

While the above description might make it seem that this volume is made up of disparate articles that have little to do with one another, the reality is quite different. As one reads the entire manuscript, certain themes emerge that bind these works together in a mosaic that tells a story of the current efforts of social work researchers studying GLBT populations. Of course, all of these themes do not appear in all of the manuscripts. But the congruence of thought apparent in a number of articles suggests issues that are important to the field as it pursues future research endeavors with these populations.

In reading this volume, one caveat should be kept in mind. Social science research on GLBT populations is in its infancy, with the first important studies appearing less than 50 years ago (D'Augelli).[1] The social sciences, particularly psychology, produced important information about gay (and to a lesser degree, lesbian) populations during the 1980s, and the AIDS epidemic led to a burgeoning literature on a variety of issues related to it in the late 1980s. However, descriptive articles and research aimed at the *social service* needs of GLBT populations found a home less than ten years ago with the publication of the first issue of the *Journal of Gay & Lesbian Social Services* in 1993. The first issue of that Journal dedicated specifically to research issues appeared in

1995, and focused solely on lesbians (Tully, 1995). And the first major summary of methodological and ethical issues in research with lesbians and gay men appeared in the social work literature only very recently (Martin & Knox, 2000). Thus, social work has lagged behind the social sciences in the development of a unique knowledge base about these populations, and the research issues faced by other social scientists in past decades are only now being identified and addressed by human service professionals. What are these issues?

The Importance of the Ecological Perspective

Social workers have long recognized the ecological perspective as a comprehensive way of understanding human behavior. It is therefore not surprising that numerous authors in this volume note the importance of looking beyond individual factors, to the ways in which individuals interact with others and with their environments, in order to gain a fuller understanding of the phenomena under study. Swindell and Pryce note that personal contexts shape lesbians' understanding of and reactions to their sexual identities, and that factors both within and outside the person influence their reaction to coming out. Gorman states that we must not only understand why gay men use drugs, but also "the people with whom they . . . [are] using, and the circumstances under which they . . . [are] using" if we are to design interventions that decrease the incidence of unprotected sex. And Wheeler notes that this perspective is particularly important when studying Black and African American GLBT persons, for it demands that researchers "examine individual and environmental forces in the process of scientific inquiry" and "incorporate sociocultural, structural, and behavioral variables into [their] research."

Swann and Anastas make an even more cogent argument for incorporating the ecological perspective into research with GLBT populations. Not only do they state that "social, political, and cultural contexts shape individuals' understandings of their sexual identities," but they add that cohort effects may be highly salient in research with lesbian (and by extension GBT) populations. These authors acknowledge the "significant political changes made within the past 20 years," and note that "lesbians coming out today. . . are more likely to have access to positive role models . . . [and] social service and community-based agencies . . . [that] affirm young lesbian identities." Because of these changes in the environment, "existing models need to be empirically tested . . . as societal attitudes and beliefs . . . impact the identity development process."

The Need for Complexity

In the Foreword of this volume, D'Augelli makes the point that descriptive research in this field has helped to eradicate stereotypes about same-sex couples, GLBT youth, and older adults. Likewise, Swindell and Pryce note that much of what we know about GLBT communities is based on descriptions of behavioral patterns, often focusing on problems such as substance abuse, mental illness, and suicide, and their apparent higher incidence among GLBT people than among heterosexuals.

A number of authors in this volume comment that such simple description, while important, is only a first step in the development of knowledge. For example, D'Augelli states that description should be undertaken only with an eye toward eventual explanation of the phenomena found. Swindell and Pryce echo this sentiment, and call for us to move beyond simple description to the use of complex models, containing mediating and moderating variables, in order to understand the presence of problems experienced by members of these populations. They contend that a fuller understanding of the reasons why self-destructive behaviors occur among members of GLBT communities can lead to preventive and ameliorative interventions that foster resilience.

In a similar vein, Swann and Anastas call for greater complexity in the conceptualization of key concepts. They show how testing a theoretically derived measure of a concept as seemingly linear as identity formation can result in a more complex construct that better explains this process. They state that it is critical to test the ways in which these more complex conceptualizations interface with cultural, racial, ethnic, and socioeconomic forces to see how the coming out process varies among people with different characteristics in diverse circumstances.

Within Groups Variations

The need to test conceptualizations and research findings with various subgroups points to the fact that GLBT populations are far from monolithic, an assumption often made by those doing research in the field. Wheeler makes this point when he notes that even within more marginalized subgroups important variations exist; all Black and African American gay men do not experience their sexual orientation or relate to the world in the same way. Similar points are made by Swann and Anastas regarding differences in the way lesbian identities are formed, and by Swindell and Pryce in terms of the coming out process. Sullivan and Losberg sum up the risks of such thinking eloquently when they state "aggregation without awareness of the differences between people included in research samples runs the risk of producing conclusions that are misleading or simplistic."

The Need for Improved Samples

Many of the authors in this volume discuss the difficulties in sampling members of GLBT populations. According to Sullivan and Losberg, "sampling is fraught with dilemmas, particularly with populations that are difficult to define, hard to reach, or resistant to identification because of potential discrimination, social isolation or other reasons that are relevant to lesbian, gay, bisexual, and transgender (LGBT) populations." Such difficulties and dilemmas are exacerbated when one desires to study hard-to-locate subgroups that are not part of mainstream GLBT communities, or to broaden their studies to be more inclusive. Those who are hard to locate and difficult to engage in research include: members of transgender and bisexual populations in general; those who do not identify with a GLBT community; youth who are questioning or who have not disclosed to their parents; older or nonwhite GLBT people; poor and poorly-educated GLBT people; isolated GLBT people who often live in rural areas; and GLBT drug abusers and others who engage in marginalized behaviors (Elze; Gorman; Hash & Cramer; Swann & Anastas; Wheeler). There is a need to move away from research that includes only "easy to find" samples (e.g., urban, male, middle and upper class), who self-identify as gay or lesbian, are connected to a GLBT community and its organizations and media outlets, and are present at pride celebrations (Elze; Hash & Cramer; Gorman; McClennen; Swann & Anastas; Wheeler).

A number of the authors whose work appears in this volume used new and innovative techniques to overcome some of these problems. Beyond snowball sampling, which was a method of choice in some of the studies reported, some researchers used the internet or specifically targeted people of color or those who report same-sex sexual attractions and behaviors but do not identify as gay or lesbian. Others used toll-free phone lines and school-based personnel in their sampling strategies.

But no matter how widely the net is cast, non-probability samples will never be generalizable, and numerous replications of studies will always be necessary to confirm knowledge claims. Sullivan and Losberg suggest a number of ways that might produce more representative samples, including random digit dialing. However, they note that strategies for obtaining representative samples are costly and very complex, and that only two of the studies they reviewed used them.

Perhaps the best way to obtain truly representative samples is to include questions about sexual orientation and gender expression in the census and in ongoing surveys that draw large representative samples. Those who identify as GLBT could then be extracted and compared with the remaining group to analyze similarities and differences (D'Augelli; Elze). As D'Augelli notes, "Once sexual orientation items are routinely collected as sociodemographic characteristics required to understand any sample, progress [in understanding and knowledge building] can occur remarkably quickly. Consider, for instance, how much we would learn if the U.S. Census had questions about sexual orientation."

Protection of Research Participants

In their manuscript, Martin and Meezan go beyond the obvious acknowledgement that steps normally taken to protect human participants must always be applied in research on GLBT populations. They assert that protection of these participants requires special attention and vigilance, given past travesties and societal attitudes that maintain their marginalization and vulnerability to exploitation.

Beyond standard precautions, researchers in this volume have suggested two ways to protect the safety and confidentiality of GLBT people who participate in social research. Martin and Meezan suggest obtaining a Certificate of Confidentiality to prevent researchers from being compelled to identify participants in their study under any circumstances. Elze suggests protecting underage adolescents in research by having agency personnel or participant advocates serve *in loco parentis* when obtaining parental consent would jeopardize their safety.

There are other, less formal, ways to protect research participants. Martin and Meezan argue for the use of anonymous surveys, but acknowledge that this methodology may not be appropriate for all research questions. LaSala and Martin and Meezan both suggest that maintaining appropriate boundaries and avoiding dual relationships are important for protecting participants and the professional nature of the research relationship. And Wheeler urges us to consider other ways in which confidentiality can be breached within the context of a specific study, and to devise ways to protect against them with the help of those who will participate in the study. He recommends that we avoid setting up an "us-them" dichotomy in the process of protecting participants, since "the emphasis on protecting subjects could seem paternalistic and patronizing to some populations." Instead, he suggests that research should aim for "participation, collaboration, and mutuality," and that researchers should use the form and content of the consent agreement as "a way of spelling out their obligations to the partnership, in addition to enumerating the protections available to potential participants."

Moving Toward Participatory, Inclusive Research

Wheeler's idea of collaborating with one's research participants is echoed in a number of the other papers in this volume, and collaboration with research participants is seen by many authors as something that should span the entire research enterprise. Martin and Meezan note that one way of avoiding harm to research participants is to consult with them. Dodd and Meezan claim that nonhierarchical agency settings, in which evaluation research with GLBT populations often takes place, call for egalitarian research strategies that match these agencies' characteristics. They warn that top-down approaches to evaluation can alienate and disempower the organization, its staff, and clients, and lead to resistance to the evaluation process. Both McClennen and Hash and Cramer suggest that top-down approaches to research may alienate participants.

The call for participatory, inclusive research methods applies to all of the stages of the research process addressed in this volume. Dodd and Meezan suggest a comprehensive model for these methods in their article on the evaluation of AIDS service organizations. According to Gorman, research questions should be informed by consumers, while Wheeler underscores the need to collaborate with research participants in order to ask appropriate questions in appropriate ways. Both McClennen and Wheeler discuss ways in which those being researched can be included in the design of instruments. Elze discusses ways in which respondents can help to increase sample size and ensure more representative samples. Both LaSala and Hash and Cramer discuss the involvement of participants in assessing the clarity and accuracy of conclusions drawn from research data. Hash and Cramer and Wheeler discuss the involvement of participants in the dissemination of findings.

In order to assure that research is inclusive, some authors (Dodd & Meezan; McClennen) suggest the use of formal committees to advise those conducting studies. Wheeler recommends that agency personnel have ongoing input in each of the major phases of the research process. Still others (Gorman; Hash & Cramer; LaSala) suggest that hierarchical approaches to research are broken down through the use of qualitative methods, where the purpose of the research is to understand the complexity of phenomena through the discovery of themes, patterns, and meanings which emerge and are checked with informants; where methods are flexible rather than predetermined; and where detailed data are collected in order to gain a depth of understanding. No matter what mechanism is used, most authors in this volume attempt to redefine researchers as teachers, facilitators, and learners, rather than "experts."

McClennen states that "adopting innovative, unconventional methodologies is necessary if research on sensitive topics within stigmatized populations is to be relevant and useful."

Debate on the Insider Perspective

Few authors in this volume would disagree that members of the GLBT communities start with certain advantages when they conduct research within their group. LaSala, like Cramer and Hash, Gorman, and McClennen, acknowledges many of them when he recognizes that GLBT researchers may formulate research questions that might not occur to outsiders; that they may be more likely to gain entry into settings where GLBT people congregate; that they may have greater knowledge on where and how to find and reach their samples; and that participants may be more open to engaging in research, and be more honest in their reporting, when they know that the researcher is a member of their group.

However, several authors, including LaSala, note that being an insider may also present problems: that due to the great variability of GLBT communities, they might not understand the terms, constructs, or meanings of responses when it is assumed that they would; that they might fail to notice the obvious and familiar in their work; that objectivity might be lost in these situations; and that the information they are given might be contaminated by response biases due to participants' concerns that the researcher will judge them negatively or compromise their anonymity. According to Wheeler, being an insider does not give a researcher *carte blanche* for accessing groups that research has exploited in the past, nor does it guarantee a productive, working relationship; trust must be gained even by GLBT researchers studying populations to which they belong.

Although researchers who lack knowledge about the group they are studying can cause harm (Martin & Meezan), those who discuss this issue generally feel that entry to GLBT populations, and access to reliable and valid data, can be gained by non-GLBT researchers. In order to do so, they should immerse themselves in the culture of the people they are studying, be appropriately prepared and knowledgeable about them, have "guides" who can explain behaviors or responses they don't understand, and be respectful of those from whom they wish to gather data (LaSala; McClennen). While some GLBT research participants may be reluctant to share information with non-GLBT researchers, they appear to be a minority; most seem willing to cooperate in research that they see as beneficial to their community. As one of McClennen's participants put it, "We're not the ones who discriminate."

The Uses of Research

While all of the authors would agree that the general purpose of research with GLBT populations is to build knowledge about these marginalized or ignored groups, some authors see other purposes as well. Dodd and Meezan contend that research should be used for program improvement and organizational learning about the best ways to deliver services. Hash and Cramer and McClennen see advocacy and social justice issues, including the equitable distribution of resources, as an important purpose of research. They also see research as a way to empower participants and give them "voice." At the very least, research must be socially responsible. As Martin and Meezan note, "Researchers must think very seriously about the possible consequences [of the research], especially when participants or stakeholders are members of vulnerable GLBT populations."

CONCLUSIONS

In their review of articles in the *Journal of Gay & Lesbian Social Services*, Sullivan and Losberg note that basic demographics were often missing from many studies they examined, response rates were only sporadically reported, basic concepts were not defined adequately or were defined inconsistently across studies, few authors used established measurements, and most samples were unrepresentative and biased toward whites and the middle class. While not embracing any research paradigm or methodology, they call for greater consistency in the ways in which methodologies and samples are reported in the research literature. We could not agree more, for if social work is to build a unique knowledge base in this area, social work researchers must be able to understand, replicate, and build on each other's work.

There is also a need for more social workers to do research on GLBT populations. If Sullivan and Losberg's findings are generalizable, and more research appearing in this *social work* journal was completed by psychologists than by social workers, there is clearly a gap that needs to be filled. While all social scientists can contribute to the general knowledge base about GLBT populations, social work's unique mission is to do research that will improve social services, and through this work the lives of the people it studies.

Despite the potential consequences, research on doubly stigmatized GLBT populations must move forward. While some segments of GLBT communities may be reluctant to expose the existence of individuals who break social norms, abuse drugs, and engage in risky sexual behaviors (Gorman), or batter their partners (McClennen), it is within these subpopulations that the need for intervention may be most pronounced. In addition, many GLBT sub-populations who have long been ignored, particularly members of ethnic minority communities, deserve considerably greater research attention given the known correlations between minority status and a host of undesirable social conditions in the general public (Wheeler). We must also learn the needs of those who carry out responsibilities typically associated with families, such as caregiving, without the availability of social supports or services (Hash & Cramer).

And we must extend our research concerns to groups about whom we currently know little. Transgender populations are only marginally represented in this volume, reflecting the virtual absence of social work research on them. Non-research writings describe the extreme prejudice and massive discrimination suffered by these populations (e.g., Mallon, 1999), with all of the destructive and self-destructive consequences such forces are known to lead to within the gay and lesbian community. These writings also describe the unique strengths of transgender individuals (e.g., Feinberg, 1996). The need for social work research on transgender populations is both significant and immediate, given the lack of appropriate services available to them. However, members of these communities are likely to be at least as wary of researchers as are members of gay and lesbian communities. Researchers who do not belong to transgender communities should carefully follow the recommendations of several authors in this volume regarding preparation for such work (LaSala; McClennen), the protection of participants from harm (Martin & Meezan), and the use of participatory, inclusive methods (Dodd & Meezan; Gorman; Hash & Cramer; Wheeler).

Similarly, social work research has thus far given inadequate attention to the experiences and needs of those who we might classify as bisexual, and this volume addresses them only indirectly. The belief that sexual orientation is categorical might be as limited as the belief that gender is binary. Research indicates that women's sexuality tends to be more fluid than men's (Golden, 1996), even though they might not be any more likely to endorse bisexual identities. And men of color are less likely to self-identify as gay even if they have sex with other men (Hunter, Shannon, Knox, & Martin, 1998). In order to obtain research samples that are diverse in gender, ethnicity, and social class, at the very least researchers should make sure their selection criteria do not reflect white, male, or middle class constructions of identity. Like transgender populations, bisexual populations are inadequately addressed by social services. Careful description of these populations by social work researchers, including their variability and commonalities, problems, strengths, and needs, is a necessary step toward improving the services available to them.

Finally, we must resist pressures, both within and outside GLBT communities, not to ask certain questions about certain people, or not to report findings that some consider embarrassing, threatening, or dangerous to the general well-being of GLBT populations. And we must accept rational findings from carefully designed and executed studies that do not support dominant views. According to Martin and Meezan, in their article on ethics, the belief that studies should not be conducted simply because their subject matter is taboo, "or because they might provide 'ammunition' for opponents of GLBT rights," is likely to prevent the development of knowledge that challenges existing social and political structures. As such, this belief is not consistent with either social work's or psychology's ethical principles. As Eileen Gambrill (1997) has written, "We must shift from being believers to being questioners. . . . There must be no sacred cows in a profession dedicated to helping clients, especially when the sacred cows get in the way of helping clients and avoiding harm" (p. 322, 325).

NOTE

1. Unless otherwise noted, all references are to manuscripts that appear in this volume.

REFERENCES

Feinberg, L. (1996). *Transgender warriors: Making history from Joan of Arc to Dennis Rodman*. Boston: Beacon Press.

Gambrill, E. (1997). Social work education: Current concerns and possible futures. In M. Reich & E. Gambrill (Eds.), *Social work in the 21st century* (pp. 317-327). Thousand Oaks, CA: Pine Forge Press.

Golden, C. (1996). What's in a name? Sexual self-identification among women. In R.C. Savin Williams & K.M. Cohen (Eds.), *The lives of lesbians, gays, and bisexuals* (pp. 229-249). Fort Worth, TX: Harcourt Brace.

Hunter, S., Shannon, C., Knox, J., & Martin, J.I. (1998). *Lesbian, gay, and bisexual youths and adults: Knowledge for human services practice*. Thousand Oaks, CA: Sage.

Mallon, G.P. (1999). Practice with transgendered children. *Journal of Gay & Lesbian Social Services, 10(3/4)*, 49-64.

Martin, J.I., & Knox, J. (2000). Methodological and ethical issues in research on lesbians and gay men. *Social Work Research, 24*, 51-59.

Tully, C.T. (Ed.) (1995). *Lesbian social services: Research issues*. Binghamton, NY: Harrington Park Press. Co-published simultaneously as the *Journal of Gay & Lesbian Social Services, 3(1)*.

When Interviewing "Family": Maximizing the Insider Advantage in the Qualitative Study of Lesbians and Gay Men

Michael C. LaSala

SUMMARY. Lesbian and gay investigators who study lesbians and gay men may bring special knowledge and understanding to their research, which can facilitate data collection and analysis. However, inside investigators may mistakenly assume common cultural understandings with interviewees and fail to explore their respondents' unique perceptions. Furthermore, social desirability effects can bias respondent reports. Using illustrations from the author's research, this article describes the strengths and potential weaknesses of having an inside perspective when conducting qualitative research with gay men and lesbians. Maintaining self-awareness, peer debriefing, and prolonged engagement are offered as ways to maximize the advantages and avoid the potential biases of the insider position. *[Article copies available for a fee from The Haworth Document Delivery Service: 1-800-HAWORTH. E-mail address: <getinfo@haworthpressinc.com>*

Michael C. LaSala, MSW, PhD, LCSW, is Assistant Professor, School of Social Work, Rutgers, The State University of New Jersey, New Brunswick, NJ.

Address correspondence to: Dr. Michael C. LaSala, School of Social Work, Rutgers, The State University of New Jersey, 536 George Street, New Brunswick, NJ 08901-1167 (E-mail: mlasala@rci.rutgers.edu).

[Haworth co-indexing entry note]: "When Interviewing 'Family': Maximizing the Insider Advantage in the Qualitative Study of Lesbians and Gay Men." LaSala, Michael C. Co-published simultaneously in *Journal of Gay & Lesbian Social Services* (Harrington Park Press, an imprint of The Haworth Press, Inc.) Vol. 15, No. 1/2, 2003, pp. 15-30; and: *Research Methods with Gay, Lesbian, Bisexual, and Transgender Populations* (ed: William Meezan, and James I. Martin) Harrington Park Press, an imprint of The Haworth Press, Inc., 2003, pp. 15-30. Single or multiple copies of this article are available for a fee from The Haworth Document Delivery Service [1-800-HAWORTH, 9:00 a.m. - 5:00 p.m. (EST). E-mail address: getinfo@haworthpressinc.com].

KEYWORDS. Inside research, social desirability, qualitative research, emic and etic, gay men and lesbians

Lesbian and gay male investigators who do qualitative research with other lesbians and gay men have an inside perspective, which can benefit but also bias their research. In this article, I will discuss the advantages and possible problems that can emerge when lesbians and gay men do interview research with other lesbians and gay men. I will also offer several suggestions for minimizing the weaknesses and maximizing the strengths inherent in this type of research.

THE RESEARCHER'S PERSPECTIVE

The terms emic and etic describe the different perspectives used to understand groups or communities that are the focus of social science research (Pike, 1967, 1990). The emic perspective is the viewpoint of the members of the group or culture being studied. Behavior and events are described strictly in terms of what they mean to the informants. From the etic or outsider standpoint, behavior is explained using theories that are thought to be applicable to all groups and cultures. Good research incorporates an integration of both etic and emic perspectives (Lett, 1990; Pike, 1990; Sands & McClelland, 1994). For example, gay men in non-monogamous couples might state that they engage in extra-relational sex because, as gay men, they need sexual variety, and therefore it is impossible or unrealistic to stay monogamous with one partner. This idea represents an emic view. From an etic perspective, a researcher might relate this behavior to theories and research which suggest that, due to biological evolutionary factors, men tend to cognitively separate sex from love (Buss & Schmitt, 1993; Townsend, 1995). A reasonable balance of these perspectives would suggest that even though evolutionary theories might be applicable, the belief among gay men that they have unique sexual needs should be considered and perhaps further explored.

In isolation, emic and etic viewpoints each have their own heuristic weaknesses, and if one is favored over the other, the research can seem shortsighted or biased (Sands & McClelland, 1994; Simon, 1966; Wimsatt, 1980, 1986). Although social scientists have been interested in the emic perspectives of their informants, etic perspectives have been historically overemphasized.

Western European and American ethnographers left their countries to study "primitive" or indigenous people in other geographic regions (Aguilar, 1981; Chilungu, 1976; Hayano, 1979; Srinivas, 1967). White, Anglo, heterosexual sociologists in the U.S. studied "deviance" among African Americans, Latinos, and gay men (Humphreys, 1975; Parades, 1977; Staples, 1976). Critics noticed that when these investigators studied other cultures or groups, they seemed to evaluate their informants' reports and behaviors against standards of white, Western European or American culture (Fine, 1994; Haraway, 1988). Social scientists were criticized for failing to capture the perspectives of their respondents, and for overlooking how respondents' reports to researchers representing dominant or oppressive groups might have been less than honest (Blauner & Wellman, 1973; Goodson-Lawes, 1994; Ohnuki-Tierney, 1984; Parades, 1977; Staples, 1976; Warren, 1977; Zinn, 1979). This failure to recognize and control for the biases related to an emic under-emphasis led to studies which seemed to stereotype third world and colonized people, as well as people of color in the United States (Aguilar, 1981; Chilungu, 1976; Ladner, 1971; Lewis, 1973; Moynihan, 1966; Rosaldo, 1993; Staples, 1976). An uncritical acceptance of the mid-twentieth century etic view that homosexuality was pathological, along with a failure to procure the emic perspective of a non-clinical sample of lesbians and gay men, led to a series of study findings that portrayed homosexuality as a mental illness (Apperson-Behrens & McAdoo, 1968; Bieber et al., 1962; Loney, 1973; O'Connor, 1964; Thompson, Schwarz, McCandless, & Edwards, 1973; West, 1959).

Up until the mid-twentieth century, it was believed that insiders could not perform unbiased research within their own groups. It was thought that the feelings and commitments of inside investigators to fellow group members would interfere with their ability to remain objective (Aguilar, 1981; Chilungu, 1976; Hayano, 1979; Merton, 1978; Srinivas, 1967). It was also believed that only a stranger was capable of noticing what was important within a particular group or culture (Aguilar, 1981; Merton, 1978). The special advantages insiders might have in capturing emic perspectives were not widely acknowledged.

ADVANTAGES OF THE INSIDER POSITION

The Inside Researcher's Perspective

Qualitative researchers who are members of the groups or communities they study may have a unique ability not only to elicit emic perspectives, but also to understand their importance. Insider researchers' personal familiarity with issues affecting their respondents' lives may enable them to formulate research questions and hypotheses that might not occur to outsiders (Staples,

1976; Zinn, 1979). For example, because I am a gay man, I am conscious of how commonly held ideas about relationships may not fit everyone. I have met coupled gay men who have chosen to establish and maintain sexually non-monogamous relationships, and therefore I am open to the idea that non-monogamous relationships can be functional for some gay men. Unless heterosexual investigators know many gay men, they may not have had the same opportunity to see the assumed connection between monogamy and relationship satisfaction challenged. As a result, heterosexual researchers who encounter open gay male couples might assume that they are dysfunctional. Incorporating an emic perspective, I might be more likely to investigate how and under what conditions these relationships succeed. Lacking this emic perspective, a heterosexual researcher might instead choose to study the causes and implications of a presumed lack of intimacy among open gay male couples. In this way, divergent insider and outsider perspectives could result in strikingly different studies of the same phenomenon, and lead to markedly different conclusions being drawn from similar data.

Data Collection

Because they live in the same world as their respondents, inside investigators often have special knowledge about how and where to collect a sample. Gwaltney (1981), an African American ethnographer of urban Black culture, has discussed how he tapped into his own social networks to find his sample. Gay men and lesbians are not consistently identifiable, and despite increasing societal tolerance in recent years, many remain hidden from the larger society. Gay or lesbian researchers are often familiar with newsletters, organizations, listservs, chat rooms, and social networks where they can advertise for respondents. Lesbian and gay researchers might also know lesbian and gay acquaintances who can refer "friends of friends." Such sources might not be known or available to heterosexual investigators.

Oppressed minority respondents may want to participate in research done by an inside investigator because they perceive that the researcher shares their desire to rectify societal misconceptions of their group (Gwaltney, 1980; Maykovich, 1977). Indeed, many of the respondents I interviewed stated that they volunteered for my study because they believed that, as a gay man, I could be trusted to accurately portray their lives (LaSala, 1998, 2000, 2001). Thus, gay and lesbian respondents may be more likely to participate in research conducted by a lesbian or gay man because they believe the researcher is committed to deconstructing societal misperceptions about who they are.

The ability to communicate the expressions, sentiments, and goals of the group can be used to engage informants and establish the rapport necessary for honest reporting (Cornwall, 1984; Davis, 1997; Hayano, 1979; Rhodes, 1994).

Lesbian and gay male researchers share experiences such as coming out with their gay and lesbian informants. This familiarity enables gay and lesbian investigators to communicate a special empathy that, in turn, can encourage respondent trust and honesty (LaSala, 1998, 2001).

There is an additional way inside familiarity can help the lesbian or gay researcher gather data. As a gay man, I am aware of the variety of subtle ways parents might manifest disapproval toward a son or daughter's homosexuality. As I interviewed lesbians and gay men about their intergenerational relationships, I knew to inquire whether the partner was included in family celebrations, introduced by relatives to extended family, or sent a birthday card by the respondent's parents. Thus, gay or lesbian researchers studying their own groups can use their emic understanding of the studied phenomenon to develop appropriate interview questions.

POTENTIAL LIMITATIONS OF THE INSIDER POSITION

Not Noticing the Familiar

Research performed by an insider is not immune to potential biases related to the perspective of the investigator. When inside researchers excessively emphasize the emic perspective over the etic, they may fail to notice what is unique and informative about their own group or culture. For example, it was not until I taught family therapy to a class of predominantly heterosexual social work students that I realized it might not be commonly known that many gay men establish couples that are sexually non-monogamous. The students' reactions of surprise upon hearing this information led me to do research which explores this unique aspect of gay male life.

The inside investigator's proneness to overemphasize emic perspectives could result in research that seems biased or limited. One example would be uncritically accepting non-monogamous gay male relationships as functional, without somehow addressing the etic idea that monogamy is essential to intimacy (Pittman, 1990). On the other hand, non-monogamous gay male relationships may have something to teach people of all sexual orientations about intimacy, couple satisfaction, and sex. By not sufficiently considering the etic perspective, the researcher loses the opportunity to use emic information to build upon or modify existing etic theories.

Inside investigators might fail to adequately explore certain respondent perceptions because they take for granted that they understand how their informants view common cultural phenomena (Aguilar, 1981; Hayano, 1979; Kanuha, 2000). An indigenous Hawaiian lesbian investigator (Kanuha, 2000) who interviewed other indigenous lesbians reported that, when respondents discussed situations that she found familiar, she "did not pursue vague statements, generalities, or even participant-initiated leads with follow-up probes" (p. 442). Although it is unclear whether such oversights affected the trustworthiness of her findings, the potential for bias did exist. During my own research examining the relationships between gay men and their parents, one respondent stated, "My Dad is a real Army honcho." Another described his mother as "really Catholic." Without exploring these answers, I assumed that the respondents were trying to explain the magnitude of their parents' homophobia and, as I will describe later, this assumption was not entirely accurate.

Investigator Reactions

Laslett and Rapoport (1975) have noted how psychodynamic concepts might be applied to the interviewer-respondent relationship. They have suggested that researchers can develop countertransference reactions toward their interviewees which, if not recognized, might distort investigators' interpretations. If they share common experiences, researchers might mistakenly project their own feelings about these experiences onto their respondents, which could bias data collection and analysis. For example, when I interviewed lesbian and gay respondents about their perceptions of their parents' feelings regarding their sexual orientation, many reported that their parents were "fine" (LaSala, 1998, 2000, 2001). However, several of the same respondents gave responses later in their interviews that indicated that their parents still harbored disapproval. Remembering my own difficult experiences with my family, I would find myself growing impatient and irritated at the interviewees for what I perceived to be their unwillingness to face "reality." These feelings threatened to interfere with my ability to accurately interpret my respondents' reports.

Respondent Reactions

Even though lesbian and gay researchers may have a special advantage in establishing rapport with lesbian and gay respondents, it is important to note that interviewee reactivity is still a possibility. Gay male and lesbian informants can be suspicious of inside researchers, and this distrust could bias their interview responses. Researchers who interview members of their own communities have noted that respondents sometimes fear investigators will use their information to gossip (Aguilar, 1981; Rhodes, 1994). Such fears might surface when gay men or lesbians interview informants who live in their own regions. Even in large, gay-friendly cities like New York, Los Angeles, and San Francisco, gay and lesbian communities can seem small and insular. Respondents may have concerns about their anonymity or about disclosing personal information to a member of the same social circle, and such misgivings could affect their willingness to be candid during interviews.

Respondents might also be reluctant to admit vulnerabilities or difficulties to a member of her/his group for fear of "loss of face" (Padgett, 1998, p. 66) or because they want to put forth "the best face" possible (Laslett & Rapoport, 1975, p. 973). Applying a psychodynamic perspective, Laslett and Rapoport (1975) have suggested that, like clients, research respondents can experience a kind of transference whereby they project their feelings about previous relationships onto the investigator. The tendency to identify with, or to project feelings onto, the researcher might be more likely when the investigator and respondent share important characteristics.

In my own research, certain responses suggested that my status as a gay man did have an impact on respondents. For the past year, I have been interviewing coupled gay men about their extradyadic sexual agreements and behavior. Several times during interviews with men in monogamous relationships, respondents would say, "You must think we are really boring." When I probed such statements further, these interviewees would state how they felt embarrassed because they believed the other gay men I was interviewing were having more eventful sex lives. In addition, one man who claimed he was completely monogamous, discussed how on camping trips, he and his friends would "fool around," meaning perform mutual masturbation and oral sex. A week after his interview, he contacted me to say "I want you to know, I'm not crazy"; he knew he was having sex outside of his relationship, yet he still considered himself monogamous because he was not engaging in extrarelational anal intercourse. Though these examples do not unequivocally indicate a social desirability effect, they do suggest that respondents, fearing researcher disapproval, might engage in some type of impression management that could affect the trustworthiness of their reports. Clearly, more research is needed which compares the reports of lesbian/gay respondents to lesbian/gay versus heterosexual investigators.

The Outside Insider

Several writers and investigators have questioned whether there is such a thing as a complete inside or native researcher (Aguilar, 1981; Messerschmidt, 1981; Narayan, 1993; Srinivas, 1967; Yang, 1972). Though researchers and respondents may share characteristics such as sexual orientation, in order to become an investigator one must step outside of his or her home community for training and education (Messerschmidt, 1981; Narayan, 1993). Problems can arise if, in the process, the insider loses sight of the emic perspective and adopts etic ideas that may not fit the realities of the respondents. For example, a gay male social worker wishing to do meaningful research in the gay male community attends graduate school and learns theoretical perspectives as well as research skills. During his education, he may have learned theories that emphasize sexual monogamy as an important component of couple intimacy and satisfaction (Pittman, 1990). However, if he rigidly adopts this etic perspective without considering the viewpoint of his respondents, he might not recognize how non-monogamous relationships might be functional for some gay male couples.

Certainly, lesbian and gay respondents who notice differences between themselves and their interviewers on gender and economic status may not consider the researcher a true insider. Minority respondents often do not fully trust an investigator who has acculturated to the dominant group enough to become a social scientist (Aguilar, 1981; Parades, 1977). Furthermore, it is possible that gay or lesbian respondents might want to impress gay men or lesbians of high status by giving socially desirable, rather than honest, responses. Of course, this tendency could bias respondent reports.

STRENGTHENING "INSIDER" QUALITATIVE RESEARCH WITH LESBIANS AND GAY MEN

Lesbians and gays who do qualitative interview research with lesbians and gay men can maximize the trustworthiness of their research by reassuring respondents of confidentiality, developing and maintaining self-awareness, avoiding dual relationships, using peer debriefing, and maintaining prolonged engagement with informants.

Confidentiality

Of course, it is always important to keep confidential an informant's research participation and responses. However, it is important to recognize that when respondents participate in gay or lesbian research, they are identifying themselves as lesbian or gay. If their participation becomes public, so does their sexual orientation, leaving them open to discrimination and harassment. Although most of my respondents were out of the closet, several were not. Thus, it is essential to take all necessary precautions to protect lesbian and gay male respondents' confidentiality.

If respondents are concerned that an investigator from their community is going to gossip, they might censor their responses. Therefore, at the start of each interview, lesbian and gay male investigators from the same community as their respondents should verbally reassure them that their confidentiality will be maintained, even if this protection is clearly described in the consent form. Interviewers and respondents might also plan for possible social encounters. In my own experience, I have found that sometimes respondents do not maintain confidentiality, and tell their friends and family about their research participation. Nevertheless, I explicitly state to respondents that I will never reveal their identities as research participants. I tell them that if we encounter each other socially, I will not greet them first. Rather, I will wait for them to initiate greetings, or introduce their friends or partners. In this way, I let the respondents decide whether they want to break confidentiality. Stressing the strictly confidential nature of their participation hopefully reassures respondents who are willing to disclose the personal information that is the target of the research.

Self-Awareness

Ohnuki-Tierney (1984) urges inside investigators to acknowledge the ways they are similar to and different from the groups they are studying. Certainly, lesbian and gay social work researchers doing insider research need to think about their relationships to the gay/lesbian community, the social work profession, the social science community, and society as a whole. As stated earlier, despite sharing their sexual orientation with respondents, gay or lesbian researchers will, in some ways, always be outsiders. However, from this partial outsider position, investigators can remain distant enough to notice what is unique and informative about their own group. From an etic perspective, inside researchers can become aware of what information heterosexual social workers and social work students need in order to effectively assess and intervene with lesbians and gay men. Developing and maintaining an awareness of the various ways they are both insiders and outsiders can help gay or lesbian investigators achieve the balance of emic and etic perspectives believed necessary for knowledge building (Lett, 1990; Pike, 1990; Sands & McClelland, 1994).

As previously mentioned, the similarities between the investigator and the respondent could lead to a countertransference reaction, which could bias the research findings. However, if acknowledged and examined, the emotional reactions of the investigator to either the respondents or the research experience might prove informative, and may ultimately enrich the findings (Kondo, 1986). I stated earlier that when I asked respondents how they thought their parents felt about their sexual orientation, many answered "fine" or "OK," only to give answers later in their interviews that suggested otherwise. After growing increasingly irritated with what I believed were the respondents' denials, I decided to explore the apparent inconsistencies. In response to my clarifying probes, some said that, in the course of the interview, they began to realize that their parents still disapproved. Others responded that as long as their parents included their partner in family events, any other ways their parents communicated disapproval were unimportant. Thus, acknowledging and exploring my own feelings led me to clarify many of the respondents' reports, which in turn helped me to further understand the complex dynamics of their family relationships. Therefore, it might be a good idea for investigators to maintain an awareness and respect for their feelings during the research.

Researchers must also be conscious of how their presence can impact respondents. As stated previously, respondents can be overly concerned with the interviewer's impressions, which could affect what they report. In addition, informants could project their own feelings onto the investigator. Investigators need to be aware of these potentials and minimize them by communicating a nonjudgmental openness. As mentioned previously, during my study of extradyadic sexual agreements among gay male couples, men in strictly monogamous relationships worried that I might think they were boring. Men in monogamous couples, who had covert sex outside of their relationships, believed I would disapprove. Because of these reactions, I decided to begin interviews citing previous results (Blasband & Peplau, 1985; Kurdek, 1988; McWhirter & Mattison, 1984) as well as my own preliminary findings, which suggested that a surprising variety of relationships may be functional for gay men, including those in which a partner is "cheating." This seemed to help respondents feel more relaxed and may have led them to be more honest in discussing their own relationships.

The Potential for Dual Relationships

Because lesbian and gay researchers and respondents share important characteristics and experiences, investigators might be tempted to develop social or even sexual or romantic relationships with certain respondents. On several occasions, my research assistants and I met respondents who seemed as if they would make desirable friends. I have been invited to dinner several times and have even been asked to a sex party! It is not uncommon for minority informants to invite the inside researcher to overstep the boundaries of the investigator-participant relationship (Kanuha, 2000; Zinn, 1979). I prefer to be very clear about the research relationship boundaries and to graciously decline such invitations, explaining that engaging in any personal relationship with respondents would violate research ethics. Strom-Gottfried and D'Aprix (2001) recommend that investigators apply NASW Code of Ethics (1996) standards governing worker-client relationships to investigator-respondent interactions, and avoid any involvement with respondents that could lead to dual relationships.

However, there is an alternative perspective. In doing inside research among native Hawaiian lesbians, Kanuha (2000) described the cultural importance of accepting a dinner invitation from a respondent. She found that maintaining looser boundaries than those prescribed for practitioner-client relationships put her respondents at ease and enhanced her data-gathering efforts.

I strongly recommend that the decision to accept a social invitation from a respondent be based on whether such social interaction would benefit the research effort. In addition, researchers must be sure that such action does not exploit respondents' willingness to be of service to the study, nor gives the false impression that they are friends.

Peer Debriefing

Reviewing parts or all of one's data and interpretations with a peer can help researchers identify personal feelings and their impacts on data collection and analysis (Lincoln & Guba, 1985). Padgett (1998) proposes the use of peer debriefing as a primary mechanism for guarding against bias. As I previously described, it was while reviewing my data and findings with a gay male colleague that I realized that I was unconsciously generalizing my own experiences with my parents to those of my respondents. Thus, gay and lesbian researchers may want to establish a network of other researchers with whom they can review their data for potential biases.

To guard against potential biases of the emic perspective, it might be advisable to include "outsiders" or heterosexual colleagues as part of the peer debriefing process. Outsiders can help inside investigators balance emic and etic perspectives by pointing out how emic information fits or refutes existent etic theories. In addition, outsiders can identify areas where the inside investigator assumed common understandings with the respondents without sufficient exploration. As stated previously, a respondent in my own research stated, "My Dad is a real Army honcho." Another described his mother as "really Catholic." Without adequately exploring these statements, I assumed that the respondents were explaining the depth of their parents' homophobia, and my gay and lesbian peers who I consulted agreed with my assumptions. It was not until I reviewed the data with heterosexual colleagues, who expressed curiosity about these responses, did I realize that these statements could have several different meanings. As I recontacted respondents and clarified these statements, I discovered that my perception regarding the respondent's Catholic mother was accurate. However, the other interviewee explained that because his "Army honcho" father was very masculine, he had feared this parent's reaction before he came out. Once he disclosed his sexual orientation, he was relieved that his father did not reject him. Upon coming out, the respondent learned that his father knew several gay men while in the Army. As a result, this parent was more knowledgeable and tolerant than the respondent originally anticipated. Thus, through the debriefing process, a trusted group of "outsider" peers can help the lesbian or gay male inside investigator gain sufficient distance to determine whether taken-for-granted common understandings should be further explored.

Prolonged Engagement

Repeated contacts with respondents, also known as member checks (Lincoln & Guba, 1985; Padgett, 1998), offer the opportunity for researchers to clarify issues and explore initially neglected areas, including those identified during peer debriefing. During member checks with my respondents, I was able to get more information about issues that I failed to explore sufficiently during my first contacts, and this additional data helped me capture a richer description of my respondents' relationships with their parents.

In addition, member checks and lengthy interviews can minimize the social desirability and respondent reactivity effects that can emerge when lesbian and gay male investigators interview lesbians and gay men. According to Padgett (1998), the more contact the respondent has with the researcher, the more likely the respondent will get accustomed to the researcher's presence. As she states, "Lengthy interviews make it hard to maintain an untruthful story for long" (p. 96). Spending extended time with my respondents, and asking similar questions in several different ways, helped me identify inconsistencies in their responses. For example, some of my respondents, who said that their parents fully accepted their same-sex relationships, stated later that their parents either did not introduce their partners to extended family or friends, or introduced them as roommates. Extended engagement and asking similar questions in different ways enabled me to identify and clarify such discrepancies, and to gain a richer understanding of the respondents' perceptions of parental feelings.

CONCLUSION: LINKS BETWEEN INSIDE AND OUTSIDE

Establishing and maintaining links to both inside and outside worlds can help lesbian and gay male investigators balance etic and emic perspectives in their work. Lesbians and gay men have a lot to teach the world about stigma, sexual behavior, sex roles, and relationships. Gay male and lesbian investigators who can integrate emic and etic viewpoints can use their respondents' experiences to modify existing theories that have traditionally ignored or excluded the realities and perspectives of these groups.

Narayan (1993) suggests that all researchers are simultaneously insiders and outsiders to varying degrees. Lesbian and gay male researchers who are mindful of their concurrent insider and outsider positions in various contexts may be especially able to recognize and describe this similar complexity in their respondents' lives. This special perspective can greatly enhance the ability of lesbian and gay researchers to perform meaningful research with lesbian and gay respondents. By maintaining awareness of their insider and outsider roles, and by balancing etic and emic perspectives, lesbian and gay male researchers can ensure that the inherent benefits of the insider position are maximized. Social workers, mental health providers, family scholars, and society at large could benefit from further research done by lesbian and gay investigators who are able to sensitively portray the lives of their lesbian and gay respondents from this balanced insider perspective.

REFERENCES

Aguilar, J. L. (1981). Insider research: An ethnography of a debate. In. A. Messerschmidt (Ed.), *Anthropologists at home in North America: Methods and issues in the study of one's own society* (pp. 15-26). New York: Cambridge University Press.

Apperson-Behrens, L., & McAdoo, G. (1968). Parental factors in the childhood of homosexuals. *Journal of Abnormal Psychology, 73*, 201-206.

Bieber, I., Dain, H., Dince, P., Drellich, R., Grand, H., Gundlach, R., Kremer, M., Rifkin, A., Wilbur, C., & Bieber, T. (1962). *Homosexuality: A psychoanalytic study*. New York: Basic Books.

Blasband, D., & Peplau, L. (1985). Sexual exclusivity versus openness in gay male couples. *Archives of Sexual Behavior, 14*, 395-412.

Blauner, R., & Wellman, D. (1973). Toward the decolonialization of social research. In J.A. Ladner (Ed.), *The death of white sociology* (pp. 310-321). New York: Random House.

Buss, D.M., & Schmitt, D.S. (1993). Sexual strategies theory: An evolutionary perspective on human mating. *Psychological Review, 100*, 204-232.

Chilungu, S.W. (1976). Issues in the ethics of research method: An interpretation of the Anglo-American perspective. *Current Anthropology, 17*, 457-481.

Cornwall, J. (1984). *Hard earned lives: Accounts of health and illness from East London*. London: Tavistock Publications.

Davis, D.W. (1997). The direction of race of interviewer effects among African-Americans: Donning the black mask. *American Journal of Political Science, 41*, 309-322.

Fine, M. (1994). Reinventing the self and other in qualitative research. In N.K. Denzin & Y.S. Lincoln (Eds.), *Handbook of qualitative research* (pp. 70-82). Thousand Oaks, CA: Sage.

Goodson-Lawes, J. (1994). Ethnicity and poverty as research variables: Family studies with Mexican and Vietnamese newcomers. In E. Sherman & W.J. Reid (Eds.), *Qualitative research in social work* (pp. 21-31). New York: Columbia University Press.

Gwaltney, J.L. (1980). *Drylongso: A self-portrait of Black America*. New York: Random House.

Gwaltney, J.L. (1981). Common sense and science: Urban core black observations. In D.A. Messerschmidt (Ed.), *Anthropologists at home in North America: Methods and issues in the study of one's own society* (pp. 46-61). New York: Cambridge University Press.

Haraway, D. (1988). Situated knowledges: The science question in feminism and the privilege of partial perspective. *Feminist Studies, 14,* 575-599.

Hayano, D.M. (1979). Auto-ethnography: Paradigms, problems and prospects. *Human Organization, 38,* 99-104.

Humphreys, L. (1975). *Tearoom trade: Impersonal sex in public places.* Chicago: Aldine.

Kanuha, V.K. (2000). "Being native" versus "going native": Conducting social work research as an insider. *Social Work, 45,* 439-447.

Kondo, D.K. (1986). Dissolution and reconstitution of self: Implications for anthropological epistemology. *Cultural Anthropology, 27,* 74-88.

Kurdek, L. (1988). Relationship quality of gay and lesbian cohabitating couples. *Journal of Homosexuality, 15(3/4),* 93-118.

Ladner J. (1971). *Tomorrow's tomorrow.* Garden City, NY: Doubleday.

LaSala, M.C. (1998). Coupled gay men, parents and in-laws: Intergenerational disapproval and the need for a thick skin. *Families in Society, 79,* 585-595.

LaSala, M.C. (2000). Gay male couples: The importance of coming out and being out to parents. *Journal of Homosexuality, 39(2),* 47-71.

LaSala, M.C. (2001). The importance of partners to lesbians' intergenerational relationships. *Social Work Research, 25,* 27-35.

Laslett, B., & Rapoport, R. (1975). Collaborative interviewing and interactive research. *Journal of Marriage and the Family, 37,* 968-977.

Lett, J. (1990). Emics and etics: Notes on the epistemology of anthropology. In T.N. Headland, K.L. Pike, & M. Harris (Eds.), *Emics and etics: The insider outsider debate* (pp. 127-142). Newbury Park, CA: Sage.

Lewis, D. (1973). Anthropology and colonialism. *Current Anthropology, 14,* 581-602.

Lincoln, Y.S., & Guba, E.G. (1985). *Naturalistic inquiry.* Beverly Hills, CA: Sage.

Loney, J. (1973). Family dynamics in homosexual women. *Archives of Sexual Behavior, 2,* 343-350.

Maykovich, M.K. (1977). The difficulties of a minority researcher in minority communities. *Journal of Social Issues, 33,* 108-119.

McWhirter, D.P., & Mattison, A.M. (1984). *The male couple: How relationships develop.* Englewood Cliffs, NJ: Prentice-Hall.

Merton, R.K. (1978). Insiders and outsiders: A chapter in the sociology of knowledge. *American Journal of Sociology, 78,* 9-47.

Messerschmidt, D.A. (1981). On anthropology "at home." In D.A. Messerchmidt (Ed.), *Anthropologists at home in North America: Methods and issues in the study of one's own society* (pp. 3-14). New York: Cambridge University Press.

Moynihan, D.P. (1966). *The Negro family: The case for national action.* Washington, DC: U.S. Department of Labor, Government Printing Office.

Narayan, K. (1993). How native is a "native" anthropologist? *American Anthropologist, 95,* 671-686.

National Association of Social Workers (1996). *Code of ethics.* Washington, DC: Author.

O'Connor, J. (1964). Aetiological factors in homosexuality as seen in the Royal Air Force psychiatric practice. *British Journal of Psychiatry, 5,* 85-97.

Ohnuki-Tierney, E. (1984). Critical commentary: "Native anthropologists." *American Anthropologist, 11,* 584-585.

Padgett, D.K. (1998). *Qualitative methods in social work research: Challenges and rewards.* Thousand Oaks, CA: Sage.

Parades, A. (1977). On ethnographic work among minority groups: A folklorist's perspective. *New Scholar, 6,* 1-53.

Pike, K.L. (1967). *Language in relation to a unified theory of the structure of human behavior.* The Hague, The Netherlands: Mouton.

Pike, K.L. (1990). On the emics and etics of Pike and Harris. In R.G. Headland & M. McClelland (Eds.), *Emics and etics: The insider/outsider debate* (pp. 28-47). Newbury Park, CA: Sage.

Pittman, S. (1990). *Private lies: Infidelity and the betrayal of intimacy.* New York: W.W. Norton.

Rhodes, P.J. (1994). Race-of-interviewer effects: A brief comment. *Sociology: The Journal of the British Sociological Association, 28,* 547-549.

Rosaldo, R. (1993). *Culture and truth: The remaking of social analysis.* Boston: Beacon Press.

Sands, R.G., & McClelland, M. (1994). Emic and etic perspectives in ethnographic research on the interdisciplinary team. In E. Sherman & W.J. Reid (Eds.), *Qualitative research in social work* (pp. 32-41). New York: Columbia University Press.

Simon, H.A. (1966). Scientific discovery and the psychology of problem solving. In R.G. Colodny (Ed.), *Mind and cosmos: Essays in contemporary science and philosophy* (pp. 22-40). Pittsburgh: University of Pittsburgh Press.

Srinivas, M.N. (1967). *Social change in modern India.* Los Angeles: University of California Press.

Staples, R. (1976). *Introduction to Black sociology.* New York: McGraw-Hill, Inc.

Strom-Gottfried, K., & D'Aprix, A.S. (2001, March). Ethics for academics. Paper presented at the 47th Annual Program Meeting, Council on Social Work Education, Dallas, TX.

Thompson, N.D., Schwarz, B., McCandless, B., & Edwards, D. (1973). Parent-child relationships and sexual identity in male and female homosexuals and heterosexuals. *Journal of Consulting and Clinical Psychology, 41,* 120-127.

Townsend, J.M. (1995). Sex without emotional involvement: An evolutionary interpretation of sex differences. *Archives of Sexual Behavior, 24,* 173-206.

Warren, C.A. (1977). Fieldwork in the gay world: Issues in phenomenological research. *Journal of Social Issues, 33,* 93-107.

West, D. (1959). Parental figures in the genesis of male homosexuality. *International Journal of Social Psychiatry, 5,* 85-97.

Wimsatt, W.C. (1980). Reductionistic research strategies and their biases in the units of selection controversy. In T. Nickles (Ed.), *Scientific discoveries: Case studies* (Vol. 60, pp. 213-259). Boston: Reidel Publishing Co.

Wimsatt, W.C. (1986). Heuristics and the study of human behavior. In D.W. Fiske & R.C. Shweder (Eds.), *Metatheory in social science* (pp. 293-314). Chicago: The University of Chicago Press.

Yang, M.M. (1972). How "A Chinese Village" was written. In S.T. Kimball, & J.B. Watson (Eds.), *Crossing cultural boundaries: The anthropological experience* (pp. 63-73). Scranton, PA: Chandler Publishing Co.

Zinn, M.B. (1979). Field research in minority communities: Ethical methodological and political observations by an insider. *Social Problems, 27*, 209-219.

Researching Gay and Lesbian Domestic Violence: The Journey of a Non-LGBT Researcher

Joan C. McClennen

SUMMARY. The purpose of this article is to present the author's personal journey as a heterosexual woman conducting research on domestic violence within the LGBT community. The contributions of these studies to the theoretical and knowledge base of this social problem provide evidence of the ability of a nonaffiliated member to produce meaningful and sensitive research within an oppressed population even on a sensitive topic. In this article the author presents her rationale, as an outsider, for being interested in the LGBT community and, more importantly, her adoption of eight innovative strategies to overcome methodological barriers. These strategies emerged from her initially designing these studies based on the feminist participatory research model. Each strategy is discussed with particular attention paid to the one that most influenced her life–immersion into the culture. Also presented are the exchanges of rigor for relevance in her research, and her perceptions of the costs and benefits of conducting research within a stigmatized population. *[Article copies available for a fee from The Haworth Document Delivery Service: 1-800-HAWORTH. E-mail address: <getinfo@haworthpressinc.com>*

Joan C. McClennen, MSW, PhD, is Associate Professor, School of Social Work, Southwest Missouri State University, Springfield, MO.

Address correspondence to: Dr. Joan C. McClennen, School of Social Work, Southwest Missouri State University, 901 S. National Avenue, Springfield, MO 65804 (E-mail: jcm334f@smsu.edu).

[Haworth co-indexing entry note]: "Researching Gay and Lesbian Domestic Violence: The Journey of a Non-LGBT Researcher." McClennen, Joan C. Co-published simultaneously in *Journal of Gay & Lesbian Social Services* (Harrington Park Press, an imprint of The Haworth Press, Inc.) Vol. 15, No. 1/2, 2003, pp. 31-45; and: *Research Methods with Gay, Lesbian, Bisexual, and Transgender Populations* (ed: William Meezan, and James I. Martin) Harrington Park Press, an imprint of The Haworth Press, Inc., 2003, pp. 31-45. Single or multiple copies of this article are available for a fee from The Haworth Document Delivery Service [1-800-HAWORTH, 9:00 a.m. - 5:00 p.m. (EST). E-mail address: getinfo@haworthpressinc.com].

31

KEYWORDS. Domestic violence, gay, lesbian, feminist participatory research, research methodology

Debate exists about the ability of nonaffiliated group members to do meaningful and sensitive research within oppressed populations. This ability is further challenged when the topic is of a sensitive nature. As a heterosexual woman, I have spent over six years investigating domestic violence within the lesbian, gay, bisexual, and transgender (LGBT) community. Adoption of innovative strategies assisted me in overcoming many methodological challenges, thereby producing quantitative studies that contribute to the knowledge base of this social problem. The purpose of this article is to share these strategies with others who are researching relatively unexplored social problems within oppressed populations for the ultimate purpose of overcoming social injustices. Rather than concentrating on my research results, I request that you accompany me on my journey as a stranger in a foreign land.

CHALLENGES OF NONAFFILIATED VERSUS AFFILIATED RESEARCHERS

If they are to produce meaningful results, nonaffiliated researchers within the LGBT community (as well as other oppressed populations) need to overcome the methodological challenges of theoretical approaches, gaining access to the community, and maintaining their professional ethics (Jacobson, 1995; Zinn, 1979). Because theoretical approaches are largely established using majority populations, and thus are not generalizable to minority cultures, researchers need to approach the LGBT community with alternative theoretical frameworks. Gaining initial access to the community, and securing the ongoing cooperation of its members, require researchers to adopt culturally-sensitive strategies enabling them to be considered as other than intrusive outsiders (Park, 1992). Nonaffiliated researchers are particularly suspect of violating their professional ethics by using studies of the LGBT community in order to enhance their own careers, rather than for reducing social injustices (Gorelick, 1991). Inability to overcome these challenges tends to result in oversimplification and overgeneralization of findings, creating a disservice to the oppressed community (Mindel & Kail, 1989; Warren, 1977).

The argument that affiliated members of the LGBT community have fewer problems in producing meaningful research has not held true. Although initial access to the community is more easily obtained, feelings of obligation and apprehension about public intervention may bias their work and preclude these researchers from accessing the inner circle of the community. Although affiliated researchers may have different problems in overcoming barriers to producing meaningful research, their problems are equally severe (Maykovich, 1977; Zinn, 1979). Both nonaffiliated and affiliated members of oppressed populations continue to search for strategies that will help them to overcome barriers to producing meaningful research.

PARTICIPATORY RESEARCH

Participatory research models have proven effective for qualitative researchers in overcoming various methodological challenges (theories, access, and ethics) by breaking many of the barriers that are present between themselves and members of oppressed populations (Denzin & Lincoln, 1998; Stoecker & Bonacich, 1992). The feminist participatory research model provides guidelines for both qualitative and quantitative researchers in producing meaningful results through the combination of investigating problems of concern to the LGBT population, approaching the study as an educational process for the researchers and the participants via collective interaction, and using the results of the study for social change (Park, 1992; Renzetti, 1995). Despite progress in reducing methodological challenges through the adoption of numerous models, current strategies remain insufficient for empowering the oppressed to break the barriers between themselves and the society that oppresses them (Gorelick, 1991).

Typically, researchers do not detail the specific strategies they use to generate knowledge in their writings. Instead, their focus is on the problems tackled, the general methods used, and the results obtained. Sufficient explanations of methods for obtaining the results are provided to assure scientific rigor within the investigation process. Understandably, this primary focus is based on researchers' ties to academia and the conventional norms of academic writing (Zinn, 1979). So, too, in researching same-gender domestic violence, I have journal articles reporting the outcomes of my studies, but until now, I have not written a detailed account of the strategies used to reach these findings.

In this article, I report my strategies for overcoming the challenges I faced in my work. In essence, this is a documentary of a heterosexual woman's journey within the LGBT community while conducting research on the sensitive subject of domestic violence. The hope is for this story to assist other non-LGBT researchers to produce empirical information aimed at reducing social injustices within the LGBT community.

MOTIVATION FOR RESEARCHING LGBT DOMESTIC VIOLENCE

My entrance to academia followed over 20 years of being a social worker, principally within the areas of family violence and mental health. Being a survivor of domestic violence, my interest in conducting research on this topic was natural. During the exploration of the domestic violence literature, a traumatic event occurred within my family; my brother's partner of 15 years, Jim, died of a heart attack. In the aftermath of his death, the two issues of domestic violence and same-gender relationships merged as a topic to which I began to dedicate my research. I reflected on the struggles my brother (who I will call Lee) had experienced during his life. While in a heterosexual marriage, he served his country and had three children. Following his divorce, he experienced many broken heterosexual relationships. In time, he began living with a man and identifying with the same-gender community. I observed my family's reactions to my brother's changed life. Mostly, silence prevailed as if nothing had occurred. I had my own inner turmoil in accepting Lee's changed life, due to belief in my church's doctrine. Despite all the feelings that haunted me, I remained silent. Prejudice rejoices in denial.

The silence between Lee and me ended with the family's trauma of a series of deaths, with Jim's being the final breaking point. Preceding Jim, within a four-year period, was the death of our parents, my sister's husband, and my husband. Lee and I shared the same sorrow in the loss of our loved ones. It was during this time, when we shared the same grieving process and inner battles, that I truly started to realize the similarities, rather than the differences, between same gender-oriented and opposite gender-oriented people.

As a professor, I wrote articles and taught classes about family violence. But I had read almost nothing about domestic violence between same-gender partners, nor had I given it much thought. Even though no problem of this nature had existed within Lee's relationship, Jim's death brought the question to my mind: "What about domestic violence between same-gender couples?" Soon finding that research on this topic was scarce, I continued my pursuit to answer this question. Although apprehensive about gathering information from members of a community about which I knew virtually nothing, this relatively unique topic fascinated me. Thus, my area of research was born. In time, I became a living testimony of Gorelick's (1991) findings–in participatory studies the researcher is transformed in the process as she influences and is influenced by those being researched.

Research Projects

With co-authors, I conducted two research projects; one addressed abuse between lesbian partners and the other between gay male partners. The purpose of the research with lesbians was to design a scale that assessed power imbalance resulting in abuse between partners. Based upon the available theoretical and empirical evidence (Coleman, 1996; Davies, 1995; Renzetti, 1992, 1996), factors were identified that could potentially be used to define and identify power imbalances. Convenience sampling techniques were implemented. Collected data were factor analyzed. The resulting Lesbian Partner Abuse Scale-Revised (LE-PAS-R) is a 25-item assessment tool having concurrent and construct validity. Further details of its construction are presented elsewhere (McClennen, Summers, & Daley, 2002).

The purpose of our research on gay male partner abuse was to obtain empirical evidence regarding the dynamics (forms, patterns, and frequencies), help-seeking behaviors, and correlates of this social problem. Methodological procedures were implemented to answer seven research questions. Data collected on a convenience sample were analyzed and compared with data from two other studies on same-gender partner abuse (Merrill & Wolfe, 2000; Renzetti, 1992). Results of this study are also presented elsewhere (McClennen, Summers, & Vaughan, 2002).

LEARNING MY WAY AROUND: THE JOURNEY

Following the Feminist Participatory Research Model

Considering that Renzetti (1992) was the first empirical article I read on same-gender partner abuse, I tended to follow many of her methods, including the adoption of the feminist participatory research model. With the intent of having this model help me overcome major methodological barriers, I followed its guiding principles: (a) a critical examination of cultural insensitivity within the research process; (b) giving voice to the members of the marginalized population; (c) rejecting the hierarchical relationship between the researcher and the researched in favor of acting in mutual relationship; (d) making a political and moral commitment to reducing social inequality; and (e) taking action on this commitment (Cancian, 1992 as cited in Renzetti, 1995).

I began to sensitize myself to the LGBT culture by performing volunteer services within it. I formed two research teams comprised of LGBT members to give voice to the community being researched and to break hierarchical relationships between the researchers and those being researched. I made a conscious commitment to the LGBT community to use the research findings toward overcoming social injustices. Had I known of the depth of the commitment needed to continue my research, I doubt that I would have had the courage to begin this journey.

Emerging Strategies

As I continued toward gaining acceptance, trust, support, and entrée into the same-gender oriented community, various strategies for overcoming methodological barriers emerged: (a) becoming educated about the culture; (b) preparing for objections; (c) incorporating instruments designed by those being researched; (d) implementing various sampling techniques; (e) engaging affiliated members for assistance; (f) becoming immersed in the culture; (g) collaborating with scholars and other professionals; and (h) triangulation in data collection. Specifics about each of these strategies are presented to assist future researchers in overcoming the barriers they will face in conducting research with these and other marginalized populations.

Becoming educated about the culture was a slow, arduous, continuous process. Through continually searching library holdings and making contacts following any leads, I read the classics on the topic of same-gender partner abuse (Island & Letellier, 1991; Lobel, 1989; Renzetti, 1992). And, using the snowball technique, I spoke with individuals throughout the United States who were interested in this topic.

I formed a Lesbian Advisory Committee consisting of a dozen lesbians and lesbian-friendly women. These women initially met at my home on a Saturday afternoon to give their opinions regarding my conducting research within their community, and after supporting this idea, to help design the Lesbian Partner Abuse Scale. Other contacts were made by telephone, through e-mail, and in person.

I worked with a less formalized group of gay men to assist in the study within their community. A gay male friend made possible my invitation to visit the group during one of their weekly meetings. The purpose of the visit was to obtain their opinions and sanction for my conducting research within their community. Being supportive, they acted in an advisory capacity during the project's design and implementation. Contacts were also maintained with members of this group throughout the study.

Attendance at a meeting of Parents and Friends of Lesbians and Gay Men (PFLAG) and at a national conference targeting LGBT issues proved educational. At both meetings I made presentations about my research and was able to obtain feedback:

Preparing for objections helped to reduce my anticipatory stress. During the beginning years of my research, a few members of the same-gender oriented community raised objections. Two poignant objections were my being opposite-gender oriented and my use of politically incorrect phrases (e.g., alternative lifestyle). I attempted to overcome these objections by relying on the advice of the same-gender oriented individuals who supported me, continuing my involvement with the community, and being truly committed to the cause of using my research to reduce social injustices within this community.

These objections helped prepare me for the rejection I expected from a large portion of the LGBT community. The reality was quite different. For the most part, I was accepted and patiently educated by the people with whom I had contact. When I asked one person if I had an opportunity to be accepted, the unforgettable reply was, "We're not the ones who discriminate." I have received complimentary advertising, booths, meals, and board. Most of all, I received patience, kindness, cooperation, and psychological support.

Incorporating instruments designed by those being researched is presupposed within the feminist participatory research model. Systematic error from using culturally inappropriate instruments can cause immeasurable harm. The instrument designed by Renzetti (1992) to gather data from lesbians experiencing partner abuse served as a model in designing the instruments for my two studies. The two advisory groups–one of lesbians and one of gay men–assisted in content validation of the instruments.

Implementing various sampling techniques was essential for obtaining respondents. Initially, we randomly selected 300 therapists to mail our instruments for the construction of the Lesbian Partner Abuse Scale, and another 300 to mail instruments for obtaining data on gay male partner abuse. Our efforts met with dismal results; the total response was 17 (2.8%) out of the 600 requests.

As alternative techniques for obtaining respondents, we used purposive, snowball, and convenience sampling. Ironically, the failure of our original data gathering method led to enriching experiences in the LGBT community and the commitment needed to continue my research. The most effective source of data came from person-to-person contacts, including those with individuals at PRIDE festivals, professionals at conferences, and members of the local community. In addition, advertisements were placed in LGBT-oriented magazines, and counselors, administrators, friends, and family members knowing of potential respondents were mailed packets of information.

Engaging affiliated members for assistance began with two individuals–one lesbian and one gay man. As a former victim of domestic violence, the woman allowed me to tape an interview for use in my presentation at a national conference. She was my access to many of the women who served on the lesbian advisory committee, to volunteer opportunities with the LGBT community, and to other persons within the community.

A gay man who expressed interest in the research was invited to assist in its implementation. He became my advocate and teacher, as he shared information about the community and accompanied me to various events and locations (e.g., restaurants and libraries) that targeted the LGBT community. Having these closely affiliated members to assist me in the research process was immeasurably helpful.

Becoming immersed in the culture required a multifaceted approach. Becoming immersed tends to overlap with other strategies (e.g., becoming educated); however, the experiences are more intense in the immersion process. During the immersion process I not only came to know about the LGBT community, but to socialize in it and form friendships with its members.

My attendance at the national conference targeting the LGBT community and at several PRIDE festivals was quite valuable. Although the initial intent of attending these events was research oriented–to present the studies and to collect data–these encounters helped to immerse me in LGBT culture. These immersion experiences were open, honest, and sincere efforts to understand a culture unfamiliar to me by getting to know people within it. Approaching these events as a researcher would not have resulted in the same outcome.

My male partner, Ivan, attended most of these events with me. His experiences, coupled with mine, changed our attitudes toward persons seemingly different from ourselves; they therefore changed our lives as well. These experiences, which influenced us emotionally and spiritually, were far beyond the mere cognitive domain of educational events. Although not considered homophobic, Ivan had been relatively uninterested in discussing any topic about same-gender oriented individuals. In time, and with his interaction with attendees at the conference and festivals, he was transformed into an ardent advocate for the rights of LGBT people. His transformation was evidence for the assertion that lack of understanding should not be confused with intolerance (Smith & Dale, 1999).

The PRIDE festival within my own urban/rural community led to my meeting and identifying with a largely closeted group of individuals who seemed equally surprised to see me in attendance. Word of mouth continued to assist in my connecting professionally and socially with LGBT individuals and their advocates. The conference and other PRIDE festivals were held in metropolitan cities. Most of the time, Ivan and I were on our own in these unfamiliar environments; we became the "minority." Most people sensed we "looked lost." Rather than discriminating against us, people went out of their way to help us feel comfortable and welcomed.

The following encounters, although they may seem trite to others, were exceedingly personal and life-changing to us:

- At the conference, we had the opportunity to speak with innumerable individuals about health care and related issues. We asked questions about medications being displayed for HIV-positive individuals and about other personal issues. While people around us were discussing the various options, we had no clue what they were talking about; it was a foreign language. Although feeling somewhat embarrassed by my unending, seemingly ignorant questions of the most intimate nature, no one laughed; they enthusiastically helped us to learn.
- At one dinner, our gay male friend informed us that he was surprised we did not mind being seen with him, since many people would not want to share dinner with a gay man. Ivan and I had not given this a second thought; he was our friend!
- During a walk to observe contributions to the AIDS Memorial Quilt, I could barely hold back the tears as I thought of all the young men who had died so tragically and senselessly; as my lesbian acquaintance shed tears, we formed a bond.
- Before Ivan saw the Quilt, a man had informed him that one reason we were having so much trouble finding gay male respondents was because many of them had died from AIDS. The actual experience of seeing and reading squares of the quilt embedded in Ivan's psyche the overwhelming truth of this statement. To him, this was an emotional and spiritual awakening.
- At one of the festivals, we became acquainted with a man whose booth was next to ours. He was a volunteer at a shop supplying donated items for members of the LGBT community, especially those suffering from HIV and AIDS. For years after that event, Ivan and I would attempt to take items to this man and keep in touch by telephone; numerous failures, we believe, came from his increasing health problems.
- At PRIDE festivals Ivan sat and had drinks with gay men; his initial intent was to discuss my research and elicit their assistance. Their conversations lasted for hours and touched on an endless number of subjects, similar to his conversations with his opposite-gender oriented friends. Gay men became just "men."

Aside from these experiences, Ivan and I went with my brother Lee and his new partner (who I will call Mitch) to various LGBT bars. We danced, socialized, and celebrated one New Year's Eve in a gay male bar. We also accompanied Lee and Mitch to numerous church services. My most emotionally intense experience was sharing communion with the two of them and a minister as we prayed before Lee's surgery. The tears I shed heightened my commitment to my research despite my adversaries, and to its ultimate use to alleviate social injustice.

All these experiences served to immerse me in the LGBT community. I became sensitized to the similarities rather than the differences between members of the opposite-gender and same-gender oriented communities. Cultural immersion included my participation on a website advocating LGBT issues and writing proposals to obtain funding for further research and services.

Collaborating with scholars and other professionals researching or employed in the LGBT community established relationships that assisted me in gathering information about LGBT culture and about available services throughout the U.S. These individuals also helped me to locate respondents. Some were researchers who willingly shared the results of their studies even prior to their publication, thus helping to keep us aware of the latest findings. I had the privilege of joining the Editorial Board of a same-gender oriented professional journal and of serving on a doctoral committee at another university; the student had heard of my research and contacted me for assistance. I continue to receive e-mail from across the U.S. and am able to share information about research and services. These ongoing contacts maintain a feeling of camaraderie among individuals interested in helping the LGBT community to alleviate the problem of partner abuse.

Triangulation in data collection enhanced the cooperation of respondents at PRIDE festivals by having at least two trained individuals collecting data who were different in style and gender. During these festivals, Ivan and I circulated to recruit respondents. Although we asked the same questions, we had two different styles–he as an extrovert salesman and I as a more introverted professor. The higher comfort level between him and gay men was balanced with my higher comfort level with lesbians. Together, we were able to obtain the interest and involvement of both men and women. Had we obtained additional grant funding, we could have hired members of the LGBT community to assist in data gathering at these events.

Obtaining gay male respondents was more difficult than obtaining lesbian respondents. At the festivals, lesbians were more receptive to discussing our research. This experience supported the literature about the "veil of secrecy" (Montero, 1977, p. 5) gay men maintain about partner abuse to protect their community from further stigmatization.

Thus, in the debate regarding the need for researchers to be affiliated members of the community under study, I side with those who believe that being knowledgeable, sensitive, and culturally unbiased can compensate for this cultural difference. To a great extent, I was able to conduct my research by adopting the feminist participatory research model and by implementing innovative strategies for overcoming methodological challenges.

APPROPRIATE USE OF RESEARCH FINDINGS

According to the feminist participatory research perspective and the National Association of Social Workers' Code of Ethics (NASW, 1996), research findings are to be used for the reduction of social injustices. Researchers, especially those studying sensitive issues within stigmatized populations, must not lose sight of those who would misuse their findings to increase the stigma. Both same-gender and opposite-gender oriented persons can condemn researchers publishing about same-gender partner abuse by accusing them of "fueling heterosexism" (Renzetti, 1999, p. xi). The more stigmatized the population being researched, the more sensitive researchers need to be in relating findings.

Overgeneralizing findings tends to oversimplify problems. Many research studies on same-gender partner abuse use a small number of respondents from a relatively homogeneous group; most respondents are from the middle and upper class (Merrill & Wolfe, 2000; Renzetti, 1992). My respondents were no exception. In generalizing from our findings, researchers must be specific as to who their samples were and how they were chosen. This is not to diminish the importance of these studies' findings. Each piece of the puzzle helps to put together the whole picture of same-gender partner abuse. The nature of partner abuse is as complex as the people involved. The more the problem is understood, the faster prevention and intervention strategies can be implemented.

Appropriate use of findings involves communicating these findings to other researchers interested in the issue. It also demands remaining politically and morally committed to the use of research findings for reducing social inequality in the population under study (Stoecker & Bonacich, 1992).

COSTS TO RESEARCHERS CONDUCTING STUDIES ON STIGMATIZED POPULATIONS

Straight researchers of LGBT populations need to be aware of the potential personal and professional costs of being identified with the population under study. The same environmental pressures placed on the stigmatized community, such as individual and institutionalized homophobia, are placed on them (Montero, 1977; Warren, 1977). If researchers are willing to assume these pressures, they need to develop strategies to cope with them.

Some of the pressures I have had to endure in order to study same-gender partner abuse included: (a) upon reading that my research was being partially funded by the University, two prominent citizens contacted the University administration and questioned its quality and appropriateness; (b) being untenured at the time, I became apprehensive about continued employment because of my topic of research, which proved to be unnecessary since university personnel remained supportive; (c) the prejudices of many of my family members caused me to have to refrain from discussing my work; and (d) innuendoes of my being lesbian were spread to students, faculty, and to my male partner.

The strategies we developed to overcome these environmental pressures were based on our making a conscious decision as to the amount of personal and professional risk I was willing to take to continue my research. We prepared for potential negative professional consequences, trusted in the support provided by colleagues and administrators, sought a church that was nondiscriminatory toward same-gender oriented persons, and maintained a veil of silence toward family members and acquaintances who were offended by my work. Undertaking and continuing research of stigmatized populations requires commitment to the ethical contract that exists between the researcher and those being researched.

RIGOR VERSUS RELEVANCE IN STUDYING STIGMATIZED POPULATIONS

Rigor, the extent to which methodology has been followed, is emphasized in quantitative research. Relevance, the extent to which a study is useful for developing theory or social policy, is the emphasis of qualitative research. Rather than being seen as a dichotomy, research can be conceptualized as existing on a continuum, with exchanges between rigor and relevance (Denzin & Lincoln, 1998). The feminist participatory research model is a paradigm falling midway on the quantitative-qualitative continuum. My two research projects reported quantitative outcomes. However, the methodology required the flexibility necessary to follow the model's guiding principles.

The innovative techniques implemented in conducting my studies inevitably detracted from their internal and external validity. Respondents self-identifying as victims of partner abuse may actually be perpetrators who think they are or were victims; volunteers may be different from non-volunteers; and non-random selection of respondents limits generalizability. However, adopting innovative, unconventional methodologies is necessary if research on sensitive topics within stigmatized populations is to be relevant and useful (Jacobson, 1995; Roffman, Picciano, Wickizer, Bolan, & Ryan, 1998). Researchers need to make conscious decisions regarding the exchange between rigor and relevance. In essence, I made a decision to trade some rigor for relevance in order to decrease the social injustices suffered by members of the LGBT community experiencing partner abuse.

BENEFITS OF "DOING IT MY WAY"

The purposes of research are to develop theory, to increase the knowledge base of our profession, to improve the effectiveness of our interventions with clients, and to reduce social injustices (Grinnell, 1997). The products of my research within the LGBT community can assist professionals in: approaching this problem from different theoretical perspectives; improving their skills through the use of screening instruments to detect potential abuse; continuing their efforts to further comprehend the dynamics of this social problem; advocating to reduce social injustices based on my findings; and empowering members of the LGBT community (McClennen, 1999; McClennen & Gunther, 1999).

We must never lose sight of the reasons we dedicate ourselves to chosen endeavors at the cost of alternative activities. As I continue on my journey, I am asked to contemplate, in retrospect, the benefits gained in conducting my research the way I thought was right, despite any criticisms of over-involvement in the community or of the exchange between rigor and relevance. In addition to professional satisfaction, my benefits are personal. Through this process, my theological and psychological foundations were shaken, torn apart, and rebuilt. I have gained in spiritual peace within myself and through fellowship with others who are open to diverse populations. Peace within oneself is an invaluable benefit. I have watched my partner shed his prejudicial feelings, and he continues on this journey with me. Having someone on a journey makes it less lonely and deepens the bond between the travelers. I came to an awareness of my unconscious prejudice and have overcome it. Having brought it out of its closet, it no longer exists. Lack of prejudice opens the gate for exciting new experiences of life. As a professor, I share my experiences with my students. If nothing else, this forces them to think critically about their choices in life. Many have thanked me for my openness, whether or not they agree with me. These are some of the small rewards of teaching.

However, the ultimate benefit of making a journey to a strange land is enlightenment. In my case, the enlightenment was filled with new dimensions of love for life.

REFERENCES

Coleman, V.E. (1996). Lesbian battering: The relationship between personality and the perpetration of violence. In L.K. Hamberger & C. Renzetti (Eds.), *Domestic partner abuse* (pp. 77-102). New York: Springer.

Davies, L.V. (1995). Domestic violence. In R.L. Edwards (Ed.), *Encyclopedia of social work* (19th ed.) (pp. 780-795). Washington, DC: NASW Press.

Denzin, N.K., & Lincoln, Y.S. (1998). Introduction. In N.K. Denzin & Y.S. Lincoln (Eds.), *Strategies of qualitative inquiry* (pp. 1-34). Thousand Oaks, CA: Sage.

Gorelick, S. (1991). Contradictions of feminist methodology. *Gender & Society, 5(4),* 459-477.

Grinnell, Jr., R.M. (1997). *Social work research & evaluation: Quantitative and qualitative approaches.* Itasca, IL: F.E. Peacock.

Island, D., & Letellier, P. (1991). *Men who beat the men who love them: Battered gay men and domestic violence.* Binghamton, NY: The Haworth Press, Inc.

Jacobson, S. (1995). Methodological issues in research on older lesbians. *Journal of Gay & Lesbian Social Services, 3(1),* 43-46.

Lobel, K. (Ed.) (1989). *Naming the violence: Speaking out about lesbian battering.* Seattle: Seal Press.

Maykovich, M.K. (1977). The difficulties of a minority researcher in minority communities. *Journal of Social Issues, 33(4),* 108-119.

McClennen, J.C. (1999). Prevailing theories regarding same-gender partner abuse: Proposing the feminist social-psychological model. In J.C. McClennen & J. Gunther (Eds.), *A professional guide to understanding gay and lesbian domestic violence: Understanding practice interventions* (pp. 3-12). Lewiston, NY: The Edwin Mellen Press.

McClennen, J.C., & Gunther, J. (Eds.) (1999). *A professional guide to understanding gay and lesbian domestic violence: Understanding practice interventions.* Lewiston, NY: The Edwin Mellen Press.

McClennen, J.C., Summers, A.B., & Daley, J.G. (2002). The Lesbian Partner Abuse Scale. *Research on Social Work Practice, 12(2),* 277-292.

McClennen, J.C., Summers, A.B., & Vaughan. C. (2002). Gay men's domestic violence: Dynamics, help-seeking behaviors, and correlates. *Journal of Gay & Lesbian Social Services, 14(1),* 23-50.

Merrill, G.S., & Wolfe, V.A. (2000). Battered gay men: An exploration of abuse, help seeking, and why they stay. *Journal of Homosexuality, 39(2),* 1-30.

Mindel, C.H., & Kail, B.L. (1989). Issues in research on the older woman of color. *Journal of Drug Issues, 19(2),* 191-206.

Montero, D. (1977). Research among racial and cultural minorities: An overview. *Journal of Social Issues, 33(4),* 1-20.

National Association of Social Workers. (1996). *Code of ethics.* Washington, DC: Author.

Park, P. (1992). The discovery of participatory research as a new scientific paradigm: Personal and intellectual accounts. *American Sociologist, 23,* 29-42.

Renzetti, C. (1992). *Violent betrayal: Partner abuse in lesbian relationships.* Newbury Park, CA: Sage Publications.

Renzetti, C.M. (1995). Studying partner abuse in lesbian relationships: A case for the feminist participatory research model. *Journal of Gay & Lesbian Social Services, 3(1),* 29-42.

Renzetti, C.M. (1996). The poverty of services for battered lesbians. In C.M. Renzetti & C.H. Miley (Eds.), *Violence in gay and lesbian domestic partnerships* (pp. 61-68). Binghamton, NY: Harrington Park Press.

Renzetti, C.M. (1999). Preface. In J.C. McClennen & J. Gunther (Eds.), *A professional guide to understanding gay and lesbian domestic violence: Understanding practice interventions* (pp. ix-xiii). Lewiston, NY: The Edwin Mellen Press.

Roffman, R.A., Picciano, J., Wickizer, L., Bolan, M., & Ryan, R. (1998). Anonymous enrollment in AIDS prevention telephone group counseling: Facilitating the participation of gay and bisexual men in intervention and research. *Journal of Social Service Research, 23(3-4),* 5-22.

Smith, R., & Dale, O. (1999). The evolution of social policy in gay/lesbian/bisexual domestic violence. In J.C. McClennen & J. Gunther (Eds.), *A professional guide to understanding gay and lesbian domestic violence: Understanding practice interventions* (pp. 257-276). Lewiston, NY: The Edwin Mellen Press.

Stoecker, R., & Bonacich, E. (1992). Why participatory research? *American Sociologist, 23(4),* 5-14.

Warren, C.A. (1977). Fieldwork in the gay world: Issues in phenomenological research. *Journal of Social Issues, 33(4),* 93-107.

Zinn, M.B. (1979). Field research in minority communities: Ethical, methodological, and political observations by an insider. *Social Problems, 27(2),* 209-219.

Empowering Gay and Lesbian Caregivers and Uncovering Their Unique Experiences Through the Use of Qualitative Methods

Kristina M. Hash
Elizabeth P. Cramer

SUMMARY. Studies over the last two decades have greatly advanced knowledge about gay and lesbian aging. These studies have also discovered the challenges involved in studying older gay and lesbian populations. The study described in this article adds to this knowledge by examining the caregiving experiences of this "hidden" population. It describes the research process used in the study, and advocates for the use of qualitative methods to empower study respondents and uncover their

---

Kristina M. Hash, MSW, PhD, LCSW, is Assistant Professor, West Virginia University, School of Social Work and Public Administration, Division of Social Work, Morgantown, WV. Elizabeth P. Cramer, MSW, PhD, LCSW, ACSW, is Associate Professor, Virginia Commonwealth University School of Social Work, Richmond, VA.

Address correspondence to: Kristina M. Hash, West Virginia University, School of Social Work and Public Administration, Division of Social Work, P.O. Box 6830, Morgantown, WV 26506-6830 (E-mail: hash-k@lycos.com).

This article is based upon dissertation research conducted by Kristina Hash. Special appreciation is given to the nineteen study participants for their willingness to share their stories and contribute to the study methodology.

[Haworth co-indexing entry note]: "Empowering Gay and Lesbian Caregivers and Uncovering Their Unique Experiences Through the Use of Qualitative Methods." Hash, Kristina M., and Elizabeth P. Cramer. Co-published simultaneously in *Journal of Gay & Lesbian Social Services* (Harrington Park Press, an imprint of The Haworth Press, Inc.) Vol. 15, No. 1/2, 2003, pp. 47-63; and: *Research Methods with Gay, Lesbian, Bisexual, and Transgender Populations* (ed: William Meezan, and James I. Martin) Harrington Park Press, an imprint of The Haworth Press, Inc., 2003, pp. 47-63. Single or multiple copies of this article are available for a fee from The Haworth Document Delivery Service [1-800-HAWORTH, 9:00 a.m. - 5:00 p.m. (EST). E-mail address: getinfo@haworthpressinc.com].

47

unique experiences. It also presents the challenges faced, strategies employed, and lessons learned from the study. *[Article copies available for a fee from The Haworth Document Delivery Service: 1-800-HAWORTH. E-mail address: <getinfo@haworthpressinc.com> Website: <http://www.HaworthPress.com> © 2003 by The Haworth Press, Inc. All rights reserved.]*

KEYWORDS. Qualitative research, caregiving, aging, gay men, lesbians

Since the 1970s, researchers have studied the unique issues gay men and lesbians face in aging. Overall, these studies have found that older gay men and lesbians are psychologically well adjusted, have high levels of self-acceptance, have strong friendship ties, and tend to couple with same-aged peers (Berger, 1982; Dorfman, Walters, Burke, Hardin, & Karanik, 1995; Quam & Whitford, 1992). Some advantages to aging among gay men and lesbians have also been found, such as the ability to manage stigma, learning self-reliance at a younger age, and gender role flexibility (Berger, 1982; Friend, 1980; Kehoe, 1988).

Although several studies have focused attention on the issues facing gay men and lesbians in older adulthood, very few researchers have sought out the experiences of gay men and lesbians in midlife. As a result, very little is known about the midlife experience of this population. Existing studies seem to suggest that midlife lesbians develop a solid sense of self and receive strong support from female friendship networks (Sang, 1991; Weinstock, 2000). As compared to their heterosexual counterparts, midlife lesbians may be more accepting of the physical changes of aging, but they may also experience greater financial challenges (Bradford & Ryan, 1991; Sang, 1991). Most researchers looking at gay men in midlife have either included them in studies of older gay men (Berger, 1982; Gray & Dressel, 1985), or have based their conclusions solely upon theory (Kimmel & Sang, 1995; Kooden, 1997).

Aside from the HIV/AIDS literature (e.g., Folkman, Chesney, & Christopher-Richards, 1994; Turner, Catania, & Gagnon, 1994), and one survey of gay and lesbian caregivers (Frederikson, 1999), non-normative life events such as chronic illness and caregiving are not addressed within this population. Even when addressing caregiving issues, studies largely exclude the experiences of gay men and lesbians over 50. The traditional elder caregiving literature (e.g., Cantor, 1983; Poulshock & Deimling, 1984; Zarit, Todd, & Zarit, 1986) that addresses caregiving among persons over 50 describes the experiences of caregivers who are adult daughters and (presumably) heterosexual spouses. As a result, very little is known about caregiving among midlife and older gay men and lesbians.

To address the need for research in this area, this qualitative study was conducted to uncover the unique aspects of the caregiving experiences of midlife and older gay men and lesbians who provide care to chronically ill partners. It chronicles the researcher's exploration of this little-known phenomenon and highlights the opportunities involved in conducting qualitative research with a population that lacks sufficient voice in the literature. Challenges in conducting research in this area, and strategies used to overcome the challenges, are also discussed. Finally, the lessons learned through this process, and suggestions for future studies, are shared.

THE CURRENT STUDY

The aim of the current study was to add to the existing knowledge base by illuminating the unique caregiving experiences of midlife and older gay men and lesbians. It also sought to understand their experiences in the "post-caregiving" period, or following the cessation of care. Toward this aim, a qualitative approach was employed. Before providing a rationale for and a detailing of the specific methods used, it is first necessary to clarify what is meant by a "qualitative approach."

Although various traditions of qualitative research exist, qualitative inquiry usually involves a few common elements. To begin, qualitative methods are often used when a topic is exploratory in nature and ideologically in line with the phenomenological or interpretive paradigm, which is subjective and which seeks to understand the complexity of phenomena (Maykut & Morehouse, 1994). These methods also use the researcher as the data collection instrument, and the data collection occurs in the naturalistic settings of the respondents (Lincoln & Guba, 1985). Through data collection, the researcher seeks to discover meanings, or how people make sense out of the world and of events in their lives (Bogdan & Bilken, 1998). Data analysis is inductive, without regard for preconceived hypotheses, and themes and patterns emerge from the data or words of the study respondents (Patton, 1990). The overall design is emergent, and it evolves as the study progresses (Lincoln & Guba, 1985). Methods are flexible and may change during the course of the study (Patton, 1990).

Qualitative methods were therefore appropriate for addressing the topic of the present study. Because it involved an area in which very little is known, an exploratory study with an emergent design was desired. An additional attraction to qualitative inquiry was based on its potential to empower study respondents. In light of this aspect, Rubin and Rubin (1995) note that the qualitative interview allows respondents to tell their story, and it sends them the message that others care about and value their experiences. They further assert that talking about difficult experiences can help respondents make meaning out of their suffering and allow them to gain new insights and understandings of their experiences.

Qualitative research can be especially empowering for members of oppressed groups and marginalized populations. Lincoln (1995) describes qualitative inquiry as involving a commitment that "enables and promotes social justice, community, diversity, civic discourse, and caring" (p. 6). LeCompte (1993) asserts that there is a duty to involve marginalized populations in qualitative research, and he encourages qualitative researchers to "seek out the silenced" (p. 10) for inclusion in research. This "seeking out" of the experiences of "the silenced" echoes the perspective held by many qualitative researchers that qualitative inquiry should give "voice" to those whose views and experiences are not typically captured in traditional research (Lincoln, 1995).

Not only did qualitative inquiry provide appropriate methods to answer the study's research questions, but it also promoted social justice by giving voice to the experiences of caregivers who are members of a marginalized population and whose stories are not told in the traditional literature. In addition, this study uncovered the injustices respondents experienced in their interactions with professionals and organizations, and it sought their suggestions regarding individual, organizational, and societal changes that could remedy such injustices.

In addition to the potential to empower study participants, qualitative inquiry also allowed for the use of specific methods to match the needs of the study. For the present study, it was decided not to align with a particular qualitative research tradition (such as constructivism, phenomenology, and grounded theory). Instead, as Patton (1990) suggests, the study methodology reflected a "pragmatic" approach to qualitative research. Using this approach, the researcher is concerned more with the appropriateness of specific methods rather than choosing methods based upon adherence to a paradigm or research tradition. Patton calls this a "paradigm of choices," which "recognizes that different methods are appropriate for different situations" (p. 39). In this case, the methods one uses are based upon the study's purpose and research questions, as well as the time and money available.

SPECIFIC METHODS EMPLOYED

Several qualitative methods were used in the conduct of the present study. Sampling was purposive, meaning subjects were chosen based on the purpose of the study and the researcher's knowledge about the population of interest (Rubin & Babbie, 1997). Recruitment strategies included the use of known community agencies, the gay and lesbian media, and contacts in the gay/lesbian community. The study employed in-depth interviews to collect data from the 19 study respondents. An interview guide was used to ensure that key topics were addressed with each respondent. As new topics and themes emerged, the interview guide was revised for subsequent interviews. The interview guide contained questions related to these topics: caregiving and post-caregiving experiences; encounters with formal and informal support persons; plans and decision-making processes; and suggestions for sampling this study population.

Data from these interviews were analyzed using a constant comparison method, which involves the unitizing of data, the identification and refinement of themes, and the simultaneous processes of coding and analyzing data (Taylor & Bogdan, 1998). Analysis began with reading and re-reading interview field notes and replaying audiotapes of the interviews for further clarification. During this process, data were divided into units of meaning. These units varied in length from one word to one paragraph, and were assigned topics that described their content. Units were compared and contrasted, and organized into categories representing topic meanings. Categories were compared and contrasted, resulting in the identification of patterns among the categories. Finally, an integrative diagram was developed to visually display these patterns and show relationships among categories (McMillan & Schumacher, 1997).

Several techniques were used to ensure rigor in the study, including the use of thick description of findings and the maintenance of a field journal and field log. The field journal included observations of emerging themes, issues of validity, and questions for future interviews. The field log consisted of dates, times, and strategies used to attain respondents. A database was developed and maintained for this purpose.

Member checking was also applied and involved seeking feedback from study participants about the data and conclusions (Lincoln & Guba, 1985). Member checking can be solicited in a variety of ways and during different stages of a study. In this study, five respondents served as member checkers and were given a draft of the study findings for review. These respondents were asked to assess the accuracy and clarity of main points, conclusions, and interpretations. In general, peer debriefers found the write-ups to be very engaging and comprehensive. There were only a few recommendations for changes to content, which usually involved placing greater emphasis on certain findings discovered in the data analysis. Some commented on how the use of rich narration and quotations made the findings more "real" than those found in traditional (quantitative) studies. A few also mentioned that they were very taken with the comments and experiences of the other respondents and truly empathized with them.

Peer debriefing was also used to ensure rigor, and involved engaging a colleague to play "devil's advocate" and check on the inquiry process (Lincoln & Guba, 1985). The peer debriefer was a classmate who met with the researcher to confer about methods and the evolution of the study. Issues discussed during peer debriefing sessions included sampling strategies, and the use of the Internet, data analysis, and self-disclosure.

METHODOLOGICAL CHALLENGES AND STRATEGIES USED TO OVERCOME THEM

In conducting the present study, several methodological challenges arose. However, due to the flexibility of the study design, the researcher was able to employ certain strategies to overcome them. The foremost challenges were related to sampling and the role of the researcher.

Sampling

In conducting the study, the most significant challenge was recruiting a diverse and numerically adequate sample. This challenge was expected, as numerous other researchers have noted the difficulty of collecting adequate and diverse samples within this population (Berger, 1984; Jacobson, 1995; Kehoe, 1988; Quam & Whitford, 1992). As a result, samples have tended to overrepresent younger (ages 50-60), male, white, middle to upper class, urban members. Some believe the difficulty in sampling is due to the "invisibility" of older gay men and lesbians (Berger, 1982; Kehoe, 1988). Older lesbians may not identify themselves as "lesbian," which compounds these sampling difficulties (Jacobson, 1995; Kehoe, 1988).

The initial sampling strategy involved advertising in a limited geographical area; four respondents were recruited using this strategy. To recruit a larger and more diverse sample, the researcher decided to expand the area of recruitment to attract persons in other parts of the country. Once the geographic area of recruitment was expanded, telephone interviews became a necessary means of data collection for the respondents who lived more than a few hours away.

This expanded recruitment strategy was accomplished mostly through advertising on the Internet and in gay and lesbian newspapers with large circulations. To recruit additional respondents, the researcher also made more of an effort to develop personal contacts. These contacts were made at conferences and through gay and lesbian organizations. The expanded sampling strategy yielded 15 additional respondents.

Snowball sampling was also attempted, as it has been noted to be a method that works well in identifying members of a population who are hard to reach (Rubin & Babbie, 1997). In using snowball sampling, participants are asked to identify other potential participants who they know. Unfortunately, no additional participants were obtained through the use of this method, even though a few respondents did mention that they would pass along information about the study to friends who had been caregivers.

To recruit the sample, approximately 1,000 flyers and advertisements were distributed to 175 individuals and organizations in 15 states, mostly in the Southern and Northeastern U.S. and the District of Columbia. Advertisements were placed in the gay and lesbian media (including independent newspapers) and in the bulletins of gay and lesbian social, political, and spiritual organizations. Flyers were sent to gay and lesbian organizations, bookstores, social groups, groups for gay and lesbian cultural minorities, and support groups, as well as hospice agencies and support groups for persons with HIV/AIDS. They were also sent to university women's centers and to personal contacts of the researcher.

Several ads were placed on Internet message boards. Most of these boards were specifically for older gay men and lesbians. Most of the inquiries received from these ads were from women. Unfortunately, only three persons (out of 12) recruited through this means followed through and returned the consent form, and only two of them went on to participate in an interview. Some stopped contact with the researcher at the point when they learned that they would need to complete a consent form or that the interview would be conducted in person or over the telephone. From e-mail contacts with these persons, it seems that many were interested in remaining anonymous, and preferred to fill out an online survey or to be asked questions via an e-mail or chat room medium.

Chatroom and e-mail interviews were not conducted for two reasons. The first was out of concern for the respondent's privacy, as there is no way to prevent others from viewing the often-sensitive content of an interview in such media. The second was the desire for uniformity across interviews, as an electronic media interview does not allow for the vocal variations and gestures that exist within the context of face-to-face and phone interviews.

Another interesting aspect of respondent recruitment was that the initial contact between the majority ($n = 16$; 84%) of respondents and the researcher was through e-mail. This is intriguing, since the flyers and ads that were not posted on the Internet included both a phone number and an e-mail address. This significant use of e-mail may have been due to the efficiency of this method or may have occurred because it is a less revealing form of communication. Interestingly, the two respondents who heard about the study on the Internet made additional e-mail inquiries with the researcher prior to their agreeing to participate in the study. This may be because material placed on the Internet is perceived as being suspicious.

Due to the difficulty in sampling this "hidden population," the researcher solicited feedback from the respondents about the best ways to recruit older gay and lesbian caregivers for the study. Most of the suggested avenues for recruitment had already been explored by the researcher, including Metropolitan Community Churches, HIV/AIDS services, and gay and lesbian newsletters. A few novel sampling strategies were uncovered in this process, including advertising in the general media, contacting "Gay AA" groups, and distributing flyers to services in cities that have a high percentage of gay and lesbian retirees.

The researcher also discussed the difficulty of sampling this population with the study respondents. Respondents agreed that gay men and lesbians over 50 would be very difficult to recruit, and some suggested that particular segments of this population are even harder to reach, such as lesbians over 70, older gay men and lesbians of color, those involved in gay spiritual organizations, and those in the South.

Of the 19 study respondents, four were recruited through agencies that specifically served older gay men and lesbians, and three were recruited through social and political organizations that cater to this group. Six were attracted to the study through ads in gay and lesbian newspapers. Three were recruited through ads on gay and lesbian message boards on the Internet. Two respondents were recruited through personal contacts of the researcher, and one was recruited through a Metropolitan Community Church. No participants were recruited by referral from general health care or social service support groups or agencies.

The respondents included nine women and 10 men who ranged in age from 50-77 ($M = 60$). Many lived in the Northeast and South. All but five had at least a four-year college degree, and all but one appeared to be at least middle class in terms of income. Although many efforts were made to recruit nonwhite participants, the final sample contained only two persons of color.

Researcher Role

The researcher role also presented challenges during the course of the study. The researcher role is described as the "social relationship" that the researcher has with the study respondents (McMillan & Schumacher, 1997). In line with in-depth interviews, the relationship with the majority of respondents was brief but personal (Marshall & Rossman, 1995). In the present study, the researcher's self-disclosure of sexual orientation was a critical issue and challenge.

During the initial interviews, a few respondents were interested in knowing the sexual orientation of the researcher prior to completing the interview. After the researcher disclosed to a male respondent that she was a lesbian, he then mentioned the fact that he was a teacher and did not want to be "outed" in his workplace. Others mentioned that some people may be afraid to be "outed" by responding to an ad for this type of study. Because the sexual orientation of the researcher seemed to matter to a few of the early respondents, she changed the flyer and advertisements to include a statement that she was "involved in the gay community." It was thought that, in some cases, self-disclosure would facilitate a more trusting and comfortable environment, and that respondents would find that a gay or lesbian researcher would better understand challenges they faced related to their sexual orientation.

To further investigate the issue of her sexual orientation, the researcher began asking respondents (during the interviews) whether it mattered to them if a researcher conducting this kind of study was gay or lesbian. All of the respondents who were asked this question claimed that the sexual orientation of the researcher did not matter to them. As one respondent stated, "The way I look at it, if you're brave enough to ask, I'm brave enough to tell." Another respondent claimed, "There are a lot of people who think if you are not [gay/lesbian] you couldn't understand and I am not so sure that is true."

Disclosure also proved to be problematic in some interviews. The respondent's feeling of being understood can, at times, complicate the research process. For example, in some instances it was clear that respondents assumed that because the researcher was a lesbian, she understood a particular term they used or situation they described. Some, then, seemed surprised when the researcher probed for further explanation. One respondent attributed a particular lack of understanding as a generational difference, and said that "polyamory" (a committed relationship among more than two people) was a "thing of the 60s" that was somewhat common in the gay community. The respondent graciously pointed the researcher to literature on the topic and mentioned that she knew of a polyamorous caregiving relationship among three older gay men. To combat this challenge, the researcher was careful not to assume the respondent's meanings and made it a point to ask for clarification.

STUDY FINDINGS

Through the use of qualitative methods and strategies used to overcome methodological challenges, a great deal was learned about caregiving and post-caregiving for midlife and older gay men and lesbians. The study found respondents to have had similar experiences in caregiving as those in previous studies, including managing caregiving responsibilities, experiencing emotional and physical strains, and conflicts with employment responsibilities. Similarly, respondents experienced loneliness and depression following the loss of the caregiving role, and faced the challenge of moving on with their lives after the loss of their partners.

Unique aspects of respondents' experiences involved their interactions with formal and informal support persons and services, and their long-term planning and decision-making processes. Persons outside of the partner relationship had the potential to greatly affect the caregiving and post-caregiving experiences. Respondents were often faced with family and coworkers who were not accepting of their relationship and, as a result, did not provide the level of support needed during caregiving or post-caregiving. While some had family and coworkers who were unsupportive, others had the advantage of a strong network of friends and family members who were supportive of the relationship.

Although homophobic attitudes were not overtly expressed by professionals very often, they were at times apparent through slighting remarks or rude or hostile behavior toward the couple or caregiving partner. Some organizational policies and practices were unsupportive of same-sex couples, often insisting that "next of kin" did not include a partner. Unfortunately, support was generally not anticipated from others, and respondents expected to be faced with insensitive individuals. In fact, some drafted advanced directives to assure that professionals and family members would respect their wishes.

Respondents also had unique challenges in disclosing the nature of their same-sex relationship to family, professionals, and coworkers, and in reconstructing their lives following the cessation of care. Some maintained a "don't ask, don't tell" practice of disclosure, while others advocated direct communication of the nature of the partner relationship. In post-caregiving, many also faced the challenge of reengaging in the gay and lesbian community and establishing new romantic relationships. The caregiving and post-caregiving experiences also affected their lives in extraordinary ways; some became involved in activism in the gay community and/or became more open about who they were, while others changed vocations to help other caregivers.

In light of their experiences, respondents offered suggestions for changes in health and human services and larger systems. Many believed that professionals should treat all consumers as individuals, whether heterosexual or gay/lesbian, and spend more time getting to know their special needs. They also believed professionals should be more open to receiving training related to diversity in human relationships. A few respondents also asserted that public policies and the attitudes of the larger society must change before they can expect their relationships to be respected by professionals and organizations. Some also believed that gay men and lesbians themselves should be more up front with professionals about the nature of their relationships, and that the larger gay community should be more available to provide support to caregiving couples.

LESSONS LEARNED AND RECOMMENDATIONS FOR FUTURE RESEARCH

It was not only the unique aspects of caregiving and post-caregiving that were uncovered in the present study. Several research lessons were learned that can inform future studies in this area. These lessons are related to the benefits of qualitative methods, sampling strategies, the use of technology, and the personal investment of respondents.

Benefits of Qualitative Methods

As this study demonstrated, qualitative methods can offer many benefits to researchers in the area of gay and lesbian aging. To begin with, an emergent and flexible design is a benefit in studying a topic about which very little is known. This is certainly the case when studying a population of caregivers whose experiences are very likely to depart from those in the "traditional" literature. Taking a pragmatic approach and following a "paradigm of choices" (Patton, 1990) can increase the flexibility of the study design and the options for overcoming challenges that may arise.

As an added benefit, the in-depth nature of the qualitative interview allows for the collection of very rich and detailed data. Instead of relying on quantitative scales that were validated on "traditional" caregivers, study respondents were able to describe the experiences during caregiving and following the cessation of care. Dialogue between the researcher and the respondents also allowed for questioning and probing that facilitated a deeper understanding of the respondents' experiences.

The empowerment aspect stands as the primary advantage of qualitative inquiry with midlife and older gay men and lesbians. Seeking out and shedding light on the experiences of those who have gone unnoticed in the traditional literature can promote social justice for oppressed populations. In this type of research, the study respondents were able to see that a researcher valued their experiences and wanted to share their unique stories and issues with others. In sharing their experiences, the researcher can promote an understanding of, and sensitivity to, their special issues and concerns; a few respondents specifically mentioned their excitement that this topic was finally being addressed, and that they hoped it would produce change in the attitudes of others who did not recognize the legitimacy of their partner relationships and the strength of their commitments.

Sampling Strategies

This study reached the majority of its participants through the gay and lesbian media, including newspapers and newsletters. With this population, it is important to advertise nationwide in order to attract an adequate number of participants. As a result, gay and lesbian newspapers with a large circulation seemed to be especially effective. The electronic media, including gay and lesbian websites, also appeared promising since it allowed us to reach persons from all over the country. Unfortunately, many of them lost interest after discovering that the study did not involve an anonymous survey.

The mainstream media may be an untapped resource in sampling this population. This was not an avenue that was thoroughly explored in the conduct of the present study, but those who are not likely to read gay and lesbian newspapers may read a local mainstream paper on a regular basis. Some larger newspapers have special health care inserts once a week that include numerous ads for studies. Although far more costly than placing an ad in a gay and lesbian publication, an ad in such an insert may increase sample size.

Whether mainstream or gay and lesbian media, writing up preliminary results in a newsletter or newspaper may attract additional study respondents. In this case, an ad requesting additional study participants can be placed within the article. One respondent mentioned that such an article written by the researcher attracted him to the study. As mentioned by the respondent, this is a way to convey the study's importance and the researcher's credibility. Readers' interest in participating may also be sparked by their ability to relate to the experiences of the initial study participants. It is likely that this type of advertisement would also decrease suspicion among potential respondents who fear being outed.

One of the most important lessons learned in the conduct of this study was that connections are essential in sampling this hard-to-reach population. Connections can be made with leaders in national organizations that serve this particular population, as well as by attending national conferences related to this population. These connections can help get the word out, often at a national level, that a study is being conducted. Making personal contacts with local health and human service agency staff may also be important. Although this approach did not help in obtaining respondents for this study, it may be beneficial in other studies.

It is not clear why in-person or mail contacts to agencies and agency staff did not produce interest in study participation. Perhaps agency personnel did not feel comfortable in approaching gay and lesbian clients (or those they suspected to be gay or lesbian) to participate in the study. Maybe they feared outing these clients within the agency or making them feel uncomfortable. An alternative could be choosing not to confront individual clients, but placing study flyers on a bulletin board or on a table in the organization. However, this type of recruitment is clearly less direct, which introduces additional sampling hurdles. In comparison, when respondents learn of a study through a newspaper or website, they can personally and anonymously decide whether they will make contact with the researcher. Although snowball sampling did not prove effective in the present study, it does hold promise for other studies. As evident in this study, it is very likely that respondents will know others who could participate.

The present study made some progress in understanding sampling issues among midlife and older gay men and lesbians. Despite this progress, challenges remain in recruiting racial minorities, persons of lower economic statuses and education levels, and persons residing in rural areas. Better representation of these populations can only strengthen the knowledge base in this area of research.

Technology

In the future, technology may be a strong ally in conducting research with this population. Technology presents exciting new avenues for recruiting study respondents and for collecting data. As this study shows, many midlife and older gay men and lesbians are online. As was mentioned, the majority of respondents e-mailed the researcher as their first correspondence related to the study, even though they did not learn of the study on the Internet. Although somewhat evident in the present study, the Internet is fast becoming a way for gay men and lesbians of all ages to find community and support.

The Internet may have great potential for survey research with gay men and lesbians of all ages. Posting advertisements on popular websites that link directly to a survey that can be completed online and submitted electronically and anonymously, may prove to be a very successful strategy to collect data. A chatroom format that could guarantee privacy, security, and anonymity could also be effective. In addition, mixed methodology that includes anonymous surveys and in-depth interviews could produce a larger study sample.

With the advent of webcams (cameras which attach to a computer and allow for video phone conversations), electronic interviews may also become more feasible and successful with midlife and older gay men and lesbians. In this way, respondents can be interviewed economically across long distances. In addition, this type of interview would have many of the same advantages as face-to-face interviews, including the ability to observe gestures and environmental surroundings. However, webcams and other technologies may limit samples to those who are technologically sophisticated and who can afford the latest equipment. Thus, using technology alone is not recommended; multiple sampling methods are suggested.

Personal Investment of Respondents and Collaboration

From the beginning, it was very clear that several of the respondents had a vested interest in the study and its findings. Several commented on the importance of this type of study, and one mentioned that she had been "waiting" for someone to research this topic area. In addition to their belief in the importance of the study, a few respondents also wanted to have access to, and input into, the presentation of the study findings. This was apparent in their interest in seeing the findings. One respondent, who had participated in other gay and lesbian aging studies, commented that study respondents should have "editorial say" in the write-up of the results because some studies of which she was aware were "horrendous" in how they represented the experiences of the study participants. Others were also interested in where the results would be disseminated. A few respondents specifically asked about "where" the results "would go." Many hoped that the results would be available to health and human service professionals in order to effect changes in current practices, and to increase knowledge of and empathy for this population. Others also hoped that the findings would be available to other gay men and lesbians who are going through the same experience. As one respondent explained, "It is important for people to share their stories and for other people to hear their stories. It's important for people to know that they are not alone."

Because of the investment and concern of the participants, dissemination of findings for this type of study is particularly important. Dissemination should include journals, newsletters, and organizations that reach professionals whose practice could benefit from knowledge of this population. As mentioned by one respondent, it is also important to disseminate to places where other midlife and older gay men and lesbians can benefit from the results. Dissemination should certainly involve providing copies of the completed findings to the study respondents.

When possible, respondents should be engaged as collaborators in the research process. As collaborators, respondents have a great deal to offer. As this study showed, they are wonderful resources for sampling and dissemination of findings. They can also be of tremendous help with study implications–who better to ask about what changes should be made than someone who has experienced a situation? Collaboration is especially important for members of oppressed populations like gay men and lesbians, who have not been given the opportunity to share their unique experiences or insights. Member checking is important in this regard, to ensure that an accurate story is being told for persons who have not previously had a voice in the traditional literature.

Self-disclosure may also be important in researching this particular area. As evident in this study, some respondents may be interested in knowing that the researcher is gay or lesbian before proceeding with the interview. It is possible that some may be worried about being "outed" as a result of their participation or contact with the researcher. In these cases, self-disclosure may facilitate a more trusting and comfortable environment for some study participants. Respondents may also find that a gay or lesbian researcher may better understand challenges they face related to their sexual orientation. In addition, reiterating confidentiality may be especially important in research with this population.

It is unclear whether the sexual orientation of a researcher significantly impacts the conduct of this type of study. Although it seemed to make a difference in rapport with some respondents, others reported that the sexual orientation of the researcher was not a factor in their willingness to share their experiences. For some respondents, it may be enough to know that the researcher is understanding and is interested in learning about their unique experiences and challenges.

CONCLUSION

Clearly, the present study added to knowledge in the area of caregiving among midlife and older gay men and lesbians. In addition, many lessons were learned through the conduct of the study that can inform future research with this population. As the study revealed, qualitative inquiry holds great promise for research with midlife and older gay men and lesbians. The emergent design allowed the researcher the flexibility to employ various strategies to answer the research questions. In addition, the potential to empower respondents through this type of research cannot be overstated, and is certainly an area that warrants further exploration.

Although future researchers may expect to be faced with challenges related to sampling and the role of the researcher, they may also benefit from the expertise of respondents who are personally invested in the findings and the possibilities for change. Additionally, the advancement of technology offers exciting opportunities for future research with these and other hard-to-reach populations. Despite these opportunities, the challenge of recruiting diverse study respondents remains. The influence of the researcher's sexual orientation on the research process is also an issue that deserves continued investigation. In effect, there is still a great deal to learn about and from this special population. Hopefully, future studies will continue to advance the knowledge of methods that can elicit its unique experiences and personally empower its members.

REFERENCES

Berger, R.M. (1982). *Gay and gray: The older homosexual man.* Urbana, IL: University of Illinois Press.

Berger, R.M. (1984). Realities of gay and lesbian aging. *Social Work, 29,* 57-62.

Bogdan, R.C., & Bilken, S.K. (1998). *Qualitative research for education: An introduction to theory and methods* (3rd ed.). Needham Heights, MA: Allyn & Bacon.

Bradford, J., & Ryan, C. (1991). Who we are: Health concerns of middle-aged lesbians. In B. Sang, J. Warshow, & A.J. Smith (Eds.), *Lesbians at midlife: The creative transition* (pp. 147-163). San Francisco: Spinsters Book Company.

Cantor, M.H. (1983). Strain among caregivers: A study of the experience in the United States. *Gerontologist, 23(6),* 597-604.

Dorfman, R., Walters, K., Burke, P., Hardin, L., & Karanik, T. (1995). Old, sad and alone: The myth of the aging homosexual. *Journal of Gerontological Social Work, 24(1/2),* 29-44.

Frederikson, K.I. (1999). Family caregiving responsibilities among lesbians and gay men. *Social Work, 44,* 142-155.

Friend, R.A. (1980). Gayging: Adjustment and the older gay male. *Alternative Lifestyles, 3(2),* 231-248.

Gray, H., & Dressel, P. (1985). Alternative interpretation of aging among gay males. *Gerontologist, 25,* 83-87.

Jacobson, S.A. (1995). Methodological issues in research with older lesbians. *Journal of Gay & Lesbian Social Services, 3(1),* 43-56.

Kehoe, M. (1988). Lesbians over 60 speak for themselves. *Journal of Homosexuality, 16(3/4),* 1-111.

Kimmel, D.C., & Sang, B.E. (1995). Lesbians and gay men in midlife. In A.R. D'Augelli & C.J. Patterson (Eds.), *Lesbian, gay, and bisexual identities over the lifespan: Psychological perspectives* (pp. 190-214). New York: Oxford University Press.

Kooden, H. (1997). Successful aging in the middle-aged gay man: A contribution to developmental theory. *Journal of Gay & Lesbian Social Services, 6(3),* 21-43.

LeCompte, M.D. (1993). A framework for hearing silence: What does telling stories mean when we are supposed to be doing science? In D. McLaughlin & W.G. Tierney (Eds.), *Naming silenced lives: Personal narratives and processes of educational change* (pp. 9-27). New York: Routledge.

Lincoln, Y.S. (1995). *Emerging criteria for quality in qualitative and interpretive research.* Paper presented at the Annual Meeting of the American Educational Research Association, San Francisco, CA.

Lincoln, Y.S., & Guba, E.G. (1985). *Naturalistic inquiry.* Newbury Park, CA: Sage.

Marshall, C., & Rossman, G.B. (1995). *Designing qualitative research* (2nd ed.). Newbury Park, CA: Sage.

Maykut, P., & Morehouse, R. (1994). *Beginning qualitative research: Philosophic and practical guide.* London: Falmer Press.

McMillan, J., & Schumacher, S. (1997). *Research in education: A conceptual introduction* (4th ed.). New York: Longman.

Patton, M.Q. (1990). *Qualitative evaluation and research methods.* Newbury Park, CA: Sage.

Poulshock, S.W., & Deimling, G.T. (1984). Families caring for elders in residence: Issues in the measurement of burden. *Journal of Gerontology, 39,* 230-239.

Quam, J.K., & Whitford, G.S. (1992). Adaptation and age-related expectations of older gay and lesbian adults. *Gerontologist, 32,* 367-374.

Rubin, A., & Babbie, E. (1997). *Research methods for social work* (3rd ed.). Pacific Grove, CA: Brooks/Cole Publishing.

Rubin, H.J., & Rubin, I.S. (1995). *Qualitative interviewing: The art of hearing data.* Thousand Oaks, CA: Sage.

Sang, B.E. (1991). Moving toward balance and integration. In B. Sang, J. Warshow, & A.J. Smith (Eds.), *Lesbians at midlife: The creative transition* (pp. 206-214). San Francisco: Spinsters Book Company.

Taylor, S.J., & Bogdan, R.C. (1998). *Introduction to qualitative research: A guidebook and resource* (3rd ed.). New York: John Wiley & Sons.

Turner, H.A., Catania, J.A., & Gagnon, J. (1994). The prevalence of informal caregiving to persons with AIDS in the United States. *Social Science and Medicine, 38,* 1543-1552.

Weinstock, J.S. (2000). Lesbian friendships at midlife: Patterns and possibilities for the 21st century. *Journal of Gay & Lesbian Social Services, 11(2/3),* 1-32.

Zarit, S.H., Todd, P.A., & Zarit, J.M. (1986). Subjective burden of husbands and wives as caregivers: A longitudinal study. *Gerontologist, 26,* 260-266.

Methodological Issues in Conducting Community-Based Health and Social Services Research Among Urban Black and African American LGBT Populations

Darrell P. Wheeler

SUMMARY. Health and social service utilization experiences of disenfranchised groups have recently gained renewed public attention. Reducing and eliminating racial disparities in health care has become a major national agenda. While a fairly substantial literature on Black and African American health outcomes and social service utilization does exist, and may help to influence interventions to reduce disparities, there is no comparable literature for Black and African American lesbian, gay, bisexual, and transgender (LGBT) persons. In this article the author examines factors affecting research with urban Black and African American LGBT populations. A brief case study is included that demonstrates the viability of the recommended research methods and discusses the

Darrell P. Wheeler, MSW, MPH, PhD, ACSW, is a visiting faculty member, Hunter College School of Social Work, City University of New York, New York, NY.

Address correspondence to: Dr. Darrell P. Wheeler, Hunter College School of Social Work, City University of New York, 129 E. 79th Street, New York, NY 10021 (E-mail: darrell.wheeler@hunter.cuny.edu).

[Haworth co-indexing entry note]: "Methodological Issues in Conducting Community-Based Health and Social Services Research Among Urban Black and African American LGBT Populations." Wheeler, Darrell P. Co-published simultaneously in *Journal of Gay & Lesbian Social Services* (Harrington Park Press, an imprint of The Haworth Press, Inc.) Vol. 15, No. 1/2, 2003, pp. 65-78; and: *Research Methods with Gay, Lesbian, Bisexual, and Transgender Populations* (ed: William Meezan, and James I. Martin) Harrington Park Press, an imprint of The Haworth Press, Inc., 2003, pp. 65-78. Single or multiple copies of this article are available for a fee from The Haworth Document Delivery Service [1-800-HAWORTH, 9:00 a.m. - 5:00 p.m. (EST). E-mail address: getinfo@haworthpressinc.com].

65

possible negative consequences of deviating from these methodological suggestions. *[Article copies available for a fee from The Haworth Document Delivery Service: 1-800-HAWORTH. E-mail address: <getinfo@haworthpressinc. com> Website: <http://www.HaworthPress.com> © 2003 by The Haworth Press, Inc. All rights reserved.]*

KEYWORDS. Black, African American, research methods, lesbian, gay, bisexual, transgender

The health and social service utilization experiences of disenfranchised groups have recently gained renewed public attention. Before leaving office, President Clinton made the elimination of health disparities a major national priority. The growing concern for the health and social well-being of the U.S. populace across racial and ethnic spectra translates into a need to develop effective and efficient mechanisms for delivering services that produce desired outcomes.

While a fairly substantial literature on Black and African American health outcomes and social service utilization does exist (Clark, Anderson, Clark, & Williams, 1999; Coates, 1990; Marin, 1996; Smith, 1999; Williams, 2000), a comparable literature examining the experiences of Black and African American lesbian, gay, bisexual, and transgender (LGBT) persons does not. One reason for this situation is the social stigma associated with LGBT issues, both in Black and African American communities and in America in general. A second reason is that researchers have not gained entry, support, or trust in these communities. A third reason is the extent to which investigators have considered research among Black and African American LGBT persons unimportant.

In this article I examine factors affecting research with urban Black and African American LGBT populations. The primary focus will be on identifying methods and processes that can facilitate meaningful research with and for urban Black and African American LGBT communities. The article begins by examining issues affecting the interaction between researchers and subject or target groups. This is followed by a discussion of key substantive and methodological factors that shape the research agenda and the experiences of those who work with this population. A brief case study is then presented to demonstrate the application of the recommended research methods, and to identify their potential strengths and weaknesses.

SELF-AWARENESS AS A FIRST STEP

Interactions between researchers and the subjects of their research can significantly impact the research process. This is not a new or startling proclamation. However, inattention to these factors, particularly when researching groups that have experienced adverse impacts of research in the past, is an egregious error on the part of researchers. Even when researchers are members of the target group, based upon demographics or other characteristics, the process of conducting the research places them in somewhat of an "other" role (Dozier & White, 1998). This is important to acknowledge, for it keeps investigators more objective and reminds them that membership in a group does not give them *carte blanche* for accessing that group for research purposes, nor does it guarantee the development of a productive working relationship with its members.

Thus, a critical first step in successfully engaging historically "hard to engage" communities in the research process involves researchers taking an inventory of their own motives for conducting the research and the ways in which the research will be used (Dozier & White, 1998). For the purposes of this article, critical self-examination would include attention to the researcher's own understanding of race and racism, sexual identity, class, and social oppression. Preliminary findings from a recent study suggest that researchers' own awareness of these issues can facilitate deeper, more meaningful, and attentive focus on contextual understanding and interpretation of the subjects' situations. Such attention to contextual understanding and interpretation has been found to be associated with positive perceptions of researchers by subjects, and an increased willingness to work with them (Wheeler, 2001).

While a full review of the self-awareness literature is not possible here, it should be noted that this literature does suggest that the development of self-awareness increases one's ability to see difference as "difference," and not jump to the conclusion that differences are pathological (Harris, 1997; Harry, 1992; MacDougall & Arthur, 2001; Richardson & Molinaro, 1996). As we consider the issues of research within urban Black and African American LGBT communities, this will be an important assertion to remember, not only in terms of the substantive aspects of the research, but for methodological and ethical considerations as well.

WHY FOCUS ON URBAN BLACK AND AFRICAN AMERICAN LGBT COMMUNITIES?

What makes research on urban Black and African American LGBT communities so critical? Why must we devote attention to the specifics of methods and processes in these populations? In its simplest form, the answer is that while LGBT populations in the U.S. are oppressed and disenfranchised, the intersection of sexual orientation, gender, race, and ethnicity compounds their marginalization. Researchers must realize that the effects of these interactions are more likely to be geometric than additive. Attempts to study LGBT populations, or develop interventions designed to help overcome health and social service disparities, that fail to take this contextual reality into consideration will miss a critical factor in the more than 300 years of polarization between Blacks and Whites (and by parallel argument, LGBT communities). To construct an LGBT health and social service research and program development agenda that does not include, or actively excludes, race and ethnicity as salient variables, underestimates the societal reality that remains prevalent in today's political, economic, social, and health arena (Wheeler, 1999; Williams, 2000).

THE IMMUTABLE CONSTRUCT OF RACE
IN AMERICAN RESEARCH

The labels used to describe racial groups in research efforts are usually constructed to be mutually exclusive (i.e., White/Caucasian, Asian/Pacific Islander, Native American/Alaskan, Black). These categorical labels have substantial historical and sociological meaning in the U.S. A detailed examination of this construction is not possible here. However, racial labeling has been used historically to exclude groups from access to services and the benefits of scientific inquiry. Some would argue that this pattern continues today (Williams, 2000). One of the many limitations of oversimplified labeling of groups based on color gradations is the homogenization of diverse people into a single constructed group. The construct of Black or African American is used to embody any number of biological, physiological, psychological and/or sociological elements. It does away with the need to understand individuals with all of their complexities and exceptions to the (presumed) norms. It allows researchers to group and objectify differing individuals. Further, the labels Black or African American signify that people meeting these categorical criteria are NOT White or Caucasian, an important demarcation in a society that has historically struggled with issues of social oppression and discrimination.

Throughout this article I use the term "Black and African American." I have purposively used this terminology to underscore the diversity among persons of African ancestry who now reside in the U.S. It has been my experience in conducting research with Black and African American LGBT communities that individuals use various terms to describe themselves racially and/or ethnically. Some individuals reject the need for such labeling. For others, these labels provide a sense of collective identity and pride. Allowing respondents to self-identify, and not being offended by it, can reduce unnecessary conflicts within the research process and can, in turn, reduce difficulties in conducting the research. It can also reduce negative feelings and outcomes for the community participants.

A parallel argument can be made for the categorical labeling of sexual identities (i.e., heterosexual, homosexual, and bisexual). That is, the use of these labels reduces category members to the simplest aspects of their complex selves. As I will illustrate in the case study that follows, the oversimplification of race and sexual identity, the presumed neutrality of the researcher, and the presumed benign nature of research itself, can collude to make research efforts within these communities onerous and even impossible to conduct.

HEALTH AND SOCIAL SERVICE DISPARITIES IN URBAN BLACK AND AFRICAN AMERICAN COMMUNITIES

There is insufficient evidence to suggest that Black and African American LGBT persons have significantly different health and social service experiences than non-LGBT Blacks and African Americans. However, there is evidence from a nascent body of inquiry that suggests that persons who do not possess positive gay and racial identities are at increased risk for psychological stress and other health and social anomalies (Clark, Anderson, Clark, & Williams, 1999; Walters, 1998).

There is also substantial evidence of significant differences in the health and social service experiences of Blacks and African Americans in the U.S. when compared to White and European Americans. Whether in terms of infant and maternal mortality, obesity, diabetes, or HIV/AIDS, the theme is the same; there are differences in outcomes based on or linked to race (Centers for Disease Control and Prevention, 2001). The disparities are also seen in service utilization statistics where, for example, Blacks and African Americans are more likely to use emergency rooms for primary medical needs, have increased contact with child welfare service providers, and be more involved with the criminal justice system and correctional facilities than White and European Americans (Pequegnat & Stover, 1999; Smith, 1999; Williams, 2000).

In social work education we are taught to understand the "person-in-environment" or "person-in-situation." The emphasis is on the need to examine and understand the interface between individuals and their way of viewing a problem situation in order to formulate meaningful interventions. This perspective has significant utility when conducting research with Black and African American LGBT persons. It is from this perspective that researchers are called to examine individual and environmental forces in the process of scientific inquiry. Applying this perspective leads us to incorporate sociocultural, structural, and behavioral variables into our research.

HEALTH AND SOCIAL SERVICES RESEARCH
FOR LGBT PERSONS

During the past 20 years, researchers have given increased attention to the health and service needs of LGBT persons. This increase has been propelled as much by the HIV/AIDS epidemic as by an interest in developing knowledge about LGBT persons and their issues. Much of this work has been aimed at providing data that can be used to change risk-taking or strengthen health promoting behaviors. Such research has influenced the development and delivery of health and human services in many areas of interest and concern to LGBT populations, such as aging, domestic violence, child care, and HIV/AIDS (Adams & Kimmel, 1999; D'Augelli & Garnets, 1995; Tafoya, 1997; Walters, 1998; Wheeler, 1999). Given this interest in, and growing acceptance of, LGBT issues as a viable, valid, and important research agenda, one might expect to see greater use of racial, economic, geographic or gender-specific categories in the psychological, sociological, and health and human service literature. Unfortunately, this is not yet the case.

Research reported in many journals and texts tends to emerge from academic or other institutional settings. This research tends to focus on urban or suburban populations, and men's health issues, specifically HIV/AIDS and other sexually transmitted diseases. Although increasing in recent years, few studies have been focused on the needs of transgender populations. Fewer studies have focused on Southern populations, and especially rural communities in that region. And although racial and ethnic inclusiveness and diversity appear in many research efforts, published reports all too often contain the familiar disclaimer that due to limited numbers of Blacks and African Americans included in the study, further investigations focusing on these populations are warranted.

Such deficiencies in research raise serious concerns about the appropriateness and utility of research findings to the lives of Blacks and African Americans (as well as other under-studied and neglected groups), and it perpetuates the perception that research is neither for nor about them. There is a definite need for research that is relevant to the lives and needs of Black and African American LGBT populations, and researchers must develop methods of scientific investigation that provide as much to Black and African American LGBT communities as they take from them.

METHODOLOGICAL ISSUES

Rather than presenting a global discussion of research in Black and African American LGBT communities, I will focus on five aspects of the research process: confidentiality and the protection of human subjects; study design and the introduction of the study; sampling; instrumentation; and dissemination. These aspects were selected for two primary reasons. First, each is an important component of the research process. Second, they have emerged from my own research experience as critical areas that require specific attention in both conceptualizing and conducting research within these communities. By sharing these experiences, I hope that others will avoid the pitfalls that I have encountered in the past.

Confidentiality and the Protection of Human Subjects

When planning a study, researchers should consult with an indigenous expert, especially regarding the ways in which confidentiality could be breached in the target population, ways to avoid such breaches, and the implications of the study findings for those who have participated in the research. By consulting with indigenous experts, researchers can develop a richer contextual understanding of the target population and of ways to facilitate the investigative process.

Another consideration is the use of consent forms. Of course, subject protection and confidentiality are essential in research. There are many institutional and legal safeguards in place to protect research subjects. Researchers employ painstaking measures to move through Human Subject and Institutional Review Board (IRB) processes, checking and re-checking their consent and confidentiality forms. However, the very construction of the "subject-researcher" sets up an "us-them" dichotomy. This dichotomy, and its meaning, should not be overlooked in work with Black and African American LGBT communities.

For example, researchers should ask whether their consent form is going to serve primarily to protect subjects or to spell out their obligations and commitments to potential participants. This is not a subtle distinction. In the former, the language of subject and researcher sets up a dichotomy that is inherently rigid and hierarchical. Further, the emphasis on protecting subjects could seem paternalistic and patronizing to some populations. In the latter, the focus is on participation, collaboration, and mutuality. In such cases researchers use the document as a way of spelling out their obligations to the partnership, in addition to enumerating the protections available to potential participants. While this way of approaching interactions might be typical in clinical settings, it is not always employed in the research process. The expert indigenous consultant can help to reframe the dichotomous "researcher-subject" paradigm as a more inclusive and participatory one, an approach suggested for any researcher regardless of race, ethnicity, or sexual orientation.

Study Design and the Introduction of the Study

Researchers should ask why they are studying this particular group at this particular point in time. This question cuts to the issue of the researcher's authenticity and genuineness, as seen by members of the target population. Inattention to these questions, and an unsatisfactory resolution of them with members of the population to be studied, can result in unresolved suspicions, denial of entry to the particular community, and social desirability bias in participants' responses. Such problems can sabotage the process of research and the utility of its findings.

In constructing the study design and introducing it to the target population, researchers should partner with members of the target population. Early partnering will provide researchers with a clearer understanding of the views held about the research among members of the target population, and will suggest ways of communicating authentic and genuine investment in conducting meaningful and respectful research. This collaboration can also facilitate access to the target population itself.

One issue that has repeatedly emerged in my own research efforts is the epistemological dialectic of research as a process or research as a product. For some members of the target population, the fruits of research are in the challenge of unlocking hidden mysteries and in contributing new knowledge. For others in the target population, research is a process, sometimes an onerous one, used to point out their faults and shortcomings. Developing clarity about the target population's understanding of the research is important. The researcher does this not only to allay concerns about the research, but also to plan the design and implementation of the study.

In addition to considering how the target population sees the research effort, researchers should address the issues of trust and distrust when working with Black and African American LGBT groups. A commonly cited aspect of traditional African American experience is the expressive nature of personal interactions and communications. Effective communication is crucial in the research process with such groups, particularly when introducing the study to potential participants. Using words and symbols that do not alienate or patronize is of utmost importance. To coin a contemporary phrase, by "keeping it real" researchers can convey their research plans without being off-putting.

Anyone who is interested in conducting research with Black and African American LGBT persons should understand that for many in the Black and African American community, research (especially health care research) is not always viewed as beneficial to the individual or to the community. The

Tuskegee syphilis study and its legacy are often cited as contributing to this situation and to the distrust often present among Blacks and African Americans of health care services, health care providers, and biomedical and other forms of research. As Thomas and Quinn (1991) remind us, the Tuskegee Syphilis Study (1932-1974) allowed this disease to go untreated among Blacks in the rural South, so that scientists could document its natural progression through its end stage (death), despite treatments being available.

Sampling

Researchers should avoid making assumptions about the meaning and understanding of being Black and African American or LGBT. According to Walters (1998), sexual and racial identities exist on continua that intersect at various points. Understanding the complexities of these intersections allows researchers to see beyond simple categorizations about urban Black and African American LGBT identities. Recognizing that sexual and racial identities are but two of the multiple identities and statuses Black and African American LGBT persons have is important. The impact of social class, religion, marital or partner status, and health status may need to be considered when investigating any issue in this population.

Of course, including additional or more complex variables increases the number of participants needed for the investigative work. Because locating Black and African American LGBT participants is a challenge for research, the desire for complexity presents a conundrum for researchers. In HIV/AIDS research this conundrum is exemplified by the use of terms such as "nongay-identified Men Who Have Sex With Men" (MSM) and, in the popular media, as "men on the down-low" and "homo-thugs." When developing a sampling strategy in work with Black and African American LGBT populations, researchers must decide whether to use simple categorical self-definitions that risk the loss of meaningful information or to create more exhaustive categories that require larger samples. Another possibility is not to employ any categories at all, letting respondents describe their racial and ethnic identification as well as their sexual orientation and gender identification.

The use of the label "Persons of Color" (POC) is one strategy taken by some researchers. While it is broadly inclusive and socially compelling, it does not allow for the uniqueness of cultural, social, political, and/or historical experiences among Blacks and African Americans. Instead, it relegates all POC to a homogenous group. It also begs the question of what a person of "no color" is.

There is probably no simple resolution to this methodological dilemma. Researchers will have to make critical decisions based on their skills, resources, intent, passions, and convictions, in partnership with members of the study population. My experiences have led me to recognize that in developing a sampling strategy I must be mindful of at least three things: the need for inclusion; the need to avoid tokenism; and the need for statistical power.

When sampling Black and African American LGBT populations, researchers should consider the full range of potential participants and seek breadth to the extent possible and necessary to answer the research questions. They should, whenever possible, avoid selection of "model" representatives who either meet their expectations or are the most accommodating. Finally, quantitative researchers have to examine their samples for statistical power, which might bring them back to using tried and true methods for capturing adequate numbers of subjects.

Instrumentation

I have come to realize that multiple methods of measurement provide the clearest picture of whatever phenomena are being studied. Although this concept is not new, it is often short-circuited in research on urban Black and African American LGBT populations. For example, I have begun to use more than one construct to examine sexual identity, as I have realized that the sexual self is often viewed as consisting of a sexual orientation, a sexual label, and a behavioral component. By examining these three components, we may develop a more complete and valid picture of the sexual self.

Similarly, in seeking to develop a more contextually valid understanding of the role of race and ethnicity, I have begun to examine not just the self-categorization but also the significance of race and ethnicity to the person. Miller and MacIntosh (1999) provide an example of this application in their examination of the role of racial socialization on the lives of urban African American adolescents. What their work illustrates is that within African American groups there is diversity in the degree to which ethnicity is internalized and is seen as salient to the individual. This self-perception may be a more valid measure of racial and ethnic identity than the simple selection of a racial category.

In addition to employing these approaches, using existing measures or developing measures that are consistent with indigenous markers of success, well-being, and pathology, are critically important. Researchers should allow for participant groups to inform the research concerning what is and is not meaningful, appropriate, and relevant from their perspective. This strategy ensures that critical constructs are appropriately captured, critical variables are included, and the researcher's understanding of the participants is enriched.

Dissemination

Researchers are ethically obligated to report the findings of their work. However, the way in which the findings are reported, and to whom they are reported, might not be consistent with participants' views and needs. In work with Black and African American LGBT communities, researchers must anticipate these issues and be prepared to respond to questions about them.

In addition to professional and academic journals, researchers working with Black and African American LGBT persons should consider disseminating their findings in the popular and contemporary media. Having partnered with members of the community from the outset, researchers should have identified the most important sources of information in the community. For some groups it might be a community newspaper, while for others it might be a national magazine.

The voices of participant-partners are crucial in the dissemination process. These voices will need to be clearly heard if the dissemination is to be meaningful to the target audience. Further, collaboration in dissemination can be demonstrated through coauthoring and copresenting of findings. Such coauthoring and copresenting should not be relegated to dissemination in the popular media; participant-partners should be offered shared billing on all products of the research. After all, without the "subjects" there would be no findings.

CASE STUDY

I will now present a brief case study to illustrate many of the points made throughout this paper. The case study is drawn from my work as a consultant to a New York City AIDS Service Organization (ASO). I had been approached to facilitate the process of collecting information about HIV/AIDS treatment and education among HIV-positive persons in northern Manhattan. I accepted the task and was eager to begin the work. Having done community collaborative research before, and feeling comfortable in this community, I felt prepared to do it.

I began by meeting with the administrators of the ASO, and by getting a sense of their expectations for the project. The full staff complement was not in place; the project director had not yet been hired. Nevertheless, time was ticking away and I felt compelled to produce the requested work. I returned to my "ivory tower" and examined the relevant literature. I eventually developed what I thought to be a reasonable survey instrument. By the time the first draft was finished, the project director was in place. When she and I met, she let me know that the document that I had produced would not only net zero responses, but it would jeopardize the reputation of her program because people would view the program as a research study and not a community resource. This was a subtle distinction that I had failed to grasp.

I went back to the drawing board and came back with a revised version. Further discussion and more editing followed. After a couple more iterations, the director and I agreed to a version that was appropriate for review, but not piloting, by the rest of the staff. The staff reviewed the document with keen eyes and found additional things that needed to be changed. Each revision strengthened the collaborative work.

During the process of developing the instrument we also constructed the consent forms. It was here that I learned about the meaning of Tuskegee to this community. In these discussions, many of the staff did not know the specific details of this atrocity, but understood the ways in which this study influenced people's understanding of research and their decision about whether to engage in it. It was during this period that I realized that we were "participant-partners" and collaborators in the research effort; that all involved had expertise and all of us needed to be heard. Even though I was a member of the community in many ways, I was operating as an outsider looking in.

Like the survey instrument, the consent form went through several iterations that involved extensive participation by the staff. During this process I discovered that there was great interest among the staff in the process of research. In response, we implemented a mini-introductory research course that I taught. As staff gradually expressed their increased confidence, they began to take more responsibility and ownership for the project. In fact, the staff took leadership roles during the data collection phase. In the analysis of the data I worked closely with the staff and project director. Under our dissemination plan, we first reported the findings to the local community, and only then to the scientific community. In both cases, dissemination was handled jointly and in partnership.

DISCUSSION

This case illustrates a number of concepts that are explicated in the article. First, critical self-assessment is a necessity when conducting research on Black and African American LGBT populations. Second, researchers must develop partnerships with members of the community from the outset of the enterprise. Third, investigators must develop cogent ways of reaching the populations of interest. Fourth, researchers must develop appropriate instrumentation. Finally, dissemination of the findings should be handled collaboratively with members of the community.

It is apparent that research on issues affecting Black and African American LGBT groups lags behind research among White LGBT groups. This gap is likely to impact the type and quality of services that are offered to Black and African American LGBT communities. Researchers have an obligation to contribute new knowledge that will lead to the development of new and better services. I hope that attention to establishing more appropriate and effective research methods will result in rich and important contributions.

REFERENCES

Adams, C.L., & Kimmel, D.C. (1999). Exploring the lives of older African American gay men. In B. Greene (Ed.), *Ethnic and cultural diversity among lesbians and gay men* (pp. 132-151). Thousand Oaks, CA: Sage.

Centers for Disease Control and Prevention (2001). National Center for Health Statistics: Fast stats A to Z. Retrieved November 12, 2001 from www.cdc.gov/nchs/fastasts.

Clark, R., Anderson, N.B., Clark, V.R., & Williams, D.R. (1999). Racism as a stressor for African-Americans: A biopsychosocial model. *American Psychologist, 54,* 805-816.

Coates, T.J. (1990). Strategies for modifying sexual behavior for primary and secondary prevention of HIV disease. *Journal of Consulting and Clinical Psychology, 58,* 57-69.

D'Augelli, A.R,. & Garnets, L.D. (1995). Lesbian, gay, and bisexual communities. In A.R. D'Augelli & C.J. Patterson (Eds.), *Lesbian, gay and bisexual identities over the lifespan: Psychological perspectives* (pp. 293-320). New York: Oxford.

Dozier, C.D., & White, G.J. (1998). The more things change, the more they stay the same: A framework for effective practice with African Americans. In *Cultural competence for health care professionals working with African-American communities: Theory and practice* (DHHS Publication No. 98-3238) (pp. 107-128). Center for Substance Abuse Prevention, Health Resources & Services Administration, U.S. Department of Health and Human Services.

Harris, M.S. (1997). Developing self-awareness/racial identity with graduate social work students. *Smith College Studies in Social Work, 67,* 587-607.

Harry, B. (1992). Developing cultural self-awareness: The first step in values clarification for early interventionists. *Topics in Early Childhood Special Education, 12,* 333-350.

MacDougall, C., & Arthur, N. (2001). Applying racial identity models in multicultural counseling. *Canadian Journal of Counselling, 35,* 122-136.

Marin, B.V. (1996). Analysis of AIDS prevention among African Americans and Latinos in the United States. In American Psychological Association Office on AIDS, *The effectiveness of AIDS prevention efforts: HIV prevention: State of the science* (pp. 124-158). Washington, DC: U.S. Congressional Office of Technology Assessment.

Miller, D.B., & MacIntosh, R (1999). Promoting resilience in urban African American adolescents: Racial socialization and identity as protective factors. *Social Work Research, 23,* 159-169.

Pequegnat, W., & Stover, E. (1999). Considering women's contextual and cultural issues in HIV/STD prevention research. *Cultural Diversity and Ethnic Minority Psychology, 5,* 287-291.

Richardson, T.Q., & Molinaro, K.L. (1996). White counselor self-awareness: A pre-requisite for multicultural competence. *Journal of Counseling and Development, 74,* 238-242.

Siegel, K., Karus, D., & Schrimshaw, E.W. (2000). Racial differences in attitudes toward protease inhibitors among older HIV-infected men. *AIDS Care, 12,* 423-434.

Smith, D.B. (1999). *Health care divided: Race and healing a nation.* Ann Arbor, MI: University of Michigan Press.

Tafoya, T. (1997). Native gay and lesbian issues: The two-spirited. In B. Greene (Ed.), *Ethnic and cultural diversity among lesbians and gay men* (pp. 1-10). Thousand Oaks, CA: Sage.

Thomas, S.B., & Quinn, S.C. (1991). The Tuskegee Syphilis Study, 1932 to 1972: Implications for HIV education and AIDS risk education programs in the Black community. *American Journal of Public Health, 81,* 1498-1504.

Walters, K.L. (1998). Negotiating conflicts in allegiances among lesbians and gays of color: Reconciling divided selves and communities. In G.P. Mallon (Ed.), *Foundations of social work practice with lesbian and gay persons* (pp. 47-76). New York: Harrington Park Press.

Wheeler, D.P. (1999). Cultural competence in community evaluation and collaboration: A case example. *The Community Psychologist, 32(1),* 32-34.

Wheeler, D.P. (2001). Patient-provider relationship: A critical variable in treatment for HIV among African American and Black gay men. Unpublished manuscript.

Williams, D.R. (2000). Race, stress and mental health. In C.J. Hogue, M.A. Hargraves, & K.S. Collins (Eds.), *Minority health in America: Findings and policy implications from the Commonwealth Fund Minority Health Survey* (pp. 209-243). Baltimore: Johns Hopkins University Press.

Research with Gay Drug Users and the Interface with HIV: Current Methodological Issues for Social Work Research

E. Michael Gorman

SUMMARY. Studying the co-occurrence of drug use and sexual risk behaviors among gay men poses special challenges for research. The importance of conducting such research, however, is underscored by current trends in the gay community, including increases in methamphetamine and club drug use. This increase has been associated with high-risk behavior for the transmission of HIV and other diseases (e.g., hepatitis B and hepatitis C). The author describes methodological issues related to initiating and conducting research among gay male drug users, and discusses how such research can guide more effective prevention, treatment, and policy initiatives related to drug abuse and HIV/AIDS. *[Article copies available for a fee from The Haworth Document Delivery Service: 1-800-HAWORTH. E-mail address: <getinfo@haworthpressinc.com> Website:*

E. Michael Gorman, MSW, MPH, PhD, is Assistant Professor, College of Social Work, San Jose State University, San Jose, CA.

Address correspondence to: Dr. E. Michael Gorman, College of Social Work, San Jose State University, San Jose, CA 95192-0124 (E-mail: emg3@sjsu.edu).

The author wishes to express his grateful appreciation for the editorial assistance of Keith Nelson, MSW.

[Haworth co-indexing entry note]: "Research with Gay Drug Users and the Interface with HIV: Current Methodological Issues for Social Work Research." Gorman, E. Michael. Co-published simultaneously in *Journal of Gay & Lesbian Social Services* (Harrington Park Press, an imprint of The Haworth Press, Inc.) Vol. 15, No. 1/2, 2003, pp. 79-94; and: *Research Methods with Gay, Lesbian, Bisexual, and Transgender Populations* (ed: William Meezan, and James I. Martin) Harrington Park Press, an imprint of The Haworth Press, Inc., 2003, pp. 79-94. Single or multiple copies of this article are available for a fee from The Haworth Document Delivery Service [1-800-HAWORTH, 9:00 a.m. - 5:00 p.m. (EST). E-mail address: getinfo@haworthpressinc.com].

KEYWORDS. Gay men, HIV/AIDS, drug use, sexual risk taking, research methods

What important or useful methodological insights might be gleaned from examining the issue of substance abuse, especially illicit drug use, among gay and bisexual men in relation to HIV? This paper will discuss important aspects of this research, and convey an understanding of some of the challenges that are present when conducting research on this particular population. It also suggests why it is important to study this population from a social work policy perspective.

There are several reasons to engage in this endeavor. The most important has to do with the still disproportionate burden of HIV and AIDS among gay and bisexual men (often referred to as "men who have sex with other men" or MSM in the United States), and the particular role that drug abuse plays with respect to both HIV transmission and treatment within this population. In addition, social workers have historically been on the front lines of the battle against HIV and substance abuse (Straussner, 2001). Thus, it is instructive to reflect on the current state of research efforts by social workers, and the challenges they face in working with hidden and very high-risk populations. Finally, by describing methodological issues with respect to a gay or bisexual population such as this one, a number of important lessons can be learned about the dynamics of the research process.

THE SCOPE OF THE PROBLEM

As noted, gay and bisexual men have been disproportionately affected by the HIV/AIDS epidemic in the United States. In the case of AIDS-related mortality, out of some 435,000 deaths attributed to HIV/AIDS in the U.S. over the first two decades of the pandemic, approximately 250,000 were among men classified by the U.S. Centers for Disease Control and Prevention as MSM; in other words, gay or bisexual men (CDC, 2001).

Historically, the preponderance of HIV infection among MSM was attributed to sexual transmission. However, drug use, including injection drug use, has also played a significant role in the HIV/AIDS epidemic in this population (e.g., Diaz et al., 1994; Gorman, Morgan, & Lambert, 1995; Ostrow, 1996;

Paul, Stall, Crosby, Barrett, & Midanik, 1994; Stall, & Purcell, 2000; Sullivan, Nakashima, Purcell, & Ward, 1998). Approximately one in seven AIDS patients with a history of injection drug use has been a gay or bisexual male (CDC, 2001). In the western U.S. and certain other American urban areas, that proportion has been much higher. For example, nearly 35% of California's AIDS-intravenous drug using (IDU) patients between 1994 and 2000 were gay or bisexual men. An additional number of AIDS cases and HIV infections were likely to have resulted from sexual exposure while under the influence of one or more illicit substances or alcohol (Cabaj, 1989; Gorman, 1996; Gorman & Carroll, 2000; Ostrow, 1996; Paul et al., 1994; Paul, Stall, & Davis, 1993; Peterson, Coates, & Catania, 1992).

A substantial prevalence of use of both licit and illicit substances has been documented in gay/bisexual men (e.g., Paul et al., 1993; Stall & Wiley, 1988). Chief among the former has been alcohol, but there has also been a long history of other drug use, including amyl nitrite (poppers), marijuana, MDMA (ecstasy), cocaine, methamphetamine (crystal), ketamine (special K), and gamma hydroxil butyrate (GHB).

Methamphetamine is one the most potent of these drugs. Methamphetamine initially produces feelings of heightened alertness, strength, and productivity, in addition to its aphrodisiac properties. It can be snorted, smoked, injected, or ingested orally. Smoking and injection are the most addictive forms of ingestion, and they are the ones most associated with the strong sex-enhancing properties of this drug. This stimulant has been associated with numerous negative mental health, health, and social health consequences, including sexually transmitted diseases (STDs), paranoia, depression, dehydration, dental problems, and drug dependency (Anderson & Flynn, 1997; Gorman & Carroll, 2000; National Institute on Drug Abuse [NIDA], 1998). The association of methamphetamine with HIV-related risk behaviors has also been reported. Methamphetamine injectors in one study were reported to have had four times the HIV seroprevalence as heroin injectors after controlling for sexual orientation (Harris, Thiede, McGough, & Gordon, 1993).

The HIV/AIDS epidemic has been a catalyst for the development of important new research initiatives within gay, lesbian, bisexual, and transgender (GLBT) communities. Within social work, heretofore overlooked research topics have been recognized, among them the often hidden topic of GLBT substance abuse (Cabaj, 1989; Gorman, 1996; Ostrow, 1996; Stall & Ostrow, 1989). GLBT drug users constitute a doubly stigmatized and historically underserved population that needs to be better understood, since they constitute a critically important population in terms of HIV prevention, outreach, intervention, and treatment.

CHALLENGES

The challenges faced when undertaking research with this population fell into two broad categories. The first set of challenges was external, and related to the legitimacy of working with gay/bisexual drug users. For example, justifying the need for research in terms of HIV risk, in addition to competing for federal, state or local funding, was necessary to legitimize working with this very stigmatized population.

The second set of challenges, which were internal, had to do with the nature of the research process itself. Issues arose regarding the framing of the research problem, the formulation of the research questions, the design of the research, the sampling methodologies used, the data collection methods employed, and the analytic approaches undertaken.

External Challenges

It took some time for public health officials, policy practitioners, and researchers to appreciate the need for work with this particular population. This situation may have been due to several factors. First, research on GLBT substance abuse issues has always been sparse. While the bar was often identified as the quintessential gay institution in many communities, the impact of alcohol, much less illicit drugs, on gays, lesbians, and bisexuals was virtually ignored. It was only after several years of the HIV/AIDS epidemic that some researchers (e.g., Stall & Wiley, 1988) began to articulate the need for more systematic investigations addressing this issue. This interest was sparked by a growing awareness of the association between HIV and problematic use of both licit and illicit substances among many HIV risk populations, including gay and bisexual men. Although anecdotal and clinical information had been available for years, it took until the 1990s for researchers to begin to publish findings on this topic (e.g., Gorman, 1996; Gorman & Carroll, 2000; Ostrow, 1996; Paul, Stall, & Davis, 1993; Weinberg, 1994).

Among the reasons why it took so long for appropriate concerns to be raised was the fact that there were few data on gay, lesbian, or bisexual substance abusers. And the data that were available were not collected in a systematic or compelling way. Thus, it was difficult to estimate the magnitude and gravity of the situation.

In addition, the subject presented political challenges. In the wake of HIV/AIDS, it is fair to say that many GLBT people were reluctant to open another Pandora's box of stigmatized and stigmatizing investigations into their own community. This may have been the case especially with respect to illicit drug use, particularly injection drug use. The specter of injection drug users in a community already marginalized was not an easy one to contemplate for those trying to promote the "normality" of gay, lesbian and bisexual men and women. It took a fairly detailed reanalysis of HIV/AIDS incidence and prevalence data, combined with strong ethnographic research, to put the problem into perspective and onto the radar screen of GLBT researchers. Even then, there was considerable regional variation, so that it was difficult to make generalizable statements about the scale of the problem or its specificity.

Related to these considerations was the fact that the population of HIV/AIDS-impacted drug users (DU) lay at the intersection of several service sectors, and presented severe challenges to an already taxed system of service provision. It also lay at the intersection of several different research agendas. This added to the perception that MSM-DU were anomalies; not important, or even damaging to "mainstream" GLBT research.

Because MSM-DU spanned risk populations (including MSM, injection drug users, women, children, and those who became infected via transfusion or needle stick), they challenged individuals and systems that had developed their own research agendas and funding streams. Because MSM-DU spanned categories, they came to be viewed by some as "illegitimate" competitors for scarce service or research dollars. It took until the early 1990s for a strong enough case to be made in the HIV/AIDS context that gay/bisexual drug users constituted a population of sufficient risk and sufficient numbers to merit research resources.

In the end, these external obstacles were addressed by a combination of dogged persistence on the part of researchers, and the efforts of agency providers and community advocates who brought service delivery questions and a research agenda about this population to the table. They were able to shift the dominant paradigm sufficiently to allow for a broader inclusion of hidden, at-risk populations, including MSM-DU, into ongoing discussions of issues facing the LGBT community. This educational, community-based effort included many presentations, community meetings, organizing efforts, and exchanges with congressional representatives over a several-year period. It ultimately succeeded in legitimizing the problem and the need to address it through both service and research efforts.

Internal Challenges

One must remember that the most compelling rationale for placing this problem on the research agenda had to do with the nature of the HIV epidemic itself. As noted earlier, over time it became obvious that there was a large population of gay and bisexual men, not all of whom were gay identified, who were both at risk of HIV and contributing to the transmission of HIV through their substance-using and unsafe sexual behaviors. Those who were HIV positive were often receiving HIV/AIDS related services, yet their concurrent drug use was frequently not addressed because it was not disclosed (Gorman & Carroll, 2000). It therefore became an important public health issue to understand this population better, especially the drugs they were using (singly and in combination), the reasons why they were using, the people with whom they were using, and the circumstances under which they were using. All of these factors were seen as potential correlates of unprotected sex.

How does one study such an issue? Since my own prior research training had been in social anthropology and social epidemiology, I made the decision to utilize an ethnographic approach, albeit one framed by certain epidemiological parameters. I also chose this approach because I believed that it would best answer the salient research questions in the most efficient way.

This decision was based in part on work being undertaken by ethnographers in the area of drug abuse, which I felt might provide useful models for exploring hidden, marginalized gay and bisexual populations (e.g., Agar, 1986, 1996; Bernard, 1988; Koester, 1995; Padgett, 1998; Sterk-Elifson, 1995; Trotter, 1995). The primary aim of ethnographic research is to develop a theoretical framework grounded in data. This is especially the case in exploratory studies of hidden populations; ethnography has proven effective in describing the structure and function of small, atypical social environments that are hidden from usual observation. It entails labor-intensive fieldwork, under the rubric of participant observation, usually with in-depth individual interviews and focus groups.

Ethnographers draw from multiple methods that differ according to their focus, degree of researcher control, and recording strategy. They then analyze the data using a dialectical logic model aimed at constructing a coherent explanation of the phenomenon being studied (Agar, 1986). Descriptions can then be analyzed using inferential methods, and triangulated with other data in order to capture the context and meaning of behavior better than might be obtained by purely quantitative methods.

While quantitative methods usually aim for a higher degree of researcher control, and often allow for greater specificity of findings, they often lack the flexibility of method and depth of findings available through qualitative methods. Phenomena related to socially undesirable behaviors like the ones we studied (i.e., drug abuse in naturalistic settings) would be difficult to accurately capture using only quantitative methods. Precisely because ethnographic methods aim for a high degree of subject input, differences often emerge between researcher expectations and the obtained data. The resolution of such differences results in thematic coherences that can be used to build a new conceptual framework that enables further understanding of the phenomena. Given the sometimes personal nature of the research questions, a properly enacted ethnography can elicit a rich quantity of data, with the resulting interpretations bridging the gap between those studied, the researchers, and the research audience (Agar, 1986).

Research questions. The fact that there were so few available data on this population made the choice of research questions very challenging; it was hard to decide where to begin. My colleagues and I were fortunate to be able to draw upon the experiences, insights, and information collected by those working in the field, including outreach workers at the local health department. In addition, the presence of drug-specific epidemiological, treatment, and needle exchange data was useful, since it helped to point us in specific directions regarding important research questions. These data also suggested that we might be looking at several related but different populations–populations that may have shared drugs and had sex with each other, but which were otherwise quite different from one another. We thus speculated that these different but related populations might come from several communities that shared some, but not all, of the same social institutions.

The general research questions chosen concerned information about the population of MSM-DU in one (and later two) particular locales. It included information about their socio-demographic characteristics, the context of their daily lives, their communities and social networks, and their presumed high-risk behaviors. We were interested in learning whether there were several subgroups of MSM-DU in greater Seattle (and subsequently San Jose, California); the specific contexts of drug use in those specific geographic and cultural settings; the role of community culture in the initiation and continuation of drug use, alcohol misuse, and concomitant HIV sexual risk behaviors; the context of the lives of these men with regard to such domains as identification with "mainstream" gay communities and other ethnic or geographical or cultural communities; their experience with the stigma associated with sexual orientation, behavior, and/or race/ethnicity; the impact of such stigma on associations and experiences with families, and other social systems; and the specific barrier and access issues related to the delivery of community-based AIDS education, prevention, drug abuse treatment, and health care programs. We wondered whether it would be possible to establish close enough working relationships with members of this population to obtain sufficient baseline data.

Study design. We developed a research design for the study, named Substance Use Risk Exploration (SURE), that was ethnographic in many of its basic approaches and nested in an overarching epidemiological paradigm informed by extant county and state level data. Once we felt that we had developed a certain basic overview, we proceeded to undertake investigations that incorporated both individual and focus group interviews with three levels of participants. The first level consisted of key public health officials, agency administrators, and community leaders. The next level focused on community gatekeepers, including service providers, outreach workers, and knowledgeable community members. The third level focused on the target population of drug users.

The target population was located through multiple methods. These included direct recruitment by ethnographers, referrals from service providers, snowball methods, and advertisements in community newspapers and on posters distributed in the local community. We initially paid subjects $20 for interviews that were typically an hour or two in length; this incentive was later increased to $25. Interviews were audiotaped unless the subject requested otherwise, and were anonymous in that we collected no information that might identify subjects. Each subject was assigned a pseudonym and case number. All subjects were at least 18 years of age.

To enhance the overall quality of our data, and to increase its trustworthiness, we recruited an experienced multidisciplinary team that included health educators, anthropologists, a psychologist, social workers, and masters-level social work students. They were all trained in methods of ethnographic fieldwork (specifically contextual observation) and in taking field notes and coding data. However, in order to enrich the study, we encouraged each member of the team to maintain his or her own disciplinary perspective.

In addition, we specifically recruited individuals who "looked" like members of the populations we sought to recruit (gay men), and who might have insight into the organizational and social dynamics of those we wanted to better understand. In addition, we also recruited lesbians and heterosexual women and men in an effort to further enhance the credibility of the observations and interviews that were undertaken.

Sampling. Ethnographic research typically utilizes non-probability approaches in selecting and recruiting subjects. In addition, as Padgett (1998) emphasizes, the intent is one of "flexibility and depth, rather than on mathematical probability and generalization" (p. 50). A primary goal of ethnographic research is to maximize the veracity of data; to accurately depict the phenomena being studied (Stewart, 1998). Thus, ethnographic samples tend to be smaller than samples used in quantitative research, and produce data characterized by careful description and richness of detail. However, this sampling methodology prevents these data from being generalizable to the larger populations.

In the exploratory ethnographic research that was undertaken, our goal was to select specific kinds of subjects (gay and bisexual men who had used specific drugs in the relatively recent past), guided by certain judgments that were theoretically and experientially informed (Johnson, 1990). In other words, we had certain kinds of knowledge and experience about this population that we sought to enhance in our first and second level interviews (Honigman, 1970). We then used that information to select subjects according to age, location, race/ethnicity, social class, sexual identity, and other characteristics, in order to gain as much knowledge as we could about the range and types of MSM-DU and the contexts in which they lived. We hoped that these lessons could be used to inform social service and public health outreach efforts, and to generate research hypotheses testable in future studies.

Among the non-probability sampling strategies that we used was purposive or judgment sampling, in which we specified the purpose we wanted our subjects to serve. In our study we sought to interview three different levels of individuals, each of which contributed specific kinds of information about our ultimate target, MSM-DU. At each level of inquiry we targeted subjects with a particular purpose in mind, informed by our prior clinical work and pilot research with this population. For example, at the third level we sought to recruit men who had sex with another man in the previous three months who had also used one or more illicit substances during that same period. We made particular efforts to recruit nongay-identified men and men of color.

We also utilized snowball sampling, in which the subjects were asked to refer people like themselves to the study. Since MSM-DU often constituted themselves in small networks of people who were difficult to find, this method proved useful. We found that our sampling strategy provided a rich, informative, and somewhat surprising picture of a far more complex world of drug use among gay and bisexual men than we had anticipated. This world was characterized by many overlapping social circles and networks, and it had a variety of distinct subpopulations.

Data collection. Data were collected over a period of more than two years. In part, this was done to provide prolonged engagement with the population over time, another way of increasing the trustworthiness of the data (Stewart, 1998). We collected observational data from unobtrusive observations that were written up in the form of field notes, as well as individual interviews and focus groups. Most individual interviews and focus groups were audiotaped and then transcribed as soon as possible.

The contextual observations occurred in a variety of community settings including bars, clubs, coffeehouses, parks, and alleyways, and at public community events and private parties. Members of the ethnographic team were instructed to identify themselves as researchers, but their observations were often fairly unobtrusive. Team members also went into gay bathhouses, sex clubs, and other places in an effort to document whether drug use was occurring in such settings and to gain a better sense of the context of such behavior.

In recent years there has been a considerable expansion of ethnographic endeavors in clandestine settings such as these, where HIV-related risk behaviors and illegal drug-related activity occurred (e.g., Clatts, Davis, & Atillasoy, 1995; Koester, 1995; Needle et al., 1998; Needle, Ashery, & Lambert, 1995; Sterk-Elifson, 1995). As in all such settings, we were interested in maintaining the highest professional research standards. To that end, we worked with staff to maintain professional and ethical standards as a matter of commitment to the project and as a condition of employment. We followed the rigorous ethical standards of the American Anthropological Association for conducting ethnographic research.

Although our primary focus in the field was data collection, we also provided referral information regarding STD and HIV testing and counseling, and information about HIV services and substance abuse treatment. Therefore, we had to address a dilemma regarding the specific role of team members in such settings–team members were not there as clinicians, nor were they just disembodied observers of a scene. Rather, in addition to providing documentation for the record, they were also there to provide prevention education and to serve as sources of contact for members of the target populations.

Thus, one of the project goals was to establish professional relationships between team members and target population members (e.g., Agar, 1980), and to build trust. Indeed, it seemed that team members did come to be recognized as sources of help, and they were able to provide referrals. Thus, while the primary goal of the project was research, that role did not preclude engagement with regard to prevention and treatment opportunities.

Data analysis. After transcribing all interviews, investigators coded the results using *EZ-Text*, a qualitative database developed by the CDC. *EZ-Text's* ability to capture a significant amount of diverse/detailed information in an easily retrievable format makes it an excellent tool for initial descriptive analyses. Also, *EZ-Text* greatly aids in achieving a high level of inter-coder reliability; the degree of specificity that can be achieved in the individual codes through this program helps to ensure reliability when data is being coded by a large number of people.

The coding scheme was developed using a four-tiered process designed to ensure maximum input from ethnographic field interviewers, the coding team, and other project staff. At each tier, the coding scheme was reviewed for omissions and redundancies in salient domains.

Development of the coding scheme began with discussions with the ethnographic field interviewers. A preliminary coding scheme containing 29 general cultural domains resulted from this discussion. The coding team then tested the coding scheme's structure on several completed interviews. Next, the coding team and ethnographic field interviewers reviewed the results of this test and suggested changes. The final coding scheme was then developed, incorporating the diverse views of the ethnographic field interviewers, coders, and analysts.

The final code set was comprised of 104 specific codes (e.g., text related to the dynamics and effects of drug use on subjects' primary partner). These codes were contained in 31 subsets (e.g., text related to the history of the relationship between subject and primary partner). These subsets were conceptualized as belonging to five very broad cultural domains: subjects' personal history and background; causes, effects, and patterns of drug use; drug manufacturing and distribution; sex, drugs, and HIV knowledge and risk behavior; and social services and other prevention/treatment programs.

FINDINGS

This study confirmed the notion articulated by major national and international health agencies, such as the CDC and the World Health Organization, that the HIV/AIDS epidemic is composed of diverse multiple sub-epidemics that vary over time by region, community populations, and risk factors. Through this project, we found that the interface of high-risk drug use and high-risk sexual practices coincided in a variety of situations for quite diverse reasons. Many different subgroups of gay/bisexual drug users were identified, and are described elsewhere (Gorman, Barr, Hansen, Robertson, & Green, 1997). The use of methamphetamine as a sex drug, especially among MSM-DU, was quite common. Reasons for use varied considerably: some identified the socially empowering effects of methamphetamine as its primary attraction, while others were first introduced to the drug by sexual partners.

Many physical and mental health problems were documented among users. Methamphetamine (often in combination with club drugs) and alcohol appeared to affect all of the users' relationships. Due to the stigma attached, especially if the user was injecting, the habit was often hidden from partners and friends.

It was quite common for use to progress to heavier levels, with increasing social costs to the user. Many of the users also reported being victims of violent behavior, including domestic violence and street assault; others were engaged in violent activities related to drug acquisition. Quite a few indicated that they had been involved in drug dealing, and a few in drug manufacturing.

Most respondents reported problems with available methamphetamine treatment programs and/or difficulties in gaining access to such programs. For example, they reported that many, if not most, of the existing drug treatment programs were homophobic, AIDS phobic, or both.

RESEARCH LESSONS LEARNED

As principal investigator, my own sense was that the overall operation of the project ran well enough, although certainly not without its management and logistical challenges. Although we anticipated many of them, we faced more than a few that were not anticipated. Tasks accomplished included recruiting and training a multidisciplinary research/outreach team, and gaining access to requisite epidemiological data and key experts at various levels. We were successful in entering into a challenging netherworld of stigma and clandestine behaviors that included the use, manufacture, and selling of drugs. We were able to recruit research subjects in accordance with our project goals, and to conduct numerous contextual observations in a variety of locales. In all, the team conducted and transcribed approximately 175 interviews.

The project likewise experienced its share of difficulties. Initially, we assumed it would be relatively easy to recruit anthropologists or others with background and training in qualitative methods. To the contrary, this proved to be difficult until we were well along in the project; many of the most desirable candidates were already employed, and we eventually had to turn to younger and less experienced individuals who had to be trained.

An explicit goal had been to use social work students as team members. This was difficult at first because of my academic appointment in an alcohol and drug abuse research institute rather than a school of social work. While the project was explicitly about social work, it was more popular with students than with social work faculty, other than field or practicum faculty. In the end, the project was designated as a research practicum under the auspices of the school of social work. We found second-year MSW students and doctoral students to be more appropriate than first-year MSW students, perhaps because of the unique demands of the project and the need for more experienced and autonomous workers. The project also recruited master's level public health and nursing students.

In addition to the staff recruitment challenges already described, the project faced such mundane challenges as competing with others for limited space, and developing training materials and protocols. Other more important challenges included establishing viable working relationships with agencies and developing appropriate timetables.

In such a context, I learned a great deal about myself as a researcher-manager. It was challenging to wear so many hats, including those of social scientist, recruiter, trainer, teacher, mentor, manager, community liaison, data analyst, and policy analyst. Simply stated, there were few models to prepare me adequately; I learned to respond to the various challenges as they emerged.

Not too far into the project, I realized that all was not going well. Feelings of awkwardness had developed in team meetings and debriefings; difficulties developed in communication. Initially, I tended to remove myself somewhat from the day-to-day exigencies of the field office, retreating to the quiet of my research desk and leaving day-to-day operations to a program manager. It soon became abundantly clear that this strategy did not work, as a morale problem developed among the staff. As a multidisciplinary HIV field project targeting a new and potentially difficult-to-reach population, there needed to be a project leader who was accessible and as flexible as possible. As the Principal Investigator, I had to reframe the role in order to incorporate "best" community social work practice with ethnographic, project managerial, and policy level expertise.

In the end, whatever success the project may have had was due primarily to the remarkable team that came together and worked so hard. The men and women who became expert ethnographers, who made the contacts, observed the scenes, interviewed, transcribed, coded, and helped analyze the data, made the study. It was their commitment, their professionalism, and their sense of the mission for this project that prevailed. In the end, I think we all found it to be a rich and satisfying personal and professional experience.

IMPLICATIONS

With respect to HIV, the project findings underscored initial assumptions regarding the wide-ranging prevention, intervention, and related social service needs of this population, which we found to be comprised of overlapping social networks and mini-ecologies. Not only were MSM-DU hidden and marginalized, they were skeptical about being given a "fair hearing" by health care providers. This skepticism often prevented the disclosure of important personal information when they did encounter the health care system (Gorman & Carroll, 2000).

Lessons learned from the project strongly suggested that much more had to be done regarding this issue in order to increase the effectiveness of HIV prevention efforts with this population. Also, we found methamphetamine and club drug use by themselves, or in combination with sex, to constitute significant health and mental health problems that should be of concern to social workers. In particular, the growing popularity of circuit parties, rave scenes, and the general perception of greater tolerance of illicit drug use generally in many GLBT communities should be cause for concern.

The reality is that both direct and indirect associations with such drug-using populations heavily influence successful prevention and intervention dynamics. Innovative community assessment and outreach projects can assist in contributing to better social work practice by facilitating entrée into hidden, marginalized, at-risk populations and their social networks. They can also help to gain a better understanding of salient risk factors and the context and meaning of risk engagement. By utilizing a traditional "person-in-environment" framework, such efforts can provide useful information in the development of appropriate treatment programs, referrals, and the dissemination of drug- and behavior-specific information to use. Such projects may provide useful models for social workers engaged at the micro, mezzo and macro levels in a variety of cultural settings, with a variety of at-risk populations including GLBT populations. They might also provide opportunities for the development of hands-on, applied, community-based research experience.

FINAL THOUGHTS

Social work research is rooted in the National Association of Social Workers' Code of Ethics (NASW, 1996), which articulates six values: service, social justice, dignity of the person, importance of human relationships, integrity, and competence. The SURE project attempted to incorporate these values by identifying and clarifying a given need in a population that was not well understood and that suffered from discrimination and social injustice. We attempted to respect the dignity of subjects by providing opportunities for their voices to be heard and by respecting their boundaries. Our goal was NOT to "get them into treatment," but to try and build relationships with them. We attempted to meet them where they were and to listen to them. We attempted to emphasize the importance of the relationship between ethnographer and subject, and between community and project. Finally, under the domain of competence, we drew upon the experience of a number of drug researchers, HIV experts, social work researchers, and GLBT community members to develop the highest level of competence possible. In a unique, multifaceted, and multidisciplinary project such as this one, such a task could be daunting, in part because there weren't any "best practices" *per se*. In that regard, we hope this project will be a catalyst for others attempting to do similar, difficult work with this and other hidden, stigmatized populations.

REFERENCES

Agar, M. (1980). *The professional stranger*. New York: Academic Press.

Agar, M. (1986). *Speaking of ethnography*. Newbury Park, CA: Sage.

Agar, M. (1996). Recasting the "ethno" in epidemiology. *Medical Anthropology, 16,* 391-401.

Anderson, R., & Flynn, N. (1997). The methamphetamine-HIV connection in Northern California. In H. Klee (Ed.), *Amphetamine misuse: International perspectives on current trends* (pp. 181-196). Amsterdam: Harwood Academic Publishers.

Bernard, H.R. (1988). *Research methods in cultural anthropology.* Newbury Park, CA: Sage.

Cabaj, R. (1989). AIDS and chemical dependency: Special issues and treatment barriers for gay and bisexual men. *Journal of Psychoactive Drugs, 21,* 387-393.

Centers for Disease Control (2001, June). *HIV/AIDS surveillance report* (vol. 13, no. 1). Atlanta: Author.

Clatts, M.C., Davis, W.R., & Atillasoy, A. (1995). Hitting a moving target: The use of ethnographic methods in the development of sampling strategies for the evaluation of AIDS outreach program for homeless youth in New York City. In R. Needle, R. Ashery, & E. Lambert (Eds.), *Qualitative methods in drug abuse and HIV research: National Institute on Drug Abuse Research Monograph Series, 157,* 117-135. Washington DC: National Institute on Drug Abuse.

Diaz, T., Chu S.Y., Byers, R.H., Hersh, B.S., Conti, L., Rietmeijer, C., Mokotoff, E., Fann, A., Boyd, D., Iglesias, L., Checko, P., Frederick, M., Hermann, P., Herr, M., & Samuel, M. (1994). Types of drugs used by injection drug users with HIV/AIDS in a multisite surveillance project: Implications for intervention. *American Journal of Public Health, 84,* 1971-1975.

Gorman, E.M. (1996). Speed use and HIV transmission. *Focus, 11(7),* 4-6.

Gorman, E.M., Barr, B., Hansen, A., Robertson, B., & Green, C. (1997). Speed, sex, gay men and HIV: Ecological and community perspectives. *Medical Anthropology Quarterly, 11,* 505-515.

Gorman, E.M., & Carroll, R. (2000). The interface of substance abuse and HIV: Considerations regarding methamphetamines and other "party drugs" for nursing practice and research. *Journal of Nursing and AIDS Care, 11(2),* 51-62.

Gorman, E.M., Morgan, P., & Lambert, E.Y. (1995). Qualitative research considerations and other issues in the study of methamphetamine use, qualitative methods in drug abuse and HIV research. In R. Needle, R. Ashery, & E. Lambert (Eds.), *Qualitative methods in drug abuse and HIV research: National Institute on Drug Abuse Research Monograph Series, 157,* 157-181. Washington, DC: National Institute on Drug Abuse.

Harris, N., Thiede, H., McGough, J., & Gordon, D. (1993). Risk factors for HIV infection among injection drug users: Results of blinded surveys in drug treatment centers, King County, Washington, 1988-1991. *Journal of Acquired Immune Deficiency Syndromes, 6,* 1275-1282.

Honigman, J.J. (1970). Sampling in ethnographic fieldwork. In R. Naroll & R. Cohen (Eds.), *Handbook of methods in cultural anthropology* (pp. 255-281). New York: Columbia University Press.

Johnson, J.C. (1990). *Selecting ethnographic informants.* Newbury Park, CA: Sage.

Koester, S. (1995). Applying the methodology of participant observation to the study of injection related HIV risks. In R. Needle, R. Ashery, & E. Lambert (Eds.), *Qualitative methods in drug abuse and HIV research: National Institute on Drug Abuse Research Monograph Series, 157,* 84-99. Washington, DC: National Institute on Drug Abuse.

National Association of Social Workers (1996). *Code of ethics.* Washington, DC: Author.

National Institute on Drug Abuse (1998). *Methamphetamine abuse and addiction–research report series* (NCADI Publication No. PHD756). Retrieved Oct. 21, 2001 from *http://www.nida.nih.gov.*

Needle, R., Ashery, R., & Lambert, E. (Eds.) (1995). *Qualitative methods in drug abuse and HIV research*: *Research Monograph Series*, *157*, Washington, DC: National Institute on Drug Abuse.

Needle, R.H., Coyle, S., Cesari, H., Trotter, R., Clatts, M., Koester, S., Price, L., McLellan, E., Finlinson, A., Bluthenthal, R.N., Pierce, T., Johnson, J., Jones, T.S., & Williams, M. (1998). HIV risk behaviors associated with the injection process: Multiperson use of drug injection equipment and paraphernalia in injection drug user networks. *Substance Use and Misuse*, *33*, 2403-2423.

Ostrow, D.G. (1996). Substance use, HIV, and gay men. *Focus*, *11(7)*, 1-3.

Padgett, D. (1998). *Qualitative methods in social work research*. Thousand Oaks, CA: Sage.

Paul, P., Stall, R., Crosby, M., Barrett, D.C., & Midanik, L.T. (1994). Correlates of sexual risk-taking among gay male substance abusers. *Addiction*, *89*, 971-983.

Paul, P., Stall, R., & Davis, F. (1993). Sexual risk for HIV transmission among gay/bisexual men in substance abuse treatment. *AIDS Education and Prevention*, *5*, 11-24.

Peterson, J., Coates, T., & Catania, J. (1992). High risk sexual behavior and condom use among African-American gay and bisexual men. *American Journal of Public Health*, *82*, 1490-1494.

Stall, R., & Ostrow, D.G. (1989). Intravenous drug use, the combination of drugs and sexual activity and HIV infection among gay and bisexual men: The San Francisco Men's Health Study. *Journal of Drug Issues*, *19(1)*, 57-73.

Stall, R., & Purcell, D. (2000). Intertwining epidemics: A review of research on substance abuse among MSMS. *AIDS and Behavior*, *4(2)*, 181-92.

Stall, R., & Wiley, J. (1988). A comparison of alcohol and drug use patterns of homosexual and heterosexual men: The San Francisco Men's Health Study. *Drug and Alcohol Dependence*, *22*, 63-73.

Sterk-Elifson, C. (1995). Determining drug use patterns among women: The value of qualitative research methods. In R. Needle, R. Ashery, & E. Lambert (Eds.), *Qualitative methods in drug abuse and HIV research*: *National Institute on Drug Abuse Research Monograph Series*, *157*, 65-83. Washington, DC: National Institute on Drug Abuse.

Stewart, A. (1998). *The ethnographer's method*. Thousand Oaks, CA: Sage.

Straussner, S.L. (2001). The role of social workers in the treatment of addictions: A brief history. *Journal of Social Work in the Addictions*, *1(1)*, 3-9.

Sullivan, P.S., Nakashima, A.K., Purcell, D.W., & Ward, J.W. (1998). Geographic differences in noninjection and injection substance use among HIV seropositve men: Western US vs. other regions. *Journal of Acquired Immune Deficiency Syndrome*, *19*, 266-273.

Trotter, R.T. (1995). Drug use, AIDS, and ethnography: Advanced ethnographic research methods exploring the HIV epidemic. In R. Needle, R. Ashery, & E. Lambert (Eds.), *Qualitative methods in drug abuse and HIV research*: *National Institute on Drug Abuse Research Monograph Series*, *157*, 38-64. Washington, DC: National Institute on Drug Abuse.

Weinberg, T.S. (1994). *Gay men, drinking, and alcoholism*. Carbondale, IL: Southern Illinois University Press.

Self-Disclosure Stress:
Trauma as an Example
of an Intervening Variable
in Research with Lesbian Women

Marian Swindell
Jo Pryce

SUMMARY. To date, research on lesbians has been primarily descriptive and has focused mainly on studies of the coming out process, identity formation, and the psychosocial problems and self-destructive behaviors manifested in this population. The authors contend that research within lesbian populations has too often been simplistically conceptualized, lacking models with mediating and moderating variables that might help to explain the occurrence of specific phenomena within its members. This paper identifies trauma, through constructivist self-development theory, as a potentially important framework for understanding the impact of and responses to the coming out process among lesbians, and calls for the de-

---

Marian Swindell, MSW, PhD, is Assistant Professor of Social Work, Mississippi State University-Meridian, Meridian, MS. Jo Pryce, MSW, PhD, is Associate Professor, University of Alabama School of Social Work, Tuscaloosa, AL.

Address correspondence to: Dr. Marian Swindell, Mississippi State University-Meridian, 1000 Highway 19 North, Meridian, MS 39307 (E-mail: Mswindell@meridian.msstate.edu).

[Haworth co-indexing entry note]: "Self-Disclosure Stress: Trauma as an Example of an Intervening Variable in Research with Lesbian Women." Swindell, Marian, and Jo Pryce. Co-published simultaneously in *Journal of Gay & Lesbian Social Services* (Harrington Park Press, an imprint of The Haworth Press, Inc.) Vol. 15, No. 1/2, 2003, pp. 95-108; and: *Research Methods with Gay, Lesbian, Bisexual, and Transgender Populations* (ed: William Meezan, and James I. Martin) Harrington Park Press, an imprint of The Haworth Press, Inc., 2003, pp. 95-108. Single or multiple copies of this article are available for a fee from The Haworth Document Delivery Service [1-800-HAWORTH, 9:00 a.m. - 5:00 p.m. (EST). E-mail address: getinfo@haworthpressinc.com].

95

velopment of more complex models of behavior as a way to further our knowledge of the experience of lesbians. *[Article copies available for a fee from The Haworth Document Delivery Service: 1-800-HAWORTH. E-mail address: <getinfo@haworthpressinc.com> Website: <http://www.HaworthPress.com> © 2003 by The Haworth Press, Inc. All rights reserved.]*

KEYWORDS. Lesbian, coming out, trauma, psychological stress

A plethora of research exists that focuses on the psychosocial problems and self-destructive behaviors manifested in lesbian populations. Three large, well-designed studies have found that lesbians attempt suicide two to seven times more often than heterosexual comparison groups (Bradford & Ryan, 1988; Gibson, 1989; Saunders & Valente, 1987). The National Lesbian Health Survey (Bradford & Ryan, 1988) reported that more than 50% of the lesbian participants had suicidal ideation at some time in their lives, and that 18% had attempted suicide.

A majority of suicide attempts by lesbians and gay men occur during their youth, and lesbian and gay youths are two to three times more likely to attempt suicide than other young people. This population may comprise up to 30% of completed youth suicides annually, and it reportedly accounted for approximately one-third of all teenage deaths between 1950 and 1980 (Gibson, 1989). Suicidal gestures of gay and lesbian teens, as measured in one study, were more severe than those of other adolescents (Jones, 1978).

Lesbians have been reported to have significantly higher occurrences of risk factors related to suicide, including suicide attempts, substance abuse, interrupted social ties, chronic depression, truancy, school failure, sexual promiscuity, early relationship conflicts, and having to survive on their own prematurely (Gibson, 1989; Saunders & Valente, 1987). For example, substance abuse has been reported to be two to three times higher among lesbian and gay youths than among their heterosexual counterparts (Sears, 1991).

Negative responses to the discovery of one's own lesbianism may well be exacerbated by the reactions of others, especially family members. Many lesbian children face hostile and rejecting reactions from their parents, with parents reporting feeling guilt, embarrassment, and shame surrounding their children's lesbianism (LaSala, 2001). Gibson (1989) found that nearly one-half of gay and lesbian adolescent clients experienced violence inflicted by family members. Almost 30% of these clients were forced to leave their homes and schools because of their sexual orientation.

Based on our reading of the literature, we have concluded that research with this population has been primarily descriptive, and it has focused on topics such as dysfunctional behavior (suicide rates, mental illness including depression, substance abuse), discrimination, identity formation, and the coming out process. We believe that there has been too little research that offers complex explanations of dysfunctional behaviors within lesbian populations, or why they might occur at disproportionately higher rates among them than among heterosexual populations. It is our contention that research within lesbian populations has too often been simplistically conceptualized, lacking models with mediating and moderating variables that might help to explain the occurrence of specific phenomena. We propose that more complex conceptual models be tested in order to understand the presence of the simple descriptive relationships found to date.

Toward that end, this paper introduces the concept of trauma surrounding the coming out process as a variable that might be considered in order to gain a fuller understanding of the troubling behavior that is more likely to occur among lesbians than among straight women. The concept of trauma was chosen for exploration because all of the negative behaviors described may be symptomatic of cognitive stress, which can either be caused by or lead to trauma. Thus, while this paper is about trauma, it uses this construct to call for increased complexity in the conceptualization of research problems with lesbian (and, by extension, with gay, bisexual, and transgender) populations. The article thus explores trauma and its potential relationships with specific variables that have been examined in the literature as impacting the well-being of lesbians as they come out of the closet and face the world.

COMING OUT

"Coming out of the closet," or "coming out" refers to the progression of verbally and/or behaviorally acknowledging oneself as being lesbian. When a lesbian decides to come out, the process involves several simultaneous processes in which a woman self-identifies as a lesbian and then shares this knowledge with others, e.g., family, friends, co-workers, community, acquaintances. Two researchers, Cass (1979) and Coleman (1982), described the coming out process as a time when lesbian women begin to reevaluate their lives and shed a stigmatized identity in favor of a more positive sense of self. Thus, it is a time when a recognized sexual orientation is incorporated into other aspects of their identity.

Usually, the coming out process is neither easy nor short. For many lesbians, it can be emotionally painful, psychologically stressful, and challenging. Gramick (1984) characterized the process of coming out as one of "reality shock," which is often accompanied by guilt, confusion, and alienation, as some women recognize that they are members of a stigmatized group. For others, coming out can be a natural process involving self-growth; many women experience this process as empowering.

There is no correct way to come out, with each person coming out for different reasons and to different people. There is also no correct time to come out. For some people, the decision to come out takes place later in life. For others, the process happens as early as adolescence. According to Jay and Young (1992), it generally takes between one to two years for a person to come out to friends, family, coworkers and acquaintances.

D'Augelli (1996) found that lesbian youths and young adults were able to disclose to multiple, sometimes overlapping, audiences that include family of origin (parents, siblings, extended family), friends (ranging from casual acquaintances to close friends), and additional important others in their social networks (coworkers, religious leaders, teachers, and others). However, first disclosures were usually made to the safest and most supportive person they knew. According to D'Augelli and Hershberger (1993), 73% of lesbian youths came out to a friend first. Savin-Williams (1995, 1998) obtained similar findings, noting that first disclosures were usually made to a best friend or the opposite-sex person they were dating.

Some youths tend to experience the coming out process as a monumental event. They are often able to recall exact dates, times, and places when they first revealed their sexual orientation, their feelings about this self-revelation, and the reactions of their confidants (Savin-Williams, 1998). Since recall of events can be symptomatic of an experience being cognitively traumatizing (McCann & Pearlman, 1990), it may be that an understanding of the degree of trauma suffered during the coming out experience can help to explain both the reaction to coming out and the behavioral consequences of it. Thus, an exploration into the trauma associated with coming out may be a useful mediating and moderating variable to explore when looking at developmental outcomes for lesbians.

CONSTRUCTIVIST SELF-DEVELOPMENT THEORY

As lesbians experience life, they construct representational models of the world. During the coming out event, which presents new information and can induce stress, lesbians may be unable to "think through," explain, accommodate, or assimilate the reasons or characteristics of the event into their worldview. This is known as "cognitive disruption." When a traumatic event causes a disruption that cannot be accommodated, psychological growth is temporarily disrupted, and certain traumatic stress symptoms are exhibited. They might include lack of sleep, anxiety, headaches, nausea, reliving the event, avoidance of situations that remind the person of the event, rumination, intrusive thoughts about the events, numbness, and feelings of unreality. However, not all people experience the same reactions or symptoms with the same degree of intensity (McCann & Pearlman, 1990).

One possible theory explaining the degree of trauma associated with the disclosure process and its behavioral outcomes within lesbian populations is Constructivist Self-Development Theory (CSDT) (McCann & Pearlman, 1990). This theory blends object relations, self psychology, and social cognition theories. It is based upon a constructivist view of trauma, in which peoples' unique histories shape their reactions and define how they adapt to the experience.

This theory posits that the experience of trauma begins with exposure to a non-normative or highly distressing event or series of events that potentially disrupts the self. The individual's unique response to this trauma is a complex process that includes the personal meanings and images of the event, extends to the deepest parts of a person's inner experience of self and world, and results in an individual adaptation (McCann & Pearlman, 1990).

CSDT has considerable potential for providing a theoretical basis for explaining the traumatic stress that might be present in the process of coming out. A primary advantage of applying this theory to the self-disclosure process is that it allows for individualized reactions to stressful events by way of examining the way the event is experienced based on two major factors: the person's temperament and the context in which the event occurs (see Figure 1). Thus, the theory is compatible with social work's ecological perspective, since it explores both personal and environmental factors that may lead to behavioral outcomes among lesbians. By understanding these factors, we may be able to devise interventions that prevent, understand, and decrease the harmful behaviors that might be associated with the stress of coming out.

The theory posits four sub-domains within the temperamental domain. The first sub-domain proposes that individuals react to stressful events by drawing on the internal organization of the self, including self-capacities, ego resources, psychological needs, and cognitive schemas about the world. The second sub-domain may be labeled "developmental stage and current emotional health." According to McCann and Pearlman (1990), people react differently to different situations according to their psychological development at the time of the stress-inducing event, any pre-existing pathology, their past experiences, and the magnitude of the stressful event. The third sub-domain deals with the adaptive mechanisms at the person's disposal, including current positive adaptations to the world, the drive for personal growth, and the presence of self-protective judgements. The final sub-domain is locus of control, or people's perception of control over their ultimate destiny.

FIGURE 1. CSDT Overview

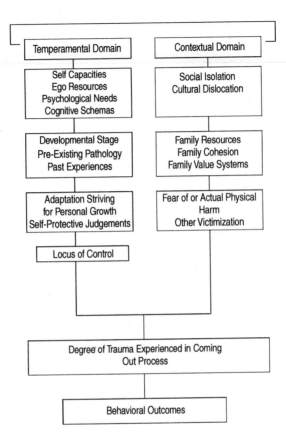

The contextual domain focuses attention on the stress present in the individual's person-situation interactions. There are three sub-domains within this domain. The first deals with the social isolation and cultural dislocation that coming out might involve. The second deals with family reactions to the self-disclosure, which may be shaped by the availability of family resources, the cohesion of the family of origin, and the family's value system. The final sub-domain is concerned with the social environment in which the lesbian lives, and the degree of potential physical harm or other victimization that is present within it.

While it is not shown in Figure 1, in addition to these temperament and contextual factors, CSDT considers the lesbian to be an active agent in creating, modifying, and changing her view of the world. CSDT thus provides a viable framework for understanding the impact of trauma on the self by emphasizing the importance of the individual's psychological experience of the trauma, rather than focusing primarily on the external nature of the traumatic event.

The field of stress and trauma has not yet explored the relationships between the coming out process and the stress factors associated with it (J. Wilkerson, Sidran Traumatic Stress Institute, personal communication, January 17, 2002). However, this model has potential for helping us to understand the sequelae of the coming out process based on the domains posited above. As suggested, inner resources and the traumatic factors surrounding the coming out process (including rejection from family members and society, internalized homophobia, fear of physical harm, and social isolation) may well shape the way in which this event is perceived by individuals and their response to it.

Many lesbians whose experience of coming out was stressful to the point of traumatizing have learned to cope and find meaning in their experience, continuing on with their lives without being haunted by the memories of those negative reactions. This does not mean that the traumatic or stressful events surrounding their coming out have gone away or go unnoticed. When a lesbian is traumatized, her psychological developmental stage, and temperamental and contextual factors, determine the defenses she employs. Thus, depending on predisposing, vulnerability, and other factors, lesbians will vary greatly in their psychological responses to the coming out process. We believe that CSDT, which considers traumatic impact as arising from aspects of the event in interaction with individual factors, may be a fruitful framework for understanding these differences. Toward this end, we now turn to each of the elements in Figure 1 for a fuller discussion.

Temperamental Domain

Internal organization. CSDT explains aspects of the self that are impacted by trauma, including the self and one's frame of reference. The self is conceptualized as the "hypothetical construct used to describe the psychological foundation of the individual" (McCann & Pearlman, 1990, p. 90). It comprises: (1) basic capacities whose function is to maintain an inner sense of identity and positive self-esteem; (2) ego resources, which serve to regulate and enhance one's interactions with the world outside oneself; (3) psychological needs, which motivate behavior; and (4) cognitive schemas, which are the conscious and unconscious beliefs, assumptions, and expectations through which individuals interpret their experiences (McCann & Pearlman, 1990). One's frame of reference refers to the way in which people view themselves and the world based on these four constructs.

According to CSDT theory, people who are strong in these areas, including a positive frame of reference, are less likely to be traumatized by the coming out process, and more likely to have positive behavioral outcomes, than those who do not. For example, ego resources, which influence the interpretation of events and promote adaptation, may be disrupted when disclosure is stressful. These resources include intelligence, introspection, willpower, initiative, the ability to strive for personal growth, and an awareness of one's psychological needs. They also include the ability to view oneself and others from more than one perspective, to foresee consequences, to establish mature relations with others, to be aware of and establish personal boundaries between self and others, and to make self-protective judgments.

Similarly, the trauma surrounding reactions during and after the coming out event can also result in disruption of self-capacities. McCann and Pearlman (1990) describe self-capacities as: the ability to tolerate and regulate strong affect without self-fragmentation or acting out; the ability to be alone without being lonely; the ability to calm oneself through processes of self-soothing; and the ability to moderate self-loathing in the face of criticism or guilt.

Developmental stage and current emotional health. The point in the life cycle at which a particular crisis occurs impacts how the event is perceived. Research in the area of lesbian identity development indicates that lesbians have a subjective awareness of being "different" in early childhood. It is the cognitive labeling of these differences, and an attribution to sexuality, that usually occurs during adolescence (Van Wormer, Wells, & Boes, 2000). The earlier youths are aware of their sexual orientation and identify themselves as lesbian, the greater the conflicts they might have, since they may lack world experience and coping skills.

These conflicts become even more traumatic for teens who are subjected to severe peer pressure, physical and verbal abuse, and rejection or isolation from family. Due to a lack of social support, many lesbian youths often feel totally alone, and they may withdraw socially due to fear of adverse consequences, which results in increased stress (Van Wormer et al., 2000). In addition, lesbian youths may face problems in accepting themselves due to a lack of accurate information about homosexuality, internalization of a negative self-image, or preexisting pathologies. Such conditions often lead to assaults on self-esteem and other ego resources.

If a lesbian blames herself for her same-sex orientation, or is unable to cope with negative reactions to it, there is a greater probability of her experiencing psychological difficulties. And when a traumatic or stressful event occurs suddenly, as sometimes occurs in the coming out process, it is more likely to threaten her psychological well-being (McCann & Pearlman, 1990).

Adaptive mechanisms. When traumas are addressed by confronting them, constructive living and psychological growth are possible. Meaning can be attributed to traumatic events, which can subsequently become opportunities for growth (Averill & Nunley, 1992), but only when self-protective and adaptive mechanisms are either in place or are developed as a result of the experience. Shostrom (1983) noted that "most people who become self-actualizing do so as a result of a struggle to overcome a problem in their lives" (p. 311). As noted above, although a traumatic or stressful event can suddenly threaten psychological well-being, it can also provide an opportunity to achieve psychological adjustment if the appropriate positive psychological mechanisms (and external supports) are in place (McCann & Pearlman, 1990).

Locus of control. One quality of traumatic and stressful events is the perceived lack of control over them (Slaby, 1989). Individuals can control many events (e.g., the decision to self-disclose or not), but those that cannot be controlled (i.e., the reactions from others after the disclosure) can cause them to experience powerlessness and helplessness. Such feelings are likely to challenge psychological well-being (McCann & Pearlman, 1990).

Events that are out of the ordinary are also more likely to be difficult for individuals to handle, as are events that create long-lasting problems (Davidson, Fleming, & Baum, 1986). Many problems in life are potentially reversible, such as failing a class, having an argument, and getting the flu. However, coming out is irreversible because it entails revealing one's true self to oneself and others at a given point in time. Because of this, it is imperative that individuals have as much control as possible over the coming out process.

Contextual Domain

Social isolation and cultural dislocation. Neither peer nor family support can be presumed to follow disclosure. On the contrary, lesbians, especially adolescent lesbians, may find themselves alienated and alone. They may believe themselves to be outsiders within their home, their school, and among their friends and families. D'Augelli (1996) found that initial disclosure often involved a risk of rejection, particularly when the individual was without access to social support networks or helping resources.

Moving into a lesbian culture sometimes involves a loss of reference groups (e.g., family of origin, friends, coworkers and relatives), feelings of belonging, pride, and a shared sense of reality. Additionally, one's identity can become threatened when exposed to homophobic and heterosexist remarks, or when conflicts over values and beliefs occur with others (Atkinson, Morten, & Sue, 1993; Ruiz, 1990). Thus, entering a lesbian culture may require learning new rules of behavior and the recognition that sexual minorities are punished and undervalidated. Moving into the new culture often engenders a need to find positive role models and affiliations.

During the coming out process, lesbians may experience a phenomenon that has been called "cultural dislocation." That is, lesbians are usually raised in a heterosexually-oriented culture, but upon awareness of same-sex orientation they must begin adjusting to a lesbian culture while still belonging to the heterosexual world. This movement from the familiar to the foreign often involves complex, diverse, multifaceted experiences, and significant psychological adjustment. Culture shock and discouragement may accompany such drastic changes in the individual's social environment and life-style (Furnham & Bochner, 1986).

Family. Coming out to parents is the most difficult part of the coming out process for many lesbians, and it is the disclosure most likely to evoke the greatest fear. Knowing that it will probably upset parents and other family members, young people usually engage in intense internal debates about whether to disclose. The anticipated negative consequences of disclosure to family members include rejection, scorn, ridicule, alienation (Wells & Kline, 1987), parental disillusionment, loss of emotional support, and subsequent isolation (Myers, 1982). Garnets and Kimmel (1993) noted that lesbians who disclosed to their parents usually did so only after first disclosing to others. Woodman (1985) observed that comments such as "It will devastate my parents" or "If I come out to them I will lose my parents" suggest that some lesbians know how difficult it may be for parents to accept their same-gender sexual orientation. Brown (1989) stated that most lesbians agonize over telling their parents. It is thus not surprising that parents were often the last persons told.

Although disclosure to parents and other family members more often than not results in negative reactions (Garnets & Kimmel, 1993), families display different ranges and intensities of responses (Green & Herek, 1994). According to Strommen (1990), families' stereotypes about same-gender sexual orientation and their value systems influence both the form and intensity of their reactions to the disclosure.

Among family members, parental reactions to disclosure are the best documented; few studies have reported on disclosure to other relatives (Garnets & Kimmel, 1993). What is known is that when most or all family members know about a lesbian family member, existing family alignments and relationships may break apart (De Vine, 1984; Strommen, 1989), and divisions can occur among family members because of differences in values and their subsequent responses to the disclosure.

Physical harm and other victimization. Hate crimes, defined here as crimes in which the perpetrator intentionally selects victims because of their actual or perceived sexual orientation, send a message that certain groups of people are neither welcome nor safe in a particular community. In 2000, there were 211 specific anti-lesbian hate crimes reported in the U.S. Twenty-four (11%) of these offenses were aggravated assaults, 51 (24%) simple assaults, and 82 (38%) incidents of intimidation. There were over 1,486 gay and lesbian-oriented incidents in 2000 (Federal Bureau of Investigation, n.d.). The personal and social costs of hate crimes are incalculable. And other types of victimization–discriminatory business practices, unequal insurance accessibility, and lack of legal protections–add to these costs and send the message that lesbians are not welcome within certain milieus.

BEHAVIORAL OUTCOMES

We believe that the individual elements in the CSDT model, its two major domains, and the model as a whole should be tested to determine the extent to which it explains why certain dysfunctional behaviors occur within the lesbian population at disproportionately higher rates. Lesbians vary in their psychological responses to the coming out process, and such differences may be due to predisposing factors, vulnerability factors, contextual factors, and/or other issues. If this is indeed the case, lesbians with healthy temperamental dispositions, living in healthy and supportive contexts, would be less traumatized by the coming out process and would adjust to their new sexual identity more positively than lesbians whose temperament and/or contexts are less supportive of healthy development. For example, if a lesbian does not have strong internal protective factors she might act out, withdraw, experience self-doubt or self-loathing, be unable to think coherently or view herself as a worthwhile individual in society, and have impaired functioning at home and/or at work. In the extreme, self-destructive behaviors such as suicide, substance abuse, truancy, and sexual promiscuity could result from an inability to compensate for missing self-capacities and ego resources.

Similarly, lesbians who come out in hostile contexts may suffer significant trauma and experience adjustment problems. When lesbians who come out to their friends and family experience the trauma of rejection and isolation, the resulting cognitive disruption may lead to subsequent coping mechanisms that include a myriad of negative behaviors.

Even when their families are supportive, adjusting to a new cultural system may lead lesbians to experience inner conflicts, since their identity and sense of belonging may be threatened in the new culture (Arredondo, 1984). Therefore, feelings of cultural dislocation, loneliness, self-doubt, and identity confusion may emerge. And when the new cultural system involves an increased potential for physical harm or other victimization, the process of coming out can be even more traumatic. Bart (1998) reported that one in six gay and lesbian students are beaten so badly that they require medical attention, and that the drop-out rate for gay and lesbian students has been estimated at three times the national average.

By contrast, lesbians whose inner defenses are strong, and whose environments are supportive of healthy development, may come through the coming out process without significant trauma. For these women, the positive outcomes of coming out may include increased self-esteem, greater honesty in their lives, greater freedom of self-expression, and a greater sense of personal integrity. Such women often experience a release of tension when they stop trying to deny or hide this important aspect of their lives. Women who come out within positive contexts can find that previous feelings of isolation and alienation are reduced as a result of increased support from families and friends (Jordan & Deluty, 1998).

CONCLUSIONS

We believe that research has thus far relied upon inadequately developed and insufficiently complex explanations of self-destructive behaviors among lesbians. This paper presented an example of a more complex theoretical framework that focused on traumatic stress in the coming out process, and which included a variety of mediating and moderating variables. Self-disclosure of sexual orientation by lesbians might not be traumatic in and of itself. Rather, the anticipated and actual reactions to that disclosure, and the inability to process them in a positive way, might be what is traumatizing.

Adding greater complexity to the research enterprise is imperative, for it is disrespectful to lesbians to simply describe their circumstances without understanding them. Simple descriptions suggest that problems lie within individuals themselves; more complex conceptualizations shed light on the many contextual factors that might better explain them. Through greater complexity, research can help society to better understand the circumstances that lead to dysfunctional behaviors among lesbians and stop "blaming the victims."

REFERENCES

Arredondo, P. (1984). Identity themes for immigrant young adults. *Adolescence, 19,* 978-993.

Atkinson, D., Morten, G., & Sue, D. (1993). *Counseling American minorities: A cross-cultural perspective.* Madison, WI: Brown and Benchmark.

Averill, J., & Nunley, E. (1992). *Voyages of the heart.* New York: Free Press.

Bart, M. (1998). Creating a safer school for gay students. *Counseling Today, 26*, 36-39.

Bradford, J.B., & Ryan, C. (1988). *The National Lesbian Health Care Survey: Final report*. Washington, DC: National Lesbian and Gay Health Foundation.

Brown, L. (1989) Lesbians, gay men and their families: Common clinical issues. *Journal of Gay & Lesbian Psychotherapy, 1(1)*, 65-77.

Cass, V. (1979). Homosexual identity formation: A theoretical model. *Journal of Homosexuality, 4(3)*, 219-235.

Coleman, E. (1982). Developmental stages of the coming out process. In W. Paul, J. Weinrich, J. Gonsiorek, & M. Hotvedt (Eds.), *Homosexuality: Social, psychological and biological issues* (pp. 149-157). Beverly Hills, CA: Sage.

D'Augelli, A.R. (1996). Enhancing the development of lesbian, gay, and bisexual youths. In E.D. Rothblum & L.A. Bonds (Eds.), *Preventing heterosexism and homophobia: Primary prevention of psychopathology* (pp. 124-150). Newbury Park, CA: Sage.

D'Augelli, A.R., & Hershberger, S. (1993). Lesbian, gay, and bisexual youth in community settings: Personal challenges and mental health problems. *American Journal of Community Psychology, 21*, 421-448.

Davidson, L., Fleming, I., & Baum A. (1986). Post-traumatic stress as a function of chronic stress and toxic exposure. In C. Figley (Ed.), *Trauma and its wake, Vol. 2: Traumatic stress theory, research and intervention* (pp. 57-77). New York: Brunner/Mazel.

De Vine, J. (1984). A systematic inspection of affectional preference orientation and the family of origin. *Journal of Social Work and Human Sexuality, 2*, 9-17.

Federal Bureau of Investigation (n.d.). *Uniform crime reports*. Retrieved January 14, 2002, from *http://www.fbi.gov/ucr/cius_00/hate00.pdf.*

Furnham, A., & Bochner, S. (1986). *Culture shock: Psychological reactions to unfamiliar environments*. New York: Methuen.

Garnets, L., & Kimmel, D. (1993). Introduction. In L.D. Garnets & D.C. Kimmel (Eds.), *Psychological perspectives on lesbian and gay male experiences* (pp. 1-51). New York: Columbia University Press.

Gibson, P. (1989). Gay male and lesbian youth suicide. In M. Feinleib (Ed.), *Report of the Secretary's Task Force on Youth Suicide, Vol. 3: Preventions and interventions in youth suicide* (pp. 110-142) (DHHS Publication No. ADM 89-1623). Washington, DC: U.S. Government Printing Office.

Gramick, J. (1984). Developing a lesbian identity. In T. Darty & S. Potter (Eds.), *Women-identified women* (pp. 31-44). Palo Alto, CA: Mayfield.

Green, B., & Herek, G. (Eds.) (1994). *Lesbian and gay psychology: Theory, research, and clinical applications*. Thousand Oaks, CA: Sage.

Jay, K., & Young, A. (Eds.) (1992). *Out of the closets: Voices of gay liberation*. New York: Jove.

Jones, G. (1978). Counseling gay adolescents. *Counselor Education and Supervision, 18*, 144-152.

Jordan, K.M., & Deluty, R.H. (1998). Coming out for lesbian women: Its relation to anxiety, positive affectivity, self-esteem, and social support. *Journal of Homosexuality, 35(2)*, 41-63.

LaSala, M. (2001). The importance of partners to lesbians' intergenerational relationships. *Social Work Research, 25*, 27-36.

McCann, L., & Pearlman, A. (1990). Vicarious traumatization: A framework for understanding the psychological effects of working with victims. *Journal of Traumatic Stress, 3,* 131-149.

Myers, M. (1982). Counseling the parents of young homosexual male patients. *Journal of Homosexuality, 7(2/3),* 131-143.

Ruiz, A. (1990). Ethnic identity: Crisis and resolution. *Journal of Multicultural Counseling and Development, 18,* 26-40.

Saunders, J., & Valente, S. (1987). Suicide risk among gay men and lesbians: A review. *Death Studies, 4,* 1-23.

Savin-Williams, R.C. (1995). Lesbian, gay male and bisexual adolescents. In A.R. D'Augelli & C. Patterson (Eds.), *Lesbian, gay, and bisexual identities over the lifespan* (pp. 165-190). New York: Oxford University Press.

Savin-Williams, R.C. (1998). *"...and then I became gay": Young men's stories.* New York: Routledge.

Sears, J. (1991). *Growing up gay in the south: Race, gender, and journey of the spirit.* New York: Harrington Park Press.

Shostrom, E. (1983). *From manipulator to master.* New York: Bantam Books.

Slaby, A. (1989). *Aftershock.* New York: Random House.

Strommen, E. (1989). "You're a what"?: Family members' reaction to the disclosure of homosexuality. *Journal of Homosexuality, 18(1-2),* 37-58.

Strommen, E. (1990). Hidden branches and growing pains: Homosexuality and the family tree. *Marriage & Family Review, 14,* 9-34.

Van Wormer, K., Wells, J., & Boes, M. (2000). *Social work with lesbians, gays, and bisexuals: A strengths perspective.* Boston: Allyn and Bacon.

Wells, J., & Kline, W. (1987). Self-disclosure of homosexual orientation. *Journal of Social Psychology, 127,* 191-197.

Woodman, N. (1985). Parents of lesbians and gays: Concerns and interventions. In H. Hidalgo, T. Peterson, & N. Woodman (Eds.), *Lesbian and gay issues: A resource manual for social workers* (pp. 21-32). Silver Spring, MD: National Association of Social Workers.

Dimensions of Lesbian Identity During Adolescence and Young Adulthood

Stephanie K. Swann

Jeane W. Anastas

SUMMARY. As knowledge about gay, lesbian, bisexual, and transgender people continues to mature, social work research must address the complexity of key issues, including sexual identity. The present study examined dimensions of sexual identity among young women who identify as questioning or lesbian, and it illustrates the progress being made in conceptualization and measurement in this area.

Three distinct dimensions of lesbian identity were found: "New Identity Possibilities," "Consolidation and Fulfillment," and "Stigma and Mistreatment Management." For these young women, individual and social dimensions of identity development were not distinct as had been previously hypothesized. These findings are discussed in relation to theory and future research that attends to the intersection of gender, age, and sexual identity. *[Article copies available for a fee from The Haworth Document Delivery Service: 1-800-HAWORTH. E-mail address: <getinfo@haworthpressinc.com> Website: <http://www.HaworthPress.com> © 2003 by The Haworth Press, Inc. All rights reserved.]*

Stephanie K. Swann, MSW, PhD, LCSW, is Assistant Professor, School of Social Work, University of Georgia, Athens, GA. Jeane W. Anastas is Professor, Shirley M. Ehrenkranz School of Social Work, New York University, New York, NY.

Address correspondence to: Dr. Stephanie K. Swann, University of Georgia, School of Social Work, Tucker Hall, Athens, GA 30602 (E-mail: skswann@arches.uga.edu).

[Haworth co-indexing entry note]: "Dimensions of Lesbian Identity During Adolescence and Young Adulthood." Swann, Stephanie K., and Jeane W. Anastas. Co-published simultaneously in *Journal of Gay & Lesbian Social Services* (Harrington Park Press, an imprint of The Haworth Press, Inc.) Vol. 15, No. 1/2, 2003, pp. 109-125; and: *Research Methods with Gay, Lesbian, Bisexual, and Transgender Populations* (ed: William Meezan, and James I. Martin) Harrington Park Press, an imprint of The Haworth Press, Inc., 2003, pp. 109-125. Single or multiple copies of this article are available for a fee from The Haworth Document Delivery Service [1-800-HAWORTH, 9:00 a.m. - 5:00 p.m. (EST). E-mail address: getinfo@haworthpressinc.com].

KEYWORDS. Lesbian, identity development, factor analysis, measurement

As theory and research addressing lesbian, gay, bisexual, and transgender (LGBT) issues has matured since the mid-1950s, the conceptualization of key concepts used to understand the lives of LGBT people has become more complex. This greater complexity has arisen for a number of reasons, including paradigm shifts in psychological and social theory in general, the emergence of queer theory and queer studies within the academy, and a growing (although still inadequate) appreciation of the diversity among LGBT people and communities.

With this greater complexity of understanding, however, have come new methodological challenges. The ways that social, political, and cultural contexts shape individuals' understandings of their sexual identities have been essential themes in recent scholarship (Foucault, 1978). As theorists have developed a more sophisticated comprehension of sexual identity, it has become necessary in empirical studies to clearly identify what aspect of sexuality is being measured (e.g., emotional attraction, sexual fantasy, or sexual behavior) as well as the social, political, and psychological components of people's experiences of their sexual identity. Without this clarification, the same terms can mean very different things, both conceptually and operationally across studies, making it difficult to compare and synthesize theoretical models and study findings. A more complex understanding of identity issues is also essential to capture the diversity within LGBT populations, where people's experiences of their sexual identity may vary based on their gender, race, ethnicity, and/or age.

This paper will focus on measurement issues, specifically the measurement of lesbian sexual identity development. It will show how theory and measurement in this specific area have evolved in recent decades. Selected findings will be examined from a recent study of identity development in a sample of young women aged 16-24, who identify as lesbian, bisexual, or questioning (Swann, 2001). The findings of this study are relevant to the current issues in theory and research on lesbian identity development, and the implications of the findings for future research will be discussed.

THE EVOLUTION OF THEORY RELATED
TO LESBIAN IDENTITY DEVELOPMENT

Models of gay and lesbian identity development have traditionally conceptualized identity formation as a unitary or singular process (e.g., Cass, 1979;

Coleman, 1982; Troiden, 1979). In such models, sexual identity development is viewed as a staged process involving both personal acceptance and social or group identity development. Sexual identity development is thought to progress through five stages: (1) an initial vague awareness of difference; (2) a process that leads to understanding oneself as lesbian; (3) disclosure of one's new identity to non-heterosexuals; (4) disclosure of one's identity to heterosexuals; and (5) identification with lesbians as a group or community. In this model, separating internal acceptance from disclosure is thought to be difficult, as both are considered to be essential and to be highly influential upon one another (Falco, 1991). Newer models of identity development have tried to address this assumption of traditional models (McCarn & Fassinger, 1996).

The limitations of traditional models may arise for a number of reasons. First, the data used to develop many of these models were derived from mostly white, middle class, male samples (e.g., Maylon, 1982; Minton & McDonald, 1984; Troiden, 1979); it is only recently that models have been developed that focus on the ways in which specific cultural, ethnic, racial, class, and socioeconomic factors interface with an individual's coming out process (e.g., McCarn & Fassinger, 1996). Second, studies used to develop these models were limited to samples of people who self-identified as gay or lesbian to the researcher. Third, as Boxer and Cohler (1989) point out, the use of retrospective data in the development of identity formation models can be limited by distortions in the memories of childhood and adolescent sexual experiences. These limitations point to the need for further research on the models, utilizing diverse samples of adolescent and young adult females.

Model development has also been hampered by difficulties in obtaining a sufficient number of participants who are in the early stages of gay and lesbian identity formation. Neither Levine (1997) nor Brady and Busse (1994) were able to report any findings on the early stages of development due to their limited sample sizes and compositions. In addition, Brady and Busse (1994) have postulated that people in the earlier stages of identity formation may not view themselves as gay or lesbian, may have negative feelings about their homosexual feelings, or may be reluctant to be part of a research study. Thus, research on early stages of gay and lesbian identity is particularly lacking.

Specific to lesbian identity, several theorists have pointed to the fluidity in women's sexual development and identity (Brown, 1995; Golden, 1987; Sophie, 1985/1986). Stage models of lesbian identity development are not able to account for this fluidity. There is an implicit assumption within stage models that the process of sexual identity formation has one acceptable outcome. Furthermore, most models of lesbian identity development assume that sexual identity is a dichotomous phenomenon, since many of the models were derived at a time in history when bisexuality was considered a phase in the transition from a heterosexual identity to a gay or lesbian identity. Women who identify as lesbian and then move to an identity of either bisexual or heterosexual were either understood to be experiencing identity foreclosure (Cass, 1979), or not understood at all and therefore ignored (Brown, 1995).

Lesbian identity development research has utilized a lesbian-identified sample to test the applicability and utility of existing models of homosexual identity formation (Faderman, 1984; Levine, 1997). For example, Levine's (1997) study of 118 women who self-identified as either lesbian or as questioning their sexuality provided support for the utility of Cass' model of homosexual identity formation. The results of Levine's (1997) study indicated that there was congruence between self-reported and assigned stages of homosexual identity formation, and that participants moved through critical developmental tasks in the order predicted by Cass' model.

Sophie (1985/1986) utilized the existing literature on homosexual identity development to create the first known model specific to women. Sophie synthesized six theories of homosexual identity formation to create a general stage theory of lesbian identity development that included the following: (1) awareness of difference; (2) testing and exploration; (3) identity acceptance; and (4) identity integration. Using this general model, Sophie conducted a qualitative study with 14 women who were "confused about their sexuality or going through changes in their sexuality" (p. 42). Although the sample was small, it did contain at least some women who fit into all four stages.

Sophie (1985/1986) identified a number of problems that resulted from conceptualizing lesbian identity formation as a linear process. Although some of her participants followed the progression predicted by the stage model, others did not. For example, two of the participants who initially declared pride in a lesbian identity rejected that identity in later interviews. One participant demonstrated a later interest in men that could be understood through the use of Cass' (1979) concept of foreclosure. But Sophie had assessed that participant's self-acceptance of her lesbian identity as high, which is inconsistent with foreclosure. She also described other women in her sample who did not follow the accepted homosexual identity formation pathway.

According to stage models, disclosure is an event that should occur late in the developmental process. However, Sophie found that disclosure occurred anywhere from the first stage through the fourth stage. Overall, Sophie found that the general model she constructed was unable to explain all the individual variations in development due to the assumption of linearity present in all homosexual identity formation models. She concluded that the idea of linear progression in identity formation needed to be exchanged for recognition of sexual identity development as a flexible process.

Most recently, McCarn and Fassinger (1996) introduced a new model of lesbian identity development that was derived from models of female identity development and racial/ethnic identity development. Although linear, this model conceptualizes sexual identity formation as having two separate but interrelated processes (or dimensions): individual sexual identity development and group membership identity development. Whereas the processes of personal acceptance and reference group orientation were conflated in earlier models (e.g., Cass, 1979), McCarn and Fassinger separated them. Consequently, each process is seen as independent of the other, and a deficiency in one does not necessarily compromise the other. In other words, McCarn and Fassinger posited a model that ultimately allows for greater focus on the formation of an internally coherent sense of self, while minimizing the effect of viewing public disclosure as a manifestation of this process.

Currently, there continues to be debate as to whether lesbian identity can be understood from a theoretical position that uses linear stage models (Bohan & Russell, 1999). Although McCarn and Fassinger's (1996) model remains in this tradition, they have developed a model that allows for the separate examination of two distinct dimensions of identity: group membership and individual sexual identity. The theoretical rationale that underlies this model creates space for the experiences of diverse lesbians who may not have the freedom or may not choose to develop an identity with the larger lesbian community.

While there is now more research available on lesbian identity development, and more recent models tend to be more complex than those developed in the past, lesbian youths continue to be understudied (Levine, 1997). Furthermore, since most of the models of gay and lesbian identity formation were developed during the 1970s and 1980s (e.g., Cass, 1979; Coleman, 1982; Maylon, 1982; Minton & McDonald, 1984; Troiden, 1979), cohort effects may limit their usefulness with lesbians of the 21st century. For example, there have been significant political changes made within the past 20 years. Lesbians coming out today, whether during adolescence or young adulthood, are more likely to have access to positive role models via the media, arts, and politics. In conjunction with this increased exposure, a number of social service and community-based agencies have opened in large metropolitan areas to affirm young lesbian identities. Because of these recent and significant changes, existing models need to be empirically tested with current cohorts of lesbian youths, as societal attitudes and beliefs are understood to impact the identity development process.

Overall, adolescence has long been accepted as the time frame in which identity development becomes paramount (Blos, 1968; Erikson, 1968; Freud, 1958). Adolescent lesbian identity development is unique in that this process includes not only negotiating the complex tasks of overall identity formation, but coming to understand and accept an aspect of identity that is both stigmatized and largely misunderstood (Deisher, 1989). Rich (1980) wrote "The lesbian experience [is] a profoundly female experience" (p. 650). Furthermore, the experience of being a lesbian youth is profoundly adolescent. It is not sufficient to apply theoretical and empirical data collected with adult women to the experience of adolescent females.

THE PRESENT STUDY

Because adolescence is a time when young women need the approval of peers, and because young people may not have the same opportunities to seek out affirming social contacts, this seemed to be an interesting and important group through which to examine the McCarn and Fassinger (1996) identity formation model. As part of a larger study, the present study examines whether there is evidence of two distinct dimensions of lesbian identity development–individual sexual identity and group identification–among lesbian and questioning adolescents and young adults using the Lesbian Identity Questionnaire (LIQ; Fassinger & McCarn, 1997).

Study Sample

The sample consisted of 205 females ranging in age from 16 to 24 who defined their sexual orientation as "lesbian" or "questioning." By allowing this flexibility, the study attracted females from across a wide spectrum of lesbian identity development. Other studies have found that limiting the sampling criteria to "lesbian" resulted in most participants falling into one of the more advanced phases of development (Levine, 1997; R. Savin-Williams, personal communication, August 13, 1999).

Participants were recruited through a variety of sources in an attempt to obtain a diverse sample. Overall, 56% of the participants were recruited while attending a gay pride event in a southeastern city. Another 22% of the sample were recruited via an Internet site for LGBT and questioning youth. Through the use of the Internet, it was possible to approach youth who may identify as questioning or lesbian but were not connected to a lesbian community–a group not usually available to researchers in the past.

After reading about this study, participants contacted the principal investigator at her e-mail address, and research packets were mailed to the residences of these potential volunteers (there was an 83% return rate). An additional 9% of the sample came from an LGBT and questioning youth organization. These youths responded to a flyer left at a center that included the nature of the study and the principal investigator's e-mail address and telephone number.

In addition to these three sampling strategies, snowball sampling was used to reach lesbian or questioning youth who were not affiliated with the LGB youth community or connected to a virtual community. Snowball sampling remains the method of choice with hidden groups such as lesbian individuals (Anastas & MacDonald, 1994). Participants were asked to give the investigator's e-mail address to potential participants who otherwise would not have been recruited through the other strategies. Overall, 13% of the sample were obtained using this technique.

The mean age of the 205 participants in this study was 20 (*SD* = 2.3, range = 16-24). Twenty-two percent were between the ages of 16 and 18, and 44% of the participants were between 19 and 21. The remaining 35% of participants were between the ages of 22 and 24.

Although other specific additional attempts were made to recruit young women of color, the sample ultimately had little racial diversity. Overall, 81% of the participants identified as white, not of Hispanic origin. African Americans were the next most frequently represented group (5%), followed by Latinas (3%), Native Americans (2%), and Asian Americans (2%). Six percent of the participants identified as either biracial or multiracial.

Location of participants was coded as city, suburb, town, or rural. Fifty-six percent of the participants reported residing within a city, 24% classified their location as suburban, and 14% reported living in a town. Only 6% of the participants lived in rural areas. The majority of participants lived with one or more roommates (36%) or still lived with their family of origin (36%). Sixteen percent lived with a current girlfriend/partner, and 11% lived alone. Only one (0.5%) of the participants identified herself as homeless, and six participants (3%) identified themselves as "in transition."

The largest percentage (39%) of participants were currently in college. Twenty-three percent had completed college and were currently employed or in graduate school. In addition, 13% had attended college but had not completed their education and were not currently attending school, and 13% were currently in high school. Only 2% of the sample reported dropping out of high school, a percentage lower than that reported in other studies of gay and lesbian youth (Mallon, 1997).

Data Collection

Participants were asked to sign a consent form and then to complete a set of self-report questionnaires. Participants first completed a background questionnaire asking about demographics, education level, religious affiliation (current and past), sexual orientation and milestones related to the development of sexual orientation, gender identity, use of mental health services, and history of violence and harassment. In addition, participants completed the Lesbian Identity Questionnaire (Fassinger & McCarn, 1997).

Lesbian Identity Questionnaire (LIQ). The LIQ is a 40-item measure of sexual identity development that utilizes a seven-point Likert scale ranging from (1) disagree strongly to (7) agree strongly (Fassinger & McCarn, 1997). The LIQ was derived from McCarn and Fassinger's (1996) model of lesbian identity formation. The questionnaire items identify the current beliefs and feelings respondents have about their sexual identity. There are five items for each of the eight phases that are included in the model. Four phases are associated with individual sexual identity development and four phases are associated with group membership identity development. The phases for both branches include: (1) awareness, (2) exploration, (3) deepening/commitment, and (4) internalization/synthesis.

The model from which the LIQ was developed was originally tested through the use of the Q-sort method with 38 women ranging in age from 20 to 42 ($M = 30$) (McCarn, 1991). The women in that sample differed from previous research (e.g., Cass, 1979; Troiden, 1979) in that they were diverse in race and ethnicity. After developing the LIQ, the scale's author modified its items to make them relevant to gay men as well (Fassinger & Miller, 1996). Because of the small sample sizes used in the initial stages of scale development, there has been no prior study of the LIQ using factor analysis.

Results

In the present study, dimensions of lesbian identity were examined through the use of factor analysis of respondents' answers to the items on the LIQ. An initial principal components factor analysis was performed on the LIQ using an eigenvalue cutoff of 1.0 and Cattell's Scree test to determine the final number of factors (Kline, 1994). There is general agreement among factor analysts that when too few factors are rotated, broad second-order factors tend to emerge; when too many factors are rotated, factors split up. Cattell's Scree test was adopted as the best solution for choosing the correct number of factors (Kline, 1994).

Eight possible factors were extracted in the unrotated solution using both criteria. A value of $r > .30$ was used to determine which LIQ items loaded on each factor. This was appropriate, for when samples are large (at least 100 respondents), a factor loading of .3 is considered salient, as it accounts for at least 9% of the variance associated with the factor (Kline, 1994). In this analysis, only three out of 40 LIQ items did not load more strongly (> . 40) on one of the three factors generated in the rotated solution.

The majority of the original 40 items loaded on two main factors (Table 1). Most of the items loading on these two factors related to the individual sexual identity dimension and ranged across all four phases. Nine items loaded on a third factor, and the remaining factors (4 to 8) had fewer than five items loading on each. The hypothesized two-dimensional model was not supported by the results.

Using the recommendations summarized by Kline (1994), Varimax rotation of a three-factor solution was performed. Rotation was achieved in five iterations (Table 2). However, the three-factor solution that emerged from these data reflected a different but very interesting picture of the dimensions of lesbian identity development.

New Identity Possibilities. Factor one was labeled "New Identity Possibilities," in which respondents considered the potential and feasibility of a sexual identity other than heterosexual. Seventeen of the 40 LIQ items loaded on factor one, with 13 items loading exclusively on this factor. Three of the items with loadings greater than .70 reflected the substance of this factor: "Recently I have found myself wondering what it would be like to be with a woman"; "Recently I have become aware of a strong desire to kiss another woman"; and "Recently, I have discovered that there may be people out there like me who aren't trying to live as heterosexuals." Of the 17 items that loaded on factor one, six were originally labeled by group membership, and the remaining 11 were originally labeled as individual sexual identity items. Four of the six group membership items loaded exclusively, whereas nine of the 11 individual sexual identity items loaded exclusively on factor one. Although both individual and social in nature, the items on this factor all seemed related to experiences and feelings that other models viewed as earlier stages of identity development.

Fulfillment and Consolidation. Factor two was labeled "Fulfillment and Consolidation" and reflected a commitment to a psychological and social identity as a lesbian. There has been a successful exploration of the new possibilities for a different sexual identity and there is a settling into a new understanding of oneself. With this consolidation, there is increased comfort in relating to the larger society as a lesbian. Seventeen of the 40 LIQ items loaded on factor two, with 13 items loading exclusively on this factor (four group membership and nine individual sexual identity items). Three of the items on factor two with loadings greater than .70 reflected the essence of this factor: "My lesbianism is now an integrated part of my social and public life"; "I now fully accept my emotional and sexual preference for women"; and " I have finally successfully incorporated my intimacy with women into my overall

TABLE 1. Factor Analysis of Items Measuring Lesbian Identity Formation (Principal Component Analysis)[1]

Item	Factor Loading							
	1	2	3	4	5	6	7	8
1) I am getting to know GLB people for the first time	.60							
2) My lesbianism is now an integrated part of who I am		.74						
3) I am just realizing that I want to date women	.62							
4) By my choices I'm expressing a preference for women		.65						
5) I'm aware I've been mistreated because of my lesbianism			.51				.38	
6) I'm noticing GLB people everywhere		.45				.53		
7) More sexually and emotionally intimate with women		.73						
8) Heterosexuality is not all there is	.70							
9) The way I feel about women may mean something	.53							
10) Heterosexuals are accepting			−.64					.30
11) The way I feel means I'm in love with a woman		.50						
12) I'm undergoing a liberation-involvement in GLB community		.41		.41				
13) As lesbian I can relate comfortably to both hetero and GLB		.49	−.51					
14) Lately, very important for me to meet GLB people	.37		.42					
15) I'm just realizing I am different from other women	.62							
16) I realize I have been conditioned to view GLB negatively	.48		.42					
17) I notice I have strong desire to touch a woman's body	.47	.36						
18) I realize many heteros don't know GLB people exist			.39					.49
19) I realize I am a woman who has intimate relations with women		.56			.37			
20) Lately, I am withdrawing from hetero world	.38	.30		.45				
21) I'm just realizing I am willing to live with a female lover	.61							
22) Lately, I'm angry at how heteros treat GLB people				.35	.66			
23) I'm consistently doing as I want in love and sex		.58						
24) I feel pulled toward women in ways I don't understand	.64							
25) I'm comfortable with my lesbianism no matter where I am		.65						

Item	Factor Loading							
	1	2	3	4	5	6	7	8
26) I discovered there are others not trying to live as hetero	.75							
27) Recent awareness of strong desire to kiss another woman	.78							
28) I would probably not consider men as intimate partners	.47	.45						
29) I can't imagine what a room of GLB people would be like		.38		−.40				.33
30) I feel deep contentment about my love for a woman		.67						
31) I notice for the first time I feel nervous around women	.69							
32) Lately, I only feel at ease in GLB surroundings	.36						−.50	
33) I'm wondering what it's like to be romantic with a woman	.69							
34) I mostly rely on GLB for support/have hetero friends too				.43			−.33	−.34
35) Now accept my emotional and sexual preference for women		.82						
36) The way I feel–I want to be sexual with a woman	.74							
37) I had no idea before now there were GLB people out there	.37		.50					
38) I feel fulfilled in relationship with women		.76						
39) I have been duped into thinking everyone is hetero	.56		.36					
40) I've incorporated intimacy with women into overall identity		.70						

[1] Items drawn from the Lesbian Identity Questionnaire (Fassinger & McCarn, 1997).

identity." Although both individual and social in nature, the items on this factor all seemed to reflect feelings and experiences commonly described as characteristic of "later" or "higher" levels of identity development.

Stigma and Mistreatment Management. Factor three was labeled "Stigma and Mistreatment Management." This factor consisted of nine items, all originally labeled as group membership (five loaded exclusively on factor three). Typical items from this factor included "I'm aware I've been mistreated because of my lesbianism" and "I realize I have been conditioned to view GLB negatively." Whereas factor one and two seemed to reflect different phases of the same process, the fundamental and "advanced" phases of lesbian identity development, factor three related more specifically to stigma management.

TABLE 2. Factor Analysis of Items Measuring Lesbian Identity Formation (Rotation Method: Varimax with Kaiser Normalization)[1]

	Factor 1: New Identity Possibilities	Factor 2: Fulfillment Consolidation	Factor 3: Management of Stigma and Mistreatment
1) I'm getting to know GLB people for the first time	.62		
2) Lesbian identity is an integrated part of who I am		.76	
3) Just realizing I want to date women	.67		
4) I'm expressing a preference for women		.66	
5) I'm aware I've been mistreated because of my lesbianism			.44
6) Noticing GLB people everywhere			.43
7) More sexually and emotionally intimate with women		.73	
8) Heterosexuality is not all there is	.68		
9) The way I feel about women may mean something	.53		
10) Heterosexuals are accepting			−.66
11) The way I feel means I'm in love with a woman		.52	
12) I'm undergoing a liberation-involvement in GLB community		.43	
13) As lesbian I can relate comfortably to both hetero and GLB		.45	−.58
14) Lately, very important for me to meet GLB people			
15) I'm just realizing I am different from other women	.59		
16) I realize I have been conditioned to view GLB negatively	.31		.57
17) I notice I have strong desire to touch a woman's body	.38	.40	
18) I realize many heteros don't know GLB people exist			.41
19) I realize I am a woman who has intimate relations with women		.59	
20) Lately, I am withdrawing from hetero world		.34	.33
21) I'm just realizing I am willing to live with a female lover	.61		
22) Lately, I'm angry at how heteros treat GLB people			
23) I'm consistently doing as I want in love and sex		.56	
24) I feel pulled toward women in ways I don't understand	.72		
25) I'm comfortable with my lesbianism no matter where I am		.63	
26) I discovered there are others not trying to live as hetero	.73		
27) Recent awareness of strong desire to kiss another woman	.79		
28) I would probably not consider men as intimate partners	.39	.48	
29) I can't imagine what a room of GLB people would be like	.33		
30) I feel deep contentment about my love for a woman		.67	
31) I notice for the first time I feel nervous around women	.71		
32) Lately, I only feel at ease in GLB surroundings			.35
33) I'm wondering what it's like to be romantic with a woman	.77		
34) I mostly rely on GLB for support/have hetero friends too			
35) Now accept my emotional and sexual preference for women		.82	
36) The way I feel–I want to be sexual with a woman	.78		
37) I had no idea before now there were GLB people out there			.61
38) I feel fulfilled in relationship with women		.76	
39) I have been duped into thinking everyone is hetero	.40		.52
40) I've incorporated intimacy with women into overall identity		.71	

[1] Items drawn from the Lesbian Identity Questionnaire (Fassinger & McCarn, 1997).

Because a lesbian identity is not fully accepted by the dominant culture, learning to manage a stigmatized identity is an integral aspect of identity development. However, according to the way in which this sample of young women responded on the LIQ, stigma management appeared to be understood as a separate process. In other words, in this sample the only aspect of lesbian identity development that did not have both individual and group elements was the dimension related to stigmatization and mistreatment.

DISCUSSION

The individual and group dimensions identified by McCarn and Fassinger (1996) are not as distinct as had been expected among this sample of young women identifying as lesbian or questioning. There are several possible explanations for these findings. The first is that the idea posited by McCarn and Fassinger (1996) of separate dimensions–individual and group–might be invalid, at least for young lesbians and questioning women. The ideas reflected in earlier stage models (e.g., Cass, 1979; Troiden, 1979)–that there are concurrent and inseparable social experiences, personal thoughts, and feelings about oneself as other than heterosexual–were validated in the current study. The findings from the factor analysis suggest that respondents answered the questions in ways that distinguished between an early stage of development (New Identity Possibilities) and a more advanced stage of development (Fulfillment and Consolidation). Items described as "individual" and "group" were not understood as separate dimensions of these stages of development but were found to load on both factors. The third factor, here labeled "Stigma and Mistreatment Management," was comprised of LIQ items that were only "social" in original conception, but did not include all of the items originally classified by McCarn and Fassinger (1996) as social.

In Western culture, sexual orientation is a component of identity development that is thought to become salient during adolescence. Identity development during adolescence happens through the identification with a peer group. Therefore, as lesbian adolescents search to understand themselves, they, like their heterosexual peers, need a peer group that can mirror and affirm their sexual orientation. Frankel (1998) acknowledged the potential for isolation and despair that can result from a lesbian adolescent having no peer group with whom to identify, as well as the psychological transformation that can occur when the adolescent discovers that such a group exists. In fact, self-in-relation theory situates the female core self-structure in a relational context (Kaplan, Klein, & Gleason, 1991). For the development of an authentic self to continue, the female adolescent faces the challenge of finding a peer group through which she is able to come to understand and validate her true self (Gilligan, 1988). Hence, social and individual identity are linked.

Scholars have suggested that LGBT adolescents are less likely to emerge with a closely related and integrated personal and social identity than their heterosexual peers. This is understood to be largely due to the fact that LGBT youths have to struggle with a stigmatized sexual identity that can lead to internal conflict, and the need to compartmentalize some aspects of identity (Hunter & Mallon, 2000; Hunter & Schaecher, 1995; Schneider, 1989). However, participants in this study responded to the LIQ as if they, too, experienced an integrated process of personal and social identity formation.

The sample of women that was utilized in the development of McCarn and Fassinger's (1996) model, from which the LIQ was constructed, was significantly older than the participants in this study (McCarn, 1991); by adulthood, women have had more time and opportunity to develop significant relationships and to develop self-images in relation to other components of identity (e.g., occupational, philosophical, political, religious). With the establishment of relationships comes the opportunity for identification with non-LGBT groups. Time to reflect on who one has become may enable adult women to consciously understand the development of a lesbian identity as a process that involves both an internal process and a process of identifying with a larger group. Adult women may be better equipped developmentally to choose whether to see themselves as a member of the larger LGBT group. Conversely, if there is little or no opportunity for membership due to conflicting identities (e.g., being a woman of color or being involved in a religious group), adults may be able to continue their individual sexual identity development separately from forming identification with an LGBT group.

It is also possible that younger lesbians are experiencing more mistreatment at school and within their families than older women who are less dependent on or less directly involved with their families of origin (Kimmel, 2000). Adult lesbians may have had the opportunity to develop communities of support and families of choice that validate their sexual orientation in ways that adolescents and young adults have not. The presence of the third factor in this study (Stigma and Mistreatment Management) suggests that participants acknowledged experiences of mistreatment and separatism but understood them to be a management task separate from any stage of identity development.

In addition, the methods used in this study–a sample of young white women and factor analysis–were different from those used in McCarn and Fassinger's (1996) earlier work, which used a sample of lesbians who were older and a Q-sort methodology. In addition, despite efforts to recruit diverse respondents, this study sample was largely homogenous with regard to race. Perhaps inclusion of the experiences of young women of color might have resulted in alternative findings. Hence the difference in results could be an artifact of different samples or different methods of analysis. However, since McCarn and Fassinger's (1997) scale development did use a phase model, although on distinct dimensions, it is not entirely surprising that some version of a phase model was found here.

Given differing empirical findings on the nature of lesbian identity development, how useful is any phase-based model of lesbian identity development? Are there entirely different theoretical paradigms that should be considered in future research? For example, as Eliason and Morgan (1998) explain it, queer theory "suggest[s] that lesbians are just one variety of a larger category called 'queer,' which consists of [men and] women, and more ambiguously sexed and/or gendered people who differ from the mainstream by their sexual practices or identities" (p. 48). How sexism may differentiate the experiences of lesbians from other queer people may not be addressed through such a theory, and there are conceptual and political tensions that arise when trying to encompass such a diverse group of people within a single conceptual label.

However, a major contribution of queer theory is to draw attention to the varieties of lesbianism that do exist, as well as the degree of "otherness" that they all share. In this framework, a lesbian identity is viewed as a social construction, a script that is authored, not an internal essence waiting to be discovered and revealed. In fact, there is evidence to suggest that lesbians define their identities in a variety of ways (Bohan & Russell, 1999; Eliason & Morgan, 1998). It is these more complex understandings that must inform our conceptualization and measurement of lesbian identity in future research in order to reflect the creativity and diversity of lesbian life today.

REFERENCES

Anastas, J.W., & McDonald, M.L. (1994). *Research design for social work and the human services*. New York: Macmillan, Inc.

Blos, P. (1968). Character formation in adolescence. In R.S. Eisler, A. Freud, H. Hartmann, & M. Kris (Series Eds.), *Psychoanalytic study of the child: Vol. 23* (pp. 245-263). New York: International Universities Press.

Bohan, J.S., & Russell, G.M. (1999). Conceptual frameworks. In J.S. Bohan & G.M. Russell (Eds.), *Conversations about psychology and sexual orientation* (pp. 11-30). New York: New York University Press.

Boxer, A.M., & Cohler, B.J. (1989). The life course of gay and lesbian youth: An immodest proposal for the study of lives. In G. Herdt (Ed.), *Gay and lesbian youth* (pp. 315-355). New York: Harrington Park Press.

Brady, S,. & Busse, W. (1994). The Gay Identity Questionnaire: A brief measure of homosexual identity formation. *Journal of Homosexuality, 26(4)*, 1-22.

Brown, L. (1995). Lesbian identities: Concepts and issues. In A.R. D'Augelli & C. Patterson (Eds.), *Lesbian, gay, and bisexual identities over the lifespan* (pp. 3-23). New York: Oxford University Press.

Cass, V.C. (1979). Homosexual identity formation: A theoretical model. *Journal of Homosexuality, 4(3)*, 219-235.

Coleman, E. (1982). Developmental stages of the coming-out process. *Journal of Homosexuality, 7(1)*, 31-43.

Deisher, R.W. (1989). Adolescent homosexuality: Preface. In G. Herdt (Ed.), *Gay and lesbian youth* (pp. xiii-xv). New York: Harrington Park Press.

Eliason, M.J., & Morgan, K.S. (1998). Lesbians define themselves: Diversity in lesbian identification. *Journal of Gay, Lesbian, and Bisexual Identity, 3(1)*, 47-63.

Erikson, E.H. (1968). *Identity: Youth and crisis.* New York: Norton Press.

Faderman, L. (1984). The "new gay" lesbians. *Journal of Homosexuality, 10(3/4)*, 85-95.

Falco, K.L. (1991). *Psychotherapy with lesbian clients.* New York: Bruner/Mazel.

Fassinger, R E., & McCarn, S. (1997). Lesbian Identity Questionnaire. Unpublished Scale, University of Maryland, Baltimore.

Fassinger, R.E., & Miller, B.A. (1996). Validation of an inclusive model of sexual minority identity formation on a sample of gay men. *Journal of Homosexuality, 32(2)*, 53-78.

Foucault, M. (1978). *The history of sexuality: Vol. 1.* New York: Vintage Books.

Frankel, R. (1998). *The adolescent psyche: Jungian and Winnicottian perspectives.* London: Routledge.

Freud, A. (1958). Adolescence. In R.S. Eisler, A. Freud, H. Hartmann, & M. Kris (Series Eds.), *Psychoanalytic study of the child, Vol. 13* (pp. 255-278). New York: International Universities Press.

Gilligan, C. (1988). Adolescent development reconsidered. In C. Gilligan, J.V. Ward, & J.M. Taylor (Eds.), *Mapping the moral domain* (pp. iii-xxxix). Cambridge, MA: Harvard University Press.

Golden, C. (1987). Diversity and variability in women's sexual identities. In Boston Lesbian Psychologies Collective (Eds.), *Lesbian psychologies: Explorations and challenges* (pp. 18-34). Urbana, IL: University of Illinois Press.

Hunter, J., & Mallon, G. (2000). Lesbian, gay, and bisexual adolescent development: Dancing with your feet tied together. In B. Green & G. L. Croom (Eds.), *Education, research, and practice in lesbian, gay, bisexual, and transgendered psychology: A resource manual* (pp. 226-243). Thousand Oaks, CA: Sage.

Hunter, J., & Schaecher, R. (1995). Gay and lesbian adolescents. In R.L. Edwards (Ed.), *Encyclopedia of social work* (pp. 1055-1063). Washington, DC: NASW Press.

Kaplan, A.G., Klein, R., & Gleason, N. (1991). Women's self development in late adolescence. In J. Jordan, A.G. Kaplan, J.B. Miller, I.P. Striver, & J.L. Surrey (Eds.), *Women's growth in connection* (pp. 122-144). New York: Guilford Press.

Kimmel, D.C. (2000). Including sexual orientation in lifespan development psychology. In B. Green & G.L. Croom (Eds.), *Education, research, and practice in lesbian, gay, bisexual, and transgendered psychology: A resource manual* (pp. 59-73). Thousand Oaks, CA: Sage.

Kline, P. (1994). *An easy guide to factor analysis.* New York: Routledge.

Levine, H. (1997). A further exploration of the lesbian identity development process and its measurement. *Journal of Homosexuality, 34(2)*, 67-78.

Mallon, G.P. (1997). When schools are not safe places: Gay, lesbian, bisexual, and transgendered young people in educational settings. *Reaching Today's Youth, 2(1)*, 41-45.

Maylon, A.K. (1982). Biphasic aspects of homosexual identity formation. *Psychotherapy: Theory, Research and Practice, 19(3)*, 335-340.

McCarn, S.R. (1991). *Validation of a model of sexual minority (lesbian) identity development.* Unpublished master's thesis, University of Maryland at College Park.

McCarn, S.R., & Fassinger, R.E. (1996). Revisioning sexual minority identity formation: A new model of lesbian identity and its implications for counseling and research. *The Counseling Psychologist, 24*, 508-534.

Minton, H.L., & McDonald, G.J. (1984). Homosexual identity formation as a developmental process. *Journal of Homosexuality, 9(2/3)*, 91-104.

Rich, A. (1980). Compulsory heterosexuality and lesbian existence. *Signs, 5*, 631-660.

Schneider, M. (1989). Sappho was a right-on adolescent: Growing up lesbian. In G. Herdt (Ed.), *Gay and lesbian youth* (pp. 111-130). New York: Harrington Park Press.

Sophie, J. (1985/1986). A critical examination of stage theories of lesbian identity development. *Journal of Homosexuality, 12(2)*, 39-51.

Swann, S. (2001). *Understanding the dimensions of lesbian identity development during adolescence and young adulthood.* Unpublished doctoral dissertation, Smith College School for Social Work, Northampton, MA.

Troiden, R.R. (1979). Becoming homosexual: A model of gay identity acquisition. *Psychiatry, 42*, 362-373.

8,000 Miles and Still Counting . . . Reaching Gay, Lesbian and Bisexual Adolescents for Research

Diane E. Elze

SUMMARY. Major challenges in conducting research with sexual minority adolescents include difficulties in finding large samples of youths under 18, particularly young women, diverse in their stages of coming out, and not associated with organized groups. Institutional review boards may prohibit the participation of youths for whom parental consent cannot safely be obtained. This paper discusses the strategies employed to recruit a sample of 184 self-identified gay, lesbian and bisexual adolescents (mean age = 16.6), of which 62% were female, 56% resided

---

Diane E. Elze, MSSA, PhD, is Assistant Professor, George Warren Brown School of Social Work, Washington University, St. Louis, MO.

Address correspondence to: Dr. Diane Elze, George Warren Brown School of Social Work, Campus Box 1196, Washington University, St. Louis, MO 63130 (E-mail: delze@gwbmail.wustl.edu).

This research was supported by grant #R03MH5898201 from the National Institute of Mental Health.

The author wishes to thank the youths and adults of Portland-OUTRIGHT, Midcoast OUTRIGHT, Milford Area Gay and Lesbian Youth (MAAGLY), Concord OUTRIGHT, Seacoast OUTRIGHT, Manchester OUTRIGHT, Framingham Regional Alliance of Gay and Lesbian Youth (FRAGLY), Supporters of Worcester Area Gay and Lesbian Youth (SWAGLY), OUTRIGHT Vermont, Coastal OUTRIGHT, Downeast OUTRIGHT, OUTRIGHT/Lewiston-Auburn, OUTRIGHT TOO, Youth Aware, Umbrella and Sisters United of Bangor, Maine.

[Haworth co-indexing entry note]: "8,000 Miles and Still Counting . . . Reaching Gay, Lesbian and Bisexual Adolescents for Research." Elze, Diane E. Co-published simultaneously in *Journal of Gay & Lesbian Social Services* (Harrington Park Press, an imprint of The Haworth Press, Inc.) Vol. 15, No. 1/2, 2003, pp. 127-145; and: *Research Methods with Gay, Lesbian, Bisexual, and Transgender Populations* (ed: William Meezan, and James I. Martin) Harrington Park Press, an imprint of The Haworth Press, Inc., 2003, pp. 127-145. Single or multiple copies of this article are available for a fee from The Haworth Document Delivery Service [1-800-HAWORTH, 9:00 a.m. - 5:00 p.m. (EST). E-mail address: getinfo@haworthpressinc.com].

in rural areas or small towns, 23% were not associated with organized groups, and, using participant advocates, 65% participated without parental consent. It also reports on some findings from a larger study using data collected from this sample. *[Article copies available for a fee from The Haworth Document Delivery Service: 1-800-HAWORTH. E-mail address: <getinfo@haworthpressinc.com> Website: <http://www.HaworthPress.com> © 2003 by The Haworth Press, Inc. All rights reserved.]*

KEYWORDS. Gay, lesbian and bisexual, adolescents, sampling, research methodology

Researchers interested in conducting studies with gay, lesbian, and bisexual (GLB) adolescents face major challenges in finding large samples of youths diverse in their processes of sexual questioning, disclosure to others, and openness about their sexual orientation. Most studies with this population have been conducted with extremely small, predominantly male, convenience samples of youths drawn from metropolitan or college-based support groups. Such samples are biased towards those most open, visible and resolved about their sexual orientation, or those most active in gay and lesbian organizations. Savin-Williams (2001) recently noted the unlikelihood of a youth's first disclosure being to a researcher, rather than to a best friend. Existing recruitment methods usually result in samples of GLB adolescents who have self-disclosed to friends and/or family members. Findings typically cannot be generalized to youths not connected with organized groups; youths who experience same-sex attractions but do not identify as gay, lesbian or bisexual; or youths unwilling to disclose to others.

D'Augelli and colleagues (Hershberger & D'Augelli, 1995; Hershberger, Pilkington, & D'Augelli, 1997) suggested that youths attending organized groups may differ in other important ways from gay, lesbian and bisexual adolescents who do not attend such groups. Those who seek out gay- and lesbian-identified settings may feel more positive and exhibit greater openness about their sexual orientation than youths who choose not to participate in or cannot access such groups, or they may be open about their sexual orientation at earlier ages. However, Savin-Williams (1994) suggested that the youths who participate in research studies are those who may be the most psychologically, physically and socially troubled. Previous research has found that heightened risk accompanies greater openness, identifying more family-, school-, and community-based victimization among the more open, visible youths (Pilkington & D'Augelli, 1995). No study to date, however, has examined whether GLB adolescents who attend gay- and lesbian-identified agencies or groups are psychosocially different from the young people who do not.

An additional challenge facing researchers is that university institutional review boards (IRBs) may prohibit the participation of youths for whom parental consent cannot safely be obtained. Such policies, in effect, exclude the majority of GLB adolescents from research participation. Previous research with GLB youths indicates that disclosure of sexual orientation to family members is often associated with verbal and physical abuse and threats of violence (D'Augelli, Hershberger, & Pilkington, 1998; Pilkington & D'Augelli, 1995). Some young people risk eviction from their homes upon disclosure (Herdt & Boxer, 1993; Hunter, 1990). Youths refrain from disclosing out of fear of rejection, ridicule, and verbal and physical abuse, and experience the prospect of disclosure as emotionally troubling (D'Augelli et al., 1998; Pilkington & D'Augelli, 1995). Youths who have disclosed to one parent often fear abuse or ridicule from the other. Even when parents are aware of the youth's sexual orientation, the family may be unable to discuss the topic without verbal and/or physical fighting or extreme stress and discomfort. To understand the diverse experiences and needs of sexual minority adolescents, it is important that research studies include young people who have not yet disclosed their sexual orientation to parents, or whose parents know but are unaccepting.

This paper discusses the recruitment methods and the procedures to protect human subjects that were used to secure a sample of 184 self-identified GLB adolescents, ages 13 to 18, for a cross-sectional investigation of risk and protective factors associated with their mental health and behavioral functioning. It should be immediately acknowledged that limiting a sample to only self-identified youths excludes adolescents who experience same-gender attractions and/or sexual behaviors but do not self-identify as gay, lesbian or bisexual (Savin-Williams, 2001). However, through the methods and procedures employed, the investigator hoped to recruit a substantial proportion of self-identified youths not connected to organized youth groups, diverse in their degree of openness with friends and family members, where youths under 18 and females were well represented. This paper also examines whether GLB adolescents connected to organized groups differ on key psychosocial characteristics from youths who have never accessed a sexual minority youth group. The strengths and limitations of this sample are compared to those of previous samples, and the implications of using such a sample on research findings are discussed.

HUMAN SUBJECTS CONSIDERATIONS

Federal regulations governing the protection of children and adolescents in the conduct of research mandate the informed consent of parents or legal guardians (Putnam, Liss, & Landsverk, 1996). However, under these regulations, a waiver of parental consent is possible, pursuant to 45 CFR 46.408(c), if securing parental consent would jeopardize the participants' welfare or violate a teenager's privacy. Under such a waiver, alternative procedures are utilized to protect the participants (Fisher, 1993; Fisher, Hoagwood, & Jensen, 1996). Due to the psychosocial or physical risks posed to some GLB adolescents should their parents discover their sexual orientation, this waiver provision should be considered when proposing research on sexual minority youths to university IRBs. Decisions to waive parental consent, however, should always be based on the best interests of the participants rather than for the convenience of the researcher (Fisher, 1993). Some university IRBs have waived parental consent for GLB adolescent participants, allowing agencies serving these youths to act *in loco parentis* (e.g., Rosario, Hunter, & Gwadz, 1997; Rotheram-Borus et al., 1994), or requiring the presence of a participant advocate (e.g., A. R. D'Augelli, personal communication, August 28, 2000; D'Augelli & Hershberger, 1993).

Federal regulations require a participant advocate when children and adolescent research subjects are wards of the state; however, the procedure is also recommended for other situations when an IRB approves a waiver of parental consent, such as research with maltreated children (Fisher, 1993; Fisher et al., 1996). Participant advocates have also been used in previous studies with sexual minority adolescents (e.g., D'Augelli & Hershberger, 1993; Fisher et al., 1996) and juvenile detainees (Fisher et al., 1996).

In the present study, the IRB required that an individualized determination be made with each study participant on the appropriateness of securing parental consent. On the assent form, youths checked off one of the following statements, choosing the one most applicable to their situation: (a) "I state that, due to the gay, lesbian, and bisexual content of this project, talking to my parent/legal guardian about this would create problems in my relationship with them. Therefore, I request that you accept my assent without contacting them"; and (b) "My parent/legal guardian knows about my sexual orientation and it is alright if you contact them about my participation in this project."

In lieu of universal parental consent, an advocate was utilized to protect the participants (Fisher, 1993). The advocates were social workers or counselors with expertise in working with youth. As recommended, the advocates verified the youths' understanding of the assent procedures and ensured that: (a) the youths' participation was voluntary; (b) they fully understood their rights as participants; and (c) the post-survey debriefing addressed all their questions and concerns (Fisher, 1993).

Because of the investigator's network of contacts with adolescent mental health providers and other youth workers in northern New England, the site of the study, the process of finding advocates for youths not connected to organized groups, although time-consuming and challenging, was achievable. Trusted teachers, guidance counselors, mental health clinicians, and parents also functioned as advocates.

Sixty-five youths, out of 135 under 18, indicated that their parents could be contacted, and written, informed consent was obtained. No legal guardian refused consent. It must be acknowledged, however, that this consent procedure placed responsibility on the youths to accurately assess their parents' awareness of and anticipated reaction to their sexual orientation.

RECRUITMENT PROCEDURES

Data collection occurred in northern New England (Maine, New Hampshire, Vermont, and Massachusetts) between July and October, 1998. This area was chosen because of the proximity of both rural and urban areas and the potential to access youths in rural areas. Additionally, the investigator was the founder of and advised the first support and social group for sexual minority adolescents in Maine between 1987 and 1992, and therefore had a network of contacts that would potentially refer youths to the study. The investigator temporarily relocated to New England for the fieldwork period. Self-report questionnaires were administered directly by the investigator.

Youths were recruited through multiple methods. Previous research with gay and bisexual male adolescents demonstrated successful recruitment of subjects using multiple methods, with advertisements yielding 14%; peers and professionals 13%; social groups 44%; and 29% from multiple sources (Remafedi, 1994). For this study, the following recruitment methods were utilized:

1. *Community-based support groups.* A network of youth groups exists for sexual minority adolescents under 21 years old in northern New England. Letters of introduction, a resume, and an overview of the study were sent to nine youth groups seven months prior to the fieldwork period, followed by a phone call two weeks later. By the end of the fieldwork period, 15 support groups had served as recruitment sites. Relationships with these groups were built and maintained by keeping them informed about the study's progress. At least one week prior to data collection, meetings were held with the adult facilitators and youth participants to establish the logistics of data collection and to provide the youths with an opportunity to get acquainted with the investigator and ask questions about the study. Youth assent and parental consent procedures were explained and parental consent forms were distributed. Youths were also

asked to bring GLB friends with them when they came to complete the questionnaire. Pizza was provided as an additional incentive.

2. *Youth friendship networks.* The support groups constituted a starting point from which snowball sampling was used to reach youths who did not attend the groups but who belonged to the friendship networks of the attendees. Additionally, brightly-colored, wallet-sized cards, containing a brief, non-stigmatizing description of the project and the investigator's name and contact information, were distributed to youth participants who were asked to pass cards on to their GLB friends and acquaintances.

3. *Adolescent service providers.* The adult facilitators of the support groups, as well as other adolescent service providers (e.g., multiservice youth agencies, independent living programs, family planning agencies, private schools, teen peer advising programs, and youth employment programs) were asked to post flyers and distribute cards to sexual minority adolescents they knew.

4. *Outreach activities.* Information was distributed about the study at special youth group functions, and a toll-free line was established to facilitate contact with the investigator by youths, parents, and professionals. Additionally, other potential referral agents were contacted, such as Parents and Friends of Lesbians and Gays (PFLAG) and the Gay, Lesbian, and Straight Educators Network (GLSEN).

5. *Internet and other media.* To reach more isolated youths, notices were posted on Maine GayNet, an internet site accessed by GLB and transgender people in Maine. An advertisement was placed in a GLB publication in Vermont, *Out in the Mountains.* To reach parents and professionals, an article about the project appeared in *The Maine Times*, a statewide weekly newspaper.

6. *Monetary incentive.* As an additional incentive, youths were paid $20 for participating.

Recruitment and data collection were labor and travel intensive, adding 9,000 miles to an odometer within four months. Building relationships and arranging for data collection with several youth groups required multiple trips. Several long trips were also conducted to gather data from youths not connected to organized groups. For example, data collection with four youths from Maine's northernmost county required an 11-hour round-trip excursion.

Sixty-one percent of the youths were recruited through the community-based support groups and pizza parties, with an unknown number of those youths coming via friends who brought them. Twenty-six percent were recruited through friends, with seven youths' participation facilitated by the parent of a mutual friend who informed them about the study (the parent hosted a gathering at her home). Nearly 10% were recruited through teachers, guidance counselors, school nurses, social workers, family planning educators and other adolescent service providers, and 2.7% through ads or posted flyers.

SAMPLE CHARACTERISTICS

The study used a self-labeling definition (Martin & Knox, 2001) for the population of interest, assessing sexual identity with two questions: (1) "If you had to identify yourself as one of the following, which one would you pick?" with response choices being "gay," "lesbian," "bisexual," and "unsure" and; (2) "How would you describe your sexual orientation?" with response choices being (a) 100% gay or lesbian; (b) mostly gay or lesbian, a little heterosexual; (c) bisexual, equally gay/lesbian and heterosexual; (d) mostly heterosexual, a little gay or lesbian; or (e) 100% heterosexual." These latter response options were revisions of those used in prior studies (D'Augelli & Hershberger, 1993; Remafedi, Resnick, Blum, & Harris, 1992; Remafedi, 1994). To examine within-group variability (Savin-Williams, 2001), and to tap the complexity of sexual orientation (Gonsiorek, Sell, & Weinrich, 1995; Laumann, Gagnon, Michael, & Michaels, 1994), additional questions asked about gender of sexual partners (lifetime and past year) and romantic feelings and sexual attractions towards both men and women. Unlike previous studies with this population (e.g., D'Augelli & Hershberger, 1993), the youths identifying as "mostly heterosexual," "a little gay/lesbian," and "unsure" were retained in this sample because they reported at least some same-sex romantic feelings and sexual interests.

Of the 184 study participants, 62% were female, 56% resided in rural areas or small towns, and 23% had never attended a youth group (an additional 16% attended youth group meetings less than six times a year). With the use of a participant advocate (Fisher, 1993), 65% participated without parental consent. The mean age of the youths were 16.6. The majority of youths lived with one or more parents (72.3%) and were still in high school (73.9%). Over three-quarters (77%) of the youths perceived their families to be middle class (17.2% upper middle class, 44.1% middle class, and 16.1% lower middle class), followed by low income or poor (11.3%), and working class (10.8%). Less than 1% identified their families as rich. Twenty-five percent of the youths identified as lesbians, 25.5% as gay males, 36% as bisexual females, 12% as bisexual males, and 1.5% as unsure.

Most youths (73.4%) had disclosed their sexual orientation to at least one parent (biological, adopted, or stepparent), with no gender differences reported (71% of the girls and 77% of the boys); 44.6% had disclosed to more than one parent. Despite their disclosures, however, 45% rated themselves below the midpoint on overall openness with family. Self-disclosure is not synonymous with openness or comfort for many gay, lesbian and bisexual adolescents. Although adolescents may tell their parents about their sexual orientation, they cannot comfortably talk about their daily lives. Sixty-two percent of the youths reported feeling uncomfortable within their family as a GLB individual, nearly half of whom felt "very" or "extremely" uncomfortable. Nineteen percent had not yet disclosed their sexual orientation to any family member.

Overall, the youths were more open with their friends than with their family. Only five youths said their sexual orientation was completely hidden from their friends, and 32% said all their friends knew about their sexual orientation. However, over one-third (35%) said that half or more of their friends thought they were heterosexual, and approximately one-quarter (26.1%) rated themselves below the midpoint on overall openness with friends. Only three youths had not yet disclosed their sexual orientation to anyone–friend or family member.

MEASUREMENTS

A variety of standardized and other instruments were used to measure youths' mental health and emotional problems and other psychosocial characteristics.

Attendance at Youth Group

The frequency of youths' attendance at a GLB and transgender youth group was measured with one item on a six-point Likert scale, ranging from 0 (never) to 5 (once a week or more), that asked how often they attended such a group. For some analyses, a dichotomous variable was created; not ever attending a youth group was coded 0, and attending one or more times was coded 1.

Developmental Milestones Related to Sexual Orientation

Youths were asked to report the ages at which they first thought they were gay, lesbian or bisexual, and when they knew about their sexual orientation.

Emotional and Behavioral Problems

Emotional and behavioral problems were assessed with the Youth Self-Report (YSR) (Achenbach, 1991), the self-rating version of the Child Behavior Checklist for adolescents ages 11 to 18. The YSR is a standardized self-report of feelings, behaviors, problems and emotional difficulties within the past six months. In this study, the internalizing and externalizing scales had Cronbach's alpha coefficients of .89 and .84, respectively, indicating good internal consistency.

Current depression was measured with the Center for Epidemiologic Studies Depression Scale (CES-D), a 20-item, widely-used self-report developed by the National Institute of Mental Health (Radloff, 1977), and used in several studies with adolescents (Garrison, Addy, Jackson, McKeown, & Waller, 1991). Youths reported the extent to which they experienced each symptom during the past week on a four-point scale, ranging from 0 (rarely or none of the time) to 3 (most or all of the time). In this study, Cronbach's alpha was .90.

Openness About Sexual Orientation

Participants rated their openness about their sexual orientation using two seven-point scales, ranging from 0 (not open at all) to 6 (totally open). One item measured the degree of openness with family and the other with friends. A higher score indicated greater openness.

Social Integration

Social integration with heterosexual peers was measured with four questions that asked youths about the number of close heterosexual friends (and those not so close) who were aware of the youths' sexual orientation, and the number of close heterosexual friends (and those not so close) with whom the youths could be themselves. These items used a six-point response scale, ranging from 0 (none) to 5 (over 20). The items were summed, constituting a composite score of social integration. The internal consistency coefficient was .81 for this study.

Feelings About Sexual Orientation

Youths' feelings about their sexual orientation were measured with 15 items on a six-point Likert scale, ranging from 0 (never) to 5 (all of the time). Seven items were similar to items in Nungesser's (1983) Homosexual Attitudes Inventory; the investigator developed eight items with the assistance of two focus groups comprised of sexual minority adolescents in St. Louis, Missouri. Examples of items are: (a) "My life will be fulfilling as a gay, lesbian or bisexual person"; (b) "I'm not really normal because I'm gay, lesbian or bisexual"; (c) "I feel proud about being gay, lesbian or bisexual"; and (d) "I am afraid that being gay, lesbian or bisexual means I have an emotional or mental problem." A higher score indicated more positive feelings. The Cronbach's alpha coefficient was .87 for this study.

Self-Esteem

Self-esteem was measured with the Rosenberg Self-Esteem Scale (Rosenberg, 1965), a 10-item instrument frequently used to measure adolescent self-esteem, including sexual minority adolescents' self-esteem (e.g., D'Augelli & Hershberger,1993; Savin-Williams, 1990). Cronbach's alpha was .90 for this study.

Family Attitudes About Sexual Orientation

Participants rated their perceptions of their parents' and other family members' actual or anticipated reactions to their sexual orientation on a six-point scale, from 1 (very supportive) to 6 (rejecting). These items were used in previous studies (D'Augelli & Hershberger, 1993; Remafedi, 1994; Savin-Williams, 1990), though with fewer response choices. Response choices were added based on focus groups conducted with sexual minority adolescents in St. Louis. Negative items were reverse scored; a higher score indicated more positive attitudes. A composite score was derived by summing the responses and dividing by the number of family members. The Cronbach's alpha coefficient was .82 in the current study.

Victimization

School and community victimization were measured with 18 items that asked youths the frequency with which they experienced nine forms of violence within their schools and communities in the last six months because of their sexual orientation, ranging from 0 (never) to 3 (3 or more times). Types of victimization included: (a) verbal insults; (b) threats of violence; (c) having objects thrown at you; (d) having personal property damaged or destroyed; (e) being chased or followed; (f) being spat upon; (g) being punched, kicked, hit, or beaten; (h) sexual assault; and (i) assault with a weapon. Using Dean, Wu, and Martin's (1992) categorization, the nine forms of violence were aggregated into three variables representing three escalating levels of violence: Level I (verbal insults, threats of violence), Level II (objects thrown, personal property damaged, being chased, followed, or spit on), and Level III (being punched, kicked or beaten, sexually assaulted, or assaulted with a weapon). These categories have been used in previous research with GLB adolescents (Hershberger & D'Augelli, 1995: Pilkington & D'Augelli, 1995). For each setting, each youth received a composite score for each level of violence, calculated by averaging the frequency scores of the specific items in each category. The distributions were so skewed, and not sufficiently improved by transformations, that a dichotomous variable was created for each setting, with no victimization coded 0 and victimization coded 1.

RESULTS

Over three-fourths (77.6%) of the youths had attended an organized youth group at least once. No gender differences were found in the likelihood of youths ever attending a group, or in the frequency of their attendance. However, youths who had attended a group were significantly more likely to identify as gay or lesbian (58.4%), while those who never attended were more likely to identify as bisexual (76.2%), (χ^2 (1) = 15.56, $p \leq .001$). They were also more likely to have disclosed their sexual orientation to a parent than were the youths who never attended a group (78.9% versus 54.8%), (χ^2 (1) = 9.64, $p \leq .01$).

More frequent group attendance was associated with more positive feelings among the youths about their sexual orientation, greater openness with their parents, and greater integration with heterosexual peers as openly GLB people (see Table 1). However, their feelings about their orientation were more strongly associated with their openness with friends ($r = .54, p \leq .0001$) and family members ($r = .43, p \leq .0001$), and their integration with heterosexual peers ($r = .31, p \leq .0001$) (results not shown in table), than with the frequency of their group attendance.

The frequency of youths' attendance at organized groups was also associated with a heightened risk for anti-gay victimization within their communities. A logistic regression analysis demonstrated that group attendance remained significant even after controlling for youths' openness about their sexual orientation (see Table 2). For every unit increase in the youths' frequency of attendance, they were 1.3 times as likely to report community victimization (Wald $\chi^2 = 9.23$, $p \leq .01$).

DISCUSSION

The sample in this study stands out from other samples of GLB youths of comparable size, specifically in its distributions of age, gender and sexual orientation. This study also recruited over one-third (38.6%) of the participants from places other than organized groups for gay, lesbian and bisexual adolescents. Nearly one-quarter (23%) had never attended such a group, allowing for

TABLE 1. Correlation Between Youths' Characteristics and Their Frequency of Attending GLBT Youth Groups ($n = 184$)

Youths' Characteristics	Frequency of Group Attendance
Internalizing problems	−.06
Externalizing problems	−.06
Current depression	−.07
Age first thought was g/l/b	.00
Age knew was g/l/b	−.01
Positive feelings about sexual orientation	.23**
Self-esteem	.10
Openness about sexual orientation with family	.24**
Social integration with heterosexual peers	.43***
Openness about sexual orientation with friends	.14
Family attitudes about sexual orientation	.06
Victimization in community	.25**
Victimization in school	.06

*$p \leq .01$. **$p \leq .001$. ***$p \leq .0001$.

an investigation of the psychosocial differences between youths who have attended gay- and lesbian-identified groups and those who have not.

Compared to most previous research, this sample was younger and comprised of a greater proportion of females and bisexual youths. Nearly three-fourths of the youths (73.4%) were under 18 years old, compared to 6% (Savin-Williams, 1990) and 15% (Hershberger & D'Augelli, 1995) of other samples. In previous studies that included both male and female youths, mean ages ranged from 18.3 to 19.2 (D'Augelli & Hershberger, 1993; Herdt & Boxer, 1993; Rosario et al., 1996, 1997). Diamond (1998) reported a mean age of 20 in her study of sexual identity and attractions among 89 young women. The youths in the present study were slightly younger than that of the young males recruited from the Hetrick-Martin Institute by Rotheram-Borus and colleagues (mean age = 16.8; $SD = 1.4$) (e.g., Rotheram-Borus, Hunter, & Rosario, 1994).

TABLE 2. Logistic Regression Analysis Predicting Community Victimization ($n = 184$).

Predictor Variables	β	Wald χ^2	Odds Ratio
Openness with family	$-.03$	.11	1.0
Openness with friends	.10	1.03	1.1
Frequency of group attendance	.27*	9.23	1.3

*$p \leq .01$.

With few exceptions (e.g., Rosario et al., 1996, 1997; Waldner-Haugrud & Magruder, 1996), young lesbian and bisexual women have been under-represented in studies that have recruited both male and female adolescents. Young women, however, were well-represented in this study, constituting the majority of the participants (62%), compared to 20% to 35% in other studies (e.g., D'Augelli & Hershberger, 1993; Grossman & Kerner, 1998; Herdt & Boxer, 1993; Savin-Williams, 1990).

The age and gender distributions of the sample may account for the larger proportion of youths that identified as bisexual (47.3%), particularly bisexual females (35.3%), when compared to previous studies. Although D'Augelli and Hershberger (1993) found that comparable proportions of males (25%) and females (26%) identified as bisexual, nearly three times as many females than males in this sample identified as bisexual.

Several possible explanations exist for this gender difference. Previous research suggests that males are aware of their same-sex attractions, act on them, and disclose them to others at an earlier age than females (Garnets & Kimmel, 1993). However, this was not true of the youths in this study; no significant differences by gender were found on their age of awareness, self-identification, same-gender sexual involvement, or disclosure to others. Second, males may be less likely to identify as bisexual than females, and more likely to identify as gay, because of more rigid societal expectations of males around sexuality and sexual behavior, or for some other reason. Research has found that women's sexuality tends to be more variable than men's (Golden, 1996; Kitzinger & Wilkinson, 1995; Rust, 1993). Diamond (2000) found that young sexual minority women, while stable in their sexual attractions over a two-year-period, reported greater fluidity in their sexual identities and behaviors, with 50% reporting multiple changes in identity. For males, a bisexual identity may tend to be temporary while they consolidate a gay identity, while females may tend to retain a bisexual identity into adulthood. Savin-Williams (1998) found that nearly 25% of the gay-identified adolescent and young adult males across three studies reported going through a bisexual stage on their way to a self-identification as gay. However, longitudinal research is needed to examine youths' changes or stability in their sexual identities over time.

An affiliation with organized gay- and lesbian-identified groups likely draws young people to activities and events where they experience both the joys and the risks of greater visibility as gay, lesbian and bisexual people living openly and proudly within their communities. The findings of this study reveal that the youths who sought services from the organized youth groups were not more emotionally or behaviorally troubled than the youths who had never connected with such groups, but they did report greater community victimization. Although youths may come to organized youth groups seeking support because they have been victimized, it is more plausible that their vulnerability to community victimization increases when they affiliate with organized groups and participate in gay- and lesbian-identified community events. The cross-sectional nature of this study precludes knowing the direction of this relationship with full certainty. However, if victimization causes youths to seek out youth groups, we probably would have seen a significant association between school victimization and group attendance, since school is a common place for youths to experience persistent victimization (Pilkington & D'Augelli, 1995). Without longitudinal research, however, we will not fully understand the temporal sequence of the events in young people's lives.

For the youths in this study, their self-acceptance was more strongly associated with their openness with family and their integration with heterosexual peers than it was with the frequency of their group attendance. These results suggest that the young people who more frequently attend organized groups may receive the emotional support and guidance that assists them in opening up to family members and behaving more authentically with their peers. Through their involvement with sexual minority youth support groups, young people may learn accurate information about homosexuality, solidify their identity, begin to demand validation from their friends and family members, and develop coping strategies to utilize in stressful situations related to coming out. Of course, an alternative explanation is that greater openness with family and friends allows young people to access the groups more easily, particularly if their parents monitor their whereabouts, establish a curfew or must provide transportation, or if they rely on their friends for rides. Without longitudinal studies, however, we can only conjecture about the sequence of events that leads to their positive feelings about their sexual orientation.

Although the findings add to the knowledge base about GLB adolescents, the study has several limitations. Despite the multiple methods of recruitment and the intensive fieldwork period, this sample, like the majority of samples with this population, is a small convenience sample of predominantly white youths, the majority of whom had disclosed their orientation to at least one parent and several friends. Only three participants had not yet disclosed their sexual orientation to anyone. Thus, findings cannot be generalized to sexual minority adolescents of color, those who have not yet disclosed their sexual orientation to others, or to youths too fearful of stigmatization to come forward. Reaching a more hidden, undisclosed population of sexual minority adolescents may take more time, financial resources, and different recruitment methods. This sample was also limited to adolescents residing in northern New England who may differ in important ways (e.g., existence of gay and lesbian civil rights protections, visibility of gay and lesbian issues, and availability of youth resources) from adolescents in other geographical regions.

A larger, more diverse sample could have resulted if collaboration building had begun earlier with other adolescent service providers, if recruitment and data collection had occurred during the school year, and if the wealth of internet resources had been tapped. Service providers other than the youth groups were not contacted until the fieldwork period. The pool of available youths at several youth groups was smaller than expected, as attendance dwindled during the summer months because of vacations and competing activities.

That GLB adolescents continue to fear negative repercussions from increased visibility must be acknowledged. Community- and school-based organizations for GLB youths do not eradicate youths' fears of exposure and stigmatization, presenting a challenge for even the most sensitive of researchers. Youths frequently reported that friends were too nervous to participate, even with the option of completing the instrument with only the researcher and an advocate present, and the investigator's credible reputation among the youth groups. At the time of the study, the members of one youth group in a small Maine town all lived in neighboring towns; no youths attended from the town in which the group met. Instead, those youths met informally with a school guidance counselor. A young lesbian in a school with a gay-straight alliance (GSA) described herself as the GSA's "token lesbian." A few young people from Maine attended a youth group in New Hampshire, rather than risk being visible in their own community.

Until questions about sexual orientation and same-gender attractions and behaviors appear routinely in national probability studies of adolescents, we will continue to gather data from the most visible, highly disclosed youths. We will not know whether the vast majority of GLB adolescents experience quite average lives in their families, schools and communities, or whether they experience greater hardship than their school-aged peers. With few exceptions (e.g., DuRant, Krowchuk, & Sinal, 1998; Garofalo, Wolf, Wissow, Woods, & Goodman, 1999; Remafedi, French, Story, Resnick, & Blum, 1998), most states do not incorporate questions about same-gender sexual behavior or sexual identity into their Youth Risk Behavior Surveillance System (CDC, 1998). When questions are included, they fail to tap the complexity of youths' sexual attractions, behaviors and identities. The National Longitudinal Study of Adolescent Health (Resnick et al., 1997) is the first nationally representative study of adolescents in the United States to include information on same-gender romantic attractions.

Despite its limitations, this study's sample allows for a beginning examination of the psychosocial differences between youths who have attended gay- and lesbian-identified groups and those not connected with such groups. The methods used in this study were also successful in recruiting more young women and youths residing outside urban areas. With female and bisexual adolescents well represented, this sample also permits an examination of within-group variations by gender and sexual identity.

Researchers committed to studying this population must be creative in devising strategies to reach a diversity of GLB adolescents. Expanded use of the Internet and targeted outreach to particular populations of GLB adolescents (e.g., youth of color, young women) and to gay- and lesbian-affirming youth organizations, such as the National Conference of Community and Justice's Anytown program, may result in more diverse non-probability samples. Further, as Savin-Williams (2001) noted, "far more youths have same-sex attractions, desires behaviors, or romantic relationships than report that they are lesbian, gay or bisexual" (p. 10). Researchers interested in adolescents' developmental pathways should consider recruiting young people who may not self-identify as gay, lesbian or bisexual, but who may endorse same-sex sexual attractions or behaviors.

REFERENCES

Achenbach, T.M. (1991). *Manual for youth self report and 1991 profile*. Burlington, VT: University of Vermont Department of Psychiatry.

Centers for Disease Control (1998). Youth risk behavior surveillance-United States, 1997. *Morbidity and Mortality Weekly Report, 47* (No. SS-3).

D'Augelli, A.R., & Hershberger, S.L. (1993). Lesbian, gay, and bisexual youth in community settings: Personal challenges and mental health problems. *American Journal of Community Psychology, 21*, 421-448.

D'Augelli, A.R., Hershberger, S.L., & Pilkington, N.W. (1998). Lesbian, gay, and bisexual youth and their families: Disclosure of sexual orientation and its consequences. *American Journal of Orthopsychiatry, 68,* 361-371.

Dean, L., Wu, S., & Martin, J.L. (1992). Trends in violence and discrimination against gay men in New York City: 1984 to 1990. In G.M. Herek & K.T. Berrill (Eds.), *Hate crimes: Confronting violence against lesbians and gay men* (pp. 46-64). Newbury Park, CA: Sage.

Diamond, L.M. (1998). Development of sexual orientation among adolescent and young adult women. *Developmental Psychology, 34,* 1085-1095.

Diamond, L.M. (2000). Sexual identity, attractions, and behavior among young sexual-minority women over a 2-year period. *Developmental Psychology, 36,* 1-10.

DuRant, R.H., Krowchuk, D.P., & Sinal, S.H. (1998). Victimization, use of violence, and drug use at school among male adolescents who engage in same-sex sexual behavior. *Journal of Pediatrics, 132,* 113-118.

Fisher, C.B. (1993). Integrating science and ethics in research with high-risk children and youth. *Social Policy Report: Society for Research in Child Development, 7(4),* 1-27.

Fisher, C.B., Hoagwood, K., & Jensen, P.S. (1996). Casebook in ethical issues in research. In K. Hoagwood, P.S. Jensen, & C.B. Fisher (Eds.), *Ethical issues in mental health research with children and adolescents* (pp. 135-266). Mahwah, NJ: Lawrence Erlbaum Associates.

Garnets, L.D., & Kimmel, D.C. (1993). Introduction: Lesbian and gay male dimensions in the psychological study of human diversity. In L.D. Garnets & D.C. Kimmel (Eds.), *Psychological perspectives on lesbian and gay male experiences* (pp. 1-51). New York: Columbia University Press.

Garofalo, R., Wolf, R.C., Wissow, L.S., Woods, E.R., & Goodman, E. (1999). Sexual orientation and risk of suicide attempts among a representative sample of youth. *Archives of Pediatric and Adolescent Medicine, 153,* 487-493.

Garrison, C.Z., Addy, C.L., Jackson, K.L., McKeown, R.E., & Waller, J.L. (1991). The CES-D as a screen for depression and other psychiatric disorders in adolescents. *Journal of the American Academy of Child and Adolescent Psychiatry, 30,* 636-641.

Golden, C. (1996). What's in a name? Sexual self-identification among women. In R.C. Savin-Williams & K.M. Cohen (Eds.), *The lives of lesbians, gays, and bisexuals: Children to adults* (pp. 229-249). Fort Worth, TX: Harcourt Brace College Publishers.

Gonsiorek, J.C., Sell, R.L., & Weinrich, J.D. (1995). Definition and measurement of sexual orientation. *Suicide and Life-Threatening Behavior, 25 (Suppl.),* 40-51.

Grossman, A.H., & Kerner, M.S. (1998). Self-esteem and supportiveness as predictors of emotional distress in gay male and lesbian youth. *Journal of Homosexuality, 35(2),* 25-39.

Herdt, G., & Boxer, A. (1993). *Children of Horizons: How gay and lesbian teens are leading a new way out of the closet.* Boston: Beacon Press.

Hershberger, S.L., & D'Augelli, A.R. (1995). The impact of victimization on the mental health and suicidality of lesbian, gay, and bisexual youths. *Developmental Psychology, 31,* 65-74.

Hershberger, S.L., Pilkington, N.W., & D'Augelli, A.R. (1997). Predictors of suicide attempts among gay, lesbian, and bisexual youth. *Journal of Adolescent Research, 12,* 477-497.

Hunter, J. (1990). Violence against lesbian and gay male youths. *Journal of Interpersonal Violence, 5,* 295-300.

Kitzinger, C., & Wilkinson, S. (1995). Transitions from heterosexuality to lesbianism: The discursive production of lesbian identities. *Developmental Psychology, 31,* 95-104.

Laumann. E.O., Gagnon, J.H., Michael, R.T., & Michaels, S. (1994). *The social organization of sexuality: Sexual practices in the United States.* Chicago: University of Chicago Press.

Martin, J.I., & Knox, J. (2000). Methodological and ethical issues in research on lesbians and gay men. *Social Work Research, 24,* 51-59.

Nungesser, L.G. (1983). *Homosexual acts, actors, and identities.* New York: Praeger.

Pilkington, N.W., & D'Augelli, A.R. (1995). Victimization of lesbian, gay, and bisexual youth in community settings. *Journal of Community Psychology, 23,* 34-56.

Putnam, F.W., Liss, M.B., & Landsverk, J. (1996). Ethical issues in maltreatment research. In K. Hoagwood, P.S. Jensen, & C.B. Fisher (Eds.), *Ethical issues in mental health research with children and adolescents* (pp. 113-132). Mahwah, NJ: Lawrence Erlbaum Associates.

Radloff, L.S. (1977). The CES-D scale: A self-report depression scale for research in the general population. *Applied Psychological Measurement, 1,* 385-401.

Remafedi, G. (1994). Cognitive and behavioral adaptations to HIV/AIDS among gay and bisexual adolescents. *Journal of Adolescent Health Care, 15,* 142-148.

Remafedi, G., French, S., Story, M., Resnick, M.D., & Blum, R. (1998). The relationship between suicide risk and sexual orientation: Results of a population-based study. *American Journal of Public Health, 88,* 57-60.

Remafedi, G., Resnick, M., Blum, R., & Harris, L. (1992). Demography of sexual orientation in adolescents. *Pediatrics, 89,* 714-721.

Resnick, M.D., Bearman, P.S., Blum, R.W., Bauman, K.E., Harris, K.M., Jones, J., Tabor, J., Beuhring, T., Sieving, R.E., Shew, M., Ireland, M., Bearinger, L.H., & Udry, R.J. (1997). Protecting adolescents from harm: Findings from the National Longitudinal Study on Adolescent Health. *Journal of the American Medical Association, 278,* 823-832.

Rosario, M., Hunter, J., & Gwadz, M. (1997). Exploration of substance use among lesbian, gay, and bisexual youths: Prevalence and correlates. *Journal of Adolescent Research, 12,* 454-476.

Rosario, M., Meyer-Bahlburg, H.F., Hunter, J., Exner, T.M., Gwadz, M., & Keller, A.M. (1996). The psychosexual development of urban lesbian, gay, and bisexual youths. *The Journal of Sex Research, 33,* 113-126.

Rosenberg, M. (1965). *Society and the adolescent self-image.* Princeton, NJ: Princeton University Press.

Rotheram-Borus, M.J., Hunter, J., & Rosario, M. (1994). Suicidal behavior and gay-related stress among gay and bisexual male adolescents. *Journal of Adolescent Research, 9,* 498-508.

Rotheram-Borus, M.J., Rosario, M., Meyer-Bahlburg, H.F., Koopman, C., Dopkins, S.C., & Davies, M. (1994). Sexual and substance use acts of gay and bisexual male adolescents in New York City. *Journal of Sex Research, 31,* 47-57.

Rust, P.C. (1993). Coming out in the age of social constructionism: Sexual identity formation among lesbian and bisexual women. *Gender & Society, 7(1),* 50-77.

Savin-Williams, R.C. (1990). *Gay and lesbian youth: Expressions of identity.* New York: Hemisphere Publishing.

Savin-Williams, R.C. (1994). Verbal and physical abuse as stressors in the lives of lesbian, gay male, and bisexual youths: Associations with school problems, running away, substance abuse, prostitution, and suicide. *Journal of Consulting and Clinical Psychology, 62,* 261-269.

Savin-Williams, R.C. (1998). *". . . And then I became gay": Young men's stories.* New York: Routledge.

Savin-Williams, R.C. (2001). A critique of research on sexual-minority youths. *Journal of Adolescence, 24,* 5-13.

Waldner-Haugrud, L.K., & Magruder, B. (1996). Homosexual identity expression among lesbian and gay adolescents: An analysis of perceived structural associations. *Youth & Society, 27,* 313-333.

A Study of Sampling in Research in the Field of Lesbian and Gay Studies

Gerard Sullivan

Warren Losberg

SUMMARY. This article examines the various types of sampling techniques used to research gay, lesbian, bisexual, and transgender issues. Sample characteristics, sample sizes, response rates, and methods of obtaining samples for studies published in the *Journal of Gay & Lesbian Social Services* (*JGLSS*) between 1997 and 2000 were studied. Questions about sampling issues that characterize this field of study are discussed, and suggestions for improving sampling and reporting practices are offered. Author characteristics, the topics of research published in *JGLSS*, and data collection techniques used are also summarized. *[Article copies available for a fee from The Haworth Document Delivery Service: 1-800-HAWORTH. E-mail address: <getinfo@haworthpressinc.com> Website: <http://www.HaworthPress.com> © 2003 by The Haworth Press, Inc. All rights reserved.]*

KEYWORDS. Gay, lesbian, transgender, sampling, content analysis

Gerard Sullivan, Dip Ed, MA, PhD, is Associate Professor and Head of the School of Policy and Practice, Faculty of Education, University of Sydney, Sydney, Australia. Warren Losberg, M. Behave. Health Sci., is a PhD candidate, School of Policy and Practice, Faculty of Education, University of Sydney, Sydney, Australia.

Address correspondence to: Dr. Gerard Sullivan, Faculty of Education, University of Sydney, Sydney NSW 2006, Australia (E-mail: G.Sullivan@edfac.usyd.edu.au).

[Haworth co-indexing entry note]: "A Study of Sampling in Research in the Field of Lesbian and Gay Studies." Sullivan, Gerard, and Warren Losberg. Co-published simultaneously in *Journal of Gay & Lesbian Social Services* (Harrington Park Press, an imprint of The Haworth Press, Inc.) Vol. 15, No. 1/2, 2003, pp. 147-162; and: *Research Methods with Gay, Lesbian, Bisexual, and Transgender Populations* (ed: William Meezan, and James I. Martin) Harrington Park Press, an imprint of The Haworth Press, Inc., 2003, pp. 147-162. Single or multiple copies of this article are available for a fee from The Haworth Document Delivery Service [1-800-HAWORTH, 9:00 a.m. - 5:00 p.m. (EST). E-mail address: getinfo@haworthpressinc.com].

Three overarching research paradigms have been used in gay and lesbian social research in the last decade. These are quantitative research, qualitative research, and queer studies. Each methodology has used different criteria for collecting and analyzing data for use in research projects. This article examines the characteristics of sampling procedures used in the first two of these research paradigms.

Sampling design is essentially the way in which cases are selected from a specific population. The representativeness of samples drawn from that population is the major concern in this process. Researchers who want to generalize their findings from the samples they use to the population they are researching need to use probability sampling. In practice, however, sampling is fraught with dilemmas, particularly with populations that are difficult to define, hard to reach, or resistant to identification because of potential discrimination, social isolation or other reasons that are relevant to lesbian, gay, bisexual, and transgender (LGBT) populations. Non-probability sampling is often used in response to some of these difficulties. While studies using samples selected in this manner can provide depth of insight into the people and topics they examine, the extent to which they are representative of LGBT people remains an issue.

Some of the difficulties in sampling LGBT populations have been the subject of previous articles. Joyce and Schrader (1999) conducted a bibliometric study of the first 24 volumes of the *Journal of Homosexuality* (*JH*), from 1974 to 1993. Reflecting their backgrounds in library and information studies, the authors specifically examined bibliographic citations in the source articles to determine the scholarly nature of the *JH*. This analysis included the articles' length, number of citations, and sexual tenor, and touched on sampling issues. The taxonomy they developed for the various methodological approaches of the source articles was divided into "empirical research," "theory-social science," "analysis-historical," "analysis-literary," "analysis-post-structural," "reviews of literature," and "other." Joyce and Schrader found that *JH* was comprised mainly of "empirical research" (30%), "theory-social science" (22%), and "analysis-historical" (17%). They noted that both historical and post-structural analysis had made significant inroads over the 20-year period despite the prominence of empirical research. This was attributed to the incorporation of post-structural theories into most of the social sciences and humanities by the early 1990s.

Examining studies included in *Medline*, Sell and Petrulio (1996) considered the representativeness of samples of homosexuals, bisexuals, gays, and lesbians used in public health research. They examined how populations were conceptually and operationally defined, the setting from which samples were selected, and the use of probability sampling to select subjects. They found that articles rarely conceptually defined the population they were sampling, used a range of divergent methods to identify and select subjects, sampled from settings representative of dramatically different populations, and rarely used probability sampling.

Of initial importance to the issue of sampling in lesbian and gay studies is disclosure behavior. For example, Laumann, Gagnon, Michael, and Michaels (1994) note that women's willingness to report homosexual behavior is strongly correlated with socioeconomic status. Because of such factors, identification of LGBT people and populations, and access to participants for research, are among the largest challenges to researchers in LGBT studies.

Because non-probability sampling does not involve the identification of large sampling frames or use random selection of participants in research, which would allow for the calculation of sampling error, questions of sampling bias arise (Greenwood, 1999). While probability sampling is preferred by statisticians, the use of other types of sampling is usually more appropriate for qualitative research (Llewellyn, Sullivan, & Minichiello 1999), or more practical when selecting participants from populations about which parameters are unknown.

In an attempt to overcome the difficulties in identifying gay or bisexual men, and in order to choose a representative sample, Meyer and Colten (1999) tested Random Digit Dialing (RDD) of phone numbers in gay-identified areas of New York City. The RDD technique identified gay/bisexual men who were qualitatively different from gay/bisexual men contacted using standard non-probability techniques. The RDD technique produced samples in which men were less likely to feel connected to the gay community and had higher levels of internalized homophobia (a predictor of mental health problems and AIDS-related high-risk sexual behaviour). However, this technique did not produce samples that differed widely in terms of their demographic characteristics. The authors acknowledged that RDD would be of limited use in less densely populated areas. This is because the cost of locating gay/bisexual men where they are widely spread may be prohibitive due to the low number of calls in a general population to gay-identifying households. Meyer and Colten conclude that while RDD can improve the representation of respondents in most research settings, alternative methods of sampling are generally more practical.

Other strategies used by researchers to improve representativeness in LGBT samples (e.g., Blair, 1999; Harry, 1986) have included the use of complex two-stage telephone survey designs, using data from the early stages of a survey to improve the efficiency of subsequent stages. While most of these studies attempt to include a random component in their sampling methodology, many are costly to implement and therefore impractical.

Each type of sampling design has its own distinctive advantages. Accordingly, no one sampling design is inherently preferable over others. A number of factors affect which type of sampling design will be chosen (Singleton & Straits, 1999). Estimating sample precision is usually unimportant in exploratory and qualitative research (Llewellyn, Sullivan, & Minichiello, 1999). Representative samples are more important in large-scale, "fact-finding" studies that provide input for major policy decisions when a carefully controlled probability sample is necessary to ensure sample precision (Schofield & Jamieson, 1999).

METHOD

The present study examines sampling strategies and data collection techniques used in research in the field of gay and lesbian studies related to social work, as represented in publications appearing in the *Journal of Gay & Lesbian Social Services (JGLSS)*. This journal was selected because of its prominence in the field of lesbian and gay studies and because of its influence in social work and other health and human service professions. *JGLSS* is one of the newer journals in the field of gay and lesbian studies, and it has not yet been the subject of a sampling analysis. In addition, we examined the characteristics of authors and the topics they investigated.

Content analysis was used to examine articles published in the four-year period from 1997 to 2000. All articles published in the *JGLSS* from Volume 7, Number 1 to Volume 11, Numbers 2/3 were examined. The analyses excluded introductions, prefaces and forewords, program/practice/research notes, news and views, poems, and book and video reviews.

Initially, approximately 25 articles from *JGLSS* were examined to devise a coding system. This process generated a large number of variables that proved to be unwieldy and cumbersome, as only some of the variables were used in multiple studies. Accordingly, we reduced the number and type of variables used for data collection by deleting or combining several of the initial variables. The main reason for deleting or collapsing variables was a lack of data falling within particular categories. Examples of demographic variables that were deleted or combined with others due to inadequate data were the duration of cohabitation and occupation.

Data that were collected and coded during the content analysis included information about:

- sample size (i.e., the total number of people invited to participate by the authors of a research project or, if the number of people invited was not reported, the actual number of participants);

- response rate (i.e., the proportion of the initial sample from which data were obtained);
- source of participants;
- characteristics of samples, including sexual orientation, sex and/or gender, residential patterns, family status, educational level, employment, ethnicity, age and income.

In addition, information was collected about the number and sex of the authors, the principal discipline they represented, and topics of the research (e.g., domestic violence, gay youth).

RESULTS

Omitting the exclusions mentioned above, 103 articles were published in the five volumes of the *JGLSS* that were examined in this study. The articles were divided into 37 research articles, which were empirically-based and involved sample selection, and 66 professional articles, which were mainly descriptions of professional practice and professional education that relied on the author's personal experience and client vignettes. Thus, over one-third of the articles (35.9%) were research oriented.

The majority of articles (71.8%) were written by single authors. Research articles were more likely to involve collaboration than professional articles. One hundred and fifty authors (84 women and 65 men) wrote the 103 articles examined. Only five of the articles were co-authored by a woman and a man together. Women were more likely to co-author than men; 19.6% of the articles involving women were co-authored versus 3.6% of the articles involving men. The most frequent academic credential among the authors of both research and professional articles was PhD (45.7%) followed by MSW and MSW candidates (14.1%).

The author's affiliation was coded based on the discipline of the first author's current employment or, where this information was unavailable, on the academic discipline of the first author's highest qualification. If the field of study could not be determined, then the background of the second author was used. The most common field of study was social work (34%), followed by psychology (25.2%) and health (10.7%). Social work dominated the professional articles (39%), but psychology was the most prevalent discipline represented in the research articles (38.5%).

The primary topic of each article was determined from the article title and abstract. Some articles were about more than one topic. For example, an article with a title like "The Social Support Needs of Older Lesbians, Gay Men, and

Bisexuals" was classified with a primary topic of social support and a secondary topic of older gays and lesbians. The most reported primary topic was gay and lesbian widowers (11.3%), followed by HIV-related research (8.5%), mental health (7.5%), violence towards gays and lesbians (6.7%), gay youth (5.7%), and gays and lesbians as parents (5.7%). Social support and couples were topics that often appeared in the research articles (10.8% each). The most common secondary topics were therapeutic practice and violence towards gays and lesbians (both 9.8%), followed by transgender issues (7.8%), family issues (7.8%), and program evaluation (7.8%).

Most of the professional articles were oriented towards professional education about client groups. Many of them included guidelines for professional practice or described the personal experience of the authors. Among the professional articles, self-narratives and case studies were the most common type of evidence used to support conclusions, followed by literature reviews and policy and practice analysis.

In the research articles, quantitative research designs occurred with the same frequency as qualitative research designs (both 48.6 %). A wide range of data collection techniques were employed. As might be expected, survey was the most common method used; interviews, case studies, and field observations were also commonly employed. About one-fifth of the 37 research articles (21%) used established scales in their data collection. Not infrequently, they were modified to suit the purposes of the research. Only one scale, the Attitudes Toward Lesbians and Gay Men scale (Herek, 1988), was used in more than one study, and then only twice.

SAMPLING TECHNIQUES AND SAMPLE CHARACTERISTICS IN THE RESEARCH ARTICLES

Sample Size

Authors defined sample size as either the total number of people invited to participate by the authors of a research project or, if the number of people invited was not reported, the total number of participants who actually participated. Using the first definition, only 27% of the research articles ($n = 10$) provided information on the number of people invited to participate and those who actually did (response rate). The mean sample size, defined as the number of participants invited to participate in a study, was 860.8 ($SD = 1393.9$; range = 24-1925). Response rates in these 10 research articles varied from 20% to 92%, with an average of 53.2%. Fifty-nine percent of the articles ($n = 22$) did not report the number of people who declined to participate in the research, and only mentioned the number of participants, which varied from 3 to 829 ($M =$ 93.9; $SD = 272.1$). Five studies did not report the number of participants in the research, but one of these reported a response rate of 20%.

Sample Type

Six research articles did not provide any details about the way in which participants were selected. Only two studies reported using probability samples. One of them reported using a random sampling design, and the other did not specify the type of probability sample used. The remainder of the studies examined here (78.4%) used some form of purposive or haphazard sampling technique, and nine of these included an element of snowball sampling to locate participants.

Sources of Data

Most of the 37 research articles (64.1%) relied on more than one source for obtaining study participants. Of the 70 reports of participant sources, friendship networks, gay and lesbian social spaces, and gay and lesbian organisations were among the most common, presumably because they offered relatively easy access to participants (see Table 1).

Country of Origin

Most of the research published in the *JGLSS* was based in the mainland United States (79.5%, $n = 29$). The vast majority of articles did not specify the nationality of participants in the research. However, it may be reasonably inferred that where this information was not included, the sample was selected from the same country as the authors' place of employment. Very few authors were based outside the United States, but these authors invariably specified the location from which the sample was drawn. Four articles (10.8%) were about gay and lesbian social services in Thailand, one article was about Canada, and another about Puerto Rico. Only two articles (5.4%) involved cross-national comparisons.

Sexual Orientation and Gender

Research published in the *JGLSS* reflects the complexity of sexual orientation and gender identity. While it might be argued that transgenderism is an issue of gender rather than sexual orientation, a number of authors did not make this distinction. One article dealt exclusively with transgenderism, but the samples of four other studies mixed transgender with gay, lesbian, and bisex-

TABLE 1. Sources of Data: Research Articles Published in the *Journal of Gay & Lesbian Social Services* 1997-2000

	N	*%**
Friendship Networks	15	40.5
Gay and Lesbian Social Spaces[1]	12	32.4
Gay and Lesbian Organisations	10	27.0
Gay and Lesbian Media[2]	4	10.8
Students[3]	4	10.8
Clients of Authors	3	8.1
Professional Workers[4]	3	8.1
Community Events[5]	3	8.1
AIDS Organisations	2	5.4
Other[6]	8	21.6
Not Reported	6	16.2

* Column totals equal more than 100% due to multiple responses
[1] includes resorts, gyms, beaches, parks, book stores, etc.
[2] includes newspapers and the Internet
[3] includes students of any sexual orientation
[4] mainly social workers and psychologists
[5] includes Dignity conventions, Gay Pride picnics, etc.
[6] includes bars, sex venues, and official records

ual participants. The collective term LGBT is common in the field and was used by several authors.

Some studies did not report the number of participants of particular sexual orientations, but did report the percentage of the sample with particular sexual orientations (see Table 2). For example, authors might report that 5% of the sample was transgender, but not provide information about the total sample size, making it impossible for readers to calculate the number of transgender participants. In addition, 16.2% of all the research articles either did not report or imprecisely reported the sexual orientation of participants. Lesbians constituted the sexual orientation most frequently researched in the *JGLSS* (25.6% of the research articles). Only two of the research articles contained samples consisting solely of gay men. The remaining articles used samples with a variety of sexual orientations or gender identifications.

TABLE 2. Sexual Orientation of Participants: Research Articles Published in the *Journal of Gay & Lesbian Social Services* 1997-2000

	N	%	Mean Sample Size	Minimum	Maximum
Lesbian	10	27	209	3	1925
Gay	2	5.4	17	14	20
Gay/Lesbian/Bisexual (GLB)*	3	8.1	75	7	170
Transgender	1	2.7	not reported		
Lesbian and GLB**	1	2.7	21		
Gay and GLB	1	2.7	273		
Lesbian and Gay	3	8.1	121	81	151
Lesbian, Gay, and GLB	4	10.8	122	34	262
Gay and Transgender	2	5.4	21		
Gay, Transgender, and GLB	1	2.7	122		
Heterosexual	1	2.7	226		
GLB and Heterosexual	1	2.7	56		
Lesbian and Heterosexual	1	2.7	829		
Gay, Lesbian, GLB, Transgender, and Heterosexual	1	2.7	not reported		
Not or imprecisely reported	5	13.5	-		
Total	37	100			

* The GLB category was used to code samples in which differentiation was not made between homosexuals and bisexuals. This category did not necessarily involve both men and women. For example, articles about men who have sex with men (MSM) were coded in this category.
** Where GLB occurs with another category it refers to bisexuals only.

Sex of Participants

In contrast to the field of lesbian and gay studies in general, in which research about gay men predominates, research articles published in the *JGLSS* were more likely to involve women. This may, in part, reflect the gender composition of social work and human service professions. Given this finding, it is not surprising that women were recruited more often than men as participants. Only two articles exclusively involved gay men, while 10 had only lesbian participants. When bisexuals and heterosexuals were considered, 12 (32.4%) of the studies were about women only, and three (8.1%) were about men only (excluding transgender). Five studies (13.5%) included transgender participants. Eleven (29.7%) studies included men and women in their samples (see Table 3).

Ethnicity

The majority of research articles (74.4%) reported information about the ethnicity of participants, but practices varied widely. Some authors only reported the number and/or percent of Caucasian participants. Commonly, others reported the number of Caucasians and African Americans, and sometimes Hispanic participants. Less commonly reported were participants of Asian ancestry and, in a few cases, other categories such as Native Americans. In all studies involving multiracial samples, Caucasians were the most numerous group. One study involved Hispanic participants exclusively, and four studies that were part of a special issue on Thailand included Asian participants only. Relative to their proportion in the overall population, racial minorities were poorly represented in almost all research articles with multiracial samples in the U.S.

Education

There was no consistency in the research articles in the reporting on educational attainment of participants. Sixty-two percent ($n = 23$) of the studies did not report any data on educational attainment, while 18% ($n = 7$) provided incomplete data. For example, one study reported that two participants had only completed high school. Other studies only reported the percent of participants who were college graduates. Some reported the mean years of schooling, and a few studies provided a detailed breakdown of participants' educational attainment (i.e., number and percent completing graduate degrees, college, or high school). A number of studies combined college graduates with participants who had completed some college.

Employment

Sixty-five percent of the research articles ($n = 24$) did not report any information about the employment status of participants. Practices varied widely among the remaining research articles for reporting employment statistics. Many authors did not differentiate between full-time and part-time employment, and very few consistently provided detailed information about the type of employment held by participants. Some authors indicated the percent of participants who were in professional occupations but rarely provided definitions of such designations.

TABLE 3. Sex of Participants: Research Articles Published in the *Journal of Gay & Lesbian Social Services* 1997-2000

	<u>N</u>	<u>%</u>	<u>Mean Sample Size</u>	<u>Minimum</u>	<u>Maximum</u>
Female	14	37.8	221.3	3	1925
Male	8	21.6	94.9	14	273
Male and Female	11	29.7	161.5	34	492
Transgender	1	2.7			
Not reported/imprecisely reported	3	8.1			
Total	37	100			

Age

Most research articles (74%) provided information about the age range of participants, which was the most common format for reporting age. The age of participants varied enormously between the studies. Forty-nine percent reported the mean age of participants in their samples. A few studies reported median age. Twenty-six percent of articles did not report any information about the age of their participants, while one study made imprecise references to the age of its participants.

Living Situation, Family Status, Income, and Religious Affiliation

Only 12 research articles (32.4%) reported on the living situation of participants (i.e., living alone, living with partner). Over half (56.8%) of the research articles either did not report or imprecisely reported the relationship status of their participants (see Table 4). Nine of the studies based in the U.S. reported some information about the income of participants. Only four studies reported mean or median income. All those reporting income provided a range. A minority of studies reported information about the religious affiliation of participants, but there was no consistency in how this information was reported.

DISCUSSION

The most obvious finding was the differentiation of articles into research articles and those oriented specifically toward professional practice in the social services sector. The latter frequently involved reports about professional prac-

TABLE 4. Family Status: Research Articles Published in the *Journal of Gay & Lesbian Social Services* 1997-2000

	<u>N</u>	<u>%</u>	<u>Mean No. Participants</u>	<u>Minimum</u>	<u>Maximum</u>
Not reported/imprecisely reported	21	56.8	-		
Couples	6	16.2	78	13	190
Children present	5	13.5	42	10	85
Single	2	5.4	22	14	43
Singles and Couples	3	8.1	94	59	129
Total	37	100			

tice with particular types of LGBT clients (such as couples, youths, or those living with HIV/AIDS). Most of these articles were oriented toward education about these groups, relevant policy analysis, or providing guidelines for professional practice. While these articles often provided descriptions and analysis of case studies, rarely was any information provided about how or why particular participants were selected for inclusion, and how they may have been similar or different from others in the category under discussion. Nevertheless, these articles have an important role in the development of social work and related professions, since they provide insight to readers who may be assisted by learning about professional practices of colleagues.

One-third of the articles published were classified as research oriented, so defined because they described sample selection and the use of specific research methods. Research articles were more likely to be co-authored than were professional articles, and more likely to be authored by women than men, in contrast to the professional articles. Research articles were equally likely to be quantitative (mostly using survey methods) as qualitative. Only one-quarter of the research articles provided information about response rates, and many authors were vague about the sampling techniques that they used. Given the populations being studied, use of quantitative sampling techniques that are random or "representative" is likely to be difficult, expensive, or impossible for reasons outlined earlier in the article. Hence, we are likely to see the continued use of haphazard, purposive, and snowball sampling techniques (Greenwood, 1999; Llewellyn et al., 1999).

It is typical of social sciences research to use a range of incomparable methods to identify and select subjects, not to use probability sampling, or to sample from settings representative of dramatically different populations. The results of this study are consistent with the findings of Sell and Petrulio (1996). We conclude that LGBT research is not particularly deficient when compared to social science research involving many other populations. However, Sell and Petrulio's concern that LGBT research rarely conceptually defined the populations being studied is one about which the field needs to be especially concerned. The sexual orientation of those sampled in the research articles examined here is indicative of this issue. For example, men who have gay identities, men who participate in the gay community, men who are bisexual, and men who have sex with men but do not see themselves as gay, are sometimes differentiated and sometimes unthinkingly aggregated under the label of "gay" men. In other studies, gay men and lesbians are aggregated. Wahler and Gabbay (1997) make a case for separating the two groups:

> Gay men and lesbians are more different from one another than they are similar, both in their orientation and in their gender. . . . Thus any attempt to join them for the purpose of sociological research is both artificial and misleading. Joining them under one umbrella of research on "homosexuals" has the effect of diluting our understanding of each and trivializing the experience of both. (p. 2)

Wahler and Gabbay (1997) go on to remind us of a very complex research environment in which care needs to be taken to disaggregate data on a range of other variables as well:

> Sexual orientation exists on a continuum from exclusively heterosexual to exclusively homosexual, with a continuous middle range which represents permutations of the variables of behavior, fantasy, exclusivity, opportunity, and choice, among others. . . . The experience of gay men is qualitatively different as a result of their sexual orientation than that of heterosexual or bisexual men. . . . Gay identity represents an interplay between internal drives and needs and interpersonal socio-systemic interaction and feedback. This varies *across* individuals, with historical time, culture and ecological circumstance, and *within* individuals as a function of development and experience . . . (p. 2)

Consideration of all these factors would make research enormously complex and, in many cases, probably defeat the enterprise entirely. However, aggregation without awareness of the differences between people included in research samples runs the risk of producing conclusions that are misleading or simplistic.

We found great variety in the range of demographic characteristics reported by authors of research articles. While the age and ethnicity of participants in research is usually reported, the reporting format is often inconsistent, making it difficult to compare samples. Authors do not always report both the number and percent of subgroups, and they vary enormously in how subgroups are identified. Although the great majority of research articles published in *JGLSS* are based in the U.S., the identification of ethnic groups is inconsistent. Some authors identify two or three racial groups, while others may include Asian Americans and/or Native Americans. Similarly, while the age range of samples is commonly reported, the mean age was reported in only half of the research articles.

The limited information provided by authors about the age, education, income, employment, living situation, family status, and religious affiliation of participants does not allow us to make any useful comments about these sample characteristics. It was common for authors to only partially report data on a particular characteristic. For example, one author might report on the percentage of her sample who had a partner, while another might report the number of participants who had a partner, and a third author may include both percentage and number of participants who were living alone or who had partners. Only five authors were comprehensive in their reporting of the various living arrangements of participants, and included both percent and number.

It may be more or less appropriate to report the social class (as indicated by education and income), domestic arrangements (e.g., family status or cohabitation) and/or personal characteristics (e.g., religious affiliation) of participants in research, depending on the topic being investigated.

RECOMMENDATIONS

Based on the preceding analysis, we make the following recommendations for journal editors and research authors:

1. We suggest that the *Journal of Gay & Lesbian Social Services* (and other journals that link research and professional practice) differentiate between research and professional articles in their tables of contents. Editors should provide more guidance to the authors of research articles in relation to reporting the details of study designs and results.
2. All authors should be encouraged to describe how samples were selected, and to acknowledge or comment on the character of the sample and potential sampling bias.
3. Authors should be encouraged to think carefully about sampling design before beginning a study, and journal editors should require authors to

report details of the methods used before articles are accepted for publication. These issues apply to both qualitative and quantitative research.

4. Authors need to think carefully about the sexual orientation and other characteristics of those invited to participate in research, to make this explicit for readers, and to be careful about drawing conclusions about the LGBT community in general.

5. Authors should provide detailed information about the gender and sexual orientation of participants in the research.

6. If the findings from this journal review are typical of those of others dealing with LGBT populations, editors should develop guidelines for authors to follow when reporting the age and ethnicity of research participants. Not only would this provide readers with useful information and improve the academic standard of the journal, it would potentially allow for the comparison of results of various research reports.

7. Although we do not think that authors should be required to collect or report data on social class (as indicated by education and income), domestic arrangements (e.g., family status or cohabitation) and/or personal characteristics (e.g., religious affiliation), it may be appropriate for editors of LGBT journals to devise guidelines for authors who wish to report this information, so that it is done in a standard format that would allow the results of various research reports to be compared.

REFERENCES

Blair, J. (1999). A probability sample of gay urban males: The use of two-phase adaptive sampling. *The Journal of Sex Research, 36*, 39-44.

Greenwood, K.M. (1999). The logic and need for statistics. In V. Minichiello, G. Sullivan, K. Greenwood, & R. Axford (Eds.), *Handbook of research methods in health sciences* (pp. 463-478). Sydney: Addison-Wesley.

Harry, J. (1986). Sampling gay men. *The Journal of Sex Research, 22*, 21-34.

Herek, G.M. (1999). Heterosexuals' attitudes toward lesbians and gay men: Correlates and gender differences. *The Journal of Sex Research, 25*, 451-477.

Joyce, S., & Schrader, A.M. (1999). Twenty years of the *Journal of Homosexuality:* A bibliometric examination of the first 24 volumes, 1974-1993. *Journal of Homosexuality, 37(1)*, 3-24.

Laumann, E.O., Gagnon, J.H., Michael, R.T., & Michaels, S. (1994). *The social organization of sexuality: Sexual practices in the United States.* Chicago: The University of Chicago Press.

Llewellyn, G., Sullivan, G., & Minichiello, V. (1999). Sampling in qualitative research. In V. Minichiello, G. Sullivan, K. Greenwood, & R. Axford (Eds.), *Handbook of research methods in health sciences* (pp. 173-199). Sydney: Addison-Wesley.

Meyer, I.H., & Colten, M.E. (1999). Sampling gay men: Random Digit Dialing versus sources in the gay community. *Journal of Homosexuality, 37(4)*, 99-110.

Schofield, M., & Jamieson, M. (1999). Sampling in quantitative research. In V. Minichiello, G. Sullivan, K. Greenwood, & R. Axford (Eds.), *Handbook of research methods in health sciences* (pp. 147-172). Sydney: Addison-Wesley.

Sell, R.L., & Petrulio, C. (1996). Sampling homosexuals, bisexuals, gays, and lesbians for public health research: A review of the literature from 1990 to 1992. *Journal of Homosexuality, 30(4)*, 31-47.

Singleton, R.A., & Straits, B.C. (1999). *Approaches to social research* (3rd ed.). Oxford: Oxford University Press.

Wahler, J., & Gabbay, S. (1997), Gay male aging: A review of the literature. *Journal of Gay & Lesbian Social Services, 6(3)*, 1-20.

Matching AIDS Service Organizations' Philosophy of Service Provision with a Compatible Style of Program Evaluation

Sarah-Jane Dodd

William Meezan

SUMMARY. The purpose of this paper is to outline the unique features of AIDS Service Organizations (ASOs) that should be considered when developing an evaluation strategy. It describes current evaluation approaches used by ASOs which are incongruent with the service philosophy of these organizations and the drawbacks these current evaluation efforts present. It then describes an alternative evaluation approach that better matches ASOs' philosophy of service delivery with the evaluation process. An illustrative case example is used to show how a more participatory approach can be used in an ASO and why such an approach is

Sarah-Jane Dodd, MSEd, MSW, PhD, is Assistant Professor, Hunter College School of Social Work, City University of New York, New York, NY.

William Meezan, MSW, DSW, is the Marion Elizabeth Blue Professor of Children and Families, University of Michigan School of Social Work, Ann Arbor, MI.

Address correspondence to: Dr. SJ Dodd, Hunter College School of Social Work, City University of New York, 129 E. 79th Street, New York, NY 10021 (E-mail: sdodd@hunter.cuny.edu).

[Haworth co-indexing entry note]: "Matching AIDS Service Organizations' Philosophy of Service Provision with a Compatible Style of Program Evaluation." Dodd, Sarah-Jane, and William Meezan. Co-published simultaneously in *Journal of Gay & Lesbian Social Services* (Harrington Park Press, an imprint of The Haworth Press, Inc.) Vol. 15, No. 1/2, 2003, pp. 163-180; and: *Research Methods with Gay, Lesbian, Bisexual, and Transgender Populations* (ed: William Meezan, and James I. Martin) Harrington Park Press, an imprint of The Haworth Press, Inc., 2003, pp. 163-180. Single or multiple copies of this article are available for a fee from The Haworth Document Delivery Service [1-800-HAWORTH, 9:00 a.m. - 5:00 p.m. (EST). E-mail address: getinfo@haworthpressinc.com].

163

more likely to produce meaningful data that will be utilized for program development and refinement. *[Article copies available for a fee from The Haworth Document Delivery Service: 1-800-HAWORTH. E-mail address: <getinfo@haworthpressinc.com> Website: <http://www.HaworthPress.com> © 2003 by The Haworth Press, Inc. All rights reserved.]*

KEYWORDS. Evaluation research, participatory evaluation, AIDS Service Organizations (ASOs), research methodology

Throughout their two decades of service, AIDS Service Organizations (ASOs) have taken a community-based, grassroots approach to service delivery (Wilson, 1995). This approach, championed by the gay community, was a necessary response to the lack of action taken by governmental and non-profit organizations to address the medical and social services needs brought on by the AIDS pandemic (Penner, 1995; Wilson, 1995). Ironically, however, program evaluations within these organizations have tended to take on a more bureaucratic and "top-down" approach (Miller & Cassel, 2000), which appears to be in conflict with the philosophy of both AIDS Service Organizations and the lesbian, gay, bisexual and transgender (LGBT) community that feels ownership of them. The purpose of this paper is to outline the unique features of ASOs that should be considered when developing an evaluation strategy, current evaluation approaches, drawbacks to these current efforts, and an alternative approach that matches ASOs' philosophy of service delivery with the evaluation process.

HISTORY OF AIDS SERVICE ORGANIZATIONS

The development of ASOs as a grassroots movement in the early 1980s can be attributed to two key factors. First, AIDS, in its early years, was associated with three strongly stigmatized groups: gay men, IV drug users, and prostitutes. The association of HIV with such stigmatized groups meant political support and assistance from the public purse was extremely limited (Shilts, 1987). It has been argued that the fact that "HIV/AIDS primarily affected stigmatized and marginalized populations underscored the need for grassroots, community-based approaches" (Wilson, 1995, p. 125). Second, existing service organizations were often unwilling to adjust their service provision to accommodate people with HIV or AIDS. Lack of knowledge and understanding of the disease and its transmission led to widespread fear of contagion, which caused resistance to service provision within existing service organizations (Finch, 1992; Wilson, 1995).

While this initial inaction by government and service providers created a need for specialized services, the sudden increase in infection rates during the mid-1980s amplified service deficiencies (Finch, 1992). The response of many gay communities was to create ASOs offering services specifically designed for people with HIV/AIDS. The ASOs were designed to have three major functions: to respond to broad public policy issues relevant to HIV/AIDS; to promote education and prevention efforts within the community; and to provide social services specifically for people with AIDS (PWAs) (Wilson, 1995). In keeping with their grassroots foundation, ASOs' mission statements often included "themes of social justice, social change, and self empowerment" (Finch, 1992, p. 79). In fact, individuals (usually volunteers) working with PWAs often focused on service strategies and interventions that fostered autonomy and empowerment (Lopez & Getzel, 1987).

ASOs first developed in the areas hardest hit by the pandemic: New York, San Francisco and Miami (Fleishman, Piette, & Mor, 1990). Many of the early ASOs were created by a "small, cohesive cadre of committed volunteers" (Fleishman et al., 1990, p. 35), who were directly affected and impacted by the epidemic (Finch, 1992; Fleishman et al., 1990; Wilson, 1995).

Thus, it was members of gay and lesbian communities who rose to the challenge presented by the need for increased services. It was these same communities, and the organizations that they formed, that also became more politically active and visible as a means of countering society's homophobic response to AIDS (Taylor-Brown, 1995). Indeed, in many areas during the late 1980s and early 1990s, lesbian and gay communities took on increased ownership of both AIDS and ASOs (Schneider, 1997).

As the number of people infected and affected by HIV and AIDS continued to rise, the demand for needed services escalated. In fact, the "continued lack of a vaccine or cure shifted community HIV organizations from a voluntary, short-term perspective to a more long-term, institutionalized structure" (Penner, 1995, p. 218). In an attempt to meet the needs of an increasing caseload and respond to the changing reality of the nature of the pandemic, some of the larger ASOs moved away from dependence on a core volunteer staff and increasingly employed professional staff supported through external funding (Botnick, 2000).

The continual increase in demand for services also resulted in a constant struggle for financial support, which in turn created a high degree of uncertainty within these organizations (Finch, 1992). In order to accommodate their rapid growth, many organizations tended to become more bureaucratic in nature (Cain, 1997; Finch, 1992; Fleishman et al., 1990). Facing a desperate need for funding and an ever spreading epidemic, AIDS activists worked hard to make AIDS not "just" a gay disease. This effort to reduce the stigma and increase funding further distanced ASOs from their roots and resulted in parts of the gay community withdrawing some of their initial support.

Yet despite these pressures and trends, some ASOs attempted to remain true to their grassroots beginnings. Some have "sought to [continue to] share power by emphasizing and maintaining a non-hierarchical, collaborative, and egalitarian structural framework" (Finch, 1992, p. 82). Others continually struggle to maintain a balance between their size and the scope of their services and their community roots. Almost all continue to have PWAs in powerful staff and Board positions, in part to give voice to their clients in agency decision-making.

As is common in all social service sectors, increased reliance on external funding has led to an increased demand for evaluations to justify program continuation. In ASOs, the shift in organizational structure and funding, from grassroots, "democratic," voluntarily-supported organizations to more hierarchical, bureaucratic, governmentally-funded organizations, has been reflected in the types of evaluation approaches used in this service arena.

CURRENT THINKING REGARDING THE EVALUATION OF HIV/AIDS PROGRAMS

Members of the Centers for Disease Control and Prevention (CDC) Division of HIV/AIDS Prevention-Intervention Research and Support Department recently discussed an evaluation strategy for HIV prevention programs based on an evaluation pyramid (Davis et al., 2000). The pyramid depicts seven different evaluation types, each with a different function. The seven evaluation types are: community planning for prioritizing the HIV comprehensive plan; intervention planning for planning effective intervention; process monitoring for documenting the people served, services provided and resources used; process evaluation for determining whether the intervention is implemented as intended; outcome monitoring for determining if the intervention achieves its outcome objectives; outcome evaluation for determining if the intervention works; and impact evaluation to determine broader effects (Davis et al., 2000). While this evaluation pyramid is helpful in guiding the choice of evaluation questions appropriate to the phase of the particular program under study, it does not address how to implement the evaluation in a way that honors the philosophy and roots of the ASO or how to reduce staff resistance to the evaluation and maximize organizational learning.

In addition to this classification of research types within the AIDS prevention field, a nationwide effort has been made to coordinate and prioritize a research and evaluation agenda for HIV service delivery. This effort has taken place with participation from the Health Resources and Service Administration, the Agency for Health Care Policy and Research, and the National Community AIDS Partnership (Weissman et al., 1994). But, as with the CDC classification of evaluation questions/types, these groups have made no effort to determine the most appropriate approach to the evaluation process.

Thus, while consensus has been reached as to the types of research that should be conducted, and the substantive priorities for evaluative efforts, no guidelines have been provided regarding how best to conduct these evaluations in order to achieve accurate and meaningful data upon which to make appropriate program decisions. The CDC has attempted to ensure the quality of HIV- related evaluations by publishing two guidebooks to assist in the evaluation of CDC-funded HIV prevention programs within health departments (CDC, 1999a, 1999b). In addition, it offers technical assistance to CDC grantees in evaluation methodology (Davis et al., 2000). However, since not all ASOs are CDC grantees, this technical assistance is not universally available.

Consequently, current evaluation strategies vary widely in purpose, methodology, scope, approach, and sophistication. And despite the generation of the CDC pyramid of evaluation research questions, many ASO evaluations focus on prevention outcomes (especially condom use) (Crosby, 1998), with surprisingly little emphasis on service planning, program implementation, program monitoring, or the achievement of psychosocial outcomes.

CURRENT EVALUATION APPROACHES

The way that one conceives evaluation impacts the purpose, nature, and process of the evaluation, and evidence suggests that most ASO evaluations employ a fairly traditional evaluation approach (Miller & Cassel, 2000). In these traditional approaches, research constructs are adapted to the organizational setting, the evaluation is designed and conducted by an "objective" social scientist, and the evaluation is used to determine whether a program is "effective" and therefore should be continued. This approach is still suggested in many evaluation texts. For example, Rossi, Freeman and Lipsey (1999) define evaluation research as the "use of social research procedures to systematically investigate the effectiveness of social intervention programs" (p. 4). They suggest that evaluators should "use social research methods to study, appraise and improve social programs in all their important aspects" (p. 4). This definition suggests that evaluation is done *to* a program rather than in collaboration *with* it. And this most recent definition has been significantly tempered by the authors who, in earlier writings, used words such as "assess" and "judge" (Rossi & Freeman, 1993, p. 5) rather than "investigate" and "appraise" when discussing the purpose of evaluation and the role of the evaluator.

While traditional evaluation approaches, which utilize "top-down" decision-making and place the evaluator in the role of "expert," may be appropriate in some limited circumstances, the unique histories of ASOs suggest that this approach may be incompatible with the missions of these organizations, their organizational structures, and/or their methods of service delivery. In fact, they may be so incompatible that a "culture clash" occurs, leading to situations where evaluation is seen as burdensome and irrelevant rather than helpful. Such clashes almost guarantee that the design, execution, and utilization of evaluation results will be compromised.

INCOMPATIBILITY OF CURRENT EVALUATION APPROACHES

Traditional evaluation approaches–those imposed by outside funding agencies without agency input into the identification of program goals and objectives, the measurements used, or the methods of data collection–often encounter resistance in social service agencies. The fact that such evaluations are often designed by "outsiders" to "judge" the worth of a program with which they might be unfamiliar has resulted in evaluation being feared by social service programs and their staff. Indeed, traditional evaluation is often associated with the idea of the "program termination squad" (Patton, 1997, p. 10). As Reed and Collins (1994) have noted, "if evaluation reveals services to be ineffective according to arbitrary research criteria, this would require changes in the agency and might endanger funding" (p. 75). Such consequences would limit the ability of the agency to deliver what are perceived to be necessary and important services in a manner consistent with the needs of their service population and their agency philosophy.

Resistance to traditional evaluation approaches may be heightened in ASOs for a number of reasons. First, such evaluations are perceived as an imposed burden that detracts from the agency's mission (Reed & Collins, 1994). Resources that could be used to provide services are seen as being diverted to a less important function as a matter of compliance rather than of choice. Evaluation is thus perceived as an activity that diverts resources from the program's critical function of providing services to a highly stigmatized population that other providers would rather ignore.

Second, resistance to traditional evaluations within ASOs is heightened by the fact that service providers in these settings are deeply invested in their clients–clients who are often part of their "community." In addition, some of the service providers are HIV+ like their clients. Thus, negative evaluation results are perceived not only to attack to program effectiveness, but they can be experienced as an attack on service recipients, the individual service providers, agencies based in and supported by the LGBT community, and the LBGT community itself. Thus, evaluations of programs within ASOs may have political consequences that reach well beyond the specific program being evaluated.

Third, the assumptions and approaches used in traditional evaluations seem particularly incompatible with ASOs. Alkin (1990) has argued that "imposed research questions, methodology and procedures work in concert to alienate and disempower the organization being evaluated" (p. 2). Thus, traditional evaluation approaches may be especially troublesome for ASOs, with their histories of power sharing, consumer involvement and empowerment, grass-roots control, and non-judgmental attitudes toward the disenfranchised.

Fourth, Cherin and Meezan (1998) note that traditional evaluation approaches can create an atmosphere where agencies are forced to "protect and defend their current practices in reaction to the 'auditor' spirit of the evaluation process" (p. 2). Evaluations whose primary purpose is to judge the worthiness of a program may be especially troublesome for ASOs, whose clients are frequently judged. And summary judgements about programs have little to do with building useful knowledge for program development and improvement. Such judgements do little to explain which elements of the program might be working for different clients under varying circumstances, whether the program is meeting unmeasured objectives that might be critical to key stakeholders, or whether there are issues of program integrity and fidelity that might first be addressed in order to increase program success.

Fifth, traditional evaluations that are done *to* rather than *with* agencies, in a "top-down" manner by someone outside the AIDS community, are likely to be resisted. It should be remembered that members of the LBGT community formed these organizations to take care of their own. Outsiders, particularly those who are not members of LBGT communities, who attempt to dictate their evaluation wishes on ASOs, are likely to find it difficult to successfully implement their evaluation plans.

Given these particular incompatibilities between traditional evaluation approaches and ASOs, the developmental stage and changing nature of programs within ASOs (particularly given new AIDS-impacted populations), as well as the usual difficulties present in successfully executing an outcome evaluation, it should not be surprising that, to date, evaluations in this field have not been able to contribute significantly to program knowledge or improvement. For example, Fullerton, Holland and Oakley (1995) reviewed 114 reports of evaluations of HIV/AIDS prevention interventions and found that in only a small proportion of cases was it possible to "come to reliable conclusions about demonstrated effectiveness" (p. 103). In addition, Miller and Cassel (2000) assert that "although more programs are being evaluated, few evaluations have been conducted with sufficient skill and rigor to result in useful information" (p. 22). As a result, some have claimed that "inefficient duplication of poorly evaluated services is common" (Reed & Collins, 1994, p. 75).

Along with the lack of definitive findings has come a lack of utilization of evaluation results. Extending beyond the usual reasons cited in the literature for the lack of utilization of research findings (Alkin, 1990), the incompatibility between the research produced and the information needs of ASOs, and the absence of useful evaluation findings in the field (Weissman et al., 1994), may also be at play.

Miller and Cassel (2000) suggest four reasons for substandard evaluations of HIV/AIDS programs: (1) limited resources; (2) lack of personnel skilled in program evaluation causing poor methodology and questionable validity of sensitive data; (3) incongruent models of program evaluation; and (4) politics affecting the rigor and usefulness of the evaluation. Citing these issues, many of which were described above, they call for the creation of evaluation departments within ASOs as a way of combating this problem.

For many ASOs, however, creating and supporting evaluation departments can be a daunting and expensive task, and some of the largest ASOs (e.g., Gay Men's Health Crisis in New York) have disbanded their internal research and evaluation efforts. It is our assertion that there is a viable alternative to this solution–the use of an alternative approach to program evaluation in ASOs. Such an approach would embody the values of ASOs and enhance organizational learning through the use of more inclusive evaluation methodologies. Such an approach would redefine the role of the evaluator from expert to facilitator, and change the function of the evaluation from one which judges the program's "success" to one which garners understanding about the program and uses it for systematic improvement and enhancement (Altpeter, Schopler, Galinsky, & Pennell, 1999; Secret, Jordan, & Ford, 1999).

AN ALTERNATIVE APPROACH TO PROGRAM EVALUATION IN ASOs

There is a growing consensus in the professions concerned with the delivery of social services that if evaluations are to be successfully planned, executed, and utilized to improve service delivery, members of the organization must be involved from the very beginning of the process and fully engaged in the planning and execution of the evaluation. Research conducted on the impact of participation of agency personnel on evaluation utilization (Nay, Scanlon, Schmidt, & Wholey, 1976; Rothman, 1980; Wholey, 1991) has concluded that the degree of participation by organizational personnel in evaluation routines (including objective setting, choice of design and methodology, research implementation, and data analysis) has the greatest impact on the acceptance of the evaluation process and the utilization of evaluation results.

Given the history and nature of most ASOs, taking such an evaluation approach makes both intuitive and logical sense–evaluations that are conducted using processes compatible with the philosophy of the host organization enhance the chances that the evaluation will be designed and executed in a meaningful way. ASOs, founded on premises of self-empowerment, and structured in ways that embrace collaborative and non-hierarchical organizational arrangements, could be expected to gravitate toward evaluation approaches that are inclusive, collaborative, and respectful of input from a variety of sources. Spiers (1991), recognizing the grassroots nature of ASOs, suggests that community involvement in research decisions would be in keeping with the tradition of these organizations. He also suggests that notions of consultation and self-empowerment within ASOs are congruent with the AIDS communities' efforts to ensure medical self-empowerment for PWAs.

It is our contention that shifting towards a more collaborative process of program evaluation would not only lead to better designed, executed, and more useful evaluations, but would also act as a catalyst towards greater program ownership by agency staff and clients. In fact, appropriately designed and executed evaluations could foster an improved sense of community, something that has begun to disappear from within ASOs (Botnick, 2000).

The following is an attempt to describe an evaluation process and approach that would dovetail with the service philosophy and historical roots of ASOs. The proposed process combines aspects of a number of newer evaluation approaches, including utilization-focused evaluation (Patton, 1997), empowerment evaluation (Fetterman, Kaftarian, & Wandersman, 1996), participatory evaluation (Cousins & Earl, 1995), and the notion of double-loop learning (Cherin & Meezan, 1998). Within this process it is assumed that the evaluation can and should be a learning opportunity for the agency, and that it should be a participatory process. The evaluation is a collaborative process done with an ASO, and can thus foster both self-determination and program improvement simultaneously (Fetterman et al., 1996).

Secret et al. (1999) detail the usefulness of empowerment evaluation for HIV prevention programs, while also recognizing some of its weaknesses. In the evaluation approach described here, the strengths of the empowerment evaluation (and their compatibility with the ASOs' philosophy) are maintained while the weaknesses are minimized by the careful inclusion of a trained evaluator throughout the process. However, this evaluator is not seen as "expert," but rather as a teacher/collaborator who facilitates sound decision-making by those involved in the evaluation planning and implementation. By working with a skilled evaluator who assumes the teacher/collaborator role, ASOs can be helped to understand and utilize (if they choose) sophisticated research designs and methodologies while, at the same time, issues of trust are diffused and organizational ownership is enhanced (Wang, Siegal, Falck, Carlson, & Rahman, 1999).

Cherin and Meezan (1998) outline an approach to program evaluation that allows organizations to turn the evaluation process into an opportunity for learning, where "new information becomes a stimulant to rethink the norms of the organization and the way in which it delivers service" (p. 10). Within this process of evaluation are five overlapping phases: "discovering, refining, launching the evaluation, utilizing, and archiving" (Cherin & Meezan, 1998, p. 11). Using the five-stage process that they developed (see Figure 1), it is possible to outline a hypothetical evaluation for an ASO.

Discovering

The initial phase in the process is a time of information gathering regarding the program and the service delivery process. Tasks at this phase include determining program goals in an effort to begin to formulate general research questions, and surveying the relevant literature to help determine whether these questions are appropriate. It is important to note that "this phase is an iterative process, with full give-and-take between the researcher and organizational personnel" (Cherin & Meezan, 1998, p. 12). One useful way of reducing feelings of judgement and increasing the investment by workers is to have the program personnel involved in generating the evaluation questions.

Deciding the key questions of an ASO evaluation should be a collaboration among all stakeholders, including community members, agency personnel at all levels, clients, and funders, with the evaluator facilitating the retrieval of information. Patton (1997) suggests that evaluators use their expertise not to provide questions but to assist others in question generation. In this way, the evaluation will have meaning for all of the stakeholder groups involved. Reed and Collins (1994) noted a similar process when they developed a model for HIV mental health research and service delivery that included collaboration between researchers, community-based organizations, and persons living with HIV and AIDS. One of their reasons for recognizing the need for this collaborative approach was that "as professionals (researchers), we had assumed that

FIGURE 1. Cherin and Meezan's (1998) Action Evaluation Model

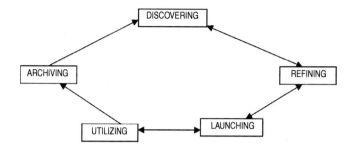

Reprinted with permission of The Haworth Press, Inc. From Cherin, D., & Meezan, W. (1998). Evaluation as a means of organizational learning. *Administration in Social Work, 22(2)*, 1-21.

we knew what was best for people living with HIV and AIDS, that we knew better than they what questions research should address" (Reed & Collins, 1994, p. 72). Experience with the AIDS community while planning an annual conference on HIV and AIDS research led them to abandon this position.

Refining

In this phase the research questions are refined by developing an understanding of both what is known and what needs to be known about the program and its method of service delivery. In addition, a tentative evaluation process is developed for distribution throughout the organization. This process is used to gain insight and develop ownership of the evaluation within the organization.

Inherent within the system of empowerment evaluation is an attempt to sufficiently demystify the evaluation process so that the organization can eventually become self-evaluating. Such a process leads to the situation where the conceptualization and execution of the evaluation remain largely in the hands of program personnel (Fetterman et al., 1996). Similar strategies are used in participatory evaluation (Cousins & Earl, 1995) to achieve the same purpose.

The process of refining supports the achievement of this goal by involving the entire organization in the process reviewing the evaluation plan. Close consultation with evaluators is maintained during this phase to help ensure that the potential benefits from this process occur, for through their role evaluators educate those involved around critical methodological issues and discuss with the program stakeholders the costs and benefits of making certain decisions. Involving all stakeholders in this process, and improving their understanding of the evaluation process, may help to overcome some of the resistance toward evaluation displayed by the AIDS community.

In noting problems encountered in their study, Fleishman, Mor, Cwi and Piette (1992) recognized difficulties arising from "staff's lack of time and from the low(er) priority staff gave to the evaluation than to providing direct service" (p. 402). It is therefore essential to use the refining phase to develop an understanding with key stakeholders that the results of the evaluation will have a direct impact on the way in which services are delivered. It should be emphasized at this time that the intention of the evaluation is to both acknowledge what is going well and improve client services where appropriate. While engaging in this process is time consuming (Cherin & Meezan, 1998), the potential benefits outweigh these costs, as it helps to ensure the eventual utilization of evaluation findings.

Launching the Evaluation

The third phase involves revising, finalizing, and implementing the evaluation design. It is during this phase that the "sense of the evaluation belonging to the organization is cemented" (Cherin & Meezan, 1998, p. 13). Brown (1995) and Patton (1997) both recommend the use of multiple methods and multiple data sources or measures to ensure that appropriate information is matched to the appropriate questions. Whether quantitative or qualitative methods are used, either independently or together, is dependent upon the evaluation's goals and the specific research questions to be addressed.

The appropriate methodology may also relate directly to the stage of development of the program. For example, qualitative methods may be more appropriate for the evaluation of developing programs or for process evaluations, while quantitative methods may be more appropriate for the evaluation of established programs and outcome evaluations (Patton, 1997). Thus, during this phase, particular attention must be paid to the stage of development of the program and its host organization. The evaluator's role at this stage is to ensure that the learning needs of the agency are addressed through the research that is undertaken, a process that is enhanced by gathering feedback from as many program stakeholders as possible. It is also at this time that the evaluation team grapples with the need to balance scientific rigor against that which is "doable" and "meaningful" for the organization/program. For example, it may be easy and accurate to count the number of people that attend an HIV prevention program. However, that does not provide any information about whether the material presented was accurate, whether the participants understood it, and ultimately whether it had an impact on risk behaviors.

In addition, decisions have to be made regarding whether knowing if the program was "successful" is enough, or whether there is a need to know for whom the program was successful, and under what circumstances success occurred (which requires the collection of a significant amount of additional information). It should be remembered that the traditional emphasis has been on the accomplishment of measurable outputs, but such information does not address why the program was or was not successful. Such "narrow" knowledge does not facilitate program improvement, for important information is missing. Therefore, one must balance the need to generate knowledge about measurable outputs with a focus on generating meaningful information that can be used for program design and change.

Of particular concern for AIDS program evaluations during this phase are sampling issues. Problems with access, concerns regarding confidentiality, and high mortality rates have all created cause for concern regarding the validity of research and evaluation results (O'Connell, 2000). In addition, inability to develop probability samples has limited the generalizability of findings, and subsequently the transfer of knowledge between programs (Fleishman et al., 1992). The collaboration of program staff and clients is essential in generating a sampling plan that is both useful and feasible. Without the support of both staff and clients, developing a representative sample is not possible. A combination of organizational ownership and methodological consultation is key to success at this stage in the process.

Utilizing

During this phase, the information learned as a result of the evaluation is disseminated in a way that maximizes the potential for its utilization within the organization and the wider AIDS community. AIDS program evaluations have been particularly unsuccessful at securing useful and usable results that can be utilized by the program involved (Fullerton et al., 1995; Weissman et al., 1994). This five-stage process of program evaluation helps to foster increased utilization of results in two major ways. First, it involves program personnel and other stakeholders in all the major decisions regarding the evaluation process, which increases their investment in the results. Second, it involves program personnel in assembling the results and developing the materials for dissemination, which increases their investment in utilization of findings.

Archiving

The final phase, which is ongoing throughout the evaluation, involves documenting the actual evaluation process (as opposed to the evaluation results) and making this record available to other programs within the agency and other ASOs. The face of HIV and AIDS is rapidly changing. In response, ASOs themselves and the services that they offer are changing (Cain, 1997). Careful documentation of the evaluation process undertaken allows the organization to build on previous efforts while responding to dynamic circumstances. Lessons learned in earlier research efforts are clearly documented for improvement and refinement as the process begins again with new or refined programs.

APPLICATION OF THE MODEL

To help the reader understand how this model of evaluation can be applied in ASOs and their programs, Figure 2 hypothetically applies this five-stage approach to the evaluation of an outreach and education program aimed at increasing awareness of HIV transmission.

As can be seen, the "Discovering" stage involves gathering program information, reading relevant literature, and tentatively formulating the program's goal, which in this example addresses the need to decrease risk behaviors. The "Refining" phase specifies program objectives and research questions, and ensures that program elements are present to meet the objectives of the program. Thus, questions such as whether participation in the program increases knowledge of HIV transmission routes are appropriate to include at this point in the process. The "Launching" phase involves coming to consensus regarding the methodology to be used in the evaluation. Stakeholders here have to address issues of design, sampling, measurement, and data collection strategies. The "Utilizing" phase involves data analysis, data presentation, and dissemination of the results. Data analysis, of course, is dependent on the design chosen by the stakeholders in the previous phase of the evaluation. The final phase, the "Archiving" phase, ensures that information about the process is made available to others in the ASO and other ASOs, so that the organization can begin to develop the capacity to conduct such studies without the constant help of an outside evaluator.

CONCLUSIONS

The changing face of HIV means that now, more than ever, there is a need for meaningful evaluation data that are utilized by ASOs. This paper has suggested that matching the evaluation process more closely to the grassroots nature and philosophy of ASOs can serve the multiple functions of generating

FIGURE 2. Application of Five-Phase Evaluation Approach to an HIV Prevention Program

Phase	Tasks	Program Process and Response
Discovering	Gathering program information	Learn about the program and the organization.
	Initial formulation of program goals and objectives in order to generate initial research questions	Decrease behaviors known to be risk factors in the transmission of HIV.
	Reading relevant program and evaluation literature	Thorough review of the literature, by members of the staff, regarding identification of risk factors related to transmission of and resistance by the community to behavior change.
Refining	Specifying program goals and objectives	Increase awareness of HIV rates; decrease belief in myths associated with "immunity" from HIV/AIDS; increase knowledge of HIV transmission routes; decrease HIV risk behaviors.
	Refining research questions	Develop research questions related to each specified objective.
	Ensuring program elements are appropriate to meet given objectives	Ensure that program content matches desired objectives, and that there is a program activity for each objective. Ensure program space is conducive to creating a safe environment. Refine outreach to potential program participants to ensure appropriate participants.
Launching the Evaluation	Design	Choosing between descriptive (e.g., pre-test/post-test), quasi-experimental (e.g., case overflow) and experimental design (random assignment to various groups) and determining whether there will be a follow-up period.
	Sample	All program participants identified.
	Measures	Survey instrument designed to specifically address knowledge of issues of HIV transmission, myths commonly voiced in the community, and participation in specific risk behaviors. Information regarding demographic information and program participation would also be gathered. Self-administered survey completed in person pre- and post-education workshop, and by mail at 6-month follow-up.
	Data gathering strategy	Self-administered survey, completed in person, at appropriate times depending on the design chosen.
Utilizing	Analysis of data	Data analysis would focus on both changes in attitudes and behavior from pre- to post-test and other appropriate research questions depending on the research design chosen. Participant demographic and service utilization information would be used to determine with whom the program was most effective and the service components that seemed to contribute to program effectiveness.
	Presentation of data	Program staff would be involved in strategizing methods for data presentation and for intra-agency dissemination.
Archiving	Documentation of process	One member of the program staff would be responsible for keeping a journal documenting the entire process. Materials gathered during the process would be kept as supplementary information. The archived material would be made available to all programs within the organization to inform future evaluation efforts.

meaningful evaluation results, creating investment in evaluation utilization, and providing an opportunity for organizational learning. In addition, the evaluation process presented in this paper has the potential to combat disenfranchisement and may facilitate the re-ownership of ASOs by the LBGT communities in which they operate. Thus, this more inclusive approach to evaluation might allow ASOs not only to meet their accountability requirements and improve the quality of services provided to clients, but to help reengage LBGT communities in the battle against AIDS through the empowerment of both individuals and the organizations that serve them.

REFERENCES

Alkin, M. (1990). *Debates on evaluation.* Newbury Park, CA: Sage Publications.

Altpeter, M., Schopler, J.H., Galinsky, M.J., & Pennell, J. (1999). Participatory research as social work practice: When is it viable? *Journal of Progressive Human Services, 10(2),* 31-53.

Botnick, M. (2000). Gay community survival in the new millennium, part 3: A community divided. *Journal of Homosexuality, 38(4),* 103-132.

Brown, P. (1995). The role of the evaluator in comprehensive community initiatives. In J. Connell, A. Kubisch, L. Schorr, & C. Weiss (Eds.), *A new approach to evaluating community initiatives: Comprehensive community initiatives* (pp. 201-225). Washington, DC: The Aspen Institute.

Cain, R. (1997). Environmental change and organizational evolution: Reconsidering the niche of community-based AIDS organizations. *AIDS Care, 9,* 331-344.

Centers for Disease Control and Prevention (1999a). *Evaluating CDC-funded health department HIV prevention programs. Volume 1: Guidance.* Atlanta, GA: Author.

Centers for Disease Control and Prevention (1999b). *Evaluating CDC-funded health department HIV prevention programs. Volume 2: Resources.* Atlanta, GA: Author.

Cherin, D., & Meezan, W. (1998). Evaluation as a means of organizational learning. *Administration in Social Work, 22(2),* 1-21.

Cousins, J.B., & Earl, L.M. (1995). *Participatory evaluation in education: Studies in evaluation use and organizational learning.* London: Falmer Press.

Crosby, R. (1998). Condom use as a dependent variable: Measurement issues relevant to HIV prevention programs. *AIDS Education and Prevention, 10,* 548-557.

Davis, D., Barrington, T., Phoenix, U., Gilliam, A., Collins, C., Cotton, D., & Chen, H. (2000). Evaluation and technical assistance for successful HIV program delivery. *AIDS Education and Prevention, 12 (Suppl A),* 115-125.

Fetterman, D., Kaftarian, S., & Wandersman, A. (Eds.) (1996). *Empowerment evaluation: Knowledge and tools for self-assessment and accountability.* Thousand Oaks, CA: Sage Publications.

Finch, W. (1992). Alternative service organizations: The AIDS community. In H. Land (Ed.), *AIDS: A complete guide to psychosocial intervention* (pp. 79-87). Milwaukee: Family Service America.

Fleishman, J.A., Mor, V., Cwi, J.S., & Piette, J.D. (1992). Sampling and accessing people with AIDS. *Evaluation and the Health Professions, 15*, 385-404.

Fleishman, J.A., Piette, J.D., & Mor, V. (1990). Organizational response to AIDS. *Evaluation and Program Planning, 13(1)*, 31-38.

Fullerton, D., Holland, J., & Oakley, A. (1995). Towards effective intervention: Evaluating HIV prevention and sexual health education interventions. In P. Aggelton, P. Davies, & G. Hart (Eds.). *AIDS: Safety, sexuality and risk* (pp. 90-108). London: Taylor & Francis.

Lopez, D., & Getzel, G. (1987). Strategies for volunteers caring for persons with AIDS. *Social Casework, 68*, 47-53.

Miller, R., & Cassel, J.B. (2000). Ongoing evaluation in AIDS-Service Organizations: Building meaningful evaluation activities. *Journal of Prevention & Intervention in the Community, 19(1)*, 21-39.

Nay, J.N., Scanlon, J.W., Schmidt, R., & Wholey, J. (1976). If you don't care where you get to then it doesn't matter which way you go. In C. Abt (Ed.), *The evaluation of social programs*. Beverly Hills, CA: Sage Publications.

O'Connell, A.A. (2000). Sampling for evaluation: Issues and strategies for community-based HIV prevention programs. *Evaluation and the Health Professions, 23(2)*, 212-234.

Patton, M. (1997). *Utilization-focused evaluation* (3rd ed.). Thousand Oaks, CA: Sage Publications.

Penner, S. (1995). A study of coalitions among HIV/AIDS service organizations. *Sociological Perspectives, 38*, 217-239.

Reed, G.M., & Collins, B.E. (1994). Mental health research and service delivery: A three communities model. *Psychosocial Rehabilitation Journal, 17(4)*, 69-81.

Rossi, P., & Freeman, H. (1993). *Evaluation: A systematic approach* (5th ed.). Newbury Park, CA: Sage Publications.

Rossi, P.H., Freeman, H.E., & Lipsey, M.W. (1999). *Evaluation: A systematic approach* (6th ed.). Newbury Park, CA: Sage Publications.

Rothman, J. (1980*). Using research in organizations: A guide to successful application.* Beverly Hills, CA: Sage Publications.

Schneider, B.E. (1997). Owning an epidemic: The impact of AIDS on small city lesbian and gay communities. In L. Martin, P. Nardi, & J. Gagnon (Eds.), *In changing times: Gay men and lesbians encounter HIV/AIDS* (pp. 145-169). Chicago: University of Chicago Press.

Secret, M., Jordan, A., & Ford, J. (1999). Empowerment evaluation as a social work strategy. *Health & Social Work, 24(2)*, 120-127.

Shilts, R. (1987*). And the band played on: Politics, people and the AIDS epidemic.* New York: St. Martin's Press.

Spiers, H.R. (1991). Community consultation and AIDS clinical trials: Part III. *IRB: A Review of Human Subjects Research, 13(5)*, 3-7.

Taylor-Brown, S. (1995). Foreword. In G. Lloyd & M. Kuszelewicz (Eds.), *HIV disease: Lesbians, gays and social services* (pp. xiii-xvii). New York: Harrington Park Press.

Wang, J., Siegal, H.A., Falck, R.S., Carlson, R.G., & Rahman, A. (1999). Evaluation of HIV risk reduction intervention programs via latent growth model. *Evaluation Review, 23(6)*, 648-662.

Weissman, G., McClain, M., Hines, R., Harder, P., Gross, M., Marconi, K., & Bowen, G.S. (1994). Creating an agenda for research and evaluation: HIV service delivery, the Ryan White CARE Act, and beyond. *Journal of Public Health Policy, 15,* 329-344.

Wholey, J.S. (1991). Evaluation for program improvement. In W. Shadish, T. Cook, & L. Leviton (Eds.), *Foundations of program evaluation: Theories of practice* (pp. 225-269). Newbury Park, CA: Sage Publications.

Wilson, P.A. (1995). AIDS service organizations: Current issues and future challenges. In G. Lloyd & M. Kuszelewicz (Eds.), *HIV disease: Lesbians, gays and social services* (pp. 121-144). New York: Harrington Park Press.

Applying Ethical Standards to Research and Evaluations Involving Lesbian, Gay, Bisexual, and Transgender Populations

James I. Martin
William Meezan

SUMMARY. This manuscript examines the application of ethical standards to research on LGBT populations and the evaluation of programs and practices that impact them. It uses social work's Code of Ethics (National Association of Social Workers, 1996) and psychology's Ethical Principles of Psychologists and Code of Conduct (American Psychological Association, 1992) to examine specific ethical issues as they pertain to research involving LGBT populations. It notes that when conducting studies with these populations, researchers may need to take additional

James I. Martin, MSW, PhD, is Associate Professor, Shirley M. Ehrenkranz School of Social Work, New York University, New York, NY. William Meezan, MSW, DSW, is Marion Elizabeth Blue Professor of Children and Families, University of Michigan, School of Social Work, Ann Arbor, MI.

Address correspondence to: Dr. James I. Martin, Shirley M. Ehrenkranz School of Social Work, New York University, 1 Washington Square North, New York, NY 10003 (E-mail: james.martin@nyu.edu).

[Haworth co-indexing entry note]: "Applying Ethical Standards to Research and Evaluations Involving Lesbian, Gay, Bisexual, and Transgender Populations." Martin, James I., and William Meezan. Co-published simultaneously in *Journal of Gay & Lesbian Social Services* (Harrington Park Press, an imprint of The Haworth Press, Inc.) Vol. 15, No. 1/2, 2003, pp. 181-201; and: *Research Methods with Gay, Lesbian, Bisexual, and Transgender Populations* (ed: William Meezan, and James I. Martin) Harrington Park Press, an imprint of The Haworth Press, Inc., 2003, pp. 181-201. Single or multiple copies of this article are available for a fee from The Haworth Document Delivery Service [1-800-HAWORTH, 9:00 a.m. - 5:00 p.m. (EST). E-mail address: getinfo@haworthpressinc.com].

measures to protect participants from harm and to ensure the relevance and usefulness of their findings. In addition, heterosexist and genderist biases are examined as ethical issues, as is the tension between scientific objectivity and values in research involving LGBT populations. *[Article copies available for a fee from The Haworth Document Delivery Service: 1-800-HAWORTH. E-mail address: <getinfo@haworthpressinc.com> Website: <http://www.HaworthPress.com> © 2003 by The Haworth Press, Inc. All rights reserved.]*

KEYWORDS. Ethics, research, professional codes of ethics, research bias, gay, lesbian, bisexual, transgender

Cournoyer and Klein (2000) defined professional ethics as principles of conduct, based on a specific set of values, that guide appropriate professional behavior. Because personal and professional values inform nearly every choice made when engaging in both research and practice, the main professional organizations for social workers and psychologists have codified their core values into specific standards of ethical conduct. They are the National Association of Social Workers' (NASW) *Code of Ethics* (1996) and the American Psychological Association's (APA) *Ethical Principles of Psychologists and Code of Conduct* (1992). Although the standards of these two organizations are not exactly the same, they have many similarities.

Members of NASW and APA are expected to abide by their respective Codes when engaging in research and practice. Adherence to these Codes, and the standards that derive from them, are expected to protect the public from potential harm when receiving services and participating in research and evaluation studies.

Hardly any of the numerous elaborations, explanations, and applications of ethical standards in social work and psychological research (e.g., Kendler, 1993; McHugh, Koeske, & Frieze, 1986; Padgett, 1998; Reamer, 1998; Royse, Thyer, Padgett, & Logan, 2001) identify the unique ethical dilemmas that may arise in the conduct of research with lesbian, gay, or bisexual populations or explain the application of ethical standards in these situations (see Herek, Kimmel, Amaro, & Melton, 1991; Martin & Knox, 2000; Woodman, Tully, & Barranti, 1995). None examine the application of ethical standards to research involving transgender populations.

Lesbian, gay, bisexual, and transgender (LGBT) populations are marginalized in American society, and their members are at risk for experiencing violence, discrimination, and exploitation in a variety of contexts (Herek, Gillis, Cogan, &

Glunt, 1997; Hunter, Shannon, Knox, & Martin, 1998) and the subsequent negative effects of these experiences (Clements-Nolle, Marx, Guzman, & Katz, 2001; Diaz, Ayala, Bein, Henne, & Marin, 2001; Herek, Gillis, & Cogan, 1999; Hershberger & D'Augelli, 1995; Meyer, 1995; Savin Williams, 1994). Because research involving LGBT populations always occurs within this context, there may be greater potential for exploitation and harm to participants and the communities they represent in these studies than in studies of less vulnerable and marginalized populations. These dangers are likely to be magnified in studies of "deviant behaviors" or social problems (e.g., alcoholism and drug abuse, intimate partner violence, HIV behavioral risk patterns) in LGBT populations. Therefore, the lack of attention in the literature to the ethical dilemmas encountered in research involving LGBT populations, or the elaboration of guidelines for protecting members of these populations in the course of research, is extremely troubling.

There is an ample history of medical and social science research involving LGBT populations that have violated contemporary ethical standards. Murphy's (1992) review of the strategies used to attempt to change the sexual orientation of men and women includes accounts of numerous studies that caused physical harm to their participants. For example, Nazi physicians studied the effectiveness of castration and subsequent hormone injections in extinguishing homoeroticism among male prisoners (Plant, 1986). Bremer (1959) reported on castration among 244 men, and concluded that although it succeeded in reducing sex drive it was not effective in changing homoerotic orientation. Owensby (1941) studied the use of pharmacologic shock in "correcting" the homosexuality of 15 men and women. Several studies (e.g., Callahan & Leitenberg, 1973; McConaghy, 1976; Tanner, 1974) have examined the effectiveness of behavior therapy in changing sexual orientation, including covert sensitization paired with contingent electric shock and apomorphine therapy, which may cause vomiting or erection depending on dosage and method of use.

There is no evidence that physical harm was caused to participants in the Bieber et al. (1962) study of the effectiveness of several years of psychoanalytic treatment on changing men's sexual orientation. However, the treatment being evaluated might have harmed participants psychologically by encouraging them to maintain futile efforts toward changing their sexual orientation, and by reinforcing guilt and shame regarding their sexual feelings. For example, after many years of psychoanalytic treatment, Duberman (1991) discussed with his psychiatrist the difficulty he had in accepting the perspective of gay liberation. He stated "I suspect it's the extent of my brainwashing–too many years hearing about my 'pathology,' and believing it" (p. 193).

In addition, by claiming success in changing men's sexual orientation based on questionable methodology, Bieber et al. (1962) undoubtedly contributed to discriminatory societal attitudes and public policies. In particular, this study, which claimed that 27 of 106 participants changed their sexual orientation to exclusively heterosexual, used a questionnaire that the participant's *psychoanalyst* completed; there was no *self-report* of either sexual behavior or fantasy included in the measurement package.

Perhaps the best known example of research that risked harming members of an LGBT population is Humphreys' (1970) *Tearoom Trade*. This study's design involved an elaborate deception in which men's same-gender sexual behaviors in a public restroom were observed and recorded. Subsequently, the auto license plates of these men were used to obtain their home addresses. They were then asked to participate in an interview in that setting, using false pretenses to help ensure their cooperation.

Because Humphreys did not obtain informed consent from participants, and especially because of the extensive deception used in all phases of the research, the men's participation in this research must be considered to have been involuntary. In addition, the study participants' privacy was obviously invaded. However, the researcher did not breach the participants' confidentiality, and there is no evidence that any of them experienced actual harm. In fact, the study was noteworthy for bringing same-gender sexual behavior among men out of the closet in a scientifically neutral, non-condemnatory manner.

In other studies of LGBT populations, the extensive measures taken to protect confidentiality reflected the magnitude of the danger participants were thought to face. For example, Hooker (1957) interviewed gay participants in her home, rather than in her university office, fearing that no one would take part in her study without such protection–study participants were well aware that their lives could be seriously damaged if their confidentiality was breached. Hooker (1993) recalled that one of them "called me long distance at frequent intervals to ask whether his tapes had been erased" (p. 451).

Some studies have caused harm to LGBT communities, rather than to their individual participants, because of the way in which their results were used. For example, Herek (1998) noted that although researchers have generally ignored the studies conducted by Cameron and his colleagues (e.g., Cameron & Cameron, 1996; Cameron, Proctor, Cobum, & Forde, 1985), these studies "have had a more substantial impact in the public arena, where they have been used to promote stigma and to foster unfounded stereotypes of lesbians and gay men as predatory, dangerous, and diseased" (p. 247). According to Herek, Cameron's studies were used to promote and defend Colorado's Amendment 2, an initiative that would have prevented any level of that state's government from prohibiting discrimination against lesbian, gay, and bisexual residents. In striking down this law, the U.S. Supreme Court ruled that it violated the Equal

Protection Clause of the United States Constitution (FindLaw Resources, n.d.).

This article will use the standards for evaluation and research (sec. 5.02) of the NASW *Code of Ethics* as a framework for examining ethical conduct with LGBT populations. Only those standards that are particularly applicable to LGBT populations will be examined. The article will also make reference to selected standards in the APA *Code of Conduct,* and it will include ethical issues that are not directly addressed by either ethical code.

ETHICAL STANDARDS FOR RESEARCH

Standard 5.02(a). Social workers should monitor and evaluate policies, the implementation of programs, and practice interventions.

Standard 5.02(b). Social workers should promote and facilitate evaluation and research to contribute to the development of knowledge.

Since the 1970s, monitoring and evaluating practice interventions and programs have become increasingly important aspects of social work practice. With the exception of some AIDS service organizations, LGBT community organizations tend to be grassroots enterprises that rarely receive funding from government agencies. When social workers are involved with such organizations, either as board members or employees, they should spearhead or encourage program monitoring and evaluation efforts. In addition, the lack of outcome information for social work interventions, as noted by Reamer (1998), is particularly serious for interventions with LGBT clients. Evaluations of programs and interventions, especially if they are published, can help to ensure that LGBT community organizations are accountable to their members and clients, and that providers' services are appropriate, effective, and efficient.

Standard 5.02(c). Social workers should critically examine and keep current with emerging knowledge relevant to social work and fully use evaluation and research evidence in their professional practice.

According to several authors, many social workers lack information or have biases about LGBT populations (Berkman & Zinberg, 1997; Martin & Knox, 2000; Morrow, 1996). Accreditation standards of the Council on Social Work Education (CSWE) that require curriculum on lesbian and gay persons and their unique issues are an attempt to rectify this problem (CSWE, 1994). In addition, there has been a major increase in the amount of published research on lesbian and gay populations, due in large part to social work faculty who are openly lesbian or gay and to the nondiscrimination policies of the educational institutions that employ them. But social work research on bisexual and transgender populations continues to lag far behind (Martin & Hunter, 2001).

Unfortunately, professional social workers may not keep up with advances in professional knowledge (Barker, 1990). This situation is particularly disturbing for LGBT persons in need, given the lack of information about LGBT populations that many social work students report receiving in their graduate programs (Berkman & Zinberg, 1997). In other words, social workers may not learn much about these populations while getting their social work degrees, and they might not learn much more after they graduate.

> *Standard 5.02(d). Social workers engaged in evaluation or research should carefully consider possible consequences and should follow guidelines developed for the protection of evaluation and research participants. Appropriate institutional review boards should be consulted.*

Research can result in both positive and negative consequences to its participants and the populations they represent. Similarly, evaluations can result in both benefits and costs to any of the program's stakeholders. Researchers must think very seriously about these potential consequences, especially when participants or stakeholders are members of vulnerable LGBT populations. In other words, social work research must be socially responsible (Padgett, 1988).

One important consideration in this regard is the way in which others might use research or evaluation findings. For example, the U.S. Secretary of Health and Human Services (HHS) recently ordered an audit of HIV prevention grants and the programs to which they have been awarded. This review was apparently prompted by an HHS report criticizing the San Francisco Stop AIDS Project, which serves a large gay population, for the use of "obscenity" and for encouraging sexual activities (Erickson, 2001). One possible use of this audit would be to withhold or withdraw funds from HIV prevention programs for gay and bisexual men. Evaluations of such programs are not inherently heterosexist, but when they are conducted within a hostile political context there is ample reason for concern. Padgett (1998) suggested that researchers take care to "frame the presentation of the [study's] results and discuss their implications" (p. 43) in ways that minimize the possibility that others could misuse them to harm the participants, the groups they represent, or those who serve them.

When psychologist Evelyn Hooker planned her study testing the assumption of psychopathology among gay men (Hooker 1957), she could not have known that it would eventually lead to the declassification of homosexuality by the American Psychiatric Association. Surely she considered the possibility of some benefit to the larger population of gay men if her sample was found to have no more psychopathology than nongay men (as it did). But if the sample were found to have more psychopathology, it might have closed off the possibility of other research on "normal male homosexuals" (Hooker, 1993, p. 451), especially considering the extremely hostile political and social environment in which the study was conducted.

Since 1974, Institutional Review Boards (IRBs), charged with ensuring the protection of research subjects from harm, have been mandated for all organizations that receive federal funds and conduct behavioral or biomedical research. The federal regulations that mandate and govern IRBs are detailed in 45 CFR 46 (U.S. Department of Health and Human Services, 1997). Needs assessments, program monitoring and evaluations, and single system studies of client outcomes are not included in the definition of "research," according to the federal regulations.

Thus, agencies engaging in these activities, but not research leading to generalizable knowledge, are not required to have IRBs (Cournoyer & Klein, 2000). Few LGBT community agencies conduct "research" as defined by federal regulations, and thus they rarely have their own IRBs. In the event that such agencies receive federal funds for "research," they must either create their own IRB or find an existing one that is willing to review their proposal and monitor the project. Thus, one benefit of agencies partnering with faculty members for research projects is the use of a university IRB.

However, best ethical practices suggest that agencies should submit proposals for evaluation studies to either an internal or external review committee. Taking such measures will help to ensure that these studies follow appropriate treatment protocols and abide by all appropriate ethical standards.

Fundamentally, IRBs base their decisions regarding proposed research according to a risk/benefit ratio in which the potential harms or costs to participants are weighed against the potential benefits to them or to society in general (Royse, 1999). In cases in which the risks appear to outweigh the potential benefits, IRBs will typically require a redesign of the study so that the potential risks are reduced or avoided (Sieber & Stanley, 1988). For example, they might require a debriefing to alleviate emotional distress engendered by participation in the study (Monette, Sullivan, & DeJong, 1998). Or they might require that the consent form used in the study include a fuller description of the potential risks of participation.

There are no specific federal regulations for research involving LGBT populations. In fact, IRBs might be more likely to reject research proposals dealing with socially sensitive topics (Sieber & Stanley, 1988) such as sexual orientation or gender expression. According to Ceci, Peters, and Plotkin

(1985), such rejections reflect the sociopolitical ideologies of IRB committee members. Researchers proposing studies involving LGBT populations must unfortunately be wary of IRB reviews conducted in institutions that do not forbid discrimination on the basis of sexual orientation and gender expression.

> *Standard 5.02(e). Social workers engaged in evaluation or research should obtain voluntary and written informed consent from participants, when appropriate, without any implied or actual deprivation or penalty for refusal to participate; without undue inducement to participate; and with due regard for participants' well-being, privacy, and dignity. Informed consent should include information about the nature, extent, and duration of the participation requested and disclosure of the risks and benefits of participation in the research.*

> *Standard 5.02(h). Social workers should inform participants of their right to withdraw from evaluation and research at any time without penalty.*

One of the main concerns of IRBs is whether studies have appropriate and sufficient procedures to ensure participants' voluntary informed consent. The Humphreys (1970) study of men's sexual behavior in public restrooms is often identified as an example of research that violated the principle of voluntary informed consent. As described above, while the confidentiality of the study's participants was never violated, their dignity and self-determination certainly were, and permission to intrude on their privacy was never obtained through informed consent procedures.

While, in general, research should be conducted only with people who have consented to participate, this principle can be ethically circumscribed in ways that may afford the research participant even greater protection. Martin and Knox (2000) recommended that gay and lesbian (bisexual and transgender should be added) research participants should remain anonymous, and noted that written consent does not afford them this added protection. They suggested that, when possible, anonymous surveys using self-administered questionnaires or phone interviews, in which consent is implied rather than written, should be used. In this way, people who wish to be excluded from the study would not fill out and return the questionnaire or complete the interview. However, use of this procedure needs to be accompanied by assurances that participants are not coerced or highly vulnerable to exploitation (Royse et al., 2001). Thus, given the vulnerability of LGBT populations, the use of implied consent should be carefully scrutinized to make sure participants are not exploited or subject to coercion.

In addition to these points, the APA Code also states that informed consent procedures should "use language that is reasonably understandable to research participants" (Sec. 6.11(a)). Researchers should not assume that GLBT participants are all well-educated, middle-class, English-speaking individuals. Forms should be in participants' native language, and they should be written at a reading level that is not too high. According to the National Institutes of Health Office of Human Subjects Research (2000), consent forms should generally be written below a high school graduate's level of comprehension. As such, they should not contain words with more than three syllables, scientific terms, or lengthy sentences. In addition, consent procedures should avoid language that is likely to offend or be misinterpreted by prospective participants. For example, using the term "homosexual" instead of "gay and lesbian," or referring to both gay men and lesbians as "gay," could be offensive to some participants.

The APA Code also warns psychologists not to use inducements for participation in studies that are excessive or inappropriate. Such inducements could have a coercive effect on prospective participants (Sec. 6.14(b)), which would undermine informed consent procedures. Researchers must be particularly careful about excessive monetary inducements when prospective LGBT participants, especially youth, are financially unstable or impoverished.

As indicated by *5.02(h),* the consent form must inform participants of their right to withdraw from the study at any time without penalty. Related to this point, the form should explain that refusal to participate in a study, or a decision to withdraw from it, will not result in differential treatment by any agency associated with the study.

Under these procedures, participants could decide that their discomfort with, or other negative reactions to, the study outweighs any benefits they had expected to receive when they first agreed to participate. For example, LGBT participants could become uncomfortable with what they perceive to be the biased or heterosexist language, or assumptions used on a questionnaire or in an interview. Or they might find that a questionnaire takes much longer or is more difficult to complete than they had expected. An explicit statement regarding participants' right to withdraw minimizes the possibility that they will feel coerced to remain in the study against their wishes.

Standard 5.02(f). When evaluation or research participants are incapable of giving informed consent, social workers should provide an appropriate explanation to the participants, obtain the participants' assent to the extent they are able, and obtain written consent from an appropriate proxy.

Because people younger than 18 cannot legally give consent in the U.S., studies of LGBT youth must involve additional measures to assure that their participation is voluntary. Participants under the age of consent must give written "assent." But this does not substitute for the written consent of their parents or guardians, which researchers must also obtain whenever possible. However, obtaining consent from parents or guardians can be dangerous when the underaged participants are LGBT. As noted by Elze (this volume), 45 CFR 46.408(c) allows minors to participate in research without parental or guardian consent if obtaining it would compromise their safety or welfare. This is most likely to be the case among youths living in abusive households or those who have not disclosed their sexual orientation to parents or guardians. In such cases, researchers can use independent advocates to assure participants' rights (e.g., D'Augelli & Hershberger, 1993). Alternatively, IRBs can declare sponsoring agencies to be acting *in loco parentis* by allowing youths to participate in a study (e.g., Rosario, Hunter, & Gwadz, 1997).

> *Standard 5.02(g). Social workers should never design or conduct evaluation or research that does not use consent procedures, such as certain forms of naturalistic observation and archival research, unless rigorous and responsible review of the research has found it to be justified because of its prospective scientific, educational, or applied value and unless equally effective alternative procedures that do not involve waiver of consent are not feasible.*

Social work ethics do not prohibit the use of naturalistic or participant observation. But because these methods involve nondisclosure and perhaps deception, they conflict with the ethical principles of self-determination and privacy. Researchers planning to use these methods must justify them on the grounds of the expected value of the study and its findings, the lack of alternative methods (Cournoyer & Klein, 2000), and the assurance that no harm will be caused to the unsuspecting participants. As suggested by Padgett (1998), researchers should obtain permission from the appropriate gatekeepers before engaging in research in agency settings, particularly when using these methods. Doing so is especially important when the research sites are LGBT agencies, since many of their stakeholders are likely to be suspicious of being exploited by researchers or harmed by research findings. Failing to do so would probably doom the project and make it more difficult for other research to occur in that setting. The APA Code is more explicit about this point, stating that prior to conducting a study psychologists should provide host institutions and organizations with complete information in order to obtain their approval (Sec. 6.09).

Standard 5.02(i). Social workers should take appropriate steps to ensure that participants in evaluation and research have access to appropriate supportive services.

Standard 5.02(j). Social workers engaged in evaluation or research should protect participants from unwarranted physical or mental distress, harm, danger, or deprivation.

Researchers should not design studies in which participants are knowingly harmed, particularly when such harm or distress is not scientifically justified. In such cases, the risk/benefit ratio of the research, mentioned above, cannot be justified.

Although participants in social work research are unlikely to experience physical harm, psychological harm can occur. As Padgett (1998) noted, interviews that touch upon painful life events may generate considerable emotion and even distress. And studies using self-administered questionnaires do not ensure the absence of harm or distress. For example, studies asking participants to recall incidents of intimate partner violence among lesbian or gay couples, or of hate violence among transgender individuals, could re-traumatize participants by focusing their attention on reactions to events that they have not yet resolved.

In the event that participants do experience psychological distress, researchers are ethically obligated to provide them with, or refer them to, supportive services. When participants are members of LGBT populations, researchers must be particularly careful that such services are culturally competent. Even in the largest cities, culturally competent services for transgender participants might not be readily identified. Finding appropriate resources even for lesbian, gay, and bisexual participants could be difficult outside of major cities. But without the presence of such services, a study that poses even minor risk for causing psychological harm or distress to its LGBT participants should not go forward.

Standard 5.02(l). Social workers engaged in evaluation or research should ensure the anonymity or confidentiality of participants and of the data obtained from them. Social workers should inform participants of any limits of confidentiality, the measures that will be taken to ensure confidentiality, and when any records containing research data will be destroyed.

Standard 5.02(m). Social workers who report evaluation and research results should protect participants' confidentiality by omitting identifying information unless proper consent has been obtained authorizing disclosure.

Because of the heightened importance of confidentiality in studies of LGBT populations, researchers conducting studies in which participation is not anonymous must take all possible steps to ensure that the identities of participants are never revealed. Such breaches of confidentiality could occur if proper precautions are not taken or if a court issues a subpoena for the research data.

Researchers should take several measures to protect participants' identities and the confidentiality of the data collected from them. They should replace participant names with identification numbers on questionnaires as soon as possible. They should prevent unauthorized access to data files by using password protections. Diskettes, completed questionnaires, tapes, and client or researcher logs should be secured in a locked file cabinet to which only the researcher has the key (Reamer, 1998).

With the exception of consent forms, all materials that would make identification of participants possible should be destroyed prior to publishing data based on the study. Consent forms should be maintained securely and in such a way that they cannot be linked to individual participants through the presence of a corresponding identification number. After removing any information that could identify participants, researchers should keep data for five years in case any questions arise regarding the analysis or the conduct of the study.

When conducting longitudinal studies, researchers must maintain the "translation" of identification codes to participants' identities in a separate locked file cabinet. An alternative strategy requires participants to make up their own unique identification code, which they will remember throughout the course of the study. This strategy eliminates the need for a "translation" file altogether.

To prevent the possibility that sensitive data could be subpoenaed, researchers should obtain a Certificate of Confidentiality from the U.S. Public Health Service before they begin collecting data. When a Certificate of Confidentiality is granted, the researcher cannot be compelled to identify participants by any judicial or legislative body. Certificates may be issued for research on sensitive topics, particularly those having to do with mental health and HIV/AIDS. Studies do not have to be federally funded in order to qualify (Levine, 1991).

> *Standard 5.02(n). Social workers should report evaluation and research results accurately. They should not fabricate or falsify results and should take steps to correct any errors later found in published data using standard publication methods.*

There may be a heightened danger of intentionally or unintentionally misrepresenting, fabricating, or falsifying findings when the researcher is strongly motivated to find certain results. According to Martin and Knox (2000), "researchers with strong political or personal views supporting or opposing [LGBT people] should refrain from engaging in research on [them] unless they are willing to accept that the results might not support their views" (p. 52). In addition, researchers conducting evaluations of programs within an LGBT community of which they are also a member might experience internal or external pressure not to report negative findings.

Another section of the NASW Code states that social workers should "honestly acknowledge the work of and the contributions made by others" (Sec. 4.08(a)), and take "responsibility and credit . . . only for work they have actually performed and to which they have contributed" (Sec. 4.08(b)). In addition, the APA Code states that psychologists must never misrepresent data as being original if it has been published previously (Sec. 6.24). Social workers must meet this additional ethical standard when publishing in APA journals.

Standard 5.02(o). Social workers engaged in evaluation or research should be alert to and avoid conflicts of interest and dual relationships with participants, should inform participants when a real or potential conflict of interest arises, and should take steps to resolve the issue in a manner that makes participants' interests primary.

According to Woodman, Tully, and Barranti (1995), lesbian researchers conducting studies in the communities in which they live may encounter ethical dilemmas involving dual relationships. For example, a researcher might be the "therapist, professor, friend, co-worker, or teammate" (p. 62) of one or more study participants. This ethical challenge might also occur in transgender or bisexual communities, which can be quite small even in major cities, or in close-knit communities of gay men. Woodman et al. (1995) suggested expanding the sampling frame to include participants outside the researcher's community as a way of lessening this ethical challenge. However, this strategy would not remove the possible problem of having dual relationships with at least some of the study's participants.

The current version of the NASW Code of Ethics, which was published after this strategy was proposed, is quite clear that social workers should avoid all dual relationships in research. It is extremely difficult to guarantee either the participants' privacy or the confidentiality of the information provided when there is a dual relationship with the researcher. In addition, participants could easily feel coerced to involve themselves in the study, and the information they provide might very well be contaminated by an acquiescent response bias.

The safest solution to these issues would be to scrupulously avoid recruiting participants with whom there is any possibility of a dual relationship. These include persons with whom the researcher has a social or familial relationship, or patrons of a bar the researcher frequents. In the same vein, evaluators employed within an agency should be careful not to recruit their own clients as study participants.

> *Standard 5.02(p). Social workers should educate themselves, their students, and their colleagues about responsible research practices.*

Although this standard does not state explicitly that "responsible research practices" should include cultural competence regarding the populations under study, the APA Code directs psychologists to "consult those with expertise concerning any special population under investigation or most likely to be affected" (Sec. 6.07(d)) when planning and conducting a study. This is a good guideline for both LGBT and non-LGBT researchers when studying LGBT populations. Because these populations are so diverse, even researchers with extensive personal or professional knowledge are unlikely to be expert about every LGBT subgroup. For example, one might have expertise concerning gay men but not lesbians, lesbians but not women of transgender experience, or African American but not Mexican American bisexual men. In many cases experts could be members of the community one wishes to study, as they were for McClennen (this volume). Beyond relying on such experts for education about the population of interest, some authors (e.g., Bowman, 1983; Green & Mercer, 2001; Renzetti, 1995) recommend involving them on a more ongoing basis throughout all phases of the research process: planning, implementation, data collection, and the interpretation of findings, and in the dissemination process.

OTHER ETHICAL ISSUES

In addition to these specific standards for ethical research and evaluation, there are two additional ethical issues that researchers conducting studies on LGBT populations must consider. They concern biases at all stages of the research process and the tension between objectivity and values in scientific research.

Heterosexist and Genderist Biases in Research

Although the NASW Code does not specifically address the problem of biases in research, it contains several statements that do so indirectly. In particular, Sec. 6.04(c) states that "social workers should promote conditions that encourage respect for cultural and social diversity within the United States and globally," and Sec. 6.04(d) states that "social workers should act to prevent and eliminate domination of, exploitation of, and discrimination against any person, group, or class. . . ." The APA Code states explicitly that "psychologists try to eliminate the effect on their work of biases . . . and they do not knowingly participate in or condone unfair discriminatory practices."

The APA's Committee on Lesbian and Gay Concerns (1991) asserted that professional writing "should be free of heterosexual bias" (p. 974), and it provided several strategies for meeting this expectation. One was that stigmatizing or pathologizing language should be avoided, including language that communicates assumptions of psychopathology or moral turpitude. Another was that any groups to which comparisons with lesbians or gay men are made should be parallel (e.g., lesbians should be compared to heterosexual women, when appropriate, not to "the general public" or "normal women"). *The Publication Manual of the American Psychological Association* (2001) contains more extensive guidelines for reducing the use of biased language in research.

Biases represent shared assumptions among members of particular groups of people (McHugh et al., 1986) which can affect research at any stage of the process (Martin & Knox, 2000), often unintentionally. For example, many people assume that gender is binary. This assumption, labeled here as "genderist," might lead to research that negatively impacts transgender populations. Perhaps most obviously, demographic questions that ask whether participants are male or female (with no alternative category) communicate this bias, especially when the study makes comparisons between male and female participants. Similarly, studies communicate heterosexist biases when they fail to ask about participants' sexual orientation or assume that people's marital status is equivalent to their relationship status.

Biases can also enter the research process in less obvious ways: in the theories underpinning the study; the framing of the research questions; the sampling strategy; the construction or selection of measurement instruments; and the analysis of data (Herek et al., 1991; Martin & Knox, 2000). Extending the examples provided by Herek et al. (1991), research questions have heterosexist or genderist biases if they ignore the existence of LGBT people, devalue or stigmatize them, or assume that negative characteristics observed in them are caused by their sexual orientation or gender identity/expression.

To reduce the possibility of heterosexist and genderist biases in studies, researchers should take care not to use samples that lack representativeness or diversity, or data collection instruments that assume heterosexuality or binary gender. In addition, they should never report results without sufficiently acknowledging their limitations, or without anticipating and confronting ways in which the popular media or public might distort or misinterpret them.

CHOOSING THE RESEARCH QUESTION

According to Yegidis and Weinbach (2002), research problems for which there is little potential for positive utilization of the findings or recommendations should be a low priority in social work. In addition, the NASW Code states that helping people in need, addressing social problems, and challenging social injustice are primary ethical principles in social work. These principles should guide social work research as well as practice. Therefore, social workers who conduct research that may hurt people in need, or support existing social injustices, are acting contrary to the profession's ethical principles. However, Rubin and Babbie (2001) warned that such strong ethical imperatives may be counterproductive, biasing research and distorting truth.

The tension between research as a method for advocating for moral principles and research as a value-free quest for truth is longstanding (see Kendler, 1993), and it periodically erupts when research challenges existing norms or exacerbates conflicts between opposing groups of people. Because issues of sexual orientation and gender expression often serve as social and political flashpoints, research on LGBT populations can easily fan the flames of this divide.

One recent example from psychological research concerns the debate surrounding Rind, Tromavitch, and Bauserman's (1998) meta-analysis of studies of the effects of child sexual abuse on college-age young adults and Rind's (2001) later examination of the effects of gay and bisexual adolescents' sexual experiences with men. In the earlier paper, Rind and his associates concluded that child sexual abuse does not necessarily cause lasting harm, particularly among boys. Furthermore, they recommended that the term "abuse" should be used for sexual encounters between adolescents or even younger children only if the "young person felt that he or she did not freely participate in the encounter and if he or she experienced negative reactions to it" (p. 35).

This paper set off a professional and political firestorm that involved critiques on both methodological and moral grounds (e.g., Dallam et al., 2001; Ondersma, 2001), attacks in the media, a resolution in the U.S. House of Representatives condemning the article, and a resolution by the American Psychological Association explaining that it remained strongly against child sexual abuse. Rind (2000) charged that critics of the study conflated morality with science.

Rind published the second paper (Rind, 2001) in the midst of this conflict. It showed that, contrary to young women, who more consistently experience sex with an older person as traumatic, gay male adolescents and young adults frequently recalled early sexual experiences with older men as consensual and positive; many reported that they had actually initiated them. Rind suggested that the pathologizing and criminalizing of all sexual interactions between adult men and adolescent boys might be far more harmful to young gay and bisexual men than the sexual experiences themselves.

This paper is likely to anger many groups of people, including mainstream GLBT organizations, which have long since distanced themselves from advocates of "man-boy" sexual contact, child welfare organizations that are committed to protecting children from abuse, police, and many legislators. Some people might even assert that this study should not have been conducted because the subject is simply taboo, or because it might provide "ammunition" for opponents of LGBT rights. However, others might argue that assumptions about the negative impact of sexual experiences between boys and adult men are heterosexist in that they presume that all children are heterosexual, and that the process of sexual development among gay and bisexual boys–if it is different from that of heterosexual boys–must be bad. Therefore, using scientific research to examine these assumptions would be consistent with social work's and psychology's ethical principles.

CONCLUSION

Researchers must be careful to adhere to the ethical principles of their profession when conducting research on LGBT populations, especially because such studies always occur within a complex, changing, and often hostile sociopolitical environment. A primary purpose of these principles is to protect research participants from exploitation and harm. Because of their marginalized and devalued position in society, LGBT populations are particularly vulnerable to these harms. This article explained specific ways in which standards having to do with research in NASW's Code of Ethics (NASW, 1996), and to a lesser extent APA's Ethical Principles of Psychologists and Code of Conduct (APA, 1992), may be applied in research on LGBT populations. In many cases, such research requires additional measures in order to ensure the safety of participants and the relevance and usefulness of the study's findings.

REFERENCES

American Psychological Association (1992). *Ethical principles of psychologists and code of conduct* [Online]. Retrieved March 14, 2002, from *http://www.apa.org/ethics/code.html#6.21.*

American Psychological Association (2001). *Publication manual of the American Psychological Association* (5th ed.). Washington, DC: Author.

American Psychological Association Committee on Lesbian and Gay Concerns (1991). Avoiding heterosexual bias in language. *American Psychologist, 46*, 973-974.

Barker, R.L. (1990). Continuing education: A neglected component of competent practice. *Journal of Independent Social Work, 4(3)*, 1-5.

Berkman, C.S., & Zinberg, G. (1997). Homophobia and heterosexism in social workers. *Social Work, 42*, 319-332.

Bieber, I., Dain, H.J., Dince, P.R., Drellich, M.G., Grand, H.G., Gundlach, R.H., Kremer, M.W., Rifkin, A.H., Wilbur, C.B., & Bieber, T.B. (1962). *Homosexuality: A psychoanalytic study.* New York: Basic Books.

Bowman, P.J. (1983). Significant involvement and functional relevance: Challenges to survey research. *Social Work Research and Abstracts, 19(4)*, 21-26.

Bremer, J. (1959). *Asexualization: A follow-up study of 244 cases.* New York: Macmillan.

Callahan, E.J., & Leitenberg, H. (1973). Aversion therapy for sexual deviation: Contingent shock and covert sensitization. *Journal of Abnormal Psychology*, 81, 60-73.

Cameron, P., & Cameron, K. (1996). Do homosexual teachers pose a risk to pupils? *Journal of Psychology, 130*, 603-613.

Cameron, P., Proctor, K., Cobum, W., & Forde, N. (1985). Sexual orientation and sexually transmitted diseases. *Nebraska Medical Journal, 70*, 292-299.

Ceci, S.J., Peters, D., & Plotkin, J. (1985). Human subjects review, personal values and the regulation of social science research. *American Psychologist*, 40, 994-1002.

Clements-Nolle, K., Marx, R., Guzman, R., & Katz, M. (2001). HIV prevalence, risk behaviors, health care use, and mental health status of transgender persons: Implications for public health intervention. *American Journal of Public Health, 91*, 915-921.

Council on Social Work Education (1994). *Curriculum Policy Statement for master's degree programs in social work education* [Online]. Retrieved March 14, 2002, from *http://www.cswe.org/mswcps.htm.*

Cournoyer, D.E., & Klein, W.C. (2000). *Research methods for social work.* Boston: Allyn and Bacon.

Dallam, S.J., Gleaves, D.H., Cepeda-Benito, A., Silberg, J.L., Kraemer, H.C., & Spiegel, D. (2001). The effects of child sexual abuse: Comment on Rind, Tromavitch, and Bauserman (1998). *Psychological Bulletin, 127*, 715-733.

D'Augelli, A.R., & Hershberger, S.L. (1993). Lesbian, gay, and bisexual youth in community settings: Personal challenges and mental health problems. *American Journal of Community Psychology, 21*, 421-448.

Diaz, R.M., Ayala, G., Bein, E., Henne, J., & Marin, B.V. (2001). The impact of homophobia, poverty, and racism on the mental health of gay and bisexual Latino men: Findings from 3 US cities. *American Journal of Public Health, 91*, 927-932.

Duberman, M. (1991). *Cures.* New York: Dutton.

Erickson, E. (2001). Audit calls into question funding for sexually explicit AIDS prevention programs for gays. *New York Blade News*, November 30, p. 7.

FindLaw Resources (n.d.). *Romer v. Evans* [Online]. Retrieved March 13, 2002 from *http://caselaw.lp.findlaw.com/scripts/getcase.pl?court=US&vol=000&invol=U10179.*

Green, L.W., & Mercer, S.L. (2001). Can public health researchers and agencies reconcile the push from funding bodies and the pull from communities? *American Journal of Public Health, 91*, 1926-1929.

Herek, G.M. (1998). Bad science in the service of stigma: A critique of the Cameron group's survey studies. In G.M. Herek (Ed.), *Psychological perspectives on lesbian and gay issues: Vol. 4. Stigma and sexual orientation: Understanding prejudice against lesbian, gay men, and bisexuals* (pp. 223-255). Thousand Oaks, CA: Sage Publications.

Herek, G.M., Gillis, J.R., & Cogan, J.C. (1999). Psychological sequelae of hate-crime victimization among lesbian, gay, and bisexual adults. *Journal of Consulting and Clinical Psychology, 67,* 945-951.

Herek, G.M., Gillis, J.R., Cogan, J.C., & Glunt, E.K. (1997). Hate crime victimization among lesbian, gay, and bisexual adults. *Journal of Interpersonal Violence, 12,* 195-215.

Herek, G.M., Kimmel, D.C., Amaro, H., & Melton, G.B. (1991). Avoiding heterosexist bias in psychological research. *American Psychologist, 46,* 957-963.

Hershberger, S.L., & D'Augelli, A.R. (1995). The impact of victimization on the mental health and suicidality of lesbian, gay, and bisexual youths. *Developmental Psychology, 31,* 65-74.

Hooker, E. (1957). The adjustment of the male overt homosexual. *Journal of Projective Techniques, 21,* 18-31.

Hooker, E. (1993). Reflections of a 40-year exploration. *American Psychologist, 48,* 450-453.

Humphreys, L. (1970). *Tearoom trade: Impersonal sex in public places.* Chicago: Aldine.

Hunter, S., Shannon, C., Knox, J., & Martin, J.I. (1998). *Lesbian, gay, and bisexual youths and adults: Knowledge for human services practice.* Thousand Oaks, CA: Sage.

Kendler, H.H. (1993). Psychology and the ethics of social policy. *American Psychologist, 48,* 1046-1053.

Levine, C. (1991). AIDS and the ethics of human subjects research. In F.G. Reamer (Ed.), *AIDS & ethics* (pp. 77-104). New York: Columbia University Press.

Martin, J.I., & Hunter, S. (2001). *Lesbian, gay, bisexual, and transgender issues in social work: A comprehensive bibliography with annotations.* Alexandria, VA: Council on Social Work Education.

Martin, J.I., & Knox, J. (2000). Methodological and ethical issues in research on lesbians and gay men. *Social Work Research, 24,* 51-59.

McConaghy, N. (1976). Is a homosexual orientation irreversible? *British Journal of Psychiatry, 129,* 556-563.

McHugh, M.C., Koeske, R.D., & Frieze, I.H. (1986). Issues to consider in conducting nonsexist psychological research. *American Psychologist, 41,* 879-890.

Meyer, I.H. (1995). Minority stress and mental health in gay men. *Journal of Health and Social Behavior, 36,* 38-56.

Monette, D.R., Sullivan, T.J., & DeJong, C.R. (1998). *Applied social research: Tool for the human services* (4th ed.). Fort Worth, TX: Harcourt Brace.

Morrow, D.F. (1996). Heterosexism: Hidden dimension in social work education. *Journal of Gay & Lesbian Social Services, 5(4),* 1-16.

Murphy, T.F. (1992). Redirecting sexual orientation: Techniques and justifications. *Journal of Sex Research, 29,* 501-523.

National Association of Social Workers (1996). *Code of ethics.* Washington, DC: Author.

National Institutes of Health Office of Human Subjects Research (2000). *Guidelines for writing informed consent documents* [Online]. Retrieved March 15, 2002, from *http://ohsr.od.nih.gov/info/finfo_6.php3.*

Ondersma, S.J., Chaffin, M., Berliner, L., Cordon, I., Goodman, G.S., & Barnett, D. (2001). Sex with children is abuse: Comment on Rind, Tromavitch, and Bauserman (1998). *Psychological Bulletin, 127,* 707-714.

Owensby, N.M. (1941). The correction of homosexuality. *Urologic and Cutaneous Review, 45,* 494-496.

Padgett, D.K. (1998). *Qualitative methods in social work research: Challenges and rewards.* Thousand Oaks, CA: Sage.

Plant, R. (1986). *The pink triangle.* New York: Henry Holt.

Reamer, F.G. (1998). *Ethical standards in social work: A critical review of the NASW Code of Ethics.* Washington, DC: NASW Press.

Renzetti, C.M. (1995). Studying partner abuse in lesbian relationships: A case for the Feminist Participatory Research Model. *Journal of Gay & Lesbian Social Services, 3(1),* 29-42.

Rind, B. (2000). Condemnation of a scientific article: A chronology and refutation of the attacks and a discussion of threats to the integrity of science. *Sexuality and Culture, 4(2),* 1-62.

Rind, B. (2001). Gay and bisexual adolescent boys' sexual experiences with men: An empirical examination of psychological correlates in a nonclinical sample. *Archives of Sexual Behavior, 30,* 345-368. Retrieved March 8, 2002, from *http://proquest. umi.com.*

Rind, B., Tromavitch, P., & Bauserman, R. (1998). A meta-analytic examination of assumed properties of child sexual abuse using college samples. *Psychological Bulletin, 124,* 22-53. Retrieved March 8, 2002, from *http://www.psycinfo.com/ftdocs/ bul/1998/july/bul124122.html.*

Rosario, M., Hunter, J., & Gwadz, M. (1997). Exploration of substance use among lesbian, gay, and bisexual youths: Prevalence and correlates. *Journal of Adolescent Research, 12,* 454-476.

Royse, D. (1999). *Research methods in social work* (3rd ed.). Chicago: Nelson-Hall.

Royse, D., Thyer, B.A., Padgett, D.K., & Logan, T.K. (2001). *Program evaluation: An introduction* (3rd ed.). Belmont, CA: Wadsworth.

Rubin, A., & Babbie, E. (2001). *Research methods for social work* (4th ed.). Belmont, CA: Wadsworth.

Savin Williams, R.C. (1994). Verbal and physical abuse as stressors in the lives of lesbian, gay male, and bisexual youths: Associations with school problems, running away, substance abuse, prostitution, and suicide. *Journal of Consulting and Clinical Psychology, 62,* 261-269.

Sieber, J.E., & Stanley, B. (1988). Ethical and professional dimensions of socially sensitive research. *American Psychologist, 43,* 49-55.

Tanner, B.A. (1974). A comparison of automated aversive conditioning and a waiting list control in the modification of homosexual behavior in males. *Behavior Therapy, 5(1),* 29-32.

U.S. Department of Health and Human Services (1997). *Federal Policy for the Protection of Human Subjects* [Online]. Retrieved March 14, 2002, from *http://ohrp. osophs.dhhs.gov/humansubjects/guidance/45cfr46.htm#46.102.*

Woodman, N.J., Tully, C.T., & Barranti, C.C. (1995). Research in lesbian communities: Ethical dilemmas. *Journal of Gay & Lesbian Social Services, 3(1),* 57-66.

Yegidis, B.L., & Weinbach, R.W. (2002). *Research methods for social workers* (4th ed.). Boston: Allyn and Bacon.

Index

*A Professional's Guide to
    Understanding Gay and
    Lesbian Domestic Violence:
    Understanding Practice
    Interventions,* xv
Acquired immunodeficiency syndrome
    (AIDS), LGBT populations
    with, ASOs for, 163-180. *See
    also* AIDS service
    organizations (ASOs)
Adolescence, dimensions of lesbian
    identity during, 109-125
    study of, 114-121,118t-120t
    data collection in, 115-116
    LIQ in, 116
    results of, 116-121,118t-119t
    sample in, 114-115
Adolescent(s), GLB, researching
    concerning, 127-145. *See
    also* Gay, lesbian and
    bisexual (GLB) adolescents
*Affilia: The Journal of Women in
    Social Work,* xiii
African Americans, LGBT populations
    of, community-based health
    and social services research
    among, methodological
    issues in, 65-78
African Americans, LGBT populations
    of, community-based health
    and social services research
    among, methodological
    issues in. *See also under*
    Lesbian, gay, bisexual, and
    transgender (LGBT)
    populations
Age, as factor in LGBT populations
    study, 157

Agency for Health Care Policy and
    Research, 167
Aging, gays and lesbians issues related
    to, 48
AIDS. *See* Acquired
    immunodeficiency syndrome
    (AIDS)
AIDS Education and Prevention, xiv
AIDS Memorial Quilt, 39
AIDS service organizations (ASOs),
    4-5,10,75
    described, 164
    evaluation of
        approaches to, 167-168
            incompatibility of, 168-170
        archiving of, 175-176
        launching of, 174-175
        refining in, 173-174
        utilization of, 175
    history of, 164-166
    model of, application of, 176,177f
    service provision of, evaluation of,
        163-180
Alkin, M., 169
American Anthropological
    Association, 88
American Psychiatric Association
    (APA), 187
American Psychiatric Association
    (APA) Code, 182,185,189,
    190,193,195,196
American Psychological Association
    (APA), 182,185,193, 95,197
Anastas, J.W., xiii, 4,6,7,109
APA. *See* American Psychiatric
    Association (APA);
    American Psychological
    Association (APA)

APA Code, 182,185,189,190,193,195, 196
APA's Committee on Lesbian and Gay Concerns, 195
ASOs. *See* AIDS service organizations (ASOs)
Attitudes Toward Lesbians and Gay Men scale, 152
Awareness, in qualitative research on gays and lesbians, 23-24

Babbie, E., 196
Barrnati, C.C., 193
Bart, M., 105-106
Bauserman, R., 196-197
Behavioral problems, in GLB adolescent research, 134-135
Berger, R., xxiii
Bieber, I., 183-184
Bisexual(s), researching concerning, 127-145. *See also* Gay, lesbian and bisexual (GLB) adolescents, researching concerning
Blacks, LGBT populations of, community-based health and social services research among, methodological issues in, 65-78. *See also under* Lesbian, gay, bisexual, and transgender (LGBT) populations
Boxer, A.M., 111
Brady, S., 111
Bremer, J., 183
Brittenback, W.M., xxiii
Brown, P., 174
Busse, W., 111

Cameron, P., 184
Caregiver(s), of gays and lesbians, empowering of, 47-63

future research recommendations for, 57-61
study of, 49-57
described, 49-50
findings of, 55-57
lessons learned from, 57-61
methodological challenges and strategies in, 52-55
methods in, 50-52
personal investment of respondents and collaboration in, 60-61
qualitative methods in, 57-58
researcher's role in, 54-55
sampling in, 52-54
sampling strategies in, 58-59
technology in, 59-60
Carlin, A., xxiii
Cass, V.C., 97, 112
Cassel, J.B., 170
Cattell's Scree test, 116
Ceci, S.J., 187-188
Center for Epidemiologic Studies Depression Scale (CES-D), 135
Centers for Disease Control and Prevention (CDC) Division of HIV/AIDS Prevention-Intervention Research and Support Department, 166
Certificate of Confidentiality, 9, 192
CES-D. *See* Center for Epidemiologic Studies Depression Scale (CES-D)
Cherin, D., 169,172, 173f
Child Behavior Checklist, 134-135
Children & Schools, xiv
Code of Conduct, 5
Code of Ethics, NASW, 5,24,41,92, 182,185,193,194-196,197
Cohler, B.J., 111
Coleman, E., 97
Collins, B.E., 168, 172
Colten, M.E., 149

"Coming out," 97

"Coming out of the closet," 97

Community Psychologists, xvi

Community-based health and social services research, among urban Black and African American LGBT populations, 65-78. *See also under* Lesbian, gay, bisexual, and transgender (LGBT) populations

Complexity, in LGBT population research, 7

Confidentiality
in qualitative research on gays and lesbians, 22-23
in study of community-based health and social services research among urban Blacks and African American LBGT populations, 71

"Consolidation and Fulfillment," 109

Constructive self-development theory (CSDT), 98-105, 100f
adaptive mechanisms in, 103
contextual domain in, 103-105
cultural dislocation in, 103-104
developmental stage and current emotional health in, 102
family in, 104
internal organization in, 101-102
locus of control in, 103
overview of, 100f
physical harm and other victimizations in, 104-105
social isolation in, 103-104
temperamental domain in, 101-103

Council on Social Work Education (CSWE), 185

Cournoyer, D.E., 182

Cramer, E.P., xiii, 10, 11, 12, 47

Criminal Justice and Behavior, xiii

CSDT. *See* Constructive self-development theory (CSDT)

CSWE. *See* Council on Social Work Education (CSWE)

Cwi, J.S., 174

D'Aprix, A.S., 24

D'Augelli, A.R., xxi, 7, 9, 98, 103, 128, 139

Dean, L., 136

Debriefing, peer, in qualitative research on gays and lesbians, 25-26

Diamond, L.M., 138, 139-140

Dodd, S-J, xiii-xiv, 4, 10, 12, 163

Domestic violence, among gays and lesbians, research on, 31-45
costs to researchers conducting studies on stigmatized populations, 41-42
emerging strategies in, 36-41
findings of, 41
motivation for, 34-35
nonaffiliated vs. affiliated researcher in, challenges facing, 32-33
participatory research models, 33-34
rigor vs. relevance in studying stigmatized populations, 42-43

Drug use, among gays, HIV infection related to, research with, 79-94. *See also* Human immunodeficiency virus (HIV) infection, gay drug users and, interface of

Dual relationships, in qualitative research on gays and lesbians, 24-25

Duberman, M., 183

Ecological perspective, in LGBT population research, 6

Education, in LGBT populations study, 156

Eliason, M.J., 123

Elze, D.E., xiv, 4, 127, 190

Emotional issues, in GLB adolescent research, 134-135

Employment, in LGBT populations study, 156

Equal Protection Clause of the United States Constitution, 184-185

Ethical Principles of Psychologists, 5

Ethical Principles of Psychologists and Code of Conduct, 182,185, 193,195,197

Ethical standards, in research and evaluation of LGBT populations, 181-201. *See also* Lesbian, gay, bisexual, and transgender (LGBT) populations, research and evaluation of, ethical standards in

Ethnicity, in LGBT populations study, 156

EZ-Text, 88-89

Families in Society, xv, xvi

Family Process, xv

Family status, in LGBT populations study, 157, 158t

Fassinger, R.E., 113,116,121,122

Fleishman, J.A., 174

Frankel, R., 121

Freeman, H.E., 167

"Fulfillment Consolidation," 117-118

Fullerton, D., 170

Gabbay, S., 159

Gagnon, J.H., 149

Gambrill, E., 14

Garnets, L., 104

Gay, Lesbian, and Straight Educators Network (GLSEN), 132

lesbian and bisexual (GLB) adolescents, research concerning, 127-145

attendance at youth group in, 134

discussion of, 137-142

emotional and behavioral problems associated with, 134-135

human subjects' considerations in, 129-131

measurements of, 134-137

recruitment procedures in, 131-133

results of, 137,138t,139t

sample characteristics of, 133-134

self-esteem in, 136

sexual orientation in developmental milestones related to, 134

family attitudes about, 136

feelings about, 135-136

openness about, 135

social integration in, 135

victimization in, 136-137

Gay(s). *See also* Lesbian, gay, bisexual, and transgender (LGBT) populations

aging issues facing, 48

caregivers of, empowering of, 47-63. *See also* Caregiver(s), of gays and lesbians, empowering of

domestic violence among, 31-45. *See also* Domestic violence, among gays and lesbians, research on

drug use among

HIV infection related to, research with, 79-94. *See also* Human immunodeficiency

virus (HIV) infection, gay
   drug users and, interface of
   prevalence of, 81
   types of drugs in, 81
qualitative study of, insider advantage
   in, 15-30
   confidentiality in, 22-23
   data collection in, 18-19
   investigator reactions in, 20
   limitations of, 19-22
   outside insider in, 21-22
   peer debriefing in, 25-26
   perspective on, 17-18
   potential for dual relationships
      in, 24-25
   prolonged engagement in, 26
   researcher's perspective on, 16-17
   respondent reactions to, 20-21
   self-awareness in, 23-24
   strengthening of, 22-26
research concerning, 127-145. *See
   also* Gay, lesbian and
   bisexual (GLB) adolescents,
   research concerning
study of, 147-162. *See also* Lesbian,
   gay, bisexual, and transgender
   (LGBT) populations
*Gay and Lesbian Asia: Culture
   Identity, Community,* xvi
Gay Men's Sexual Stories, xvi
Gay-straight alliance (GSA), 141
Gender identity, in LGBT populations
   study, 153-154, 155t
Gibson, P., 96
GLB adolescents. *See* Gay, lesbian and
   bisexual (GLB) adolescents
GLSEN. *See* Gay, Lesbian, and Straight
   Educators Network (GLSEN)
Gorelick, S., 34
Gorman, E.M., xiv, 3, 10, 11, 79
Gramick, J., 97-98
Group variations, in LGBT population
   research, 7-8
GSA. *See* Gay-straight alliance (GSA)
Gwaltney, J.L., 18

Hash, K.M., xiv-xv, 10, 11, 12, 47
*Health and Social Work, Employee
   Assistance Quarterly,* xiv
Health Resources and Service
   Administration, 167
Herek, G.M., 184
Hershberger, S.L., 98, 139
Hetrick-Martin Institute, 138
HHS. *See* U.S. Secretary of Health and
   Human Services (HHS)
HIV infection. *See* Human
   immunodeficiency virus
   (HIV) infection
HIV/AIDS programs, evaluation of,
   current thinking regarding,
   166-167, 170-176, 173f
Holland, J., 170
Homosexual Attitudes Inventory, 135
Hooker, E.A., xix, xxi, 184, 186-187
Human immunodeficiency virus (HIV)
   infection
gay drug users and, interface of,
   79-94
   problems associated with, 80-81
   research with
      challenges facing, 82-89
      data analysis in, 88-89
      data collection in, 87-88
      findings of, 89
      implications of, 91-92
      lessons learned from, 90-91
      questions in, 85
      study design in, 85-86
      study sampling in, 86-87
LGBT populations with, ASOs for,
   163-180. *See also* AIDS
   service organizations (ASOs)
Humphreys, L., 184, 188

Income, in LGBT populations study,
   157
*Individual Differences in Cognitive
   Stress Associated with
   Self-Disclosure,* xvi-xvii

Institute Review Board (IRB)
    processes, 71
Institutional review boards (IRBs), 4,
    129,187
*International Journal of Adolescent
    Medicine & Health,* xiv
IRBs. *See* Institutional review boards
    (IRBs)

Jay, K., 98
JGLSS. *See Journal of Gay & Lesbian
    Social Services (JGLSS)*
JH. *See Journal of Homosexuality (JH)*
Journal of Applied Social Sciences, xvii
*Journal of Gay & Lesbian Medical
    Association,* xiii
*Journal of Gay & Lesbian Social
    Services (JGLSS),* xiii,xiv,xv,
    xvi,xvii,xxiii,4,5,12,147,150,
    153,154,154t,155,155t, 160
*Journal of Gay & Lesbian Social Work
    and Human Services,* xiii
*Journal of Gerontological Social
    Work,* xv
Journal of Homosexuality (JH), 148
Journal of Lesbian Studies, xiv
*Journal of Marital and Family
    Therapy,* xv
*Journal of Multicultural Social Work
    Practice,* xvii
Journal of Nursing and AIDS Care, xiv
Journal of Psychoactive Drugs, xiv
Journal of Public Health Management,
    xvii
Journal of Social Service Research, xvi
*Journal of Social Work Practice in the
    Addictions,* xiii, xiv
Joyce, S., 148

Kanuha, V.K., 25
Kimmel, D., 104
Kinsey Institute, xix-xx

Kinsey reports, xix
Klein, W.C., 182
Kline, P., 117
Knox, J., 188,193

*Lady Boys, Tom Boys, Rent Boys:
    Male and Female
    Homosexuality in
    Contemporary Thailand,* xvi
LaSala, M.C., xv, 2,9,10,11,15
Laslett, B., 20
Laumann, E.O., 149
LeCompte, M.D., 50
LE-PAS-R, 35
Lesbian(s). *See also* Lesbian, gay,
        bisexual, and transgender
        (LGBT) populations
    aging issues facing, 48
    caregivers of, empowering of,
        47-63. *See also* Caregiver(s),
        of gays and lesbians,
        empowering of
    domestic violence among, 31-45.
        See also Domestic violence,
        among gays and lesbians,
    research on
        identity of
            during adolescence and
                young adulthood, 109-125.
                See also Adolescence,
                dimensions of lesbian
                identity during; Young
                adulthood, dimensions of
                lesbian identity during.
            development of, evolution of
                theory related to, 110-114
        qualitative study of, insider
            advantage in, 15-30
            confidentiality in, 22-23
            data collection in, 18-19
            investigator reactions in, 20
            limitations of, 19-22
            outside insider in, 21-22
            peer debriefing in, 25-26
            perspective on, 17-18

potential for dual relationships
in, 24-25
prolonged engagement in, 26
researcher's perspective on,
16-17
respondent reactions to, 20-21
self-awareness in, 23-24
strengthening of, 22-26
research concerning, 127-145. *See
also* Gay, lesbian and
bisexual (GLB) adolescents,
research concerning
study of, 147-162. *See also*
Lesbian, gay, bisexual, and
transgender (LGBT)
populations
trauma in, 95-108. *See also*
Self-disclosure stress
Lesbian, gay, bisexual, and
transgender (LGBT)
populations, 110
research on
complexity in, 7
current themes in, 1-14
debate on insider perspective in,
11
ecological perspective in, 6
and evaluation of
ethical standards in, 181-201
heterosexist and genderist
biases, 194-195
research questions in,
selection of,
196-197
future of, xix-xxvii
groups variations in, 7-8
improved samples in, 8-9
participants in, protection of, 9
participatory inclusive research,
10-11
recurring themes in, 5-12
uses of, 12
study of, 147-162
age as factor in, 157
country of origin in, 153

discussion of, 157-160
education in, 156
employment in, 156
ethnicity in, 156
family status in, 157, 158t
gender identity in, 153-154,155t
gender of participants in,
155-156,157t
income in, 157
living situation in, 157
method of, 150-151
religious affiliation in, 157
results of, 151-152
sample characteristics in,
152-157, 54t,155t,157t,158t
sample size in, 152-153
sample type in, 153
sampling techniques in,
152-157,154t,155t,157t,158t
sexual orientation in, 153-154,
155t
sources of data in, 153,154t
urban Black and African American
community-based health and
social services research
among
case study of, 75-76
construct of, 68-69
described, 70
health and social service
disparities in, 69
methodological issues in,
65-78
reasons for, 67-68
study of
confidentiality in, 71
design of, 72-73
discussion of, 76-77
dissemination in, 75
instrumentation in, 74
introduction to, 72-73
methodological issues in,
70-75
sampling in, 73-74
subjects' protection in, 71
self-awareness of, 66-67

Lesbian Advisory Committee, 36
Lesbian identity questionnaire (LIQ), 116
Lesbian Partner Abuse Scale, 37
Lesbian Partner Abuse Scale-Revised
    (LE-PAS-R), 35
Levine, H., 111, 112
LGBT populations. *See* Lesbian, gay,
    bisexual, and transgender
    (LGBT) populations
Lincoln, Y.S., 50
Lipsey, M.W., 167
LIQ. *See* Lesbian identity
    questionnaire (LIQ)
Living situations, in LGBT
    populations study, 157
Losberg, W., xv, 4, 7,8,12

MacIntosh, R., 74
Martin, J.I., xxiii,1,5,9,10,12,14,136,
    181,188,193
McCann, L., 99, 102
McCarn, S.R., 113,116,121,122
McClennen, J.C., xv-xvi, 3,10,11,12,
    31,194
Medline, 148
Meezan, W., xxiii, 1,4,5,9,10,12,14,
    163,169,172,173f,181
Men Who Have Sex With Men
    (MSM), 73
Methamphetamine use, among gays,
    HIV infection related to,
    research with, 81
Meyer, I.H., 149
Michael, R.T., 149
Michaels, S., 149
Miller, D.B., 74
Miller, R., 170
Mor, V., 174
Morgan, K.S., 123
MSM. *See* Men Who Have Sex With
    Men (MSM)
*Multicultural Queer: Australian
    Narratives,* xvi
Murphy, T.F., 183

Narayan, K., 27
NASW. *See* National Association of
    Social Workers (NASW)
National Association of Social
    Workers (NASW), Code of
    Ethics of, 5, 24, 41, 92, 182,
    185, 193, 194-196, 197
National Community AIDS
    Partnership, 167
National Conference of Community
    and Justice's Anytowon
    program, 142
National Institutes of Health Office of
    Human Subjects Research,
    189
National Lesbian Health Survey, 96
Natonal Longitudinal Study of
    Adolescent Health, 142
"New Identity Possibilities," 109,117
New York University, xxiii
*Not Just a Passing Phase: Social Work
    with Lesbian, Gay and
    Bisexual People,* xiii
Nungesser, L.G., 135

Oakley, A., 170
Ohnuki-Tierney, E., 23
Owensby, N.M., 183

Padgett, D.K., 25,26,86,186,190, 191
Parents and Friends of Lesbians and
    Gay Men (PFLAG), 36, 132
Participatory research models, in
    domestic violence among
    gays and lesbians, 33-34
    following of, 35-36
Patton, M.Q., 50, 172,174
Pearlman, A., 99, 102
Peer debriefing, in qualitative research
    on gays and lesbians, 25-26
Pennsylvania State University, xxi
"Persons of Color" (POC), 73

Peters, D., 187-188
Petrulio, C., 148, 159
PFLAG. *See* Parents and Friends of
      Lesbians and Gay Men
      (PFLAG)
Piette, J.D., 174
Plotkin, J., 187-188
POC. *See* "Persons of Color" (POC)
PRIDE festivals, 37,38,39,40
Pryce, J., xvi, 4,6,7,95

Quinn, S.C., 73

Random Digit Dialing (RDD), 149
Rapoport, R., 20
RDD. *See* Random Digit Dialing
      (RDD)
Reamer, F.G., 185
Reed, G.M., 168, 172
Religious affiliation, in LGBT
      populations study, 157
Renzetti, C.M., 35, 37
*Research Design for Social Work and
      Human Services,* xiii
Research on Social Work Practice, xv
Rind, B., 196-197
Rosenberg Self-Esteem Scale, 136
Rossi, P.H., 167
Rotheram-Borus, M.J., 138
Rubin, A., 196
Rubin, H.J., 49
Rubin, I.S., 49

San Francisco Stop AIDS Project, 186
Savin-Williams, R.C., 98,128,140,142
Schrader, A.M., 148
Secret, M., 171-172
Self-awareness
   among urban Black and African
      American LGBT populations,
      66-67

in qualitative research on gays and
      lesbians, 23-24
Self-development theory,
      constructivist, 98-105,100f
Self-disclosure stress, 95-108
Self-esteem, in GLB adolescent
      research, 136
Sell, R.L., 148,159
Sexual orientation
   in GLB adolescent research
      developmental milestones
         related to, 134
      family attitudes about, 136
      feelings about, 135-136
      openness about, 135
   in LGBT populations study,
      153-154, 155t
*Sexual Preference: Its Development in
      Men and Women,* xx
Shostrom, E., 103
Social integration, in GLB adolescent
      research, 135
Social Policy Journal, xiv
Social Work Research, xiv,xv
*Social Work Research, Tulane Studies
      in Social Welfare,* xvi
Sophie, J., 112
Spiers, H.R., 171
"Stigma and Mistreatment
      Management," 109,119,121
Stress, self-disclosure, 95-108. *See
      also* Self-disclosure stress
Strom-Gottfried, K., 24
Strommen, E., 104
Substance Use Risk Exploration
      (SURE), 85
Sullivan, G., xvi, 4, 7, 8, 12
SURE. *See* Substance Use Risk
      Exploration (SURE)
Swann, S.K., xvi,4,6,7,109
Swindell, M.L., xvi-xvii, 3-4,6,7,95

Tearoom Trade, 184
The Maine Times, 132

*The Publication Manual of the
    American Psychological
    Association,* 195
"The Social Support Needs of Older
    Lesbians, Gay Men, and
    Bisexuals," 151-152
Thomas, S.B., 73
Tong, Y.L., xxiii
Trauma, as example of intervening
    variable in research with
    lesbian women, 95-108. *See
    also* Self-disclosure stress
Tromavitch, P., 196-197
Tully, C.T., 193
Tuskegee Syphilis Study, 73

U.S. Census, xxi, 9
U.S. Centers for Disease Control and
    Prevention, 80
U.S. House of Representatives, 196
U.S. Public Health Services, 192
U.S. Secretary of Health and Human
    Services (HHS), 186

Victimization, in GLB adolescent
    research, 136-137

Violence, domestic, among gays and
    lesbians, research on, 31-45.
    See also Domestic violence,
    among gays and lesbians,
    research on

Wahler, J., 159
Walter, K.L., 73
Weinbach, R.W., 196
Wheeler, D.P., xvii, 3,9,10,65
Woodman, N.J., 104,193
Wu, S., 136

Yegidis, B.L., 196
Yong, A., 98
Young adulthood, dimensions of
    lesbian identity during,
    109-125
    study of, 114-121,118t-120t
        data collection in, 115-116
        LIQ in, 116
        results of, 116-121,118t-119t
        sample in, 114-115
Youth Risk Behavior Surveillance
    System, 142
Youth Self-Report (YSR), 134-135
YSR. *See* Youth Self-Report (YSR)